Handbook of
LGBT-Affirmative
Couple and
Family Therapy

Handbook of
LGBT-Affirmative Couple and Family Therapy

Edited by

Jerry J. Bigner and Joseph L. Wetchler

Routledge
Taylor & Francis Group
New York   London

Routledge
Taylor & Francis Group
711 Third Avenue
New York, NY 10017

Routledge
Taylor & Francis Group
27 Church Road
Hove, East Sussex BN3 2FA

Printed in the United States of America on acid-free paper
Version Date: 20120308

International Standard Book Number: 978-0-415-88359-7 (Hardback)

Library of Congress Cataloging-in-Publication Data

Handbook of LGBT-affirmative couple and family therapy / edited by Jerry J. Bigner, Joseph L. Wetchler.
  p. cm.
  Includes bibliographical references and index.
  ISBN 978-0-415-88359-7 (hardback : alk. paper)
  1. Family psychotherapy. 2. Marital psychotherapy. 3. Couples--Psychology. 4. Sexual minorities--Mental health. I. Bigner, Jerry J. II. Wetchler, Joseph L.

RC488.5.H3345 2012
616.89'1562--dc23
                                                   2011043028

Visit the Taylor & Francis Web site at
http://www.taylorandfrancis.com

and the Routledge Web site at
http://www.routledgementalhealth.com

This book is dedicated to Jerry Bigner, who passed away during the final revisions of this manuscript. Jerry was a long-standing mentor, colleague, and friend to many. He provided phenomenal leadership and mentorship in the development of LGBT scholarship and was an important advocate for LGBT rights. All of us associated with this book mourn his loss, as do the many others whose lives he touched. This book is one more addition to his legacy. May it serve as one of many tributes to his life and all he stood for. Heaven is where all humans are equally accepted and valued.

Contents

Acknowledgments

I wish to thank all authors of this handbook for their excellent contributions. Their works represent the latest and most current updates on their particular topics as well as insights from years of experience in working with LGBT couples and their families. We are entering an historic era in the United States when more favorable and accepting attitudes toward members of the LGBT communities are evident—in the increased number of states that legalize same-sex marriages, civil unions, and domestic partnerships; in the numbers of individuals who see our communities as valuable and contributing members of society; in the changes in government policies regarding the inclusion of members of our communities in the armed forces; in being designated beneficiaries; and in adoption and foster care issues. In accordance with these kinds of changes, it is likely that therapists who provide emotional support and care for our communities will, in the future, see changes in the need for the different types of support that are discussed in this text. More than likely, it is certain that there will be a shift from providing the major focus of assistance to those who experience the ill effects of homophobia and heterosexism to providing increased guidance in parent–child relationships, improving communication between couples, and resolving conflicts in families. The chapters of this text represent an update in methods and skills needed by therapists to provide competent care and best practices in new ways with members of our communities. Newly minted therapists may gain expertise, and those with years of experience will gain new insights in these methods. All this that is seen here could not happen without the diligence of Joe Wetchler, who provided the impetus to gain the support of the publisher of this material. His dedication to being a strong and valiant ally of our communities is evident, again, in this text.

Jerry J. Bigner

I also wish to thank the chapter authors for their excellent work. Editing their contributions was like being in an advanced professional seminar. My hope is that their work will be the launching point for the next level of research and practice to emerge in their areas of expertise. These certainly are optimistic times, but we are still early in the move toward social justice and total equality and acceptance for all members of the LGBT communities. These chapters not only represent the most up-to-date information on their topics but also are statements of political activism. Each chapter makes a compelling argument for how current societal beliefs and practices impinge on the emotional and developmental well-being of the LGBT communities. With that in mind, I given grateful thanks to the staff at Routledge Press, who believed in this project and provided excellent assistance in bringing it to fruition. I also wish to thank Ray Yang and Duane Farnell for making this final manuscript possible by going through Jerry Bigner's computer to salvage the chapters he edited.

I give special thanks to my family members, Bernie, Jorie, Diane, and Sherry, for their love and support as well as for teaching me the importance of diversity and equality. All my love and gratitude go to my wife, Carole, for her multitude of gifts. Special thanks and love go to Carole's and my children, Jessica Marie, Ryan, and Jessica Lily. Each is an amazing adult with much to offer others.

Joseph L. Wetchler

Editors

Jerry J. Bigner, PhD, was Professor Emeritus, Department of Human Development and Family Studies, Colorado State University, Fort Collins. He was the editor of *Journal of GLBT Family Studies*, published by Taylor & Francis. He was a member of the editorial board of the *Journal of Couple and Relationship Therapy*. His principle research area was in parent–child relations with an emphasis in GLBT parenting. He was the author of *Parent–Child Relations* (8th edition; Prentice Hall, 2009) and two life-span development texts. He had more than 50 research publications and 20 chapters in texts relating to parent–child relations as well as gay and lesbian family issues. He provided expert testimony in the Canadian same-sex marriage litigation, and his research served as part of the plaintiff's cases in the Hawaii, Massachusetts, and Vermont same-sex marriage litigations. He was a research member of the American Family Therapy Academy and was a member of the National Council on Family Relations. Dr. Bigner was a 2005 Centennial Laureate Award recipient of the College of Human Sciences, Florida State University. He also was the 2007 Distinguished Alumni Award recipient of the College of Human Sciences, Florida State University.

Joseph L. Wetchler, PhD, is professor and director of the Marriage and Family Therapy Program at Purdue University Calumet, Hammond, Indiana. He is a clinical member and Approved Supervisor of the American Association for Marriage and Family Therapy, a member of the American Family Therapy Academy, and a member of the International Family Therapy Association. Dr. Wetchler was the recipient of the 2007 American Association for Marriage and Family Therapy Award for Training, the 2004 Purdue University Calumet Outstanding Faculty Scholar Award, and the 1997 Indiana Association for Marriage and Family Therapy Award for Outstanding Contribution to Research in Family Life. He served as editor of the *Journal of Couple and Relationship Therapy* from 1999 through 2008 and is an associate editor of the *Journal of GLBT Family Studies*. He has also served on the editorial boards of the *American Journal of Family Therapy*, the *Journal of Family Psychotherapy*, the *Journal of Feminist Family Therapy*, the *Journal of Marital and Family Therapy*, and the *Journal of Clinical Activities, Assignments & Handouts in Psychotherapy Practice*. Dr. Wetchler is editor of *Handbook of Clinical Issues in Couple therapy* (2nd edition; Routledge, 2011), *Handbook of Clinical Issues in Couple Therapy* (1st edition; Routledge, 2007), a coeditor (with Fred Piercy and Katherine Hertlein) of *Handbook of the Clinical Treatment of Infidelity* (Routledge, 2005), a coeditor (with Jerry Bigner) of *Relationship Therapy With Same-Sex Couples* (Routledge, 2004), a coeditor (with Volker Thomas and Terri Karis) of *Clinical Issues With Interracial Couples* (Routledge, 2003), a coeditor (with Lorna Hecker) of *An Introduction to Marriage and Family Therapy* (Routledge, 2003), and a coauthor (with Fred Piercy and Douglas Sprenkle) of *Family Therapy Sourcebook* (2nd edition; Guilford Press, 1996). In addition, he is also the author of numerous journal articles on family therapy supervision, family therapy for child and adolescent problems, couple therapy for substance abuse, and the self of the therapist. Dr. Wetchler has been a coinvestigator on a large project funded by the National Institute on Drug Abuse to study couple therapy approaches for substance-abusing women. He regularly consults to social service agencies and therapists in private practice and also maintains an active couple and family therapy practice in northwest Indiana. Dr. Wetchler is a licensed marriage and family therapist in Indiana.

Contributors

Sandra C. Anderson, PhD
School of Social Work
Portland State University
Portland, Oregon

Michele Angello, PhD
Human Sexuality Program
Widener University
Philadelphia, Pennsylvania

Marysol Asencio, DrPH
Department of Human Development and
    Family Studies
University of Connecticut
Storrs, Connecticut

John A. Blando, PhD
Department of Counseling
San Francisco State University
San Francisco, California

Thomas O. Blank, PhD
Department of Human Development and
    Family Studies
University of Connecticut
Storrs, Connecticut

Mary Bradford, PhD
Women's Therapy Center
Berkeley, California

Tiffany B. Brown, PhD
Couples and Family Therapy Program
University of Oregon
Eugene, Oregon

Thomas Stone Carlson, PhD
Department of Human Development
    and Family Science
North Dakota State University
Fargo, North Dakota

Krista Chronister, PhD
Counseling Psychology Program
University of Oregon
Eugene, Oregon

Marla Cobin, PhD
Human Sexuality Program
Widener University
Philadelphia, Pennsylvania

Colleen M. Connolly, PhD
Texas State University
San Marcos, Texas

Deborah Coolhart, PhD
Community and Human Services
Empire State College
East Syracuse, New York
and
Department of Marriage and Family
    Therapy
Syracuse University
Syracuse, New York

Lara Descartes, PhD
Division of Sociology and Family Studies
Brescia University College
London, Ontario, Canada

Linda Stone Fish, PhD
Department of Marriage and Family
    Therapy
Syracuse University
Syracuse, New York

Rashmi Gangamma, PhD
Department of Human Development
    and Family Science
The Ohio State University
Columbus, Ohio

Shawn V. Giammattei, PhD
Rockway Institute
Alliant International University
San Francisco, California

Mark Gianino, PhD
School of Social Work
Boston University
Boston, Massachusetts

Erika L. Grafsky, PhD
Department of Human Development and
    Family Science
The Ohio State University
Columbus, Ohio

Robert-Jay Green, PhD
Rockway Institute
Alliant International University
San Francisco, California

Carol Grever, MA
Straight Spouse Connection
Boulder, Colorado

Jack Grote, BA
Emory University School of Law
Emory University
Atlanta, Georgia

Amney Harper, PhD
Department of Professional Counseling
University of Wisconsin–Oshkosh
Oshkosh, Wisconsin

Rebecca G. Harvey, PhD
Marriage and Family Therapy Program
Seton Hill University
Greensburg, Pennsylvania

Steven D. Johnson, MSW
Department of Psychiatry
University of Kentucky
Lexington, Kentucky

Shoshana D. Kerewsky, PsyD
Counseling Psychology and Human Services
    Department
University of Oregon
Eugene, Oregon

Katherine Kuvalanka, PhD
Department of Family Studies and Social
    Work
Miami University
Oxford, Ohio

Arlene Istar Lev, MSW
Choices Counseling and Consulting
Albany, New York

Deanna Linville, PhD
Couples and Family Therapy Program
University of Oregon
Eugene, Oregon

Janie K. Long, PhD
Center for LGBT Life
Duke University
Durham, North Carolina

Jeff Lutes, MS
Austin, Texas

Jean Lynch, PhD
Department of Sociology and Gerontology
Miami University
Oxford, Ohio

Kevin P. Lyness, PhD
Department of Applied Psychology
Antioch University New England
Keene, New Hampshire

Maeve Malley, DPsychotherapy
Oxleas NHS Foundation Mental
    Health Trust
Kent, United Kingdom

Jean Malpas, MA
Ackerman Institute for the Family
New York, New York

Mary Marsiglio, MS
Counseling Psychology Program
University of Oregon
Eugene, Oregon

Marsha McDonough, PhD
Austin, Texas

Christi R. McGeorge, PhD
Department of Human Development and
Family Science
North Dakota State University
Fargo, North Dakota

Kathy McMahon-Klosterman
Department of Sociology
Miami University
Middletown, Ohio

Valory Mitchell, PhD
California School of Professional Psychology
Alliant International University
San Francisco, California

Michelle Novelle, MSW
Joint Program in Sociology and Social Work
Boston University
Boston, Massachusetts

Corinne Reczek, PhD
Department of Sociology
University of Cincinnati
Cincinnati, Ohio

Ellen D. B. Riggle, PhD
Department of Gender and Women's Studies
University of Kentucky
Lexington, Kentucky

Damien W. Riggs, PhD
School of Social and Policy Studies
Flinders University
Adelaide, Australia

Sharon Scales Rostosky, PhD
Department of Educational, School, and
Counseling Psychology
University of Kentucky
Lexington, Kentucky

Esther Rothblum, PhD
Women's Studies Department
San Diego State University
San Diego California

Philip A. Rutter, PhD
Human Sexuality Program
Widener University
Philadelphia, Pennsylvania

Shannon Sennott, MSW
Translate Gender, Inc.
Brooklyn, New York

Julianne M. Serovich, PhD
Department of Human Development
and Family Science
The Ohio State University
Columbus, Ohio

Anneliese A. Singh, PhD
Department of Counseling and Human
Development Services
University of Georgia
Athens, Georgia

Fiona Tasker, PhD
Department of Psychological Sciences
Birkbeck University of London
London, United Kingdom

Gil Tunnell, PhD
AEDP Institute
and
Department of Counseling and Clinical
Psychology
Teachers College, Columbia University
New York, New York

Introduction

We are pleased to present this new reference text that updates current best practices for therapists and those in training who wish to work effectively with LGBT clients, couples, and families. Earlier, we developed a text that presented comprehensive information of the time on clinical issues affecting couples within these communities in 2004, *Relationship Therapy With Same-Sex Couples*, published by Haworth Press. This book, as the one we now present, serves to update clinicians following the earlier publication of Green and Laird's (1996) text, *Lesbians and Gays in Couples and Families: A Handbook for Therapists*, the first such publication of its kind.

There have been numerous positive changes and developments affecting the LGBT communities in the years since these works have appeared. For example, there are now six states, in addition to the District of Columbia, that have legalized same-sex marriages, and at least 13 others in which domestic partnerships and civil unions are recognized legally. The federal government of the United States has recently repealed the "Don't Ask Don't Tell" law that has kept gay, lesbian, and bisexual individuals from openly serving in the military forces. Adoption of children by same-sex couples and lesbian or gay individuals is illegal now only in a few of the U.S. states, with Florida being the most recent state to rescind laws prohibiting such adoptions. Discrimination in the workplace and in other essential areas of life affecting LGBT individuals has been outlawed at many more local, state, and federal levels. Many universities now offer coursework in LGBT studies, and several mental health training programs have begun to offer LGBT-affirmative curriculums.

Although there have been many positive changes, LGBT communities continue to be affected by other factors that generate problems in daily living. Indeed, LGBT individuals, couples, and their families experience discrimination and the effects of what are called microaggressions at home, school, and the workplace that continue to generate stressful scenarios for these sexual minorities. Homonegativity as well as homophobia and heterosexism continue to plague these communities today. Seventeen states have passed "defense of marriage acts," prohibiting same-sex individuals from marrying. In addition, two states, California and Maine, recently overturned their laws allowing same-sex marriage. The California ban is now being battled in the legal system and appears headed for the U.S. Supreme Court. Further, some academic programs have been sued for teaching LGBT-affirmative curriculums.

Of great concern is the continuing problem faced by therapists who wish to provide affirmative therapeutic programs for their clients of these communities. Training of therapists in every helping field has improved in recent years in providing more than just passing reference for working with clients of these communities. However, researchers who report on training issues continue to observe deficits in training programs in failing to adequately prepare trainees. Our text, while being very comprehensive in the nature of the chapters offered to all therapists, is but the beginning of the foundation that therapists need in their training experiences.

The comprehensive nature of this text is perhaps its greatest strength. We begin by providing a much needed chapter on the history of couple and relationship therapy as applied to working with same-sex, bisexual, and transgender couples and their families. We then introduce six separate sections of the text in which issues of best care practices are explored in greater detail. In Section I, "Clinical Issues With LGBT Couples," issues and treatment models for LGBT couples are explored in separate chapters devoted to one specific group within the LGBT community rather than lumping the issues together in a single chapter. Section II, "Sex Therapy With LGBT

Couples," is unique to the LGBT literature because whereas some books have just a chapter or two, this book has an entire section that is divided into chapters on gay male sex therapy, lesbian female sex therapy, and transgender sex therapy. Also unique in many ways is Section III, "Clinical Issues With LGBT Families," because it is the first overview of LGBT treatment with an entire section devoted to family issues. Several issues that are typically lumped together are broken down for purposes of specificity (e.g., separate chapters are presented for working with LGBT parents and working with children of LGBT parents). This section also covers the life span with chapters devoted to raising LGB children, raising transgendered children, and working with elderly LGBT couples and individuals. The next part, Section IV, "Ethical Issues in LGBT Couple and Family Therapy," is the first review of LGBT clinical issues, presenting an entire section devoted to ethical issues with chapters debunking the research on reorientation therapy, helping individuals and families recover from reorientation therapy attempts, and examining the ethics of same-sex marriage. Section V, "Special Issues," covers numerous concerns faced by therapists in LGBT couple and family therapy. Here, chapters are broken out into discrete topics for purposes of specificity and because sufficient literature now exists to warrant individual chapters. Chapters that have received little coverage to date examine spiritual issues with LGBT couples and families, domestic violence with LGBT couples, and substance abuse and LGBT couples and families. Further, the chapter on LGBT couple enrichment programs is the first to address the issue of enrichment. The final part, Section VI, "Training Issues," features chapters on training issues related to learning to work with LGBT couples and families. This section is unique in that separate chapters are devoted to training straight therapists and training LGBT therapists. The training literature to date has focused primarily on the issues of straight therapists but overlooked the issues of LGBT therapists. Also covered in this section are the unique issues that exist for LGBT therapists.

We present this more inclusive text as a handbook of concise information on this particular subject of working effectively to provide affirmative therapeutic programming for LGBT and, yes, even Q(uestioning) individuals, couples, and their families. We believe that our contributors, who are the recognized experts in their particular niche of the therapy world, have addressed the most significant points needed to help practitioners provide best care practices for these particular communities. We want to emphasize that these clients, who are like all other clients but are also uniquely different in their particular needs, deserve therapeutic attention from providers who recognize their own need for additional training and experiences in order to provide affirmative care of the highest order.

Jerry J. Bigner, PhD

Joseph L. Wetchler, PhD

1

LGBTQ Couple and Family Therapy

History and Future Directions

SHAWN V. GIAMMATTEI and ROBERT-JAY GREEN

In this chapter we provide a comprehensive overview of the history and trends in couple and family therapy with lesbian, gay, bisexual, transgender, and queer (LGBTQ) people. We first describe the history and impact of homophobia, heterosexism, and heteronormativity on sexual and gender minority couples and families, with a focus on the effects of minority stress, relational ambiguity, internalized homonegativity, and lack of social supports. We then discuss some of the special challenges faced by LGBTQ couples, LGBTQ parents raising children, bisexuals in couple and family relationships, and transgender people in couples and families. Turning to treatment, we review the relative usefulness of current couple and family therapy models. We conclude by making suggestions for improving the cultural competence of practicing clinicians and those in training.

Dominant definitions of relationship and family have historically not included sexual and gender minorities. This silence, which has its roots in heterosexism and homophobia, continues to have a profound impact on LGBTQ individuals, couples, and families. The field of couple and family therapy has, more often than not, mirrored public sentiment and helped perpetuate this silence. The following quotes, taken from some of the most widely read and influential books in the field of family therapy, are illustrative of the heterosexist, homophobic, and pathologizing views of several of the field's founders and leading theoreticians:

> This is also the problem of the homosexual who longs for an intense relationship with a "real" male, only to find that the latter is always, must always be, another homosexual. (Watzlawick, Helmick Beavin, & Jackson, 1967, p. 200)

> The failures of parents to maintain boundaries between generations and to adhere to their gender-linked roles led to incestuous problems, gender-identity confusions, and homosexual tendencies in both parents and offspring. (Lidz, 1969, p. 239)

> All psychiatric diagnoses, in fact, can be conceptualized on this continuum of adaptiveness or differentiation. The age of onset, severity, and impairment of life functioning associated with all psychiatric diagnoses can be understood in the context of the multigenerational emotional process. The most extreme forms of manic-depression, alcoholism, obsessive-compulsive neurosis, and homosexuality, for example, develop over the course of at least several generations. (Kerr & Bowen, 1988, p. 241)

The first two quotes mirror the psychoanalytic view of homosexuality in the 1960s and, though disturbing, are not surprising, given that homosexuality was still considered a mental illness at the time these passages were written. Probably the most disturbing is the last quote, which came from one of the most well-known and influential leaders in the field of couple and family therapy, Murray Bowen, who founded the Georgetown Family Center and was the first president of the American Family Therapy Academy (AFTA), and his protégé Michael Kerr in their description of the intergenerational impact of lack of differentiation. Unlike the previous quotes, this passage was published 15 years after homosexuality was removed as a diagnostic category of mental illness by the American Psychiatric Association (1974) and 2 years after ego-dystonic homosexuality was removed from the DSM (Gonsiorek, 1991). In a footnote explanation, they state that a person with "a pronounced homosexual lifestyle" is suffering from extreme levels of anxiety and undifferentiation that are the result of similar levels of parental anxiety and differentiation and that the "basic levels of differentiation are generations deep" (Kerr & Bowen, 1988, p. 241).

These quotations imply that homosexuality is inherently pathological, a sign of lack of differentiation of self, and that the "most extreme forms" of this pathology take multiple generations to develop in families, thus making families responsible for the development of homosexuality. Furthermore, there is the implication that gay men in particular not only are delusional about the possibility of finding love with each other but also are not *real* men, which is only the domain of heterosexual men. All these quotations are mired in the belief that pathology is inherent in families that do not subscribe to the patriarchal, heterosexual norm of distinct sex roles for men and women. Given that the quoted authors trained thousands of therapists and published writings that were widely read from the founding of the field through the 1990s, the impact of these ideas on the field of couple and family therapy cannot be overestimated (Bowen, 1985; Jackson, 1968; Kerr & Bowen, 1988; Lederer & Jackson, 1968; Watzlawick et al., 1967).

Most of the leaders in the field of couple and family therapy, though not blatantly homophobic, have taken a heteronormative stance and remained silent on the topic of LGBTQ couples and families. On a refreshing note, Salvador Minuchin, the founder of structural family therapy, as well as many prominent feminist family therapy scholars, had refrained from these pathologizing dialogues and have on several occasions briefly referred to gay and lesbian couples in normalizing ways (Imber-Black, 1988; McGoldrick, 1988; Minuchin & Fishman, 1981).

Review of Couple and Family Therapy Literature

A review of the mainstream literature in the field of marital or couple and family therapy reveals that progress regarding the recognition of LGBTQ couples and families often mirrors public opinion. Historically, family therapy was seen as a viable method to help convert homosexuals and cross-dressers, usually males, to gender-normative heterosexuality (Rutledge, 1975; Schwartz & Masters, 1983; Thorne, 1967). In the early 1970s, following the removal of "homosexuality" from the list of psychiatric disorders (American Psychiatric Association, 1974), a few case studies of "marital" therapy with same-sex couples began to appear in mainstream family therapy journals (Osman, 1972; Pendergrass, 1975). In addition, there were a few articles that focused on parents dealing with gay or lesbian children and on husbands in heterosexual marriages coming out as gay (Bozett, 1982; Coleman, 1981; Myers, 1981). This lack of inclusion of sexual orientation in mainstream family therapy literature was quantified by Clark and Serovich's (1997) content analysis of 20 years of family therapy journal articles from 1975 to 1995. These authors found that only 77 (.006%) articles out of more than 13,000 contained content related to sexual orientation or LGB issues. When same-sex couples were included, they were often viewed through a heterosexist lens that privileged gender conformity and traditional gender roles. For example, Krestan and Bepko's (1980) article on lesbian fusion put forth the notion that lesbian couples were fused and gay couples were disengaged. By overgeneralizing gender conformity theory and applying it without respect to the distinct differences in lesbian relationships, these authors engaged in gender stereotyping that resulted in a pathologizing of same-sex relationships that still continues (see the critique in R.-J. Green, Bettinger, & Zacks, 1996).

In the mid- to late 1980s, feminist family therapists began to include brief references to lesbian couples and families in their texts and journals, which ranged from a few lines acknowledging their existence to a single chapter or article (Brown, 1989; Evans, 1990; Laird, 1994; McGoldrick, 1988; Roth, 1985). At this same time, literature involving gay couples began to appear in mainstream journals and texts (Bahr & Weeks, 1989; Butler & Clarke, 1991; Carl, 1986; Keller & Rosen, 1988). Roth's (1985) article, which brought a contemporary gender and social justice perspective to working with lesbian families, represented a positive breakthrough in the field and challenged family therapists to move away from traditional notions of gender when working with lesbian couples. In the mid-1990s, much more was being written about lesbian and gay couples and families, although relatively little was published in mainstream family therapy journals. Most of the information was to be found in journals specifically focusing on lesbian and gay issues and did not necessarily focus on clinical applications with same-sex couples. The first clinical handbook to focus on lesbian and gay couples and families was published in 1996 (Laird & Green); until the publication of the current volume, it was the only applied text dealing with both lesbians and gay men in family relationships.

Since the publication of Clark and Serovich's review (1997), there has been a growing body of clinically oriented works for professionals that depict couples and families living outside the bounds of heterosexuality (e.g., Bigner, 2006; Bigner & Wetchler, 2004; R.-J. Green, 2001; R.-J. Green & Mitchell, 2008; Greenan & Tunnell, 2003; Laird, 1999; LaSala, 2001; Lev, 2004; Stone Fish & Harvey, 2005; Kranz & Daniluk, 2006; *Journal of Marital and Family Therapy*, 2000). These authors and journals have urged family therapists to develop family environments that acknowledge the unique experiences of LGBTQ people, and more recently to nurture queerness, thus challenging the field of couple and family therapy to rethink its notions of what constitutes *normal* and *healthy*. Despite this forward movement, however, the literature and training in the field of family therapy are still primarily situated in the paradigm that privileges heterosexuality.

While specialty LGBT journals and books have begun to address the full scope of the LGBTQ community, mainstream family therapy journals have continued to remain relatively silent with respect to experiences and treatment of bisexual, mixed-orientation, and transgender couples and families. Although the terms *bisexual* and *transgender* may be included in the titles of articles and chapters, often these issues are not addressed in the text or, when included, are often assumed to be the same as the lesbian and gay experience. The bisexual experience appears to be the most misunderstood in both the mainstream family therapy and LGBTQ literature, with transgender couples and families falling to a close second. Both these groups challenge the binary notion of sexuality and gender, which makes many people, including many gay men and lesbians, feel threatened.

Heterosexism and Heteronormativity

The words *marriage* and *family* are central to some of the most fiercely debated issues of our time. In the last 10 years, we have seen several countries around the world embrace same-sex couples as equal citizens as they legalize marriage for all people regardless of gender, and unprecedented numbers of other countries have legally created civil union/registered partner rights for same-sex couples (R.-J. Green & Mitchell, 2008; International Lesbian, 2010, p. 102; Marriage Equality, 2010). At the same time, we have witnessed religious conservatives and conversion therapy proponents help fuel fear, hatred, and condone violence against LGBTQ people. This fight in the public forum by LGBTQ couples and families to be recognized as legitimate and healthy family forms has its parallels in the field of couple and family therapy.

Despite increased visibility, the fact that millions of children in the United States are being raised by LGBTQ parents (Doherty & Simmons, 1996; Patterson, 2006), and evidence that children in these families are doing well (Biblarz & Stacey, 2010; Crowl, Ahn, & Baker, 2008; Gartrell & Bos, 2010; Tasker & Patterson, 2007; Wainright & Patterson, 2008; Wainright, Russell, &

Patterson, 2004), there remains no definition of family in the public consciousness that refers to same-sex, mixed-orientation, or transgender couples with children. In fact, the propaganda often used to instill fear in the public blatantly states that same-sex couples present a harm to children. Until fairly recently, the notions of lesbian mother, gay father, or lesbian or gay family would have been nonexistent and the constitutive terms seen as mutually exclusive (Hudak & Giammattei, 2010). Currently, this is still true of bisexual and transgender parents, couples, and families, rendering them invisible in both lesbian and gay and heterosexual communities. Although the public has begun to view same-sex couples with children as families, according to a recent opinion poll, this view does not hold true for same-sex couples without children (Crary, 2010).

The institutionalization of heterosexism and homophobia in Western culture has had a significant impact on the development and implementation of couple and family therapy theories and techniques. Heterosexism is the continued promotion by the major institutions in society that perpetuate the belief in the *superiority* of heterosexuality while simultaneously denigrating any nonheterosexual form of behavior or relationship (Anderson & Holliday, 2008; Herek, 1996; Kitzinger, 1996). According to Neisen (1993), "Heterosexism is based on prejudices just as racism, sexism, etc. When our institutions knowingly or unknowingly perpetuate these prejudices and intentionally or unintentionally act on them, heterosexism is at work" (p. 50).

An aspect of heterosexism and arguably the most powerful ideology supporting homophobic actions is society's belief in the normativity of traditional gender roles and gender expression. Gender is the socially constructed set of characteristics that define femininity and masculinity in a given cultural context. Gender expression refers to how one outwardly performs gender, whereas gender roles are the societal expectations about how people should perform their gender and what behaviors are deemed appropriate given one's biological sex. The reinforcement of traditional gender roles and intolerance for gender nonconformity are integral parts of heterosexism, thus stigmatizing those who are nonconforming in behavior or appearance, regardless of sexual orientation (Anderson & Holliday, 2008).

Heteronormativity, the dominant, pervasive, and subtle belief that a viable family consists of a heterosexual mother and father raising heterosexual children together (Gamson, 2000; Hudak & Giammattei, 2010), is differentiated from heterosexism by its uncritical adoption of heterosexuality as an established norm or standard, whereas the latter assumes that heterosexuality is superior, more natural, dominant, and the only acceptable and viable life option (Perlesz et al., 2006). Heteronormativity is an organizing principle that shapes and constrains family therapy theory, practice, research, and training; it is the measuring stick for what is considered normal and healthy for all individuals, couples, and families. Therefore, it has a profound impact on the current field of couple and family therapy and the subsequent treatment of LGBTQ couples and families (Hudak & Giammattei, 2010).

Well-meaning clinicians who neither hold nor endorse homophobic or heterosexist beliefs can get caught in the web of heteronormativity because it is a system of privilege that is often invisible to those who hold to it (Oswald, Blume, & Marks, 2005). This invisibility inevitably results in *microaggressions*, "the brief and commonplace daily verbal, behavioral, and environmental indignities, whether intentional or unintentional, that communicate hostile, derogatory, or negative slights" against LGBTQ individuals, couples, and families (Sue, 2010). The relative lack of mainstream applied clinical literature that considers LGBTQ couples and families in descriptions of treatment provides strong evidence that heteronormative beliefs have had an impact on the treatment of LGBTQ couples and families.

Notwithstanding some notable exceptions (Gottman, Levenson, Swanson, et al., 2003), much of the family therapy and research literature has taken an individual approach that reads as if LGBTQ people live in bubbles without partners, spouses, or families. This assumption stems, more often than not, from the heteronormative belief that couples and families are the domain of heterosexuals and that the primary issues for which LGBTQ clients enter therapy are related to their sexual orientation and/or gender identity rather than to more universal problems.

Despite the current positive cultural shifts and increase in available literature, the field of couple and family therapy continues to engage in heteronormative discourses. This is evidenced by the frequency with which the concepts of marriage, couple, and family are used in research, theory, training, and conference presentations without specifically naming heterosexuality, even though heterosexuality seems the taken-for-granted reference point in these contexts. Most of the past and current literature on couple and family therapy shows a consistent presumption of heterosexuality as the norm of couples and families seeking treatment (Hudak & Giammattei, 2010). The same is true for all but one of the couples and family therapy training tapes (Patten, 1997), a primary learning tool in psychotherapy, which use exclusively heterosexual couples, families, or youth as examples of clients. Unspecified heterosexuality maintains it as the default position, a position of dominance and superiority that continues to marginalize LGBTQ couples and families and render them invisible (Sue, 2010). One consequence of this silence is that many couple and family therapists are uncertain about how to conceptualize and intervene actively in the problems of LGBTQ and mixed-orientation couples and families. Furthermore, because many clinicians, regardless of their sexual orientation, have not addressed or even become aware of their own heteronormative bias, they often perpetuate this bias in their treatment of LGBTQ clients (Messinger, 2006). Therefore, even those clinicians who identify as highly qualified providers for LGBTQ couples and families may, despite their best intentions, often perpetuate a heteronormative bias in their treatment (Anderson & Holliday, 2008).

Central Issues

Over the last 20 years, the research on lesbian, gay, and bisexual (LGB) couples and families has revealed a few central issues with which these families must contend that their heterosexual counterparts do not. Although similarity in experience has been assumed, there are currently little to no data on the experience of couples and families where one or more of the members is transgendered (Nealy, 2008), and very little on the experience of bisexuals or their partners and children (Biblarz & Savci, 2010). What we know is that even in the most liberal communities, all LGBTQ people must deal with societal oppression and the extraordinary vulnerability and risk of claiming socially stigmatized or pathologized identities. These experiences can have a profound impact on all aspects of their lives and relationships.

The research on same-sex couples reveals that they generally want the same things that heterosexual couples want and struggle with similar issues. In some reports, same-sex couples actually seem to be faring better (Gottman, Levenson, Gross, et al., 2003), report more satisfaction (R.-J. Green et al., 1996), and are raising children who function better on mental health indices (Gartrell & Bos, 2010). Most same-sex couples navigate the adversity they face very well and are able to create lasting, healthy relational bonds (Gottman, Levenson, Gross, et al., 2003). When they do seek therapy, they generally come in with many of the same issues as heterosexual couples. They struggle with communication, finances, sex, parenting, and division of labor (R.-J. Green & Mitchell, 2008), and they are more likely to seek out therapy for these issues than for issues directly related to being LGB. At the same time, there are several key differences, both helpful and challenging, that clinicians need to understand and address when treating LGBTQ couples and families (Gottman, Levenson, Swanson, et al., 2003). Some of these differences are a result of discrimination, homo-, bi-, or transphobia, and heteronormativity, whereas others relate more to the specific dynamics that are often present between same-sex, mixed-orientation, and transgender couples (Connolly, 2004).

Discrimination and Prejudice

The discrimination and prejudice LGBTQ people experience have far-reaching effects. It influences not only how society treats them but also how families treat their LGBTQ children and how LGBTQ individuals treat themselves, their partners, and their own children. The degree this impacts the lives of LGBTQ people is dependent on the sociopolitical climate in which they live and the subculture or groups (e.g., ethnic, racial, or religious) to which they may belong (Goldberg, 2010). Discrimination, anti-LGBTQ attitudes, and the absence of legal and social supports not only make it difficult to connect but also serve to undermine the commitment that sexual minorities make to each other and invariably threaten their emotional and relational well-being.

Anti-LGBTQ Attitudes   Whether or not LGBTQ people experience discrimination and prejudice directly or vicariously (by identifying with others who have experienced discrimination or through antigay policies and political rhetoric), they are unlikely to escape internalizing some negative attitudes and shame (R.-J. Green, 2008). The internalization of anti-LGBTQ attitudes has been termed *internalized homophobia* (sometimes referred to as *internalized homonegativity*). For some sexual minorities, this antagonism appears in the form of internalized heteronormativity. Thus, individuals may be proud of being lesbian, gay, bisexual, or transgender, but they still hold beliefs that privilege heterosexuality, especially in the creation of couples and families. For example, a same-sex couple may be open about and proud of their relationship and still hold the belief that having children is the domain of only heterosexual couples.

Effects of Minority Stress   In addition to the experience of blatant homonegativity, the daily barrage of microaggressions most LGBTQ people endure creates a level of minority stress that has been shown to have deleterious emotional and physical effects. Although studies on minority stress have not included the transgender population, many studies have noted the life-long negative experiences many transgender and gender-variant people experience (Edney, 2004; Gordon & Meyer, 2007; Grossman, D'Augelli, Howell, & Hubbard, 2005; Grossman et al., 2009; Lombardi, Wilchins, Priesing, & Malouf, 2001; Mizock & Lewis, 2008) as well as the negative impact these experiences have on their mental and physical health (Clements-Nolle, Marx, & Katz, 2006; Grossman & D'Augelli, 2006, 2007). Therefore, the likelihood that this group has higher levels of stress-related symptoms than does the general population, as well as the LGB population, is extremely high. The studies exploring the effects of minority stress on LGBTQ individuals as compared to heterosexuals reveal significantly higher rates of many mental health concerns, notably depression, suicidal ideation, substance abuse, and anxiety, as well as participation in sexually risky situations (Goodman, 2005; Lewis, Derlega, Brown, & Rose, 2009; Meyer, 2003). Furthermore, the odds of having any psychiatric disorder were significantly increased in individuals reporting day-to-day experiences with discrimination (Levitt et al., 2009). Recent studies have shown that LGB individuals living in states that passed a marriage amendment reported significantly more minority stress (i.e., exposure to negative media messages and negative conversations, negative amendment-related affect, and LGB activism) and higher levels of psychological distress (i.e., negative affect, stress, anxiety, and depressive symptoms) than did heterosexuals or LGB individuals living in the other states (Hatzenbuehler, McLaughlin, Keyes, & Hasin, 2010; Rostosky, Riggle, Horne, & Miller, 2009). In fact, Hatzenbuehler et al. (2010) found that during the 2004 and 2005 elections, psychiatric disorders increased significantly for LGB individuals in states where marriage bans were instituted; the increases reported ranged from 36.3% for mood disorders to an alarming 248.2% for anxiety-related disorders. This increase in psychiatric disorders invariably puts more stress on couple and family relationships. Without legal recognition of their relationships, LGBTQ couples and their children become vulnerable in times of crisis.

LGBTQ Youth: Coming Out to Family of Origin

The cultural and religious contexts of families of origin have the potential to significantly impact LGBTQ youths' choice to come out and the experiences they may have as a result. Those families who live in very conservative or rural areas and/or belong to conservative religious organizations that condemn homosexuality and gender-variant behavior may have a much more difficult time coming to terms with and learning to support a LGBTQ child (Connolly, 2005; Stone Fish & Harvey, 2005). Families with homonegative attitudes often feel it is their responsibility to teach and enforce heterosexuality and often leave LGB youths without a safe place to deal with the harassment, discrimination, or invisibility they are experiencing (Nealy, 2008). The result for many youths is an experience of profound and pervasive isolation (Garnets & D'Augelli, 1994).

Coming out to parents is often one of the most difficult issues for LGBTQ youths, especially if they have grown up hearing negative messages about LGBTQ people. As a result, parents are often the last to find out that their child is LGBTQ (D'Augelli, Omoto, & Kurtzman, 2006; Savin Williams, 2005). Many LGBTQ youths will wait until they are no longer dependent on their parents for financial support before coming out, and some may never come out to their families out of a very real fear of rejection and loss of social support. Others, especially those youths who are gender nonconforming, will not have the choice about coming out, making them more likely to be victimized by teachers, peers, and family members regardless of their sexual orientation (D'Augelli, Grossman, & Starks, 2006).

Unlike racial and ethnic minorities, LGBTQ youths are usually raised by parents who are not like them and rarely have knowledge of what it is like to be LGBTQ; even in the most supportive families, the parents are unaware of the level of daily harassment these youths may endure and therefore do not know how to buffer their children from the discrimination they will experience (LaSala, 2010). Those individuals who are out often find that their identities are questioned or not taken seriously; they may be told their orientation is a phase or that it is unacceptable. Some youths may be hospitalized or forced into conversion therapies by families who have been convinced they can change.

Even in families that are accepting, LGBTQ youth are left out of common dating rituals and often have to hide their same-sex interests. Their relationships are not celebrated or even allowed expression publicly without threat of backlash. In some cases, because of society's focus on the sexual behavior of LGBTQ people, their relationships may become sexualized in ways that heterosexual youths' relationships are not. For example, if a young gay adolescent were to hold his boyfriend's hand or sit close on the couch while watching a movie, the parent may see that behavior as evidence of a sexual relationship, whereas they are less likely to make the same assumptions when his heterosexual sister shows similar affection toward her boyfriend.

There is a significant amount of evidence, such as the recent rash of *bullycides* (being bullied to the point of taking one's life) being reported in the media, that the effects of minority stress on LGBTQ youths can often be intolerable. Without positive role models, parental and family support, and resources to combat the harassment and discrimination, these young people are left with a burden that appears insurmountable. Studies consistently show that LGBTQ youth, especially those who are gender nonconforming, who have suffered significant harassment at school or at home have much higher rates of depression, suicide attempts, substance abuse, homelessness, high-risk sexual behavior, and school absenteeism or dropouts (Grossman & D'Augelli, 2007; National Gay & Lesbian Task Force, 2010; Ryan, Huebner, Diaz, & Sanches, 2009). In contrast, LGBTQ youths who have family support and positive role models are better able to navigate the discrimination and have significantly better mental and physical health outcomes (Erich, Tittsworth, Dykes, & Cabuses, 2008; Grossman et al., 2005; LaSala, 2010; Ryan et al., 2009).

LGBTQ youths are not the only ones who have to deal with LGBTQ discrimination; families and parents who support their LGBTQ children are themselves frequently ostracized from community, friends, and sometimes even extended family. They may be blamed for creating their child's sexual orientation or gender variance as a result of their poor parenting. Such isolation is especially true for those individuals who live in conservative, rural areas or attend conservative religious organizations. Parents often need to reconcile their beliefs, understand their fears, and grieve the loss of any heteronormative dreams they may have had for their child before they can come to a place of acceptance and learn to truly nurture their LGBTQ child (Brill & Pepper, 2008; LaSala, 2010; Stone Fish & Harvey, 2005).

Same-Sex Couples

The sociopolitical climate has a profound influence on how same-sex couples meet and how their relationships develop. Historically, they had limited places to meet each other and interact. More often than not, these meetings occurred in gay bars, especially for men. Women, on the other hand, were more likely to meet at work or through friends (Bryant & Demian, 1994). With the growth of LGBTQ social activities outside of bars and the increased visibility of the LGBTQ community, especially in urban environments, the possible ways to meet partners have exploded. Internet dating and social networking websites have made it much easier for potential partners to find each other without the risks inherent in other venues. This has been particularly valuable to people living in communities and social contexts where homophobia is rampant, where the LGBTQ community is invisible or hard to find and where finding partners and dating are difficult and often clandestine.

Relational Ambiguity   After meeting each other, same-sex couples may face potential issues that can arise as a result of the stigmatized nature of their relationship and the lack of a normative or legal template for creating couple bonds or families. Unlike heterosexual couples, same-sex couples have no culturally defined way of being and becoming a couple. As a result, how the relationship unfolds, the decisions around who does what within the context of the relationship, levels of monogamy or nonmonogamy, financial obligations to one another, and future intentions are often left to the couple to create on their own. Although this lack of template allows them healthy flexibility, it also creates a higher level of relational ambiguity than is experienced by most heterosexual couples who can, through engagement and marriage, bring greater legal and emotional clarity to their couple commitment (R.-J. Green & Mitchell, 2008). This ambiguity not only is confusing for same-sex couples but also profoundly impacts the level of social support available to them through their families, friends, and communities. For example, many families do not acknowledge the significance of a same-sex partner, recognize the couple's status, or consider the partner a family member despite the couple's many years of living together, engaging in ceremonies to proclaim their commitment, and attending family events.

Internalized Homophobia and Levels of Coming Out   An issue that is directly related to both external and internalized homophobia is whether or not the partners are out as lesbian, gay, or bisexual and how out the couple is in particular social venues. When partners have differing levels of being out, there is a potential for conflict and hurt feelings. The reasons for staying "in the closet" are many. For some people, being out means risking the loss of their job, their home, their children, their families, their social standing, and in some social contexts their physical safety or life. In such cases as these, staying closeted is a functional and protective strategy. At the same time, the psychological effect of staying in the closet can reduce one's sense of well-being. If one partner is in the closet and the other is partially or completely out, conflicts invariably arise. Closeted partners may feel threatened by their out partners' activities, whereas the out partners may feel that closeted partners do not value them or the relationship, especially if closeted partners are not out to their families. For mixed-orientation and transgender couples where the stigma may be different for each partner, this issue can become even more complex (Buxton, 2006; Lev, 2004; Malpas, 2006), especially if one partner comes out as a LGBT after the relationship is established. Furthermore, the difficulties couples experience with respect to coming out has the potential to become exacerbated in political climates where LGBTQ civil rights are being hotly debated.

Limited Social Support   One of the most difficult issues for sexual minority couples is their lack of social support. Unlike heterosexual couples who receive a lot of family and community support, sexual minority couples are more likely to find a complete lack of support and even resistance from heterosexual parents, their own families, and sometimes even the LGBTQ community. Such life transitions as commitments and marriage, parenthood, raising adolescents, empty nests, aging, and health issues are stressful for all couples, but for LGBTQ couples the lack of social support can make these stressful events even more difficult. Without support, many couples do not survive these transitions intact.

Often, LGBTQ people are not fully embraced by their families of origin. Even when LGBTQ individuals are included in family events, their relationships are often not given the same recognition as are those of their heterosexual family members. Some couples find that this neglect shifts when they bring children into the relationship. It may be that the act of having children, which is a heterosexual relationship rite of passage, lessens the ambiguity of the LGBTQ relationship and puts it in a context that heterosexuals family members can understand. Furthermore, LGBTQ people are also less likely to have interconnected social networks than are heterosexual couples and often have to go through much more effort to create these connections. Couples who successfully navigate issues around discrimination, internalized homophobia, and relational ambiguity have been able to create a network of social supports often referred to as "family of choice." These social supports help all couples navigate life's crises and celebrate life's joys (Goldberg, 2010; R.-J. Green & Mitchell, 2008).

Parenting and the Creation of Families

The sociopolitical climate, legal and social support, and level of internalized homophobia have a significant influence on a LGBTQ person's decision to consider parenthood. It also impacts LGBTQ parents already raising children as well as influences the amount of contact they have with their families of origin (Goldberg, 2010).

Despite much evidence to the contrary (Biblarz & Stacey, 2010; Crowl et al., 2008; Gartrell & Bos, 2010; Tasker & Patterson, 2007; Wainright & Patterson, 2008; Wainright et al., 2004), many LGBTQ people who deal with internalized homophobia and heteronormative assumptions may question whether it is harmful for them to raise children. Parents raising children from previous heterosexual relationships may try to hide their sexuality from the children, giving them the message there is something wrong with the parent and thereby denying the children a space to talk about experiences in school or things they hear about in the media. Others, who choose to become parents after coming out, may have difficulty finding resources and medical professionals to help them become parents. Many sexual minorities who are unable to conceive children on their own may find that other methods of bringing children into their lives are cost prohibitive even if they can find services willing to work with them. Furthermore, adoption agencies may not be willing to place children with them or will do so only if they remain in the closet and one parent adopts the child. In addition, many states do not allow second-parent adoptions, leaving one parent without any parental rights. Even for those LGBTQ individuals who do reside in states where second-parent adoption is legal, other states may not recognize them as a legal parent and leave these families incredibly vulnerable when they travel or if they separate and one partner relocates to another state.

Lack of legal recognition for sexual minority families puts both the children and parents in these families at great risk. For couples where the children came from a previous heterosexual relationship, there is always a risk of being denied access to their children by homophobic families, ex-spouses, and family courts. In cases of divorce or death, a nonbiological parent may have his or her parental rights challenged, risk losing the family home, and lack access to recourse in case of wrongful death or if the ex-partner tries to keep the nonbiological parent from seeing the children. In other cases, a nonbiological parent may not be able to advocate for his or her child in the schools or regarding medical care. The children are sometimes left feeling as if there is something wrong with their families.

Lack of social support is particularly difficult when trying to raise children. Having grandparents and siblings available to help with child care and lend moral or financial support in tough times is invaluable to most families. Yet LGBTQ family members often do not receive the same level of emotional support that their heterosexual siblings do. Children in these families can be left with little connection to their extended family, or they can be put in situations where they hear negative comments about their parents' sexuality by people they love and trust (Goldberg, 2010).

Bisexual Couples and Families

Very few studies have examined bisexual or mixed-orientation couples, and even fewer have investigated their families. Generally it is assumed they are the same as other couples. In other words, it is assumed that in such couples, one partner is either gay or lesbian, or heterosexual, depending on the sex of the other partner. Bisexuals in same-sex relationships deal with biphobia in both the heterosexual and LGT communities (Dodge & Sandfort, 2007), as well as, many of the same issues dealt with by lesbian and gay couples and families. Out of all the groups under the umbrella labeled *queer*, bisexuals are probably the most misunderstood and the most invisible. They often receive the message that bisexuality does not exist or that bisexuals are promiscuous, carriers of sexually transmitted diseases (STDs), unable to be monogamous, and generally harmful to both the heterosexual and the lesbian and gay communities (Beaber, 2008; Firestein, 2007; Rust, 2007). As a result, many bisexuals "stay in the closet" with their partners and communities for fear of being condemned, ostracized, and abandoned.

Often feeling isolated, bisexuals experience relatively high levels of depression and self-harming behaviors (Dodge & Sandfort, 2007). The resulting impact on the couple and family can be a distancing between the couple, infidelity, and feelings of betrayal, confusion, and hurt if the bisexual partner discloses after the relationship is established. Partners often feel betrayed, even if there has been no infidelity. The cultural messages around bisexuality and biphobia have a profound impact on how same-sex and other-sex partners handle this information and their decision to stay with the bisexual partner (Buxton, 2006; Carlsson, 2007). These couples often find themselves without community support, especially if they try to make their relationship work. Many of the opposite sex, mixed-orientation couples in which the male partner comes out as bisexual do not stay together (Buxton, 2006). This consequence may partly be attributable to the social isolation and biphobia that results from the heteronormative ideas around what constitutes a couple or a family and how those relationships are supposed to play out, in addition to the ability of the two individuals to work things out (Wolkomir, 2009).

Transgender Couples and Families

Transgender couples and families are only slightly more visible than bisexual and mixed-orientation couples. Families with transgender children have become much more visible lately as a result of several popular, gender-affirming documentaries. The impact of these media depictions has been an increase in understanding of gender issues in adults. Yet, society continues to support rigid gender prescriptions and fear of anything outside the binary norm of male/female. As a result, when it becomes apparent that a family member, partner, or spouse is transgender, the family is thrown into a crisis. How members of the family they deal with this revelation depends on their own notions of gender, parenting, and level of social support. Parents who accept their transgender child may find themselves ridiculed and ostracized in their own communities for not *properly* parenting their children (Brill & Pepper, 2008; Lev, 2004).

Transgender couples come in all sorts of configurations and sexual orientations. In many cases where the couple looks heteronormative or gay or lesbian, they are assumed to be like every other couple in their community and may live an invisible existence similar to that of bisexuals, with similar benefits and costs (Denny, 2007). When one or both partners in the couple are obviously transgender, they are at risk for ostracism from their communities and families, and they become targets for violence and discrimination.

Many transgender couples go through a coming-out process because often transpeople enter relationships without acknowledging their struggles around gender. Sometimes this concealment is conscious, but often it is not. When a partner comes out as transgender, and especially if he or she intends to transition, the couple is thrown into a crisis. This result often happens even if a nontransgender partner knows about the gender issues going into the relationship. Issues around identity, community, sexuality, sexual orientation, and much more become central for both partners (Malpas, 2006; Raj, 2008; Samons, 2009). The issues differ significantly from those faced by partners who come out as LGB in a relationship because generally the partners of the latter do not question their own gender and sexual identity. In the case of couples with a transgender partner, individuals in the relationship need to navigate all these areas. It is a testament to the strength of such couples that despite the transphobia and upheaval, many are able to stay together through the transition (Malpas, 2006; Mason, 2007).

It appears that the farther individuals, couples, and families get from the binary notions of gender and sexuality, that is, from heteronormative notions of what constitutes a couple, a family, and a healthy relationship, the more likely they are to experience discrimination; internalized homo-, bi-, and transphobia; and minority stress. They are also much less likely to have a social support system to help them deal with these issues. For those individuals who also deal with multiple levels of oppression (age, ability, race or ethnicity, etc.), these issues can become compounded and their resources even more limited (Long, Bonomo, Andrews, & Brown, 2006). At the same time, given the number of long-term happy relationships in evidence, there is also an incredible amount of resilience to be found in LGBTQ families and communities (Long & Andrews, 2007).

LGBT Elders

LGBT elder couples and their families are faced with a much higher level of heterosexism and homonegativity than are younger cohorts. Many LGBT elders find that they are forced to go back into the closet in order to access medical care and housing. Couples are often torn apart as they begin to require more care but the facilities designed to address these issues do not accommodate same-sex couples (Balsam & D'Augelli, 2006). As they become more dependent on others, LGBT individuals find that their connection with family becomes much more important (Cook-Daniels, 2006; Kimmel, Rose, Orel, & Green, 2006). Legal documentation and financial planning are much more significant issues for LGBT elders because their partners and families are not guaranteed access to the same resources as are those of non-LGBT elders (Cook-Daniels, 2006; Dworkin, 2006; Kimmel et al., 2006). Despite many of these difficulties, community organizations geared toward LGBT seniors are becoming more widely available, and gerontologists are beginning to recognize that there are LGBT seniors with specific needs (Kimmel et al., 2006). Therefore, it is highly likely that LGBT people who are currently middle-aged may have a very different experience as they reach retirement than had those elders who came before them.

Current Trends and the Future Directions

Couple and Family Therapy

As of this writing, there are no known couple or family therapy treatment protocols that have been empirically validated with sexual and gender minority couples and families. Most family therapy texts and treatment manuals do not discuss the viability of treatment with LGBTQ clients or assume that treatment protocols that work for heterosexual couples translate easily to working with LGBTQ couples. When such couples are included, the literature usually refers only to lesbian and gay couples (Dodge & Sandfort, 2007). Despite this lack of validated treatment methods, several authors have made compelling arguments for the usefulness of various mainstream treatments with this population (Balsam, Martell, & Safren, 2006; Bettinger, 2004; Butler, 2009; Coates & Sullivan, 2005; Deacon, Reinke, & Viers, 1996; Greenan & Tunnell, 2003; Josephson, 2003; Knudson-Martin & Laughlin, 2005; Long et al., 2006; Martell, Safren, & Prince, 2004; Negy & McKinney, 2006; Saltzburg, 2007; Szymanski, 2005; Treyger, Ehlers, Zajicek, & Trepper, 2008). The influence of feminist family therapists has certainly moved the treatment models forward with respect to gender and power, which adds support to these arguments. The most often noted systemic models that have been discussed when working with same-sex couples and families are structural, feminist, narrative, emotion-focused, solution-focused, and cognitive-behavioral therapies. There have also been texts that recommend integration of several of these treatment styles to address the various issues that come up with LGBTQ clients (Coates & Sullivan, 2005; Lev, 2004; Stone Fish & Harvey, 2005).

The clinical literature that explores the use of specific couples and family models with same-sex couples generally begins with a discussion of the notable differences between these couples and heterosexual couples. The primary differences noted are the effects of discrimination and minority stress; the experience of biculturalism; partner cultural and stage differences; coming out in relationships; gender differences regarding monogamy; emotional intimacy and sex; issues around gender role socialization; invalidation of the couple and loss of heterosexual privilege in families of origin; and the lack of role models, which is closely tied to the concept of relational ambiguity. The models are then presented, more often than not, with heterosexual couples, after which the differences are explored using the model with LGB couples. A notable exception to this is Long et al.'s (2006) description of the prominent systemic models and their potential use with LGBTQ clients wherein each model's strengths and weaknesses are explored through brief clinical vignettes with LGBTQ couples and families.

Currently, there is a dearth of literature exploring the usefulness of mainstream family and couple treatment protocols with transgender couples and families and very little that addresses the issues of bisexual and mixed-orientation couples in same-sex relationships. Most of the literature on these families is focused on the unique issues that a couple's therapist will more than likely encounter when working with a mixed-orientation or transgender couple. In addition to dealing with the differences outlined for same-sex couples, these couples have to negotiate the differences in their identities, the betrayal often experienced by the non-LGBT spouse or partner, the possible renegotiation of their sex lives, and, in some cases, shifts in sexual and social orientation (Buxton, 2004, 2006; Malpas, 2006; Raj, 2008; Treyger et al., 2008). Treyger et al. (2008) have recommended a solution-focused approach when working with mixed-orientation couples, whereas those researchers who have addressed the use of clinical models for working with transgender couples and families have introduced either an integration of different theories (Malpas, 2006) or an entirely new model (Raj, 2008).

Regardless of the model used, it is important that it address the issues presented by the couple or family without inadvertently blaming the clients for the impact of discrimination and internalized homonegativity. Such postmodern and social constructionist models as feminist and narrative approaches have been used in this arena because they directly address the system from a sociopolitical perspective.

It is important that clinicians maintain an awareness of the heteronormativity inherent in the models they use, address these issues, and modify the protocols accordingly. For example, most couple and family therapy models consider nonmonogamy detrimental to the maintenance of a relationship. Although this model may hold true for most heterosexual couples, it may not be true for LGBTQ couples, many of whom have come to define fidelity much more flexibly, including the possibility of sexual nonexclusivity or polyamory. Furthermore, structural family therapy, which is very helpful with families raising children as well as with couples, may focus on hierarchies that do not resonate for LGBTQ couples, especially with respect to gender roles and distribution of labor. Many of the family therapy models may have the same pitfalls, especially if practiced by a clinician who holds heteronormative views around gender and gender roles. If, however, one is focused on the experience of the clients rather than gendered notions of how people are supposed to behave, many of these models may prove to be quite useful.

The significant differences found with regard to emotional experiences, relationship satisfaction, and dissolution that have been found between lesbian, gay, and heterosexual couples (Gottman, Levenson, Gross, et al., 2003; Gottman, Levenson, Swanson, et al., 2003) need to be clearly accounted for within any couple's treatment protocol. For example, treatment should address that same-sex couples experience lower satisfaction and show a higher risk of dissolution with low levels of physiological arousal (the opposite of heterosexual couples). Furthermore, gay male couples may be less effective in repairing an interaction if it becomes negative, and lesbians tend to feel supported more by affection than validation, whereas the reverse may be true for gay men (Gottman, Levenson, Gross, et al., 2003).

Gottman, Levenson, Gross, et al. (2003) have suggested that treatment focusing on emotional connection as opposed to the level of positivity or negativity in interactions may be more helpful for same-sex couples. Furthermore, with gay male couples, interventions focusing on processes that may interfere with their ability to repair negative interactions may help them better maintain stability. It may be that emotion-focused couple therapy, which is based on attachment and emotion, could be particularly applicable, given the findings of Gottman, Levenson, Gross, et al. (2003) and the high potential for ruptures to attachment as a result of discrimination and internalized homonegativity.

A very promising move in family therapy, not only for LGBTQ clients but also for all couples and families, is the "queering" of family therapy. Stone Fish and Harvey (2005) describe a model that successfully merges queer theory, postmodern approaches, and family therapy in a way that is respectful of all people, yet addresses heteronormativity head on, not only for LGBTQ clients but for everyone. Rather than taking the stance that having a queer family member is something to *cope* with, family therapy should take the radical stance that diversity is normative and should uphold the value and beauty of nonheterosexual or gender-variant family members not *in spite of* their identity but because of it (Hudak & Giammattei, 2010). This model is based in the reality that societal notions around gender, gender roles, and sexual orientation have affected everyone, and all people should have the opportunity to deconstruct these ideas and evaluate whether or not they work in the best interest of their relationships.

Training of Couple and Family Therapists

The importance of training couple and family therapists to work affirmatively with sexual and gender minority clients cannot be overstated. Studies have shown that 70–90% of couple and family therapists work with LGB clients (Godfrey, Haddock, Fisher, & Lund, 2006). Furthermore, the ethical codes for all mental health practitioners have an expectation that clinicians will "do no harm" and maintain a level of cultural competence when working with minority groups. Among others, the National Association of Social Workers, American Association for Marriage and Family Therapy (AAMFT), and American Psychological Association have statements about appropriate treatment of LGBTQ clients that include having knowledge of the LGBTQ experience, understanding one's own biases, providing respectful treatment that includes avoiding heterosexist assumptions, and seeking continuing education to work with these groups. Despite this requirement, many couple and family therapists are not well trained and do not feel equipped to treat sexual minority clients.

Graduate-Level Training   In 1996, half of the AAMFT clinical members did not feel competent working with lesbian and gay clients (Doherty & Simmons, 1996). Although a more recent study of Master's in social work (MSW) students showed that there has been some improvement, with clinicians showing lower levels of homophobia than in past years, low levels of competence and high levels of bi- and transphobia remain (Logie, Bridge, & Bridge, 2007). Social workers were often uninformed regarding relevant issues or inadequately prepared for working with these populations. Forty-two percent of the students expressed that they lacked knowledge about the issues and challenges facing LGBTQ populations and had a low level of competence in working with them.

A recent survey of couple and family therapists revealed that students may be hearing about heterosexism or heterosexual privilege, but this training does not seem to influence their beliefs in the existence of heterosexism as a social structure that oppresses LGBTQ-identified individuals (Rock, Carlson, & McGeorge, 2010). This study found that over 60% of the participants reported they had received no training on affirmative therapy practices and no training on LGB identity development models. Nevertheless, participants perceive themselves to be "somewhat competent" when working with LGB clients and have low levels of self-reported homophobia. Although they indicated a moderate level of understanding of how heterosexism and discrimination impact clinical practice, they do not feel highly competent in the skills needed to treat LGBTQ clients. Overall, more coursework in affirmative therapy practices was predictive of students' overall self-reported clinical competency related to working with LGB clients, whereas the number of weeks that were dedicated to LGB identity development models was not predictive.

A similar study of marriage and family therapist (MFT) attitudes and knowledge (M. S. Green, Murphy, Blumer, & Palmanteer, 2009) found that 95% reported that they learned about gay and lesbian persons through clinical experience; less than 65% reported learning in graduate school; 46% report they learned through supervision during graduate training; and 89% learned about gay and lesbian persons through personal connections. Female clinicians reported feeling more comfortable than males working with lesbian or gay people; both were more comfortable working with lesbians.

It is clear that generalist family therapy training is not sufficient for working with the LGBTQ population and may actually be harmful to LGB couples and families because of the inherent heteronormative bias (Godfrey et al., 2006; Perosa, Perosa, & Queener, 2008). Recent studies support the previously held notion that becoming a LGB affirmative therapist requires an understanding of the realities of homophobia and heterosexism and the influences each has on the lives of therapists and clients alike (Bernstein, 2000; Godfrey et al., 2006; Long & Serovich, 2003). Also, increased contact with LGB people and their lives reduces homophobia and increases positive attitudes about LGB people (S. K. Green & Bobele, 1994; Long & Serovich, 2003). Regardless of sexual orientation or gender identity, it is important that clinicians who work with sexual and gender minorities pay attention to the self-of the-therapist, engage in deconstructing their own biases, and come to understand themselves as gendered and sexual beings (Long, 1996; Long & Bonomo, 2006). Furthermore, working from a systemic, contextual perspective that helps clients see the sociopolitical issues that affect their lives is an important component of treatment (Godfrey et al., 2006).

Training Guidelines   Given that therapists are not immune to the dominant homophobic and heterosexist assumptions in our society (Long & Serovich, 2003) and that the ethical guidelines for all clinicians prescribe a certain level of cultural competence when working with LGBTQ clients, graduate training programs have an obligation to help students learn the basics neces-sary to work affirmatively with LGBTQ clients. It is possible for graduate training programs and clinical supervision to serve as an opportunity for self-exploration and self-awareness in regard to a variety of diversity issues, including sexual orientation and gender identity. The research suggests that more training in regard to diversity not only would have the potential to increase self-awareness, which may increase comfort levels in working with this population, but also may help mental health clinicians feel more prepared in working with LGBTQ clients (M. S. Green et al., 2009; Rock et al., 2010).

There are several areas that programs and supervision need to focus in order to help therapists become better equipped to work with LGBTQ clients. The most important work for clinicians is to pay close attention to self-of-the-therapist (Godfrey et al., 2006). It is imperative that trainees examine their own beliefs, values, comfort levels, biases, prejudices, and so on about sex, gender, and sexual orientation. They need not only to understand their obvious biases but also to chal-lenge their own heteronormative beliefs, especially around what constitutes a couple or fam-ily, as well as sexual behavior and notions around gendered behavior (Long & Bonomo, 2006). This awareness can begin by helping trainees deconstruct their own experiences of heterosexual privilege, gender, sexual orientation, and gender roles, noting how society has enforced certain rules around these. This self-examination is an important exercise for all clinicians regardless of gender identity and sexual orientation. Clinicians who have not done this work are at risk for inadvertently breaking the therapeutic alliance with their clients and using therapeutic tech-niques that perpetuate heterosexist and heteronormative biases.

Trainees also need to understand the experience and effects of prejudice and discrimination on LGBTQ clients and the resulting impact on the formation and maintenance of couple and family relationships. Clinicians unaware of these experiences may, as a result of their lack of insight, pathologize clients for the oppression they experience in society and thus perpetuate myths about LGBTQ individuals, couples, and families (Herek, 2007; Rye & Meaney, 2009). Clinicians can learn through reading the vast amount of literature on these topics, by speaking with LGBTQ people about their experiences, and by participating in cultural activities within the community, especially politically related gatherings.

Several researchers have suggested that trainees need to learn to work with LGBTQ clients from a systemic perspective (Godfrey et al., 2006; R.-J. Green, 2008; Piper & Mannino, 2008; Rock et al., 2010). Clinicians risk pathologizing their clients for the psychological effects of dis-crimination, homonegativity, and heteronormativity and may inadvertently harm their clients in the process. It is very important that clinicians and clients look at the sociopolitical context in which the clients live and the effects this context may be having on the client's mental health and relationships.

Many studies have found that homonegativity decreases when a person knows someone personally who is a sexual minority and that clinicians who know LGB people feel much better equipped to work with them as clients (Pettigrew & Tropp, 2000; Rye & Meaney, 2009) and are much less likely to hold "overly pathologized views of their capacities and possibilities" (Bernstein, 2000, p. 445). Trainees avoid this pitfall by establishing relationships with LGBTQ colleagues and connecting with family members who may be LGBTQ, as well as engaging in social and political activities alongside LGBTQ people.

Graduate training programs and supervisors can require trainees to interview LGBTQ people who are not clients in order to get the inside, qualitative perspective on ordinary LGBTQ lives and relationships. Furthermore, it is most important that trainees have supervisors who have expertise in supervising LGBTQ cases and have done their own work around deconstructing gender and sexual orientation (Godfrey et al., 2006; Long & Bonomo, 2006). Finally, graduate programs could increase the cultural competence of future clinicians in working with LGBTQ clients if they were to incorporate accurate information into all courses and not leave it to students to take a special course on LGBTQ issues to garner this information.

Where Do We Go From Here?

Although many advances have been made in our understanding of LGBTQ clients, we still have a long way to go before these clients are represented appropriately in the literature. There are still many holes in our knowledge base. Mainstream couple and family researchers need to become more aware of the heteronormative bias in their studies and, at the very least, include items on their demographic questionnaires inquiring about research participants' sexual attractions, behaviors, orientation identities, and gender-related behaviors and identities. More studies are needed that focus on the experience of same-sex mixed-orientation and transgender couples, as well as the families they create. Furthermore, studies are needed that validate the treatment models we are using with LGBTQ couples and families.

Evidenced-based treatments need to be developed with LGBTQ individuals, couples, and families that directly address the distinct issues with which they are dealing, among them differences in emotional experience, minority stress, and internalized homonegativity, anxiety, depression, and substance abuse. By far, the most important thing that needs to be resolved is the lack of cultural competency around LGBTQ issues expressed by clinicians in the field, especially those still in graduate school. Training programs need to address the relevant issues faced by LGBTQ clients. The continued invisibility of LGBTQ people in training programs only serves to perpetuate the marginalization and discrimination of LGBTQ clients and inherently causes harm.

References

American Psychiatric Association. (1974). Position statement on homosexuality and civil rights. *American Journal of Psychiatry, 131*, 497.

Anderson, S., & Holliday, M. (2008). How heterosexism plagues practitioners in services for lesbians and their families. *Journal of Gay & Lesbian Social Services, 19*(2), 81–100.

Bahr, J. M., & Weeks, G. R. (1989). Sexual functioning in a nonclinical sample of male couples. *American Journal of Family Therapy, 17*(2), 110–127. doi:10.1080/01926188908250758

Balsam, K. F., & D'Augelli, A. R. (2006). The victimization of older LGBT adults: Patterns, impact, and implications for intervention. In D. Kimmel, T. Rose, & S. David (Eds.), *Lesbian, gay, bisexual, and transgender aging: Research and clinical perspectives* (pp. 110–130). New York, NY: Columbia University Press.

Balsam, K. F., Martell, C. R., & Safren, S. A. (2006). Affirmative cognitive-behavioral therapy with lesbian, gay, and bisexual people. In P. A. Hays & G. Y. Iwamasa (Eds.), *Culturally responsive cognitive-behavioral therapy: Assessment, practice, and supervision* (pp. 223–243). Washington, DC: American Psychological Association.

Beaber, T. (2008). *Well-being among bisexual females: The roles of internalized biphobia, stigma conscious-ness, social support, and self-disclosure.* 69, ProQuest Information & Learning. Available from EBSCOhost psyh database. Retrieved from http://0-search.ebscohost.com.library.alliant.edu/login.aspx?direct=true&db=psyh&AN=2008-99200-543&site=ehost-live&scope=site

Bernstein, A. C. (2000). Straight therapists working with lesbians and gays in family therapy *Journal of Marital & Family Therapy, 26,* 443–454.

Bettinger, M. (2004). A family systems approach to sex therapy with gay male couples. *Journal of Couple & Relationship Therapy, 3*(2–3), 65–74.

Biblarz, T. J., & Savci, E. (2010). Lesbian, gay, bisexual, and transgender families. *Journal of Marriage & Family, 72*(3), 480–497. doi:10.1111/j.1741-3737.2010.00714.x

Biblarz, T. J., & Stacey, J. (2010). How does the gender of parents matter? *Journal of Marriage & Family, 72*(1), 3–22. doi:10.1111/j.1741-3737.2009.00678.x

Bigner, J. J. (2006). *An introduction to GLBT family studies.* New York, NY: Haworth Press.

Bigner, J. J., & Wetchler, J. L. (2004). *Relationship therapy with same-sex couples.* New York, NY: Haworth Press.

Bowen, M. (1985). *Family therapy in clinical practice.* New York, NY: Aronson.

Bozett, F. W. (1982). Heterogenous couples in heterosexual marriages: Gay men and straight women. *Journal of Marital and Family Therapy, 8*(1), 81–89.

Brill, S., & Pepper, R. (2008). *The transgender child: A handbook for families and professionals.* San Francisco, CA: Cleis Press.

Brown, L. S. (1989). New voices, new visions: Toward a lesbian/gay paradigm for psychology. *Psychology of Women Quarterly, 13*(4), 445.

Bryant, A. S., & Demian. (1994). Relationship characteristics of American gay and lesbian couples: Findings from a national survey. *Journal of Gay & Lesbian Social Services, 1,* 101–117.

Butler, C. (2009). Sexual and gender minority therapy and systemic practice. *Journal of Family Therapy, 31*(4), 338–358. doi:10.1111/j.1467-6427.2009.00472.x

Butler, M., & Clarke, J. (1991). Couple therapy with homosexual men. In D. Hooper & W. Dryden (Eds.), *Couple therapy: A handbook* (pp. 196–206). Maidenhead, Berkshire, England: Open University Press.

Buxton, A. P. (2004). Works in progress: How mixed-orientation couples maintain their marriages after the wives come out. *Journal of Bisexuality, 4*(1/2), 57–82. doi:10.1300/J159v04n01_06

Buxton, A. P. (2006). Counseling heterosexual spouses of bisexual men and women and bisexual heterosexual couples: Affirmative approaches. *Journal of Bisexuality, 6*(1/2), 105–135. doi:10.1300/J159v06n01_07

Carl, D. (1986). Acquired immune deficiency syndrome: A preliminary examination of the effects on gay couples and coupling. *Journal of Marital and Family Therapy, 12*(3), 241–247.

Carlsson, G. (2007). Counseling the bisexual married man. In B. A. Firestein (Ed.), *Becoming visible: Counseling bisexuals across the lifespan* (pp. 108–126). New York, NY: Columbia University Press.

Clark, W. M., & Serovich, J. M. (1997). Twenty years and still in the dark? Content analysis of articles pertaining to gay, lesbian, and bisexual issues in marriage and family therapy journals. *Journal of Marital & Family Therapy, 23*(3), 239–253.

Clements-Nolle, K., Marx, R., & Katz, M. (2006). Attempted suicide among transgender persons: The influence of gender-based discrimination and victimization. *Journal of Homosexuality, 51*(3), 53–69.

Coates, J., & Sullivan, R. (2005). Achieving competent family practice with same-sex parents: Some promising directions. *Journal of GLBT Family Studies, 1*(2), 89. doi:10.1300/J461v01n02¬ï06

Coleman, E. (1981). Bisexual and gay men in heterosexual marriage: Conflicts and resolutions in therapy. *Journal of Homosexuality, 7*(2–3), 93–103. doi:10.1300/J082v07n02_11

Connolly, C. M. (2004). Clinical issues with same-sex couples: A review of the literature. In J. J. Bigner & J. L. Wetchler (Eds.), *Relationship therapy with same-sex couples* (pp. 3–12). New York, NY: Haworth Press.

Connolly, C. M. (2005). A process of change: The intersection of the GLBT individual and their family of origin. *Journal of GLBT Family Studies, 1*(1), 5. doi:10.1300/J461v01n01¬ï02

Cook-Daniels, L. (2006). Trans aging. In D. Kimmel, T. Rose, & S. David (Eds.), *Lesbian, gay, bisexual, and transgender aging: Research and clinical perspectives* (pp. 21–35). New York, NY: Columbia University Press.

Crary, D. (2010). Who's a family? New study tracks shifting US views. *Assocated Press.* Retrieved from http://www.google.com/hostednews/ap/article/ALeqM5j96YLum-LHJDA5DT1skwQ8CR2zngD9I84AAO1

Crowl, A., Ahn, S., & Baker, J. (2008). A meta-analysis of developmental outcomes for children of same-sex and heterosexual parents. *Journal of GLBT Family Studies, 4*(3), 385–407.

D'Augelli, A. R., Grossman, A. H., & Starks, M. T. (2006). Childhood gender atypicality, victimization, and PTSD among lesbian, gay, and bisexual youth. *Journal of Interpersonal Violence*, *21*(11), 1462–1482. doi:10.1177/0886260506293482

D'Augelli, A. R., Omoto, A. M., & Kurtzman, H. S. (2006). Developmental and contextual factors and mental health among lesbian, gay, and bisexual youths. In A. M. Omoto & H. S. Kurtzman (Eds.), *Sexual orientation and mental health: Examining identity and development in lesbian, gay, and bisexual people.* (pp. 37–53). Washington, DC: American Psychological Association.

Deacon, S. A., Reinke, L., & Viers, D. (1996). Cognitive-behavioral therapy for bisexual couples: Expanding the realms of therapy. *American Journal of Family Therapy*, *24*(3), 242–258.

Denny, D. (2007). Transgender identities and bisexual expression: Implications for counselors. In B. A. Firestein (Ed.), *Becoming visible: Counseling bisexuals across the lifespan* (pp. 268–284). New York, NY: Columbia University Press.

Dodge, B., & Sandfort, T. G. M. (2007). A review of mental health research on bisexual individuals when compared to homosexual and heterosexual individuals. In B. A. Firestein (Ed.), *Becoming visible: Counseling bisexuals across the lifespan* (pp. 28–51). New York, NY: Columbia University Press.

Doherty, W. J., & Simmons, D. S. (1996). Clinical practice patterns of marriage and family therapists: A national survey of therapists and their clients. *Journal of Marital and Family Therapy*, *22*, 9–25.

Dworkin, S. H. (2006). The aging bisexual: The invisible of the invisible minority. In D. Kimmel, T. Rose, & S. David (Eds.), *Lesbian, gay, bisexual, and transgender aging: Research and clinical perspectives* (pp. 37–52). New York, NY: Columbia University Press.

Edney, R. (2004). To keep me safe from harm? Transgender prisoners and the experience of imprisonment. *Deakin Law Review, 9*, 327–338.

Erich, S., Tittsworth, J., Dykes, J., & Cabuses, C. (2008). Family relationships and their correlations with transsexual well-being. *Journal of GLBT Family Studies*, *4*(4), 419–432.

Evans, B. K. (1990). Mothering as a lesbian issues. *Journal of Feminist Family Therapy*, *2*(1), 43–52.

Firestein, B. A. (2007). Cultural and relational contexts of bisexual women: Implications for therapy. In B. A. Firestein (Ed.), *Becoming visible: Counseling bisexuals across the lifespan* (pp. 127–152). New York, NY: Columbia University Press.

Gamson, J. (2000). Sexualities, queer theory, and qualitative research. In N. Denzin & Y. Lincoln (Eds.), *Handbook of qualitative research* (2nd ed., pp. 347–365). Thousand Oaks, CA: Sage.

Garnets, L. D., & D'Augelli, A. R. (1994). Empowering lesbian and gay communities: A call for collaboration with community psychology. *American Journal of Community Psychology*, *22*(4), 447.

Gartrell, N., & Bos, H. (2010). US national longitudinal lesbian family study: Psychological adjustment of 17-year-old adolescents. *Pediatrics*, *126*(1), 28–36. Epub Jun 2010.

Godfrey, K., Haddock, S. A., Fisher, A., & Lund, L. (2006). Essential components of curricula for preparing therapists to work effectively with lesbian, gay, and bisexual clients: A Delphi study. *Journal of Marital & Family Therapy*, *32*(4), 491–504.

Goldberg, A. E. (2010). *Lesbian and gay parents and their children: Research on the family life cycle.* Washington, DC: American Psychological Association.

Gonsiorek, J. C. (1991). The empirical basis for the demise of the illness model of homosexuality. In J. C. Gonsiorek & J. D. Weinrich (Eds.), *Homosexuality: Research implications for public policy* (pp. 115–136). Newbury Park, CA: Sage.

Goodman, M. (2005, August). *Minority stress and psychological distress of lesbian and gay persons.* Presented at the Annual Conference of the American Psychological Association, Washington, DC.

Gordon, A. R., & Meyer, I. H. (2007). Gender nonconformity as a target of prejudice, discrimination, and violence against LGB individuals. *Journal of LGBT Health Research*, *3*(3), 55–71. doi:10.1080.15574090802093562

Gottman, J. M., Levenson, R. W., Gross, J., Frederickson, B. L., McCoy, K., Rosenthal, L., … Yoshimoto, D. (2003). Correlates of gay and lesbian couples' relationship satisfaction and relationship dissolution. *Journal of Homosexuality*, *45*(1), 23–43.

Gottman, J. M., Levenson, R. W., Swanson, C., Swanson, K., Tyson, R., & Yoshimoto, D. (2003). Observing gay, lesbian and heterosexual couples' relationships: Mathematical modeling of conflict interaction. *Journal of Homosexuality*, *45*(1), 65–91.

Green, M. S., Murphy, M. J., Blumer, M., & Palmanteer, D. (2009). Marriage and family therapists' comfort level working with gay and lesbian individuals, couples, and families. *American Journal of Family Therapy*, *37*(2), 159–168.

Green, R.-J. (2001). Interventions with multicultural families: Coming out to family … in context. *Family Psychologist*, *17*(2), 11–14.

Green, R.-J. (2008). Gay and lesbian couples: Successful coping with minority stress. In M. McGoldrick & K. V. Hardy (Eds.), *Re-visioning family therapy: Race, culture, and gender in clinical practice* (2nd ed., pp. 300–310). New York, NY: Guilford Press.

Green, R.-J., Bettinger, M., & Zacks, E. (1996). Are lesbian couples fused and gay male couples disengaged? Questioning gender straightjackets. In J. Laird & R.-J. Green (Eds.), *Lesbians and gays in couples and families: A handbook for therapists* (pp. 185–230). San Francisco, CA: Jossey-Bass.

Green, R.-J., & Mitchell, V. (2008). Gay and lesbian couples in therapy: Minority stress, relational ambiguity, and families of choice. In A. S. Gurman (Ed.), *Clinical handbook of couple therapy* (4th ed., pp. 662–680). New York, NY: Guilford Press.

Green, S. K., & Bobele, M. (1994). Family therapists' response to AIDS: An examination of attitudes, knowledge, and contact. *Journal of Marital and Family Therapy, 20,* 349–367.

Greenan, D. E., & Tunnell, G. (2003). *Couple therapy with gay men.* New York, NY: Guilford Press.

Grossman, A. H., & D'Augelli, A. R. (2006). Transgender youth: Invisible and vulnerable. *Journal of Homosexuality, 51*(1), 111–128.

Grossman, A. H., & D'Augelli, A. R. (2007). Transgender youth and life-threatening behaviors. *Suicide and Life-Threatening Behavior, 37*(5), 527–537.

Grossman, A. H., D'Augelli, A. R., Howell, T. J., & Hubbard, S. (2005). Parents' reactions to transgender youths' gender nonconforming expression and identity. *Journal of Gay & Lesbian Social Services, 18*(1), 3–16. doi:10.1300/J041v18n0102

Grossman, A. H., Haney, A. P., Edwards, P., Alessi, E. J., Ardon, M., & Howell, T. J. (2009). Lesbian, gay, bisexual and transgender youth talk about experiencing and coping with school violence: A qualitative study. *Journal of LGBT Youth, 6*(1), 24–46. doi:10.1080/19361650802379748

Hatzenbuehler, M. L., McLaughlin, K. A., Keyes, K. M., & Hasin, D. S. (2010). The impact of institutional discrimination on psychiatric disorders in lesbian, gay, and bisexual populations: A prospective study. *American Journal of Public Health, 100*(3), 452–459.

Herek, G. M. (1996). Heterosexism and homophobia. In R. P. Cabaj & T. S. Stein (Eds.), *Textbook of homosexuality and mental health* (pp. 101–113). Washington, DC: American Psychiatric Press.

Herek, G. M. (2007). Confronting sexual stigma and prejudice: Theory and practice. *Journal of Social Issues, 63*(4), 905–925.

Hudak, J., & Giammattei, S. V. (2010). Doing family: Decentering heteronormativity in "marriage" and "family" therapy. *American Family Therapy Academy: Monograph Series, Expanding our social justice practices: Advances in Theory and Training* [Monograph] (Winter), 49–55.

Imber-Black, E. (1988). Normative and therapeutic rituals in couples therapy. In E. Imber-Black, J. Roberts, & R. A. Whiting (Eds.), *Rituals in families and family therapy* (pp. 113–134). New York, NY: Norton.

International Lesbian, G., Bisexual, Trans and Intersex Association. (2010). Marriage and substitutes to marriage Retrieved June 5, 2010, from http://ilga.org/ilga/en/index.html

Jackson, D. D. (1968). *Communication, family, and marriage: Human communication* (Vol. 1). Palo Alto, CA: Science and Behavior Books.

Josephson, G. J. (2003). Using an attachment-based intervention with same-sex couples. In S. M. Johnson & V. E. Whiffen (Eds.), *Attachment processes in couple and family therapy* (pp. 300–317). New York, NY: Guilford Press.

Journal of Marital and Family Therapy. (2000). Special section: Lesbian, gay, and bisexual issues in family therapy, 26(4).

Keller, D., & Rosen, H. (1988). Treating the gay couple within the context of their families of origin. *Family Therapy Collections, 25,* 105–119.

Kerr, M. E., & Bowen, M. (1988). *Family evaluation: An approach based on Bowen theory.* New York: Norton.

Kimmel, D., Rose, T., Orel, N., & Green, B. (2006). Historical context for research on lesbian, gay, bisexual, and transgender aging. In D. Kimmel, T. Rose, & S. David (Eds.), *Lesbian, gay, bisexual, and transgender aging: Research and clinical perspectives* (pp. 2–19). New York, NY: Columbia University Press.

Kitzinger, C. (1996). Heteropatriarchal language: The case against "homophobia." In L. Mohin (Ed.), *An intimacy of equals: Lesbian feminist ethics* (pp. 34–40). New York, NY: Harrington Park Press.

Knudson-Martin, C., & Laughlin, M. J. (2005). Gender and sexual orientation in family therapy: Toward a postgender approach. *Family Relations, 54*(1), 101–115.

Kranz, K., & Daniluk, J. (2006). Living outside of the box. *Journal of Feminist Family Therapy, 18*(1–2), 1–33.

Krestan, J. A., & Bepko, C. S. (1980). The problem of fusion in the lesbian relationship. *Family Process, 19*(3), 277–289.

Laird, J. (1994). Lesbian families: A cultural perspective. In M. P. Mirkin (Ed.), *Women in context: Toward a feminist reconstruction of psychotherapy* (pp. 118–148). New York, NY: Guilford Press.

Laird, J. (1999). Gender and sexuality in lesbian relationships. In J. Laird (Ed.), *Lesbians and lesbian families: Reflections on theory and practice* (pp. 47–90). New York, NY: Columbia University Press.

Laird, J., & Green, R.-J. (Eds.). (1996). *Lesbians and gays in couples and family therapy: A handbook for therapists.* San Francisco, CA: Jossey-Bass.

LaSala, M. C. (2001). Monogamous or not: Understanding and counseling gay male couples. *Families in Society, 82*(6), 605–611.

LaSala, M. C. (2010). *Coming out, coming home: Helping families adjust to a gay or lesbian child.* New York, NY: Colombia University Press.

Lederer, W. J., & Jackson, D. D. (1968). *The mirages of marriage.* New York, NY: Norton.

Lev, A. I. (2004). *Transgender emergence: Therapeutic guidelines for working with gender-variant people and their families.* Binghamton, NY: Haworth Clinical Practice Press.

Levitt, H. M., Ovrebo, E., Anderson-Cleveland, M. B., Leone, C., Jeong, J. Y., Arm, J. R., … Horne, S. G. (2009). Balancing dangers: GLBT experience in a time of anti-GLBT legislation. *Journal of Counseling Psychology, 56*(1), 67–81. doi:10.1037/a0012988 10.1037/a0012988.supp (Supplemental)

Lewis, R. J., Derlega, V. J., Brown, D., & Rose, S. (2009). Sexual minority stress, depressive symptoms, and sexual orientation conflict: Focus on the experiences of bisexuals. *Journal of Social & Clinical Psychology, 28*(8), 971–992.

Lidz, T. (1969). The influence of family studies on the treatment of Schizophrenia. *Psychiatry, 32,* 237–251.

Logie, C., Bridge, T. J., & Bridge, P. D. (2007). Evaluating the phobias, attitudes, and cultural competence of master of social work students toward the LGBT populations. *Journal of Homosexuality, 53*(4), 201–221.

Lombardi, E. L., Wilchins, R. A., Priesing, D., & Malouf, D. (2001). Gender violence: Transgender experiences with violence and discrimination. *Journal of Homosexuality, 42*(1), 89.

Long, J. K. (1996). Working with lesbians, gays, and bisexuals: Addressing heterosexism in supervision. *Family Process, 35*(3), 377–388.

Long, J. K., & Andrews, B. V. (2007). Fostering strength and resiliency in same-sex couples: An overview. *Journal of Couple & Relationship Therapy, 6,* 153–165.

Long, J. K., & Bonomo, J. (2006). Revisiting the sexual orientation matrix for supervision: Working with GLBTQ families. *Journal of GLBT Family Studies, 2*(3/4), 151–166. doi:10.1300/J461v2n03_08

Long, J. K., Bonomo, J., Andrews, B. V., & Brown, J. M. (2006). Systemic therapeutic Approaches with sexual minorities and their families. *Journal of GLBT Family Studies, 2*(3/4), 7–37. doi:10.1300/J461v2n03_02

Long, J. K., & Serovich, J. M. (2003). Incorporating sexual orientation into MFT training programs: Infusion and inclusion. *Journal of Marital & Family Therapy, 29*(1), 59–67.

Malpas, J. (2006). From otherness to alliance: Transgender couples in therapy. *Journal of GLBT Family Studies, 2*(3/4), 183–206.

Marriage Equality. (2010). International progress towards marriage equality. Retrieved from http://www.marriageequality.ie/download/pdf/progress_towards_marriage_equality.pdf

Martell, C. R., Safren, S. A., & Prince, S. E. (2004). *Cognitive-behavioral therapies with lesbian, gay, and bisexual clients.* New York, NY: Guilford Press.

Mason, M. E. (2007). The experience of transition for lesbian partners of female-to-male transsexuals. *Dissertation Abstracts International Section B The Sciences and Engineering, 68,* 3403.

McGoldrick, M. (1988). The joining of families through marriage: The new couple. In B. Carter & M. McGoldrick (Eds.), *The changing family life cycle: A framework for family therapy* (2nd ed., pp. 209–233). New York, NY: Gardner Press.

Messinger, L. (2006). A historical perspective. In L. Messinger & D. F. Morrow (Eds.), *Sexual orientation & gender expression in social work practice: Working with gay, lesbian, bisexual, & transgender people* (pp. 18–42). New York, NY: Columbia University Press.

Meyer, I. H. (2003). Prejudice, social stress, and mental health in lesbian, gay, and bisexual populations: Conceptual issues and research evidence. *Psychological Bulletin, 129*(5), 674–697. doi:10.1037/0033-2909.129.5.674

Minuchin, S., & Fishman, H. C. (1981). *Family therapy techniques.* Cambridge, MA: Harvard University Press.

Mizock, L., & Lewis, T. (2008). Abuse in special populations. *Journal of Emotional Abuse, 8*(3), 335–354.

Myers, M. F. (1981). Counseling the parents of young homosexual male patients. *Journal of Homosexuality, 7*(2/3), 131–143.

National Gay and Lesbian Task Force (NGLTF). (2010, October). High rates of bullying, suicide attempts among transgender and gender non-conforming people. Retrieved from http://www.thetaskforce.org/press/releases/pr_100710

Nealy, E. C. (2008). Working with LGBT families. In M. McGoldrick & K. V. Hardy (Eds.), *Re-visioning family therapy: Race, culture, and gender in clinical practice* (2nd ed., pp. 289–299). New York, NY: Guilford Press.

Negy, C., & McKinney, C. (2006). Application of feminist therapy: Promoting resiliency among lesbian and gay families. *Journal of Feminist Family Therapy, 18*(1/2), 67–83. doi:10.1300/J086v18n01-03

Neisen, J. H. (1993). Healing from cultural victimization: Recovery from shame due to heterosexism. *Journal of Gay & Lesbian Psychotherapy, 2*(1), 49–63.

Osman, S. (1972). My stepfather is a she. *Family Process, 11*, 209–218. doi:10.1111/j.1545-5300.1972.00209

Oswald, R. F., Blume, L. B., & Marks, S. R. (2005). Decentering heteronormativity: A model for family studies. In V. L. Bengtson, A. C. Acock, K. R. Allen, P. Dilworth-Anderson, & D. M. Klein (Eds.), *Sourcebook of family theory & research.* (pp. 143–165). Thousand Oaks, CA: Sage.

Patten, J. (1997). The girl in the sunflower hat [Video]. *Master's Series.* Alexandria, VA: AAMFT.

Patterson, C. J. (2006). Children of lesbian and gay parents. *Current Directions in Psychological Science, 15*, 241–244.

Pendergrass, V. E. (1975). Marriage counseling with lesbian couples. *Psychotherapy: Theory, Research & Practice, 12*(1), 93–96.

Perlesz, A., Brown, R., Lindsay, J., McNair, R., de Vaus, D., & Pitts, M. (2006). Family in transition: Parents, children and grandparents in lesbian families give meaning to "doing family." *Journal of Family Therapy, 28*(2), 175–199.

Perosa, L. M., Perosa, S. L., & Queener, J. (2008). Assessing competencies for counseling lesbian, gay, bisexual, and transgender individuals, couples, and families. *Journal of LGBT Issues in Counseling, 2*(2), 159–169. doi:10.1080/15538600802125613

Pettigrew, T. F., & Tropp, L. R. (2000). Does intergroup contact reduce prejudice? Recent meta-analytic findings. In S. Oskamp (Ed.), *The Claremont symposium on applied social psychology: Reducing prejudice and discrimination* (pp. 93–114). Mahwah, NJ: Erlbaum.

Piper, J., & Mannino, M. (2008). Identity formation for transsexual individuals in transition: A narrative family therapy model. *Journal of GLBT Family Studies, 4*(1), 75–93.

Raj, R. (2008). Transforming couples and families: A trans-formative therapeutic model for working with the loved-ones of gender-divergent youth and trans-identified adults. *Journal of GLBT Family Studies, 4*(2), 133–163. doi:10.1080/15504280802096765

Rock, M., Carlson, T. S., & McGeorge, C. R. (2010). Does affirmative training matter? Assessing CFT students' beliefs about sexual orientation and their level of affirmative training. *Journal of Marital & Family Therapy, 36*(2), 171–184. doi:10.1111/j.1752-0606.2009.00172.x

Rostosky, S. S., Riggle, E. D. B., Horne, S. G., & Miller, A. D. (2009). Marriage amendments and psychological distress in lesbian, gay, and bisexual (LGB) adults. *Journal of Counseling Psychology, 56*(1), 56–66. doi:10.1037/a0013609

Roth, S. (1985). Psychotherapy with lesbian couples: Individual issues, female socialization, and the social context. *Journal of Marital and Family Therapy, 11*(3), 273–286. doi:10.1111/j.1752-0606.1985.tb00620.x

Rust, P. C. R. (2007). The construction and reconstruction of bisexuality: Inventing and reinventing the self. In B. A. Firestein (Ed.), *Becoming visible: Counseling bisexuals across the lifespan* (pp. 3–27). New York, NY: Columbia University Press.

Rutledge, A. L. (1975). Treatment of male homosexuality through marriage counseling: A case presentation. *Journal of Marital and Family Therapy, 1*(1), 51–62.

Ryan, C., Huebner, D., Diaz, R. M., & Sanches, J. (2009). Family rejection as a predictor of negative health outcomes in White and Latino lesbian, gay, and bisexual young adults. *Pediatrics, 123*, 346–352.

Rye, B. J., & Meaney, G. J. (2009). Impact of a homonegativity awareness workshop on attitudes toward homosexuality. *Journal of Homosexuality, 56*(1), 31–55.

Saltzburg, S. (2007). Narrative therapy pathways for re-authoring with parents of adolescents coming-out as lesbian, gay, and bisexual. *Contemporary Family Therapy, 29*(1–2), 57–69.

Samons, S. L. (2009). Can this marriage be saved? Addressing male-to-female transgender issues in couples therapy. *Sexual and Relationship Therapy, 24*(2), 152–162. doi:10.1080/14681990903002748

Savin Williams, R. (2005). *The new gay teenager.* Cambridge, MA: Harvard University Press.

Schwartz, M. F., & Masters, W. H. (1983). Conceptual factors in the treatment of paraphilias: A preliminary report. *Journal of Sex & Marital Therapy, 9*(1), 3–18.

Stone Fish, L., & Harvey, R. G. (2005). *Nurturing queer youth: Family therapy transformed.* New York, NY: Norton.

Sue, D. W. (2010). *Microaggressions in everyday life: Race, gender, and sexual orientation.* Hoboken, NJ: Wiley.

Szymanski, D. M. (2005). A feminist approach to working with internalized heterosexism in lesbians. *Journal of College Counseling*, 8(1), 74–85.

Tasker, F., & Patterson, C. J. (2007). Research on gay and lesbian parenting: Retrospect and prospect. *Journal of GLBT Family Studies*, 3(2/3), 9–34.

Thorne, M. Q., Jr. (1967). Marital and LSD therapy with a transvestite and his wife. *Journal of Sex Research*, 3(2), 169–177

Treyger, S., Ehlers, N., Zajicek, L., & Trepper, T. (2008). Helping spouses cope with partners coming out: A solution-focused approach. *American Journal of Family Therapy*, 36(1), 30–47. doi:10.1080/01926180601057549

Wainright, J. L., & Patterson, C. J. (2008). Peer relations among adolescents with female same-sex parents. *Developmental Psychology, 44*, 117–126.

Wainright, J. L., Russell, S. T., & Patterson, C. J. (2004). Psychosocial adjustment, school outcomes, and romantic relationships of adolescents with same-sex parents. *Child Development*, 75(6), 1886–1898. doi:10.1111/j.1467-8624.2004.00823.x

Watzlawick, P., Helmick Beavin, J., & Jackson, D. D. (1967). *Pragmatics of human communication: A sudy of interactional patterns, pathologies, and paradoxes*. New York, NY: Norton.

Wolkomir, M. (2009). Making heteronormative reconciliations: The story of romantic love, sexuality, and gender in mixed-orientation marriages. *Gender & Society*, 23(4), 494–519.

Section I
Clinical Issues With LGBT Couples

2

Gay Male Couple Therapy
An Attachment-Based Model

GIL TUNNELL

Although the cultural wars over same-sex couples are far from finished, battles have been won that have already led to greater societal recognition and increased tolerance. A growing number of countries and several states in the United States now grant legal status to gay couples as marriage or civil union.[1] Some religions allow commitment ceremonies to be performed on sacred grounds by their priests, ministers, and rabbis. Gay male couples in many locales can conceive through surrogacy and more easily adopt children. Not all gay couples have these options, but the mass media convey to same-sex couples everywhere that they have gained far greater societal visibility if not full acceptance. If the two decades following the Stonewall Rebellion in 1969 were about individuals coming out of the proverbial gay closet, the last two decades have been about gay couples coming out and living openly in society.

In *Couple Therapy With Gay Men* (Greenan & Tunnell, 2003), a key theme was that given how society marginalizes same-sex couples, who, in turn, internalize their "inferior" status, successful treatment must include the therapist's validating the legitimacy of the relationship. As a result of the recent extraordinary societal changes, the issue of legitimacy has shifted somewhat in the therapy room from the couple dealing with the stress of marginalization and invisibility, to taking the relationship more seriously and deepening their emotional commitment. Still, society's increased recognition of same-sex relationships (a) does not banish overnight the effects of internalized homophobia and male gender-role socialization that wreck havoc on achieving intimate connections between gay men (T. W. Johnson & Keren, 1996; Mohr, 1999), and (b) brings entirely new challenges: How comfortable are we in being more fully out of the closet? For many gay couples, there was a certain adventure and devious delight in being "alternative" (Warner, 1999). If we can legally marry, will we do so (Belluck, 2003; Rothblum, 2005)? If we make an "official" public commitment, do we adopt the scripts of traditional marriage, particularly the vow of "forsaking all others"? Now that we can more easily have children, do we want to? How do we raise them with two dads and no mom? Who are our role models? At the same time, there is a rise of interest in "polyamorous relationships," in which individuals are sexually and emotionally engaged with multiple partners (Bettinger, 2005; Nelson, 2010).

It is an exciting time to be working with gay male couples. What do these societal changes mean for our models of clinical work? With culture now more on their side, male couples can be helped by their therapists to deepen their emotional bonds and to clarify their "relational

---

[1] At the time of writing in 2011, in the United States, the District of Columbia and six states (Connecticut, Massachusetts, New Hampshire, New York, Vermont, and Iowa) can legally perform same-sex marriages (and several other states legally recognize out-of-state marriages). The following countries allow same-sex marriage: The Netherlands, Belgium, Spain, Canada, South Africa, Norway, Sweden, Portugal, Iceland, and Argentina.

ambiguity," which so often permeates and undermines their relationships. Green and Mitchell (2002) define relational ambiguity as a relationship with "no givens—no preordained expectations, mutual obligations, or contracts" (p. 551), and more specifically, no automatic presumption of "monogamy, pooled finances, caring for each other through serious illness, moving together for each other's career advancement, providing and caring for each other's families in old age, mutual inheritance, health care power-of-attorney rights" (p. 553). Without legalized commitments, these real-world issues force gay men in coupled relationships to figure out their emotional commitment to each other time and time again.

On the one hand, being in an "ambiguous" relationship offers the men freedom to give it their own structure. Not confined to traditional scripts of marriage, gay partners write their own, creatively experimenting to determine what works for them, often defying convention (Kooden, 2000; Nimmons, 2002). However, lacking the structures of marriage and traditional marital roles, gay couples must build their own idiosyncratic structures from scratch and from *within* their relationship, a process that is at once liberating and stressful. The external structure of marriage holds and contains heterosexual couples during stressful upheavals; the difficulty of divorce functions as a built-in incentive to try to stay together. When severe stress occurs in gay male couples, breaking up is often the first option (Greenan, 2010).

In short, the ties that bind male couples are not all that binding: The partners in a gay male couple are continuously testing whether their attachment is sufficiently strong and secure to endure over the "long haul." In treating male couples, the couple therapist needs to address the presenting issues in a way that not only validates their relationship but also helps the men make their attachment bond more secure.

Three Fundamental Tasks of Coupling and How Gay Men Are Different

To make it over the long haul, all couples—straight and gay—have a minimum of three fundamental tasks to accomplish (Tunnell & Greenan, 2004): (1) creating a boundary around them, (2) dealing with individual differences and conflict, and (3) regulating closeness and distance. The vast majority of couples accomplish the tasks on their own; couples often seek treatment when they confront difficulty with one or more tasks. Each is much more complicated for gay male couples than for married heterosexual couples.

Creating a Boundary Around the Couple

Every couple must create a structure that establishes it as a functioning social dyad (Nichols & Minuchin, 1999). This task essentially involves reducing relational ambiguity both for the couple and for others. For heterosexual couples, the act of marriage makes the boundary. On their wedding day, legal and religious systems, families, and friends all come together to confer legitimacy onto the couple. The couple's relationship changes status, in a matter of hours, from ambiguous to clear.

Lacking a marriage or commitment ceremony witnessed by others, gay male couples (as well as unmarried straight couples) go about boundary making in fits and starts. Sexual encounters are the way many gay men first meet (Garnets & Kimmel, 1993). To become a couple, the men must transition from being "fuck buddies" to "dating" to becoming "partners," "boyfriends," "mates," "spouses," or "significant others."

As a couple goes about creating a couple boundary, a major difference between heterosexual and male couples is sexual monogamy (Green & Mitchell, 2002; T. W. Johnson & Keren, 1996; Shernoff, 2006). Unlike heterosexual married couples, gay male couples do not simply assume sexual exclusivity. Moreover, almost without exception, when a therapist asks a male couple about monogamy, they are not reticent to discuss it as an issue that has been, or is being, negotiated. Many male couples are remarkably adept at developing and refining rules and structures that deal with sexual nonmonogamy, separating it from emotional fidelity (Green & Mitchell, 2002; Shernoff, 2006).

In my own practice, most male couples report having sexually closed the relationship initially, but many retained the option to renegotiate monogamy in the future. Some couples decide to open their relationships, with success depending on their ability to "negotiate non-monogamy" (Shernoff, 2006). LaSala (2004) has found no differences in relationship satisfaction between monogamous and nonmonogamous male couples.

The gay community itself does not universally value long-term relationships or monogamy (Green & Mitchell, 2002; Greenan & Tunnell, 2003). Many gay men are skeptical about long-term relationships, believe they will not last more than a few years, and may view them as a restraint on their sexual freedoms. It is common for partners in a gay male couple to be approached sexually, either individually or as a couple, by a third party with full knowledge they are coupled. The couple must then decide whether to keep the boundary.

Dealing With Differences and Conflict

The honeymoon "idealization" phase in any relationship eventually ends, and the partners realize that they have different ideas, opinions, or values. Males in general find interpersonal conflict more physiologically arousing and distressing than females do (see Gottman & Gottman, 2008, for a review). Getting a man "to stay in the ring" long enough to air the differences, understand the other person's perspective, and negotiate a joint solution acceptable to both parties and not just to him can be a formidable task, but one that may be doubly difficult when the other party is a man. Men seem neither biologically disposed nor socialized to defer to another man (Tunnell, 2006a). In couples observed fighting in session, male couples are far more likely to escalate a conflict than are heterosexual couples. When fighting becomes too intense in heterosexual couples, the man eventually shuts down; whereas in male couples, the men continue to fight as though it would be shameful to back down to another man.

Regulating Closeness and Distance

Couples go in and out of states of emotional attunement. Largely through trial and error, couples who stay together find their own rhythm—their unique balance of closeness and distance—and learn to transition smoothly from one state to the other.

For gay male couples, the regulation of emotional closeness may be the most daunting of all three tasks for two reasons: male gender acculturation and the residual effects of growing up gay (Tunnell, 2006a). Gender acculturation socializes men to be more comfortable with autonomy, separateness, and emotional self-reliance (Chodorow, 1978; Gilligan, 1982), and less comfortable with emotional connection that involves sharing deep feelings with another man. Males have often been shamed, especially by other males, for being "too" emotional. To protect themselves from shaming experiences, most males learn to keep their emotional lives private from other males. Gay men are no exception and, in fact, may overvalue emotional autonomy (Tunnell, 2006a), more so than straight men, in order to protect the secret of their homosexuality. If gay men were still financially and emotionally dependent on their family when they realized their attraction to other males, most coped by leading a secretive, double life and developing a "false self" in interacting with others, keeping their "true self" private (Greenan & Tunnell, 2003; Tunnell, 2006a). When they did subsequently come out as gay, an ingrained pattern remained to keep their innermost feelings secret. At the same time, most gay men long for an emotional connection that a long-term relationship can provide (Green & Mitchell, 2002).

For male couples, the tendency to withhold affect is especially problematic because it undermines forming more secure attachment bonds, since attachment bonds require shared emotional experience in order to develop (Fosha, 2000; S. M. Johnson, 2004, Solomon, 2009).

A couple can exist indefinitely without having formed a secure attachment bond, and for many couples seeking therapy, insecure attachment is the underlying problem. Couples in therapy are often seeking a more secure attachment: "empathy, listening, touching, dyadic resonance, a sense of seeing and being seen by each other, and ultimately, an opportunity to be in touch with core emotions while remaining present with each other" (Solomon, 2009, p. 232). Couple therapy can provide that opportunity for shared affective experiences, both positive and negative, that lead to stronger attachment bonds.

Attachment-Based Therapy as a New Therapeutic Frame

The therapeutic model presented in *Couple Therapy With Gay Men* (Greenan & Tunnell, 2003) was an adaptation of structural family therapy (Minuchin, 1974) to male couples. The primary adaptations were (a) sensitizing therapists to how the developmental path of acquiring a false self early in life complicates forming intimate attachment bonds in adult relationships; and (b) challenging male couples to be more interdependent and emotionally connected, rather than disengage. The model of treatment, however, remained the three-stage structural model that emphasizes challenge and confrontation (Nichols & Minuchin, 1999). The most significant change to the traditional model was an extended period of "joining" (Stage 1) by validating the gay couple and asking questions that conveyed the therapist's understanding of gay issues. In Stage 2, the therapist instructs the men to engage in "enactments" (where the men speak directly to each other) so that the therapist can observe their complementarity dynamics, followed by the therapist "unbalancing" (Stage 3) the couple, that is, challenging one or both men to change their complementarity.

In structural family theory, the fundamental mechanism of change is challenge and confrontation of the couple's behaviors (Nichols & Minuchin, 1999). To change relational dynamics, the partners are made to feel anxious about their dynamic. That is, structural treatment is purposely designed to raise anxiety to effect change (Tunnell, 2006b). Unbalancing interventions do not always succeed. To counter the couple's resistance, within a single session as well as over the course of several sessions, the structural therapist alternates between joining and challenging; Minuchin has described these interventions as a combination of "stroke and kick." If and when the couple change their behaviors, the therapist shifts to a more supportive stance to consolidate and maintain the change (Greenan & Tunnell, 2003).

In training with Minuchin, I had particular difficulty with the unbalancing (or "kicking") stage of treatment (Tunnell, 2006b). In an effort to change me to become more confrontational with couples, Minuchin directly challenged my "softness," believing that challenge, and specifically raising anxiety, is the only effective way to change both couples and therapists in training. Taking into account my "soft" therapeutic style, Minuchin talked about the possibility of "soft" challenges, although he clearly preferred the "hard" variety. Hard or soft, *challenge* is the operative word in structural family therapy; without it, no real change occurs.

In my own experience practicing family therapy and from observing and supervising numerous sessions on videotape and behind one-way mirrors, I have observed that challenging patients more often leads to increased resistance and defensiveness, rather than breakthrough moments of change. I believe now this result has less to do with my inability to challenge patients effectively than with failing to tap into our patients' biologically based strivings to expand, grow, and be transformed (Fosha, 2008). Even more important, if the therapist's goal is to encourage emotional interdependency and to develop more secure attachment, the last thing gay male couples need are therapists who relentlessly challenge them. Many gay males already feel bad about themselves and their struggles to maintain long-term intimate relationships (Tunnell, 2006a); to shame them further seems counterproductive, even if it is in the service of improving their relationship.

For several years, I have been applying to couples (Tunnell, 2006a) an individual treatment model, accelerated experiential dynamic psychotherapy (AEDP; Fosha, 2000), that does not require the therapist to take adversarial positions but instead builds attachment into the patient–therapist relationship to enable the patient to uncover and process warded-off emotions.

To create the therapeutic attachment bond, the AEDP therapist explicitly expresses affirmation, empathy, and compassion for the patient from the very first session onward. In using an experiential therapy, the AEDP therapist actively helps the patient—by creating safety and providing continual emphatic support—to access "core affects" physically in his body (sadness or despair, fear, anger, joy, pleasure, shame, disgust). The overriding goal of AEDP, applied to individuals or couples, is to help the patients become emotionally engaged and function less defensively.

Although core affects are naturally occurring, universal, and hard wired into our physiological systems (Tomkins, 1962, 1963), many individuals as children learned to repress them in order to maintain an attachment relationship with one or both parents. Sacrificing emotional authenticity for attachment security, they learned not to express feelings that could upset the attachment figure on whom they depended (Fosha, 2000). To cope, they developed an "affect phobia" (McCullough, 1997), or defenses against feeling in general, and a reticence to express emotion to intimate others in particular. Although the defenses may have been partly adaptive then, they also deprived the individual of adaptive action tendencies that core affects provide (Fosha, 2000). That is, whether or not one acts on his or her feelings, being "emotionally mindful" is an essential part of living and an important guide to effective decision making (Frederick, 2009). More significant, defenses against feeling deprived the individual of developing close, intimate bonds with others, since out of deep emotional experiences with others attachment bonds are formed. For gay men especially, this was the common childhood scenario: Fearing that their gayness might be discovered by their families and peers if they revealed too much of their "true" selves, many gay males learned to be emotionally self-reliant and not to "open up" to others, especially other males, all the while longing to do so.

The goal of AEDP is to help the patient open up and gain direct access to deep affect. Through moment-to-moment tracking of nonverbal signs that the patient is experiencing emerging signs of affect (e.g., a sigh, a change in facial expression, wetting of the eyes, a shift in gaze, nervous twitching, clenching a fist), the AEDP therapist attempts to reduce the anxiety sufficiently and bypass the patient's usual defenses, so that he begins to experience his core emotions to the fullest. Unlike the parent reproachful of the child's affects, the AEDP therapist encourages the patient to connect with his body physiologically, describe the somatic sensations verbally, and express the emotion in its entirety—for example, cry in response to sadness, feel the anger in the body, and thus release the emotion completely. In AEDP's technical terms, this sequence in which the therapist actively helps the patient access, express, and manage warded-off emotional states is called "dyadic regulation of affect" (Fosha, 2001). The emotional experience is processed to completion and shared with the therapist.

As the wave of fully expressed emotion subsides, Fosha (2000, 2005) discovered that patients almost always enter a transformation she called the "core state," where feelings of tranquility, mastery, and relatedness spring forward, along with a new openness to experience completely free of anxiety and defense. This final core state transformation is profoundly calming and positive. As Fosha (2005) has written, all emotional experiences, if processed to completion, end in positive affect states.

In AEDP, having an emotional breakthrough in the presence of an empathic other is by itself insufficient to effect lasting character change. The emotional experience must also be reflected upon and integrated. To accomplish this stage, the AEDP therapist is continuously *intrapsychically metaprocessing* with the patient to reflect on the emotional experience that has occurred

("What was that like for you just now?"), thereby cognitively integrating (in the analytical left brain) what is happening affectively (in the emotional right brain). The therapist also engages the patient in *relational metaprocessing* ("What is it like to have this experience with me?"). The patient's response to the relational question is invariably positive. Relational metaprocessing is critical for strengthening attachment bonds because it draws the patient's attention to the fact that he was able to experience deep emotion safely and completely with another person, an experience that not only had no negative consequences but also, in fact, produced positive feelings of connection, closeness, and attachment.

In summary, as an individual treatment, AEDP engages the patient in an in vivo "corrective emotional experience" where warded-off feelings are felt in the body and expressed in the presence of a caring and encouraging attachment figure. Emotional release occurs, and the patient–therapist attachment bond is strengthened further. Affective competence—the ability to have a complete emotional experience (Fosha, 2000)—and attachment bonds thus develop in tandem, each building upon the other (Lipton & Fosha, 2011).

Although Fosha (2000) maintains that the attachment bond between therapist and patient is the secondary mechanism by which the primary therapeutic goal of deep emotional processing is accomplished, applying AEDP to couples flips the priorities: Helping partners experience deep emotion together in session is the secondary mechanism by which the primary goal of strengthening the attachment bond is achieved.

In contrast to structural family therapy, which emphasizes challenge and confrontation, AEDP applied to couples is an unquestionably softer way to effect changes in relational dynamics and rarely, if ever, requires the therapist to take an adversarial position. Throughout the entire treatment, the AEDP therapist remains in an affirming, supportive position. From the first session onward, the AEDP couple therapist explicitly affirms and supports the couple as a unit, much as the AEDP individual therapist does with his or her patient. Although some attachment by the couple to the therapist occurs, the primary goal is to help the men become more securely attached to each other by having emotional experiences together. In brief, if therapists want men to be gentler, kinder, and softer with each other, should not the therapy itself be of that ilk?[2]

The Importance of Attachment Bonds

Why should attachment bonds be the focus of couple treatment? The short answer is that attachment bonds are the fundamental building blocks in dyadic intimate relationships that allow both individuals to fulfill their inborn needs for both connection and autonomy. In its original form, attachment theory (Bowlby, 1969/1982, 1973) offered an elegant account of how infants become attached to their primary caregivers, a process that, when it went well, culminated in the child's ability to be separate and autonomous, as well as the ability to be relational and dependent. Bowlby believed that secure attachment had two equally important outcomes—autonomy and connection. The infant learns to trust the caregiver to care for its physical needs and to provide a reassuring emotional presence that minimizes fear and anxiety. From this context of feeling the caregiver's physical presence and emotional engagement through eye contact, voice, and touch (all right-brain–to–right-brain phenomena), the infant feels safe enough to explore the outside world, with the caregiver encouraging the infant's

---

[2] There are other modalities of couple treatment that do not emphasize challenge and, when necessary to confront couples, use softer methods of confrontation. Several of these models have been applied to working with gay male couples, for example, Bowenian family-of-origin therapy (T. W. Johnson & Colucci, 2005) and emotionally focused therapy (EFT; S. M. Johnson, 2004; Josephson, 2003). Greenan (2010) has also softened the structural model by including mindfulness and affect-based techniques.

natural desire to separate and be autonomous, welcoming the infant back from its independent exploration to reconnect with him or her (Cassidy, 2001). As in AEDP treatment, a "good enough" caregiver also engages in "dyadic regulation of affect" to help the infant manage and make sense of rudimentary emotional states that would be difficult or unbearable to experience on its own. In Fosha's theory, a trauma can result from the individual's having to bear, or not bear, intense emotional states alone.

Over time, an attachment bond is created between parent and child, with four defining characteristics (Ainsworth, Blehar, Waters, & Wall, 1978): (1) *proximity maintenance*, where both parties desire to be near each other; (2) *separation protest*, where each dislikes lengthy periods of separation; (3) *secure base*, where the infant feels psychologically cared for by an older and wiser adult (even when the adult is not physically present); and (4) *safe haven*, where the infant feels protected. Again, secure attachment not only results in the individual's ability to be autonomous and independent but also enables him to enjoy connecting with others and to turn to them when in emotional distress.

These two seemingly opposite motivations—the need for autonomy and the need for connection—are universal to all human beings (Angyl, 1951; Bakan, 1966), even though gender-role socialization emphasizes the development of autonomy in males and connection in females (Chodorow, 1978). For Murray Bowen (1966), one of the founders of family therapy, these two characteristics were central to his concept of differentiation, which is not only about being separate and autonomous but also about staying related and connected while doing so. Salvador Minuchin (1974) recognized these two characteristics of systems in their extreme forms as "disengaged" versus "enmeshed" but argued that in their less extreme forms, each was necessary in healthy family and couple functioning (Nichols & Minuchin, 1999). Although both Bowen and Minuchin argued theoretically that both autonomy and connection were required for healthy relationships, in practice their respective therapies privileged autonomy over connection. That is, both Bowen and Minuchin developed far more clinical interventions designed to help family members become more autonomous and less enmeshed.

Following gender-role socialization, it is probably no accident that Murray Bowen and Salvador Minuchin as men valued autonomy over connection in their therapeutic models and that as women Diana Fosha, Sue Johnson, and Marion Solomon (see Fosha, Siegel, & Soloman, 2009) have placed greater value on developing emotional connection than on fostering individual autonomy. Of interest is that research on secure mother–infant attachment, which has received far more attention than father–infant attachment, suggests that mothers play a greater role in soothing the child when distressed; whereas in secure father–infant attachment, fathers foster the child's exploration and autonomous strivings by being sensitive when the child becomes frustrated in new play situations, offering support and encouragement rather than ridicule, and showing delight in the child's efforts at mastery (Grossmann, Grossmann, Kindler, & Zimmermann, 2008). Here, one sees clearly how connection with the caregiver enables greater autonomy and how successful autonomy creates greater connection. In secure attachment, connection and autonomy expand and enrich each other in a circular process. As the research illustrates and as Bowlby believed, the child forms multiple attachments, responding to parents and other caregiving adults who are responsive and sensitive to the child (Cassidy, 2008).

Taking seriously Bowlby's dictum that attachment is a life-long phenomenon lasting from "cradle to grave," social and developmental psychologists began in the late 1980s applying attachment theory to adult romantic relationships (e.g., Feeny, 1999, 2008; Hazen & Shaver, 1987), with some research suggesting that childhood attachment styles are relatively stable over a lifetime unless the individual has a new in vivo emotional experience with the other (Scharfe,

2003), which can change insecure attachment to secure or vice versa.[3] As researchers applied attachment theory to adult romantic relationships, there were caveats that the parallels are not perfect: (a) Unlike parent–child attachment where the parent is the older, wiser attachment figure, the attachment relationship in healthy adult relationships is reciprocal, with each adult serving as an attachment figure to the other; and (b) In typical adult romantic bonds, there is an erotic sexuality that is acted on, unlike in parent–child attachment bonds. Yet the parallels remain striking: As in parent–child attachment bonds, in healthy love relationships there exist adult versions of proximity maintenance, separation protest, secure base, and safe haven. As a gay patient once expressed in couple therapy, "When I'm feeling right with Jonathan, I can take on the world. I feel he has my back."

A gay man may have particular difficulty forming an attachment bond with another man because in his development he has very likely had experiences with his father and male peers that taught him that men are not safe. Attachment theory postulates that children, based on their experiences with their primary attachment figures, form "internal working models" of how close, intimate relationships are supposed to function. When gay male adults form romantic attachments, they rely on their working models to predict how they are likely to be treated by other men. Many gay males were shamed and shunned by their fathers for exhibiting any kind of weakness, softness, femininity, or emotional vulnerability (Isay, 1989). In turn, the gay son steered clear of the father to avoid further shaming experiences (Tunnell, 2006a). For these boys, fathers were not a secure base nor was proximity to them sought. Mothers may or may not have offered their gay son nurturance and support. Mothers, as well as fathers, in warding off recognition that their son might be gay may have scorned any behavior suggestive of femininity (read: homosexuality). The gay boy was typically left all alone to deal with complex feeling states and did not have an "empathic other" to help him sort them out. Realizing that one is gay is not necessarily traumatic, but dealing with it alone can be (Greenan & Tunnell, 2003).

As society increasingly accepts homosexuality, this narrative of gay male development may change. Recently I worked with a straight father in individual therapy. Apart from the issues he sought help with, he spoke of his despair watching his 8-year-old son shy away from rough-and-tumble sports, how he tried to teach him how to throw a ball and in general "butch him up," and how he and his wife worried about the boy's preoccupation with *The Little Mermaid* and other feminine interests. But a remarkable thing happened: As the child became depressed about being different and not fitting in, the father (on his own, without any prompting from me) began talking to him explicitly about how all people are different, and that he was perfect the way he was and was loved for his specialness. When the son later expressed interest in ballet, the father enrolled him in a prestigious dance school for children and proudly attended his performances. This sensitive and responsive father intuited that his son was most likely gay, even though he felt the son had little conscious awareness of that, only that he was different and did not fit in.

Most gay men do not have such fathers. Instead, they develop early attachment injuries that interfere with forming romantic relationships and fear being shamed yet again by another man (Siegel & Walker, 1996): On the one hand is a yearning to bare their darkest core feelings with someone and be accepted as lovable (Solomon, 2009), and on the other hand is a fear of whether another man can really be trusted. In addition, any unresolved internalized homophobia—that

---

[3] Three "insecure" attachment styles have been delineated based on studying toddlers in the "strange situation": (1) avoidant, characterized by limited emotional connection and withdrawal in the face of heightened affect; (2) ambivalent, characterized by an intense pursuit of connection with limited autonomy; and (3) disorganized, characterized by simultaneously pursuing and rejecting connection (Ainsworth et al., 1978). An example of disorganized attachment is a toddler who, after being left without the caregiver in a strange situation, reaches out its hands to the caregiver while simultaneously backing away. Disorganized attachment is believed to be an outcome of a child's having been abused by the caregiver.

it is simply "wrong" to be sexually or emotionally intimate with a man—contributes to avoiding intimate closeness and interferes with developing trusting attachment bonds (Mohr, 1999). A major objective of AEDP with male couples is to help men overcome their fear of being emotional and vulnerable with each other by creating an in vivo therapeutic experience that demonstrates to them that they can be safe havens and secure bases for each other.

Clinical Application of AEDP to Gay Male Couple Therapy

In helping couples master the three fundamental tasks of coupling, an attachment-based AEDP treatment proceeds quite differently from structural family therapy. For each of the three tasks—creating firmer boundaries, dealing with conflict, and regulating closeness and distance—the structural model's mechanism of change is challenge and confrontation. Just as structural therapy's premise is that no real change happens without pressure, AEDP's premise is that "no real change ... is going to take place until we deal with our feelings" (Frederick, 2009, p. xvi). Again, the structural therapist raises the couple's anxiety by pushing "interactions beyond their usual homeostatic cutoffs" (Nichols & Minuchin, 1999, p. 134), where the couple is forced to try new behaviors. In contrast, the AEDP couple therapist approaches all three tasks by being particularly affirming, compassionate, and supportive to the couple as a unit as well as to each individual. The AEDP therapeutic stance attempts to lower the couple's anxiety, bypass defensive behaviors, and encourage emotional connection. By sharing affective experience, the couple is helped to strengthen their attachment bond.

Creating a Boundary Around the Couple

More important than creating an external boundary around the couple that others recognize—which, if not present, a structural therapist would challenge the men to do—an AEDP approach seeks to build a secure attachment bond within the relationship. Once the partners have made a stronger emotional commitment to each other—and then reveal to family, friends, neighbors, and colleagues that they are a couple—creating external boundaries follows more easily and naturally.

Simply because two men say they are coupled does not mean they have formed an attachment bond. If the relationship is newer than 6 months, the couple have probably not established a secure base and a safe haven, which form only when each partner experiences the other as emotionally present when one is vulnerable (S. M. Johnson, 2004). Indeed, creating those experiences becomes the primary work of the therapy. However, even during the initial "joining" phase of treatment when the therapist elicits the couple's relationship history, it is important to get beneath the "facts" of how they met, what attracted each to the other, who made the first move, and so on, by asking such affect-evoking questions as "What was that like emotionally when he came over to speak with you at the party?" or "How did it feel when this man you found so handsome asked for your number?" Similar to how the AEDP individual therapist affirms the patient in the very first session, the AEDP couple therapist in the first session not only affirms the couple but also actively helps the partners affirm each other. As with parent–child attachment, couples first become attached by sharing positive affective experiences. It is therefore essential in the early stage of couple therapy to elicit positive affects, which almost always existed at the beginning of the relationship.

Dealing With Differences and Conflict

Most couples present with conflict. The structural therapist typically has the men discuss the conflict in session with each other as the therapist observes, creating an enactment so that the therapist can hypothesize about their complementarity dynamics. Rather than respond to the content of the argument, the structural therapist tracks the nonverbal communication between the couple. The structural therapist observes, for example, that one man is more dominant and active in tone and style whereas the other is more submissive and passive and, after witnessing the enactment, makes an unbalancing intervention that challenges their style of communication.

In the AEDP approach, the therapist also tracks the nonverbal communication between the couple; but unlike the structural therapist, the AEDP therapist does not use his or her observations to criticize or confront the couple. Instead, AEDP, like emotionally focused therapy for couples (EFT; S. M. Johnson, 2004), gently helps the couple explore what emotions, particularly attachment-related emotions, are triggered by the argument. As an attachment-based therapy, AEDP recognizes that unresolved conflict can seriously threaten a relationship, particularly for same-sex couples, who, lacking the external constraint of marriage, find it easier to break up and move on. Following an attachment framework, AEDP tries to delve beneath the surface content of the argument to explore the deeper feelings being aroused and to engage the partners themselves in dyadic regulation of affect.

A major difficulty in applying dyadic regulation of affect to couples experiencing conflict is that the therapist cannot count on the observing partner to be empathically present as his partner drops his defenses to express deeper affect, let alone encourage him, as a trained AEDP therapist would, to go deeper into the feeling. That is, AEDP therapists are specifically trained in dyadic regulation of affect, how to help the individual "drop down" to a feeling state, sidestepping defenses and minimizing anxiety. Once the patient begins to experience signs of affect in the body, the AEDP therapist actively helps the patient elaborate the affect to its full expression, going deeper and deeper into it. Although the ultimate goal is to have the partners in the couple themselves engage in dyadic regulation of affect with each other, the AEDP therapist, like an EFT therapist who serves as a "surrogate" attachment figure (S. M. Johnson, 2008), must usually do it first with each of them before they can do it with other other.

What typically happens as the therapist begins helping one man become more connected to his affect is that the observing partner grows anxious and may attempt to sabotage the process, either by prematurely reassuring the sharing partner (e.g., "Don't worry, everything will be okay") or expressing disgust that the sharer is so emotionally needy (e.g., "Buck up! Be a man!"). The therapist must then actively modulate the observing partner's anxiety while helping the one experiencing the core affect complete the experience. To reduce the observing partner's anxiety, the therapist asks him simply to listen and stay engaged by looking at his partner; the therapist also reminds the observer that his turn will come. Throughout this process, the therapist encourages the men to maintain eye contact as much as possible because mutual gaze is a right-brain–to–right-brain mechanism to increase connection and security (Beebe, Lachmann, & Jaffee, 1997), especially as they discuss difficult issues and feelings. As an observer and coach to the man beginning to get in touch with his feeling, the AEDP therapist paraphrases what the speaker is saying, adding in more emotional terms, leading him to uncover whatever core feeling is being triggered by the conflict. Once the breakthrough to core affect occurs, the listening partner almost always responds with compassion and empathy. Just as structural therapy counts on more adaptive behaviors to emerge as a result of the couple being challenged (Genijovich, 1994), AEDP counts on the empathy of the other to kick in when the individual expresses deep feeling. If empathy does not kick in, the therapist may self-disclose his own affirming, empathic reaction, saying, for example, "I don't know about you, but I was very moved by your partner's courage in telling you how alone he feels in your relationship." Such statements help the partner develop more empathy as well as provide on-the-spot empathy and support to the person who has risked revealing himself.

When the process goes well—one man reaches core feeling and the other responds with empathy—it is very important for the therapist to initiate relational metaprocessing back and forth between the two partners, saying, for example, "What is it like for you to hear your partner express his feeling?" or "What is it like for your partner to be so supportive of you?" This reflective and integrative left-brain processing helps the emotional connection deepen and entrains more secure attachment.

Often, when the emotions underlying the argument are revealed, a solution is more easily reached. If the conflict is resolved successfully or dissipates, the members of the couple move naturally to greater emotional closeness and more secure attachment. To consolidate greater attachment security, however, the therapist should continue to relationally metaprocess their success, saying, for example, "What is it like for you two to have resolved this issue together?" or "How is it for the two of you that you mastered the problem together?"

Regulating Closeness and Distance

Regulation of closeness and distance refers to the dance of attunement all couples do in terms of how close or distant each partner prefers to be in any given moment, as well as over time. This task involves finding the right balance of autonomy and connection, experimenting with the right rhythm for the partners as a couple, and learning how to manage and respect each other's preferences for autonomy and connection. Although individuals vary enormously in how much emotional connection and physical separation they desire in relationships, mastering this dance of intimacy is critical in determining long-term relationship satisfaction or despair (Tunnell, 2006a). Two men who each prefer a lot of autonomy with less emotional connection can be as satisfied with the relationship as two men who like lots of emotional connection and less autonomy. That said, there must usually be a modicum of both connection and autonomy for each individual to be satisfied. However, it is not up to the therapist to determine the right balance.

Fosha (2000) has written that relational engagement is a difficult, demanding task. Although she refers here to the interplay between the individual patient and the AEDP therapist, the description might well apply to relationally engaged couples:

> The back and forth of the little-step-by-little-step process involves the capacity to express feelings directly to the person whom the feelings are about, to remain connected while taking in the other's reaction, and to sustain this emotional conversation through time. (Fosha, 2000, p. 150)

If closeness and distance regulation has become dysfunctional for the couple, it generally takes the form of "pursuer–distancer" dynamics, where the pursuer desires greater intimacy and connection. A circular dynamic is set up such that as the pursuer pursues, the distancer distances, leading the pursuer to pursue more fervently, and so on. Structural therapists typically intervene here by first challenging the pursuer to back off.

Attachment therapists view severe closeness or distance problems as a sign of an insecure attachment bond (S. M. Johnson, 2004; Solomon, 2008). That is, if the pursuer actually felt loved and was securely bonded, that is, if he felt that he was truly in the heart and mind of his partner, the exaggerated pursuit of intimacy would diminish. As an attachment therapist who is male, I am as interested in the distancer as the pursuer. Respecting separation as just as necessary for intimacy as deep connection, rather than simply as a defense against closeness, I may ask the distancing partner about his need for "down time" or solitude. Does he use solitude to gather his resources? How does the partner sometimes interfere with that? Does he need some solitude in order to connect later? Or is his distancing possibly his own way to test the security of their bond, to test his partner's desire to be with him? On the other hand, how much togetherness does he prefer? How often does he initiate togetherness?

Upon exploration, the distancer may well say he feels overwhelmed by the continually close interaction and needs a break, just as infants avert their gaze from the mother when the connection becomes too intense (Beebe et al., 1997). In attachment terms, just as an anxious mother becomes upset when the infant refuses eye contact, the adult pursuer may feel that the relationship itself is in jeopardy when the distancer simply wants space. Reacting as might an anxious mother by trying to catch the infant's eye yet again, the pursuer is, in essence, approaching the distancer for reassurance about their bond. It can thus be useful to directly ask the pursuer what, exactly, he is seeking when he wants greater closeness: Is it reassurance that he is still loved? Making this desire explicit often helps to clarify the problem. If this is so, then the distancer can be coached to provide enough reassurance to calm the pursuer, and the pursuer can be helped to view the separation as a break rather than a relationship rupture.

In essence, AEDP couple therapy normalizes the dance of closeness and distance: It is entirely natural to go in and out of states of separateness and connection; and despite its goal of creating shared affective experiences in the therapy sessions, AEDP is respectful of states of separateness. States of separation enrich states of connection. Indeed, in the individual model of AEDP, after an intense and successful session, both patient and therapist may be emotionally fulfilled but also emotionally exhausted and need a break. The AEDP couple therapist can provide the couple with psychoeducation, making clear that (a) an ebb and flow exists between closeness and separateness, (b) most people cannot sustain a deep sense of close connection indefinitely,[4] and (c) individuals vary in how much closeness or distance they can tolerate. The task becomes one of encouraging the couple to respect their individual differences and to experiment with healthier ways of transitioning between the two states of being.

Finally, given that a male couple is composed, after all, of two men each socialized to be independent, separate, and autonomous, male couples may tilt toward a balance of more distance or autonomy and less closeness or connection. Mohr (1999) has reported that gay men who have greater levels of internalized homophobia are more likely to have an avoidant attachment style, characterized by more autonomy than connection. Mohr's finding makes sense, given how some gay men become avoidant because they cannot trust other men with their feelings. On the other hand, Mohr (2008) has more recently found that gay men show higher than expected attachment anxiety and fears of abandonment. By helping gay men build more secure attachment bonds, therapists help the men become more adept at bridging and sustaining periods of distance, separation, and relative autonomy. Ultimately, secure attachment is a felt knowledge that each person exists in the heart and mind of the other. As my patient said about his partner, "I can take on the world [when] I feel he has my back."

Case Example

Jay and Robert had been coupled for 32 years after meeting in graduate school. They moved to New York City together and had been in business together for 27 years. They were out to their families, friends, and business associates. They presented with conflict around their mutual responsibilities at the office. When they began their business, Jay quickly became the "overfunctioning" partner, with Robert almost always in Jay's shadow and "underfunctioning," with all the circularity that it implies: The less Robert did, the more Jay did, causing Robert to do even less, with Jay doing even more, all the time complaining that Robert was not doing enough. As might be expected, the relationship had other characteristics that maintained the overfunctioning–underfunctioning dynamic: Jay was extroverted and socially engaging; he worked quickly and was proactive. Robert, in contrast, was shy and reserved; he worked slowly and was passive.

---

[4] Of course, there is a difference between a normal need for separation following intense close connection versus a distancer's strong defenses against any emotional closeness at all. This situation may indicate that the partners are not well matched.

In the first few months of treatment, the therapist challenged the couple's overfunctioning–underfunctioning complementarity, with the therapist at times confronting Jay to step back, be more patient, and let Robert finish tasks without taking over. At other times the therapist challenged Robert to assert himself with Jay. The couple did not change, however, and remained distressed.

In an effort to move the treatment focus away from the office and to develop more emotional communication between the partners, the therapist began tracking more closely their moment-to-moment nonverbal communication, which is how the following exchange emerged:[5]

Jay: I've about given up trying to get Robert to step up and contribute more. Recently he has developed all these physical ailments, which I believe are mostly psychosomatic and provide excuses about why he can't do more. But I can't be sure on that, and so now I am worried about Robert's physical health. My worry over him actually is causing tension in my own body.

Therapist: Oh? Where do you feel tension in your body?

Jay: In my chest, there is this tightness here, like sometimes I can't breathe.

Therapist: Are you feeling the tightness now?

Jay: Yes, I can barely breathe.

Therapist: Can you try breathing into it?

(Jay sighs heavily.)

Therapist: Mmmmm… What was that big sigh?

Jay: Resignation. I feel such resignation and despair that I am not able to help Robert. He is so passive and, I believe, depressed. I feel he lacks any purpose in his life. All my life I've tried to help him find himself.

Therapist: (to Robert, attempting to bring him into the process, and also to deepen Jay's feeling state by purposely adding the word helpless)

Did you know that Jay worries so much about you, that he doesn't know what to do anymore, and, I suppose, he just feels so helpless to help you?

Robert: No… I mean, I guess I knew that he worries, but I didn't know he felt helpless. I am sorry he worries, but I guess the worry about me is a marker of some sort that he does care.

Therapist: You didn't know that you really matter to him, in a deep way? You are together for over 30 years! My gosh!

Robert: He doesn't show that I matter. All I get from him is anger.

Therapist: And it's been years of this: Jay wanting so badly to help you find a purpose, to find some peace and happiness. And now he is expressing his frustration and absolute helplessness.

(Jay looks away and starts to tear up, which Robert doesn't notice. The therapist calls Robert's attention to it and then tracks Jay's emerging affect.)

Therapist: Robert, do you see Jay's tears?

(Robert looks alarmed but doesn't speak. The therapist senses that Robert cannot help Jay go deeper into the feeling to engage in dyadic affect regulation, so the therapist steps in.)

---

[5] The following is an edited transcript from an actual, videotaped session.

Therapist: (*speaking very quietly*)

Jay, what are the tears?

(*Jay is silent, appears embarrassed, and looks away, then begins to cry softly, a cry that turns into a deep sobbing that lasts several minutes. Robert moves closer on the couch to comfort him. The therapist waits in silence as Jay's emotional experience completes itself, observing Jay weep openly, with Robert holding him.*)

Therapist: (*attempting to get to the feeling behind the tears as Jay's crying subsides*)

You obviously have so much feeling right now. Can you put some words to it?

Jay: (*speaking unusually slowly and tentatively*)

When you said, "I didn't know what to do any more," it finally hit me. It is so frightening to acknowledge that I am helpless. Everything else I do, I succeed. I navigate around problems, I solve them, I make things happen … but with Robert, I get stuck. I can't succeed. Even worse, I fear that if Robert tried to take on more, he might fail, and that would be horrible for him. It's a no-win situation. I am totally incapacitated by this.

Therapist: You worry what will happen if Robert fails? What's that about?

Jay: Absolutely. I'm a Plan B, C, D kind of guy. What would be the backup plan if he failed? I see him out on the ledge with no protection. I want to protect him; I can't leave him on the ledge alone.

Therapist: That must be scary for you, seeing him out there on the ledge. What happens then?

Jay: I guess I rush in and do the task myself … so we never find out if Robert could have really handled something on his own. Geez, I have never said this. I didn't realize any of this. I don't know. We never talk like this.

Therapist: (*beginning relational metaprocessing*)

Well, actually, Robert hasn't said much, so let's check in: How do you feel, Robert, about everything Jay has been saying and feeling?

Robert: I'm not sure what it means, but it is obviously strongly felt. I had no idea he worried so much about me, and also that he worried I might fail. I want to allay his fears. I am more competent than he thinks.

Therapist: Can you allay his fears? Can you help him now?

Robert: I think so … (*begins to ramble*). I can understand why he'd be so concerned. I haven't done much with my life since grad school.… I have been in his shadow. He is the go-getter; I am the silent partner.

Therapist: Jay, can you look at Robert and tell him what you really need from him?

Jay: I need a sense of comfort that we are connected in our personal life and in our business. Our "brand" is the two of us; I don't want to run the business alone; I love the idea that the two of us are accomplishing the business together. But most of the time I feel alone. You don't talk to me about what is really going on with you. I want to feel that we are okay together. It hurts me to realize just now that I am actually doing harm by taking over so much. That kills me (*cries again*).

Therapist: So how could Robert really help you?

Robert: (*grabbing his turn to express his own feelings*)

What really does harm me and hurts me is how you humiliate me in front of others at the office.

Jay: (*becoming defensive*)

That's my style: I challenge the staff all the time to do better. And you know what: The staff improves every time! If I challenge you, it's an insult! I push people. Yes, I'm a taskmaster, but at the end of the day everyone does good work and is proud.

Robert: (asserting himself and fighting back)

There are other ways to help people improve! And you are right: It is absolutely insulting the way you humiliate me.

Therapist: (diffusing the emerging fight and encouraging empathy instead)

Jay, can you just sit here quietly without talking and imagine what Robert feels when you humiliate him in front of others in your office?

(Jay initially looks frustrated, then embarrassed, and averts his gaze. A long silence ensues.)

Jay: (looking into Robert's eyes)

I am sorry that I have hurt you.

(There is another very long pause as the men make prolonged eye contact and hold hands.)

Therapist: (again relational metaprocessing to help this new feeling of connection deepen)

Can I ask what it is like right now for both of you? How are you feeling as we end tonight?

Robert: Hmmmm… I never really knew the depth of Jay's worry over me. Until tonight, I guess he kept all that to himself. I didn't really feel he cared. I don't know how this is going to play out, but I do feel close to him right now, simply to know that he cares so much. I didn't really know this before.

Jay: I might be willing to let the work problems go. I don't think work is the main issue. I want to spend more quality time with Robert. I need something back from Robert. Most of the time I feel alone everywhere I go.

Therapist: Did you know this, Robert, that Jay often feels so alone? I think Jay needs you to take care of him more than he has let on.

In the next session, the therapist again metaprocessed the previous session and learned that both men believed it had provided a breakthrough of their impasse. Each reiterated that he felt closer to the other, and each had experienced a much less stressful week.

In the following weeks, the men began to change their relationship significantly. As Jay backed off pushing Robert to do more at the office, Robert began assuming more responsibilities and did not fail. But more significant improvement occurred at home, with each seeking out the other for time together (proximity maintenance restored).

Toward the end of treatment, they shared a story about how Jay had recently been honored by a professional association. Jay insisted that Robert "share the stage" with him, explaining "even though he is the 'silent partner,' he is the other half of 'our brand.'" This gesture absolutely delighted Robert. The men performed a skit reminiscent of George Burns and Gracie Allen, with Robert playing the straight man George as he set up Jay, as Gracie, to deliver the comical punch line.

Conclusion

Many gay men grow up withholding their innermost feelings and true selves while longing to reveal themselves to another man and be loved. An attachment-based model of couple therapy, developed from the individual treatment model of AEDP (Fosha, 2000), has been described in which the therapist facilitates the men's sharing of deep affects in session in order to strengthen their attachment bond. Compared to traditional structural family therapy (Nichols & Minuchin, 1999), which raises the couple's anxiety by confronting their complementarity and pressuring them to change, the AEDP approach lessens the couple's anxiety by explicitly expressing and modeling affirmation, support, and empathy to help each partner experience deep emotion in each other's presence.

An actual therapy session was presented that illustrates couple AEDP in action, showing (a) how the therapist's continual tracking of moment-to-moment affect leads to deepening affect, (b) how the therapist engages in dyadic regulation of affect with one individual while keeping the partner engaged, (c) how getting to feelings underlying the conflict can help resolve the conflict, (d) how attachment-based feelings (helplessness to help the other, not knowing the other cared, a feeling of aloneness within the relationship) can be accessed and explicitly named, and (e) how relational metaprocessing can make the couple's attachment more secure.

References

Ainsworth, M. D. S., Blehar, M. C., Waters, E., & Wall. S. (1978). *Patterns of attachment: A psychological study of the strange situation.* Hillsdale, NJ: Erlbaum.

Angyl, A. (1951). A theoretical model for personality studies. *Journal of Personality, 20,* 131–142.

Bakan, D. (1966). *The duality of human existence.* Chicago, IL: Rand McNally.

Beebe, B., Lachmann, F. M., & Jaffee, J. (1997). Mother–infant interaction structures and pre-symbolic self and object representations. *Psychoanalytic Dialogues, 7,* 133–182.

Belluck, P. (2003, November 26). Gays respond: "I do," "I might" and "I won't." *The New York Times,* p. A1.

Bettinger, M. (2005). Polyamory and gay men: A family systems approach. *Journal of GLBT Family Studies, 1,* 97–116.

Bowen, M. (1966). The use of family therapy in clinical practice. *Comprehensive Psychiatry, 7,* 345–374.

Bowlby, J. (1982). *Attachment and loss: Vol. 1. Attachment.* New York: Basic Books. (Originally published 1969)

Bowlby, J. (1973). *Attachment and loss, Vol. 2. Separation.* New York: Basic Books.

Cassidy, J. (2001). Truth, lies, and intimacy: An attachment perspective. *Attachment & Human Development, 3,* 121–155.

Cassidy, J. (2008). The nature of the child's ties. In J. Cassidy & P. R. Shaver (Eds.), *Handbook of attachment: Theory, research, and clinical applications* (2nd ed., pp. 3–22). New York: Guilford Press.

Chodorow, N. (1978). *The reproduction of mothering: Psychoanalysis and the sociology of gender.* Berkeley, CA: University of California Press.

Feeny, J. A. (1999). Adult romantic attachment and couple relationships. In J. Cassidy & P. R. Shaver (Eds.), *Handbook of attachment: Theory, research and clinical applications* (pp. 355–377). New York: Guilford Press.

Feeney, J. A. (2008). Adult romantic attachment: Developments in the study of couple relationships. In J. Cassidy & P. Shaver (Eds.), *Handbook of attachment: Theory, research, and clinical applications* (2nd ed., pp. 456–481). New York: Guilford Press.

Fosha, D. (2000). *The transforming power of affect: A model of accelerated change.* New York: Basic Books.

Fosha, D. (2001). The dyadic regulation of affect. *Journal of Clinical Psychology / In Session, 57,* 227–242.

Fosha, D. (2005). Emotion, true self, true other, core state: Toward a clinical theory of affective change process. *Psychoanalytic Review, 92,* 513–552.

Fosha, D. (2008). Transformance, recognition of self by self, and effective action. In K. J. Schneider (Ed.), *Existential-integrative psychotherapy: Guideposts to the core of practice* (pp. 290–320). New York: Routledge.

Fosha, D., Siegel, D. J., & Solomon, M. F. (2009). *The healing power of emotion: Affective neuroscience, development & clinical practice.* New York: Norton.

Frederick, R. (2009). *Living like you mean it: Use the wisdom and power of your emotions to get the life you really want.* San Francisco, CA: Jossey-Bass.

Garnets, L. D., & Kimmel, D. C. (1993). Lesbian and gay male dimensions in the psychological study of human diversity. In L. D. Garnets & D. C. Kimmel (Eds.), *Psychological perspectives on lesbian and gay male experiences* (pp. 1–51). New York: Columbia University Press.

Genijovich, E. (1994). *The impossible blended family* [Videotape]. Boston, MA: Family Studies.

Gilligan, C. (1982). *In a different voice: Psychological theory and women's development.* Cambridge, MA: Harvard University Press.

Gottman, J. M., & Gottman, J. S. (2008). Gottman method couple therapy. In A. S. Gurman (Ed.), *Clinical handbook of couple therapy* (4th ed., pp. 138–164). New York: Guilford Press.

Green, R.-J., & Mitchell, V. (2002). Gay and lesbian couples in therapy: Homophobia, relational ambiguity, and social support. In A. S. Gurman & N. S. Jacobson (Eds.), *Clinical handbook of couple therapy* (3rd ed., pp. 546–568). New York: Guilford Press.

Greenan, D. (2010). Therapy with a gay male couple: An unlikely multisystemic integration. In A. S. Gurman (Ed.), *Clinical casebook of couple therapy* (pp. 90–111). New York: Guilford Press.

Greenan, D. E., & Tunnell, G. (2003). *Couple therapy with gay men.* New York: Guilford Press.

Grossman, K., Grossman, K. E., Kindler, H., & Zimmermann, P. (2008). A wider view of attachment and exploration: The influence of mothers and fathers on the development of psychological security from infancy to young adulthood. In J. Cassidy & P. R. Shaver (Eds.), *Handbook of attachment: Theory, research, and clinical application* (2nd ed., pp. 857–879). New York: Guilford Press.

Hazan, C., & Shaver, P. R. (1987). Romantic love conceptualized as an attachment process. *Journal of Personality and Social Psychology, 52,* 511–524.

Isay, R. A. (1989). *Being homosexual: Gay men and their development.* New York: Farrar Straus Giroux.

Johnson, S. M. (2004). *The practice of emotionally focused couple therapy* (2nd ed.). New York: Brunner-Routledge.

Johnson, S. M. (2008). Couple and family therapy: An attachment perspective. In J. Cassidy & P. R. Shaver (Eds.), *Handbook of attachment: Theory, research, and clinical applications* (2nd ed., pp. 811–829). New York: Guilford Press.

Johnson, T. W., & Colucci, P. (2005). Lesbians, gay men, and the family life cycle. In B. Carter & M. McGoldrick (Eds.), *The expanded family life cycle: Individual, family and social perspectives* (3rd ed., pp. 346–361). New York: Pearson.

Johnson, T. W., & Keren, M. S. (1996). Creating and maintaining boundaries in male couples. In J. Laird & R.-J. Green (Eds.), *Lesbians and gays in couples and families: A handbook for therapists* (pp. 231–250). San Francisco, CA: Jossey-Bass.

Josephson, G. J. (2003). Using an attachment-based intervention with same-sex couples. In S. M. Johnson & V. E. Whiffen (Eds.), *Attachment processes in couple and family therapy* (pp. 300–317). New York: Guilford Press.

Kooden, H. (2000). *Golden men: The power of gay midlife.* New York: Avon Books.

LaSala, M. (2004). Extradyadic sex and gay male couples: Comparing monogamous and nonmonogamous relationships. *Families in Society: The Journal of Contemporary Human Services, 85,* 405–412.

Lipton, B., & Fosha, D. (2011). Attachment as a transformative process in AEDP: Operationalizing the intersection of attachment theory and affective neuroscience. *Journal of Psychotherapy Integration: Special Issue on Attachment, 23,* 253–279.

McCullough, L. (1997). *Changing character: Short-term anxiety-regulating psychotherapy for restructuring defenses, affects, and attachment.* New York: Basic Books.

Minuchin, S. (1974). *Families and family therapy.* Cambridge, MA: Harvard University Press.

Mohr, J. J. (1999). Same-sex romantic attachment. In J. Cassidy & P. R. Shaver (Eds.), *Handbook of attachment: Theory, research, and clinical applications* (pp. 378–394). New York: Guilford Press.

Mohr, J. J. (2008). Same-sex romantic attachment. In J. Cassidy & P. R. Shaver (Eds.), *Handbook of attachment: Theory, research, and clinical applications* (2nd ed., pp. 482–502). New York: Guilford Press.

Nelson, T. (2010, July/August). The new monogamy. *Psychotherapy Networker, 34*(4), 20–27, 60.

Nichols, M. P., & Minuchin, S. (1999). Short-term structural family therapy with couples. In J. M. Donovan (Ed.), *Short-term couple therapy.* New York: Guilford Press.

Nimmons, D. (2002). *The soul beneath the skin.* New York: St. Martin's Press.

Rothblum, E. D. (2005). Same-sex marriage and legalized relationships: I do, or do I? *Journal of GLBT Family Studies, 1,* 21–31.

Scharfe, E. (2003). Stability and change of attachment representations from cradle to grave. In S. M. Johnson & V. E. Whiffen (Eds.), *Attachment processes in couple and family therapy* (pp. 64–84). New York: Guilford Press.

Shernoff, M. (2006). Negotiated nonmonogamy and male couples. *Family Process, 45,* 407–418.

Siegel, S., & Walker, G. (1999). Connections: Conversations between a gay therapist and a straight therapist. In J. Laird & R.-J. Green (Eds.), *Lesbians and gays in couples and families: A handbook for therapists* (pp. 28–68). San Francisco, CA: Jossey-Bass.

Solomon, M. (2009). Emotion in romantic partners: Intimacy found, intimacy lost, intimacy reclaimed. In D. Fosha, D. J. Siegel, & M. F. Solomon (Eds.), *The healing power of emotion: Affective neuroscience, development and clinical practice* (pp. 232–256). New York, NY: Norton.

Tompkins, S. S. (1962). *Affect, imagery, and consciousness: Vol. 1. The positive affects.* New York, NY: Springer.

Tompkins, S. S. (1963). *Affect, imagery, and consciousness: Vol. 2. The negative affects.* New York, NY: Springer.

Tunnell, G. (2006a). An affirmational approach to treating gay male couples. *Group, 30*, 133–151.

Tunnell, G. (2006b). "The Oedipal Son" revisited. In S. Minuchin, W.-Y. Lee, & G. M. Simon (Eds.), *Mastering family therapy: Journeys of growth and transformation* (2nd ed., pp. 159–176). New York, NY: Wiley.

Tunnell, G., & Greenan, D. E. (2004). Clinical issues with gay male couples. *Journal of Couple & Relationship Therapy, 3*, 13–26.

Warner, M. (1999). *The trouble with normal: Sex, politics, and the ethics of queer life.* Cambridge, MA: Harvard University Press.

3
Lesbian Couple Therapy

COLLEEN M. CONNOLLY

Lesbian couples display remarkable determination, strength, and resilience in forming and sustaining relationships amid countless societal stressors. However, the effects of heterosexism, sexism, homoprejudice, and internalized homophobia on each partner and the couple strain relationships and can cause even the strongest of couples to falter or flounder. This chapter provides a contextual overview of lesbian couples' stressors and strengths, summarizes the identity development of couples, underscores their capacity for closeness, and highlights how female couples show innovation in creating successful and satisfying relationships. In addition, it includes clinical implications to help differentiate actual mental and relational health issues from some unique lesbian couple dynamics and culturally imposed assumptions of pathology. The use of a feminist approach underscores the value of women and their relationships; and the assessment, treatment, and engagement in the therapeutic process from a feminist and cultural perspective help to support the individual and relational health needs of clients. This approach helps clinicians resist the imposition of a heterosexual norm and provides a theoretical means to validate, strengthen, and enhance resilience for couples. Common issues and important qualities of the therapist are included, along with recommendations and conclusions to best ensure competent and affirmative lesbian couple therapy.

Lesbian couples experience countless challenges in forming, solidifying, and maintaining a relationship. To set the context for the existing environment, we will first explore the larger societal issues faced by lesbian couples. Then we will delve more into specifics about lesbian couples, their challenges, and their unique processes. Interwoven throughout is their amazing resilience. After that, we will address the issues often experienced by clinicians and look at the assessment, treatment, interventions, and therapist issues and qualities when working with lesbian couples. Finally, we will provide recommendations for future considerations in this important area.

Encountering and Maneuvering Oppression

Lesbian couples encounter insidious and pervasive impediments inherent in the current cultural system. The societal oppression based on orientation that has been noted for decades (e.g., Browning, Reynolds, & Dworkin, 1991) still exists, and legal and civil rights to validate these relationships are not universal and remain elusive to most couples. The important role that sexism plays in lesbian relationships also must be underscored, for two women continue to fight a male-dominated culture (Krestan & Bepko, 1980; Prouty Lyness & Lyness, 2007; Wright & Fish, 1997). Moreover, the triad of cultural oppression that Brown (1995) referred to—namely, heterosexism, homophobia, and an internalization of both of these processes—overlays every same-sex female relationship.

Heterosexism can be seen as a process that elevates heterosexuality while at the same time hiding, devaluing (Oswald, 2003), denigrating, and invalidating the LGBT experience (Long, 1996). As a result, a heteronormative stance has become ingrained, not only in the broader culture but also within the therapeutic professional community, as the heterosexual couple is systematically privileged and considered the social and sexual ideal (Fields, 2001). The form and appearance of these oppressive processes have changed over time; and although some of the more covert processes might not be as easily recognized by individuals outside the population, they continue to reverberate within the lesbian community. As Cowan, Heiple, Marquez, Khatchadourian, and McNevin (2005) point out, heterosexism continues to thrive, whether it is overt and demonstrated through the old-fashioned means of explicit negative attitudes and actions or is covert and enacted through modern heterosexism. This more modern evolution of heterosexism is shown through the lack of support for laws, policies, and rights that would benefit the population, and often it is couched in the language of "supporting traditional values." Regardless of the type, heterosexism denigrates, stigmatizes, and results in deleterious effects for lesbian couples and for the entire LGBT population.

Homoprejudice (Logan, 1996) refers to the prejudice exhibited and enacted against individuals who are lesbian, gay, or bisexual. Because of our cultural saturation of heterosexism and homoprejudice, fear and even hatred can be internalized individually and also infiltrate partners' images of each other (Slater, 1995). This *internalized homophobia* can be considered an inherent struggle for female couples and result in pessimistic and negative attitudes about the possibility of longevity for the relationship (Ossana, 2000). Because of the internalization of this process, mental and relational health are at risk.

For instance, higher levels of internalized homophobia was linked with lower self-esteem and associated with greater loneliness (Szymanski & Chung, 2001) and depression (Szymanski, Chung, & Balsam, 2001). Although lesbian couples in committed relationships report higher degrees of well-being and less psychological distress in the form of internalized homophobia, symptoms of depression, and stress (Riggle, Rostosky, & Horne, 2010), psychological distress in either member of the couple, even at low levels, is negatively associated with satisfaction in the relationship for both partners and may lead to an increase in conflict and a decrease in commitment to the relationship (Otis, Riggle, & Rostosky, 2006; Riggle et al., 2010). As a result, lesbian partners with higher levels of internalized homophobia and higher depressive and anxiety symptoms may internalize the negative beliefs about commitment and transfer them to the relationship (Otis et al., 2006).

These interlocking processes of heterosexism, homoprejudice, and internalized homophobia set the groundwork for the inherited lack of equal rights in our society, present incessant barriers, and can derail even the best of couples. When couples are invited to discuss the environment in which they live and feel safe enough to do so, even the healthiest of couples express feelings of being "persecuted and fearful" as they share how "dangerous and how tenuous" it can be as a lesbian couple and tell of the determination it takes to overcome the "emotionally crippling" effect of oppression (participants' words; Connolly, 2006, p. 143).

As female couples maneuver through the societal barricades, they must defend against heterosexism, homoprejudice, and internalized homophobia; manage their lesbian identity within different contexts; and create innovative relationships without a gender-role distinction. The multitude of stressors and strains contribute to real or perceived mental and relational health issues and impede the formation, maturation, and continuity of many same-sex relationships. Having current knowledge of how couples develop—that is, their identity management and development, their capacity for closeness, and their development amid socialization as gendered persons—can help guide our clinical decisions.

Couple Development

Identity Management

Despite some individuals reflecting back and saying they "always knew" their lesbian orientation, typically there is a process involving a series of coming-out events, phases, or stages to self and/or others because of the oppression. Coming out, which can be a "watershed event" for anyone (Bepko & Johnson, 2000, p. 411), is a "profoundly personal, political, and spiritual process of knowing self in relationship to other" (Halstead, 2003, p. 48). Clients might reflect on their feelings, thoughts, and experiences during the time of prediscovery or preawareness, the actual act or event of discovery, and events or interactions occurring postdiscovery (Ben-Ari, 1995), all of which might be woven into the therapeutic process.

However, individuals and couples frequently safeguard disclosures that might alter family relationships, affect social standing, or contribute to prejudice or threat (Davison, 2001). Although openness with family and in all contexts might be seen as ideal (Bepko & Johnson, 2000), it is typically life altering and can even be a life-threatening situation (Davison, 2001). As a result, individuals and couples can experience multiple identities within various relationships and contexts (Slater, 1995). They often linger between states, continually adapting based upon the changing contexts (Harry, 1993), as decisions are made about the salience (Green, 2000; Green & Mitchell, 2002) and the irreplaceability (Harry, 1993) of family, of friends, and of careers. It is important to note, however, that disclosure or lack of it is no indication of mental health or a stronger differentiation of self; rather, it might be a simple and realistic assessment of potential consequences based on that decision (Green, 2000, 2002; Green & Mitchell, 2002). For all these reasons, we might come to think in terms of *identity management* rather than focusing on the either-or, dichotomized view of disclosure, that is, either disclosing or not disclosing.

Identity Development

The formation and management of identity are unique to each individual and partner coupling. McCarn and Fassinger's (1996) lesbian identity development model provides a useful guide in stages of lesbian development. Their model is based on lesbian women being part of an oppressed group; and it is grounded in racial, ethnic, and gender identity models of development. McCarn and Fassinger's flexible phases are as follows: (a) awareness of a difference, (b) exploration, (c) deepening commitment of knowledge and possible crystallization of the identity, and (d) internalization or synthesis of the identity. When individual identity development is not matched closely enough, it can add stress to the relationship because the levels and contexts of identity management transcend the individual; they affect the couple and often require a synchronization of the partners and a mobilization of resources (Connolly, 2005; Patterson, Ciabattari, & Schwartz, 1999).

Social isolation and internalized homophobia can result in couples misinterpreting brief relational conflict as serious problems, rather than seeing them as normal developmental transitions that are inherent in all couple relationships, with many couples recognizing they have reached a transition point only when the relationship is disrupted (Berzon, 1988; Slater, 1995). Compounding the issue is the invisibility of long-term relationships to couples of shorter length, which creates difficulties with relational confidence, stirs up questions of viability, and contributes to couples viewing female couple bonds as temporary, with expectations of failure (Berzon, 1988; Connolly, 2010a; Slater, 1995; Slater & Mencher, 1991).

Capacity for Closeness

Another issue that often emerges when working with female couples is how close is close enough and how close is too close? *Merger*, also referred to as fusion and enmeshment, has been identified as a relational health issue wherein individual boundaries are blurred and togetherness and emotional closeness are prioritized (Ossana, 2000). Our understanding of merger has, however, transformed through the decades. Scholars came to understand that instead of merger being dysfunctional, it could instead be an adaptive response to adverse conditions (Biaggio, Coan, &

Adams, 2002). Closeness can be used to strengthen the couple identity within a negative culture (Biaggio et al., 2002; Ossana, 2000; Slater, 1995), and it might even be desirable when used as a means of fighting societal resistance to their coupling (Mencher, 1997).

Although lesbian couples function in a closer manner than do heterosexual couples, the emotional intensity of female relationships must not be misunderstood or automatically considered problematic, which would be setting the heterosexual standard as the norm and assuming that anything different must be dysfunctional (e.g., Biaggio et al., 2002). On the contrary, instead of what is called merger being "what's wrong" in female relationships, it may instead be "what's right" regarding women's capacity for closeness (Pardie & Herb, 1997, p. 53). Our clinical work is to determine the functionality of the couple's closeness, whether it is benefiting or impeding the relationship, and how much of that connection is based on the process of gender-role socialization.

Gender-Role Socialization

Gender-role socialization plays an important part in lesbian couple dynamics (e.g., Bepko & Johnson, 2000; Brown, 1995; Ossana, 2000; Scrivner & Eldridge, 1995). Traditional theory emphasizes autonomy, and a connected way of being in a relationship is often discouraged and marginalized in this culture (e.g., Jordan, 1992). However, women in particular value connection, are encouraged to do so, and often define themselves in terms of the relationships in their lives (e.g., Jordan, Kaplan, Miller, Stiver, & Surrey, 1991). Thus when lesbian couples experience conflicts or difficulties in a relationship, individual needs frequently become secondary to the relational needs (Littlefield, 1994).

Indeed, during times of stress, women are more likely to react in an affiliative fashion, responding in what Taylor et al. (2000) termed a *tend-and-befriend* manner rather than a fight-or-flight response. Tending can be seen as nurturing activities that promote safety and reduce distress; whereas befriending can be viewed as joining with others during stress and sharing resources and responsibilities, thereby reducing feelings of vulnerability. Taylor et al.'s work appears to provide the addition of biobehavioral research theory that mirrors clinical models of women's growth through connection rather than through autonomy (Connolly, 2005), which has been emphasized by the Stone Center theorists in the relational cultural model (see Jordan et al., 1991).

Moreover, Brown (1995) makes an important point that must be underscored: Lesbian couples are impacted by their gender-role development—times two. She contends that because two women are more than likely socialized and discriminated against in very similar patterns, they would reflect variations of the same benefits and detriments of that gender-role socialization. Thus, this mutually held socialization could be the most prominent difficulty and also the greatest strength in female dyads as the partners struggle against and struggle with each other. The challenges can actually serve to strengthen and fortify a relationship when couples forge a united front and fight together to move beyond the adverse conditions with determination and a positive perspective (Connolly, 2005).

Strength and Resilience of Lesbian Couples

Although challenges associated with being a female–female couple certainly exist, these intimate pairs also enjoy many benefits. Their similarities in gender-role socialization actually may heighten emotional expressiveness (Scrivner & Eldridge, 1995) and increase each partner's understanding of the other (Ossana, 2000). When lesbian dyads function well, couples have shown strengths in forming the initial connection and foundation for love; communicating and expressing the love throughout long-term relationships; ritualizing the love through symbolic representations, ceremony or celebration, or habitual couple rituals; and revitalizing love (Connolly, 2004). Their effective conflict resolution methods and empathic attunement might help increase satisfaction and longevity in relationships (Connolly & Sicola, 2005).

Lesbian couples are also known for many other points of strength and resilience. Lesbian couples are more prone to cohesion, intimacy, and sexual exclusivity than are other couple types, which may contribute to higher commitment, trust, and emotional intimacy between partners (Biaggio et al., 2002), with sexual exclusivity shown by one large study to be over 90% (Bryant & Demian, 1994). They show adaptability, which might be normative subculturally in addition to being adaptive psychologically (Zacks, Green, & Marrow, 1988). Furthermore, the combination of all these processes may contribute to more egalitarian (Bigner, 2000; Laird, 1993), flexible, and satisfied couplings (Green, Bettinger, & Zacks, 1996) and heighten levels of relationship quality seen with lesbian couples (Kurdek, 2008). High relationship quality appears to be related to high quality of sexual interaction, high relational commitment, low frequency of abusive behaviors, infrequent arguments, high joint income, and preparedness in legal matters (Bryant & Demian, 1994). All these processes must be taken into consideration when assessing, treating, and intervening on a therapeutic level.

Clinical Implications

The foundation of knowledge and clinical application of this profession has developed within the shadow of heterosexism (Brown, 1991; Long, 1996), and sociocultural variables at play are often the source of much of what is considered "pathology" (Negy & McKinney, 2006). In addition, diagnostic labeling and interventions, which have been enveloped in sexism and misogyny, can fall prey to dominant language patterns and behavioral nuances that might seem subtle but can have deleterious effects for women (Rampage, 1996). The ingrained heterosexism and sexism have resulted in lesbian women often being misdiagnosed and overdiagnosed (Falco, 1996). Problems persist if power issues within the therapeutic arena are not addressed (Parker, 2003); further, when heterosexism is unexamined, it can harm lesbian clients in similar ways to unexamined racism harming ethnic minorities (Long, 1996). Therefore, we must continually monitor our values and norms to ensure that the strengths of women are not covertly or overtly deemphasized, misconstrued, or overlooked (Jordan & Hartling, 2002).

There are many ways that the unique stressors experienced by lesbian couples can affect their functioning, satisfaction, and longevity, and clinicians must strive for knowledge and application of the assessment, treatment, and interventions, as well as the special therapist issues and qualities, to most effectively serve this population. Slater (1995) highlights that lesbian couples might present with stories of repeated confrontation of the same or similar stress and ensuing coping mechanisms, which can be viewed as problems in individual or couple development or defects in the couple. However, the couple's primary difficulties could instead be a result of the incontrovertible societal stressors and the challenge associated with sustaining a lesbian relationship within a continually hostile environment (Slater & Mencher, 1991).

An example of the impact of these stressors is evident in Bryant and Demian's (1994) survey of 1,749 gay men and lesbian women, which included 706 lesbian couples. The researchers found that 75% of the women reported relationship discrimination. So just viewing the prevalence of discrimination, which is embedded within the multitude of other stressors, helps us understand why lesbian women are frequent consumers of mental health services, with estimates of 75% of lesbian women being a current or past consumer of services (Bradford, Ryan, & Rothblum, 1994), and 45% of lesbian couples securing effective assistance from counselors (Bryant & Demian, 1994). Bradford et al.'s study (1994) suggests that lesbian women might seek therapy at a rate of three times that of heterosexual women, with 44% of the women reporting they sought therapy because of romantic-relationship issues.

Despite the incontrovertible stressors, lesbian couples report more satisfaction than do other types of couples (Ossana, 2000; Scrivner & Eldridge, 1995; Zacks et al., 1988). Even though lesbian couples are more satisfied, however, they are less likely to remain together in comparison with other couple types (Blumstein & Schwartz, 1983; Kurdek, 1998). As we conceptualize female couples, we might remember that because there are so few sanctions against ending a dysfunctional relationship, those dyads that do endure might be more well functioning than other types of couples (Zacks et al., 1988). Yet that does not preclude their need or desire to discover and remediate problems and/or amplify their existing strengths so as to withstand those outside stressors.

Theoretical Approach

Feminist theory offers a solid foundation for clinical work with lesbian couples. It begins with women's lives and experiences as central and valuable and reveals gaps in the existing male- and heterocentric-based knowledge (Goodrich, Rampage, Ellman, & Halstead, 1988; Halstead, 2003). Moreover, Prouty Lyness and Lyness (2007) posit that feminist therapists have broadened their analysis from how power impacts women to the myriad ways that society affects power in couples, with intersections involving race, class, ability and disability, and gender identity, in addition to orientation. As such, feminist thought influences every area of couple work; as a result, feminist couple therapy could be considered state-of-the-art.

As Negy and McKinney (2006) note, instead of feminist therapy being technique driven, it is a value-driven model and seen instead as "a sensibility" (p. 72). They contend that the essential elements of contemporary feminist sensibility include a respect for the female experience, attention to language, a commitment to social change, client collaboration, and appropriate therapist disclosure. It is a means of validating, strengthening, and promoting resilience in lesbian couple treatment. Additional areas of focus from a feminist approach involve recognizing the lesbian couple's dilemma of identity management, assessing the couple's access to social support, mobilizing the dyad's strengths and methods of coping, and confronting social injustices that compromise their functioning (Rostosky, Riggle, Gray, & Hatton, 2007).

Assessment and Treatment

Couples and therapists alike lack a clear template of what a couple "should" look like (Patterson & Schwartz, 1994), and we must strive to balance our understanding of processes that are fundamental to all couples and at the same time recognize what is particularly unique to lesbian dyads (Basham, 1999). For example, couples of all types rank-order intimacy (affection and sex) and power issues (demands and equality) as the most frequently argued points in their relationships (Kurdek, 1994). However, by understanding and recognizing the unique qualities of the lesbian relationship, we stay more intentional and resist the imposition of a heterosexual standard on female couples (Biaggio et al., 2002). As such, we remain more likely to honor their distinctive norms.

Lesbian couples can ascribe differing meanings to life processes, including sexual exclusivity, the definition of family, and the oftentimes prominent role of former partners in the couple's life, so we must resist overpathologizing what might be normative behavior in the lesbian community (Bepko & Johnson, 2000). Lesbian couples often bond with lesbian "sisters" and kindred spirits, forming together to create a much needed sanctuary (Goodrich et al., 1988). Moreover, discovering the couple's sense of family—beyond any legal- or blood-bound ties—is of the utmost importance, as often the couple's "family of choice" determines who might be included in therapy sessions (Bepko & Johnson, 2000), and it certainly guides the clinical goals and direction. In addition, lesbian couples, often marginalized within traditional religions, are often searching for alternative ways to honor and express spirituality through diverse means and rituals (Connolly, 2005).

Scrivner and Eldridge (1995) consolidated a number of recommendations for therapy. They recommend assessing the extent that the presenting problems might be related to a lesbian identity, individually assessing the stages of lesbian identity development and how it might intersect with other contextual identities, how much connection or support the clients might draw from the lesbian community, and the degree of discrimination and safety experienced. Other areas of couple assessment include assessing the amount of social validation received, possible need for positive role models, the effects of gender-role socialization, and the expectations of each partner within the relationship.

It remains important to engage in a careful and deliberate assessment of the couple dynamics and the couple's presenting concerns to determine the degree and nuance of processes and whether there are clinical implications that would lead to goals for therapy. On a deeper, more contextual level, we must assess in what ways the partners individually and the couple as a whole are impacted by heterosexism, homoprejudice, sexism, and internalized homophobia and by the sociocultural or legal discrimination they have encountered.

As we assess the lesbian identity development of each individual and the couple, some questions come to the forefront. What is their degree of internalized homophobia? How do they self-identify and manage their identity? In what contexts do the partners feel safe to be authentic? Is their lesbian identity primary or competing with other cultural identities? What is their stage of couple development? Are they matched in their actual and ideal images of themselves as partners and as a couple? Based on orientation, are their families a source of strength or an added stressor to their relationship? Have the partners found additional or alternativee sources of support in friends, created family, and the lesbian community? What is their sense of spirituality? Do they enact any rituals? These questions can inform our assessment and guide in treatment planning.

When choosing the type of intervention, practitioners might consider three strategies helpful in determining whether to focus on risks, resources, or processes. According to Masten and Coatsworth (1998), risk-focused interventions are aimed at what can be eliminated or prevented, which stressors can be averted, or how the impact of the stressors can be reduced. Resource-focused interventions are additive; they counterbalance the risk. Process-focused interventions focus on efforts to improve the relationship, and they are strongly associated to competence and focusing on strengths.

Therapeutic Process

Stressor events impacting lesbian couples are often ambiguous and nonvolitional (Boss, 1988). As a result, a unique grief process can surface for each individual, the couple, and the family; and lesbian couples might need more therapeutic relationship building, feelings of safety, and an explicit encouragement or prompt to bring the stressors and the grief into the therapeutic conversation (Connolly, 2005, 2012). The complexity of oppression and the forces of sexism can dilute and submerge couples' poignant stories of tragedies and the pain of threatened or experienced loss, resulting in the loss of opportunity to recognize and acknowledge their amazing resilience (Connolly, 2005). Naming the stressors, the strengths, and the developmental processes can be extremely useful. For instance, naming the stressors and the resulting dynamics can amplify confidence in the relationship and stabilize either the immediate crisis or the couple (e.g., Slater, 1995; Slater & Mencher, 1991). Couples often fail to realize that many of the differences can smooth out as the relationship grows and develops; they feel relief when realizing that instead of the problems being inherent flaws in the relationship, they are developmental and correctable differences in their relational maturation and growth (Mattison & McWhirter, 1987; McWhirter & Mattison, 1996).

Furthermore, we must strike a delicate and intentional balance among the affectional (Scrivner & Eldridge, 1995), affiliative (Sanders & Kroll, 2000), and sexual components of a same-sex relationship. Therapists should evaluate and expand their own ideas about sexual desire and behavior to reduce the likelihood of falsely creating problems in need of solution, possibly even redefining sex therapy with lesbian couples as relational work (Prouty Lyness & Lyness, 2007), and expanding our conceptualization of "sexual" to include physical intimacy (Connolly, 2004). Moreover, we must assess the depth and breadth of the sociopolitical, intrapsychic, and familial processes that might impact the couple while not overlooking the physiological ones (Goodrich et al., 1988).

Other therapeutic processes are important. We must resist assuming similarities in the relational capacities of lesbian partners based on their gender-role socialization because doing so hampers our ability to see individual differences and thus intervene appropriately (Murphy, 1994). If closeness does appear to be a therapeutic issue, the therapist helps the couple understand and manage the polarizing roles that develop during conflict regarding merger and separation, facilitates a greater understanding about each partner's views regarding intimacy, and fosters the skills necessary for negotiation of the problems resulting from their individual concerns in order to convert blame of each other into problems in couple dynamics (Biaggio et al., 2002). In addition, our interventions and language within session must be gender neutral, with avoidance of sexist and heterosexist language and paradigms. When sexist and heterosexual images creep into our language, immediate remediation can be powerful in identifying and naming the process and modeling active methods to fight all -isms.

Therapist Issues and Qualities

We must recognize the unique role of the therapist in lesbian couple therapy. Goodrich et al. (1988) provide a number of salient points that remain true when working with lesbian couples. We must recognize any mutually shared homoprejudice or heterosexist bias, avoid a hands-off policy or reluctance to address issues that one would address with heterosexual couples, remain cognizant of classifying clients by their presentation in therapy rather than their orientation, avoid idealizing the lesbian experience, and balance our assessment of both strengths and deficits.

When working with lesbian couples, one must be ever aware that female couples not only encounter the burdens of homoprejudice, as gay male couples do, but also confront the additive impact of maneuvering a relationship within a sexist culture (e.g., see Brown, 1995). The consequences of misogyny can appear small and personal but can have sweeping systemic ramifications, with slights that appear too small to mention resulting in enormous consequences (Goodrich, 2003). The effects of sexism, however subtle (Wright & Fish, 1997), can have overarching and devastating effects for individuals, couples, and families.

As therapists and researchers, we must continually reexamine existing models and practices for insidious and embedded sexist and heterosexist underpinnings in current psychotherapeutic theories (Halstead, 2003). This reexamination process illuminates not only gender differences but also the power of one gender over the other (Goodrich et al., 1988). However, we must always remain open to continued exploration and expansion, as even feminist therapy has privileged heterosexual couples (Rampage, 1996; Seem, 2001). Therapists often look at what health and pathology should look like and apply these paradigms to lesbian clients, who have not only distinct stressors but also unique norms and relational resilience processes (Seem, 2001).

Couples often begin, end, and negotiate major relational and life transitions without the legal protection or rituals afforded different-sex couples. Because this lack of protections and rituals can leave same-sex clients vulnerable to feelings of self-blame, shame, and helplessness, a strong therapeutic relationship can, along with externalizing these processes during the therapeutic encounter, prove invaluable (Bepko & Johnson, 2000). Forming an affiliative clinical relationship helps support a focus on strengths, resilience, and coping abilities; encourage multiple perspectives; and acknowledge power dynamics both outside and inside the therapy room (Long & Pietsch, 2004). A functional analysis by the therapist allows for an understanding of how the relationship functions and in what ways the relational patterns are helping or creating problems for the individuals and for the couple (Biaggio et al., 2002).

Furthermore, in order to provide lesbian couples effective, ethical, and affirmative therapy, therapists must know and educate themselves (Prouty Lyness & Lyness, 2007). Therapists must remain aware and responsive to personal blind spots and biases (Biaggio et al., 2002; Perez, DeBord, & Bieschke, 2000) and must actively and continuously guard against their own heterocentric bias (Green & Mitchell, 2002). They must be mindful that we are all enculturated and shaped by society, and biases can seep into the therapeutic process (Schiemann & Smith, 1996). We must strive to keep current with relevant ethical issues and consider appropriate referrals when doing so best serves the clients (Scrivner & Eldridge, 1995). Unless referrals are needed for specific mental health issues, the couple is the focus of treatment rather than the individual; but the immediate family, extended family, community, and society cannot be overlooked.

Therapists also must adopt a prochoice approach to disclosure (Green, 2002). Thus, if a client chooses not to disclose, that decision should be respected as a viable and psychologically healthy choice (Green, 2000). Some couples choose not to disclose simply because doing so is not "worth the emotional toll it would take to do it" (participant's words; Connolly, 2006, p. 147), whereas other long-term couples report the healing power of time and history with family members (Connolly, 2005).

Remaining well informed of the cultural history and setting in which issues and stressors are born and staying abreast of the cutting-edge trends in ethics, research, and practice (Perez et al., 2000) are foundational. The therapist not only should be knowledgeable about lesbian culture and relationships but also must approach the couple's perspective and experience with respect and openness (Biaggio et al., 2002). Therapists provide a powerful role in validating the couple and letting the partners know they value the struggle within this culture (Halstead, 2003). Therapists' tasks are often compensating as they help affirm the couple's legitimacy (Martin, 1998) and help couples nullify the internalized negative messages, restore and rejuvenate their relationship, and substantiate and validate their couplehood (Slater & Mencher, 1991). The bond-invalidating experiences that lesbian couples encounter are frequently the reason the partners seek therapy, especially at the early part of the relationship, when what they are actually seeking is a witnessing and validating of their coupling (Roth, 1985), which can range from joyous, to commonplace and routine, to traumatic.

Case Study

Julie and Isabella, a dual-career couple together for 12 years, had experienced stressors in the past. Although these women, ages 42 and 47 respectively, connected quickly and enjoyed the first flurry of relational excitement, after a few months they wondered whether the relationship was built on something substantial. Although some differences existed, including cultural variables, their values and interests matched well, and they began living together a few months later. The second challenging time was around Year 3. What seemed at first to be a minor flirtation for Julie had, from Isabella's perspective, turned into an emotional affair that threatened their relationship. They worked with a therapist who focused on helping the women regain and increase intimacy and communication around needs and wants within the relationship. The immediate crisis seemed to pass, and the couple ended that therapeutic relationship after a few months. Yet neither woman felt secure that they had gained solid footing as a couple.

For this third crisis, the couple found a feminist therapist who was well known in the community for her work with female couples. Julie and Isabella presented with concerns about periods of disconnection, particularly during the past few years, and the feeling that they were "sinking in quicksand" of late. Sexual and physical intimacy, which they had consistently enjoyed throughout the relationship, now felt awkward and contrived. The therapist explored perceived strengths in the relationship, which included shared values and relational commitment. When the therapist asked how the couple had managed to be sufficiently resilient to rebound from adversity as a female–female relationship, at first the couple denied any such conditions. They even provided an example of how over time Isabella's and Julie's families had learned to love and accept them as a couple. When asked specifically about managing their lesbian identity in their careers, Julie expressed total comfort. Her small group of coworkers all knew about the relationship and occasionally included Isabella in functions. Isabella's career, however, was in an ultraconservative field and company; no one at the company knew about Julie's or Isabella's relational orientation.

The therapist then asked how these differences affected them as a couple. Over the next several sessions, each partner disclosed a growing frustration over the inability to be totally open. Julie described her resentment of Isabella's increasing prioritization of work over the relationship; the more Isabella focused on work, the less important Julie felt within the relationship. Isabella shared that she did not mind the long work hours; she liked what she did. Her frustration came from how she had to almost "flip a switch" between work and home. Isabella's salary and benefits funded three quarters of the couple's living and leisure expenses; and in an effort to advance in her work environment, Isabella routinely chose to ignore prejudicial comments by coworkers and felt increasing pressure when attending company social functions alone in the sea of couples. Isabella admitted it was hard disconnecting from such an important part of herself all day long, and then coming home and shifting into a loving partner.

Over the next few months, the therapist continued naming processes and weaving in conversations around heterosexism and sexism. She helped the couple recognize ways in which prejudice had become internalized, grasp its significant impact on the relationship, and fortify their strengths to withstand inherent and ongoing stressors. Over time the couple honed skills in identifying what conditions placed them at higher risk, discussing factors that could be avoided or even changed, and creating strategies to help circumvent relational stress. Emotional intimacy increased as well as mutual and explicit appreciation of each other's strengths and complementary differences. Physical and sexual intimacy had become more frequent and spontaneous. The couple stabilized; and although they ended their regular sessions with the therapist, the couple committed to using this valuable resource as future needs arose.

Conclusion

It remains important to be aware of developmental stressor points that may emerge in relationships. McNab and Gedan (1997) identify the 3 month marker as a make-it-or-break-it point, and that rings true from my professional experience and personal observation. The intensity often presents quickly, and at that several-month point a decision is made about the suitability or viability of the relationship. In addition, Berzon (1996) identified that couples together for 3 or more years could be considered long term. However, in her clinical experience, clients have referred to that time as the point when boredom sets in; couples consider staying together too much work or they have lost their passion, such that Berzon wondered if the "three-year myth," the notion that relationships end after 3 years, has become a self-fulfilling prophecy within the lesbian community.

I initiated a qualitative research study (Connolly, 2010a) that focused on developmental stressors at the 3–4-year relational stage. Although multiple 3–4-year relationships were not sought for the study and formed no part of the study criteria, many women surprisingly reported up to four relationships of that specific length and explicitly spoke of a resigned attitude, relational fatigue, and an expectation of failure. There appears to be another critical stressor point at the 10-year milestone, wherein some couples have an anticipation, goal, and vision of reaching that milestone, but around that marker they experience significant stressors that contribute to distress within or dissolution of the relationship (Connolly, 2010b). Being attentive to the potential stressor points that could affect clients' mental health and relational well-being will be important for our clinical work.

Clinicians must be mindful of the minority stress experienced by couples, facilitate and enhance their coping skills, and approach policies perpetuating social stigma and chronic stress critically (Kurdek, 2005) and proactively. By helping couples understand the degree to which external stressors overlay and overshadow their dyadic experience, we help minimize an over-personalization of the struggles and assist them in continuing to develop creative responses for safeguarding their relationship (Slater, 1995). When working with lesbian couples, a clinician's failure to take this approach can thwart the therapeutic process and the ultimate healing for the couple.

Furthermore, because all same-sex couples are situated at an intersection of the psychological, sociological, and political, homonegativity must be seen as a societal disorder, which can be eradicated only by social change (Martin, 1998). Regardless of the dangers and risks associated with LGBT advocacy and action (Levitt et al., 2009), we must as individuals and as a broad-based community of professionals commit to this important process of working together to create safety and equality for all.

References

Basham, K. K. (1999). Therapy with a lesbian couple: The art of balancing lenses. In J. Laird (Ed.), *Lesbians and lesbian families: Reflections on theory and practice* (pp. 143–177). New York: Columbia University Press.

Ben-Ari, A. (1995). The discovery that an offspring is gay: Parents', gay men's, and lesbians' perspectives. *Journal of Homosexuality, 30*(1), 89–112.

Bepko, C., & Johnson, T. (2000). Gay and lesbian couples in therapy: Perspectives for the contemporary family therapist. *Journal of Marital and Family Therapy, 26*(4), 409–419.

Berzon, B. (1988). *Permanent partners: Building gay and lesbian relationships that last* (pp. 1–60). New York: E. P. Dutton.

Berzon, B. (1996). *The intimacy dance: A guide to long-term success in gay and lesbian relationships.* New York: Plume.

Biaggio, M., Coan, S., & Adams, W. (2002). Couples therapy for lesbians: Understanding merger and impact of homophobia. *Journal of Lesbian Studies, 6*(1), 129–138. doi:10.1300/J155v06n01_12

Bigner, J. J. (2000). Gay and lesbian families. In W. C. Nichols, M. S. Pace-Nichols, D. S. Becvar, & A. Y. Napier (Eds.), *Handbook of family development and intervention* (pp. 279–298). New York: Wiley.

Blumstein, P., & Schwartz, P. (1983). *American couples: Money, work, sex.* New York: William Morrow.

Boss, P. (1988). *Family stress management.* Newbury Park, CA: Sage.

Bradford, J., Ryan, C., & Rothblum, E. D. (1994). National lesbian health care survey: Implications for mental health care. *Journal of Consulting and Clinical Psychology, 62*(2), 228–242. doi:10.1037/0022-006X.62.2.228

Brown, L. S. (1991). Commentary on the special issue of *The Counseling Psychologist*: Counseling with lesbians and gay men. *The Counseling Psychologist, 19*(2), 235–238.

Brown, L. S. (1995). Therapy with same-sex couples: An introduction. In N. S. Jacobson & A. S. Gurman (Eds.), *Clinical handbook of couple therapy* (pp. 274–291). New York, NY: Guilford Press.

Browning, C., Reynolds, A. L., & Dworkin, S. H. (1991). Affirmative psychotherapy for lesbian women. *The Counseling Psychologist, 19*(2), 177–196.

Bryant, A. S., & Demian. (1994). Relationship characteristics of American gay and lesbian couples: Findings from a national survey. *Journal of Gay & Lesbian Social Services, 1*(2), 101–117. doi:10.1300/J041v01n02_06

Connolly, C. M. (2004). Lesbian couples: A qualitative look at long-term love. *Journal of Couple and Relationship Therapy, 3*(1), 13–26. doi:10.1300/J398v03n01_02

Connolly, C. M. (2005). A qualitative exploration of resilience in long-term lesbian couples. *The Family Journal: Counseling and Therapy for Couples and Families, 13*(3), 266–280. doi:10.1177/1066480704273681

Connolly, C. M. (2006). A feminist perspective of resilience in lesbian couples. *Journal of Feminist Family Therapy, 18*(1/2), 137–162. doi:10.1300/J086v18n01_06

Connolly, C. M. (2012). Lesbian couples and marriage counseling. In S. Dworkin & M. Pope (Eds.). *Casebook for counseling lesbian, gay, bisexual, and transgender persons and their families* (pp. 83–89). Alexandria, VA: American Counseling Association.

Connolly, C. M. (2010a). *Lesbian women: Developmental stressors at the three- to four-year relational stage.* Manuscript in preparation.

Connolly, C. M. (2010b). *A qualitative exploration of lesbian women: Critical stressors at the 10-year relational milestone.* Manuscript in preparation.

Connolly, C. M., & Sicola, M. K. (2005). Listening to lesbian couples: Communication competence in long-term relationships. *Journal of GLBT Family Studies, 1*(2), 143–168. doi:10.1300/J461v01n02

Cowan, G., Heiple, B., Marquez, C., Khatchadourian, D., & McNevin, M. (2005). Heterosexuals' attitudes toward hate crimes and hate speech against gays and lesbians: Old-fashioned and modern heterosexism. *Journal of Homosexuality, 49*(2), 67–82. doi:10.1300/J082v49n02_04

Davison, G. C. (2001). Conceptual and ethical issues in therapy for the psychological problems of gay men, lesbians, and bisexuals. *Journal of Clinical Psychology, 57*(5), 695–704.

Falco, K. L. (1996). Psychotherapy with women who love women. In R. P. Cabaj & T. S. Stein (Eds.), *Textbook of homosexuality and mental health* (pp. 397–412). Washington, DC: American Psychiatric Press.

Fields, J. (2001). Normal queers: Straight parents respond to their children's "coming out." *Symbolic Interaction, 24*(2), 165–187.

Goodrich, T. J. (2003). A feminist family therapist's work is never done. In L. B. Silverstein & T. J. Goodrich (Eds.), *Feminist family therapy: Empowerment in social context* (pp. 3–15). Washington, DC: American Psychological Association.

Goodrich, T. J., Rampage, C., Ellman, B., & Halstead, K. (1988). *Feminist family therapy: A casebook.* New York: Norton.

Green, R.-J. (2000). "Lesbians, gay men, and their parents": A critique of LaSala and the prevailing clinical "wisdom." *Family Process, 39*(2), 257–266.

Green, R.-J. (2002). Lesbians, gays, and family psychology: Resources for teaching and practice. In E. Davis-Russell (Ed.), *The California School of Professional Psychology handbook of multicultural education, research, intervention, and training* (pp. 88–105). San Francisco, CA: Jossey-Bass.

Green, R.-J., Bettinger, M., & Zacks, E. (1996). Are lesbian couples fused and gay male couples disengaged? Questioning gender straightjackets. In J. Laird & R. J. Green (Eds.), *Lesbians and gays in couples and families: A handbook for therapists* (pp. 185–230). San Francisco, CA: Jossey-Bass.

Green, R.-J., & Mitchell, V. (2002). Gay and lesbian couples in therapy: Homophobia, relational ambiguity, and social support. In A. S. Gurman & N. S. Jacobson (Eds.), *Clinical handbook of couple therapy* (3rd ed., pp. 546–568). New York: Guilford Press.

Halstead, K. (2003). Over the rainbow: The lesbian family. In L. B. Silverstein & J. T. Goodrich (Eds.), *Feminist family therapy: Empowerment in social context* (pp. 39–50). Washington, DC: American Psychological Association.

Harry, J. (1993). Being out: A general model. *Journal of Homosexuality, 26*(1), 25–39.

Jordan, J. (1992). Relational resilience. Stone Center Working Paper Series. *Work in Progress,* No. 57 (pp. 1–13). Wellesley, MA: Stone Center.

Jordan, J. V., & Hartling, L. M. (2002). New developments in relational-cultural theory. In M. Ballou & L. S. Brown (Eds.), *Rethinking mental health and disorder: Feminist perspectives* (pp. 48–70). New York, NY: Guilford Press.

Jordan, J. V., Kaplan, A. G., Miller, J. B., Stiver, I. P., & Surrey, J. L. (1991). *Women's growth in connection: Writings from the Stone Center.* New York, NY: Guilford Press.

Krestan, J. A., & Bepko, C. S. (1980). The problem of fusion in the lesbian relationship. *Family Process, 19,* 277–289.

Kurdek, L. A. (1994). Areas of conflict for gay, lesbian and heterosexual couples: What couples argue about influences relational satisfaction. *Journal of Marriage and the Family, 56*(4), 923–934.

Kurdek, L. A. (1998). Relationship outcomes and their predictors: Longitudinal evidence from heterosexual married, gay cohabiting, and lesbian cohabiting couples. *Journal of Marriage and the Family, 60*(3), 553–568.

Kurdek, L. A. (2005). What do we know about gay and lesbian couples? *Current Directions in Psychological Science, 14*(5), 251–254. doi:10.1111/j.0963-7214.2005.00375.x

Kurdek, L. A. (2008). Change in relationship quality for partners from lesbian, gay male, and heterosexual couples. *Journal of Family Psychology, 22*(5), 701–711. doi:10.1037/0893-3200.22.5.701

Laird, J. (1993). Lesbian and gay families. In F. Walsh (Ed.), *Normal family processes* (2nd ed., pp. 282–328). New York, NY: Guilford Press.

Levitt, H. M., Ovrebo, E., Anderson-Cleveland, M. B., Leone, C., Jeong, J. V., Arm, J. R., … Horne, S. G. (2009). Balancing dangers: GLBT experience in a time of anti-GLBT legislation. *Journal of Counseling Psychology, 56*(1), 67–81.

Littlefield, G. D. (1994). Common threads and themes involved in long-term lesbian relationships. *Dissertation Abstracts International: Section A. Humanities and Social Sciences, 55*(2), 394.

Logan, C. R. (1996). Homophobia? No, homoprejudice. *Journal of Homosexuality, 31*(3), 31–53.

Long, J. K. (1996). Working with lesbians, gays, and bisexuals: Addressing heterosexism in supervision. *Family Process, 35*, 377–388.

Long, J. K., & Pietsch, U. (2004). How do therapists of same-sex couples "do it"? In S. Greene & D. Flemons (Eds.), *Quickies: Brief approaches to sex therapy* (pp. 171–188). New York, NY: Norton.

Martin, A. (1998). Clinical issues in psychotherapy with lesbian-, gay-, and bisexual-parented families. In C. Patterson & A. R. D'Augelli (Eds.), *Lesbian, gay, and bisexual identities in families: Psychological perspectives* (pp. 270–291). New York, NY: Oxford.

Masten, A. S., & Coatsworth, J. D. (1998). The development of competence in favorable and unfavorable environments: Lessons from research on successful children. *American Psychologist, 53*(2), 205–220.

Mattison, A. M., & McWhirter, D. P. (1987). Stage discrepancy in male couples. *Journal of Homosexuality, 14*, 89–99.

McCarn, S. R., & Fassinger, R. E. (1996). Revisioning sexual minority identity formation: A new model of lesbian identity and its implications for counseling and research. *The Counseling Psychologist, 24*(3), 508–534.

McNab, C., & Gedan, S. (1997). *The loving lesbian.* Tallahassee, FL: Naiad Press.

McWhirter, D. P., & Mattison, A. M. (1996). Male couples. In R. P. Cabaj & T. S. Stein (Eds.), *Textbook of homosexuality and mental health* (pp. 319–337). Washington, DC: American Psychiatric Press.

Mencher, J. (1997). Intimacy in lesbian relationships: A critical reexamination of fusion. In J. Jordan (Ed.), *Women's growth in diversity: More writings from the Stone Center* (pp. 311–330). New York, NY: Guilford Press.

Murphy, B. C. (1994). Difference and diversity: Gay and lesbian couples. *Journal of Gay & Lesbian Social Services, 1*(2), 5–31. doi:10.1300/J041v01n02_02

Negy, C., & McKinney, C. (2006). Application of feminist therapy: Promoting resiliency among lesbian and gay families. *Journal of Feminist Family Therapy, 18*(1–2), 67–83. doi:10.1300/J086vl8n01_03

Ossana, S. M. (2000). Relationship and couples counseling. In R. M. Perez, K. A. DeBord, & K. J. Bieschke (Eds.), *Handbook of counseling and psychotherapy with lesbian, gay, and bisexual clients* (pp. 275–302). Washington, DC: American Psychological Association.

Oswald, R. F. (2003). A member of the wedding? Heterosexism and family ritual. *Journal of Lesbian Studies, 7*(2), 107–131.

Otis, M. D., Riggle, E. D., & Rostosky, S. S. (2006). Impact of mental health on perceptions of relationship satisfaction and quality among female same-sex couples. *Journal of Lesbian Studies, 10*(1/2), 267–283. doi:10.1300/J155v10n01_14

Pardie, L., & Herb, C. R. (1997). Merger and fusion in lesbian relationships: A problem of diagnosing what's wrong in terms of what's right. *Women & Therapy, 20*(3), 51–62. doi:10.1300/J015v20n03_04

Parker, L. (2003). Bringing power from the margins to the center. In L. B. Silverstein & T. J. Goodrich (Eds.), *Feminist family therapy: Empowerment in social context* (pp. 225–238). Washington, DC: American Psychological Association.

Patterson, D. G., Ciabattari, T., & Schwartz, P. (1999). The constraints of innovation: Commitment and stability among same-sex couples. In J. M. Adams & W. H. Jones (Eds.), *Handbook of interpersonal commitment and relationship stability.* New York, NY: Kluwer Academic.

Patterson, D. G., & Schwartz, P. (1994). The social construction of conflict in intimate same-sex couples. In D. D. Cahn (Ed.), *Conflict in personal relationships* (pp. 3–26). Hillsdale, NJ: Erlbaum.

Perez, R. M., DeBord, K. A., & Bieschke, K. J. (2000). Introduction: The challenge of awareness, knowledge, and action. In R. M. Perez, K. A. DeBord, & K. J. Bieschke (Eds.), *Handbook of counseling and psychotherapy with lesbian, gay, and bisexual clients* (pp. 3–8). Washington, DC: American Psychological Association.

Prouty Lyness, A. M., & Lyness, K. P. (2007). Feminist issues in couple therapy. *Journal of Couple & Relationship Therapy*, 6(1/2), 181–195. doi:10.1300/J398v06n01_15

Rampage, C. (1996). On being a feminist trainer in an independent institute. In K. Weingarten & M. Bograd (Eds.), *Reflections of feminist family therapy training* (pp. 7–19). New York, NY: Haworth Press.

Riggle, E. D., Rostosky, S. S., & Horne, S. G. (2010). Psychological distress, well-being, and legal recognition in same-sex couple relationships. *Journal of Family Psychology*, 24(1), 82–86. doi:10.1037/a0017942

Rostosky, S. S., Riggle, E. D., Gray, B. E., & Hatton, R. L. (2007). Minority stress experiences in committed same-sex couple relationships. *Professional Psychology*, 38(4), 392–400. doi:10.1037/0735-7028.38.4.392

Roth, S. (1985). Psychotherapy with lesbian couples: Individual issues, female socialization, and the social context. *Journal of Marital and Family Therapy*, 11(3), 273–286.

Sanders, G. L., & Kroll, I. T. (2000). Generating stories of resilience: Helping gay and lesbian youth and their families. *Journal of Marital and Family Therapy*, 26(4), 433–442.

Schiemann, J., & Smith, W. L. (1996). The homosexual couple. In H. Kessler & I. D. Yalom (Eds.), *Treating couples*. San Francisco, CA: Jossey-Bass.

Scrivner, R., & Eldridge, N. S. (1995). Lesbian and gay family psychology. In R. H. Mikesell, D. Lusterman, & S. H. McDaniel (Eds.), *Integrating family therapy: Handbook of family psychology and systems theory* (pp. 327–344). Washington, DC: American Psychological Association.

Seem, S. R. (2001). Feminist family therapy: For heterosexual couples only? In K. M. May (Ed.), *Feminist family therapy* (pp. 29–51). Alexandria, VA: American Counseling Association.

Slater, S. (1995). *The lesbian family life cycle*. New York, NY: Free Press.

Slater, S., & Mencher, J. (1991). The lesbian family life cycle: A contextual approach. *American Journal of Orthopsychiatry*, 61(3), 372–382. doi:10.1037/h0079262

Szymanski, D. M., & Chung, Y. B. (2001). The lesbian internalized homophobia scale: A rational/theoretical approach. *Journal of Homosexuality*, 41(2), 37–52. doi:10.1300/J082v41n02_03

Szymanski, D. M., Chung, Y. B., & Balsam, K. F. (2001). Psychosocial correlates of internalized homophobia in lesbians. *Measurement and Evaluation in Counseling and Development*, 34(1), 27–38. Retrieved from http://find.galegroup.com/gtx/infomark.do?&contentSet=IAC-Documents&type=retrieve&tabID=T002&prodId=AONE&docId=A74407039&source=gale&srcprod=AONE&userGroupName=txshracd2550&version=1.0

Taylor, S. E., Klein, L. C., Lewis, B. P, Gruenewald, T. L., Gurung, R. A. R., & Updegraff, J. A. (2000). Biobehavioral responses to stress in females: Tend-and-befriend, not fight-or-flight. *Psychological Review*, 107(3), 411–429. doi:10.1037/0033-295X.107.3.411

Wright, C. I., & Fish, L. S. (1997). Feminist family therapy: The battle against subtle sexism. In N. V. Benokraitis (Ed.), *Subtle sexism: Current practice and prospects for change* (pp. 201–215). Thousand Oaks, CA: Sage.

Zacks, E., Green, R., & Marrow, J. (1988). Comparing lesbian and heterosexual couples on the circumplex model: An initial investigation. *Family Process*, 27, 471–484. doi:10.1111/j.1545-5300.1988.00471.x

4

Affirmative Bisexual Couple Therapy

MARY BRADFORD

The fact that bisexuality is largely unrecognized has an impact on bisexual people's identity development and can have significant effects on their relationships. It is important for therapists working with bisexual people in relationships to understand the pressure they are under to conform to a dualistic system, as well as the cultural context of pathology, particularly the destructive effects of homophobia and biphobia. There are several ways in which bisexuality can influence the issues couples present. A partner's bisexuality may be inconsequential, might be highlighted by the presenting problem, or could be the central issue for a couple. In any of these cases, the therapeutic tasks include assessing the developmental stage of sexual identity, affirming the validity of bisexuality, providing education and resources, helping both partners come to terms with changes in the relationship, and, possibly, facilitating negotiations regarding polyamory and safer sex. When a couple is in crisis because of the discovery of bisexuality through sexual infidelity, the issues are complex and may require redefinition of the relationship. This chapter will elucidate these concerns and ways of addressing them and offer case examples to illustrate the issues.

The Experience of Bisexuality

Bisexuality is more common than most people—including perhaps most bisexuals—realize. Bisexual people are all around: single, in same-sex relationships, in heterosexual relationships, and in polyamorous relationships. They may assume lesbian or gay or straight identities, according to their current relationships, or they may say nothing at all about their sexual orientation. Many do not talk about being bisexual because bisexuality confuses or threatens people or because people just do not understand. But a typical conversation I hear is this: "I'm actually bisexual, but because I've been with Ginny for 25 years, I don't talk about it; it doesn't seem to make sense. But it's who I really am." Or another is this: "Because I'm married and a father of two and very happy in my relationship, I've never talked about it. But I'm bisexual. I won't act on it, because it would destabilize my marriage and life, but it's something true about me."

Because they are well adjusted, in healthy relationships, and have come to terms with their choices, commitments, and sacrifices, these people will not show up in your practice with problems regarding sexual orientation. You may even see them for other problems without ever knowing about this aspect of their identity. Those whom you will see are people who are conflicted—who feel forced to make choices they do not want, who have to negate part of themselves to fit into society or a subculture, who fear the loss of a relationship or security if they reveal part of their true nature, whose partners are distressed by their bisexuality, who find themselves caught between being true to their partners or to themselves, who keep part of their experience secret and live in fear of exposure, or who, unwilling to continue to hide, create crises that challenges their relationships.

Many who behave bisexually will not even identify as bisexual. They may be able to conceive of themselves only within the dichotomy of heterosexuality–homosexuality. For instance, after years of marriage, emotional attachment, and sexual satisfaction with a woman, a man may have a sexual relationship with a man and announce that he is now gay. A woman who has lived all her adult life as a lesbian, having found her identity, her sense of community, her support system, and her political values as a lesbian, may fall in love with a man and identify as "a lesbian who happens to love a man." Bisexuality may be too threatening (because of negative stereotypes of bisexuality) or too unknown (because of the lack of visibility of bisexual people, of a supportive community, or of a clear definition) to claim as an identity, especially at a time of transition, loss, and turmoil.

Overview of Bisexuality

Bisexually identified people constitute an invisible minority. The Kinsey studies of the 1940s and 1950s (Kinsey, Pomeroy, & Martin, 1948; Kinsey, Pomeroy, Martin, & Gebhard, 1953) revealed that sexuality is not restricted to the dichotomous categories of exclusive heterosexuality or homosexuality but exists on a continuum. Klein, Sepekoff, and Wolf's (1985) multidimensional model depicted sexuality as variable, complex, and fluid. However, psychological research and literature often continue to reinforce the myth of a sexual dichotomy by overlooking bisexuality or assuming it is only a state of transition or confusion. Socially, bisexual people tend to be marginalized, pathologized, and silenced. The lack of visible role models, community, and vocabulary serves to obstruct their identity development and self-definition. They experience pressure to identify in accordance with the binary system—from family, friends, and even their relational partners.

Research on bisexuality reveals that bisexual people exist in significant numbers, live a wide variety of lifestyles, are a heterogeneous population, and suffer discrimination in both the heterosexual culture and the gay and lesbian communities (Bradford, 2004a). Bisexual identity development is similar to, though perhaps more complex and less linear than, lesbian and gay identity development. It involves questioning the reality of dual attractions and struggling with doubt until fully able to affirm one's own experience; coming to terms with an identity not mirrored in the culture and finding one's own unique meaning; and then working to maintain the identity despite constant encounters with isolation, invisibility, and pressure to dichotomize (Bradford, 2004a). Unlike gay and lesbian identities, which can be strengthened by the length of time in same-sex relationships, bisexual identity can become harder to maintain the longer one is in a monogamous relationship.

There are many ways to be bisexual, many definitions of bisexuality, and many different experiences of bisexuality, all a result of the great diversity of the population (Bradford, 2004b; Goetstouwers, 2006). For the purpose of discussing issues in relationships and therapy with couples, I will use the terms *bisexual* and *bisexuality*, in the general sense, to describe both people who behave bisexually and those who identify as bisexual, and I will consider as bisexual those who have the potential for intimate romantic and sexual relationships with same-sex and other-sex people, whatever their experience of acting on that potential.

Affirmative Therapy

In just the last 40 years, psychology and psychotherapy have moved from an illness model of homosexuality and bisexuality that pathologized people, their sexual orientations, and their relationships to an affirmative model that addresses relevant concerns for lesbian, gay, and bisexual people and the therapists who work with them (Fox, 2006). It is important to establish a description of affirmative therapy that lays a framework for this work. The basis of the concept of affirmative therapy is the understanding that the difficulties gay, lesbian, and bisexual people face are culturally conferred. This means that the problems people have concerning their sexual orientations are not consequences of homosexuality or bisexuality but of homophobia and biphobia. These problems result from intolerance of difference and from ignorance.

Affirmative therapy for bisexual women and men and their partners recognizes that our dualistic system of identification is destructive; it leads to social pressure to choose between parts of the self. The invisibility of healthy models of bisexuality and the absence of validation or subculture result in damaging stereotypes, prejudice, and discrimination. These experiences lead to oppression and shame and negative coping mechanisms. Affirmative therapists understand the wounding that results from the effects of a hidden, devalued self. They help to identify the (sometimes unconscious) pressures of countering social norms, and they normalize coping strategies that are used to withstand these pressures. Affirmative therapists are nonpathologizing and are validating of bisexuality and of same-sex and mixed-orientation relationships. They encourage and allow people to form their own definitions of their sexuality. They acknowledge the courage it takes to form and maintain an identity not validated in the culture and the resilience that is gained from overcoming obstacles. They assess and reinforce their clients' strengths. Affirmative therapists educate themselves about homosexuality and bisexuality and are able to provide helpful resources,[1] including books, Internet sites, support groups, and community assistance.

Bisexuality in Couples

There are numerous relational possibilities in which bisexuality may occur: bisexual–bisexual, bisexual–straight, bisexual–lesbian, and bisexual–gay. Further variations depend on biological sex (male, female, or intersex), gender (masculine, feminine, or transgender), age (level of life experience and maturity), sexual and relationship lifestyle (monogamy, polyamory, or polyfidelity), and ethnic, racial, and cultural differences. Any of these couples may come into therapy with such common relational issues as communication problems; difficulty resolving conflicts regarding parenting, sex, money, or in-laws; adjustment to life changes; personality differences; and dissatisfaction with physical, emotional, intellectual, spiritual, or sexual levels of connection. When the presenting problem is not related to sexual orientation, it is still useful to explore the perceived differences, similarities, definitions, and meanings of the partners' sexual identities.

Exploring Differences and Meanings

My experience is that couples are not usually asked to articulate their personal definitions of sexual identity or encouraged to talk together about their feelings related to differences, and they are often relieved to be able to do so. Even members of bisexual–bisexual couples can benefit from considering together their personal experiences of and conclusions about bisexuality. Although these partners often relate joy in finding another who understands, accepts, and does not have to be educated about bisexuality, they can make assumptions from their own experiences or fail to ask questions that further their understanding of differences. In a mixed-orientation relationship, failure to explore difference eliminates an opportunity to discover important information for self and mutual understanding. Failure to acknowledge bisexuality can have the effect of reinforcing invisibility and silencing discourse, contributing to shame or disconnection. Encouraging discussion about the differences and perceived meanings of sexualities, on the other hand, can uncover hidden concerns or misconceptions and facilitate increased understanding, empathy, and connection.

---

[1] Some good bisexual resources to start with are Ochs's (2005) *Getting Bi: Voices of Bisexuals Around the World*; Hutchens and Kaahumanu's (1991) *Bi Any Other Name: Bisexual People Speak Out*; Weise's (1992) *Closer to Home: Bisexuality and Feminism*; *The Journal of Bisexuality*; and the Bisexual Resource Center (http://www.biresource.org).

When Bisexuality Is Highlighted

Sometimes one partner's bisexuality, though not the central issue, is highlighted by the presenting problem. For example, a couple's diminished emotional or sexual connection may be attributed by a straight spouse to the partner's bisexuality, accompanied by a fear that the partner is "really gay" and, therefore, uninterested in the straight spouse. A lesbian–bisexual female couple who want to explore a sexually open relationship may run into conflict over fear that the bisexual partner will be exposed to HIV/AIDS. The betrayal of trust ensuing from an affair can be further complicated by the discovery that the affair was with someone of another sex than the aggrieved partner, with whom she or he feels unable to "compete." A parent who is distressed by his or her child's coming out gay, lesbian, bisexual, or transgender may generate conflict by blaming a partner's bisexuality. In these cases, bisexuality becomes emphasized or targeted, although other issues may be equally or more significant.

When Bisexuality Is the Focus

Sometimes a couple's issues are specifically related to bisexuality. One partner's bisexuality may engender confusion about definitions and labels for each partner and for their relationship. They may grapple with disclosure within family or community and have few or no models for their relationship. For instance, a bisexual man in a long-term committed relationship with a gay man may have a secondary committed relationship with a woman that is mutually consensual and satisfactory for all three, but they may have varying levels of comfort about being out to different family members and difficulties handling decisions about holidays and family visits. In another case, one partner's bisexuality may produce insecurity in the other, based on stereotypes of promiscuity and lack of information about the meaning of bisexuality, even though the bisexual partner is unconflicted and committed to monogamy. Internalized homophobia may lead a same-sex partner to assume that a bisexual partner would leave the relationship for a "more desirable" heterosexual partner if given the chance. Because bisexual partners in mixed-orientation relationships will likely have less community support, visibility, and validation for their sexual or relational identities than their partners have, there may be an imbalance of available resources that causes conflicts in relationships.

When Bisexuality Presents a Crisis

The most highly stressed couples tend to be those in crisis because of the revelation of one partner's bisexuality long after a monogamous commitment is established, especially when the revelation comes about after the discovery of a sexual affair. These couples are often dealing with broken trust, shock, guilt, and pain. In that case, the viability of the relationship is in question, and both parties are in great distress. They are dealing with both the aftermath of the infidelity and the newly revealed sexual identity. A straight woman may be unable to come to terms with finding out that her husband has a male lover with whom he wishes to continue a relationship. A straight man may have discovered by reading his wife's e-mail that she has been carrying on a secret sexual affair with a woman whom he thought was just her friend. A gay man or lesbian woman may feel the betrayal of a partner's sexual relationship with a person of another sex both very personally and also, in a broader political context, as a homophobic wounding.

Even when the bisexual person has not acted on an attraction to someone of another sex than his or her partner's, the partner can react with great fear to the revelation of bisexuality late into the relationship. As the bisexual woman or man grapples with a hitherto unexplored path, with unfulfilled desires, with the risks of acting or not acting on this newly acknowledged inclination, the gay, lesbian, or straight partner may feel destabilized and terrified by the possibility of loss—loss of the safe containment of monogamy, or loss of the relationship itself. Despite such challenges, however, there are rich possibilities for therapeutic gains in the scenarios described.

Strengths

While addressing problems that arise for couples, it is important for therapists to remain aware of and reinforce the strengths attained by those who struggle to come to terms with marginalized identities. The challenges of forming and maintaining both a positive sense of self and healthy relationships can have the benefit of leading to increased self-confidence, self-respect, and self-reliance. Bisexual individuals and their partners who overcome cultural rejection and invalidation often find that forging their own definitions of sexual and relational identity builds resilience that serves them in all aspects of their lives. It is an experience that can lead to tolerance and compassion for others, with increased sensitivity toward those who are different or oppressed. Bisexual people report feeling that their bisexual experiences enrich their relationships and allow for a deepening of connection with their partners, often unconfined by traditional gender roles (Bradford, 1997). These strengths can be emphasized in helping couples find solutions to their conflicts.

The Therapy

Assessment

As for any couple, the therapy begins with assessment. When bisexuality is a factor, besides the usual assessment of the individuals' and the relationship's history, strengths, and stresses, it is helpful to assess the developmental stage of bisexual identity. When someone is just beginning to explore dual attractions, there may be confusion and uncertainty for both partners, and the security of the relationship may feel threatened. The bisexual partner may need acknowledgment that some people really are attracted to different genders and permission to accept the newly discovered self (Matteson, 1996). The lesbian, gay, or straight partner will need a safe place to express fears that may feel in conflict with the desire to support the bisexual partner. Both will benefit from educational and community resources for bisexuality. Someone in the later stage of established bisexual identity may be steadier but could need support and validation for maintaining the identity, including the partner's empathic understanding of his or her need for affiliation with the queer community or other-sex friendships. Someone who is visible as a bisexual activist will expose his or her partner to visibility and possible biphobia, as well, which might put a strain on the relationship.

Clarification

It is useful to help both partners explore what bisexuality means to them and to clarify assumptions and misconceptions, as well as truths. This is an opportunity to confront myths and stereotypes and to help the bisexual partner articulate a personal definition. For many people, bisexuality is experienced as a potential for attractions to any sex and may include a history of same-sex and other-sex relationships (not usually in equal numbers). Bisexuality may simply mean that the sex of a person is not a primary factor in one's choice of a partner. There is a common stereotype, which may underlie a partner's anxiety, that bisexuals can be happy only when they have partners of both genders simultaneously. It is important to differentiate between bisexuality and polyamory: They are two separate and distinct issues. Many bisexual people desire and enjoy monogamous relationships. Some bisexual people do choose polyamory to express and experience different aspects of their sexuality, just as do some straight, gay, and lesbian people.

Both parties in the couple can be helped to articulate their wishes and needs for the relationship and to hear each other with compassion. Both need support for the legitimacy of their desires, even if those desires are in conflict, before they can begin negotiating compromise and resolution.

Affirmation of Bisexuality

Any therapy with bisexual people, individually or in couples, must address the invisibility that is their constant experience (Keppel, 2006; Ochs, 1996). This means expressing sensitivity to the difficulties of developing and maintaining an identity not recognized or validated in the culture, as well as to the challenges faced by straight, gay, and lesbian partners, who often have little information other than negative stereotypes to help them understand their partners or navigate their own experiences. One of the greatest contributions a therapist can make to the well-being of a bisexual client and his or her partner is the acknowledgment of the validity of bisexuality. Many bisexual clients will have gone years without so identifying, having no models or language for their identities in a dichotomous culture. Because of the marginalization of bisexuality, such self-awareness may be repressed; as a result, many bisexual women and men tend to come out later in life than do gay and lesbian people (Fox, 1995; Weinberg, Williams, & Pryor, 1994). When they do self-disclose, they need affirmation of their identities. Their partners, perhaps not having had the information to come to this awareness gradually, may need time and patience to adjust to the disclosure.

Disclosure

The therapist should assist each partner in going through the process of coming out and in coming to terms with changes in the relationship. This process includes identifying and helping to articulate the intersection of bisexual identity with other cultural aspects of identity (Goetstouwers, 2006). The decision to disclose bisexual identity is complicated for people with multiple minority identities, especially those individuals who have already experienced marginalization and oppression and who fear isolation (Scott, 2006). Some bisexual people of minority racial or ethnic identities choose not to reveal their sexual identities, unwilling to expose themselves to another level of oppression or risk alienation from their families or cultural communities. Others feel their experiences have helped them develop the coping skills to deal with such risks. The culturally sensitive therapist can facilitate clients' considerations in weighing the risks and benefits of coming out to family or others.

Sometimes one partner chooses not to reveal his or her sexual identity to family members, whereas the other wishes to be open about it. A same-sex partner can feel rejected and closeted by this decision; an other-sex partner may feel constricted from being able to talk about the couple's situation and get support. These differences require exploration of motives, emotional needs, and fears. Empathizing with and validating both positions and mirroring the couple's dilemma can help deepen their understanding and facilitate their communication.

Negotiation

Because some bisexual clients are in or wish to explore polyamorous relationships, the therapist should be familiar with the types of polyamorous relationships, their benefits and pitfalls, and ways to help a couple consider their options (Weitzman, 2006). The discussion should include negotiations for structure, rules, limits, and ways of dealing with jealousy and trust. Any consideration of consensual nonmonogamy "requires clarifying each partner's motivations, needs, fears, expectations, and assumptions. A successful outcome demands of the partners a significant level of maturity, self-awareness, and well-developed communication skills" (Bradford, 2004b, p. 50). A polyamorous relationship presents additional challenges for an already nontraditional couple in terms of disclosure and acceptance within family and community.

Therapists need to be prepared to give these clients current and accurate information on sexually transmitted diseases and safer sex practices. This requires a nonjudgmental, accepting approach to sexuality and comfort with sexually explicit discussion. It is important for therapists to be aware and to convey to their clients that it is not bisexuality (or any sexual orientation) that spreads sexually transmitted diseases but unsafe sexual practices.

Sorting Out the Issues

Because sexuality, sexual orientation, trust, safety, and fidelity are emotionally charged and intertwined, presenting problems are often intense and complex for these couples. The therapist must help them determine what the central issues are and whether and how bisexuality actually plays a role. When bisexuality is emphasized but not central to the problem, therapy can help the couple work on the primary issues, such as intimacy or communication or processing of conflict. The difference in sexual orientation can be considered part of the diversity in the relationship, to be understood and appreciated, but not necessarily problematic. When bisexuality is the focus, the therapist may need to help the partners articulate their concerns, redefine their commitment, or negotiate their contract regarding such matters as monogamy or the handling of disclosure. When a partner's bisexuality has brought the couple to a crisis, there is an immediate need to deal with the powerful feelings—fear, confusion, or rage—and the sense of betrayal before the underlying issues can be understood and addressed in their complexity.

Couples in Crisis

Couple therapy is especially complex when one partner's bisexuality has been revealed by sexual infidelity. Homophobia and biphobia are such powerful deterrents that it is not unusual for bisexuality to be hidden, repressed, unconscious, or unexplored for years before it is expressed. It may be acted out in secret until the discovery is a catastrophic blow to the partner. The therapist must assess the strength of the foundation of the relationship and the level of damage done as well as determine each partner's degree of commitment to repairing the relationship. These couples are thrust into two different life experiences simultaneously. The bisexual partner is grappling with a newly acknowledged identity, accompanied with excitement and fear, perhaps facing homophobia directly for the first time, perhaps challenged by the potential loss of gay or lesbian support, and maybe in the thralls of infatuation. The straight, gay, or lesbian partner can be devastated—in grief, feeling sexually rejected, with damaged self-esteem—and may doubt the validity of the relationship itself. Both partners face many potential losses, including personal and financial security, home, family, and status. They will need separate resources to address their different needs (e.g., individual therapy, support groups,[2] and reading material).

Couple therapy can help these people speak openly and honestly to each other and listen empathically. It can offer them a place to consider options, including re-creating a monogamous contract and reestablishing trust, opening the relationship to the possibility of other intimate relationships, transitioning from a committed partnership to a friendship, or terminating the relationship. Some of these couples determine that their needs are incompatible and decide to separate. Many spend years sorting out alternatives but, finally, separate as well. And some commit to redefining their relationships and form strong, lasting bonds (Buxton, 2006). In addition

---

[2] Support groups for people coming out bisexual, lesbian, or gay are available at local LGBT community centers. For partners, good resources for support are Parents, Family and Friends of Lesbians and Gays (PFLAG; http://www.pflag.org) and the Straight Spouse Network (http://www.straightspouse.org).

to facilitating couples' decision making about reestablishing their relationships or dissolving them, therapists can help couples handle concerns about their children, including whether, what, and how to tell them about what the parents are going through. The choices are based on the couple's decisions about changes in the relationship and the developmental levels and needs of the children (Buxton, 2000, 2004).

Case Examples

Gwen and Stephanie: Bisexuality Highlighted by the Issues

Two young women sought couple therapy when they found their arguments over commitment escalating. Both were feeling frustrated and misunderstood in the relationship. Their history revealed that they had met online and gotten to know each other by e-mail before meeting in person. Gwen, who identified as lesbian, moved to the United States from Canada in order to live with Stephanie after only a few months of this long-distance relationship. Stephanie, who identified as bisexual, had not had a romantic relationship with a woman before. Neither had experienced living with a partner. After the excitement of a brief honeymoon period, they found themselves frequently in conflict over differences in personality, culture, habits, and communication styles. When Stephanie revealed that she was experiencing sexual attractions to men, Gwen assumed that their problems stemmed from Stephanie's bisexuality. Stephanie did not contradict that conclusion because she knew she had longings for the privileges and ease of a straight life.

In therapy, this couple was able to assess their personal histories, their individual stages of sexual identity, and the course of their relationship. As the therapist heard their stories, and as they were helped to talk and listen to each other nondefensively and empathically, it became clear that many of their problems stemmed from the haste with which they moved in together and the lack of information they had about each other. Neither woman had much relationship experience to draw upon. Gwen, though clear that she wanted to be in a relationship with a woman, had made the assumption that another woman would share her views and tastes and needs. Stephanie, in an early stage of sexual identity development, had not yet come to terms with the meaning of her bisexual attractions and was confronting homophobia and biphobia for the first time.

Both women were helped by having the time and safe place to explore their own feelings and reactions. They were given resources supportive of bisexuality and of lesbian relationships to assist them in strengthening their identities and increasing their self-esteem. They began to find a sense of community. They were encouraged to express their hopes and dreams and assumptions about relationship and to work through their disappointments. Over time, they became better able to face the reality of their differences and to process their feelings about those differences with respect and compassion and humor. They realized that bisexuality was one of the differences, but not an obstacle or deterrent to their relationship. Given the chance to back up and work through the early stages of their relationship more consciously and thoughtfully, they found that they were, indeed, compatible in many ways and wanted to be together. Therapy provided the opportunity for them to deepen their bond and form a stronger foundation from which to develop as a couple.

Ravi and Phil: Bisexuality as the Focus

Ravi and Phil came to couple therapy seeking relief from their conflicts that seemed to center on Phil's ambivalence about their relationship. They had been friends for several years before a sexual attraction developed between them. Then they were passionately drawn to each other and became sexually and emotionally intimate. For Ravi, this came easily. Having grown up in another culture where he never heard or saw evidence of homosexuality, he thrived on the freedom he experienced in a big city in the United States, where he could be openly gay. He had never discussed his sexual identity with his family, but he felt they knew and accepted him as long as he remained silent. He kept his personal and family lives separate, accepting this as the price of maintaining them both.

Phil had had positive experiences with women and assumed he was straight until he fell in love with Ravi. This compelling attraction threw him into confusion and fear. Not having any knowledge of bisexuality, Phil thought this attraction must mean he was gay. He was unable to reconcile this idea with his previous attractions to women and his sense of himself. He felt too vulnerable to expose his confusion or desires to his family, with whom he had always felt close. After an initial blissful period of exploration with Ravi, Phil withdrew and attempted to deny his attraction. He became depressed and disconnected from Ravi. There followed alternating times of closeness and distance as Phil grappled with his feelings. He gained support from the gay community but still felt in personal turmoil. This state of affairs took a toll on Ravi, who wanted a more dependable and stable relationship with Phil.

Therapy offered this couple the opportunity to hear about the reality of bisexuality and to discover whether it fit for Phil. After finding a bisexual men's therapy group and connecting with others online, he became more comfortable with his dual attractions and affirming of his feelings for Ravi. Finding language and models for his experience gave him relief and helped Ravi understand Phil's experience as well. Phil was more and more comfortable with his love for Ravi, though homophobic prejudice continued to be a stressful challenge for him. He took the risk of coming out as bisexual to his family and introducing them to his relationship with Ravi, with positive results. As Phil was more open about his bisexual identity, he faced the new challenge of biphobia in his gay community. He found himself being a spokesperson and resource for other bisexual men, which led him to start a peer support group, from which he benefited as well.

It was important in this therapy to validate the impact of many stresses on the relationship: homophobia, biphobia and bisexual invisibility, cultural and ethnic prejudice, family denial or avoidance, and intraminority group discrimination. Recognition and validation of same-sex relationships and of bisexuality, along with information and resources, were essential for Ravi and Phil. In the supportive atmosphere of couple therapy they were able to affirm their mutual caring and unite to confront the pressures they faced.

Dolores and James: Bisexuality Presents a Crisis

Married for 15 years, with two adolescent children, Dolores and James found themselves often bickering and feeling disconnected from each other. Their sex life was diminished, and they rarely made time to be alone together. Dolores found solace in a female coworker with whom she went out drinking after work and had long talks by phone. She let James know she was increasingly drawn to Lucy and felt she was falling in love. She wanted permission to explore a sexual relationship with her. James reacted with panic. He felt broadsided by the news that Dolores was not committed to monogamy, as he had assumed, and shocked that she had lesbian attractions, which she had never disclosed. He sought couple therapy in hopes of saving his marriage.

Therapy with this couple involved tracing the development of their relationship—their initial commitment and expectations, their agreements and unspoken assumptions, what they took for granted, and how they had let their connection dissolve. Understanding these aspects of their relationship helped them situate the current crisis in the context of their history. For Dolores, it was important to explore the meaning of her newly discovered sexual attractions and the shift in her identity, as well as to contemplate the risks for herself and her family of acting on this. James needed containment for his fear of loss and sense of rejection. It was important for him to clarify his emotional needs and limits. Both entered individual therapy to focus separately on self-reflection. This activity helped them to better articulate their needs and feelings when together.

Dolores recognized herself as bisexual and expressed a strong desire to experience herself in an intimate relationship with a woman. She no longer felt her bond with James was strong enough to deter her from this path. James became clear that he required the security of monogamy and could not tolerate her having a sexual relationship with Lucy. In couple therapy they grieved the loss of the relationship as they had once known it, explored the options for redefining the relationship, and contemplated the possibility of terminating it.

Bisexuality brought this couple to therapy; it was a catalyst that created a crisis. It also uncovered problems the couple faced in terms of intimacy, communication, and trust. Therapy helped Dolores and James both go through a process of self-examination to determine and define their individual needs so that they were able to consider negotiating changes in the relationship. Because Dolores had not yet acted on her attractions and was willing to postpone doing so while undergoing therapy, James was able to endure the process of examination and deliberation. In this case, because they concluded that their needs were incompatible, the couple decided to end their commitment. Therapy continued, now focused on negotiating their separation, making decisions about practical concerns, and helping their children with the changes in the family. They both wanted to reform their relationship to one of coparenting and understood the importance of collaborating in the children's best interests. The skills they gained in the therapy helped them deal with such stressful situations as deciding what information to share with family and friends about their relationship and about Dolores's new relationship with Lucy.

Role of the Therapist

In such cases, perhaps the most important characteristics for a helpful therapist are a nonjudgmental attitude and an awareness of the significant issues for bisexual people and their partners. Therapists who are informed about bisexual identity and the cultural barriers to its formation and maintenance can offer a positive therapeutic experience within which it may develop. Acceptance of the validity of bisexuality and openness to alternative lifestyles are necessary to providing clients with healing experiences of self-disclosure and visibility and a safe place for sorting out relationship issues.

It is essential that we as therapists examine and be conscious of our own homophobia and biphobia so that we are comfortable helping others do the same. Therapists must be prepared to discredit myths and negative stereotypes and to reflect positive self-images back to clients. It is very easy to fall into the dichotomous polarization of sexuality, assuming people are either gay or straight. We must continually challenge this binary categorization, by ourselves and our clients, if we are to help bisexual people and their partners and families establish and validate their identities and relationships.

Working with these couples can compel therapists to confront such difficult issues as infidelity, nonmonogamy, sexually transmitted diseases, and various sexual practices with which they may be unfamiliar. Effective and affirmative therapists will be prepared to examine their countertransference, seek consultation, and stay well informed of helpful resources to recommend when such issues arise.

Recommendations for Future Research

As exposure to diverse sexual and gender identities increases among young people and as individuals come out gay, lesbian, bisexual, and transgender at earlier ages, awareness of the issues for these populations may be increasing. Studies of bisexual identity formation in age groups younger than those studied before should be possible. In addition, we should now be able to perform longer term studies on relationships involving a bisexual partner. Research examining in depth the different relational models involving bisexuality would be a significant contribution to treatment and intervention for couples.

Conclusion

Bisexuality, like heterosexuality and homosexuality, is not inherently problematic. It is a normal and natural variation of human sexual attraction and identity. We have inherited a system, based in patriarchy and reinforced by religious dictates, that dichotomizes sexual orientation (as it does biological sex and gender) and pathologizes homosexuality (Pharr, 1988). Bisexuality remains unacknowledged in this dualism, so that bisexual behavior and identity are equated with conflict and confusion. It is important for the therapist to understand the problems people experience regarding bisexuality within this context. As is true about coming out gay or lesbian, women and men who go through a process of bisexual identity formation often acquire strengths, including resiliency, self-reliance, independence, and acceptance of and respect for diversity. Bisexual people often report enrichment of and increased satisfaction with their relationships.

In addition to helping a couple develop a positive perspective on bisexuality, the affirming therapist will attend to other, often deeper issues in the relationship. Whatever the outcome regarding bisexual behavior, both partners and the relationship benefit from the opportunity to unearth and work on these problematic dynamics. The affirmative therapist can help people understand and normalize bisexuality and draw on their strengths to work out mutually satisfying solutions.

References

Bradford, M. (1997). The bisexual experience: Living in a dichotomous culture (Doctoral dissertation, The Fielding Institute). *Dissertation Abstracts International, 58*(03B), 1520.

Bradford, M. (2004a). The bisexual experience: Living in a dichotomous culture. *Journal of Bisexuality, 4*(1/2), 7–23. Copublished simultaneously as Fox, R. C. (Ed.). (2004). *Current research on bisexuality.* Binghampton, NY: Haworth Press.

Bradford, M. (2004b). Bisexual issues in same-sex couple therapy. *Journal of Couple and Relationship Therapy, 3*(2/3), 43–52. Copublished simultaneously as Bigner, J., & Wetchler, J. L. (Eds.). (2004). *Relationship therapy with same-sex couples.* Binghampton, NY: Haworth Press.

Buxton, A. P. (2000). The best interest of children of lesbian and gay parents. In R. Galatzer-Levy & L. Kraus (Eds.), *The scientific basis for custody decisions* (pp. 319–346). New York, NY: Wiley.

Buxton, A. P. (2004). Paths and pitfalls: How heterosexual spouses cope when their husbands or wives come out. *Journal of Couple and Relationship Therapy, 3*(2/3), 95–109. Copublished simultaneously as Bigner, J., & Wetchler, J. L. (Eds.). (2004). *Relationship therapy with same-sex couples.* Binghampton, NY: Haworth Press.

Buxton, A. P. (2006). Counseling heterosexual spouses of bisexual men and women and bisexual-heterosexual couples: Affirmative approaches. *Journal of Bisexuality, 6*(1/2), 105–135. Copublished simultaneously as Fox, R. C. (Ed.). (2006). *Affirmative psychotherapy with bisexual women and bisexual men.* Binghamton, NY: Harrington Park Press.

Fox, R. C. (1995). Coming out bisexual: Identity, behavior, and sexual orientation self-disclosure (Doctoral dissertation, California Institute of Integral Studies, 1993). *Dissertation Abstracts International, 55*(12), 5565B.

Fox, R. C. (2006). Affirmative psychotherapy with bisexual women and bisexual men: An introduction. *Journal of Bisexuality, 6*(1/2), 1–11. Copublished simultaneously as Fox, R. C. (Ed.). (2006). *Affirmative psychotherapy with bisexual women and bisexual men.* Binghamton, NY: Harrington Park Press.

Goetstouwers, L. (2006). Affirmative psychotherapy with bisexual men. *Journal of Bisexuality, 6*(1/2), 27–49. Copublished simultaneously as Fox, R. C. (Ed.). (2006). *Affirmative psychotherapy with bisexual women and bisexual men.* Binghamton, NY: Harrington Park Press.

Hutchins, L., & Kaahumanu, L. (Eds.). (1991). *Bi any other name: Bisexual people speak out.* Boston, MA: Alyson.

Keppel, B. (2006). Affirmative psychotherapy with older bisexual women and men. *Journal of Bisexuality,* 6(1/2), 85–104. Copublished simultaneously as Fox, R. C. (Ed.). (2006). *Affirmative psychotherapy with bisexual women and bisexual men.* Binghamton, NY: Harrington Park Press.

Kinsey, A. C., Pomeroy, W. B., & Martin, C. E. (1948). *Sexual behavior in the human male.* Philadelphia, PA: Saunders.

Kinsey, A. C., Pomeroy, W. B., Martin, C. E., & Gebhard, P. H. (1953). *Sexual behavior in the human female.* Philadelphia, PA: Saunders.

Klein, F., Sepekoff, B., & Wolf, T. J. (1985). Sexual orientation: A multi-variable dynamic process. *Journal of Homosexuality,* 11(1/2), 35–50.

Matteson, D. R. (1996). Counseling and psychotherapy with bisexual and exploring clients. In B. A. Firestein (Ed.), *Bisexuality: The psychology and politics of an invisible minority* (pp. 185–213). Thousand Oaks, CA: Sage.

Ochs, R. (1996). Biphobia: It goes more than two ways. In B. A. Firestein (Ed.), *Bisexuality: The psychology and politics of an invisible minority* (pp. 217–239). Thousand Oaks, CA: Sage.

Ochs, R. (Ed.). (2005). *Getting bi.* Boston, MA: Bisexual Resource Center.

Pharr, S. (1988). *Homophobia: A weapon of sexism.* Inverness, CA: Chardon Press.

Scott, R. L. (2006). Promoting well-being: An ecology of intervening with African American bisexual clients. Affirmative psychotherapy with older bisexual women and men. *Journal of Bisexuality,* 6(1/2), 65–84. Copublished simultaneously as Fox, R. C. (Ed.). (2006). *Affirmative psychotherapy with bisexual women and bisexual men.* Binghamton, NY: Harrington Park Press.

Weinberg, M. S., Williams, C. J., & Pryor, D. W. (1994). *Dual attractions: Understanding bisexuality.* New York, NY: Oxford University Press.

Weise, E. R. (Ed.). (1992). *Closer to home: Bisexuality and feminism.* Seattle, WA: Seal Press.

Weitzman, G. (2006). Therapy with clients who are bisexual and polyamorous. *Journal of Bisexuality,* 6(1/2), 137–164. Copublished simultaneously as Fox, R. C. (Ed.). (2006). *Affirmative psychotherapy with bisexual women and bisexual men.* Binghamton, NY: Harrington Park Press.

5

Can Couples Change Gender?

Couple Therapy With Transgender People and Their Partners

JEAN MALPAS

This chapter articulates guidelines for providing couple therapy to transgender women and transgender men,[1] as well as to their partners. It focuses on couples formed prior to the transition of the transgender-identified partner. The first section of the chapter reviews the role that couple therapists have historically taken with transgender couples,[2] articulating the epistemological evolution of the therapeutic frameworks from a medical and pathologizing approach, to the developmental and deconstructive approaches—ones not based on the conception of transgender identity as pathological. The second section of the chapter highlights the interpersonal concerns faced by transgender people and their partners. Finally, the third section outlines a contemporary therapeutic approach specifically designed for the handling of conflict, grief, sexuality, and parenting with transgender couples. Therapeutic considerations are exemplified through vignettes of three couples in gender transition.

It would be reasonable to think that the coming out of a transgender partner in a preformed couple might be the beginning of a new chapter for each partner but the end of the story for the relationship. Although it is true that substantive empirical research is still lacking, both clinical and nonclinical narratives often highlight more hopeful outcomes (Boyd, 2003; Malpas & Davis, 2005; Erhardt, 2007; Lev, 2004; Vitale, 2004). Even though separation is a probable outcome, some couples are open to examine the potential gender transition of their relationship (Hines, 2006; Joslin-Roher & Wheeler, 2009; Malpas, 2006; Samons, 2009). Transgender men, transgender women, and their partners present to couple therapy with questions they face as a couple: What does my partner's transition mean for us? Can we transition? How will it affect our sex life and our social identity? Can we continue to parent together or will doing so harm our children? Can we remain committed while changing our sexual arrangements?

Furthermore, through the integration of queer theories (Stone Fish & Harvey, 2005) and the deconstruction of heteronormativity (Hudak & Giammattei, 2010; Lev, 2010), the field of couple and family therapy has been considering the emergence of nonnormative practices and identities not only as an opportunity for the adjustment of the "normal family" but also as a site and catalyst for transformation. Discourses on queer youth, for instance, have leaped from the notion of tolerance and acceptance of difference to the idea of nurturance and celebration of queerness and fluidity (Stone Fish & Harvey, 2005). A comparable paradigm shift might be occurring around the emergence of transgender couples. These couples are not only pointing to

---

[1] A note on language: Here I use an affirmative language and refer to individuals by the gender with which they identify, independently of their legal gender or assigned gender at birth. Since most male-to-female individuals (MTFs) identify as women, I call them transgender women; similarly, I call female-to-male individuals (FTMs) transgender men. The qualifier *transgender* is added here for clarity, to differentiate these individuals from their nontransgender partners.

[2] The expression *transgender couple* refers to a couple where at least one partner identifies as transgender or has a transgender history. The term does not imply that both partners self-identify as transgender.

and filling the blind spots of our worldviews but are also pioneering maps for the navigation of intimacy, stability, and excitement outside the heteronormative, gender-binaried, and monogamous references that have guided us thus far. Our investigation, as clinicians and theoreticians, must therefore reflect this leap: Not only are we figuring out how to help couples survive and strive in gender transition, but also we are noting the transformations of contemporary practices of partnering and couplehood in a society gradually embracing gender fluidity. Of course, our point of view should not negate the obvious and most common suffering that transgender couples face inside and outside their relationship. In fairness for this clinical diversity, this chapter incorporates both the hardship and the beautiful humanity that these couples express.

Evolution of the Role of Couple and Family Therapist With Transgender People

Medical and Pathologizing Approach

Historically, the role of the family therapist with transgender families has been rooted in the perception of transgender, or *trans*, people as pathological (Lev, 2004). In 1966, Harry Benjamin claimed that if the mind of transsexuals could not be changed—if we could not cure them of their psychiatric illness—then their body had to be the place of the cure. Granting access to sex reassignment surgery was only admitting the failure to treat the transsexual pathology (Randell, 1971), not a way to depathologize queer or trans identities. Transgender people could change sex but still had to protect the sanctity of the family from their insanity by leaving spouse and families, migrating to a community of other marginalized people. In terms of services, marriage has been considered a "contradiction to cross-sex surgery" (Randell, 1971, p. 157). "Proof of divorce" (Clemmensen, 1990, p. 124) was sometimes required to access transgender-related treatment. An either–or public health policy governed our clinical interventions. One could not be trans and in a family (Lev, 2004). Rather, one had to choose between remaining in loving relationships at the cost of suppressing one's authentic self, *or* live true to oneself, in exile. While medical research depicted wives of cross-dressers and transsexuals in the most pathologizing ways (Stoller, 1967, in Lev, 2004, p. 273), blaming their flawed and dependent character for staying with unconscionable spouses, even family therapy research remained almost silent on the issue (Lev, 2004). It is only more recently that family therapists have started to integrate transgender issues (Lev, 2004; Ma, 1997; Malpas, 2006; Rosenfeld & Emerson, 1998; Samons, 2009; Zamboni, 2006). Finally, wives and partners were excluded by therapists and gender specialists who did not consider them part of the transition process (Cole, 2000).

Normalizing Approaches

Under the influence of feminist and social justice movements, queer theorists, and transgender advocates, the role of the mental health providers has moved away from the enactment of these political sanctions toward a more affirmative position (Denny, 2004). The medical and pathologizing approach evolved into two approaches that, one, normalize and legitimize transgender identities and, two, equally important, include partners and family members (Malpas, 2006). In addition, the development of the Internet and social media has supported gender-variant people, their families, and their partners to build community (Lev, 2004). "Once able to connect and gather together, wives and partners of trans individuals reached out to support and help one another" (Cole, 2000, p. 14), rightly demanding their place at the therapeutic and community table.

Developmental Models Developmental models (Ellis & Eriksen, 2001; Kelley, 1991; Lev, 2004; Malpas, 2006; Raj, 2008; Rosenfeld & Emerson, 1998) challenge treatment practices that promote isolation. Instead, developmental models normalize the inclusion of partners and families of transgender individuals. This approach is developmental in that it positions gender fluidity as a normative possibility and gender transition as one of the journeys couples and families could face (Lev, 2004). Such models of therapy also suggest that families and couples with a transgender partner go through nonlinear stages of adjustment to the gender variance and/or transition. Ellis and Eriksen (2001), as well as Rosenfeld and Emerson (1998), find their inspiration in the similarities between these stages of adjustment and the stages of grief as outlined by Kübler-Ross (1969, in Lev, 2004). Lev's (2004) model of "family emergence" supposes that families move from the shock, betrayal, and confusion associated with the discovery of the transgender identity of a family member, through turmoil and chaotic conflict, to gradually attain the ability to negotiate with the reality of gender variance, make changes, and find acceptance and balance by integrating the transgender person and issues in the normal life of the family.

There are two potential limitations with the developmental model. First, although Lev explores the "shifting sexual identities" of couples in transition (2004, p. 301), none of these models specifically target couples and couples therapy. Second, the developmental approach's emphasis on normalization and adjustment "presents the risk of reducing the diversity of gender definitions into a binary conception, e.g. men developing into women and vice versa" (Malpas, 2006, p. 187). However, full social and anatomical transition to the "other side of the binary" is not the only treatment outcome pursued by transgender clients and their partners. It is for some members of the gender-variant community a thoughtful choice to embody a queerer form of gender (Denny, 2004; Gilbert, 2000).

Deconstructive Approaches *Deconstructive approaches* have focused on questioning the "nature of gender itself" (Dimen & Goldner, 2005, p. 96). They challenge therapists to examine their own binary conceptions of gender in order to meet transgender relationships that do not reproduce culturally defined masculinity and femininity or do not equate transition with anatomical binary sex reassignment (Caroll, 1999; Denny, 2004; Goldner, 2003; Lev, 2004; Malpas, 2006). For Goldner (2003), gender is a compromise in the politics of difference in place in each culture and, more important, in each family. Every gender behavior that does not fit within the binary injunction of parent–child attachment—"Be a boy!" or "Be a girl!"—is then buried under layers of silence and shame, leaving room for our false self to emerge, properly gendered. This constructionist therapeutic stance supports couples' and families' gender-queer identities, multiple and gender-neutral pronouns, and nonconfirming gender embodiments (Denny, 2004; Lev, 2004; Malpas, 2006; Raj, 2008). Adult attachments, whether romantic or therapeutic, do not aim at enforcing the normative imperatives of the binary but instead provide a context where gender fluidity and compromises can flourish as a relational negotiation.

As therapeutic models have diversified, so have our views on the intimate practices of transgender couples. Over the past decade, both empirical research and community narratives have brought forth more nuanced descriptions of the relational dilemmas faced by gender-variant and transgender men, women, and their partners. There is indeed a growing literature on heterosexual couples where the husband identifies as gender variant or transgender and on lesbian couples where one partner transitions to manhood. Research is yet to be done, however, on heterosexual couples where the wife decides to transition and on gay male couples where one partner transitions (Lev, 2004, p. 272).

Relational Issues Faced by Transgender People and Their Partners

Transgender People's Relational Concerns

Despite their efforts to include interpersonal concerns and loved ones (Bockting, Knudson, & Goldberg, 2006; Israel & Tarver, 1997; Korell & Lorah, 2007; Lev, 2004), mental health

treatment guidelines often give precedence to diagnostic, assessment, and individual transition issues over transgender people's relational realities. Yet, research shows that committed relationships and the sentiment of belonging are both a priority and a critical source of
emotional stability for transgender people. First, family support compensates for the negative effects of social stigma and discrimination (Bockting et al., 2006); second, involvement
in romantic relationships increases posttransition social adjustment (Huxley, Kenna, &
Brandon, 1981); and, last, relationship commitment can serve as a coping mechanism to deal
with the complex feelings around gender identity (Hines, 2006). Moreover, although the disclosure of transgender issues to a partner might create conflict, separation, or even violence
(Courvant & Cook-Daniels, 1998, in Bockting et al., 2006), transgender people's relationships
can show significant continuity, longevity, and flexibility through the challenges of transition
(Flemming, MacGowan, & Costos, 1985; Hines, 2006). Finally, clinical and nonclinical cases
debunk the myth that transgender people are too centered on their transition to take their
partners into account (Malpas, 2010a). Instead, Hines (2006) shows transgender people as
"energetic moral agents" (p. 362) negotiating gender transition reflexively, alongside commitments to family, children, and work.

On a sexual level, transgender-specific concerns can include managing gender dysphoria,
bodily acceptance, or erotic cross-dressing in a sexual relationship (Boyd, 2003; Erhardt,
2007; Hines, 2006); shifts in sexual orientation or sexual preferences as part of gender exploration; or, finally, the impact of hormonal and surgical feminization or masculinization on
sexual desire, sexual functioning, and safer sex negotiation (Bockting et al., 2006, p. 62).
Sexual orientation, which is distinct from gender identity, can evolve over the life span and
change through a gender transition. Gender-variant people are, like any other population,
known to have diverse sexual orientations. Indeed, research shows that cross-dressing men
are not systematically heterosexual and might have and want to explore bisexual or same-
gender attractions (Boyd, 2007; Bullough & Bullough, 1997). Transgender women may experience shifts in their sexual orientation and/or object of desire (S. V. Giammattei, personal
communication, June 26, 2010) as part of the emerging female gender identity or related to
the impact of female hormones (Daskalos, 1998). Transgender men describe an increased
sex drive as a result of testosterone. Some of them, who had strongly integrated lesbian
identities before transition, remain attracted to women and identify as heterosexual after
transition (Lev, 2004). Others were and remain exclusively attracted to men; their object of
desire remains masculine (S. V. Giammattei, personal communication, June 26, 2010), while
their sexual orientation changes from heterosexual to gay and bisexual through transition
(Coleman & Bockting, 1988; Bockting, Benner, & Coleman, 2009). In all cases, bisexuality of
both partners has proven to be a factor facilitating a couple's adjustment through transition
(Denny & Green, 2006).

In regard to parenting, the scarcity of data "leaves the practices of transgender parenting
relatively invisible" (J. Green, 2004; Hines, 2006, p. 363). Richard Green's studies (1978, 1998)
on same-sex and transgender parents show, however, that a parent's transgender identity does
not directly adversely impact the children. Transgender parents can remain effective parents.
In addition, according to Green (1998), "children can understand and empathize with their
transsexual parent. The cases demonstrate that gender identity confusion does not occur and
that any teasing is no more a problem than the teasing children get for a myriad of reasons." It
seems instead that the quality of the relationship between a child's transgender parent and nontransgender parent will significantly affect how the child accepts gender transformation (Hines,
2006). Children are more affected by the breakdown of their parents' relationship or by the way
their family will functionally deal with the transgender issues (White & Ettner, 2007; Lev, 2004;
Raegan, 2001) than by the issue of gender transition itself.

Relational Concerns of Transgender People's Partners

Partners and Wives of Cross-Dressing Men and Transgender Women   The most commonly studied partners are the heterosexual wives of cross-dressing men and transgender women (Boyd, 2003; Brown, 1994; Erhardt, 2007; Reynolds & Caron, 2000; Weinberg & Bullough, 1988). Male partners of transgender women remain a largely invisible and understudied population (Lev, 2004). Wives often discover that their husbands have secretly cross-dressed for years. They can present overwhelmed with shock and betrayal (Ellis & Eriksen, 2001; Erhardt, 2007). The discovery of cross-dressing and the secrecy in the marriage question the foundations of the couple's relationship and rock, at its core, the trust in the transgender spouse. Disbelief subsides as the fury at the sense of having been fooled explodes (Rosenfeld & Emerson, 1998). The one partner's declaration of gender issues is experienced by the other partner as a claim that the marriage is a fraud. Once the initial shock fades, hurt, rage, fear, anxiety, and shame can become dominant (Cole, Denny, Eyler, & Samons, 2000). Wives commonly fear that their husbands are gay, will want to transition fully, and will be rejected by extended family, social circles, and faith communities (Erhardt, 2007). Grief is a major theme throughout transition, sometimes expressed through anger and reactivity, sometimes through depression (Rosenfeld & Emerson, 1998). Wives have to deal with the obvious changes in their husbands but also face more ambiguous losses of normalcy, plans, and dreams they had for their relationship (Malpas, 2006). In addition to the questions regarding the private dilemmas they face, such as sexual compatibility, spouses are involuntarily thrown in the midst of unexpected public dilemmas. The previously invisible rug of heterosexual privilege is pulled from under their feet, and they have to face their own association with sexual minorities and figure out their own coming out (Erhardt, 2007). They too are caught in the politics of gender: If they have not themselves been stigmatized by their association with trans individuals (Califia, 1997), they may have been made invisible by trans affirmative providers who did not see them as part of the transition (Cole, 2000; Malpas, 2010a). Further, although clinical evidence shows that children can deal well with the transition of a parent (White & Ettner, 2007; R. Green, 1998), spouses experience the gender issues as potentially harmful for their families, disregarding the parenting concerns and good intentions that transgender partners continue to have (Corbett, 2001; Malpas, 2010a; Samons, 2009).

Although developmental perspectives show that some partners will be able to adjust to and accept cross-dressing or even gender transition (Ellis & Eriksen, 2001; Lev, 2004; Rosenfeld & Emerson, 1998), popular narratives are less likely to put forth the transformative experiences and the resilience that wives report as part of their own journey through transgenderism (Erhardt, 2007; Lev, 2004). Erhardt's (2007) participants show a high capacity to self-soothe and self-validate regardless of the opinions of others. Although empathic, they have good emotional boundaries (2007, p. 209). Further, many wives' stories indicate how the wives grew tremendously by staying connected to their partners at emotional and often spiritual levels. Weinberg and Bullough's (1988) research shows that wives with high self-esteem report benefiting from being married to a cross-dressing husband (Lev, 2004, p. 273). Even eroticism can be enhanced by the existence of gender variance in the relationship (Erhardt, 2007).

Among the factors that facilitate a couple's adjustment, several studies note that the intensity of a partner's reaction seems related to a large extent to how she finds out and how long the secret has been kept. Voluntary disclosure, especially early in the relationship, tends to yield a less negative response than a shocking discovery (Cole et al., 2000; Lev, 2004; Vitale, 2004). Also, the attitudes and behaviors of gender-variant spouses make a significant difference. "If they respect their partners' limits and boundaries, if they attend to their partners' needs rather than being totally self-absorbed, and if they invest time and energy in showing their devotion, their relationships stand a better chance of survival" (Erhardt, 2007, p. 210). Transparency, pacing, empathy, reciprocity, and reflexivity seem to be the keys to negotiating transgender emergence optimally as a couple. The more each partner feels met in his or her respective journey, and the more affiliated each feels with the changing relationship, the more empowered each is to transition along.

Lesbian, Bisexual, Queer, and Heterosexual Partners of Transgender Men Over the past decade, the body of knowledge about transgender men and their partners has considerably evolved. As with transgender women, women partners are far better documented than are the heterosexual and gay male partners of transgender men. In regard to transgender men and their female partners, the literature often describes the stability and longevity of their relationships (Flemming et al., 1985), as well as the positive influence of stability and longevity on posttransition outcomes (Blanchard & Steiner, 1983). Although the experience of transition of lesbian, bisexual, and queer female partners remains largely unexplored, Joslin-Roher and Wheeler's (2009) qualitative study shows that most partners experience a loss of their lesbian social identity and question their own sexual identity during their partner's transition. They feel predominantly invisible both in the heterosexual and in the LGBT communities and lack a language to describe their status and their relationship. Whereas other studies show that a transgender partner's gender dysphoria, body issue, and difficulties in engaging sexually negatively affect the female partner's body image and self-confidence (Pfeffer, 2008), other women describe their sexuality being affected positively by their partner's increased confidence as a man. Furthermore, sexual challenges and overall sense of satisfaction in the relationship do not seem to be mutually exclusive (Glassmire, 2009; Joslin-Roher & Wheeler, 2009). In a recent study comparing heterosexual couples where the male partner was either transgender or not, Kins, Hoebeke, Heylens, Rubens, and De Cuypere (2008) demonstrated that a relationship of a woman with a transgender man

> does not differ substantially from a "traditional" heterosexual relationship regarding the amount of relational and sexual satisfaction for the female partner. These women explain the success of their relationship in terms of respect, honesty, trust, love, understanding and open communication. They consider the fact that their partners know and understand women better than a biological man as the major advantage of having a transsexual partner. (p. 436)

Finally, negotiation of gender roles within the relationship remains another interesting area of adjustment for transgender men and their female partners. The largest studies on female partners to date showed that among the 50 women interviewed, most continued to carry a more important part of the household labor and emotional (care-taking) work. Contrary to reports on same-sex couples, these relationships could not be described as egalitarian (Pfeffer, 2010).

For transgender people and their partners, shared concerns and priorities seem to emerge when it comes to transitioning as a couple. First, news of a gender transition can create shock or at least confusion, propelling the relationship through conflict, communication breakdowns, and potential crisis. Underneath the initial reactivity lies a substantial and layered experience of grief, experienced by both partners. Loss of the one as we knew him or her, loss of social status or affiliation, loss of sexual and emotional connection—grieving takes many forms, some easier to identify than others. Then, obvious and anxiety provoking is the question of sexuality. Bodily discomfort and changes in preferences, in body parts, and in lovemaking scenarios turn a couple's intimacy upside down. And, last, these turpitudes cannot easily be contained to private domains. The gender variance has social and visible ramifications. Enduring stigma, rejection, and recruiting support and empowerment from families, children, schools, peers, friends, communities, and professionals influence greatly the strengths and stressors the couple can count on. But right next to these challenges emerge opportunities for transformation, affirmation of love, or even better days between two fully realized partners (J. Ariel, personal communication, July 24, 2010). Some couples find themselves satisfied, negotiating sophisticated arrangements to meet each other's needs, just as everybody else does. Only an approach that recognizes the "blessing and the curse" and the infinite potential of love and its limits, as well as these couples' hope and despair, can meet them on their journey.

Couple Therapy With Couples in Gender Transition

Contemporary Framework and Therapeutic Considerations

From a contemporary standpoint, gender fluidity is considered a normative possibility, and the emergence of a transgender member is viewed as one of many possible crises couples can face. The goal of therapy is to support couples negotiating collaboratively the emerging gender variance and, if they choose so, navigating their *relational transition*, a process by which couples find an arrangement that is congruent with each partner's gender and sexual identity. The clinical stance shifts from either/or to both/and. The therapist integrates the dilemmas of both partners and affirms the chosen gender of the transgender individual without alienating the nontransgender partner, crafting a process that affirms their attachment and acknowledges the losses and conflicts both are facing.

Assessment   Assessment is an important part of the initial stage of couple therapy (Malpas, 2006; Samons, 2009; Vitale, 2004). Assessment should include the role of the couple therapist and the expectations placed on therapy, as well as individual, sexual, gender, and marital histories. First, it is important for the therapist to evaluate his or her role in the larger mental health context in which the transgender partner might be involved . Less likely than other therapists to be identified as the primary gender therapist, couple therapists play the role of gatekeeper; that is, they are the mental health professionals to whom most individual therapists endorse their individual transgender clients (Israel & Tarver, 1997). Historically, the gatekeeper has been referred to as the mental health provider in charge of performing the psychosocial assessment that will conclude in the diagnosis of gender identity disorder and will, through a formal recommendation, grant access to medical treatment (Denny, 2004; Malpas, 2006). This issue of gatekeeping is relevant in the context of couples therapy with a transgender client as it can influence the level of comfort and transparency that clients will have with their couple therapists.

Second, it behooves treatment to clarify goals and expectations early on. Some couples come to therapy to evaluate how to navigate the gender issues, whereas others arrive with a pretty clear idea that they will need the therapist's help in separating. Although a couple's confidence in its ability to transition together can greatly increase over time, assessing whether a couple wants help in staying together or separating also gives valuable information on how deeply the gender variance is shaking the foundational narrative of the relationship. If separation ends up as the outcome of choice, treatment still allows achieving a *separation-construction*[3]— that is, a mutual and collaborative decision to part peacefully and with integrity—thereby avoiding a *separation-destruction*, which is a separation where the crisis destroys all good memory as well as any possible identification with the history of the partners' mutual love.

The third level of assessment consists of the individual and relational history. From a resilience-based perspective, valuable information is found in how the couple has handled previous crises and has coped with conflict in the past. External support, internal resources, and positive

---

[3] I am grateful to Paula Lombard for this useful conceptual distinction.

coping mechanisms will be handy when orienting the couple toward more constructive negotiation strategies. To capture the uniqueness of each couple's situation, it is also necessary to contextualize the gender variance within other independent or intersecting issues the partners are facing individually or as a family. Their cultures of origin, their notions of gender and sexuality, and the norms in their communities of affiliation will greatly influence the comfort with which they can explore gender fluidity.

Among the many contextual issues that influence a couple's possibilities, race, culture of origin, and class are important but not always deterministic factors. Although families with a greater acceptance of gender diversity may be easier to come out to than are families organized around more rigid binary and heterosexist values, I have found that families of diverse racial, class, and religious background are able to stretch and make room for many shades of gray. Exploring gender conceptions and potential homo- and transphobia and families and cultures of origin helps clinician understand the dilemmas that clients face at the intersections of their multiple social identities. Partners' age and location in the life cycle seem, however, to be a more difficult factor to deal with (Glassmire, 2009; Malpas, 2010a; Zamboni, 2006). Couples in their 30s seem to have more pressure to figure out their gender expression and sexual compatibility quickly, on time for biological reproduction. Younger couples and older couples seem to have an easier time with relational transition. When in their 20s, couples dispose of more time to explore their relational compatibility, reshape their maps of the world, and consider becoming transgender parents. Mature and post-child-bearing couples in their late 40s and 50s, might be less indebted to their families of origin, be less concerned to come out to younger children, and know that relationships are complex anyway.

Integration of Individual and Couple Sessions   The use of one or two individual sessions with each partner is recommended. Individual sessions with the transgender partner can focus on the individual's sexual history and the history of his or her gender variance, dysphoria, cross-dressing, and level of involvement with the transgender community (Samons, 2009). Although there is evidence that answers to question about an individual's history can evolve over time (Boyd, 2007), the therapist should make efforts to get clarity on how the gender-variant partner foresees the resolution of his or her gender issues. Indeed, working for a couple to integrate the contained cross-dressing behaviors of an exclusively heterosexual husband is a very different process from supporting a couple throughout full social and medical transition. Individual sessions with the nontransgender partner can also review that partner's sexual history, examine his or her belief systems related to gender normativity, and identify the challenges that the gender variance triggers in the couple's particular situation.

The ongoing use of both individual and couple sessions is indicated while requiring thoughtful considerations. Individual sessions help when such relational constraints as shame, secrets, or desire to please prevent one or both partners from expressing themselves freely. It is also indicated at the beginning of treatment when what each partner needs from therapy is diametrically different. Whereas the transgender partner might need a place to affirm and explore his or her emerging gender variance, the nontransgender partner might need to be fully heard, to have recognized his or her outrage, anger, and deep disappointment. Requiring a nontransgender individual to show full acceptance of his or her transgender partner would be as inauthentic and inappropriate as exposing the transgender individual to the nontransgender partner's virulence, disgust, or fury. I consider these individual sessions as confidential, which means that information shared by one partner does not need to be divulged to the other partner. This confidentiality, though increasing the complexity of details the couple therapist must recall, also allows for a fuller disclosure of the subjective experience of the transgender issues. The technique of "decision dialogue" (Scheinberg & True, 2008) can be used to transfer individual sessions' material to couple sessions: Thus, at the end of each individual session, a client is asked what he or she would like to bring back to the couple's process. While emphasizing couple's work as a priority, this technique allows clients to gauge and discuss with the therapist how to support the relationship to integrate their experience of the gender variance. For instance, a spouse may decide to hold back on sharing disgust and instead decide to ask for more respectful boundaries regarding cross-dressing. A lesbian partner of a transgender man may decide to ask to be better included among her partner's new transgender friends while keeping private that her partner's "top surgery" (breasts removal) is difficult to accept. This process reinforces reflexivity and emphasizes empathy in how and what partners choose to discuss.

The Self of the Therapist   Working with the transgender community obviously requires appropriate training and ability to reflect on the process of the self of the therapist (Glassmire, 2009; Lev, 2004; Malpas, 2006; Rutter & Leech, 2010; Zamboni, 2006). The central assumption that transgender individuals can transition within their romantic relationships and that partners can satisfyingly choose to stay is a necessary component to enter this process with an open mind (Malpas, 2010a). Truly holding the both/and position, affirming the transgender partner in his or her identity, and rooting for the relationship to achieve its fullest potential, instead of giving up too fast because of the lack of role models, while holding the nontransgender partner's best interest in mind can be extremely challenging. Holding multiple loyalties requires the therapist to show a great level of transparency with each partner in terms of the criteria that allow the work to be done constructively. This stance demands having clarity regarding the ethical and emotional transactions of treatment as well as being comfortable in navigating among many shades of gray.

Therapeutic Process

In order to move couples from hostility to the exploration of the transgender territory, therapists can focus on four aspects of the relational transition: (1) each partner's experience of grief, (2) the negotiation of conflict and commitment, (3) changes in the sexuality and relationship boundaries, and (4) parenting.

These therapeutic foci aim at minimizing reactivity, shutdowns, and attacks. Interventions gradually foster an empathic response that lays the foundation for reflexivity and mutuality between partners. Making room for both partners' grief as well as lessening their polarization restores connection and repairs the attachment rupture that the conflict about the gender variance has introduced into the relationship. This approach may maximize the couple's chances for integrating gender fluidity and staying together or separating constructively. Once honoring their bond and history, couples can move to a more collaborative process wherein, instead of stumbling forward through transition, they can craft solutions that work for them, their relationship, and their families.

Clinical vignettes from three couples in gender transition—Dina and Connor/Connie, Mary and Paul/Paula, and Laura and Nicole/Nick—illustrate interventions pertaining to these four themes. I have chosen these three couples because they not only represent the demographic diversity of couples in gender transition but also illustrate how therapeutic success can unfold and look very differently from one case to another.

Grief   Clinical and nonclinical evidences agree on the centrality of grief for couples in transition (Cole, 2000; Corbett, 2001; Ellis & Eriksen, 2001; Erhardt, 2007; Hines, 2006; Joslin-Roher, 2009; Kelley, 1991; Lev, 2004; Malpas, 2006; Raj, 2008; Rosenfeld & Emerson, 1998; Zamboni, 2006). The subtle ways in which grief is clinically handled can significantly influence the emergent narrative. Emphasizing the sense of betrayal and trauma can unintentionally reinforce partners' polarization into roles of victim and perpetrator. Instead, clinical interventions strive to give expression to grief, not as a source of disconnection but as an opportunity for empathy. Loss and pain point back to the depth of their bond and the complexity of their histories. "What does each partner grieve?" and "Do the partners have permission to express and be honored in their disappointment?" are some of the questions guiding my inquiry. The following vignette illustrates how Dina and Connor/Connie move beyond conflict to explore loss with mutuality and respect:

> When, 10 years ago, Connor, a 54-year-old Irish American man, met Dina, a 48-year-old Latina woman, he confided cross-dressing now and then. She grew to accept and respect it. Six years later, Connor came out as a transgender woman, insisted on wanting to be called Connie, and transitioned to full-time.
>
> As Connie transitions, Dina feels sad and at a loss: "I don't identify as a lesbian. My feelings for him, I mean for her, have not changed, but we don't have the same relationship anymore. I liked our relationship so much, how we complemented each other. I don't feel we are a couple anymore, like my parents."
>
> After having been angry for months at the changes that Connie was asking for, Dina finally expresses sadness at seeing the vision of her couple disappearing. Her relationship doesn't feel familiar anymore, and she has to reconfigure her sense of self around this unexpected change. As Dina's tone changes, Connie is able to hear her better and empathize with her. Supported by a question that makes room for her own loss, Connie is then able to share her own process.

> Therapist: And what about you? How was that for you, to build a relationship with someone you respect and you love—who also, beyond their own control, loves the masculine part that you are trying to leave behind?
>
> Connie: It is heartbreaking. I fell in love so madly for Dina. I also loved the years we had as a man–woman couple. I never thought we could be so happy and, being uncomfortable with my own body, that I could have such amazing sexual experiences. I did not want to stop that, to destroy us. I just had to become more me. If there was anything I could do to move forward without hurting her, I would.

Although frequently silenced, grief is also a critical issue for transgender people. Loss of the relationship identity and of the marital satisfaction experienced prior to coming out can be painful (Malpas, 2006). At the risk of misrepresenting their capacity for empathy with a grieving partner, however, transgender people often hide their grief from their partners and providers. Some individuals fear that doctors and mental health providers may misconstrue showing empathy or ambivalence as a lack of readiness to move forward with transition (Lev, 2004; Malpas, 2010a). When a therapist instead brings forth ambivalence and sadness as sources of connection, a more authentic and complex picture can emerge.

Grieving the losses entailed by the transition is, however, quite different from accepting the passing of a loved one. This difference is why it is relevant to investigate how couples express the ambiguous losses (Boss, 2000) that can easily beoverlooked. Shifts in sexual identities and changes in communities of affiliation create significant changes in a couple's intimacy (Lev, 2004; Malpas, 2006; Joslin-Roher, 2009).

> When Nicole took on the name of Nick and started testosterone, Laura, her girlfriend of six years, started to feel uncomfortable. While ambivalently supportive of Nick's transition, she felt strangely invisible in the lesbian community where she had been an active and well-known member.
>
> Laura: When we are out, we literally pass as a straight couple. I don't know how we crossed that line, but somehow we have. And other women (in our community) even give

> *us a weird look, even some of our friends, as if we had given up the fight, or let them down.*
>
> *As they worked on their social connections, Laura and Nick initiated poetry evenings with friends. The first one, themed "She's my boyfriend," invited their community to share experiences of transition.*

Besides providing relief for each partner and attunement within the relationship, processing grief helps each individual access the deeper existential dilemmas that gender fluidity reactivates, particularly in terms of attraction to the gender variance (J. Ariel, personal communication, July 24, 2010) and loyalties to one's family of origin.

> *Mary and Paul had been together for 8 years, had been married for 5, and had a 4-year-old son when Mary accidentally discovered Paul's desire to transition. Paul, under the name of Paula, had e-mailed a gender specialist to ask for advice and resources to deal with his gender identity issues. After months of painful fights, Mary and Paul knew therapy was giving a last chance to their relationship. Through a combination of individual and couple sessions, Mary identified how Paula's transgender identity reactivated her own dilemma with conventions. As much as she thrived to be perceived as a good and normal girl, she too had been described as a bit of a tomboy, a woman with masculine quality. She understood that their gender variance was part of what had attracted them to each other. She also understood that choosing a transgender partner would imply further questioning her loyalty to her family of origin's conventional gender norms. Although she did not mind playing with gender roles, she could not see herself living as an out lesbian in front of her family and lifelong friends.*

Negotiating Conflict and Commitment

Negotiating Conflict   Most family members and partners can experience shock and betrayal upon discovering gender issues or realizing the extent of their partner's desire to transition. Uprooted and questioned at their core, couples can enter a crisis and revert to primary survival strategies that can include misuse of power, manipulation, humiliation, sarcasm, attack, shutdown, or alliances with other family members to push or hold back the potential transition. Initial interventions aim at interrupting the negative cycle of interaction, naming the survival strategies, and redirecting the couples toward more collaborative transactions.

> *Soon after Connor expressed his desire to transition, Dina would get home to find that he had been online, chatting on transgender forums. Dina did not feel ready to implement changes yet. She also felt left out of Connor's new life and newfound excitement. Sad and angry, Dina reverted to alcohol to soothe her sorrow and to find the courage to express herself. Once drunk, she would sulk or get aggressive, hurting Connor's feelings by telling him he would never be a real woman. In therapy Dina recognized the feeling of being left out as a trigger and the drinking as a negative coping mechanism. Connor, on his end, recognized how he contributed to the situation and how he could involve Dina in his new world. The couple started researching blogs and forums for partners of transgender women, and Dina significantly cut back her drinking.*

Identifying how couples take steps forward can be used to establish better communication and more appropriate pace and limits around their exploration of gender fluidity. Out of impatience, transgender individuals might impose changes that their spouse are not ready to embrace, such as a haircut or a membership in a trans-identified space; out of grief, partners can unfairly block the conversation.

To deescalate conflict, it is often necessary to differentiate and work separately the issues related to secrecy and the issue pertaining to gender. In situations where gender identity issues have been kept secret, I invite nontransgender partners to express their sense of betrayal, anger, and disappointment, openly and constructively. The goal for transgender individuals is to be able to show their partners an understanding of the pain caused by the secrecy. Reciprocally, nontransgender partners must come to understand the shame and social stigmatization that transgender people are subjugated to as well as their fear of losing the relationship. Such an understanding will help a nontransgender partner view the untenable dilemma the spouse has faced for years. Although still hurt by the secrecy, the nontransgender partner can empathize with the fear of coming out.

Facilitating Commitment or Separation   Moreover, as much as transgender people need to take responsibility for the cost of their choices, partners also need to own their decision to stay in their relationships. The ability for partners to perceive themselves as willing participants promotes their sense of agency. Elevating the notion of choice gives partners a new normalized and empowering narrative to hold on to.

> Dina: *At some point after Connie came out, I could have said, "If you move on, I am leaving," but I did not think that was an option.*
>
> Therapist: *Why not?*
>
> Dina: *I just could not break the bond we had developed. I had to weigh all my options. I'd rather stay with somebody I love, regardless, because of our commitment. Had I walked out, it would have destroyed both of us.*
>
> Therapist: *So, what are you saying is that you made a choice? And that each choice entails losses, one of them being in a marriage that somehow in terms of identity and sexuality does not completely meet your needs, with a person that you respect, admire, and love on many other levels?*
>
> Dina: *Yes, but you could say that just about any other couple! There is always something you will miss.*
>
> As Dina concluded with a smile, Connie looked at her and joined, "That's love, meeting the other one in the middle."
>
> Shifting their narratives from victim and oppressor to mutually accountable members of the change, Dina and Connie could stop the cycle of resentment and feel proud of their progress.

Finally, and according to client-centered philosophy, clients define their vision of therapeutic success. While supporting the idea that couples can transition together, it is important to remind clients that success does not always equate saving the relationship at all costs. If separation ends up being the outcome of choice, treatment focuses on crafting a constructive goodbye rather than a destructive ending.

> After a couple of years of therapy, Mary and Paula collaboratively decided to separate. They had tried their best but felt Paula's emergent attraction for men, in addition to her gender transition, was putting too much strain on the relationship. Mary was also ready to have a second child and could not see herself in a lesbian-headed family. Their work together had, however, provided both of them with a connective narrative. They felt resolved about their choices, understood the limits of their love, and were incredibly proud to have "hung in there" as coparents.
>
> At our last meeting, Mary cried and concluded, "I am so sad but I know we did not have it all wrong."

Sexuality   Once virulent survival strategies have been abated, couples are free to explore more collaboratively the sexual ramifications of a potential change of gender. The sense of legitimacy and normalcy that couples have recovered while working on their choices and their grief lays the foundations to explore sexual arrangements as a sign of resilient creativity instead of a proof of sexual deficiency. Several clinical challenges usually arise: fear of change in sexual interests, sexual losses. and issues of sexual monogamy in the context of sexual impasses.

The Impact of Gender Dysphoria   First, the therapeutic inquiry, through individual and couple sessions, aims at understanding the impact of gender dysphoria on sex and the impact of physical and hormonal changes on sex drive as well as clarifying both partners' current sexual orientations.

> *Many spouses of transgender women are concerned that their partner may become gay. In this context, it is helpful to reduce that ambiguity. Connie, for instance, was quick to clarify that her desire for Dina had not changed at all. That she was actualizing her female identity did not mean that her sexual orientation was changing. She was still attracted to women, not to men, and still very much desired Dina.*

Facing Sexual Losses   Second, while partners realize that transitioning is not mutually exclusive with keeping the love, the friendship, or the parenting complicity that they had before, they also face sexual losses that therapy can help name and process.

> *Paula admitted that penetrating Mary was no longer comfortable, and the couple had worked on changing their erotic scripts. Mary had learned to have sex without touching Paula's penis.*
>
> Mary: *I can work on having sex differently, I understand why we try this. But I miss the feeling of him inside of me. I miss the hair on his chest, on his legs. I miss the sense of my man making love to me. Can I say that?*

Exploring Bisexuality   Finally, while bisexuality of both partners has proven to be a factor facilitating couples adjustment through transition (Denny & Green, 2006), the emergent change of sexual attraction during the transition can be difficult for partners to tolerate. Transgender men sometimes see their attraction to men as affirming of their masculinity (Bockting et al., 2009), leaving their lesbian partners confused. Transgender people's bisexuality or desire to explore new forms of sexuality, such as bisexuality, opens relationships and bondage discipline sado-masochism (BDSM), can also be part of so-called *transgender adolescence* (Malpas & Davis, 2005). Partners struggle, however, to accept at once both the gender fluidity and the sexual experimentation. For other couples, deconstructing their sexual exclusivity can be a way to rebuild coherence between opposite sexual interests and commitment as a couple. Partners who are not bisexual may feel a greater sexual dissatisfaction and can benefit from an open sexual arrangement.

> *Dina had tried to play with Connie's feminizing body. While she felt happy to satisfy Connie by touching and kissing her breasts, she still longed for the intimacy of a man. The couple worked on recognizing the limit of their sexual fit and decided to open the relationship. They collaboratively opened the boundaries of their marriage so that Dina could honor both her sexual desires and her choice to stay with Connie. In therapy, the open relationship was framed as Connie's gift to Dina and supported the narrative of unconditional love.*

As with other open relationships, it behooves couples to find a positive meaning in their decision and to explore thoughtfully the terms of their relational arrangement (Malpas, 2010b). What does each partner need to feel safe letting the other have a separate sexual experience? How can it be perceived as an act of love and generosity? Can it convey security rather than lacking in intimacy? How much of it should be shared? What are the rules about telling or privacy? How is one loyal when in an open relationship? Even further, can the outside sexual experience be used as stimulus for the couple's sex life?

Parenting   Clinicians must keep in mind that while requiring a significant adjustment from all parties, family transition should not be systematically problematized. Family transition is as much a new challenge as it is an opportunity for consolidating positive intimacy in the family, including between transgender parents and their children (Corbett, 2001; R. Green, 1998; Hines, 2006). The three couples discussed here—Dina and Connie, Mary and Paula, and Laura and Nick—examined the impact of their transition on their children or on their desire for children. These couples illustrate what research has shown (R. Green, 1998; Hines, 2006), namely, that most transgender people and their partners continue to negotiate personal, romantic, and family commitments with integrity and that children can understand and empathize with a transitioning parent.

Dina and Connie

When the couple decided that Connie would soon live full-time as a woman, they came out to the teenage daughters they each had from their previous marriages. Dina's 18-year-old daughter, Kim, welcomed the news with the typical cool of an inner-city teenager. "As long as the two of you are cool with it, I am fine. Anyway, there are plenty of gender-queer kids in my school." On the other hand, Connie and her 21-year-old daughter, Bonnie, had more work to do. Connie had left her ex-wife 11 years ago and had not been very present in Bonnie's life. Connie took her coming out to her daughter as an opportunity to make amends for her absence as a father and to express her desire to rebuild their relationship as two adults. After a couple of years of difficult conversation, Bonnie realized that Connie continuously owned her mistakes as a dad. She also began to understand what it must have felt like for Connie to keep this burning secret all her life.

Mary and Paula

Mary and Paula decided to postpone talking to Bobby, their 4-year-old son, until he had adjusted from their separation. Making Bobby feel safe during the divorce and showing him that they still loved each other as coparents was their first goal. Reading Richard Green's research and watching No Dumb Question *(Reagan, 2001), a documentary about three young girls beautifully adjusting to the transition of their uncle Bill, supported their ideas that the healthiness of their relationship would create an optimal context for telling Bobby later.*

Nick and Laura

Nick and Laura felt that transition had made them stronger as a couple, readier to have the child they had talked of having prior to Nick's transition. Laura still mourned the loss of the idea she had of two moms raising a child. She felt, however, that Nick would be a great parent.

Laura smiled and looked at Nick in one of our last sessions: "I never thought I'd say this, but I think you'll be a great dad."

"With you," Nick replied.

These examples remind us that the quality of the parental relationship significantly impacts how children are affected transgender issues. Combining family cohesion, responsible parenting, age-appropriate disclosure, and a nonjudgmental perspective on gender fluidity constitute optimal ways to handle family transitions.

Conclusions

Many issues other than grief, conflict, sexuality, and parenting are paramount to understand the complexity of helping couples in transition. Disclosures to family members, workmates, and communities, as well as medical issues and the cost of transition, make the rest of the journey just as challenging. Gender transition does not have a final end but remains a developmental task couples negotiate throughout their lives (Lev, 2004).

Mary and Paula show us that some couples do not survive transition but can negotiate separation constructively. Dina and Connie, as well as Laura and Nick, demonstrate that other couples continue to navigate the waters of complexity after facing unexpected changes and necessary transformations. Most important, they raise an interesting question: Are transgender couples that different from most other couples?

These couples' journeys have brought to light both sides of relational transition: the pain and complexity but also the triumphant plasticity of their resilience. Discovering that a partner is transgender is not only a story of loss, bitter conflict, and survival but also an amazing adventure into the heart of our stereotypes, a deconstruction of the gendered box in which we live, and a fairy tale almost of how love can transform itself over and over throughout the chapters of our lives.

References

Benjamin, H. (1966). *The transsexual phenomenon*. New York, NY: Julian Press.

Blanchard, R., & Steiner, B. W. (1983). Gender reorientation, psychological adjustment, and involvement with female partners in female-to-male transsexuals. *Archives of sexual Behavior, 12*(2), 149–157.

Bockting, W., Benner, A., & Coleman, E. (2009). Gay and bisexual identity development among female-to-male transsexuals in North America: Emergence of a transgender sexuality. *Archives of Sexual Behavior, 38*, 688–701.

Bockting, W., Knudson, G., & Goldberg, J. (2006). Counseling and mental health care for transgender adults and loved ones. *International Journal of Transgenderism, 9*(3/4), 35–82.

Boss, P. (2000). *Ambiguous losses: Learning to live with unresolved grief*. Boston, MA: Harvard University Press.

Boyd, H. (2003). *My husband Betty: Love, sex and the life e of a crossdresser*. New York, NY: Thunder's Mouth Press.

Boyd, H. (2007). *She's not the man I married: My life with a transgender husband*. Emeryville, CA: Seal Press.

Brown, G. R. (1994). Women in relationships with cross-dressing men: A descriptive study from a nonclinical setting. *Archives of Sexual Behavior, 23*(5), 515–530.

Bullough, B., & Bullough, V. (1997). Are transvestites necessarily heterosexual? *Archives of Sexual Behavior, 26*(1), 1–12.

Califia, P. (1997). *Sex changes: The politics of transgenderism*. San Francisco, CA: Cleis.

Caroll, R. (1999). Outcome of treatment of gender dysphoria. *Journal of Sex Education and Therapy, 24*, 128–136.

Clemmensen, L. H. (1990). The "real-life" test for surgical candidates. In R. Blanchard & B. W. Steiner (Eds.), *Clinical management of gender identity disorders in children and adults* (pp. 121–135). Washington, DC: American Psychological Association.

Cole, S. (2000). A transgendered dilemma: The forgotten journey of partners and families. Paper presented at the XVI Harry Benjamin International Gender Dysphoria Association Symposium. August 17–21, 1999, London, UK. Abstract at *The International Journal of Transgenderism, 4*, (1).

Cole, S. S., Denny, D., Eyler, A. E., & Samons, S. L. (2000). Issues of transgender. In L. T. Szuchman & F. Muscarella (Eds.), *Psychological perspectives on human sexuality* (pp. 149–195). New York, NY: Wiley.

Coleman, E., & Bockting, W. (1988). "Heterosexual" prior to sex reassignement—"homosexual" afterwards: A case study of a female-to-male transsexual. *Journal of Psychology and Human Sexuality, 1*, 69–82.

Corbett, S. (2001). Love in the 21st century: When Debbie met Christina, who then became Chris. *The New York Times Magazine*, October 14, 84–87.

Daskalos, C. T. (1998). Changes in the sexual orientation of six heterosexual male-to-female transsexuals. *Archives of Sexual Behavior*, *27*(6), 605–614.

Denny, D. (2004). Changing models of transsexualism. *Journal of Gay & Lesbian Psychotherapy*, *8*(1/2), 25–40.

Denny, D., & Green, J. (2006). Gender identity and bisexuality. In B. Firestein (Ed.), *Bisexuality: The psychology and politics of an invisible minority* (pp. 84–102). Thousand Oaks, CA: Sage.

Dimen, M., & Goldner, V. (2005). Gender and sexuality. In E. S. Person, A. M. Cooper, & G. O. Gabbard (Eds.), *Textbook of psychoanalysis* (pp. 95–120). Arlington, VA: American Psychiatric.

Ellis, M., & Eriksen, K. (2001, July). Transsexual and transgenderist experiences and treatment options. *Family Journal*, *10*(3), 289–299.

Erhardt, V. (2007). *Head over heels: Wives who stay with cross-dressers and transsexuals.* Binghampton, NY: Haworth Press.

Flemming, M., MacGowan, B., & Costos, D. (1985). The dyadic adjustment of female-to-male transsexuals. *Archives of Sexual Behaviorior*, *14*(1), 47–55.

Gilbert, M. (2000). What is transgender? The transgender philosopher [Special issue]. *International Journal of Transgenderism*, *4*(3). Available from http://www.symposion.com/ijt/gilbert/gilbert.htm

Glassmire, J. (2009). *The experience of transgender couples: Toward the development of couples therapy guidelines for this sexual minority population* (Unpublished dissertation). Argosy University, Washington, DC.

Goldner, V. (2003). Ironic gender/authentic sex. *Studies in Gender and Sexuality*, *4*(2), 113–139.

Green, J. (2004). *Becoming a visible man.* Nashville, TN: Vanderbilt University Press.

Green, R. (1978). Sexual identity of 37 children raised by homosexual and transsexual parents. *American Journal of Psychiatry*, *135*(6), 692–697.

Green, R. (1998). Transsexuals' children. *International Journal of Transgenderism*, *2*(4). Available from http://www.wpath.org/journal/www.iiav.nl/ezines/web/IJT/97-03/numbers/symposion/ijtc0601.htm

Hines, S. (2006). Intimate transitions: Transgender practices of partnering and parenting. *Sociology*, *40*(2), 353–371.

Hudak, J., & Giammattei, S.V. (2010, Winter). Doing family: Decentering heteronormativity in "marriage" and "family" therapy [Mongraph]. *American Family Therapy Academy*, 49–55.

Huxley, P. J., Kenna, J. C., & Brandon, S. (1981). Partnership in transsexualism: Part I. Paired and nonpaired groups. *Archives of Sexual Behavior*, *10*(2), 133–141.

Israel, G. E., & Tarver, D. E. (Eds.). (1997). *Transgender care: Recommended guidelines, practical information, and personal accounts.* Philadelphia, PA: Temple University Press.

Joslin-Roher, E., & Wheeler, D. (2009). Partners in transition: The transition experience of lesbian, bisexual and queer identified partners of transgender men. *Journal of Gay and Lesbian Social Services*, *21*, 21–30.

Kelley, T. (1991). Stages of resolution with spouses. In J. Dixon & D. Dixon (Eds.), *Wives, partners, and others* (126–133). Waltham, MA: International Foundation for Gender Education.

Kins, E., Hoebeke, P., Heylens, G., Rubens, R., & De Cuypere, G. (2008). The female-to-male transsexual and his female partner versus the traditional couple: A comparison. *Journal of Sex & Marital Therapy*, *34*, 429–438.

Korell, S. C., & Lorah, P. (2007). An overview of affirmative psychotherapy and counseling with transgender clients. In K. J. Bieschke, R. M. Perez, & K. A. DeBord (Eds.), *Handbook of counseling and psychotherapy with lesbian, gay, bisexual, and transgender clients* (pp. 271–288). Washington, DC: American Psychological Association.

Lev, A. I. (2004). *Transgender emergence: Counseling gender-variant people and their families.* Binghampton, NY: Haworth Clinical Practice Press.

Lev, A. I. (2010). How queer! The development of gender identity and sexual orientation in LGBTQ-headed families. *Family Process*, *49*, 268–290.

Ma, J. L. C. (1997). A systems approach to the social difficulties of transsexuals in Hong Kong. *Journal of Family Therapy*, *1*(1), 71–88.

Malpas, J. (2006). From otherness to alliance: Transgender couples in therapy. *Journal of GLBT Family Studies*, *2*(3/4), 183–206.

Malpas, J. (2010a, June). *Can couples change gender? Supporting couples in gender transition.* Paper presented at the American Family Therapy Academy annual meeting, Boulder, CO.

Malpas, J. (2010b, May/June). Commentary on Jeff Levy's case: "Between gay and straight: Honoring a client's multiple identities." *Psychotherapy Networker*.

Malpas, J., & Davis, C. (2005, April). *Trans-families: A relational approach to working with transgender individuals and transgender families.* Workshop presented at the Ackerman Institute for the Family, New York, NY.

Money, J., Clarke, F., & Mazur, T. (1975). Families of seven male-to-female transsexuals after 5 to 7 years: Sociological sexology. *Archives of Sexual Behavior, 4,* 187–197.

Pfeffer, C. A. (2008). Bodies in relation—bodies in transition: Lesbian partners of trans men and body image. *Journal of Lesbian Studies, 12*(4), 325–345.

Pfeffer, C. A. (2010). "Women's work"? Women partners of transgender men doing housework and emotion work. *Journal of Marriage and Family, 72,* 165–183.

Raj, R. (2008). Transforming couples and families: A trans-formative model for working with the loved-ones of gender-divergent youth and trans-identified adults. *Journal of GLBT Family Studies, 4*(2), 133–163.

Randell, J. (1971). Indications for sex reassignment surgery. *Archives of Sexual Behavior, 1*(2), 153–161.

Reagan, M. (Producer). (2001). *No dumb questions* [Documentary film]. Available from http://www .nodumbquestions.com

Reynolds, A. L., & Caron, S. L. (2000). How intimate relationships are impacted when heterosexual men crossdress. *Journal of Psychology & Human Sexuality, 12,* 63–77.

Rosenfeld, C., & Emerson, S. (1998). A process model of supportive therapy for families of transgender individuals. In D. Denny (Ed.), *Current concepts in transgender identity* (pp. 391–400). New York, NY: Garland Press.

Rutter, P., & Leech, N. (2010). Couples counseling for a transgender-lesbian couple: Student counselor's comfort and discomfort with sexuality counseling topics. *Journal of GLBT Family Studies, 6*(1), 68–79.

Samons, S. L. (2009) Can this marriage be saved? Addressing male-to-female issues in couples therapy. *Sexual Relationship Therapy, 24*(2), 152–162.

Scheinberg, M., & True, F. (2008). Treating family relational trauma: A recursive process using a decision dialogue. *Family Process, 47*(2), 73–95.

Stone Fish, L., & Harvey, R. (2005). *Nurturing queer youth: Family therapy transformed.* New York, NY: Norton.

Vitale, A. (2004). *Couples therapy when the male partner crossdresses.* Retrieved from http://www.avitale .com/cdcouples.htm

Weinberg, T., & Bullough, V. L. (1988). Alienation, self-image and the importance of support groups for wives of TV's. *Journal of Sex Research, 24,* 262–268.

White, T. J. H., & Ettner, R. I. (2007). Adaptation and adjustment in children of transsexual parents. *European Child & Adolescent Psychiatry, 16*(4), 215–221.

Zamboni, B. (2006). Therapeutic considerations in working with the family, friends, and partners of transgendered individuals. *Family Journal, 14*(2), 174–179.

Section II
Sex Therapy With LGBT Couples

6

Sex Therapy for Gay Male Couples
Affirming Strengths and Stemming Challenges

PHILIP A. RUTTER

This chapter explores the benefits of an affirmative psychotherapy approach to sex therapy with gay male couples. This integrative model fosters engaging, productive, and timely sex therapy assistance with desire disorders, sexual dysfunctions, and other unique dynamics encountered by gay males' intimate coupled relationships. Integrating narrative, feminist, and cognitive concepts and strategies coupled with systemic lenses—from either a multigenerational-Bowenian or a structural therapy approach—affirmative psychotherapy strategies can move the couple forward toward resolution, clarity, and positive individual and dyadic change.

Background: Theory and Research

To begin, the arena of sex therapy and relevant literature has its foundation in mostly psychodynamic concepts and some psychoanalytic grounding. Only recently have researchers and clinical trainers made forays into more strength based or postmodern theories as those proposed by affirmative psychotherapy (Long, Burnett, & Thomas, 2006). This chapter will cover the foundational psychodynamic approaches used in initial sex therapy models while supplementing with concepts from postmodern and family systems. Sex therapy (or relationship therapy, as oft referred) was formed out of a niche in marriage and family therapy that was lacking a true exploration of these most intimate sexual engagements that couples make or, conversely, may not make in the presence of dysfunction or desire disorders. The earliest sex therapy intervention and treatment models, books, or journal articles all tended to be heterosexist, focusing on upper-middle-class client issues, and, seemingly and operationally, patriarchal and exclusionary (Bettinger, 2004; Long et al., 2006). Although this tendency appears to have lessened in the past decade, much is to be gained by incorporating concepts and strategies of the affirmative psychotherapy model because it deconstructs dominant paradigms, confronts gender stereotypes and patriarchy, and broadens the lens of potential socioeconomic status and ethnic and cultural groups who may benefit. Further, this approach fits well with the oppressed and marginalized status frequently accompanying the experience of gay male couples.

A Google search of resources currently available on the topic of sex therapy with gay male couples brings up stereotypical "hits": gay male couples and HIV, infidelity, substance abuse, and so on. What appear to be new are more articles about the strengths of gay male couples (and lesbian couples, for that matter), inclusive of John Gottman's (2006) work on same-sex couples' engagement and commitment to maintaining their relationships.

Sex Therapy Basics

Leiblum and Rosen (2004) describe the original template(s) for sex therapy in their book *Principles and Practice of Sex Therapy*. A good resource for those considering adding this to their repertoire or clinical practice realm, the text describes the impact of psychopharmacology upon the profession while also explaining the impact of modern technology upon the provision of services (online advice sites, for example) and the impact of Internet pornography or online relationships upon the couple seeking sex therapy. Leiblum and Rosen, along with other leading clinical sexologists, urge the use of systemic strategies to treating dysfunctions and/or desire to guide a sex therapist's work with a couple presenting with desire discrepancy (Hertlein, Weeks, & Gambescia, 2009; Leiblum & Rosen, 2000). This chapter will explore the fit of this model with gay couples seeking sex therapy and will bolster the presentation with consideration of recent work on desire disorders among men, an oft-overlooked problem (Meuleman & Van Lankueld, 2004), to integrate the model with the affirmative psychotherapy approach (Bieschke, Perez, & DeBord, 2007; Bigner & Wetchler, 2004).

Historical Grounding of Counseling Models

Couple counseling with either heterosexual or homosexual clients has a historical grounding in psychodynamic (and often psychoanalytic) perspectives (Leiblum & Rosen 2000; Long et al., 2006). Prior models explored the symbolic content and utility of the symptoms or exploration of defenses and the ego's unconscious as it relates to desire disorders (Scharff & Scharff, 1987). As the reader may already know, although the groundings of early sex therapy constructs used psychoanalytic and/or object relations concepts foundations to support sex therapy approaches and interventions (Leiblum & Rosen, 2000), the psychodynamic or psychoanalytic model does not fit well when conducting sex therapy with same-sex couples (Bettinger, 2004). Given that these historical theories do not fit well, what is needed for sex therapy with same-sex couples is some type of systems theory (Hertlein, Weeks, & Sendak, 2009; Long et al., 2006). In addition, a trend to use postmodern approaches that are inclusive of social justice frames is urged in sex therapy and clinical work with same-sex couples; through these approaches, marginalized groups or previously oppressed groups (from a mental health perspective) are empowered to "reconstruct" their path through use of narrative therapy and feminist therapy (Bettinger, 2004; Long et al., 2006).

The move within the past decade is truly to gravitate toward short-term models (8–12 sessions) that are efficacious (Corey, 2009; Long et al., 2006). Again, this trend is one reason why sex therapy has moved away from the earlier psychoanalytic stance in unfolding the problem and creating treatment plans (Leiblum, 2006). The benefit of covering historical or systemic issues is, of course, to garner evidence of patterns of relating, history of abuse, or dysfunction across relationships, as well as uncovering individual issues with biological, psychological, or social functioning (Bettinger, 2004). Although the majority of sex therapy or clinical sexology literature suggests that this short-term model and postmodern theories are the norm, there are several clinicians doing good work with attachment theory (Tunnell, 2006) or approaches using psychodynamic groundings (Iasenza, 2005).

Current Counseling Approaches

Current approaches to counseling gay male couples are varied but have at their core several threads of commonality. Theories that affirm the struggle, that openly accept the unique sex lives of gay men, and that offer an empathic yet operational perspective on the presenting problem are best received and most effective (Long et al., 2006; Rutter, Estrada, Ferguson, & Diggs, 2008).

Couple counseling is by its nature systemic, but current theorists and applied researchers offer a subset of family therapy models that fit well with gay men. Structural therapy and multigenerational therapy can be integrated with other postmodern theories to challenge patterns of relating that are less functional but ingrained (Bettinger, 2004) while offering an explanation of repeating patterns that could be curtailed or modified to be curative. One example from multigenerational work conducted by Carter and McGoldrick (2009) is the use of sexual genograms. These generational diagrams are impactful ways for gay partners to see the patterns of sexual expression, dysfunction, and secrets across generations. These diagrams can often empower clients to acknowledge the pattern and stem it (ending what McGoldrick calls generational transference). Therapists using the multigenerational approach suggest that it is both illuminating and empowering for the clients served (Long et al., 2006). Structural therapy is currently integrated into same-sex relationship counseling by the clinician's use of techniques including family mapping, enactments, and unbalancing rigid structures and roles (Long et al., 2006). These techniques and their benefit will be explored in a later segment of this chapter through case presentation.

Other theories that fit well with sex therapy provision for gay couples include cognitive therapy and solution-focused therapy. Both approaches can boast significant data and studies to explain their efficacy. Both also fit what would be considered a brief-treatment model. What may come as a surprise is a change in the visibility of rational emotive behavior therapy (REBT) in its application to same-sex couples. This change may have to do with the highly expert power inherent in REBT not fitting well with sexual minority clients. My experience in serving lesbian and gay individuals and couples suggests that a more collaborative, coach-like role (as in cognitive therapy or solution-focused therapy) fits better.

Sex Therapy With Same-Sex Couples

Before strategizing sex therapy with gay male couples, therapists should realize the resilience of these couples and recognize their ability to weather the storm, so to speak. As a key marriage and family therapist and researcher phrased so eloquently, "Gay and lesbian couples are a lot more mature, more considerate in trying to improve a relationship and have a greater awareness of equality in a relationship than straight couples" (Gottman, 2006).

For these reasons and the marginalized and oppressed status of many same-sex client couples, sex therapists working with gay male couples would be well served to integrate the concepts espoused by the affirmative therapy model—namely, cognitive, solution-focused, and narrative tasks (from an individual perspective) and multigenerational or structural approaches (from a systems perspective). These theories are not, of course, integrated in tandem; but as Corey (2009) suggests, an integrative approach includes a delineation of who, when, and why questions. For all three, the foregoing theories suggest a very good fit with sex therapy for gay male couples. A final theory, or approach, that is part of the affirmative psychotherapy model is feminist therapy. Here, this theory is dealt with separately because it is probably one of the most powerful frameworks or theoretical stances that couples' counselors serving same-sex couples can hold. The significant impact of navigating internalized patriarchal messages; exploring gender roles, inclusive of gender-role analysis; and confronting gender stereotypes can prove quite beneficial when treating a desire disorder or dysfunction manifest for a gay male couple (Long et al., 2006).

Social Context for Gay Male Couples

Among the larger stressors for the current generation of gay couples—assuming a client base of 25–55-year-old clients—are the debate around same-sex marriage and the impact of the HIV/AIDS pandemic (though its prevalence among gay men has dropped dramatically in the last decade). These issues indeed impact gay male couples by relating to fidelity, monogamy, and the sanctity of their commitment. These two significant social issues are part of the gay male couples' "script." Drawing from narrative concepts, clinicians working with gay male couples ought to be aware of the messages each individual partner carries into the sexual relationship.

Areas of Vulnerability for the Gay Male Couple

A sexual dysfunction or desire discrepancy is discouraging and potentially devastating for the gay male couple. Particularly stressful is the paradigm of two men who may have acted on their mutual physical attraction and moved quickly into the realm of sexual activity early in their relationship, with less foundation on emotional and psychological connectedness (Bettinger, 2004). So when the sexual relationship has concerns, the gay male couple may falter, finding these concerns wholly distracting and challenging, and may not have the emotional or inter-dependent resources to navigate the current dilemma. Sex therapists serving gay male couples could serve clients well by exploring the *emotional* and *intellectual* attractions to buoy the couple above the current sexual disconnect (Tunnell, 2006).

Venues for Socializing

While broadening each year, the predominant social network and outlet for the gay male com-munity remains the local gay bar. Substance use and abuse is still a significant issue for gay men and lesbian women. The focus here on male same-sex couples and sex therapy offers one additional caveat that sex therapists ought to be aware of. Some gay men will tolerate the dam-age their substance abuse or alcohol use causes to their sexual relationship because they need to keep the "bar scene" a part of their ritual social outlet. It is indeed powerful to hear the cognitive distortions connected to drinking, drugging, and sexual enjoyment or dissatisfaction. Often sex therapy with gay male couples will necessitate a thorough exploration of substance use with the couple and the individual partners to determine its impact and role in their daily interactions.

A separate venue for socializing would have to include the Internet dating and sexual encoun-ter sites. Although frequenting these sites is possibly a step toward nonalcohol environments, these encounter sites promote a sexually based connection that may be stimulating or excit-ing for both partners but offers no basis for connection beyond pure sex (Bettinger, 2004). In working with gay male couples, it is important to fully explore how the partners met and in what context (club, park, through friends, online, etc.). This exploration would be important for any couple, straight or gay, but with same-sex couples it can help you in your assessment of strengths, limitations, and areas for exploration.

Also important is to recognize comorbidity concerns relevant to the gay male couple's sex therapy provision. One arena is a client's potential HIV+ status, and the other is use of recre-ational drugs. First, the therapist must recognize that a client's HIV status can cause depression, which though understandable can coincide with antidepressant medications (selective sero-tonin reuptake inhibitors) that contribute to erectile dysfunction (Meuleman & van Lankveld, 2004); or the HIV+ partner may be prescribed anabolic steroids when his T-cell count reaches a critical number, a symptom also connected with hypoactive sexual arousal disorder (HSAD; Purcell et al., 2005).

Second, in clinical intake interviews the therapist should ascertain whether the client has used recreational or illicit psychoactive substances. Purcell and colleagues (2005) examined the use of MDMA (ecstasy) among gay men who were sero-positive and found a high comborbity with erectile dysfunction, ejaculatory incompetence, and potential desire decline. The confusing element here is that MDMA use, in the moment, can actually cause stimulation and feelings of attractiveness. It is the actual "mechanics" that suffer once one is with a partner; that is, an erec-tion may be partial or absent, and ejaculate minimal or absent (Purcell et al., 2005).

Strength and Resiliency in Gay Male Couples

Although some scripts for the gay male population are laden with stereotypes and misogyny, many more gay men confront gender stereotypes and create their own templates for "normal" sexual play and creativity. Beyond the typical encounters all couples, heterosexual or homo-sexual, engage in, gay men are vastly creative! If one area of desire or dysfunction crops up for a gay male couple, these same clients are wonderfully resilient in creating alternative behaviors to express their attraction and meet their sexual needs. One vivid example is the willingness of gay male couples to broaden their definitions of monogamy or commitment. Traditional sex therapy and couple work most likely assumes that gay couples' open relationships or polyamorous systems are fragile; but in the experience of two men in romantic and sexual connection, these constructs are less daunting and damaging. The ability of gay male couples to engage or broaden their sexual repertoire through nonprimary partners is fodder for sex therapy conversations and seen as a way partners have discovered to meet their individual and dyadic sexual needs (Bettinger, 2004; Tunnell, 2006).

Strengths of Gay Male Couples' Sexual Orientation

Gay male couples (and lesbian couples, for that matter) can get quite scrappy, for lack of a clinical term, in defending and securing the couple. Given the relatively small pool of viable candidates (a direct quote from numerous couples and individuals I have counseled), gay men coming for sex therapy and relationship counseling are motivated, pure and simple, to make their relationship work. If doing so means engaging in new behaviors or deleting old ones, or potentially closing the relationship or opening it to other partners, gay clients are ultimately willing to be creative and purposeful in maintaining the couple through difficult times (Bigner & Wetchler, 2004).

Gottman (2003) elaborated on a difference in communication style that may buoy gay and lesbian couples above their heterosexual peers. It seems that for gay and lesbian couples, "positive emotions seem to have a lot more power or influence" (p. 70). In addition, Gottman's research with gay and lesbian couples offered the idea that the ways gays and lesbians resolve conflict may be the glue that maintains stability, allowing these same-sex couples to focus on positive communication that enables quicker problem solving and conflict resolution.

The creation of the gay male relationship without prescribed notions of what is normal suggests flexibility that adds actual strength to gay male couples in particular. Bettinger (2004) and Tunnell (2006) both speak to the aspect of monogamous or open systems among gay male couples and the potential benefit of choosing the best fit for the couple. Essentially, gay male couples create what fidelity means to them, whether that notion involves an exclusive relationship or an open relationship with each other as primary partners. This ability to control how they define their connection while also respecting the system as their primary focus, is a powerful example of creativity and actual security in the dyad (Tunnell, 2006).

Finally, it needs mention that humor and resilience for this population go hand-in-hand. Confronting stereotypes together, working collaboratively to present themselves to the broader population as a health-loving couple, and navigating the day-to-day stressor often found in all couples are most usually accompanied by a rapier wit, a sardonic commentary style, or a playful ability to laugh at the problem or stressor in tandem. These characteristics benefit the process of sex therapy with gay men by allowing therapists to include this strength, to use humor to confront the issue, and to band together to poke fun at it. My clinical work with gay men and couples has often included highly resilient humorous anecdotes related to their sexual lives and encounters. This ability to laugh through exploration in the process of therapy without being self-deprecating or hurtful is, in my opinion, one of the healthier coping mechanisms gay couples bring to sex therapy.

Recommendations for Assessment

The clinical literature suggests two levels of assessment, which intertwine with the actual processes of couples counseling. Initial sessions include clinical impressions, communication styles, perspectives on the problem, and previous strategies (Long et al., 2006). In my clinical sexology training classes I call this initial phase a *soft assessment*. It follows into the second set of sessions, which are held separately with each member of the system. A *second session* is an individual session where the presenting problem and relationship dynamics are explored without the partner present.

This approach is inclusive of a thorough biopsychosocial intake, essentially assessing the broader perspective on the issue at hand. One reason why the affirmative psychotherapy integrated approach works so well here is that it is, by its very nature, biopsychosocial, exploring individual, dyadic, and systemic arenas simultaneously (Hertlein, Weeks, & Sendak, 2009).

The second realm of assessment in sex therapy is often referred to as paper-and-pencil methods. These include use of a sexual history interview, either shorter versions (Kingsberg, 2006) or more elaborate versions (LoPiccolo & Heiman, 1978). The former may be considered cursory and is supplemented with additional assessment protocols (described in this chapter); the latter is quite extensive, taking approximately an hour for the client to complete (and subsequently an hour for the clinician to read through and consult upon). Both versions of paper-and-pencil assessment hold significant clinical value.

As the reader is assuredly aware, couples presenting with concerns about sexual desire or dysfunctions are often navigating layers of personal and interpersonal conflict, which are being played out in the bedroom. Gottman's (1999) approach to assessing couple functioning, though systematic and somewhat linear, is invaluable in gaining quick perspective on the couple's interaction style, blockages, and potential for positive change. Among several surveys of note are the Locke Wallace Marital Adjustment Scale, applicable to same-sex couples; the Four Horsemen; and the Repair Attempt Checklist. There are multitudes of surveys that can be used, but these three offer a decent perspective on relational patterns, communication styles, and previous problem resolution strategies.

Bettinger (2004) refers to a strategy that mirrors narrative therapy in asking gay male couples their "sex story." His approach is relevant because so many gay couples define monogamy differently, are sexually active early on in their relationship, and equate success in the dyad with success in their sexual lives. Unfortunately, in language and in constructs many sexual history interviews and surveys are geared to heterosexual married couples. Such interviews and surveys do indeed have merit, but use of the aforementioned surveys would need to be modified for same-sex couples. Aside from these limitations deserving attention, use of a paper-and-pencil survey, as well as a narrative of the couple's sex story, combines well to fully describe the journey and the obstacles encountered by gay male couples experiencing sexual dysfunction or desire disorders.

Case Presentation

A client couple, Tim (age 23) and Jeffrey (age 22), described their presenting problems as a "change in sexual frequency" and an apparently sudden desire discrepancy. When prompted to tell when the presenting problem started, Tim disclosed his HIV+ status, which had been diagnosed 2 months prior (Jeffrey is HIV–). Prior to this diagnosis, the couple had enjoyed a vibrant and open sexual relationship. Tim and Jeffrey had plans to move in together and to become partners, sealing their relationship with a commitment ceremony.

Although these plans remained focal, as part of their narrative, the decimation of their sex life because of the dwindling desire of the HIV– partner (Jeffrey) was in discord with their emotionally and socially constructed reality of "getting married" as a young gay couple. With this couple, sex therapy focused solely on the desire disorder would be fruitless. Rather, this clinician heard their sex story and socially constructed narrative and worked to deconstruct those chapters or scripts no longer helpful to the dyad. This new construction of their respective individual and systemic narratives was an imperative, given the change in HIV status and their current navigation as a sero-discordant couple. Conversations included exploring fears, hopes, expectations, wants, and needs for each other and for themselves. Using narrative questions

(Shapiro & Ross, 2002) in both couple and individual breakout sessions, we were able to gather data about the impact of this diagnosis and what it meant for the relationship and the partners moving forward. The couple held to the script of wanting to move in together because living together would test their capacity to share space. Upon exploration of their story and script, we learned the step of getting engaged or committed to each other was a familial message both partners were receiving from their parents—quite consistently and frequently, actually. Jeffery offered the insight that though he and Tim had always wanted to live together with or without a ceremony cementing their relationship, his mother looked at the wedding or ceremony as a validation of the couple. Both he and Tim assumed that this was a good narrative to follow. Only after pointed conversations and questions did they concurrently realize that the idea of having a ceremony was externally imposed.

This male couple also expressed urgency in wanting to restore their sex life and asked for specific strategies each of the first three sessions. Although sensate focus was indeed useful in slowing them down from Session 1 to Session 2, the dynamics suggested that cognitive behavioral constructs might help more. Inherent in individual breakouts with both partners were fear of contagion, diminished hope for the relationship, desire decline in the HIV− partner (who had previously been receptive), shame and self-esteem issues with Tim (because of his HIV+ status), and individually and systemically distorted assumptions. One pivotal discussion included Tim's cognitive distortion that Jeffrey no longer found him sexually attractive. When this perception was disclosed to Jeffrey, his response was a resounding yes to still being "very attracted" to Tim. They had become caught up in defining their intimate connection and attraction to mere sexual or physical parameters.

Pertinent to this point in the clinical dialogue was the depiction of Tim and Jeffrey's sex story (Bettinger, 2004) in which both partners had become set in a particular sexual role or position. Jeffrey was historically the receptive partner, with Tim being the insertive partner. Whereas they had been sexually versatile in prior relationships, now they remained in these "bottom" (Jeffrey) and "top" (Tim) roles. Utilizing feminist therapy concepts, sessions explored a gender-role analysis as it folded into sexual positions and preferences. Upon discussion, it became apparent that the bedroom was not the only gendered activity occurring in this couple. Expectations for Jeffrey to make meals, clean, and generally present as more nurturing were complimented by and contrasted with Tim's role to provide more expendable income, work on yard, and so on. Although these activities may be more shared across genders, gender-role analysis suggested that the partners in this couple had presumed much from each other and fallen into distinct patterns that were now impacting their sex lives in palpable ways.

A behavioral suggestion included trying sex toys (dildos) to explore role reversals or versatility in anal sex positions. Initially unsure of the purpose of this activity, the couple left the third session with mixed responses as to whether they could accomplish the task. Returning to the fourth session, they shared that they had not only successfully switched roles and positions but also created a replica dildo of each other's penis using a plastic cast process. The description presented that week, of the couple creating the cast from each other's erect penis, of making the new dildo from a plastic form kit, and the actual giddy presentation of "trying them on for size" was the happiest I had seen this couple present.

Once we had some successes in sessions, it seemed important to return to the systemic messages they received from parents and family of origin about coupling and intimate relationships. And the couple's earlier rigid role status suggested that a sexual genogram could be helpful. Both described a generally supportive, but often directive, connection to their mothers. Jeffrey came from an impoverished upbringing (his father left when Jeffrey was 10 years old) in a single-parent household and had a very close, open relationship with his mother—he came out to her at age 9. His mother suffered from a terminal illness, and Jeffrey was, in many ways, her apparent guardian. Conversely, Tim came from a highly affluent household and had come out to his mother only in the context of the relationship. She was accepting, however, and was promoting the commitment ceremony along with Jeffrey's mother. The context of being a single parent was explored, as well as messages about intimacy, sexual expression, and what commitment or marriage meant from a generational and now dyadic perspective.

Role of the Therapist

One significant benefit of the affirmative psychotherapy approach is the role of the therapist as nonexpert. This role matches well with marginalized or oppressed groups (Ritter & Terndrup, 2002). To be more explicit, feminist and narrative postmodern social constructionist theories operate from a low expert power role, allowing clients to describe the context of their experiences without therapists judging what is proper or improper functioning. A feminist or narrative therapist offers the gay male couple suggested directions only when the client's description suggests that the gender role or script is oppressive or antagonistic.

In addition and in accord with clients' expectations of sex therapy, the integration of slightly more directive theories can provide perspectives to initiate more immediate change. In particular, cognitive therapy does explore internal and shared distorted cognitions as they impact self-image, perceptions of a partner's behavior, and negative or inaccurate assumptions. In this role, a cognitive therapist is like a coach, with the client again learning how to address cognitions, both accurate and distorted. The use of cognitive therapy along with feminist and narrative approaches fits very well because numerous distortions accompany gender-role scripts or socially constructed norms for which gay male couples may fall prey.

Finally, systems theories, either multigenerational or structural, allow the male partners to gain historical perspectives on how others in their respective families of origin operated intimately (i.e., romantically, physically, and interdependently). Here, the clinician using either model will take the role of expert to guide the couple toward exploration of either sexual genogram patterns or boundary concerns (multigenerational) or use of enactments and unbalancing (structural) to add significant insight to the presenting problem of desire or dysfunction.

Helpful Therapist Characteristics and Therapist Issues

In working with same-sex couples, it is important to explore issues of countertransference, transference, and projection. Supervision for these cases is initially helpful if concerns around the sexual acts of two gay men would give the therapist pause or discomfort (Bettinger, 2004). One item for consideration that relates to feminist theory, for example, includes the use of disclosure. Gay and lesbian clients are more likely than their heterosexual peers to ask about the therapist's own sexual orientation or couple status. Of course, disclosure may or may not align the therapist's theoretical stance or personal style. It is important to realize, however, that gay and lesbian couples will indeed ask.

Countertransference, transference, and projection are relevant in all sex therapy work and are recommended grist for the mill in clinical supervision. If the therapist also identifies as a gay male and is working with a gay male couple, one can surely see countertransference or projection likely occurring. Several works cited in this chapter are critical readings for sex therapists wanting to serve gay male couples. Bettinger's (2004) and Tunnell's (2006) articles, for example, both speak candidly of the nature of sex therapy with two gay men, that is, of penis-to-mouth or penis-to-anus contact. Potential reactions to these behaviors or other sexual acts between two men would be an issue to discuss in supervision before ever serving a same-sex couple. As Bettinger succinctly states, "Gay men often have a finely tuned intuitive ability to sense a professional's discomfort or disapproval of their sexual choices" (2000, p. 70). In addition, Leiblum and Rosen's (2000) and Long, Burnett, and Thomas's (2006) texts offer great insight to sex therapy processes, treatment plans, and intervention styles. The former offering more systemic strategies and the latter offering the broader integrative approach used in affirmative psychotherapy.

Sex therapy with gay male couples also includes a unique variable that many clinicians may bristle at, namely, a different construction of monogamy or of what it means to be a couple. Gay male couples are sometimes mutually exclusive, other times exclusive for intercourse only. Other couples form a more polyamorous stance, in which the partner is a primary relationship and there are secondary and tertiary romantic relationships. Finally, yet other couples have a completely open relationship status. The importance of exploring how the couple partners define their intimate relationship, monogamy, and behaviors within and outside the dyad is crucial to sex therapy with gay male couples. Our impressions or judgments on closed or open systems are fodder for supervision, not for the clinical room.

Conclusions

The arena for same-sex sex therapy models and assessments has much room for improvement. Because most assessments and literature come from the marriage and family therapy camps, the language is at times laden with heterocentric terms (e.g., wife, husband, spouse, or marital discord) and at other levels riddled with sexual activities that are likewise heterocentric (e.g., focus on penis-to-vagina intercourse or assuming insertion or penetration). Finally, much literature can be found about the impact of affairs and the devastating effect upon sexual desire or sexual functioning. As mentioned earlier, gay male couples are potentially nonmonogamous, and this literature could potentially pathologize those vastly healthy same-sex couples enjoying an open relationship or those who are part of a stable, loving, polyamorous system.

Clinicians already in the field of sex therapy work may not be operating from the currently ascribed affirmative therapy model and would be well served to consider the benefits of integrating feminist, narrative, and cognitive concepts to best assist their gay male couple clients. Efficacy studies, client reports, and benefits of these affirming strength-based approaches all suggest that a primer on affirming approaches could help both seasoned sex therapists and the clients they serve.

Finally, the realm of sex therapy and the breadth of clinical backgrounds and disciplines interested in the provision of sex therapy, as well as graduate training on same, are vast, yet LGBT-affirming models are mostly absent. Sex therapist operationalizing this text and using an affirmative psychotherapy approach could move the future of sex therapy for gay male couples by (a) affirming the strengths and coping styles of gay male client couples; (b) validating their co-constructed models of intimacy and monogamy; and (c) exploring these gay male couples' gender scripts, historical narratives, and family messages as they enhance or detract from their intimate connections.

References

American Council for Drug Education (ACDE). (2010). Basic facts about ecstasy (MDMA). Retrieved from http://www.acde/drugfacts/mdma.org

Bettinger, M. (2004). A systems approach to sex therapy with gay male couples. *Journal of Couples and Relationship Therapy, 3*(2/3), 65–74.

Bieschke, K., Perez, R., & DeBord, K. (Eds.). (2007). *Handbook of counseling and psychotherapy with gay, lesbian, bisexual, and transgender clients* (2nd ed.). Washington, DC: American Psychological Association.

Bigner, J., & Wetchler, J. (2004). *Relationship therapy with same sex couples.* London, England: Haworth Press.

Carter, B., & McGoldrick, M. (Eds.). (2009). *The expanded family life cycle: Individual, family, and social perspectives.* New York, NY: Allyn & Bacon Education.

Corey, G. (2009). *Theory and practice of counseling and psychotherapy* (7th ed.). Belmont, CA: Brooks/Cole.

Gottman, J. (1999). *The marriage clinic: A scientifically based marital therapy.* New York, NY: Norton.

Gottman, J. (2006). *Same sex couples: How gay and lesbian couples can teach heterosexuals how to improve relationships.* Retrieved from http://www.gottman.com/49850/Gay--Lesbian-Research.html

Gottman, J., Levenson, R. W., Gross, J., Frederickson, B. L., McCoy, Y., Rosenthal, L., … Yoshimoto, D. (2003). Correlates of gay and lesbian couples' relationship satisfaction and relationship dissolution. *Journal of Homosexuality, 45*(1), 23–43.

Hertlein, K. M., Weeks, G. R., & Gambescia, N. (Eds). (2009). *Systemic sex therapy.* New York, NY: Routledge.

Hertlein, K. M., Weeks, G. R., & Sendak, S. K. (2009). *A clinician's guide to systemic sex therapy.* New York, NY: Routledge.

Iasenza, S. (2005). Some unconscious sources of low sexual desire in gay male and heterosexual peer marriages. *Contemporary Sexuality, 39*(7), 3–7.

Kingsberg, S. A. (2006). Taking a sexual history. *Obstetrics Gynecology Clinics of North America, 33*, 535–547.

Leiblum, S. (Ed.). (2006). *Principles and practice of sex therapy* (4th ed.). New York, NY: Guilford Press.

Leiblum, S., & Rosen, R. (Eds.). (2000). *Principles and practice of sex therapy* (3rd ed.). New York, NY: Guilford Press.

Long, L., Burnett, J. A., & Thomas, R. V. (2006). *Sexuality counseling: An integrative approach.* New York, NY: Merrill.

LoPiccolo, J., & Heiman, J. R. (1978). Sexual assessment and history interview. In J. LoPiccolo & L. LoPiccolo (Eds.), *Handbook of sex therapy* (pp. 110–123). New York, NY: Plenum Press.

Meuleman, E. J., & Van Lankveld, J. J. (2004). Hypoactive sexual desire disorder: An underestimated condition in men. *BJU International, 95,* 291–296. doi:10.1111/j.1464-410X.2005.05285.x

Purcell, D. W., Wolitski, R. J., Hoff, C. C., Parsons, J. T., Woods, W. J., & Halkitis, P. N. (2005). Predictors of the use of viagra, testosterone, and antidepressants among HIV-seropositive gay and bisexual men. *AIDS, 19*(Suppl. 1), 57–66.

Ritter, K., & Terndrup, A. (2002). *Handbook of affirmative psychotherapy with lesbians and gay men.* New York, NY: Guilford Press.

Rutter, P., Estrada, D., Ferguson, L., & Diggs, G. (2008). Sexual orientation and counselor competency: The impact of training on enhancing awareness, knowledge, and skills. *Journal of LGBT Issues in Counseling, 2,* 209–225.

Scharff, D. E., & Scharff, J. S. (1987). *Object relations family therapy.* Linham, MD: Jason Aronson, Inc.

Shapiro, J., & Ross, V. (2002). Applications of narrative theory and therapy to the practice of family medicine. *Family Medicine, 34*(2), 96–100.

Tunnell, G. (2006). An affirmational approach to treating gay male couples. *Group, 30*(2), 133–152.

7

Sex Therapy With Lesbian Couples

MARLA COBIN and MICHELE ANGELLO

Sex between women has a precarious place in history. Even today, there are plenty of "experts" who deem that sex between women is unnatural. It is not difficult to find therapists doing reorientation therapy. Women in same-sex relationships need therapy as much as anyone else. Whereas it can be difficult to find a therapist who is well versed in working with lesbians, it is even more challenging to find a therapist who is adept at working with lesbian couples. Significantly more difficult than this is finding a therapist who is trained, experienced, and competent to do sex therapy with lesbian couples. Perhaps it is for this reason that there is a paucity of empirical research and little written about sex therapy with lesbian couples. It is time for this area of the sexuality therapy field to develop so that women in same-sex relationships having sexual difficulties can more easily find the help that they need and deserve.

The dearth of reliable information with this community makes it arduous for nascent therapists to develop competency in this area. By far, the pioneer in this field is Margaret Nichols, who has been writing about the subject since the 1980s. In 1987, the book *Lesbian Psychologies: Explorations and Challenges*, edited by the Boston Lesbian Psychologies Collective, was published. Two of this groundbreaking book's chapters were written by Nichols (1987a, 1987b). Her chapter, "Lesbian Sexuality: Issues and Developing Theory," highlights what she found to be common sexual problems among lesbian couples. More recently, Leiblum (2007) wrote the chapter "Therapy With Sexual Minorities" for the popular sex therapy book she edited, *Principles and Practice of Sex Therapy*. Marny Hall (1998, 2004) has written several articles and book chapters about *lesbian bed death* and developed a four-stage model for working with lesbian couples. There are several others who have written works that include information on this subject. Many of these authors are cited throughout this chapter and deserve credit for contributing to this area of literature that is so lacking.

It should be noted that in this chapter we use the word *lesbian* when, in fact, we acknowledge that many couples made up of two women do not identify as such. Often women in same-sex relationships identify as bisexual, queer, or otherwise. As therapists, we ask clients how they identify both as individuals and as a couple in order to ensure that we utilize appropriate language throughout the therapeutic relationship.

Social Issues

Lesbians remain a marginalized group, facing continual ridicule, judgment, and sometimes violence. Homophobia and heterosexism continue to permeate society. Green (2004) outlines four challenges that may lead to problems between same-sex couples. They are societal homophobia and heterosexism, the "lack of [a] normative and legal template for same-sex couplehood," lower levels of family and social support, and the possibility of both partners conforming to "traditional gender roles" (Green, 2004, p. xv).

It is imperative to acknowledge both vulnerability and resiliency within the couple. Many women in relationships with women have been cut off from their family of origin because of the family's unwillingness to accept their orientation. This concept of being disowned can initially lead to an "us against the world" dynamic in which the couple partners insulate their relationship and deny anything but perfection with each other. Eventually this utopian mindset evolves into a more realistic view, and the couple partners can encounter difficulty acknowledging that they have differences, as do all couples. If these differences remain unacknowledged, this disconnect can lead to fusion between a couple whereby the couple partners might experience emotional distance from each other, unresolved conflict, some type of dysfunction with one or both partners, or triangulation in which a third party is involved in order to obviate blame from the couple (Green, Bettinger, & Zacks, 1996). On the contrary, the same authors acknowledged that this concept of fusion among lesbian couples may actually be considered a positive attribute because many of the couples exhibited intense closeness that manifested in intimacy, mutual engagement, and empowerment. The authors went on to say, "Our findings indicate that lesbian couples are exceptionally close and more satisfied with their relationships than gay male and heterosexual couples" (Green et al., 1996, p. 204).

Blumstein and Schwartz (1983) discussed the lack of legitimization of marriages as a contributing factor in the high dissolution rates of lesbian relationship. Another theory for the dissolution of relationship that Nichols (1987b) suggested is that women couple "prematurely," which leads to a "later falling off of sexual desire" (p. 101). She says that "only falling in love produces sexual desire, so we fall in love again, with a new partner, and the limerance of this new relationship revives our flagging sexuality" (Nichols, 1987b, p. 107). She suggests that it is important for lesbian couples to expand ways in which desire is developed (Nichols, 1987b).

Because there is another chapter in this book devoted to general therapy with lesbian couples (see Chapter 3, this volume), here we will not go into more detail about the impact of societal oppression on lesbian couples. It is important to mention, however, that such issues as homophobia, heterosexism, internalized homophobia, "coming out," and gender-role socialization may affect issues around sex and sexuality, in addition to general relationship issues, for lesbian couples (Connolly, 2004). There are myriad other issues that may also contribute to the reasons that lesbian couples seek sex therapy, including race, class, bisexuality, and gender identity.

Reasons for Treatment

Hall (2004) discussed the idea of a paradox that lesbian couples have to maneuver. On one side, lesbians are faced with a society in which many individuals, even "experts," invalidate their relationships and deem their sexual encounters unnatural and immoral. On the other side, there is research asserting that lesbians have frequent, passionate sex lives. According to Hall (2004), this confusion often leads to a disillusion of the sexual relationship, with frequency significantly declining after the first few years. Couples are then faced with emotional issues that come with low desire or desire discrepancy (Hall, 2004).

For lesbian couples seeking sex therapy the most common issue, one that has been written about for nearly 3 decades, is that of low sexual desire and sexual desire discrepancy between partners (Nichols, 1987b; Nichols & Schernoff, 2007). Nichols asserts that in the last 2 decades, the lesbian community has become more sexual (Nichols, 2005). In her more recent work, Nichols explores a variety of more current reasons that lesbian couples seek sex therapy. These include nonmonogamy, identity issues, coming-out problems, bisexuality, sadomasochism, sexual fringe issues, and desire discrepancy (Nichols & Schernoff, 2007).

Because there is so little research on this topic, many assumptions have been made. Recently, an Internet study was conducted that compared self-reported sexual problems of lesbians and other women. The results showed that "lesbians reported significantly fewer sexual problems than heterosexual women" (Nichols & Schernoff, 2007, p. 395). Among women, the most common problems, beginning with the most frequent, were lack of interest in sex and/or having lower desire than one's partner, problems with orgasm, experiencing greater desire than one's partner, difficulty lubricating, and anxiety about sex. Far fewer lesbians reported problems with lubrication as well as reaching orgasm. The reason for this may be that lesbians lubricate more and have less painful penetration than do heterosexual women, or it may be that lesbians avoid vaginal penetration and thus do not have to cope with lubrication difficulties and do not emphasize nonclitoral orgasms. The data did show that lesbians achieve orgasm more reliably than do women involved in heterosexual sexual relationships (Nichols & Schernoff, 2007).

Many authors have talked about what in the 1980s was coined *lesbian bed death*. This term refers to a common theme in literature about lesbian relationships of sex being frequent during the first few years and then tapering off significantly. More recently, this concept has been criticized and the empirical validity of the research spawning the term questioned. The concept is criticized for several reasons. The first is that mainstream theory defines sex as including genital contact with a goal of reaching orgasm. Many lesbian couples have more frequent sexual contact that may simply not include genital contact and/or orgasm than do some heterosexual couples. The second reason for criticizing mainstream theory as heterosexist is that it asserts that frequency of sex is an indicator of sexual health (Goldstein et al., 2007; Nichols & Schernoff, 2007). Finally, beyond the heteronormative undertones of this term—namely, that it is much more common for women partnered with women to have issues with sexual infrequency or low desire—it is problematic on many levels.

Low sexual desire is a common complaint of women in general, with possibly 30–40% of women reporting low desire. When to deem this as dysfunction is a source of debate (Basson, 2007). There are several possible reasons for the sexual repression or low frequency of sex displayed by lesbians that often contribute to lesbian couples' seeking sex therapy. One is that because of socialization, women may be less likely to actively request sex. Lesbians have been socialized as heterosexual women and have likely adopted certain, possibly constricting and conflicting, views about what is appropriate and acceptable (Nichols, 1987b). More recently, it was asserted that compared with women in heterosexual relationships, women in lesbian relationships are less likely to have sex solely because their partner wants it, implying that lesbian women are more empowered and say no if they do not want to have sex (Goldstein et al., 2007). Another possible reason for lesbian couples' low desire, discussed in Nichols's early work, is that often, sex and love are fused for women, making problems in the relationship a contributing factor to low sexual desire. Nichols (1987b) explains that some believe that, often, sexual contact creates fusion and that sex and desire decrease as women become "overinvolved" or "fused." Yet another issue in decreased desire may be that, based on one quarter of women having a history of sexual assault, this statistic may affect lesbian couples more than other couples, as it is more likely that one or both of the women has had a traumatic sexual experience. Internalized homophobia is another issue that Nichols (1987b) cites. Women who have not completely accepted their sexual orientation may feel sexually inhibited because of heteronormative ideas of what sex "should" consist of.

Nichols also talks about "fusion" or "merging," a notion many lesbian relationships "suffer from" (Nichols, 1987b, p. 107). She explains that some individuals believe that sexual contact creates fusion and that consequently sex and desire decrease as women become "overinvolved" or "fused" (Nichols, 1987b).

Along with low sexual desire, sexual desire discrepancy between lesbian partners is the other most common reason for seeking sex therapy as a couple (Nichols & Schernoff, 2007). Blumstein and Schwartz (1983) found that lesbians have significantly less sex than do gay male or heterosexual couples. Low desire is a common complaint for couples, with approximately 50% of heterosexual couples presenting with this as the presenting issue for sex therapy (Segraves & Segraves, 1991).

Many women are seen in sex therapy for such sexual pain issues as vaginismus and dyspareunia. According to Nichols and Schernoff (2007), such conditions are rarely seen among lesbians in sex therapy. The reason for this may not be that fewer lesbians have vulvar or vaginal pain but that if they do, it is easier, in lesbian sexual relationships, to avoid penetrative sex and simply focus on other aspects of sex that are pleasurable. This complaint could also be in part attributable to the fact that many heterosexual couples assume that penetrative sex will be a part of their sexual experience, whereas for lesbians this is not always the case.

Female orgasmic disorder was formerly categorized in the DSM-IV-TR as inhibited female orgasm. When a woman is experiencing a persistent or recurrent delay in, or absence of, orgasm, this can be an issue that brings the couple in for therapy. We have found this complaint to be less of an issue with women in relationship with other women. We suspect that perhaps the assumption in many heterosexual relationships that penile-vaginal penetration is ultimately satisfying for both partners is perhaps why more women partnered with men present with this concern.

Aversion to oral sex is a common complaint among lesbians, sometimes with both partners and sometimes with one of the partners disliking cunnilingus. It is only a problem when the couple partners believe that not participating in oral sex as part of their sexual activity will diminish their experience. Some women believe that oral sex is an important part of lesbian sex, whereas others see it as unpleasant and unimportant. Sometimes the aversion is on a physical level, whereas other times it is on an emotional level (Loulan, 1984; Ritter & Terndrup, 2002).

Role of Therapist

Many lesbians have, by the time they enter a therapist's office, already had negative, pathologizing experiences with doctors and mental health professionals. Therefore, it is critical that the stance of the therapist not be judgmental or pathologizing. Lesbians seek couples sex therapy for many of the same reasons that gay male couples and heterosexual couples do. So, sometimes sexual orientation is largely irrelevant. A difference does exists, however, in that in order for therapy to be comfortable for the clients and effective, the therapist must be "perceived as queer friendly" (Nichols & Schernoff, 2007, p. 388). Not making heterosexist assumptions and using gender-neutral language are simple but critical ways to let the clients know that the therapist has every intention of being respectful. Another issue for therapists to be mindful of is that often, lesbians, like their gay male counterparts, did not have normative adolescent experiences around sexuality and may continue to deal with such issues as secrecy, shame, and poor self-worth (Nichols & Schernoff, 2007). It is critical for therapists to leave behind any preconceived notions about what is normal when talking about sex. Judgment must not come into the therapy office (Nichols & Schernoff, 2007). Lesbians are already stigmatized, so it is essential that they are offered a safe, supportive space for couples' sex therapy.

Coming in for sex therapy can make anyone apprehensive, and certainly coming in with a significant other to discuss the sex life within your relationship can be even more anxiety provoking. It should be noted that for some same-sex couples, the additional fear that the therapist will in some way (whether overtly or not) have a moral judgment about the relationship or at least perpetuate heteronormative expectations is something the therapist should be willing to gently confront from the first session. We have several bookshelves in our offices, and we both are intentional about keeping books about sexual orientation, gender identity, and kink as visible on the shelves as those about general therapeutic issues. We also each make visible some kind of "safe space" sign as a clear indicator that we not only are open to discussing but also welcome conversation about these very important and sometimes vulnerable questions that often go unsaid because the clients are concerned about the therapist's reaction or moral judgment. Nichols points out that it is critical that when discussing sexuality, therapists working with lesbian couples be "mindful of the political implications" because women, and specifically lesbians, tend to talk about their sexuality in a political context because sexuality has been used as a form of oppression (1987b, p. 108). At the same time, therapists should not assume that all clients value egalitarianism in their relationships or that all clients are feminists. Most of the research done on lesbian couples has been on white, upper-middle-class, educated lesbians who come from a feminist perspective (Ritter & Terndrup, 2002). Therapists must be careful not to generalize and to be culturally sensitive when working with lesbians across race, class, education level, and so on.

As Nichols states in her early work, and we believe, an essential role of the therapist is to be "active and directive" (1987a, p. 245). A significant part of therapy is cognitive-behavioral in nature and may often include homework assignments. Therefore, the therapist needs to play an active role in engaging with and guiding the couple by offering insight and strategies to help improve their sexual functioning. It is also important for sex therapists who are themselves lesbians to be positive role models for lesbian couples, displaying sex-positive attitudes (Nichols, 1987a).

Of course, not all therapists providing sex therapy for lesbian couples are lesbians or even women, for that matter. There is thus important information heterosexual and other nonlesbian-identified therapists should have going into therapy with lesbian couples (Kort, 2008). It is not adequate to be gay friendly if being so implies that the therapist is simply not homophobic. Clinicians should be aware of the stages of coming out as nonheterosexual and of specific challenges that some couples face: for example, reluctance to publicly display affection for each other because there is a risk of being physically attacked, or facing issues of being disenfranchised because one's partner is not eligible for domestic partner benefits. "To be uninformed is a form of prejudice by omission" (Kort, 2008).

It is also important for therapists not to make assumptions about what is normal for any particular couple. Asking questions and learning about each client's ideas about what sex means and how sex should happen are critical. Ritter and Terndrup (2002) make the critical point that clients should be assured that there is no one way or a right way for lesbian couples to engage in sex. Sexual activity should not be based on heterosexist norms and may vary widely from one couple to another (Ritter & Terndrup, 2002).

Assessment

An important assessment tool, particularly when working with couples, is a detailed sex history. This assessment activity is done when meeting with each partner individually. Our experience has been that by the time most couples enlist the support of a sex therapist, they feel defeated and oftentimes hopeless. Reviewing their sex history can feel overwhelming to them if not handled with an appropriate amount of clinical savvy and respect for what the couple as a whole, as well as each individual, is experiencing. We find it helpful to integrate a series of nonthreatening questions regarding the couple's presenting problem(s) by "engaging in a fluid therapeutic conversation" (Iasenza, 2004, p. 18).

It is suggested that the clinician maintain the standard sex history format but also take a more broad systemic approach in gathering information. For clinicians unfamiliar with standard sex history taking, we recommend that Wincze and Carey (2001) be used as a primer. This portion of the therapeutic relationship should be done during the individual session in order to allow for the greatest amount of comfort for the client. Keeping in mind that most people presenting for therapy have had very few opportunities to openly discuss their sex history, the therapist should begin with the most nonthreatening information, such as demographics and further inquiry into what brings the client into therapy. For female clients, questions about regularity of menses and last gynecological appointment should be discussed. If there are such notable medical concerns as endometriosis, we request that the client sign a release so that we can speak to the appropriate physician to gather more information. We ask each client to talk a bit about what she considers the ideal outcome to be, as well as when the presenting issue was first experienced (to assess for lifelong versus acquired as well as generalized versus situational types). We are interested in hearing from each member of the couple how this concern is impacting the relationship. Something else that we find helpful in the sex history portion of our interview is to hear about the overt as well as covert messages regarding sex that the client received as a child. We conclude each sex history by asking if there is anything that we forgot to ask or anything the client would like to clarify. When talking about childhood, we agree with Iasensza's (2004) approach, which includes dialogue about gender roles, gender treatment, sexual feelings toward others, religiosity, race, ethnicity, and class. When discussing adolescence, in addition to standard sex history questions, Iasensza expresses interest in sexual experiences and coming out experiences. When exploring adulthood, she asks about coming-out experiences at home and work. When exploring current sexual experiences and functioning, she explores gender identity and sexual orientation, in addition to standard sex history topics. Using a multicontextual approach in taking a sex history, Iasenza includes conversation about "community contact" and "societal influences," in addition to questions about "friends and neighbors (heterosexual/homosexual); involvement in religious, educational, and government institutions and self-help groups; political activity (past and present); recreation/cultural groups; volunteer work; and any connections to the gay/lesbian community" (2004, p. 18). She also pays close attention to "political, social, and economic issues; and effects of biases based on race, ethnicity, gender, class, sexual orientation, religion, age, disability, and family form" (Iasenza, 2004, p. 18).

When meeting with the couple, it is important to talk about how each partner thinks culture and society has influenced their relationship and sexuality, both individually and as a couple. Iasensza (2004) suggests asking such questions as "How do you think growing up and living in a homophobic and sexist society has affected your relationship?" (p. 17). We include questions regarding the client's spiritual beliefs and attempt to investigate the potential connection between the presenting concern and certain faith-based groups' disparagement of same-sex relationships. For some individuals or couples, this connection is not an issue they are consciously aware of until given the opportunity to discuss the overt and covert messages they received from such groups.

Finally, it is critical for therapists to pay close attention, during the sex history, to how the client answers their questions. Many clients will be inexperienced in talking openly about sexual matters. Some will be much more comfortable than others. Observing these nuances can give the therapist important information (Ritter & Terndrup, 2002).

When meeting with the couple partners together, the therapist must look for the levels of autonomy as well as fusion. Ritter and Terndrup (2002) encourage therapists to "observe the distancing stagies used" and find out if the relationship "allows for individual friends and pursuits," as well as determine "what purpose these outside allegiances and activities serve" for both the individual and the couple (p. 351). It is also important for the therapist to learn about how the couple partners react to conflict (Ritter & Terndrup, 2002).

Therapeutic Approach

Multicontextual Approach

We believe that sex therapy with lesbian couples must involve a multicontextual approach in order to be highly effective. This means that the therapist must view presenting problems in the larger context of family, community, and society, appreciating these influences as contributing to presenting problems. Such systemic influences as homophobia and sexism often contribute to relationship and sexuality issues between couples (Iasenza, 2004). "Attention to the ways that various systemic levels help create or maintain problems" enables the therapist to "rapidly and efficiently help a couple make positive shifts that might not be possible" if the therapist were to only focus on "the presenting problem" (Iasenza, 2004, p. 19).

Feminist Approach

We choose to use a feminist approach and find it particularly useful with lesbian couples. A feminist approach is one that recognizes gender roles and inequalities; gender script; race, class, and cultural differences; and how societal inequalities affect relationships between partners. Issues of power are addressed in feminist literature and affect couples not only relationally but sexually as well (Prouty Lyness & Lyness, 2007). Feminist therapists can help couples explore how gender-role preferences and differences—including power imbalances as related to gender role, income, age, and the like—and how race, class, and cultural differences affect a couple's intimacy and views of sexuality. It is important not to ignore such differences. Doing so is equivalent to working from an ethnocentric, white, heterosexist view that not only is limited but also can be damaging. It is also important to acknowledge that lesbians automatically hold at least a dual minority status, being both women and sexual minorities. They often also hold other minority statuses based on class, race, religion, ethnicity, and the like. In addition, there are age discrepancies in lesbian couples more often than in heterosexual couples. This discrepancy brings along its own set of power imbalances and must not be ignored. All these issues are tied into power and must not be overlooked in sex therapy with lesbian couples, for such concerns can clearly affect how couples relate intimately and sexually. Feminist couples therapists can help clients redistribute power, improve communication, build increased affection and intimacy, and "broaden meanings of love" (Prouty Lyness & Lyness, 2007).

Education

One of the primary areas of need when doing sex therapy with lesbian couples is simply offering information. Women who have sex with women have grown up in a society where heteronormative assumptions permeate sex education. Therefore, many lesbians may feel that their sexual behaviors are inadequate or abnormal. Sometimes, simply educating clients and validating experiences can be enough to increase the women's comfort and confidence in their personal experiences. In our clinical practice, we have found that lesbians often need to be reassured that lesbian sexual expression is vastly different from experiences of heterosexual couples and that it can be damaging to compare their experiences or evaluate their experiences against standards based on male sexual desire and experience.

We have found that many clients come into our offices for sex therapy when, in fact, what would be more appropriate is education and assistance with the ubiquitous sex-negative messages they have learned. In these cases (and it should be noted that these are the majority in our clinical practices), we have found it judicious to begin with a four-stage model developed by Jack Annon (as cited in Leiblum & Slowinski, 1991). The model goes by the acronym PLISSIT, which stands for Permission giving (P), Limited Information (LI), Specific Suggestions (SS), and Intensive Therapy (IT). The PLISSIT model is utilized as a filter, beginning with the permission giving and limited information stages in an attempt to free one or both members of the couple of any anxieties they may have about sexual thoughts, fantasies, desires, or behaviors that are contributing to the presenting issue. If after spending time with these two components of the PLISSIT model the couple still find themselves struggling, we move onto specific suggestions.

There are a variety of common suggestions we make, but the most common is sensat- focus exercises that concentrate on sensual play that may or may not involve genital contact. There has been a great deal written about sensate-focus exercises, but the only educational tool we are aware of specific to female couples is the DVD *A Lesbian Couples Guide to Sexual Pleasure* (Schoen, 2006). Finally, after these three interventions have been completed, the clinician commences with intensive therapy with the couple.

Therapists who work with women in relationships with women should be aware of the aforementioned DVD because it not only is one of the few that is specific to same-sex couples but also includes a "Therapist's Guide" analogous to the section that is recommended to clients. It also reaffirms the more circular sexual-response models.

Narrative Therapy

We have found narrative therapy to be an effective approach for many women in relationships with women who come in for sex therapy. Developed by Michael White and David Epston (1990), this particular approach proposes that the therapist act as an investigative reporter of sorts, assisting the clients in discovering first the themes that are ubiquitous in each person's life, based on social, political, and cultural contexts in which they have lived. After the clients recognize stories or feelings that they have themselves perpetuated, stories or feeling no longer of benefit them, the therapist and couple collaborate to forge new narratives.

Treatment

Decreased Frequency, or Lesbian Bed Death

If a couple come in for therapy primarily because the frequency with which they have sex has significantly declined, it is important that the therapist normalize sexual frequency. The couple must first ask questions about what this decline means to each partner. A thorough investigation into the meaning and hypothesized reasons for sexual frequency decline must be explored in order for the therapist and the couple to understand the overall picture. It is important that the therapist not assume that the decline is problematic for the couple. The couple may simply believe that the decline is a problem because it is a drastic change, but sexual infrequency may in fact be satisfactory to both partners (Hall, 1988).

Low Desire and Desire Discrepancy

As stated earlier, we prefer to view lesbian sexuality from a feminist perspective and recognize but do not perpetuate heterosexist assumptions when exploring more traditional views of sexual dysfunction. Sometimes simply talking to clients about their own assumptions about what is normal can help resolve the sexual conflicts for which they are seeking treatment.

Loulan (1984) believes that the first step in dealing with lack of desire is for the couple to discuss their feelings with each other. Because sexual desire can be "blocked by unrecognized and unexpressed feelings towards [one's] partner," it is important to work through this difficulty and rule it out before looking at other reasons for low desire (Loulan, 1984, p. 93). Loulan (1984) points out that sometimes simply discussing feelings can unblock low desire. In her book *Lesbian Sex*, Loulan (1984) provides lists of questions for the partner with lower desire as well as the partner with greater desire. These questions can be helpful for each woman to help them understand why they feel the way they do. It can also be helpful for the couple to explore the questions and subsequent responses together to increase communication and understanding. In addition, Loulan (1984) points out that differences in class, race, age, size, disability, and the like may also need to be explored. Because these are often areas of sensitivity, having a skilled, culturally sensitive therapist may be helpful in exploring these issues.

In 1984, Loulan expanded Helen Singer Kaplan's model, which Loulan believed to be anti-lesbian. Loulan (1984) took Kaplan's three-stage model and expanded it to include six stages, beginning with willingness and ending with pleasure. In her book on lesbian sex, she outlines homework exercises for couples (Loulan, 1984). Rosemary Basson (2007) developed a more current sexual response model, asserting that Masters and Johnson's (1966) model and Helen Singer Kaplan's (1974) model were too linear and did not apply to many women. When lesbian couples come to therapy complaining about low sexual desire or sexual desire discrepancy, educating the couple about the Basson model can be helpful. In this model, Basson "incorporates the importance of emotional intimacy, sexual stimuli, and relationship satisfaction" with concepts from the previously mentioned models of sexual response (Jones, Kingsberg, & Whipple, 2005, p. 6). Using this model can help women couples with low desire or desire discrepancy. Therapy can teach the couple that often "the decision to have sex is driven by the desire for intimacy, not lust" (Nichols & Schernoff, 2007, p. 396). If a woman is receptive to sex, this will lead to sexual activity. Activity leads to arousal, which results in desire. A situation in which both women have lost desire and no one initiates sex is called the Basson-squared effect (Jones, Kingsberg, & Whipple, 2005). If only one of the women has lost desire, this woman can feel shame and worry that without desire sex will not be enjoyable. The woman who still has desire may feel rejected.

Education about the model can help the woman who has lost desire feel validated and can help the woman who feels rejected depersonalize the situation. The therapist can help the woman with low desire to challenge herself to become willing to have sexual activity without concern about lust. The couple should be encouraged not to rely on spontaneity but, rather, to schedule time for sexual activity. A couple really struggling with low desire on one or both partners can be encouraged to treat these scheduled times as actual dates. Doing so may help lead the couple to be flirtatious and seductive (Nichols & Schernoff, 2007).

Couples often believe that in order to have a successful sexual encounter, both women must reach orgasm. Therapists can help educate couples to change this belief system. Therefore, if one woman has a significantly higher libido than the other woman, they can come to see that it is okay to have sexual activity where only one of the women reaches orgasm. This can be helpful to the woman with lower desire, or anorgasmia, so that she does not feel pressured to reach orgasm every time the couple has sex. This approach may decrease her avoidance of sex by taking performance anxiety off the table. Furthermore, this approach can result in much more frequent sexual activity with much less anxiety (Nichols & Schernoff, 2007).

Another way in which therapist can help lesbian couples increase frequency of desire and frequency of sex is by helping the couple expand their definition of sex. Many couples limit themselves to oral and manual genital sex. By introducing the couple to such sex toys as vibrators, dildos, butt plugs, feathers, and different types of lubrications, the therapist helps the partners to find other ways to enjoy sexual connection, ways they might not have thought of. A way to help make sex more fun and desirable, this approach has been used by Margaret Nichols in her therapy practice to help increase frequency of sex in lesbian couples (Nichols & Schernoff, 2007).

Ritter and Terndrup (2002) encourage therapists to note the "degree of fusion and autonomy" and watch for "repeated cycles of merger and separation" when working with couples (p. 351). Although lesbian couples may be fused early in their relationships, they may, over time, find ways to distance themselves from each other. Ways in which this happens as well as how conflict is addressed can give insight into how the level of fusion in their relationship may affect their sexual relationship (Ritter & Terndrup, 2002).

Oral Sex Aversion

When a couple comes in complaining of oral sex aversion, it is important for the therapist to discover the source of the aversion. Is it societal messages? Is it based on heteronormative ideas of what sex is? Is it simply unpleasant for the individual with the complaint? Exploring what is behind the aversion and helping the members of the couple communicate with each other about it may decrease anxiety about engaging in or not engaging in the act. Although there are no studies we are aware of that speak to oral sex aversion specifically with regard to lesbian couples, research with heterosexual couples suggests that clinicians explore issues of physical or sexual trauma (Wincze & Carey, 2001). We have found that if the avoidance of oral sex is something attributable to sex-negative messages that one or both partners have incorporated into their sexual scripts, then sensate-focus exercises can be helpful.

Female Orgasmic Disorder

Many women have difficulty having orgasms during sex with their partner. This difficulty can often lead to feelings of inadequacy on the part of the woman who does not reach orgasm. Similarly, the partners of these women may also feel inadequate, blaming themselves for not being able to please their partner (Loulan, 1984).

One thing we consider when a woman presents with orgasmic disorder is whether the problem is something the woman has always experienced or one that she has acquired. We also explore whether this is an issue the woman has experienced with other partners or is exclusive to the current relationship. The information gathered during the sex history interview can give the clinician a great deal of insight into whether there may be deeper, unspoken relationship issues that are manifesting sexually.

As with all issues for which individuals and couples present, it is important to rule out biological factors. Some such considerations are "disease, injury, or disruption that affects the sympathetic or parasympathetic nervous systems" (Wincze & Carey, 2001, p. 43). Hormonal variation is also something to suggest having the client's gynecologist or endocrinologist check on. Finally, use of prescription medication is another factor that can inhibit orgasm for some women. It is commonly acknowledged that treatment with SSRIs can decrease a woman's ability to orgasm (Wincze & Carey, 2001).

Case Scenario

Casey made the initial phone call for therapy. She stated that she and Margot had been together for almost 3 years. The concern that prompted the call was that the couple could not seem to find time when each partner was interested in, or felt she had time for, sex. Casey reported that both she and Margot were getting extremely frustrated about "our sexless relationship" and wondered how to remedy it.

When Casey (age 41) and Margot (age 32) entered the office, both appeared slightly nervous and quiet. The therapist asked Margot what prompted the couple to come for therapy, and her response was essentially the same as Casey's. She stated that their sex life had been passionate when they first met and had remained so for the first few months, but it had since then waned to the point of almost being nonexistent. She said that they still very much enjoyed each other's company and were in love with each other, but both were concerned that they were getting accustomed to not having sex.

It was established by both partners that they genuinely wanted to be sexual with each other and that they were missing the passion and closeness that their sexual connection gave them. The couple came in for two sessions together, and then it was suggested that each person come in on her own. The intention behind this was to establish a sense of connection with them as individuals and also to interview each person with regard to previous sex histories, as well as to gain a greater contextual understanding of each person's life experience, including race, class, spirituality, history, and relationship with family of origin, and the experience of coming out as nonheterosexual.

Margot, who identified as bisexual, shared that this was her first long-term relationship with a woman. She said that she had experienced sexual intimacy with several different women in college but had, after graduation, found herself sexually attracted exclusively to men. She met Casey at the gym and was surprised to feel both physically and emotionally attracted to her. She said that she found herself thinking of Casey throughout the day and looking forward to the mornings when they both attended the same workout class at the gym. After several long conversations at breakfast following their workouts, Casey asked Margot if she would like to go to dinner, and Margot said that she initially froze but said, "I was so into her that I couldn't say no again." The couple had sex on their first date; and when asked why she qualified the experience by saying that it wasn't "real sex," Margot said because there was no penetration. Also worth noting during the individual interviews were answers to the family-of-origin questions. Margot had yet to articulate to her family that she and Casey are partnered and share an apartment together. She said that she assumes her family members know, but she would rather not discuss her relationship openly. Also, Margot is African American and until her relationship with Casey was very involved with a Christian church. One of the issues that Margot believes further isolates her from her family is that her family are not "particularly excited about me dating a white woman." When she began dating Casey, Margot also felt awkward continuing to attend her place of worship because it had been made clear to her that same-sex relationships were not accepted. Her family made it clear that people who do not attend church services are considered "a spiritual abomination." When asked what initially attracted her to Casey, Margot responded immediately, and without hesitation, that she found "Casey's confidence, and no-nonsense style very intriguing."

Casey came in the following week for her individual intake. She stated that she came out as a lesbian when she was 14 years old. She had been in several long-term relationships with women. She was Caucasian and grew up in what she called a "pretty traditional middle-class house with a mom, dad, and a few kids." She described her family as "more spiritual than religious." She said that she currently has a private spiritual practice. When asked what attracted her to Margot, she said that she found her "intellectually stimulating as well as really attractive." Casey said that sexually she enjoyed Margot's freedom early in their relationship, but after a few months felt as though unless she herself initiated sex, their sex life would be nonexistent. Casey's family of origin remained accepting and supportive from the moment she came out, 27 years ago.

When the couple came back together after the individual sessions, Casey mentioned that she had read something about female couples having little or no sexual relationship being common and was wondering if this state of affairs was just something they would "need to learn to live with." It is not unusual for some female couples to self-diagnose lesbian bed death, as this condition has been labeled. The therapist spent time explaining how their situation might be reframed as a desire discrepancy and not as a foregone conclusion of two women in partnership with one another. Both women seemed relieved by this explanation and also appeared anxious to move forward with treatment.

It was at this point that the therapist attempted to synthesize the contextual dynamics with which each member of the couple entered the relationship. Casey's family was supportive and accepting, and she had been out as a self-identified lesbian for most of her life. With Casey, there did not appear to be any internal conflict with regard to race, class, or spirituality. Her personality was very assertive, and she enjoyed sharing being the initiator of sexual activity. She expected Margot to feel the same. Margot was more reserved, however, and did not have explicit familial support of her relationship. She felt estranged from her family of origin since her relationship and also admitted to feeling uncomfortable confronting her family about their issue with Casey's being white. She also was experiencing unspoken discord with her family about her withdrawal from the church. Margot was comfortable with a bisexual identity; but sexually, she tended to lean toward more traditionally established gender norms of women being sexually passive. Intellectually, she acknowledged that given that Casey was a woman, she would not be expected to initiate and that this assumption that women have to be sexually passive was in conflict with her own feminist ideals. Casey expressed initial discomfort with Margot's sharing of the expectation of sexual passivity and stated that if Margot expected her to "be the man in the sexual relationship, this isn't going to work."

Since society indoctrinates a sense of heteronormativity, the therapist felt it important to explain that even though many relationships are judged by traditional assumptions about gender-role norms, same-sex relationships, as well as many different-sex relationships do not always utilize these "rules of conduct." It is important to establish a sense of normalcy that is not guided by heterosexist assumptions. We agreed to use the notions of passive and assertive with regard to the sexual roles.

We also discussed the sexual response cycle and used the Loulan and Basson models, which more than other models are focused on female sexual response. It was suggested that the couple talk openly about cultural differences. Although these are not necessarily issues that would deter more sexual activity for the couple, the therapist felt it would be myopic to strictly focus on sexuality without considering psychosocial factors that could be contributing to the relationship. It was also suggested that they each write in a journal daily with no intention of ever sharing with each other what they wrote. It was not long before Margot and Casey began coming in laughing and happily sharing things they had learned about each other through their conversations.

As the sessions progressed, the therapist recommended specific sensate-focus exercises. It was suggested that they watch *A Lesbian Couples Guide to Sexual Pleasure* (Schoen, 2006). Casey and Margot seemed to enjoy the "homework." After approximately 12 weekly sessions, they were having frequent sexually intimate experiences.

Recommended Research

As stated earlier, there is little research in the area of sex therapy with lesbian couples. Most helpful would be more empirical evidence about specific therapeutic approaches for the variety of issues lesbian couples present with in sex therapy. Giving therapists a large repertoire of clinical expertise would enable them to provide lesbian couples with comprehensive treatment that is successful. Gay-affirmative training of mental health practitioners who provide sex therapy is critical in order for women in relationships with women to receive appropriate, comprehensive, unbiased care.

Conclusion

Women who are in intimate relationships with other women face a unique challenge when seeking couple therapy. The intention of this chapter has been to discuss specific factors that the therapist must be aware of in order to provide an optimal safe space for the couples to share openly. One of these factors is the language therapists and clients use to discuss sexuality and identity, and we have suggested allowing the individuals as well as the couple to inform the therapist how they identify themselves—whether as lesbian, queer, or bisexual or another form of self-identification that feels more accurate. Because women in same-sex partnerships have been found to be particularly resilient and exceptionally bonded, therapists should certainly consider but not assume fusion within a female couple.

Other specific considerations for female couples include recognition that as children, adolescents, and even adults, many women have experienced heterosexist messages about sexuality. The authors work with myriad modalities with lesbian couple sex therapy, including the use of multicontexual, feminist approaches, narrative therapy, and a great deal of educational reframing and incorporation of sensate-focus exercises specific for women.

References

Basson, R. (2007). Sexual desire/arousal disorders in women. In S. R. Leiblum (Ed.), *Principles and practice of sex therapy* (4th ed., pp. 25–53). New York, NY: Guilford Press.

Blumstein, P., & Schwartz, P. (1983). American couples: Money, work, and sex. New York, NY: Morrow.

Connolly, C. M. (2004). Clinical issues with same-sex couples: A review of the literature. In J. J. Bigner & J. L. Wetchler (Eds.), *Relationship therapy with same-sex couples* (pp. 3–41). New York, NY: Haworth Press.

Green, R. J. (2004). Forward. In J. J. Bigner & J. L. Wetchler (Eds.), *Relationship therapy with same-sex couples* (pp. xiii–xvii). New York, NY: Haworth Press.

Green, R. J., Bettinger, M., & Zacks, E. (1996). Are lesbian couples fused and gay male couples disengaged? In J. Laird & R. J. Green (Eds.), *Lesbians and gays in couples and families: A handbook for therapists* (pp. 185–230). San Francisco, CA: Jossey-Bass.

Hall, M. (1988). Sex therapy with lesbian couples: A four stage approach. In E. Coleman (Ed.), *Integrated identity for gay men and lesbians: Psychotherapeutic approaches for emotional well-being* (pp. 137–156). New York, NY: Harrington Park Press.

Hall, M. (2004). Resolving the curious paradox of the (a)sexual lesbian. In J. J. Bigner & J. L. Wetchler (Eds.), *Relationship therapy with same-sex couples* (pp. 75–83). New York, NY: Haworth Press.

Iasenza, S. (2004). Multicontextual sex therapy with lesbian couples. In S. Green & D. Flemons (Eds.), *Quickies: The handbook of brief sex therapy* (pp. 15–25). New York, NY: Norton.

Jones, K. P., Kingsberg, S., & Whipple, B. (2005). Women's sexual health in midlife and beyond. In *Clinical Proceedings*. Washington, DC: Association of Reproductive Health Professionals.

Kaplan, H. (1974). *The new sex therapy.* New York, NY: Brunner/Mazel.

Kort, J. (2008). *Gay affirmative therapy for the straight clinician.* New York, NY: W.W. Norton.

Leiblum, S. (Ed.). (2007). *Principles and practice of sex therapy* (4th ed.). New York, NY: Guilford Press.

Loulan, J. (1984). *Lesbian sex.* San Francisco, CA: Spinsters Ink.

Masters, W., & Johnson, V. (1966). *Human sexual response.* London: Churchill.

Nichols, M. (1987a). Doing sex therapy with lesbians: Bending a heterosexual paradigm to fit a gay life-style. In Boston Lesbian Psychologies Collective (Ed.), *Lesbian psychologies: Explorations & challenges* (pp. 242–260). Urbana: Board of Trustees of the University of Illinois.

Nichols, M. (1987b). Lesbian sexuality: Issues and developing theory. In Boston Lesbian Psychologies Collective (Ed.), *Lesbian psychologies: Explorations & challenges* (pp. 97–125). Urbana: Board of Trustees of the University of Illinois.

Nichols, M. (2005). Sexual function in lesbians and lesbian relationship. In I. Goldstein, C. Meston, S. Davis, & A. Traish (Eds.), *Women's sexual function and dysfunction: Study, diagnosis, and treatment.* London, England: Taylor & Francis.

Nichols, M., & Schernoff, M. (2007). Therapy with sexual minorities: Queering practice. In S. R. Leiblum (Ed.), *Principles and practice of sex therapy* (4th ed., pp. 379–415). New York, NY: Guilford Press.

Prouty Lyness, A., & Lyness, K. (2007). Feminist issues in couples therapy. *Journal of Couple & Relationship Therapy, 6*(1/2), 181–195.

Ritter, K. Y., & Terndrup, A. I. (2002). *Handbook of affirmative psychotherapy with lesbians and gay men.* New York, NY: Guilford Press.

Schoen, M. (Prod. & Dir.). (2006). *A lesbian couples guide to sexual pleasure* [DVD]. Available from http://www.HSAB.org

Segraves, K., & Segraves, R. T. (1991). Hypoactive sexual desire disorder: Prevalence and comorbidity in 906 subjects. *Journal of Sex and Marital Therapy, 17,* 55–58.

White, M., & Espton, D. (1990). *Narrative means to therapeutic ends.* New York, NY: W.W. Norton.

Wincze, J. R., & Carey, M. P. (2001). *Sexual dysfunction: A guide for assessment and treatment* (2nd ed.). New York, NY: Guilford Press.

8

Transsexual Desire in Differently Gendered Bodies

ARLENE ISTAR LEV and SHANNON SENNOTT

The very nature of transgender "sex changes" evokes images of shifting identities, bodily alterations, and transgressive sexuality. The media sensationalizes transsexual body modification, focusing on surgical operations and physical transformations (Serano, 2007), ignoring the psychological disembodiment that compels people to publicly transition. The medical community has pathologized transsexuality, classifying it as a mental illness in need of psychological intervention (Lev, 2005; Winters, 2009) and ignoring the long history of gender variance throughout history and across diverse cultures (Blackwood & Wiering, 1999; Bullough & Bullough, 1993).

Despite the public gaze on transsexual bodies and the clinical pathologization of the transgender identities, there has been little attention paid to the actual sex lives of transgender, transsexual, and other gender-nonconforming people. Transgender eroticism is unexamined and poorly documented within the scholarly literature despite the unique experiences transgender people have of their embodiment (Lev, in press). Indeed, even in discussing transgender identity and sexuality, communication is muddied by the changing use of language for a community at the beginning of identity development. *Transgender* is generally used as an umbrella term to include all gender-nonconforming people. However, many *transsexuals*—people who have fully transitioned their sex through surgery, hormones, and legal documents—do not identify with the larger transgender umbrella. Gender-variant behavior can include a wide spectrum of human expression and behavior; hence, here we will use the term *trans* to include as many people as possible and thus, we hope, avoid offending anyone.

The lack of attention to the erotic lives of differently gendered people is hardly surprising, given the overwhelming silence regarding all serious inquiry in the sphere of human sexuality. Despite the commercial exploitation of sex in advertising and the popular media and the widespread proliferation of pornography, especially on the Internet, sexuality and eroticism remain inadequately explored areas in virtually all aspects of the social sciences and clinical research. From the societal fears of teaching sex education in public schools to inadequate funding of sexual research in higher education, discussion of human sexual response is guided by a "Don't ask, don't tell" philosophy. This is especially noteworthy in an academic context, where sexuality remains a taboo topic within psychology and social work programs devoted to marriage and family counseling (Pope, Sonne, & Greene, 2006).

The silence that surrounds all clinical studies of human sexuality grows deafening when examining trans identity. Human bodies modified by hormonal treatments and surgeries are judged as unattractive or even "deformed," with body parts that may be scarred and attributes that appear "odd." Paradoxically, trans people are summarily dismissed as "sexual perverts"— they are eroticized and exoticized—except when they are viewed as asexual, as if they have been cut off from potential human intimacy as a direct result of their gender-modified bodies.

In truth, transsexuality has been so infrequently studied that much of what is "known" is based on inference and conjecture. Since trans identities by their very nature cross the traditionally established sex binary, sexual relations frequently (though not definitively) defy traditional expectations. When congruence and embodiment must be sought and achieved, sexual exploration must negotiate complex issues of sexual orientation and passion, and erotic pleasures may be revealed that defy heteronormative expectations.

Theory and Research: Past to Present

The Conflation of the Sex and Gender Binaries

Prodigious attempts to gather research data for this chapter were met with professional silence and sometimes hostile or bemused reactions. Pairing the words *transgender* or *transsexual* with *sex*, *sexual*, or *erotic* in extensive academic interlibrary searches repeated yielded "zero results" or, occasionally, a general article on "LGBT social services," since the *T* follows the *LGB* even when the topic has nothing to do with trans issues. The same words plugged into Internet search engines revealed a colorful pornographic netherworld, displayed in overlapping pop-up windows downloading furiously to a home-based computer, initiating a sudden paralyzing fear of the potential consequences that could befall a scholar of sexuality living in a post–Patriot Act America.

There has been little substantial research on human sexual behavior (with the notable exception of Kinsey's exhaustive data collection in the mid-1940s) and transsexual practices have rarely been the focus of empirical studies. In the nineteenth century the relationship between what we now call homosexuality and transsexuality was not as clearly delineated as it is today. The emerging field of sexology as exemplified in Krafft-Ebing's seminal work *Psychopathia Sexualis* (1886/1999) viewed homosexual desire as a kind of gender dysphoria. Hekma (1994) says, "[Krafft-Ebing] assumed that men were attracted to men as if they were women, while women attracted to women should feel like men.... Homosexual preference and gender inversion were completely intertwined" (p. 226). This conflation of same-sex desire and gender nonconformity continues to challenge scholars of modern human sexuality; as we examine historical identities through a modern lens, the distinctions between sexual orientation and gender identity still baffle many clinicians today.

Medical science in the eighteenth and nineteenth centuries scrutinized, and even dissected, the bodies of intersex people, then labeled hermaphroditic, while they sought to find their "true sex" hidden in their gonads (Dreger, 1998). It was unthinkable to medical scientists that sexed bodies could exist outside of a male–female binary. In contrast, sociological and anthropological studies of cross-gendered people reveal a long historical record of human beings across the globe expressing complex and multigendered identities (Blackwood & Wiering, 1999; Bullough & Bullough, 1993; Roscoe, 1998). These studies have, however, focused more on the social identities of gender-nonconforming people rather than their sexual practices. When Freud began his explorations of human sexuality, he analyzed the sexual libido presumably hidden deep in the unconscious mind, and using psychoanalysis as his scalpel he tried to dissect human sexual response. With a probing intellect of a taboo topic, Freud was nonetheless a product of his repressive and sexist Victorian culture. His complex legacy of human sexuality does not address gendered sexuality outside the male–female binary.

Despite the seismographic cultural wave impacting sexuality in the past 60 years, including the impact of feminism and the sexual liberation movement, comprehensive scientific study into actual sexual practices has been minimal. Masters and Johnson (1966) and Helen Singer Kaplan (1974), the first modern sex researchers, presented a more expansive vision of human sexuality, yet neither mentions the existence of trans people in any depth, nor how their models of sex therapy might be adapted for people of transgender experiences. Models of human sexuality remain heteronormative in belief and practice, and "normal" human sexuality is assumed to include sexual intercourse with a penis and vagina (always leading to orgasm, of course). The "obsessive genital focus" (Tiefer, 2001, p. 39) of most research is steeped in heterosexist assumptions about the body parts people bring to bed with them and, most important when discussing trans bodies, how people experience those body parts or want to use them sexually.

The Medical Pathologization of Trans Identities and Sexualities   Contemporary research into transsexuality was developed within a medical model that has viewed trans people through a pathologizing lens. Indeed, the research participants were often people who sought medical treatment through established gender clinics (Denny, 1992). Since participants were dependent on the researchers' approval for treatments they desperately desired, it likely impacted their honesty and willingness to reveal information that might prevent them from continuing treatment. In order to receive medical treatment, participants were expected to articulate a "transsexual narrative" (Prosser, 1998), an autobiographical narrative that mirrored the trajectory of gender dysphoria outlined by Harry Benjamin (1966). These official narratives found in autobiographies (and which are now easily accessible on the Internet) became a blueprint for the only acceptable case histories with which participants could attain their treatment. It is thus no surprise that trans people seeking treatment have purposely lied to researchers (Lewins, 1995; Walworth, 1997), raising critical questions about the validity of the extant research on transgender and transsexual sexuality.

The only other avenues of research data, in addition to the information gleaned from gender clinics, are sociological studies on heterosexual cross-dressers and their wives (G. R. Brown, 1998; Doctor, 1988; Weinberg & Bullough, 1988), and sexual practices were never the primary purpose of these studies. These two threads of research focus on small population samples of White middle-class cross-dressing males and male-to-female transsexuals. There has been a paucity of studies on the masculine identities of natal females or the impact of race, ethnicity, or class on trans experience. Most of the research has focused on psychosocial adjustment, post-surgical sexual satisfaction, and the incidence of regret following transition (Pfäefflin & Junge, 1998). Complicating any analysis of research, concepts are defined and operationalized differently across studies; and given the wide diversity of people with gender-variant experience, it is difficult even to identify the parameters of who is being studied (Namaste, 2000). As mentioned earlier, even the words *transgender* and *transsexual* are used differently within different communities. Researchers do not uniformly examine the same populations; for example, have they included only those individuals who have had surgery, or have they included part-time cross-dressers or those living full-time without surgery? Despite the limitations of the research, a brief overview follows.

Studies of Transsexual Sexualities and Sexual Practices   Early research on male-to-female (MTF) transsexuals revealed that MTFs were commonly asexual, both before and after surgical reassignment (Benjamin, 1966; Person & Ovesey, 1974). Indeed, low sex drive was considered a necessary criterion for diagnosis of transsexualism (Lewins, 1995). Given the aforementioned widespread use of an approved "transsexual narrative," whether individuals were afraid to admit to erotic desires remains unclear; such an admission often raised "a red flag" as to whether the surgical candidate was really transsexual and should be considered for medical treatment (Ramsey, 1996, p. 49). Perhaps MTF transsexuals viewed their sexuality "as something that must be sacrificed in order to live in [their] chosen gender" (Tobin, 2003, para. 43, Pt. 1). Or perhaps rather than being asexual, they suffered from anatomical dysmorphia and experienced confusion or disgust regarding using their body parts sexually (Tully, 1992). The process of transitioning is a very intense time, and some people withdraw from social and familial interests to focus exclusively on their transition, which might, for some, include withdrawal from sexual activity (Devor, 1997; Lewins, 1995). Exogenous hormone treatment also impacts sexual desire and functioning for

MTF transsexuals, including causing a lowering of their sex drive and causing difficulties maintaining and achieving orgasms, which may lessen their sexual interest and activity.

Female-to-male (FTM) transsexuals, however, have been described in the literature as highly sexual, in part a result of the effects of testosterone on the human libido. Research studies and personal accounts have consistently shown that FTMs have increased sexual arousal following hormonal treatment (De Cuypere et al., 2005; Devor, 1997; J. Green, 2004; Hansbury, 2004; Valerio, 2006). Although research attests to the stability and longevity of intimate relationships for FTMs throughout their transition (Fleming, MacGowan, & Costos, 1985), there is scant research on FTM sexual practices and little attention has been paid to the process whereby couples negotiate the complexities of gender transition as it affects their sexual relationships.

Although few studies actually define sexual satisfaction, research has consistently shown that transsexual men and women identify sexual fulfillment following transition (De Cuypere et al., 2005; Pfäefflin & Junge, 1998) and that transsexual women experience orgasms following surgical transition (Lawrence, 2003; Schroder & Carroll, 1999). Sexual satisfaction and postsurgical adjustment often hinge on the success of the surgical results (Pfäefflin & Junge, 1998; Schroder & Carroll, 1999), which continues to improve as the surgical techniques for sex reassignment are refined (De Cuypere et al., 2005; Pfäfflin & Junge, 1998). This is a particularly challenging area for trans men, since genital surgeries are prohibitively expensive and surgical results for trans men are far less advanced than for trans women (Rachlin, 1999). Consequently, many FTMs do not have bottom (i.e., genital) surgeries, although genital changes, including an enlargement of the clitoris, do occur from exogenous hormone treatment for trans men.

The older research is extremely patholgizing, as exemplified in Steiner and Bernstein's (1981) statement of bewilderment as to why a "normal biological female would chose a 'penis-less man' as a partner" (p. 178). Although the majority of FTMs would likely choose to have genital surgeries if the cost were not prohibitive and the results showed greater functionality, research concludes that FTMs are able to establish stable male-gender identities (Fleming et al., 1985; Kockott & Fahrner, 1987). Trans men who for personal, medical, or financial reasons have transitioned without genital surgery have, to some extent, redefined social norms of masculinity and manhood (J. Green, 2004; Kotula, 2002; Vanderburgh, 2007) by developing satisfying sexual relationships with their partners without the presence of a phallus. It is possible that transitioning without bottom surgeries may provide more sexual consistency and familiarity for trans men's sexual partners, making it easier to adapt to the vast changes in other areas of their lives.

Emerging Perspectives of Trans Identities   In the past two decades sociocultural understanding of transgender identity underwent a paradigm shift, transforming the political landscape and heralding in a reevaluation of psycho-medical paradigms that pathologize trans identities (Denny, 2004). Treatment models are being developed that are respectful of diverse transsexual expressions, incorporate family and couple issues, and address posttransition identity and relationships (Bockting, Knudson, & Goldberg, 2006; Lev, 2004; Malpas, 2006; Raj, 2002; Vanderburgh, 2007). In 2010, the World Professional Association for Transgender Health (WPATH) released a statement urging the depsychopathologization of gender variance worldwide (WPATH, 2010); and in 2008, the American Medical Association (AMA) passed a resolution affirming the effectiveness of medical treatment for transsexuals and calling for an end to discriminatory denial of health insurance coverage for transsexual treatments (AMA, 2008). In addition to trans-positive policy statements from the American Psychological Association (APA; 2008) and the National Association of Social Workers (NASW; 2005, 2010), the Association of Lesbian, Gay, Bisexual, and Transgender Issues in Counseling (2009) developed a clinical competency statement specifically for working with transgender clients.

These vast changes in public policy and medical care are changing how trans people are viewed socially and politically, which will impact clinical care as well as research for years to come. The erotic lives of trans people is underexplored and rarely clinically examined. The research has only peripherally focused on issues related to family life, intimacy, and sexuality, but changes in the sociopolitical climate have set the stage for studies of transsexuality to begin.

Societal and Familial Stressors and Resiliencies

The Impact of Stressors on Transsexuality and Desire

There are numerous societal and familial stressors that impact the sex lives of trans people. Such stressors as dating, intimacy, forming partnerships, fertility, and transitioning within an already established relationship are specifically associated with sexuality. There are other aspects of trans people's lives that are not as directly related to their sexuality, however, but may impact it, for example, medical treatments, insurance or medical costs, work-related transition issues, parenting, and constant social scrutiny during the transition process.

The reality of violence, discrimination, and bias in the daily lives of trans people has been well documented, as has the negative impact this abuse has on their psychological stability (Lombardi, Wilchins, Priesing, & Malouf, 2001; Nuttbrock et al., 2010). Trans people face bias in child custody decisions (R. Green, 2006), for instance, and they have difficulty accessing competent and skilled health care (Kenagy, 2005). Workplace discrimination is ubiquitous; in one study, nearly 50% of trans people experienced an adverse job-related action, and 97% experienced mistreatment or harassment at work (NCTE & NGLTF, 2009). It is difficult to imagine that such daily stressors as these do not impact the sexual desires, behaviors, and experiences of trans people.

Social and familial challenges related to transitioning can cause great strain in people's lives, especially in interpersonal relationships. Friendships are tested, and intimate relationships may not survive the transition process. Frequently, it is not the transition itself that is challenging for partners and families but, rather, the immense discrimination and social stigma related to being differently gendered. Despite these challenges, many transgender and transsexual people successfully navigate the difficulties and maintain or create significant, ongoing, intimate relationships. Trans people are wives and husbands, lovers and partners, and single; and despite the outdated research, there is no reason to assume that trans people are less interested in sexual intimacy than are nontrans people. However, as Wilchins has noted, the partners of trans people "must be willing to negotiate the ambiguity of the terrain" (1997, p. 120); sadly, becaue of prejudice and transphobia, some people are not.

Trans people who are single and seek out intimate relationships may experience rejection, just as any single person might; and although there are bars, community centers, and Internet dating sites that are welcoming, isolation is an all-too-common experience. It is invaluable for trans people to have a network of friends and family to turn to for support because social prejudices are amplified when exploring dating. Even those individuals who are posttransition face questions of when and how to reveal their transition history to a new sexual partner (Vanderburgh, 2007). There are people (trans and nontrans) who are specifically eroticized by transgender bodies. Although appreciated by some trans people, this is a source of distress for others who resent having their trans status exoticized and fetishized; they want to date people who will simply honor their affirmed identity.

Historically, it was assumed that being trans was reason enough for a spouse to end a long-term marriage. Shocking to a modern viewpoint, transition protocols once expected transsexuals to divorce their spouses as part of the standard procedure to be approved for gender reassignment (Clemmensen, 1990). This clinical stance has led to increased isolation for trans people and the severing of familial ties and parental relationships. The fact that clinicians could not even imagine spouses wanting to remain together speaks to the underlying assumptions and prejudice toward differently gendered people and their intimate partners. It is only recently that narratives have been revealed and protocols been developed to assist couples with a trans partner to remain together (Erhardt, 2007; Lev, 2004; Malpas, 2006; Chapter 5, this volume).

Ways to Nurture Resilience in Transsexualities and Practices   Gender-variant people who are in the early stages of recognizing and addressing their trans identities can begin to build a support system by confiding in a loved one about the feelings they are having. Sometimes it is easier to first open up to a close friend than to an intimate partner. Support groups can also be invaluable in staving off feelings of isolation and loneliness. This process of reaching out for support can include revealing an interest in cross-dressing behavior or anatomical dysphoria, or confiding in their partners their desire to seek out gender-affirming hormones or undergo gender-affirming surgical treatments. The partner or spouse of a trans person will often move through a predictable developmental trajectory that includes a process of discovery and disclosure, turmoil, negotiation, and finding balance (Lev, 2004). Part of the negotiation stage often involves coping with the sexual aspects of intimate relationships, especially when the trans person's body is changing from the effects of exogenous hormones. The spouse or partner may be deeply disturbed and confused by feelings that can range from revulsion to arousal. Spouses who continue their exploration may find themselves sexually excited by the gender transition (Erhardt, 2007). Individual therapy, as well as support groups for partners, can be helpful; sometimes these resources and groups can be accessed through local LGBT community centers. The more awareness partners have about their own prejudices and biases related to trans identities, the more able they will be to connect with their trans partners on an intimate and sexual level.

Transgender and transsexual people represent a wide spectrum of individuals, who express diverse sexual behavior and varied sexual relationships. For some trans people, gender dysphoria interferes with their sexual expression and comfort in their bodies; for others, living in mixed-gendered bodies is experienced as sexually exciting and something to celebrate—a gender "euphoria." As is true for all individuals, there is a broad continuum of sexual behavior for gender-variant people. Some trans people are very conventional in their sexual behavior, whereas others appear more interested in atypical sexual practices. What sets trans people apart is that when they seek out sexual relationships with others they have to navigate the socially constructed assumptions and biases related to their transgender status.

Assessment and Treatment of Sexual Concerns

Understanding the Gender Identity and Sexuality

The first issue regarding assessment when working with trans people is to understand the diversity of gender presentations and identities that people can experience. Older models rely on medicalized classifications that belay the multiple and complex solutions trans people develop to understand their gender identities and express and present their gender within the social world. For example, although erotic cross-dressing in males has long been recognized, female cross-dressing has been an unacknowledged area of transgender studies; it has been suggested that this area remains unexplored because male clothing holds no erotic attraction for females (Ettner & Brown, 1999). However, the use of male clothing in lesbian culture as a way of expressing masculine identities has been consistent throughout queer and lesbian history. Female cross-dressing in the bondage, discipline, sado-masochism (BDSM) and kinky sex subcultures (Hale, 1997) and among drag kings (Volcano & Windh, 2005) is evidence that there exist erotic aspects to female masculinity and cross-dressing (Halberstam, 1998).

The predominant theory of transsexualism is based on the idea that transsexuals seek medical treatments in order to migrate from one side of the sex binary to the other. Although this is certainly a common reason to transition, emerging research shows that trans identities exist outside of a simple binary. Ekins and King (2007) discovered in their research a wide spectrum of patterns of gender mobility, including those who *mix* or *blend* gender, those who *oscillate* or move back and forth from one gender to the other, and others who attempt to *erase* their sexed body. Blending gender and expressing androgyny have been identified as emerging strategies for resolving gender dysphoria (Kane-Demaios & Bullough, 2005; Lev, 1998; Nestle, Wilchins, & Howell, 2002). As transgender communities organize and politicize (Lev, 2006), tension has developed between trans individuals with a more "traditional" understanding of their gender (i.e., crossing the binary from one sex to the other) and those who express more fluid genders (Roen, 2001). Clients present with many different ways of expressing their gender, and therapists must support trans people in determining their own gender identity and identifying their own gender expression. It is also important for therapists to advocate for people seeking medical treatments who may present outside of the traditional "transsexual narrative" (Lev, 2009).

Researchers have noted within transsexual subcultures a co-occurrence of what they call fetishistic behavior (Tobin, 2003; Tully, 1992), and personal narratives attest to BDSM sexual practices (Hale, 1997), although further study is necessary to determine the frequency and occurrence of kinky sexualities practices within various trans communities.

Until the late 1990s the bulk of the research on transgenderism focused on MTFs. Considered uncommon, FTM individuals were thought to be exclusively attracted to women, primarily heterosexual women. However, more current accounts have revealed that FTMs have a wide range of sexual attraction and behaviors, including relationships with both heterosexual and lesbian women (Devor, 1997). Further, some FTMs also recognize sexual attraction to men and identify themselves as gay or bisexual men (Coleman & Bockting, 1988). Although cross-dressers were always presumed to be heterosexual men, research shows that some cross-dressers identify as gay (Bullough & Bullough, 1997). Rankin and Beemyn's (2011) current research also reveals a wide range of sexual orientations in trans people. Approximately 32% of their respondents identified as bisexual and 30% identified as heterosexual; in addition, many identified as "other," stepping outside traditional categories of sexual orientation.

Sexual orientation can sometimes change following transition (Daskalos, 1998; Israel & Tarver, 1997; Lawrence, 2005; Schroder & Carroll, 1999), and some trans people have sexual relationships with each other (Devor, 1997), obscuring such concepts as same-sex and opposite-sex sexual orientations. Tobin (2003) has concluded, "It has become more and more clear that trans people come in more or less the same variety of sexual orientations as non-trans people" (para. 27, Pt. 1). Indeed, it is critical to not to make any assumptions about sexual orientation or sexual practices but instead embrace the multitude of possibilities for sexual desire and partnership.

The desire for particular categories of sexed or gendered people may not be the best way to describe the complexity of any human sexual desires, but the notion is especially confounding when examining the erotic and intimate relationships of gender-variant people and their sex partners. Currah (2001) states that the term *sexual orientation* "remains intelligible only if sex and gender remain relatively stable categories" (p. 182). Transgenderism disrupts this stable boundary of gender and sexual orientation, rendering such concepts as heterosexual and homosexual inadequate to describe the sexual experiences of those engaging in intimate and sexual behavior. Similarly, having a sexed body that is mixed or blended can impact sexual orientation, desire, and identity. Rankin and Beemyn's (2011) document that some of the unique sexual orientation identifications trans research participants used to describe themselves include "pansexual," "queer," "transgender lesbian," "heterosexual lesbian," lesbian with bisexual leanings," "omnisexual," "attracted to genderqueer people," and "bisexual when dressed in female clothes otherwise heterosexual." Nichols (2000) says, "There are problems inherent even in arriving at common definitions of sexual minorities, because the phenomena we are attempting to define are so variable and complex" (p. 337).

Identifying Therapeutic Needs for Trans Individuals and Their Partners

Kleinplatz (2001) critiques traditional sex therapy on a number of grounds, including stating that sex therapy tends to emphasize performance rather than subjective meaning and experience, marginalizes diversity rather than embracing it, and assumes a "norm that involves two able-bodied heterosexuals in a monogamous relationship" (p. 116). Iasenza (2008) echos Kleinplatz's concerns, saying, "Medicalization of sexual functioning promotes one-size-fits-all models of sexual response" (p. 539), illuminating the tendency to try to fit differently gendered individuals into sexual categories that are, at best, not relevant and, at worst, extremely oppressive and damaging to the therapeutic relationship. Kleinplatz challenges sex therapists not to simply "stretch our sexual norms" but to "learn from those we label as 'other' to fundamentally question and revise our conceptions of sexuality" (p. 116). This is the exciting challenge of doing sexuality work with couples where one or both partners are trans.

It is crucial when working therapeutically with trans individuals and their partners to honor and celebrate the desires of each partner equally and not to assume that relational discomfort or discontent is directly linked to the transition. Iasenza (2010) discusses the need to create "a safe holding environment" for all couples, and to "create [an] expansive erotic space by inquiring about, exploring, and, if necessary, normalizing and reframing queer experiences" (p. 298). She recognizes that gender transpositions and genderqueer fantasies, as well as internalized shame regarding these feelings, are important to explore in all sexual pairings, not just those that are identified as trans or queer. The field of sex therapy has taken a giant leap forward in recognizing the queer possibilities inherent in heterosexual, opposite-gender sexuality.

Male-to-female transsexuals in heterosexual marriages may struggle with sexual problems (Tully, 1992), related in part to their wives' reluctance to engage in "lesbian" sex. Research has shown that heterosexual wives have identified a lack of sexual arousal toward their partner's cross-dressing (Doctor, 1988), although, in one study 43% of women stated they continued to engage in sex with husbands while they were cross-dressed (Weinberg & Bullough, 1988). Some of the difficulties wives identify are related to sexual functioning; other difficulties involve frustration with the spouse's preoccupation with stereotypical femininity or his refusal to act "like a man" (Boyd, 2003). Erhardt (2007) says, "The libido of a gender-variant natal male may flourish if the wife welcomes the femme persona in the bedroom" (p. 208). The libido also might diminish, however, if she cannot welcome the persona—and she often simply cannot—leaving both partners with unmet sexual needs.

For example, Steven and Marcy had been married for over 20 years and had raised two children, now in college, when Steven revealed his transsexual identity. Although Marcy was aware that Steven enjoyed cross-dressing, she was shocked to find that "Stephanie" had been living a secret life for many years. Both were committed to maintaining their relationship and worked hard in therapy through many layers of shame, betrayal, and disclosure. Marcy identified as a heterosexual woman, and as Stephanie moved along in her transition, developing breasts and dressing publicly as a woman, Marcy was not sure how to continue a sexual relationship with Stephanie. Stephanie remained sexually attracted to women and longed for the experience of being in bed with her wife, as a woman; however, the idea of lesbian sex did not appeal to Marcy. Stephanie did not pursue sex reassignment surgery, partially because of her ambivalence about the necessity of it, and also because of the financial constraints it would place on the family. The female hormones had impacted Stephanie's ability to have or maintain an erection, and

Stephanie seemed more sexually aroused by wearing sexy lingerie than she was in pleasuring Marcy, which caused Marcy to feel rejected, angry, and "like a fool" for trying to maintain a sexual relationship with her husband's female body.

Boyd (2003) debunks the facile assumption that there are two kinds of wives, "the ones who accept their husband's cross-dressing and those who don't" (p. 52). She says that a woman may be both types "depending on the day or the week or the moment" (Boyd, 2003, p. 52). In the case of Marcy and Stephanie, it took them a series of difficult conversations in therapy for Marcy to express her anger with Stephanie. At first Stephanie could only hear Marcy's anger as rejection of her as a trans woman, but over time she was able to empathize with Marcy's situation. With Stephanie's compassion, Marcy began to grieve what she had lost because of the gender transition. As the newness of Stephanie's transition faded, she was able to become a more attentive, less self-absorbed, partner. It is unlikely that sexual intimacy will emerge unscathed by the massive changes gender transition evokes, although many transsexual women and their wives are able to develop working accommodations and maintain a positive sexual relationship.

Although trans men and their partners also experience complex relational challenges during transition, trans men commonly remain in stable relationships with female partners both during their transition and afterward (Fleming et al., 1985; Kockott, & Fahrner, 1988; Steiner & Bernstein, 1981). This pattern can be explained in part by the fact that before their transition, most FTMs expressed their gender with a masculine aesthetic, which their partners found attractive. For FTMs, there is little shift in their social gender impression or the expression of their gender within the context of their sexual relationship, unlike for the female partners of trans women who are negotiating the loss of heterosexual privilege as well as the serious social challenges invoke by their spouses' public "sex change."

Female partners of trans men are often comfortable with the public masculinity of their partners and share with them a sense of being "different" or even "queer" not only as lesbian couples but in some cases also as couples identified as butch–femme. When butch or masculine females begin to transition their sex, however, lesbian partners, especially those who are femme identified, often face unique psychological challenges to their identity (N. R. Brown, 2005; Mason, 2006). Having a partner with a male identity and who is using male pronouns can bring with it unexpected heterosexual privilege; a lesbian partner may be more likely to reject than embrace being perceived of by others as a heterosexual wife. For lesbian-identified women, losing membership in the lesbian community can be very emotionally challenging.

For example, when Lucas began his transition, his partner Sally was supportive. They had met on a butch–femme Internet community bulletin board, and their sexual attraction was built upon their erotic dance of their gender expressions. Sally was sexually excited by Lucas's masculinity and understood that he experienced some dysphoria in his body. When he decided to resolve this dysphoria by having chest reconstructive surgery and taking gender-affirming hormones (i.e., testosterone), Sally initially shared his excitement in the journey. However, as Lucas's body began to change, including the deepening of his voice and the removal of his breasts, and was consistently perceived in public as a male, Sally became withdrawn and depressed. She found his facial hair and body smells repulsive and hated being viewed as heterosexual in her daily life. She felt confused about her own sexual identity; she wondered, if she could be involved with a trans man, why not a bio man, and what did that mean for her sense of herself as a lesbian? Lucas enjoyed his changing body; and as he grew increasingly comfortable as a man, he wanted Sally to embrace his changes. He felt rejected by her resistance to his transition and her unremitting stance to identify as a lesbian.

For some lesbian identified women like Sally, negotiating sexuality across the gender binary is psychologically complicated. Adjusting to shifts in a partner's identity and body may be easier for women who are bisexual, in either identity or practice (Glassmire, 2009). It is also true that some previously lesbian-identified women have come to love, embrace, and value their partner's changing body, and they find it sexually appealing and erotic (N. R. Brown, 2005; Mason, 2006). In order to work therapeutically with Lucas and Sally as a couple, it is important to affirm their identities and aid them in recognizing that sexual identities can be fluid. Lucas has to come to accept the salience of Sally's lesbian identity—that it is more than a statement of her sexual expression; that it is, rather, a core part of her identity. Although Lucas would like to have lived his life as man and leave his lesbian history behind, he has come to understand that he cannot do that and remain lovers with Sally. Sally has had to really examine her views about men and masculinity and what it meant for her to truly love Lucas, not as he was, but for who he had become.

Although the sexual issues for trans people and their partners may be somewhat unique, as Doctor (1988) says, "they are by no means entirely different" from other issues that couples bring to therapy (p. 181). Coping with intimacy, honesty, communication, and changing bodies over time are universal concerns. Effective sex therapy with transgender people and their intimate partners must foster sexual communication that allows for the multiple experiences within changing bodies and erotic desires. The therapist must create a holding environment that can contain both the negative emotionality and anxiety caused by the changing identities and bodies, and the possibility of future sexual satisfaction.

The Therapist's Role in Treatment: Self-Awareness, Self-Education, and Transparency

Providing therapy for trans people and their partners requires an understanding of the trans person's gender emergence and the partner's experiences, as well as the dynamic relational process that emerges for the couple (Lev, 2004; Malpas, 2006). In addition, therapy based on models that incorporate empowerment, advocacy, and transfeminist principles creates a safe environment for the couple to explore the development of intimacy and sexuality (Lev & Sennott, in press).

Self-awareness on the part of the therapist is the first component of a strong therapeutic connection with differently gendered clients. It is important to be aware of one's blind spots stemming from personal beliefs. If a therapist comes to a countertransferential impasse regarding aspects of trans identities, he or she ought not subject clients to this impasse but should seek out supervision with a trained gender therapist who is also familiar with marital and family issues or refer the couple to someone who can provide affirming gender and sexuality treatment.

If the discomfort a therapist feels is based on a lack of knowledge, then self-education can be the most effective way to move forward. Being honest with a client about your level of experience is helpful, for such disclosure lets the client know that though you are not an expert in trans issues, you are willing to educate yourself on the issues and work together with the clients. Educating yourself does not mean asking the client to be the educator, however, for such a situation can feel retraumatizing for some trans people. Note that some clients might "use" the therapist's lack of knowledge to misinform the therapist or redirect the therapy away from necessary clinical explorations. A clinician's discomfort in talking openly about sex in general and transsexuality in particular can add to the oppressive dynamic in the therapeutic relationship.

It is constructive to destigmatize transsexualities with clients so they can approach communication with their partners more easily (Malpas, 2006). The therapist models a depathologizing approach, which encourages relational honesty and openness between the partners, taking a stance of affirming curiosity while mirroring the language used by the client regarding preferred name and pronouns. Using the correct pronouns with clients is not always easy; even therapists sometimes make mistakes, which should be acknowledged in the room as a step in building trust and establishing an alliance with the client. Therapists can help clients to express their feelings of betrayal when pronouns are misused and repair damage created within the therapeutic relationship; this approach also models successful communication around other difficult topics (i.e., sexuality, gender difference, and atypical sexual practices), not only in therapy but also with partners and family members. This approach reframes an individual problem into a normative relational adjustment (Malpas, 2006).

Last, when working clinically with trans and gender-nonconforming people, transparency is vital to the therapeutic alliance. After the therapist has explored issues of countertransference and has engaged in self-education, it is the relational action of transparency that indicates to clients that the therapist does not assume any specific narrative of trans lived experience (Malpas, 2006). Each couple is going to experience transition differently, in part because of the trans partner's identity and experience and in part because of the couple's particular relational dynamics. This approach will allow a more complex and individualized story to emerge and also aid in integrating past identities with present and future experiences, as well as disclosing fears about transition. The transparency of the therapist's unique reactions and experiences to the emerging narrative can communicate to clients that they do not need to fit into a typical or predetermined trans life story. Transparency with differently gendered clients is a blending of psychotherapy, notions of alliance building, and the ethics of social justice and feminist practice, that is, the transfeminist therapeutic approach (Sennott, 2011). In order to foster a trans person's self-definition of his or her own gender, therapists must be knowledgeable and supportive of diverse gender identities and expressions, as well as understand their own relationship to gender, sexuality, and identity The process of self-awareness, self-education, and transparency will enable therapists to bring language and understanding to the experiences of transition and help them communicate about sexual desires and practices within intimate relationships.

Case Scenario

Gracie and Maggie have been married for 35 years. They have three grown children who are living on their own and who were adopted as a sibling group at ages 3, 5, and 7 through the foster care system. Gracie and Maggie have always had difficulty finding time for intimacy since becoming parents of children with an extensive trauma history. Parenting took a significant focus their energy and time for nearly 20 years, and their relationship and sexuality were neglected. When Gracie, then Greg, revealed his transsexual identity 25 years into their marriage, while they were actively raising three teenagers, Maggie was shocked, having had no idea that her husband had any concerns about his gender. While the couple were managing issues of disclosure to the children, Maggie's feeling of betrayal and Gracie's emergence process became the focus of years of intensive therapy, little of which focused on their sex lives.

However, Maggie has long been concerned about their sexual difficulties, and in fact, one year before Gracie came out to Maggie as being "a trans woman, and maybe genderqueer too," Maggie had searched for a sex therapist for them to see together to discuss their lack of intimacy. Gracie avoided the appointments, making excuses and sabotaging the process because "he" was deeply struggling with his gender identity and was afraid that his life-long secret might be detected by a sex therapist. Maggie was very hurt by her husband's behavior and had begun to give up hope of having an intimate connection with him. Only after Gracie's transition and their children's launching into their own lives were they able to begin to explore their sexual desires.

Maggie is struggling on two levels in relation to her intimacy with Gracie. The first is that they have had almost no sexual connection for at least 10 years; the other is that Maggie is not sure how to understand her consistent attraction to Gracie during and after transition. Maggie had always considered herself to be a heterosexual woman but is now grappling with sexual feelings for Gracie that both surprise and amaze her and also, on a deep level, are "disgusting" to her. She is able to acknowledge that these feelings are partly her lack of understanding and familiarity about transsexualism in general and sexual minorities issues in particular. Maggie is still shocked to find herself part of an "LGBT community."

As the therapist helped Maggie explore her feelings about the "disgust" she feels, Maggie is asked "who" the disgusted voice reminds her of, and she admits that she is hearing the voices of her mother and brother, both of whom are extremely homophobic and close minded. Gracie begins to realize that she needs to stand up to her family's judgments about Gracie's transition so that their messages would hold less power and she would feel more free to explore her sexual attraction for Gracie.

Although Gracie and Maggie have lived together for over 3 decades and successfully reared into adulthood three children with challenging issues, they have not had a functioning sex life for many years despite sharing other forms of intimacy and closeness. Gracie spent years avoiding Maggie because of her own lack of embodiment. For both women there are years of distrust, betrayal, anger, and feelings of sexual rejection that must be explored. The journey toward each other will likely be slow and cautious. However, as a couple with 35 years together, having weathered the trials of foster adoption, parenting, and the emergence of transsexual identity, they have a strong foundation on which to develop a healing sexual relationship.

The therapist's reactions, conscious and unconscious, will strongly influence the success of the therapy. Certainly, education is essential regarding trans identities, couple dynamics, and sex therapy. In addition, the therapist must be cognizant of his or her own reactions to this couple's struggles. Perhaps younger therapists might find themselves surprised that a couple can neglect their sex lives for "so many years," or the therapists might even think that there is no point to work on sexuality for a couple in their 50s. Perhaps an experienced LGBTQ therapist might be annoyed or even angry at Maggie's "disgust" at her desire or frustrated with her heterosexual privilege and resistance to identifying as a member of a minority group. A heterosexual therapist might overidentify with Maggie's ambivalence, encouraging her to "go slow," perhaps mirroring the therapist's own need to go slow. For trans persons, it might be difficult to contain the relational dynamics, which might reflect their own histories and experiences, and therefore pain.

Recommendations for Future Research, Treatment, Assessment, and Intervention

As previously noted, there is scant research on trans people in general and even less on transsexuality in particular. The bulk of the extant research was completed before the rise of the transgender liberation movement and expression of genderqueer identities; it is not clear how closely the research represents modern sexual practices. With the advent of the Internet, transgender people and trans sex practices have become a somewhat more visible subculture (Lev, 2006), yet few researchers are examining trans sex lives. There is especially a dearth of research on transgender people of color, those living with disabilities, and the implications for aging trans individuals.

Summary

Trans identities by their very nature cross the traditionally established sex binary, making it easy to assume that sexual relations between trans people and their sexual partners will also defy traditional expectations. However, it is often not the transition itself that is challenging for partners and families but, rather, the immense discrimination and social stigma related to being differently gendered. Despite these challenges, many transgender and transsexual people successfully navigate through the difficulties and maintain or create significant, ongoing, intimate relationships. When working with trans people, clinicians need to understand the diversity of gender presentations and identities that people can experience. Clinicians must utilize newer models of assessment and treatment that respect the emerging paradigms of identity that trans people have developed to understand their gender. It is at the junction where gender identity and sexual orientation meet that intimacy, desire, and sexuality take shape and new language is created to describe it; this pattern may be true of those individuals who fit neatly into the gender-sex binary as well as those who are differently gendered. Effective sex therapy with trans people and their intimate partners will challenge clinicians to think differently about bodies and identities, including body modification and the complexity of sexual orientation. Trans sex therapy can foster healthy sexual communication and can cultivate erotic desires within changing bodies.

References

American Medical Association (AMA), GLBT Advisory Committee. (2008). *Removing barriers to care for transgender patients* (H-185.950). Retrieved from http://www.ama-assn.org/ama/pub/about-ama/our-people/member-groups-sections/glbt-advisory-committee/ama-policy-regarding-sexual-orientation.shtml

American Psychological Association (APA). (2008). APA Policy Statement: Transgender, Gender Identity, & Gender Expression Non-Discrimination. Retrieved from http://www.apa.org/about/governance/council/policy/transgender.aspx

American Psychological Association (APA). (2010). Transgender Identity Issues in Psychology: Resolution Supporting Full Equality for Transgender and Gender-Variant People. Retrieved from http://www.apa.org/pi/lgbt/programs/transgender/index.aspx

Association of Lesbian, Gay, Bisexual, and Transgender Issues in Counseling. (2009). *Competencies for counseling with transgender clients.* Alexandria, VA: Author.

Benjamin, H. (1966). *The transsexual phenomenon.* New York, NY: Julian Press.

Blackwood, E., & Wiering, S. E (Eds.). (1999). *Same-sex relations and female desires: Transgender practices across cultures.* New York, NY: Columbia University Press.

Bockting, W., Knudson, G., & Goldberg, J. (2006). Counseling and mental health care for transgender adults and loved ones. *International Journal of Transgenderism, 9,* 35–82.

Boyd, H. (2003). *My husband Betty: Love, sex, and the life of a cross-dresser.* New York, NY: Thunder's Mouth Press.

Brown, G. R. (1998). Women in the closet: Relationships with transgendered men. In D. Dallas (Ed.), *Current concepts in transgender identity* (pp. 353–372). New York, NY: Garland.

Brown, N. R. (2005). *Queer women partners of female-to-male transsexuals: Renegotiating self in relationship* (Unpublished dissertation). York University, Toronto, Canada.

Bullough, B., & Bullough, V. (1993). *Crossdressing, sex, and gender.* Philadelphia: University of Pennsylvania Press.

Bullough, B., & Bullough, V. (1997). Are transvestites necessarily heterosexual? *Archives of Sexual Behavior, 26*(1), 1–12.

Clemmensen, L. H. (1990). The "real-life" test for surgical candidates. In R. Blanchard & B. W. Steiner (Eds.), *Clinical management of gender identity disorders in children and adults* (pp. 121–135). Washington, DC: American Psychiatric Association.

Coleman, E., & Bockting, W. (1988). Heterosexual prior to sex reassignment, Homosexual afterward: A case study of female-to-male transsexual. *Journal of Psychology & Human Sexuality, 12,* 69–82.

Currah, P. (2001). Queer theory, lesbian and gay rights, and transsexual marriages. In M. Biasius (Ed.), *Sexual identities—Queer politics* (pp. 178–197). Princeton, NJ: Princeton University Press.

Daskalos, C. T. (1998). Changes in sexual orientation of six heterosexual male-to-female transsexuals. *Archives of Sexual Behavior, 27,* 605–613.

De Cuypere, G., T'Sjoen, G., Beerten, R., Selvaggi, G., De Sutter, P., Hoebeke, P., ... Rubens, R. (2005). Sexual and physical health after sex reassignment surgery. *Archives of Sexual Behavior, 34*(6), 679–691.

Denny, D. (1992). The politics of diagnosis and a diagnosis of politics: The university-affiliated gender clinics, and how they failed to meet the needs of transsexual people. *Chrysalis: The Journal of Transgressive Gender Identities, 1*(3), 9–20.

Denny, D. (2004). Changing models of transsexualism. In U. Leli & J. Drescher (Eds.), *Transgender subjectivities: A clinician's guide* (pp. 25–40). Binghamton, NY: Haworth Medical Press.

Devor, H. (1997). *FTM: Female-to-male transsexuals in society.* Bloomington: Indiana University Press.

Doctor, R. F. (1988). *Transvestites and transsexuals: Toward a theory of cross-gender behavior.* New York, NY: Plenum Press.

Dreger, A. D. (1998). *Hermaphrodites and the medical invention of sex.* Cambridge, MA: Harvard University Press.

Ekins, R., & King, D. (2007). *The transgender phenomenon.* London, England: Sage.

Erhardt, V. (2007). *Head over heels: Wives who stay with cross-dressers and transsexuals.* Binghamton, NY: Haworth Press.

Ettner, R., & Brown, R. (1999). *Gender loving care: A guide to counseling gender-variant clients.* New York, NY: Norton.

Fleming, M., MacGowan, B., & Costos, D. (1985). The dyadic adjustment of female-to-male transsexuals. *Archives of Sexual Behavior, 14*(1), 47–55.

Glassmire, J. (2009). The experience of transgender couples: Toward the development of couples therapy guidelines for this sexual minority population (Unpublished dissertation). Argosy University, Washington, DC.

Green, J. (2004). *Becoming a visible man.* Nashville, TN: Vanderbuilt Press.

Green, R. (2006). Parental alienation syndrome and the transsexual parent. *International Journal of Transgenderism, 9*(1), 9–13.

Halberstam, J. (1998). *Female masculinity.* Durham, NC: Duke Press.

Hale, C. J. (1997). Leatherdyke boys and their daddies: How to have sex without women or men. *Social Text, 52–53*(153/154), 223–236.

Hansbury, G. (2004). Sexual TNT. In U. Leli & J. Drescher (Eds.), *Transgender subjectivities: A clinician's guide* (pp. 7–18). Binghamton, NY: Haworth Medical Press.

Hekma, G. (1994). A female soul in a male body: Sexual inversion as gender inversion in nineteenth-century sexology. In G. Herdt (Ed.), *Third sex, third gender: Beyond sexual dimorphism in culture and history* (pp. 213–240). New York, NY: Zone Books.

Iasenza, S. (2008). Queering: The new view. *Feminism Psychology, 18*, 537–545.

Iasenza, S. (2010). What is queer about sex? Expanding sexual frames in theory and practice. *Family Process, 49*(2), 291–308.

Israel, G. E., & Tarver, D. E. (1997). *Transgender care: Recommended guidelines, practical information & personal accounts.* Philadelphia, PA: Temple University Press.

Kane-Demaios, J. A., & Bullough, V. L. (Eds.). (2005). *Crossing sexual boundaries: Transgender journeys, uncharted paths.* Amherst, NY: Prometheus Books.

Kaplan, H. S. (1974). *New sex therapy: Active treatment of sexual dysfunctions.* New York, NY: Random House.

Kenagy, G. P. (2005), Transgender health: Findings from two needs assessment studies in Philadelphia. *Health and Social Work, 30*, 19–26.

Kleinplatz, P. J. (2001). A critique of the goals of sex therapy, or the hazards of safer sex. In P. J. Kleinplatz (Ed.), *New directions in sex therapy: Innovations and alternatives* (pp. 109–131). Philadelphia, PA: Brunner-Routledge.

Kockott, G., & Fahrner, E.-M. (1987). Transexuals who have not undergone surgery: Follow-up study. *Archives of Sexual Behavior, 16*(6), 511–522.

Kotula, D. (Ed.). (2002). *The phallus palace.* Los Angeles, CA: Alyson.

Lawrence, A. A. (2003). Factors associated with satisfaction or regret following male-to-female sex reassignment surgery. *Archives of Sexual Behavior, 32*(4), 299–315.

Lawrence, A. A. (2005). Sexuality before and after male-to-female sex reassignment surgery. *Archives of Sexual Behavior, 34*, 147–166.

Lev, A. I. (1998, October). Invisible gender. *In the Family*, 8–11.

Lev, A. I. (2004). *Transgender emergence: Counseling gender-variant people and their families.* Binghamton, NY: Haworth Clinical Practice Press.

Lev, A. I. (2005). Disordering gender identity: Gender identity disorder in the DSM-IV-TR. *Journal of Psychology and Human Sexuality, 17*(3/4), 35–70.

Lev, A. I. (2006). Transgender communities: Developing identity through connection. In K. Bieschke, R. Perez, & K. DeBord (Eds.), *Handbook of counseling and psychotherapy with lesbian, gay, and bisexual clients* (2nd ed., pp. 147–175). Washington, DC: American Psychological Association.

Lev, A. I. (2009). The ten tasks of the mental health provider: Recommendations for revision of the World Professional Association for Transgender Health's Standards of Care. *International Journal of Transgenderism, 11*(2), 74–99.

Lev, A. I. (in press). Sexuality issues for transgender, transsexual and gender-nonconforming people. In S. L. Morrow & R. E. Fassinger (Eds.), *Sex in the margins: Erotic lives of sexual minority people.* Washington, DC: American Psychological Association.

Lev, A. I., & Sennott, S. (in press). Understanding gender nonconformity and transgender identity: A sex positive approach. In P. J. Kleinplatz (Ed.), *New directions in sex therapy: Innovations and alternatives*. New York, NY: Routledge.

Lewins, F. (1995). *Transsexualism in society: A sociology of male-to-female transsexuals*. South Melbourne, Australia: MacMillian Press.

Lombardi, E. L., Wilchins, R. A., Priesing, D., & Malouf, D. (2001). Gender violence: Transgender experiences with violence and discrimination. *Journal of Homosexuality, 42*(1), 89–101.

Malpas, J. (2006). From otherness to alliance: Transgender couples in therapy. *Journal of GLBT Family Studies, 2*(3/4), 183–206.

Mason, M. E. (2006). The experience of transition for lesbian partners of female-to-male transsexuals (Unpublished dissertation). Alliant International University, San Francisco.

Masters, W. H., & Johnson, V. E. (1966). *Human sexual response*. New York, NY: Bantam Books.

Namaste, V. K. (2000). *Invisible lives: The erasure of transsexual and transgendered people*. Chicago, IL: University of Chicago Press.

National Association of Social Workers (NASW). (2005). Social work speaks: Official statement concerning homosexuality from the National Association of Social Workers (7th ed.) [Abstract]. *NASW Policy Statements Abstracts*. Retrieved from http://www.socialworkers.org/resources/abstracts/default.asp

National Association of Social Workers (NASW). (2010). Social work speaks: Gender identity disorder and the DSM: Policy statement on gender identity [Abstract]. *NASW Policy Statements Abstracts*. Retrieved from http://www.socialworkers.org/diversity/new/lgbtq/51810.asp

National Center for Transgender Equality (NCTE) & National Gay and Lesbian Task Force (NGLTF). (2009, November). *National transgender discrimination survey preliminary findings*. Retrieved from http://transequality.org/Resources/NCTE_prelim_survey_econ.pdf

Nestle, J., Wilchins, R., & Howell, C. (2002). *GenderQueer: Voices from beyond the sexual binary*. Los Angeles, CA: Alyson.

Nichols, M. (2000). Therapy with sexual minorities. In S. R. Leiblum & R. C. Rosen (Eds.), *Principles and practice of sex therapy* (4th ed., pp. 353–367). New York, NY: Guilford Press.

Nuttbrock, L., Hwahng, S., Bockting, W., Rosenblum, A., Mason, M., Macri, M., & Becker, J. (2010). Psychiatric impact of gender-related abuse across the life course of male-to-female transgender persons. *Journal of Sex Research, 47*(1), 12–23.

Person, E., & Ovesey, L. (1974). The transsexual syndrome in males: I. Primary transsexualism. *American Journal of Psychotherapy, 28*, 4–20.

Pfäfflin, F., & Junge, A. (1998). Sex reassignment: Thirty years of international follow-up studies after sex reassignment surgery: A comprehensive review, 1961–1991 (Trans. R. B. Jacobson & A. B. Meier). *International Journal of Transgenderism* [Symposion electronic books]. Retrieved from http://symposion.com/ijt/pfaefflin/1000.htm

Pope, K. S., Sonne, J. L., & Greene, B. G. (2006). *What therapists don't talk about and why: Understanding taboos that hurt us and our clients*. Washington, DC: American Psychological Association.

Prosser, J. (1998). *Second skins: The body narratives of transsexuality*. New York NY: Columbia University Press.

Rachlin, K. (1999). Factors which influence individual's decisions when considering female-to-male genital reconstructive surgery. *International Journal of Transgenderism, 3*(3). Retrieved from http://www.symposion.com/ijt/ijt990302.htm

Raj, R. (2002). Towards a transpositive therapeutic model: Developing clinical sensitivity and cultural competence in the effective support of transsexual and transgendered clients. *International Journal of Transgenderism, 6*(2). Retrieved from http://www.symposion.com/ijt/ijtvo06no02_04.htm

Ramsey, G. (1996). *Transsexuals: Candid answers to private questions*. Berkeley, CA: Crossing Press.

Rankin, S., & Beemyn, B. (2011). *The lives of transgender people*. New York, NY: Columbia University Press.

Roen, K. (2001). "Either/or and both/neither": Discursive tensions in transgender politics. *Signs: Journal of Women in Culture and Society, 27*(2), 501–523.

Roscoe, W. (1998). *Changing ones: Third and fourth genders in native North America*. New York, NY: St. Martin's Press.

Schroder, M., & Carroll, R. (1999). New women: Sexological outcomes of male-to-female gender reassignment surgery. *Journal of Sex Education and Therapy, 24*, 137–146.

Sennott, S. (2011). Gender disorder as gender oppression: A transfeminist approach to rethinking the pathologization of gender non-conformity. *Women and Therapy, 34*(1/2), 93–113.

Serano, J. (2007). *Whipping girl: A transsexual woman on sexism and the scapegoating of femininity*. Emeryville, CA: Seal Press.

Steiner, B. W., & Bernstein, S. M. (1981). Female-to-male transsexuals and their partners. *Canadian Journal of Psychiatry*, *26*, 178–182.

Tiefer, L. (2001). Feminist critique of sex therapy: Foregrounding the politics of sex. In P. J. Kleinplatz (Ed.), *New directions in sex therapy: Innovations and alternatives* (pp. 29–49). New York, NY: Taylor & Francis.

Tobin, H. J. (2003, April). *Sexuality in transsexual and transgender individuals* (Honors thesis in sociology, Oberlin College). Retrieved from http://www.geocities.com/harperjeantobin/thesis/index.html

Tully, B. (1992). *Accounting for transsexualism and transhomosexuality*. London, England: Whiting & Birch.

Valerio, M. W. (2006). *The testosterone files: My hormonal and social transformation from female to male*. San Francisco, CA: Seal Press.

Vanderburgh, R. (2007). *Transition and beyond: Observations on gender identity*. Portland, OR: Q Press.

Volcano, D. L., & Windh, I. (2005). GenderFusion. In I. Morland & A. Willox (Eds.), *Queer theory* (pp. 130–142)). New York, NY: Palgrave/Macmillan.

von Krafft-Ebing, R. (1999). *Psychopathia sexualis: The classic study of deviant sex*. Burbank, CA: Bloat Books. (Original work published in 1886)

Walworth, J. (1997). Sex reassignment surgery in male-to-female transsexuals: Client satisfaction in relation to selection criteria. In B. Bullough, V. L. Bullough, & J. Elias (Eds.), *Gender blending* (pp. 352–373). Amherst, NY: Prometheus Books.

Weinberg, T., & Bullough, V. L. (1988). Alienation, self-image, and the importance of support groups for wives of TV's. *Journal of Sex Research*, *24*, 262–268.

Wilchins, R. A. (1997). *Read my lips: Sexual subversion and the end of gender*. Ithaca, NY: Firebrand.

Winters, K. (2009). *Gender madness in American psychiatry: Essays from the struggle for dignity*. Charleston, SC: BookSurge.

World Professional Association for Transgender Health. (2010, May 26). For immediate release, May 26, 2010 [Statement urging the depsychopathologisation of gender variance worldwide]. Retrieved from http://www.wpath.org

Section III
Clinical Issues With LGBT Families

9

Coming Out to Family
Adrift in a Sea of Potential Meanings

VALORY MITCHELL

Introduction

Most of us travel life's road, from beginning to end, within families—families of origin, families of creation, and families of choice. Family is also at the center of our psychological life—a recognition that psychodynamic, attachment, relational, and systemic or family approaches to therapy take as a foundation for healing. For these reasons, coming out to family is "the most important, yet frightening context" for the disclosure of an LGBT identity (Savin-Williams, 1996a, p. 154).

In helping families to find their way when adrift in the tumultuous seas of coming out, therapists will rely not only on their knowledge and skills but also on their capacity for relationship, on the strengths and resilience of the strands of the family fabric, and on each family member's need to sustain meaningful connection.

Coming out to family is frightening or dangerous to the extent that the LGBT person expects their news to evoke a negative response (Johnston & Jenkins, 2004), possibly rejection, devastation, anger, confusion, hurt, trauma, shame, blame or self-blame, guilt, disappointment, and even fear. Each of these responses makes sense only in relation to the set of meanings that being LGBT holds for the recipient of the news, often a set of meanings markedly different from the meanings held by the LGBT person (Pearlman, 2006). In the 21st century, we recognize that the meanings associated with being LGBT, like the meanings associated with all social locations, are constructed, and so they can be deconstructed and problematized. An individual's and a family's narratives can be "re-storied," "re-authored," and "re-presented" (White & Epston, 1990) in ways that legitimate and empower families that have LGBT members. Assisting the family with the intricacies of this process is at the core of the "manifest content" of therapy for families who are coming out.

Similarities and Differences

Beyond these two core premises—that family (and enduring relationship) is central to us all and that the coming-out process is profoundly shaped by the meaning that being LGBT is given—each individual's and family's experience is informed by an array of dimensions of diversity. Lesbian, gay, bisexual, and transgender people are drawn from every ethnic group, age group, race, cultural background, social class, religion, nationality, extent of ability or disability, geography and region, political perspective, and style of life. Family members' views about LGBT people come not only from the general social context but also from the specific ethnic, cultural, religious, class, and political vantage points of the family as well as from beliefs that have been passed down in the family across generations (Greene, 1994). In addition, we and our family members bring to the coming-out experience a panoply of individual characteristics: values, hopes, personality traits, strengths and weaknesses, preferences, fears and worries, accomplishments and aspirations. Successful therapy will take each of these components into consideration.

Despite the uniqueness of each family and the foregoing dimensions of variation, there is much about the coming-out experience that is shared. Accordingly, I will first briefly describe an eclectic model of intervention that is relevant to all instances of coming out to family. At the same time, important distinctions must be drawn. People come out at every age, from childhood through old age. They come out to their parents, children, siblings, wives or husbands, elderly relatives, and extended family. They come out in the context of their culture, their communities, and their values. They come out as lesbian, gay, bisexual, or transgender, and each of these identities holds different meaning sets and therefore involves different work and potential outcomes. After presenting the general model, I will address some considerations that are specific to these dimensions of diversity. Finally, 21st-century developments have markedly changed the context and worldviews that affect the coming-out process; these changes will be identified and explored.

Whether (or Not) to Come Out to Family

Before embarking on this journey, it is important to pause to consider whether one wishes to do so. In the late 20th-century struggles of gay liberation, coming out was strongly (even unequivocally) endorsed by mental health professionals as a statement of pride, a willingness to fight oppression, and a step toward greater mental health (see Green, 2000, for a critique). In the 21st-century era of gay rights, a more differentiated view prevails. As Connelly (2006) points out:

> Coming out may be beneficial or problematic. Therefore, no hard-and-fast rule exists about disclosing one's sexual orientation or gender identity to the family of origin. Both disclosure and secret-keeping can be stressful and provoke intense anxiety. Family reactions can alleviate stress or exacerbate it. [Mental health professionals can] question outcome and ask, "coming out but going where?" (p. 10)

As a result of deeply rooted homophobia or gender traditionality, some family members (though a minority today) cannot welcome the LGBT person. Several decades of research have documented traumatic responses, among them rejection, expelling children from the home, physical violence by family members (e.g., D'Augelli, 1991; Herdt & Boxer, 1993; Martin & Hetrick, 1988; cited in Savin-Williams, 1996b). Even when years pass and a modicum of tolerance allows for resumption of family obligations, the wounds of this emotional and physical abandonment may continue to take a toll (Cayleff, 2010).

Many LGBT people weigh carefully the costs and benefits of coming out; for some, deciding against doing so, or coming out to only some family members, is the healthiest choice. This decision is based on a fear of negative reprisals or a wish not to hurt family members or jeopardize their standing within their social network. Strommen (1990) described this decision as based on an understanding that stereotypes accepted by the family make being gay (or transgender) incompatible with being a family member.

Lesbian, gay, bisexual, and transgender people from ethnic communities grapple not only with homophobia and gender intolerance but also with racial prejudice and discrimination; their families are often a key source of refuge, understanding, and advocacy in the face of this oppression. Given this double and sometimes triple jeopardy (Greene, 1994), LGBT people of color may decide against coming out and risking exclusion from the family or adding to the minority stress that the family must already bear.

Unpacking Our Prejudices

Regardless of their enormous diversity, what unites LGBT people is that they are vulnerable to similar kinds of condemnation, prejudice, discrimination, and marginalization by persons and institutions both inside and outside their families. Research (see Taylor, 2002, for an overview) has documented the psychological damage that results from this. Accordingly, unpacking, becoming conscious, and dismantling homophobia, transphobia, heterocentrism, and gender traditionality are central tasks of the coming-out process for both the LGBT individual (Green & Mitchell, 2002) and the family.

To enable them to accomplish these tasks, Brown (1994) suggests that therapists help them learn skills of resistance:

> Resistance means the refusal to merge with dominant cultural norms and to attend to one's own voice and integrity … uncovering the source of distress so that this influence of the dominant can be named, undermined, resisted and subverted…. [T]eaching resistance [means] learning the ways in which each of us is damaged by our witting or unwitting participation in dominant norms, or by the ways in which such norms have been thrust upon us. (p. 25)

Tasks of Therapy

In this section, I will sketch the process of therapy. However, three goals need to be considered throughout: sustaining the self of each family member, respecting and handling different agendas, and holding the hope and remembering the love.

An essential task for the therapist is to provide psychological sustenance for all family members as they navigate this often-difficult process. Concepts from self-psychology can clarify what is needed (Mitchell, 2010). Self-psychology theorizes that psychological life is sustained by three psychological functions. We gradually internalize these functions and become able to sustain ourselves; however, we always need a bit of help from others, and especially at trying times. The first of these functions, *mirroring*, combines recognition of, interest in, and valuing of the self. The second, *idealizing*, combines soothing and giving comfort with the presence of values and a big-picture perspective. The third, *twinship*, is a sense of shared purpose and common humanity. Support of these functions provides a lighthouse beacon by which I chart my course in these stormy seas (Mitchell, 2010).

Family members come to therapy with different agendas. Some hope the LGBT person will "change their mind" (Pearlman, 2006). The LGBT person, in contrast, will be focused on gaining acceptance by the family and being seen for who he or she is. A parent, child, or spouse may be swept away by confusion and loss at the same time that the LGBT person is joyously feeling clarity and welcoming a chance to live authentically. To create a climate where communication and growth can take place, the therapist will validate each person's experience while taking care to prevent further emotional injury to individuals or relationships. Especially at first, when reactions are most raw, this validation may best be accomplished by meeting with family members individually or in subsystems.

In many therapies, the clients begin at a point of anguish, rage, or despair. While making no promises, the therapist embodies the recognition that they have come to heal deep emotional, spiritual, cognitive, and relational wounds and that, provided with support, knowledge, and encouragement, they can heal. The therapist has faith in the strength of individuals and the family system to cope constructively, to grow, to take responsibility for the quality and direction of their lives (Buxton, 2006), and to honor their connections and care for one another. I believe that therapists hold this faith for all their clients; it is no less important when the family confronts the issues of coming out.

Assessment

If contacted by the LGBT family member, it will be useful for the therapist to obtain several pieces of information: Whom have they told? Whom do they want to tell first, and why? Who is most important to tell, and why? Who is most difficult to tell, and why? (Savin-Williams, 1996b). The therapist should take stock of the LGBT family member's views of the acceptance–rejection terrain in the family (Jenkins, 2008), as well as the extent of the LGBT person's emotional, financial, social, and physical dependence on the family and vulnerability to coercion through legal consequences (e.g., custody threats or by being a legal minor) or through emotional blackmail.

If the therapist is contacted by the family, the nature of the presenting problems gives the therapist an idea of where the family is in the coming-out process and also some indication of their level of acceptance. The therapist should gather information from each family member about the family's strengths and characteristics: Is the family a source of support, a locus of ethnic or religious identity? Is it close, open, conflicted? (Green, 2000).

Laird (1996) summarizes features of this assessment:

The family's response … reflects its more enduring patterns of organization and the extent to which the … family narrative is available for rewriting. Families who tend to be inflexible concerning rules for behavior and visions for their children are often inflexible about many things. Families that have difficulty talking about sensitive or controversial issues of any kind will have more trouble talking about this one. Families … can use the convenient "red herring" of [LGBT identity] to stall their child's leaving or to insist on loyalty to traditional social, religious, or political ideas…. How well the [LGBT person] and family together are able to integrate the [LGBT] story into their lives and to embrace new definitions for couple and family life is expressive of how well parents are able to come to terms with their [children] becoming the authors of their own lives as independent [adults]. (p. 116)

Early Interventions

Early interventions will include planning for disclosure, putting out the fire, locating the love, and deciding on a considered response to the disclosure.

Planning for Disclosure   Help the LGBT family member maximize the effectiveness of the disclosure or subsequent conversations. When, where, how, and to whom will they disclose? The LGBT client should be prepared to answer questions, as well as for the possibility that their news will be entirely unexpected and met with surprise or shock or that the listener will withdraw for a while (Clunis & Green, 2003). It is helpful not to disclose prematurely; the LGBT person will want to sort out his or her own feelings before they encounter the feelings of others (Clunis & Green, 2003). Stereotypes represent lesbian and gay life as primarily focused on sex, where heterosexual life is seen in terms of families and relationships; it may thus be difficult to speak about a sexual identity in the domain of the family (Malley & McCann, 2002). Entering the coming-out experience with a big-picture perspective reminds everyone that coming out is a process and that the LGBT person is likely much farther along in that process than are others.

Putting Out the Fire   Even in an accepting family, the disclosure experience often involves shock, disbelief, confusion, and loss (Buxton, 2006), accompanied by waves of affect-laden beliefs. Individual meetings with each family member who is struggling or awash in negative affect can provide a safe, confidential place where each can vent the full range and intensity of feelings, identify concerns, and feel heard and understood. The privacy of the individual session allows family members to give voice to their reactions without inflicting their pain on the already burdened LGBT family member; this may be an especially important consideration when a child is coming out to parents. Pearlman (2006) describes the therapist as inhabiting two noncontradictory "empathic locations": The first is in deeply understanding the family member's feelings in reaction to the disclosure, and the second is in serving as a compassionate and knowledgeable advocate who can understand the LGBT person's experience and facilitate adjustment and reconciliation.

Therapists can use Minuchin's (1984) concept of reframing to see disclosure as a step not toward otherness but toward honesty and connection (Long, Bonomo, Andrews, & Brown, 2006), as a recognition rather than a sudden, unexpected change, to focus away from difference and toward locating "terms of connection" (Pearlman, 2006), noting that the LGBT person is still the same person, not some "other." Native American two-spirit people recount that "identity acquisition is really a process of becoming who they were meant to be—a process of coming home or coming in, as opposed to coming out or leaving an old identity behind to embrace a new one" (Walters, Evans-Campbell, Simoni, Ronquillo, & Bhuyan, 2006, p. 135). Supporting the shared humanity of each family member (self-psychology's twinship function) and inquiring about shared history with the LGBT person (perhaps revisiting childhood memories) help create continuity.

Where Is the Love?   Soon, the therapist will look for ways in which a family member's negative feelings are connected to that person's love for the LGBT person. For example, fears about safety or fears that being LGBT brings unhappiness (even fears about "sin") are rooted in protectiveness and concern. Guilt and self-blame are rooted in the wish to be a good parent, child, spouse, or sibling to the LGBT person. Anger and disappointment often reflect lost expectations of future times with the loved person. In this way, the therapist helps the family return to the bigger picture of connection and relationship (the soothing idealizing function of self-psychology).

The therapist can ask each person about his or her hopes. The therapist can ask, as did the early family therapist Virginia Satir, "What can make family a more comfortable place?" (cited in Long et al., 2006, p. 28). When family members apply their core values—love, authenticity, autonomy, or commitment—to the current circumstance, they can get their equilibrium back and operate out of self-respect. Deeply conservative families often prioritize family unity, and this can be a mainstay as they struggle with acceptance. The therapist who is "locating the love" is also seeing the potentials of coming out: honesty and authenticity, freedom and a sense of being oneself, genuine acceptance of a profound aspect of the self, and greater closeness and intimacy both in the present and in the future.

What Do You Really Want to Say in Response?   Even after a first response, there is time to consider, from a bigger picture perspective, what family members want to say to the LGBT family member. There is no expiration date on the usefulness of a considered response. When addressing this task, the family members must begin from the premise that the LGBT identity is here to stay; the "solution" to coming out cannot be that the LGBT individual becomes heterosexual or gender traditional.

According to Savin-Williams (1996a), "Parents can say things that can never be withdrawn or ameliorated … [and] can inflict deep wounds" (p. 174). When tossed into the sea of emotions and beliefs that sometimes come with disclosure, family members may make dramatic emotional or condemning statements. As they get their bearings, they may regret these extreme remarks and their impact. Therapists can help the family members convey their regrets and place those early evocative words in a context of alarm and turmoil, helping move them from a status of "truth" to a manifestation of "the heat of the moment."

Next Steps: The Middle Phase of Therapy

The middle phase of therapy involves working through assumptions, dealing with loss, recognizing defenses, envisioning an expanded definition of family, and interfacing with the social world.

Coming out to family must be seen from the perspective of individual, interpersonal, intergroup, and cultural and societal viewpoints (Markowe, 2002); these nested contexts (Bronfenbrenner, 1979) are the loci of potential change and also of potential prejudice and damage.

Working Through Assumptions   Therapists can draw effectively on narrative therapy to address assumptions (Long et al., 2006). Narrative therapists first externalize a problem. Here, the LGBT person or the unaccepting family member is not the problem; the problem is homophobia, heterocentrism, transphobia, or gender traditionality. Clarifying each family member's relationship to these external problems is important; by including everyone's perception, the therapist expands the way the problem is conceptualized.

Cultural representations, historically grounded in prejudicial beliefs, become the building blocks for assumptions (Taylor, 2002). What are the meanings that each family member has learned to give to a lesbian, gay, bisexual, or transgender identity? What does each member of the family believe are the implications for the personality, family relationships, or the kind of life "those people" lead? Therapists help family members, including the LGBT person, identify and articulate these assumptions and question whether they are fact or myth, much like CBT work. Problem-saturated narratives are made from prevalent myths that LGBT people live unhappy lives, cannot have lasting couple relationships, cannot have their own biological children, are betraying their ethnic community, are in constant physical danger, are self-hating, will contract HIV, will abuse alcohol or drugs, and will be lonely and isolated in their old age. "The therapist identifies with the family against those ways in which Western culture oppresses them via the media and general social milieu," suggest Long et al. (2006, p. 20). This deconstruction process creates the room to consider new meanings and narratives (Malpas, 2006) that include success, empowerment, accomplishment, and connection—and evoke very different emotions. Psycho-education is essential here. Research-based factual knowledge is particularly helpful to counteract prejudices (see Goldman, 2008, for an extensive list of resources). In this phase of the work, the therapist listens and understands but also provides information and disputes misinformation. Contacting LGBT-affirmative families through such organizations as Children of Lesbians and Gays Everywhere (COLAGE) and Parents, Family and Friends of Lesbians and Gays (PFLAG) eliminates isolation and extends the experience of validation and normalizing. Listening to others who have managed, struggled, and healed, telling their own stories, is pivotal for some families. Collaborating with the family to explore the oppressive social influences that have led them to regard an LGBT identity as sinful, disturbed, inferior, and so on (Green & Mitchell, 2002) can help family members recognize that these are the views of particular constituencies and are not "universals." Therapists neutralize these messages by viewing LGBT lives as normal human variations. To accomplish this task effectively, therapists must be aware of current social settings (both real and virtual), changing vocabulary, and changing social realities. It is imperative that therapists working with trans people and their families know about medical options, the transition experience, ways to conceptualize and express gender, and new values and philosophies about gender exploration.

Recognition of Defenses   Each family member will handle the coming-out process by relying on his or her own repertoire of coping mechanisms and defenses. Naming these and framing them in a nonjudgmental way as useful ways to cope when things get too difficult can foster open communication and empathy. All family members are encouraged to describe their strategies for coping. Once these strategies are named, now conscious and shared, family members are less likely to be hurt by them. Common defenses against disclosure include denial, withdrawal, and compartmentalization.

Dealing With Losses   Schneider (2001) points out that heterosexism, that is, the expectation that all people are heterosexual, "creates a set of roles, expectations and social pressures that must be discarded in order to … identify as gay or lesbian" (p. 84). Families of LGBT people also have heterocentric hopes and dreams that they must, sometimes painfully and reluctantly, discard. Straight spouses have a particular investment in their partners' heterosexuality and gender as complements to their own.

Because family relationships are gendered, the family of a trans person is grieving the loss of a son or daughter, sister or brother, mother or father. The formerly same-gender parent must give up the expectations of shared gender-based camaraderie that many parents treasure. Because gender is a central organizing schema, when it changes, family members are profoundly uncertain about who the trans person will become and may struggle to recognize that the trans person, who has been known to them lifelong, is and will be the same person.

The LGBT person, too, is grieving the loss of an idealized parent, partner, or child who will immediately accept and understand. It can be difficult to be patient and allow the ups and downs of the coming-out process to unfold in their own time.

Grieving these losses is best addressed by the same types of grief work that clients require in other circumstances. Since witnessing family members' grief may cause harm to the LGBT individual, therapists may consider individual sessions where grief and acceptance can exist side-by-side.

It can be useful for family members to realize, perhaps for the first time, that their LGBT loved one may have endured years of feeling different, of being alone with his or her fears, of carrying the tension of having secrets from those closest and dearest. This reconstruction of history brings both losses and gains into focus.

Envisioning an Expanded Definition of Family   As they develop shared meanings and understand how they have been damaged by myths, family members have a foundation for building a family that is a welcoming, mutually respectful, and inclusive place for all. Therapists have prepared the family for this work by noting when a family member's voice is not heard. In Bozsormenyi-Nagy's multidirectional partiality,

> the therapist validates the differing perspectives by modeling the capacity to understand and empathize with many types of experience, even those seemingly in conflict with one another. No family member is considered to have the one and only truth, but all are validated as living a truth that deserves its due. (Long et al., 2006, p. 25)

The LGBT person may be the focus, but no one should feel overlooked, uninformed, or unsupported. Buxton (2006) notes, "The effects on [family members] are generally overlooked and, if noticed, little understood by families, friends, counselors, or clergy" (p. 50). An inclusive family must have a place for everyone at the table.

The "miracle question" from solution-focused therapy (Long et al., 2006, p. 28) asks, "Suppose that one night there is a miracle, and while you were sleeping the problem that brought you to therapy is solved. How would you know? What would be different?" This question offers hope, begins the problem-solving process, highlights possible solutions that family members recognize or create, and encourages each person to speculate on what they can do differently. The family is developing alternative visions of the future, rehearsing and envisioning what this could look like in all areas of family functioning, even those that are not directly linked to coming out.

The Interface Between the Family and Their Social World   As the family comes out, it moves toward the margin because it is marginalized by a gender-rigid and homophobic culture. Family members need support to handle insults; children especially may need information that can protect them from negative reactions.

Savin-Williams (1996b) suggests that family members unobtrusively normalize the LGBT person's relationships by asking about them and that they also begin to talk with peers and others. Therapists can help the family manage and process disclosure to friends or extended family and plan for milestone events and community gatherings. When will they out the LGBT family member or out themselves as having an LGBT family member? Which family photos will be on display? Who is coming for holidays or family events? What support and strengths are in place for this family, and will these change?

Concluding the Therapy

Five tasks comprise the final phase of therapy: taking stock, coming to terms, continuing the work, consolidating gains, and moving from otherness to being allies.

Taking Stock   The family's coming-out process is not linear; in fact, it might best be described as "progressing from … a roller coaster of contradictory feelings—hurt/empathy, love/anger, fear/hope, to acknowledge and accept the new reality of their lives, and move toward transformation" (Buxton, 2006, p. 56). The therapist can give family members permission to take as much time as they need. Taking stock emphasizes the family's ability to use the skills they have acquired and to maintain ongoing momentum in addressing the tasks of coming out.

Coming to Terms   Family members may wish to be nearer to a resolution than they are. For some families, periods of adjustment may be necessary. A pattern of distancing and deterioration followed by gradual return and improvement is not unusual (Laird, 1996; Savin-Williams, 1996b). Frequent obstacles are residual shame, guilt, fear of condemnation, or concern that now others see the family unfavorably. Buxton (2006) found that progress is affected by feelings of hurt that hardens into a victim mentality, of anger that hardens into bitterness, of fear of the inability to handle unknown challenges, and by grief over the many losses that threatens to become despair. Family members seek individual therapy and can also share regrets and shortcomings. If these anguishing feelings can be accepted compassionately by the family, this sharing underscores that family is a place where members can be true to themselves in an empathic atmosphere.

Acceptance may be a matter of degree. To a large extent, it rests on such personal characteristics as personality; education; political and religious beliefs that value diversity and human rights; exposure to LGBT people; wanting a close, authentic relationship with the LGBT family member; and recognition of that person's happiness. Therapists are encouraged to help family move past a limited acceptance that contains the conflict but fosters pretense rather than true relationship (Greene & Boyd-Franklin, 1996; Pearlman, 2006). Doing this will require family members to manifest ongoing social support and affiliation, stable acceptance, disclosure to others, positive expectations, a political analysis of homophobia or transphobia, and a sense of reward being a member of the family of an LGBT person.

Lesbian, gay, bisexual, and transgender people often create a family of choice (Mitchell, 2008; Savin-Williams, 1996b), a network of relationships that provides consistent and enduring support and connection. Families of choice offer an alternative for LGBT individuals whose biological family has not been accepting or inclusive, but they can be of great value to all LGBT people (and others, too).

Continuing the Work   Several tasks still await the family. First, each family member needs to clarify what he or she wants and needs from the family now. Will coming out change the family's familiar ways? Minuchin's (1974) structural family concepts (Long et al., 2006) can help the family look at how their rules for subsystems may change or how they fear the rules will change.

Some family members may be reconfiguring their identities and belief systems. Some may seek new spiritual understandings to comprehend and accept the changes (Buxton, 2010);

nondualistic non-Western metaphysics have been valuable because sexual and gender fluidity require nondualistic ways of thinking and understanding.

Consolidating the Gains   As with any therapy termination, it is important to join the family members in looking back over their work; recognizing what they have accomplished; naming the work still to be done; and acknowledging their resilience, flexibility, enduring love, loyalty, positive intentions, and capacity to navigate rough waters and still stay afloat. The family may not be exactly what it once was, but it is now a more genuine and realistic home for all its members; Savin-Williams (1996b) talks about the gift of disclosure. Themes of agency and closeness can be contrasted with past feelings of victimization or of being misperceived and invalidated. Therapists can accentuate the family's accomplishments by providing research that shows the psychological value of being out to a supportive family. As the family members look at the work still to be done, it may be useful to frame that work as transformations that result when family members act according to their deepest values.

Moving From Otherness to Being Active Allies   The family's private struggle is embedded within a larger societal context. The therapist can help the family create a narrative of empowerment by accessing organizations of LGBT allies. Therapists, too, can take up an identity as ally (Lynch & McMahon-Klosterman, 2006) by being conscious of gender privilege and heterosexual privilege and by modeling advocacy and social action, accepting the responsibility to use their power and privilege to effect change and to speak up on behalf of LGBT people (Lynch & McMahon-Klosterman, 2006).

Dimensions of Diversity in Coming Out

The foregoing model gives an overview of the process, issues, tasks, and interventions that characterize many families' experience of the coming-out process. However, particular issues arise depending on the age, ethnicity, and identity of the LGBT individual and on each particular family relationship.

Coming Out as an Adolescent

Developmentally, adolescence is a time when all young people are at work on the psychological tasks of bringing together all that they are, synthesizing the characteristics into an identity that can carry them forward into the adult world (Erikson, 1960). Gender and sexual orientation are two components of that identity. The peer culture of adolescence is not an easy one for the LGBT youth. Because adolescents are occupied with identity issues, they are often more polarized in their gender roles than at any other time in their lives—for LGBT youth, this can lead to ostracism and rejection by peers (Long et al., 2006). Adolescents are coming out at younger ages than in the past and therefore often live at home. Their parents and siblings have the opportunity to take action as allies. Schools are often unsafe environments marred by the "overwhelming presence of homophobia and heterosexism" (King, 2008, p. 367). Family can be of great emotional and practical support by buffering the impact of harassment and intervening to ensure the emotional and physical safety of an LGBT youth. As Long et al. (2006) state, "Self-identifying is a time when one can feel very much alone because old supports do not work and new ones are not yet in place. Therefore, familial support for these adolescents is extremely important in helping them to remain resilient" (p. 14).

Coming Out as an Adult

Whereas some adults may have been aware of their LGBT identity since childhood, others may not have. Many adults experience fluidity in their sexual identity and discover same-sex attraction or gender variance in response to a changed circumstance. Falling in love with a same-sex person later in life or meeting others who do not embrace a binary approach to gender expression may bring these aspects of self into consciousness for the first time (Hunter, 2005; Savin-Williams, 1996b).

Depending on their age cohort, LGBT adults may interact with people whose ideas are associated with past eras of secrecy and oppression. Their own expectations and those of their cohort may influence their approach to disclosure in ways atypical of younger people. In addition, LGBT people in their age group may be living closeted or acting in stealth in many areas of their lives (see Hunter, 2005, for an overview of this body of research). However, as the children of older adults enter adulthood themselves, and as retirement nears, more LGBT adults become comfortable with being out. Adults come out to spouses, to children, to siblings, and to parents, often making four or more distinct decisions about disclosure. The implications of disclosure differ according to the age and circumstance of the person coming out and the person receiving the news.

Disclosure to Parents

According to Hunter (2005), "Disclosure to parents is the most difficult for LGB persons and probably evokes the greatest fear for children of any age" (p. 49). The reasons for this fear have to do with the centrality and psychological importance of parents and of children. Parenting is, for many, one of the most valued endeavors in life. Parents have hopes for their children's happiness, fulfillment, and success in life; as parents, they try to nurture these outcomes. Many parents want an ongoing closeness with their adult children and a sharing of experience across the generations. Similarly, children have hopes for their parents' happiness, fulfillment, and feelings of success and also seek an ongoing closeness and sharing. To the extent that having an LGBT identity seems to mean that these treasured goals will be compromised or thwarted, parents and children grapple with the anguished choice between authenticity and causing pain or rupture.

When doing coming-out work, therapists must keep in mind the depth of parent–child relationships, the variety and intensity of the parents' and the child's investment in each other, and the ways these play out in relation to the child's LGBT identity.

Disclosure to Siblings

Sometimes LGBT people come out to their sibling before other family members, thereby hoping for greater acceptance and also hoping for help in creating understanding from parents and other relatives (Gottlieb, 2005). Although these hopes sometimes come to pass, coming out can have immense effects on the sibling relationship. It is often an entirely idiosyncratic and unexpected event. Particularly for siblings who have played important parts in each other's lives, attempting to integrate this new information into their ongoing expression of an intimate sibling bond may be bewildering (Jenkins, 2008).

Like their LGBT brother or sister, young siblings may also be harassed; their physical and emotional safety must be a visible concern for the family. If parents offer extra support to the teen who is coming out but fail to notice the experience of siblings, resentment between siblings or across generations may result (Long et al., 2006).

Disclosure to One's Heterosexual Spouse

Buxton (2006) has described the following issues for the spouse whose partner comes out as LGBT: sexual rejection; damaged sexual self-image; challenge to redefine marriage or to divorce; worries about the impact on children; identity crisis; social stigma; isolation; feeling of deception or betrayal by the person that they trusted most; feeling used, abandoned, left out, or no longer needed; loss of self-worth and sense of confidence; questioning whether they are able to judge what is true or false about others; shattered assumptions about gender, marriage, and a shared future; destruction of the beliefs that gave meaning to the couple's lives; feeling powerless or purposeless; difficulty with the nondichotomous concepts of bisexuality or transgenderism; moral dilemmas or a crisis of faith; fear of the future; questions about what was true and what was false in the relationship; and doubting one's own orientation or that of others.

Some of these issues can be usefully addressed in the context of family work, but many of them are best suited for an ongoing individual therapy. In addition, the national Straight Spouse Network offers counseling, psycho-education, and networking.

Disclosure to One's Children

The Parenting Team   If the LGBT person has a parenting partner, as parents they will want to talk through their ideas and concerns about disclosure together before talking with their children. Parents may have different views on the value of outness, and these variant views should be recognized and discussed before taking action. Gay parents and their straight spouses often decide to tell the children in the context of divorce or because they do not want the children to hear the news from someone who may be judgmental, giving an added sense of urgency or potential danger or disruption to the disclosure experience. Buxton (2006) encourages parents to wait until they are comfortable, calm, and unified; they will want to feel able to reassure the children of their continued love and support: "Both parents become models from this point on: the parent who is being true to him/herself and the straight parent who is working to understand and, eventually, to accept" (p. 54).

Children's Concerns   Children receive the news of a parent's LGBT identity in the context of their own age and stage of development (see Snow, 2004, for children's accounts). Young children are most concerned about their parent's love and constancy. They want a safe, stable home, where LGBT-related matters do not impinge on how they live each day. For these reasons, parents are likely to find young children more accepting than are older children or teenagers (Long et al., 2006). School-aged children can become frightened or embarrassed by other children's teasing or remarks about gay or transgender people. Adolescents, who are most concerned with peer reaction, may keep silent about a parent's identity and hope that the parent will also. At the same time that adolescents may be silent, they are listening closely and are very aware of peer attitudes. Some adolescents find it painful that their parent is considering sexual identity and life goals at the same time as they are themselves engaged in this developmental process.

Parents should think ahead about the types of concerns that may surface as their children integrate the disclosure. Psycho-educational materials can help parents respond to children's questions in a way that meets them at their age and developmental level. Among the concerns reported by children of LGBT parents are worries about nonconventional sexuality or gender expression; challenges to their understanding of traditional marriage; fears of possible family breakup; threat to their existing bond with the LGBT parent; conflicting loyalties to the gay and to the straight parent; AIDS fear; difficulty embracing the LGBT parent as a nontraditional role model; peers' antigay attitudes; reevaluation or uncertainty about their own sexual and gender identity; concerns about honesty, trust, and secret keeping; and questioning of traditional concepts.

Even adult children may find that a parent's disclosure of an LGBT identity brings psychological consequences. Davies's (2010) study of adult daughters whose mothers come out later in life found that 84% had no idea that their mother was a lesbian and that 50% examined their own sexual identity after their mother's coming out.

Coming Out as Transgender

Parents of transgender youth whose children first came out as lesbian said that accepting sexual orientation was nothing compared to the task of accepting a changed gender status (Pearlman,

2006). The parents described devastation, daughter loss, a sense of the change as life altering, and a need for reconciliation. Therapists should expect family work involving disclosure of a transgender identity to be more prolonged, complex, and difficult than the integration and acceptance of a family member's sexual orientation. Societal responses to the transgender experience are reminiscent of the pathologization, invisibility, and condemnation directed at LGBT people several decades ago. Accordingly, these families may have greater struggles with isolation, stigmatization, and shame.

In addition, family members may feel that their beliefs about gender are fundamental to their understanding of who people are and how life is lived; the disruption of these beliefs can be profound. Most of today's society regards gender as a very important and foundational fact about an individual and as an organizing principle for what that person's life will (and will not) include. Traditional beliefs hold that a binary gender is discovered, not assigned, at birth and remains constant throughout life. To be transgender is to challenge all these ideas, often leaving family members' belief systems shattered. In addition, today's transgender person is less likely to be "crossing over" from one side of the binary to the other than to be trying to express and be perceived as the gender combination that he or she is. The idea of a spectrum of gender expression, rather than mutually exclusive binary categories, is foreign to many family members. Coming out moves forward when therapists help family members recognize that beliefs about gender have been key structural building blocks of their worldview. Accepting this notion allows for an honest understanding of the enormity of their tasks of separating fact from belief and of acquiring new and alternative perspectives.

Ethnic and Cultural Variations in the Coming-Out Experience

In the United States, the Euro-White family is typically conceptualized as consisting solely of parents and children. Most other U.S. ethnic communities regard the family as including a larger number of people, perhaps many households, including cousins and aunts and uncles, the extended family. The tasks and implication of coming out to family may vary as a result of differing ideas of who is included in one's definition of family. In addition, Euro-White cultural values accentuate individuality and autonomy, whereas African American, Asian American, Jewish, and Latino cultural values strongly emphasize family loyalty, honoring parents, and extended family ties (Savin-Williams, 1996a). This difference in value emphasis creates a different context of meaning for the act of claiming an individual LGBT identity that may bring shame or humiliation to the family or disappointment to particular family members.

Loyalty to one's ethnic community is sometimes associated with the expectation that all members will have children; indeed, not to do so may be considered selfish, branding the person a traitor to his or her group. The aspiration of many lesbians and gay men to have and raise children may not be legitimated or, sometimes, not even recognized. As a consequence, an LGBT identity carries for members of these communities meanings it does not have for members of other cultural groups.

Fundamentalist Christianity or Catholicism may fuel homophobia, whether in ethnic communities or among members of the dominant culture, adding to the tension and potential sense of shame felt by family members. Insofar as a religion is considered a part of one's ethnic heritage, being able to maintain a connection with one's religious community may hold special importance (Hunter, 2005). For these reasons, LGBT members of nondominant ethnic communities may make choices about when and to whom to come out that differ from the choices made by members of privileged or dominant cultural groups (Green, 2000). Family members may also erect a wall of silence for fear of embarrassing relatives or facing disapproval in their ethnic community (Savin-Williams, 1996a).

Members of nondominant ethnic communities are managing multiple minority statuses, each associated with less power and fewer resources than are available to members of the dominant or privileged groups. It is essential that the family therapist understand all families, as well as the choices made by individuals, in the context of their culture and in the context of a larger society marred by prejudice and discrimination. Failure to do so is oppressive because these decisions reflect a realistic assessment of potential consequences (Green & Mitchell, 2002).

Coming Out in the Present Sociohistorical Moment

Over the past 50 years, enormous changes in inclusion, visibility, normalization, and acceptance, though far from universal, have created drastically different contexts for LGBT lives. Today, one can meet LGBT people who experienced young adulthood in the pre-Stonewall era of isolation and silence when gay people risked forced hospitalization, arrest, and loss of jobs and housing; others who were young adults in the gay liberation era of condemnation, politicization, and fighting oppression; and still others who reached adulthood in the gay rights era of mainstreaming, validation, visibility, and expectations of acceptance (Hunter, 2005). These vast differences have suggested the existence of a "gay generation gap" (Mitchell, 2010). One component of this gap is young people's lack of experience with stigma and hiding that was typical a generation ago (Garnets & Kimmel, 2003) and may have shaped the expectations of family members and family therapists.

Child-rearing values at this time in history in the United States encourage individualism, personal gratification, self-expression, a separate identity, autonomy, independence, and choices that lead to individual happiness. Parenting ideologies emphasize attunement and gratification of the child's perceived emotional needs and encourage closeness and connection between parents and children. These parenting ideologies set the stage for expectations about family members' response to disclosures about an individual family member's identity.

Today, families dealing with coming out can easily find examples of effectively functioning gay and lesbian people in all occupations and in multigenerational families. These real-life stories are invaluable in providing evidence to contradict the stereotypic scenarios of loneliness and despair that sometimes cause a family to fear for the future of their LGBT family member. Although there is less visibility of transgender people, autobiographical accounts, photo essays, and blogs provide heartening first-person accounts. As LGBT people go on record with photographed wedding ceremonies, senior proms, and such family and cultural milestone events as the quinceañera and the bar and bat mitzvah (events often shown on Facebook or YouTube), stereotypes of gay life as not normal, as sexually preoccupied, or as isolated are challenged. In addition, the cultural, racial, class, ability, and age diversity of the LGBT community becomes irrefutable.

Widespread use of the Internet and its social networks has given LGBT people and their families ready access to others who are going or have gone through the coming-out process (see Goldman, 2008, for an extensive list of websites). Many of the sites posted online encourage interaction through chat rooms and blogs, allowing for an interflow of information and relationships. Even for families living in rural areas or conservative regions—families who have particularly struggled with isolation in the past—a sense of community is available. In addition, privacy is assured for those individuals who feel uncomfortable or endangered by becoming visible.

Everyday visibility and Internet and media access make it almost impossible for LGBT people and their families to lack for role models. The popular media provide abundant examples of LGBT celebrities in music, film, politics, and athletics; as well, films, plays, and television series include increasing numbers of LGBT characters. These models may be especially helpful in their similarity to the age, ethnicity, or class of the LGBT family member, as well as for addressing particular fears.

There is now greater acceptance and acknowledgment of lesbian, gay, and bisexual individuals' civil rights (Loftus, 2001), along with changes in law and public policy. Although struggles continue, substantial portions of the American public are accepting of lesbian, gay, and bisexual people. Nonpathologizing language has become available, and such major mainstream organizations as the American Bar Association, the American Medical Association, the American Psychological Association, and the American Psychiatric Association support lesbian and gay—and more recently bisexual and transgender—rights.

Conclusion

Although many LGBT people remain anxious about coming out, acceptance by family and friends is increasingly prevalent. Laird (1996) found that "most of us are *not* cut off from families—not forever rejected, isolated, disinherited.... Physical and emotional cut-off … from … family is much rarer than commonly assumed" (pp. 90, 99). She suggests that for most people, disconnection from family is a myth that should be considered part of the "homophobic dominant discourse" (Laird, 1996, p. 91). In truth, she finds that most LGBT people weather the tumult of coming out to their families, albeit with periods of adjustment, and maintain powerful lifelong connections. Even 20 years ago (D'Augelli, 1991) only a small minority of parents of lesbian, gay, and bisexual youths (10% of mothers and 25% of fathers) responded with rejection. Similarly, in a sample of mothers of trans men, Pearlman (2006) found that "their sense of selves as mothers and individuals was enhanced by a continuing bond with their trans son and maintaining that connection was a major source of assurance of both individual and maternal self-worth" (p. 121). Reviewing 25 years of work with parents who come out, Buxton (2006) found that most children become proud of their LGBT parent over time.

These findings diminish neither the anguish and exclusion that many LGBT people experience in relation to unaccepting family nor the tumult and pain of parts of this process; family members often have arduous, protracted, and emotionally difficult work to do. Still, the findings indicate that acceptance and inclusion of the LGBT individual are the norm. As Laird (1996) concludes, "Coming out, although it can be a painful and debilitating process for some, for others is a most self-authenticating and differentiating process that can result in very positive growth for both the individual and the family. We rarely hear about that side of family life" (p. 98).

A Case Example

David came to my office with great anxiety. He had fallen in love, and this was both wonderful and alarming for him. At age 45, David had worked hard to make a good life, a life his parents and he could be proud of; he had achieved success in his career and had a rich family life. He had married his high school girlfriend, and they were raising two boys, age 16 and 12. David valued the history and companionship he had known with his wife and was a committed father to his sons.

At the same time, throughout his adult years, David had known that he had put together a life that was built, in part, on attempting to deny the same-sex attractions he had felt since childhood. As we talked, a key question for Dave was "Why am I no longer able or willing to continue in the life I've made?" As we explored this question, we could see the influence of his changing place in the lifespan and the changing world around him. Dave's father had died a few years before, and his mother was facing early signs of dementia; neither parent would be watching him or judging, and so he could no longer disappoint them. Just as his parents had entered late adulthood, David had moved into midlife—a time where "the road not taken" can emerge as a fresh focus for a person's thoughts and feelings. At the same time, Dave recognized that the decision he thought he was making 25 years ago was between family life and parenthood, on the one hand, or gay life, on the other. In the ensuing 25 years, gay parents had been featured in newspapers and on television, and Dave was well aware that being gay and being a father was not an either/or dichotomy. A backdrop for all these changes was one thing that had not changed—Dave continued to be drawn to other men and dreamed of living with a male partner who would share his life, a life where he could feel a depth and a focus he had never known with Jeri.

David had begun to meet men online and to date. He traveled frequently for his work and saw the traveling times as opportunities to explore the gay community. On one of his travels, he met Francisco. As he continued this long-distance relationship, Dave confronted his wish to come out and to pursue the relational life that felt true to him. He seriously considered the option of "living two lives," that is, saying nothing, but continuing to live with Jeri, Ben, and Steven while creating more opportunities to "travel" with Francisco. After considerable rumination about the potential consequences, he decided that he could not continue as he was. He would tell Jeri and the boys that he was gay and that he needed to move out of the family home because he had met someone he wanted to live with as his partner.

Dave had been meeting with me to sort out his situation, and once he reached this decision, we began to consider how to begin his disclosure to his family. He would start by talking with Jeri.

Telling Jeri, His Wife

Dave and Jeri were raised in a liberal, urban Jewish community and have lived their adult lives in a college town. They are both open minded and tolerant. For Jeri it did not matter that Dave had fallen in love with a man; what mattered was that it was not her he had fallen in love with. Her initial response was to feel rejected; she was terribly hurt and felt humiliated, as if Dave were judging her and finding her wanting.

Dave suggested that they meet with me in the hope that I could offer some help to Jeri, who was devastated by Dave's news. Providing psychological sustenance for Jeri in this process would require, first, that I be able to recognize the insult she felt and offer comfort and compassion. As she felt understood and cared about, she could begin to question some of her initial ideas—that Dave no longer cared about her or the life they had made, that he was no longer interested in her or valued her. Unraveling these aspects of the relationship was difficult and painful. Jeri understood marriage to mean that she was the most important person—perhaps the one truly important person—in Dave's world. Her "fall" from this position meant to her that she was cast out into an uncaring world, very much alone and unwanted. She loved Dave and wanted to be loved by him in return. She felt so betrayed that she was initially unable to talk deeply with Dave, and so Jeri and I met individually for a time.

Eventually, and very gradually, Jeri began to believe Dave when he told her that she was still a central figure in his life. He imagined a future where they were often together, particularly as parents to their sons; and although their parenting partnership was only one aspect of the relationship she had cherished, Jeri recognized the truth of it. This work took a few years, however; and long before she had made much headway, she and Dave were faced with how to talk with their children.

Telling the Children, Ben and Steven

As we worked together to prepare for telling their sons, we found ourselves moving between two very different narratives. The first spoke to David being true to himself while also affirming the continuity and centrality of his commitment to being a "good and loving dad." The second, however, was a narrative of disruption and selfishness. Questions emerged about whether this was a "good time" for the boys to learn that their father was gay and to carry that information with them at school and with their friends or, instead, to have Dave move out of the house and not have a daily presence in their lives, or even whether the boys should be asked to meet their dad's new partner.

Finding out about the experiences of other families was invaluable to Dave and Jeri. Others' positive outcomes gave them the courage to believe that things could go well in their own family. In addition, we found videos that the boys could watch, either with their parents or on their own, that might allow them to learn about families with gay parents in a way that felt less awkward or emotional than talking with their own parents.

Dave and Jeri did not know what questions, and what fears, Ben and Steven would have, but they recognized that they should come prepared to answer questions and to address fears, so we rehearsed, role-played, and made lists of what-ifs. What they found was that the boys had markedly different responses. The older son, Ben, took a "Yeah, so what?" stance and was unfazed by his father's being gay or his departure from the family home. "Well, you travel a lot already," he said. As time has passed, in my meetings with Ben, he has maintained this position. He feels that "This is just what dad is doing now." He will visit his father's new home, spend time with Dave and Francisco, but finds his father's life peripheral to his own concerns about his senior year in high school, his choice of college, and his own move out of the house. In many respects, this self-absorption is entirely age appropriate. Steven, however, has had a very different response. He had never thought about gay people and was mystified by his father's disclosure and at a loss to grasp what it meant. With time, it has become apparent that Steven does not want to know; he has been reluctant to read or watch informational material or ask questions. Like many younger children, his experience is more about his father moving away and his mother being upset, and it has been difficult for Steven to reach an understanding of why these changes have come about or have felt necessary to Dave. As a result, Steven is reluctant to go to Dave's new home or spend time with Dave's partner, Francisco.

Redefining Family

It has been a few years since Dave came out to his family, and much has changed in all their lives. Although a lot of the work is completed, I see this family occasionally to continue the taking-stock process with them, checking to see that they have remained allies, consolidating their gains, and continuing the work.

Jeri wisely decided to enter her own individual psychotherapy to help restore her equilibrium and have a place to question her self-criticism as she undertook the divorce process. She has found therapy useful in relation to her inner critic and also as a resource while parenting two teenaged boys throughout those turbulent years.

As planned, Dave has remained a very active, involved parent. He and Jeri have been able to join together in addressing their children's needs; for example, Dave will come to Jeri's house (where he used to live) to help Steven with homework, since Steven is uncomfortable at Dave's new home. He hopes that with time, both his sons will expand their vision of family to include parents in two homes and with new partners. At the same time, he recognizes that Ben's focus is on establishing his own young adult life and Steven is immersed in high school and that spending time with parents is less interesting for both of them now. All members of Dave's family have recognized, with time, how much happier Dave has become and respect his decision to "live an honest life."

The family continues to be together for holidays, birthdays, and other landmark events; for the most part, however, they have not yet integrated Francisco into these gatherings. Although all the family members accept him as Dave's partner, his closest relationship is with Ben, and he is not regarded as a stepparent. Dave hopes that as his sons grow up and have partners of their own, his relationship with Francisco will make more sense and become more comfortable and integrated with the family. He and Jeri remain close, calling on each other as parents and also, increasingly, as helpful friends.

References

Bronfenbrenner, U. (1979). *The ecology of human development.* Cambridge, MA: Harvard University Press.

Brown, L. (1994). *Subversive dialogues: Theory in feminist therapy.* New York: Basic Books.

Buxton, A. (2006). Healing an invisible minority: How the Straight Spouse Network has become the prime source of support for those in mixed-orientation marriages. In J. Bigner & A. Gottlieb (Eds.), *Interventions with families of gay, lesbian, bisexual and transgender people: From the inside out* (pp. 49–70). Binghamton, NY: Haworth Press.

Buxton, A. (2010). Unforeseen and transformative: New dimensions in the third quarter of my life. In V. Mitchell (Ed.), *Women doing therapy in the last third of life: The long view* (pp. 118–133). New York, NY: Routledge.

Cayleff, S. (2010). Feeding the hand that bit you: Lesbian daughters at mid-life negotiating parental care-taking. In V. Mitchell (Ed.), *Lesbian family life, like the fingers of a hand: Under-discussed and controversial topics* (pp. 115–132). New York, NY: Routledge.

Clunis, D., & Green, D. (2003). *The lesbian parenting book: A guide to creating families and raising children* (2nd ed.). New York, NY: Seal Press.

Connelly, C. (2006). A process of change: The intersection of the GLBT individual and his or her family of origin. In J. Bigner (Ed.), *An introduction to GLBT family studies* (pp. 121–147). New York, NY: Haworth Press.

Davies, K. (2010). Adult daughters whose mothers come out later in life: What is the psychosocial impact? In V. Mitchell (Ed.), *Lesbian family life, like the fingers of a hand: Under-discussed and controversial topics* (pp. 133–141). New York, NY: Routledge.

Erikson, E. (1960). *Childhood and society.* New York: Norton.

Garnets, L., & Kimmel, G. (2003). *Psychological perspectives on lesbian, gay and bisexual experiences.* New York, NY: Columbia University Press.

Goldman, L. (2008). *Coming out, coming in: Nurturing the well-being and inclusion of gay youth in mainstream society.* New York, NY: Routledge.

Gottlieb, A. (2005). *Side by side: On having a gay or lesbian sibling.* Binghamton, NY: Haworth Press.

Green, R. J. (2000). "Lesbians, gay men and their parents": A critique of La Sala and the prevailing clinical "wisdom." *Family Process, 39,* 257–266.

Green, R. J., & Mitchell, V. (2002). Gay and lesbian couples in therapy: Homophobia, relational ambiguity, and social support. In A. S. Gurman & N. J. Jacobson (Eds.), *Clinical handbook of couple therapy* (3rd ed., pp. 546–568.). New York, NY: Guilford Press.

Greene, B. (1994). Ethnic minority lesbians and gay men: Mental health and treatment issues. *Journal of Consulting and Clinical Psychology, 62,* 243–251.

Greene, B., & Boyd-Franklin, N. (1996). African American lesbians: Issues in couples therapy. In J. Laird & R. J. Green (Eds.), *Lesbians and gays in couples and families* (pp. 251–271). San Francisco, CA: Jossey-Bass.

Hunter, S. (2005). *Midlife and older LGBT adults: Knowledge and affirmative practice for the social services.* New York, NY: Haworth Press.

Jenkins, D. (2008). Changing family dynamics: A sibling comes out. *Journal of GLBT Family Studies, 4*(1), 1–16.

Johnston, L., & Jenkins, D. (2004). Coming out in mid-adulthood: Building a new identity. *Journal of Gay & Lesbian Social Services, 16*(2), 19–42.

King, S. (2008). Exploring the role of counselor support: Gay, lesbian, bisexual and questioning adolescents struggling with acceptance and disclosure. *Journal of GLBT Family Studies, 4*(3), 361–384.

Laird, J. (1996). Invisible ties: Lesbians and their families of origin. In J. Laird & R. J. Green (Eds.), *Lesbians and gays in couples and families* (pp. 89–122). San Francisco, CA: Jossey-Bass.

Loftus, J. (2001). America's liberalization in attitudes towards homosexuality. *American Sociological Review, 66*(5), 762–782.

Long, J., Bonomo, J., Andrews, B., & Brown, J. (2006). Systemic therapeutic approaches with sexual minorities and their families. *Journal of GLBT Family Studies, 2*(3/4), 7–37.

Lynch, J., & McMahon-Klosterman, K. (2006). Guiding the acquisition of the therapist ally identity: Research on the GLBT stepfamily as resource. *Journal of GLBT Family Studies, 2*(3/4), 123–150.

Malley, M., & McCann, D. (2002). Family therapy with lesbian and gay clients. In A. Coyle & C. Kitzinger (Eds.), *Lesbian and gay psychology: New perspectives* (pp. 198–218). Oxford, UK: British Psychological Society.

Malpas, J. (2006). From otherness to alliance: Transgender couples in therapy. *Journal of GLBT Family Studies, 2*(3/4), 183–206.

Markowe, L. (2002). Coming out as a lesbian. In A. Coyle & C. Kitzinger (Eds.), *Lesbian and gay psychology: New perspectives* (pp. 63–80). Oxford, UK: British Psychological Society.

Minuchin, S. (1974). *Families and family therapy*. London, UK: Tavistock Press.

Minuchin, S. (1984). *Family kaleidoscope*. Cambridge, MA: Harvard University Press.

Mitchell, V. (2008). Choosing family: Meaning and membership in the lesbian family of choice. *Journal of Lesbian Studies, 12*, 301–313.

Mitchell, V. (2010). Developing the therapeutic self: Supervising therapists with lesbian, gay, bisexual and transgender clients in the 21st century. *Women & Therapy, 33*, 7–21.

Pearlman, S. (2006). Terms of connection: Mother-talk about female-to-male transgender children. In J. Bigner & A. Gottlieb (Eds.), *Interventions with families of gay, lesbian, bisexual and transgender people: From the inside out* (pp. 93–122). Binghamton, NY: Haworth Press.

Savin-Williams, R. (1996a). Ethnic and sexual minority youth. In R. Savin-Williams & K. Cohen (Eds.), *The lives of lesbians, gays and bisexuals: Children to adults* (pp. 152–165). New York, NY: Harcourt Brace.

Savin-Williams, R. (1996b). Self-labelling and disclosure among gay, lesbian, and bisexual youths. In J. Laird & R. J. Green (Eds.). *Lesbians and gays in couples and families* (pp. 153–182). San Francisco, CA: Jossey-Bass.

Schneider, M. (2001). Toward a reconceptualization of the coming-out process for adolescent females. In A. D'Augelli & C. Patterson (Eds.), *Lesbian, gay, and bisexual identities and youth: Psychological perspectives.*(pp. 71–96). New York, NY: Oxford University Press.

Snow, J. (2004). *How it feels to have a gay or lesbian parent: A book by kids for kids of all ages*. Binghampton, NY: Harrington Park Press.

Strommen, E. (1990). Hidden branches and growing pains: Homosexuality and the family tree. In F. Bozett & M. Sussman (Eds.), *Homosexuality and family relations*. Binghamton, NY: Haworth Press.

Taylor, G. (2002). Psychopathology and the social and historical construction of gay male identities. In A. Coyle & C. Kitzinger (Eds.), *Lesbian and gay psychology: New perspectives* (pp. 154–174). Oxford, UK: British Psychological Society.

Walters, K., Evans-Campbell, T., Simoni, J., Ronquillo, T., & Bhuyan, R. (2006). "My spirit in my heart": Identity experiences and challenges among American Indian two-spirit women. *Journal of Lesbian Studies, 10*(1/2), 125–150.

White, M., & Epston, D. (1990). *Narrative means to therapeutic ends*. New York, NY: Norton.

10

Working With LGBT Parents

FIONA TASKER and MAEVE MALLEY

The 21st century has seen a growth in the number of children who are parented by lesbian, gay, bisexual, or transgendered parents. The U.S. Census of 2000 has provided data on the numbers of children being raised in same-gender couple households: Of the 293,000 households headed by women, a third reported at least one child aged under 18 years old living with them, and a fifth of the 301,000 households headed by male partners similarly reported having at least one child (Simmons & O'Connell, 2003). Census data are likely to have underestimated the numbers of lesbians and gay involved in parenting because direct questions were not included on sexual orientation, neither single lesbian and gay parents nor multiparental relationships were included, and different types of involvement in nonresidential parenting were not considered. Previous estimates of the numbers of lesbian and gay men involved in parenting in the United States had come from surveys within the gay community and had estimated that around 1 in 10 gay men and 1 in 5 lesbians had parenting responsibilities (Bell & Weinberg, 1978; Bryant & Demian, 1994). Estimates of the number of bisexual or transgendered parents may be even more difficult to ascertain because bisexual or transgendered parenting may remain cloaked by heterosexual parenting, although with estimates increasing of the numbers of people identifying as bisexual (Mosher, Chandra, & Jones, 2005) or as transgendered (Olyslager & Conway, 2007; Reed, Rhodes, Schofield, & Wylie, 2008), it is likely that more parents will have a nonheterosexual identity.

Data on prevalence of LGBT parenting have been criticized as imprecise at best (Tasker & Patterson, 2007). In-depth interviews or adapted genogram techniques, which can fully explore the meaning and implications of family relationships, have had more success in revealing an array of different informal parenting or care-giving arrangements in which LGBT parents participate (Swainson & Tasker, 2005; Weeks, Heaphy, & Donovan, 2001). There are many differences between families with LGBT parents: Some will have been planned as LGBT parented families; some will have been created after the end of a previous heterosexual family relationship with the transitioned identity of the LGBT parent; other LGBT parents may have ongoing opposite-gender sexual partnerships; some parents may be single parents, whereas others will be in couple or multiparental relationships (Gross, 2006; Pallotta-Chiarolli, 2006; Tasker & Patterson, 2007). Careful and sensitive exploration of clients' backgrounds and histories makes it increasingly likely that psychotherapists will encounter and acknowledge LGBT parenting in their clinical work with adults or children.

LGBT Parents and Their Children

A variety of different reasons can bring LGBT parents or their children into psychotherapy, some of which may be connected with sexual identity. We have identified three common themes connected to LGBT parenting that challenge LGBT parents and their families: First, we consider aspects of pioneering and forming new family relationships; second, we consider issues involving appreciating similarity and respecting differences within families; and, third, we examine the challenge of connecting with others outside the LGBT parenting family circle. We draw upon clinical research and empirical studies to illustrate the issues identified by LGBT parents and professionals who have worked with them. By using research, we hope to indicate both possible problems that clients may bring to psychotherapy and potential solutions that other LGBT parents have found.

Pioneering and Forming New Family Roles

A central issue for LGBT parents is how to pioneer new parenting roles with their children. Traditional masculine and feminine gender roles still organize parenting and domestic routines for many heterosexual couples (Hawkins, Amato, & King, 2006; Yeung, Sandberg, Davis-Kean, & Hofferth, 2001). However, LGBT parents need to think outside the traditional templates provided by heterosexually gendered ascription (Demo & Allen, 1996). Freedom from traditional templates has provided many opportunities for innovative and individually tailored solutions but also may have contributed to anxiety over domestic uncertainty and conflict between parents, family members, and others outside the family circle with different expectations of family life.

In planned LGBT families, parents-to-be have already spent much time planning for parenthood, considering different options for nonheterosexual parenthood, and contending with the stress of uncertainty to finally have a baby (Mitchell & Green, 2007). In many couples or polyamorous relationships where the adults involved planned to have a child who is biologically related to at least one of them, critical decisions will have been made as to who becomes pregnant and who donates the sperm. Although personal inclination plays a big part in these pregnancy decisions, other aspects inevitably influence the decision: economic considerations connected with paid employment, such social factors as extended family considerations, and such biological factors as age and ability to conceive all have been reported to influence pregnancy decision making for lesbian couples (Herrmann-Green & Gehring, 2007; Martin, 1993; Saffron, 1994). Pregnancy decisions may then determine who can access parenting leave from paid employment and influence subsequent access to flexible employment and work-based child care schemes. Economic pressures may be acute, particularly on lesbians, who are generally lower earners than gay men (Webb & Wright, 2001). Thus pragmatic or economic considerations may need to be considered alongside expectations of equality.

Lesbian parenting couples make their journey into motherhood together and in this may feel uniquely supported by each other (Nelson, 2007). Lesbian couples parenting young children have reported dividing child care tasks and paid employment more evenly than do heterosexual couples (R. W. Chan, Brooks, Raboy, & Patterson, 1998; Patterson, Sutfin, & Fulcher, 2004; Tasker & Golombok, 1998; Vanfraussen, Ponjaert-Kristoffersen, & Brewaeys, 2003). Other studies comparing the division of domestic versus paid employment between lesbian couples with young children conceived through donor insemination (DI) have suggested that birth mothers tend to perform more child care than do comothers (Patterson, 1995). Irrespective of child care divisions, children in two-parent lesbian-led families tended to report being equally close to both of their mothers (Gartrell et al., 1999, 2000). Nevertheless, careful negotiation of child care roles may be a major consideration in same-sex parenting couple relationships when both partners have been socialized to take on similar roles.

Biblarz and Stacey (2010) have argued that comothers give children in lesbian-led families an extra boost of maternal care giving and intimacy, but the researchers also caution that asymmetries in the lesbian couples' biological and legal status with respect to their children, in addition to high standards of parenting equality, may place a strain on the couple relationship. Further research is necessary to examine whether legislative changes in the legal recognition of same-gender couple relationships through coparent adoption, same-sex marriage, and civil partnership will make a difference to social and cultural recognition of the presence and parenting contribution that coparents make.

One study that compared motherhood experiences of lesbian couples who conceived through DI with those of lesbian or heterosexual couples who adopted a child found that biological connection with the child had an ongoing influence on the parent–child relationships and the couple relationship in these families with young children (Ciano-Boyce & Shelley-Sireci, 2002). However, rather than undermine the couple relationship, the presence or absence of a biological connection may have served to explain differences in the child's relationship with its birth mother and comother and thus render biological connection less divisive. Ciano-Boyce and Shelley-Sireci further found that lesbian couples split child care more evenly than did heterosexual couples, and a nonsignificant trend indicated that lesbian adoptive parents were the most egalitarian in their division of labor. In both types of lesbian-led family, and also in heterosexual adoptive families, parents reported being preferred by their child for particular activities; usually the parent preferred for active or rough-and-tumble play was not the parent preferred for comfort. Lesbian birth mothers were more likely than non–birth mothers to be sought out by the child at bedtime, mealtime, or when the child was ill or hurt, whereas non–birth mothers tended to be preferred for rough-and-tumble play. The child's preference for a particular parent for a particular activity was more likely to be a source of tension for the couple for lesbian adoptive parents than for heterosexual adoptive parents or for lesbian couples where one mother gave birth.

Empirical studies have just begun to map out planned gay fatherhood. Gay couples with young children who had been either adopted or conceived through surrogacy arrangements tended to describe degendered or hybrid parenting roles where the couple carved up domestic duties by considering personal preferences and abilities and by applying principles of equality (Gianino, 2008; Schacher, Auerbach, & Silverstein, 2005; Silverstein, Auerbach, & Levant, 2002).

Whereas in planned LGBT families parenting roles and routines develop with the arrival of the child, LGBT parents who conceived children within a heterosexual relationship will have transitioned into LGBT parent identities and had to take on new roles and responsibilities rapidly as single parents or in new partnerships. Lynch and Murray (2000) found that most of the lesbian and gay parents and same-gender stepparents were out to their children but may previously have feared losing custody of children to an ex-spouse, been concerned about what effect having a lesbian or gay parent might have on their child, or worried about the influence of homophobia on their child and family. The parents in Lynch and Murray's study generally reported that younger children were more accepting of their parent's transitioned sexual identity than were adolescents. In the British Longitudinal Study of Lesbian Mother Families, young adults who had been brought up by their mother and her new female partner after parental divorce generally reported close relationships with their mothers' new female partners and described how their mother's female partner was integrated into family life, often more successfully than were stepfathers in heterosexual stepfamilies (Tasker & Golombok, 1997).

Findings from one of the few research studies to compare the responses of lesbian mothers with those of gay fathers suggested that gay fathers were less likely than lesbian mothers to be out to their children from a previous heterosexual relationship, perhaps because gay fathers were less likely than lesbian mothers to have their child living with them (Wyers, 1987). Research on post–heterosexual divorce gay fathering has illuminated the particular dilemmas that gay fathers face when coming out to their children. Bozett (1987) has argued that a desire for authenticity, that is, being out as a gay man as well as a father, means that fathers often want to be out to their children. However, the conflicting demands of each subcultural world have meant that this process is likely to be stressful; for example, the gay father may feel he is isolated as a man with children from a heterosexual relationship when he is with other gay men, whereas the child's mother (or other family members) may be hostile to his expression of a gay identity. Dunne (1987) has presented findings from group psychotherapy sessions with gay fathers suggesting that facilitated role-plays and group discussion made a difference in how prepared fathers felt in relation to coming out to their children from a previous heterosexual relationship. Two studies have indicated that gay men who are cohabiting with their gay partners generally felt more supported in their parenting than did single gay fathers. Barrett and Tasker (2001) reported that gay fathers in cohabiting relationships rated themselves as being more successful at managing a variety of common parenting challenges than did men without a cohabiting partner. Crosby-Burnett and Helmbrecht (1993) found that the gay fathers themselves, the father's gay partner, and the children of gay fathers were generally happier with family life if the father's gay partner was included in child-related activities.

Appreciating and Respecting Similarities and Differences

Doing family therapy for any family group is about being able to work together while also acknowledging the individuality of what family members bring to family and need from family life. Parenting for LGBT parents involves appreciating and respecting similarities and differences with their children, with partners, and with other family members.

Earlier clinical perspectives on same-gender relationships have warned against the dangers of similarity and fusion in lesbian relationships or the desire for distance and detachment in gay male relationships (Goodrich, Rampage, Ellman, & Halstead, 1988; Klinger & Stein, 1996; Krestan & Bepko, 1980) and these patterns of relating seem to leave little possibility for responsive parenting. However, subsequent authors have indicated that these patterns of emotional intimacy do not generally fit with the lived experiences of lesbian or gay relationships (Green, Bettinger, & Zacks, 1996; Hill, 1999). Moreover, empirical studies that have considered lesbian and gay parenting suggest that lesbians and gay men are just as likely as heterosexual parents to be able to be child centered in their parenting (for a review, see Tasker & Patterson, 2007). We know very little about bisexual parenting, but limited evidence suggests that bisexual parenting can be appropriately responsive to children's needs (Arden, 1996). Evidence from clinical research suggests that transgendered parents and their children will need to take time to come to terms with how a parent's transgendered identity changes parenting, but children can appreciate reassurance that a warm and loving parent–child relationship is still there (Green, 1998a, 1998b: Lightfoot, 1998; Sales, 1995). A clinical audit of cases of children with a transsexual parent found that children experienced difficulties in family relationships, namely, in relation to marital conflict between their transgendered and their nontransgendered parent (D. Freedman, Tasker, & Di Ceglie, 2002). We clearly need further research on transgendered parenting, especially research using community rather than clinic-based samples.

Parenting may involve working together with adults of the same gender, same sexual identity, and same age group, ethnicity, socioeconomic status, and ability or disability background as oneself; but it may also involve combining parenting resources across differences engendered by varying cultural perspectives and family backgrounds too. Further, although working together with someone from a similar cultural perspective may facilitate parenting, intersectionality and individual variation mean that assuming similarity from a shared gender or other particular cultural perspective is inherently problematic.

Research has suggested that many lesbian and gay parents may be particularly sensitive in appreciating similarity and difference with their children. For example, Tasker and Golombok (1997) found that the majority of children of lesbian mothers later identified as heterosexual adults themselves, although if they had experienced an attraction to someone of the same gender they were apparently more likely than peers from heterosexual family backgrounds to develop this into a same-gender relationship. Tasker and Golombok also found that compared with the sons and daughters of heterosexual mothers, the young adult sons and daughters of lesbian mothers reported having had more positive conversations with their mothers about the young person's own sexual development and relationships, whether these were same-gender or opposite-gender relationships.

Connecting With Others Outside the LGBT-Parented Family

While LGBT parents are engaged in pioneering new family relationships and roles, they are also busy dealing with the responses of others outside their family. The disclosure dilemma for LGBT parents is that in presenting their parenting relationship to others outside the family, they are exposed to the potential danger of a prejudiced response; but in not presenting their relationship to the outside world, their same-gender relationship risks being unacknowledged, undervalued, and unsupported. These pressures may be felt both in mainstream heterosexual contexts and in nonheterosexual contexts, since LGBT communities have historically not been organized around inclusion of children and parenting experiences (Week et al., 2001).

Perlesz, Brown, Lindsay, and colleagues (2006) make a useful distinction between the private (internal) and public (external) family lives of lesbian mother families and the attitudinal versus emotional responses of other family members to lesbian parenting. A close, satisfying family relationship that works well within the family may be questioned or need justifying outside the family; for example, Perlesz, Brown, Lindsay, and colleagues highlighted a family interview from their study in which an adolescent son is seen as getting on well with his divorced mother's female partner but then describes his mother's relationship as "not normal" and is wary about how he presents his family to his friends at school. Perlesz, Brown, Lindsay, and colleagues also point out the way in which extended family members may question a lesbian couple's decision to have children and yet warm to the arrival of a child and give practical support to the lesbian couple.

The difficulties of living as a marginalized family within a predominantly heterosexist world can been seen as a constant backdrop to LGBT parenting. These difficulties may be more or less pressing for LGBT parents in different cultural communities depending on the degree of acceptance of LGBT identities (C. S. Chan, 1989; Greene, 1994; Loiacano, 1989; Morales, 1990). Being a parent may obscure an LGBT identity depending on whether there is cultural pressure to pass as a single (presumed heterosexual) parent. Moving away from their cultural community is not necessarily helpful to LGBT parents because the wider society can be prejudiced about both nonheterosexuality and racial or ethnic minority groups. Indeed, LGBT parents need to be acknowledged in nonheterosexual parenting relationships, and parenthood can raise the desire to connect with cultural inheritance.

Disclosure dilemmas may be most acutely felt by LGBT parents when transitioning from a previously heterosexual identity; transitioning parents experience the social expectation that they will need to explain a changed identity or changed family circumstances, yet they may still be coming to terms with changes themselves and not be used to disclosing or dealing with the responses of others. Studies have found that lesbians parents in planned families tended to report being more open about lesbian parenting relationships to others outside their family, whereas lesbians with children from previous heterosexual families reported disclosing less often (Perlesz, Brown, McNair, et al., 2006; van Dam, 2004). Perlesz, Brown, McNair, et al. (2006) suggest that in a planned family disclosure dilemmas have been considered prior to parenthood and that a couple who planned parenthood together are more likely than those who did not to have reached a similar level of comfort with the visibility of their relationship and parenthood. In contrast, if a lesbian or gay identity is established after parenthood through a heterosexual relationship, then the implications of disclosure are more complicated in explaining this identity not only to the children but also to ex-heterosexual partners and extended family members, as well as in explaining changed family circumstances generally to others outside the family (Perlesz, Brown, McNair, et al., 2006; Tasker, Barrett, & de Simone, 2010). The results from van Dam's (2004) study revealed that although actual incidents of prejudice were low for both types of lesbian-led family, lesbian mothers with children from previous heterosexual relationships reported more incidents than did mothers in planned lesbian-led families and also perceived less support from extended family, friends, or community support groups, which may have contributed to their feeling of increased vulnerability to prejudice.

The further away the LGBT parent family appears to be from the heterosexual two-parent nuclear family, the more likely they are to experience prejudice or feel the need to be cautious and under pressure to justify family relationships. These experiences and feelings may then work to increase the invisibility of LGBT-parented families and in turn lead to a lack of external acknowledgment of family relationships. Nelson (1996, 2007, 2009) has highlighted how lesbian mothers may feel marginalized from the general community of motherhood. Nelson also indicated the increased difficulty of entering the cultural club of motherhood when a mother does not have a birth story of her own to offer; thus lesbian comothers may face particular scrutiny by other mothers and feel that their parenthood is unacknowledged. Brown and Perlesz (2007) have presented an interesting discussion of lesbian coparenting in different family circumstances and have described how using different words to describe lesbians engaged in parenting children with whom they do not have a biological connection construct, conceal, or raise the visibility of their family roles and relationships.

The gay fathers interviewed by Schacher and colleagues (2005) felt that they experienced a double prejudice from mainstream society: opposition to nonheterosexual parenting and suspicion of men who become primary caregivers. These gay fathers felt under greater scrutiny than usual in their everyday parenting and sometimes felt pressure to be "superparents" to quash negative stereotypes they encountered. Although feeling pride in their children and their own fatherhood, the gay fathers found that this extra pressure could engender personal or relationship stress as they struggled hard to prioritize their children. The gay fathers in Brinamen and Mitchell's (2008) study of planned gay parenthood often felt that they had expanded their identity and support networks through sharing common parenting experiences and generally reported feeling more connected with their own family of origin, other types of nontraditional families, and heterosexual couples with children with whom gay parents had formed new friendships. Nevertheless, the single gay fathers in Brinamen and Mitchell's study tended to be more likely than men in gay parenting couples to report that their increased support networks were offset by feelings of isolation and difference from other gay men and other (heterosexual) fathers because single gay parenting was less accepted by other heterosexual parents or by mainstream parenting services.

Considerations for LGBT Parents in Psychotherapy

The issues that bring LBGT parents to psychotherapy may be both personal and universal; that is, they may be specific to their sexuality, to their relationship, or to the reactions or presumed reactions of others. Similarly, the skills required of therapists working with these clients are both general and specific and require therapists to be able to acknowledge generality and specificity in the issues that clients present. Acknowledgment may be a key concept in this context; using psychotherapy at all can feel like an acknowledgment of difficulty or even of failure. Undergoing psychotherapy in relation to issues of parenting may give an additional sense of vulnerability; for after all, a paradoxical marker of good-enough parenting is often the sense of not being a good-enough parent! Undergoing psychotherapy as a LGBT parent can only compound this sense of vulnerability. It seems to be the nature of parenting that it is an anxiety-provoking and isolating experience in this society, and this anxiety and isolation can be greatly amplified for LGBT parents (Hargaden & Llewellin, 1996; Martin, 1993).

As we know, psychotherapy, like medicine and like other professions, is not a neutral activity, though it is often presented as such. The theory and practice of counseling and psychotherapy are pervaded by personal, societal, and cultural bias and by beliefs presented as fact or truth (Geraghty & Meddings, 1999). These beliefs, necessarily, will tend to be those of the prevailing social orthodoxy (Shamai, 1999), which will, equally, tend to be both heterosexist and homophobic (Siegel & Walker, 1996). Clients who are LGBT will be well aware of these biases, and this awareness may present a dilemma for them in terms of their undergoing psychotherapy. When LGBT clients are parents, we further suggest, beliefs and biases become more emotive: The therapist's beliefs about what is best for a child are touched upon at a time when the parent can be expected to be alert to protecting their child's best interests.

It may be useful for therapists to reflect on how their own beliefs and LGBT parents' responses to them can mirror the dilemmas that face LGBT parents outside therapy. Therapists may expect LGBT parents to hold apprehensions about societal attitudes affecting their children's life experiences. As several writers have pointed out (Blumenfeld & Raymond, 1993; M. Freedman, 1971; Margolies, Becker, & Jackson-Brewer, 1987), whereas children from many minority cultures are born into a familial context that also has minority status and therefore can teach children how best to combat and protect themselves from the consequences of minority status, this is rarely the case for lesbians and gay men (Ross, Fernandez-Esquer, & Seibt, 1996). Further, whereas all parents may wish their children to be sufficiently attached and sufficiently autonomous, sufficiently similar and sufficiently different from them, such expectations may have particular poignancy for LGBT parents. For example, on the one hand, there may be particular anxieties for parents whose children show interest in same-sex relationships or explore gendered boundaries. On the other hand, there may be concerns about how best to support a child who is identifying along conventional heterosexual, masculine, or feminine lines.

Psychotherapist Dilemmas

Psychotherapists working with LGBT parents need to have an awareness of issues specific to their clients, alongside an insight into how normative issues for parents and children—such as time, money, sex, and space considerations; inconsistencies; dilemmas involving difference versus sameness; life-cycle transitions; or reparative or replicative parental scripts—may be amplified or diminished for these clients.

The therapist will also need to have an awareness of potential wariness from clients with regard to the therapist's knowledge of issues connected with sexual identity or anxiety about negative attitudes toward LGBT sexual identity. A key issue for many clients will be whether the therapist will be able to engage in a dialogue about the respondent's sexual identity that is felt to be nonpathologizing and nonpresumptive (Malley & Tasker, 2007). Admittedly, this issue can be seen as a kind of catch-22 for therapists: If the client does not raise the issue of sexual identity, should the therapist do so? Will this be seen as the therapist assuming sexual identity to be connected with every parenting or familial issue when clients do not feel this to be the case? The confidence to raise issues of sexual identity in the same way a therapist would raise or consider other contextual issues may be lacking for many professionals.

This lack of confidence on the part of the heterosexual therapist may be manifested as the liberal "just like us" approach to LGBT clients (Kitzinger & Coyle, 1995; Tripp, 1977). Long (1997) illustrated this dilemma when she discussed supervising a heterosexual systemic therapist working with a lesbian couple. She found that her supervisee made an assumption—a good liberal, humanist assumption—that she should be working with the couple in exactly the same way that she would work with a heterosexual couple and discuss exactly the same life issues. This approach may arise for various reasons: It may chime with a sense of fairness (i.e., "I treat all my clients the same"), it may be born out of an anxiety about raising specific issues in an insensitive way, or it may be attributable to a lack of knowledge of what exactly to raise. Anxiety on the part of the therapist may compound the potential for extra anxiety from LGBT parents about being seen as good-enough parents, and therapy sessions may regularly develop into an impasse rather than progress to more helpful dialogue.

Although it is unrealistic to assume that it is possible for all clients to feel powerful, comfortable, and equal in the therapeutic context all the time—for by its very nature the experience of psychotherapy may be uncomfortable and vulnerabilizing—it is nonetheless desirable that clients feel positive about the therapeutic setting and the therapist, since it is this positivity that seems to facilitate a positive outcome for the client (Friedlander, Wildman, Hetherington, & Skowron, 1994; Lambert, Shapiro, & Bergin, 1986).

Psychotherapist Characteristics

General population studies of clinical clients, or potential clients, have found that clients most frequently wanted information about the therapists themselves, rather than about the circumstances of the therapy (appointments, confidentiality, and so on), and that the more questions people asked about the therapy and the therapist, the better they did in treatment (Braaten, Otto, & Handelsman, 1993; Seligman, 1995). Other studies have concentrated on describing various characteristics of psychotherapists that seem to be associated with client satisfaction as reported by LGBT clients. The gender of the therapist is often seen as the most important characteristic for women, but it is important also for men (Liddle, 1997). The sexuality of the therapist is also frequently cited as important by lesbian and gay male clients (M. A. Jones & Gabriel, 1999; Milton & Coyle, 1999) and the culture, nationality, or race of the therapist (Atkinson & Schein, 1986; Grant, 1994; A. Jones & Seagull, 1977; Marsella & Pederson, 1981; Sue & Sue, 1990). We suggest that for LGBT parents, as for other parents, whether the therapist is a parent may also be a salient factor in client satisfaction.

Such "hidden variables" as sexuality and parenthood may be more or less important to clients, but the clients' knowledge about whether the therapist comes from a similar or different background than they do may be constrained by the therapist's attitude toward transparency and disclosure of information about themselves. The concept of therapeutic transparency is a fraught one in that different psychotherapeutic models stand on very different points of the continuum of therapeutic opacity. Models relying on transference as a core therapeutic concept or tool see transparency in relation to disclosure as antithetic to successful practice. Other models of working (e.g., humanist, integrative, or systemic) may see transference as valid and as therapeutically and ethically important. One contested aspect of transparency is, of course, self-disclosure. There are real debates to be had about how, when, and why we in our roles as therapists and supervisors answer or decline to answer questions about our own experiences or feelings (Baldwin, 2000; Real, 1990). Our choices may be based upon our theoretical orientations, our personal histories, or our practice contexts; but the important point is that they are choices, not givens. Most therapists have a thought-out position on disclosure, but what we do and do not or would or would not disclose may say more about us and our own assumptions than about what the client experiences as most useful.

Given that LGBT family relationships may cross demographic lines, issues of appreciating and respecting perceived similarities and differences may be particularly important in psychotherapy with LGBT parents. Similarities and differences between the therapist and the client may thus be put to use in therapy sessions to explore these issues as they manifest for LGBT parents. We have found working in a demographically mixed team of systemically trained therapists to be particularly useful in this respect, together with the use of a reflecting team approach (Andersen, 1987; Andersen, Lussardi, & Lax, 1991) to aid transparency and to highlight considerate discussion of similarity and difference.

To summarize then, it is arguable that for LGBT parents, a helpful context is one that can encompass their identification as LGBT and as parents. This context may be an intersection not well reflected either by the wider LGBT community or by the community of parents. A positive experience in therapy may be more or less affected by the person of the therapist, that is, by the therapist's particular qualities or identifications; by his or her ability to engage in a dialogue about sexuality, gender, and parenting; and by his or her particular theoretical model. It is, however, equally likely that the experience in therapy will be at least as affected by the practitioner's generic therapeutic skills, that is, the ability to listen well and interact constructively and consistently.

Systemic Psychotherapy Constraints and Considerations

In terms of considering models of working that may be most useful for LGBT parents in therapy, clearly the most important factor is that the therapy should be felt to be a good fit for the parents. Most studies of therapy indicate that the most important criteria for therapeutic success is a client's perception of a benign and supportive therapeutic alliance (Friedlander et al., 1994; Lambert et al., 1986). Further, the model of working is less important than the therapist's ability to create a context that feels helpful to the client. The ability to address issues of relationship and of familial history may be less present for therapists whose theoretical models focus primarily upon the internal world of individuals. Therefore, we will examine systemic psychotherapy as a model of working that may be particularly helpful for LGBT parents because it highlights for clients the context of family relationships and the systems that surround them.

Systemic psychotherapy, the theoretical model upon which much family therapy is based, developed in the 1950s (for an overview, see Goldenberg & Goldenberg, 2008). The key tenets of systemic psychotherapy are intuitively fairly understandable: (1) human beings are relational, and relationships bring with them a process of mutual influence, and (2) we cannot understand an individual unless we understand the individual's wider context or "system," whether this is a familial, a cultural, or a peer system. Systemic psychotherapy carries a contention that our beliefs, our expectations, and our behaviors are developed within these systems and derive from the particular beliefs, expectations, and behavioral norms of these systems. There is no determinist sense that individuals cannot transcend these norms, but systemic thinking and practice does focus on how these expectations tend to be activated within our close relationships. Thus, for example, LGBT parents may have strong beliefs about how family relationships should be, but these beliefs may conflict within families and between the family and the systems that surround it, and these conflicting ideas may bring LGBT parents into therapy.

Atypically for a psychotherapeutic modality, systemic psychotherapy was developed and practiced primarily in such public-sector settings as health care and social services contexts, rather than in the private sector. Consequently, from its beginnings systemic practice and practitioners have had to factor in considerations of difference in income, education, culture, and language, all of which were apparent in client populations. Thus, systemic therapy has had increasingly to consider within the therapeutic context issues of power and access to power. Although this consideration has traditionally been from a White, liberal, humanist heterosexual position, systemic psychotherapy has had to grapple with the contradictions and dilemmas implicit in a largely middle-class, White practitioner base working with an often working-class, culturally diverse client base (Bor, Mallandain, & Vetere, 1998; Street & Rivett, 1996). It can be argued that within the context of working with a heterogeneity of family forms, systemic psychotherapy has had to be responsive to considerations of unequal power and given access to nondominant societal groups or individuals where ethnicity, gender, and culture are concerned.

Nevertheless, systemic thinking has been better, or less resistant, in considering the profound effect these normative judgments have upon women and Black and minority ethnic peoples than in considering the equally dramatic impact upon lesbians and gay men (M. A. Jones & Gabriel, 1999; Leslie, 1995; Ussher, 1991; Vessey & Howard, 1993). It could be argued that until relatively recently within much systemic practice, there would still have been a reasonable expectation of the equation of LGBT sexual identity with pathology. Systemic theory had its own ideas of what is, or what should be, normative in terms of relationship and family structure and functioning and certainly of what good-enough parenting would look like. These norms would be reflected within models of suitable parental hierarchy or roles, models of family transition (as in family life-cycle models), and models of closeness and distance in relationships and in families. Ideas of what is functional and dysfunctional in terms of family models and functioning may be strongly value laden and may all-too-easily reflect the deficit model that LGBT parents may have internalized from the wider society or from their own family templates.

As with almost all psychotherapeutic modalities, unless a consideration of LGBT identity and relationship models is interwoven into systemic training, theory, supervision, and consultancy, systemic practice and the contexts of practice are unlikely to become more informed and thus user-friendly for this client group. Systemic therapists have recently begun to discuss whether family life cycles and models of family therapy developed with heterosexuals might be extended or reevaluated to encompass the family relationships of lesbians and gay men (Carter & McGoldrick, 2005; Malley & Tasker, 1999). Including gay and lesbian family relationship models is crucial in terms of informing the knowledge base of therapists in training.

So, for therapists the dilemma is in knowing how much their therapeutic models and learning may fit lesbian and gay clients, and the only real way to know is to be as transparent as possible about assumptions and models of working or theorizing. Only then can they and their clients see the disparity between generally heteronormative models of functioning and the reality of LGBT parenting dilemmas. This approach is not simply some kind of educative or informative process for therapists at the expense of their clients: LGBT clients too will have internalized heteronormative models and templates, and their problems may lie in the poor fit between the beliefs and expectations engendered by these models and their own impulses or circumstances as parents.

Systemic therapy incorporates a concept of reparative or replicative parental or familial scripts (Byng-Hall, 1995). A *reparative script* is enacted when parents seek to create a context for their children that not only avoids the problems they experienced as children but also avoids the failings they identified in their parents' parenting. A *replicative script* sees the experience of childhood as perfect, or certainly very good, and seeks to replicate the "near-perfect" parenting remembered. Both these efforts are, of course, undermined in any family: first, by our at best incomplete ability to discern our own ways of parenting; and, second, by our inability to control how our aims are received by our children, who inevitably differ from how we were as children. Byng-Hall suggests practicing improvisational scripts to come up with parenting solutions that are both familiar to us and different from those of our parents. We suggest that considering improvisational scripts may be a useful exercise in working with LGBT parents in therapy.

Therapists helping LGBT parents with family problems may have to support them through the real pain inherent in witnessing their children's struggle in balancing loyalty to parents and accommodating to a wider societal and peer environment. There will likely be dilemmas of difference for children. Dealing with these dilemmas can be a particularly crucial task, given that one of the key aspects of parenting is to permit the adolescent child to separate from and critique his or her own family and parental context while still retaining connection to that family (Preto, 2005). When children perceive negative attitudes directed from their peer context toward their parental context, they face an impasse, which precludes their moving without too much guilt into an external world of peers and peer relationships. Children of LGBT parents thus experience a conflict of loyalty and may feel forced into an identification with the judging or judged populations. Also, the children may pressure their parents to conform to their expectations (Fitzgerald, 2010). Consequently, LGBT parents may find their children's conflict of loyalty especially painful and may feel as though it is their own sexual orientation rather than cultural prejudice per se that is causing the problem for their children. This situation can feel like a nuanced differentiation in the midst of a desire to protect their children from the awkwardness of split loyalties or painful choices.

In terms of practice, a key aspect for systemic as well as other psychotherapists is to consider and to help their clients to consider what is different for LGBT parents as compared with parents more generally. Therapists further need to consider what in their own training and their own belief structure needs to be questioned or adapted to be most useful for these clients. One of the most important things for all therapists is to feel able to risk not knowing and making mistakes. A very common failing for therapists working with clients who are either different from or similar to themselves is to assume that they know either nothing or everything about the issues these clients present. Under such circumstances, LGBT therapists and heterosexual therapists alike may feel less able to risk making a mistake or asking what they feel may be a "stupid" or presumptuous question. Therapists who do not ask questions, however, tend to fail to help clients as much as when they do ask the "unsaid" or point out the differences between their own experiences or assumptions and those of their clients or if working with more than one client highlight differences between their clients' experiences.

Case Study

Patrick and Andrew presented for help in managing the behavior of their 10-year-old son, Matthew. Patrick and Andrew had been in a relationship for 8 years and in a civil partnership for 2 years. Patrick is 38, is White Irish and works as a journalist; Andrew, aged 34 years old, is British Asian and is a teacher. Matthew is of mixed race (White Scottish and Black British). Patrick and Andrew shared parenting: Andrew worked 3 days a week, and Patrick would fit his freelance work around Andrew's regular long hours so they could both "be there" for their son, as Patrick said. When the couple both "had to work," as Andrew put it, they were usually able to get Andrew's parents in to help; but during the last year, when Andrew's parents had health problems, Patrick's mother had to come over from Ireland.

Matthew had been fostered by the couple since he was 4 years old. Matthew was the youngest child within a biological family of four children, whose parents both had substance use and mental health problems. Patrick and Andrew had applied to adopt Matthew when it became clear that Matthew would not be returning to his biological family and that his parents did not oppose the adoption. Matthew had "letterbox" contact once a year with his mother.

Patrick and Andrew were increasingly worried about Matthew's behavior both at school and at home. When the boy had first come to live with them, they had expected him to be insecure, clingy, and unhappy, and indeed he had been: He had difficulties on being left with other people, refusing to go to bed and wetting the bed. He also had early issues of school refusal. Patrick and Andrew said they were very pleased with the excellent support they had received from the school in terms of Matthew's early difficulties and felt the school had worked with them as a gay parenting couple. They had received support from Educational Psychology Services, and as a result of this Matthew saw a child psychotherapist for almost a year. Initially Matthew had poor verbal skills but caught up to standard educational levels for his age and was popular with his peers and teachers, who described him as small and endearing.

Matthew had been doing well up until 6 months prior to the start of family systemic psychotherapy appointments. However, his behavior had started to deteriorate at home and at school when, as Andrew put it, "all the old signs" had started to reappear. The reappearance of Matthew's difficult to manage behavior had been a puzzle to everyone, including Child Psychotherapy

Services, which had initiated the referral to a systemic practitioner. The couple felt that the onus was on them to "sort out Matthew's problems," as Patrick said, yet they seemed to feel deflated as parents by the setback and each was trying hard to find a solution to help Matthew, who had been difficult with each of them. Matthew's problems also seemed even more pressing because Matthew would be graduating to high school in a year, and the choices were either to enroll him in the local state school—a large comprehensive school with big classes and little pupil–teacher involvement and support—or pay for him to go to an expensive private school, entailing a long daily commute away from home.

The family members were seen for systemic therapy as a family as well as with the parents as a couple. During one of the couple sessions, when Patrick and Andrew talked about their hopes and fears for Matthew when he entered high school, it became apparent that as a couple they were having difficulty in managing their differences stemming from their individual histories within their own families of origin. It was as we explored these differences that the divergences of their beliefs about parenting Matthew became apparent. These issues are a very good example of the reparative or replicative scripts that we may carry from our own childhood that lead us to a desire to repair the areas we found difficult or problematic or to replicate a childhood we identify as desirable or ideal. Patrick and Andrew each had a sense of "not good enoughness," which would have been very difficult to discuss or acknowledge in nonsystemic therapy that was not gay informed or affirmative.

Patrick had gone to a state secondary school; he had never been particularly academic and said he had "fooled around" at school and "fallen into" sports journalism through his own sporting ability. Patrick had little belief in the value of private education and thought that Matthew would be quite intimidated by the academic approach of the private school and by the much more "conservative" social and political ethos of the school structure.

Andrew's parents had been first-generation Indian immigrants to the United Kingdom who had been brought up partly in India and partly in Kenya. When Andrew's parents had been expelled from Kenya by the Kenyan government, they had moved to London and later had sent Andrew to a private boarding school in the United Kingdom. This schooling had involved an enormous financial commitment for Andrew's parents, and Andrew felt a great debt to them for making this sacrifice. He felt that a way of repaying them was to make full use of his education, and he had a strong sense of the value of this for him and, by extension, for Matthew. It also emerged that Andrew believed that the more structured and more "conservative" approach of a richly resourced private school might be "protective" for Matthew against the vulnerabilities of his early years and against the perceived "deviance" of having gay parents, as Andrew put it. Andrew had a sense that his own academic achievement and being a "good son" had in some way "made up" to his parents for the disappointment of his sexual identity. This belief was not initially consciously held, but then it was voiced during therapy, as was Patrick's entirely opposed sense that a less structured, more "autonomous, alternative" upbringing had enabled him to care less about the level of rejection that he had experienced from his parents when he came out as a gay man.

The discussion of different life scripts helped Patrick and Andrew to make sense of the difficulties that they had in supporting Matthew. Instead of pitting their views increasingly against each other, they began to realize that they were both trying to protect Matthew from the anticipated difficulties he might face, potentially because of his early history, but also because he had gay parents. After a further session with just the couple came a session with the whole family: Patrick and Andrew brought Matthew back into the session with them. Matthew seemed much more confident than before and engaged more in conversations with his parents and the therapist, and correspondingly Patrick and Andrew seemed more content to let Matthew talk. Andrew agreed with Patrick, who said that Matthew had been much better at home, and Matthew was clearly pleased to hear this. After some discussion in the therapeutic team and with the parents, it was decided to give the family a longer interval before the next appointment. A week prior to the next meeting, Andrew phoned to say that Matthew's end-of-year grades were good and his class teacher felt that Matthew's behavior had improved, so did they need to come for the therapy session the following week. In fact, the family were seen together twice more as the therapeutic team worked with them to end the therapy sessions. As the case closed, Matthew's choice of high school did not seem to be such a loaded issue for his parents, and Matthew was himself deciding which high school to go to the following year.

Conclusion

Although a growing body of empirical research has pointed to the effective parenting skills of nonheterosexual parents and the general well-being of children growing up in their care, LGBT parents often find that mainstream society leaves them unacknowledged or misjudged in their relationships. In addition, there are as yet few LGBT community–based templates or models of how to be a successful parent. Consequently, LGBT parents may sometimes feel uncertain in their parenting, decontextualize any particular difficulties they encounter, or negatively evaluate their parenting abilities. It may be the lack of support and endorsement that they are good-enough parents that is the key issue that leads LGBT parents into therapy. We have identified three key aspects of family life that can present a challenge to LGBT parents: pioneering and forming new family relationships, appreciating similarity and respecting differences within families, and connecting with others outside the LGBT-parented family.

We have outlined key considerations in therapy with LGBT parents from the perspective of systemic psychotherapy, but psychotherapy models of whatever kind will need to acknowledge the dilemmas inherent in these transitions and negotiations and will need to have an awareness both of issues specific to LGBT contexts and of general family and relational dynamics and developmental stages. The questions that LGBT parents may feel to be most salient may bear upon issues of sexuality or gender or of the therapist's own constructions of what it means to be family or what constitutes parenting, and it is likely that the therapist's ability to address these issues will be central to the positive experience and outcome of therapy.

References

Andersen, T. (1987). The reflecting team: Dialogue and metadialogue in clinical work. *Family Process, 26*, 415–426.

Andersen, T., Lussardi, D. J., & Lax, W. D. (1991). *The reflecting team: Dialogues about dialogues about dialogues*. New York, NY: Norton.

Arden, K. (1996). Dwelling in the house of tomorrow: Children, young people and their bisexual parents. In S. Rose & C. Stevens (Eds.), *Bisexual horizons: Politics, histories, lives*. London, England: Lawrence & Wishart.

Atkinson, D. R., & Schein, S. (1986). Similarity in counseling. *The Counseling Psychologist, 4*, 319–354.

Baldwin, M. (Ed.). (2000). *The use of self in therapy* (2nd ed.). Binghamton, NY: Haworth Press.

Barrett, H., & Tasker, F. (2001). Growing up with a gay parent: Views of 101 gay fathers on their sons' and daughters' experience. *Educational and Child Psychology, 18*, 62–77.

Bell, A. P., & Weinberg, M. S. (1978). *Homosexualities: A study of diversity among men and women*. New York, NY: Simon & Schuster.

Biblarz, T. J., & Stacey, J. (2010). How does the gender of parents matter? *Journal of Marriage & Family, 72*, 3–22.

Blumenfeld, W. J., & Raymond, D. (1993). *Looking at gay and lesbian life*. Boston, MA: Beacon Press.

Bor, R., Mallandain, I., & Vetere, A. (1998). What we say we do: Results of the 1997 UK Association of Family Therapy members survey. *Journal of Family Therapy, 20*, 333–351.

Bozett, F. W. (1987). Gay fathers. In F. W. Bozett (Ed.), *Gay and lesbian parents* (pp. 3–22). New York, NY: Praeger.

Braaten, E. B., Otto, S., & Handelsman, M. M. (1993). What do people want to know about psychotherapy? *Psychotherapy, 30*, 565–570.

Brinamen, C. F., & Mitchell, V. (2008). Gay men becoming fathers: A model of identity expansion. *Journal of GLBT Family Studies, 4*, 521–541.

Brown, R., & Perlesz, A. (2007). Not the "other" mother: How language constructs lesbian co-parenting relationships. *Journal of GLBT Family Studies, 3*(2/3), 267–308.

Bryant, A. S., & Demian (1994). Relationship characteristics of American gay and lesbian couples: Findings from a national survey. *Journal of Gay & Lesbian Social Services, 1*, 101–117.

Byng-Hall, J. (1995). *Rewriting family scripts: Improvisation systems change.* New York, NY: Guildford Press.

Carter, B., & McGoldrick, M. (2005). *The expanded family life cycle: Individual, family, and social perspectives* (3rd ed.). London, England: Pearson Education.

Chan, C. S. (1989). Issues of identity development among Asian-American lesbians and gay men. *Journal of Counseling and Development, 68*, 16–20.

Chan, R. W., Brooks, R. C., Raboy, B., & Patterson, C. J. (1998). Division of labor among lesbian and heterosexual parents: Associations with children's adjustment. *Journal of Family Psychology, 12*, 402–419.

Ciano-Boyce, C., & Shelley-Sireci, L. (2002). Who is mommy tonight? Lesbian parenting issues. *Journal of Homosexuality, 43*, 1–13.

Crosby-Burnett, M., & Helmbrecht, L. (1993). A descriptive empirical study of gay male stepfamilies. *Family Relations, 42*, 256–262.

Demo, D. H., & Allen, K. R. (1996). Diversity within lesbian and gay families: Challenges and implications for family theory and research. *Journal of Personality and Social Psychology, 13*, 415–434.

Dunne, E. J. (1987). Helping gay fathers come out to their children. *Journal of Homosexuality, 14*(1/2), 213–222.

Fitzgerald, T. J. (2010). Queerspawn and their families: Psychotherapy with LGBTQ families. *Journal of Gay & Lesbian Mental Health, 14*, 155–162.

Freedman, D., Tasker, F., & Di Ceglie, D. (2002). Children and adolescents with transsexual parents referred to a specialist gender identity development service: A brief report of key developmental features. *Clinical Child Psychology & Psychiatry, 7*, 423–432.

Freedman, M. (1971). *Homosexuality and psychological functioning.* Belmont, CA: Brooks/Cole.

Friedlander, M. L., Wildman, J., Hetherington, L., & Skowron, E. A. (1994). What we do and don't know about the process of family therapy. *Journal of Family Psychology, 8*, 390–416.

Gartrell, N., Banks, A., Hamilton, J., Reed, N., Bishop, H., & Rodas, C. (1999). The National Lesbian Family Study: 2. Interviews with mothers of toddlers. *American Journal of Orthopsychiatry, 69*, 362–369.

Gartrell, N., Banks, A., Reed, N., Hamilton, J., Rodas, C., & Deck, A. (2000). The National Lesbian Family Study: 3. Interviews with mothers of five-year-olds. *American Journal of Orthopsychiatry, 70*, 542–548.

Geraghty, W., & Meddings, S. (1999). Lesbian, gay and bisexual issues in systemic therapy: Reflections on the wider context. *Context, 45*, 11–13.

Gianino, M. (2008). Adaption and transformation: The transition to adoptive parenthood for gay male couples. *Journal of GLBT Family Studies, 4*, 205–243.

Goldenberg, H., & Goldenberg, I. (2008). *Family therapy: An overview* (7th ed.). Belmont, CA: Thomson Brooks/Cole.

Goodrich, T. J., Rampage, C., Ellman, B., & Halstead, K. (1988). *Feminist family therapy.* New York, NY: Norton.

Grant, P. (1994). Psychotherapy and race. In P. Clarkson & M. Pokorny (Eds.), *The handbook of psychotherapy.* London, England: Routledge.

Green, R. (1998a). Children of transsexual parents: Research and clinical overview. In D. Di Ceglie (Ed.), *A stranger in my own body: Atypical gender identity development and mental health* (pp. 260–265). London, England: Karnac.

Green, R. (1998b, October–December). Transsexuals' children. *International Journal of Transsexualism, 2*(4). Retrieved from http://www.iiav.nl/ezines/web/IJT/97-03/numbers/symposion/ijtc0601.htm

Green, R. J., Bettinger, M., & Zacks, E. (1996). Are lesbian couples fused and gay male couples disengaged? Questioning gender straightjackets. In J. Laird & R. J. Green (Eds.), *Lesbians and gays in couples and families.* San Francisco, CA: Jossey-Bass.

Greene, B. (1994). Ethnic-minority lesbians and gay men: Mental health and treatment issues. *Journal of Consulting and Clinical Psychology, 62*, 243–251.

Gross, M. (2006). Biparental and multiparental lesbian and gay families in France. *Lesbian and Gay Psychology Review, 7*, 36–47.

Hargaden, H., & Llewellin, S. (1996). Lesbian and gay parenting issues. In D. Davies & C. Neal (Eds.), *Pink therapy: A guide for counsellors and therapists working with lesbian, gay and bisexual clients* (pp. 116–130). Bristol, PA: Open University.

Hawkins, D. N., Amato, P. R., & King, V. (2006). Parent–adolescent involvement: The relative influence of parent gender and residence. *Journal of Marriage and Family, 68*, 125–136.

Herrmann-Green, L. K., & Gehring, T. M. (2007). The German Lesbian Family Study: Planning for parenthood via donor insemination. *Journal of GLBT Family Studies, 3*, 351–395.

Hill, C. A. (1999). Fusion and conflict in lesbian relationships? *Feminism & Psychology, 9*, 179–185.

Jones, A., & Seagull, A. A. (1977). Dimensions of the relationship between the Black client and the White therapist. *American Psychologist, 32*, 850–855.

Jones, M. A., & Gabriel, M. A. (1999). Utilization of psychotherapy by lesbians, gay men, and bisexuals: Findings from a nationwide survey. *American Journal of Orthopsychiatry, 69*, 209–219.

Kitzinger, C., & Coyle, A. (1995). Lesbian and gay couples: Speaking of difference. *The Psychologist, 8*(2), 64–69.

Klinger, R. L., & Stein, T. S. (1996). Impact of violence, childhood sexual abuse and domestic violence and abuse on lesbians, bisexuals and gay men. In R. J. Cabaj & T. S. Stein (Eds.), *Textbook of homosexuality and mental health.* Washington, DC: American Psychiatric Press.

Krestan, J., & Bepko, C. (1980). The problem of fusion in lesbian relationship. *Family Process, 19*, 272–289.

Lambert, M. J., Shapiro, D. A., & Bergin, A. E. (1986). The effectiveness of psychotherapy. In S. L. Garfield & A. E. Bergin (Eds.), *Handbook of psychotherapy and behavior change* (3rd ed.). New York, NY: Wiley.

Leslie, L. A. (1995). The evolving treatment of gender, ethnicity, and sexual orientation in marital and family therapy. *Family Relations, 44*, 359–367.

Liddle, B. J. (1997). Gay and lesbian clients' selection of therapists and utilization of therapy. *Psychotherapy, 34*, 11–18.

Lightfoot, M. (1998). Issues facing the child of a transsexual parent. In D. Di Ceglie (Ed.), *A stranger in my own body: Atypical gender identity development and mental health* (pp. 275–285). London, England: Karnac.

Loiacano, D. K. (1989). Gay identity among Black Americans: Racism, homophobia, and the need for validation. *Journal of Counseling and Development, 68*, 21–25.

Long, J. K. (1997). Sexual orientation: Implications for the supervisory process. In T. C. Todd & C. Storm (Eds.), *The complete systemic supervisor resource guide.* New York, NY: Allyn & Bacon.

Lynch J. M., & Murray K. (2000). For the love of the children: The coming out process for lesbian and gay parents and stepparents. *Journal of Homosexuality, 39*(1), 1–24.

Malley, M., & Tasker, F. (1999). Lesbians, gay men and family therapy: A contradiction in terms? *Journal of Family Therapy, 21*, 3–30.

Malley, M., & Tasker, F. (2007). The difference that makes the difference: What matters to lesbians and gay men in psychotherapy? *Journal of Gay & Lesbian Psychotherapy, 11*, 93–110.

Margolies, L., Becker, M., & Jackson-Brewer, K. (1987). Internalized homophobia: Identifying and treating the oppressor within. In Boston Lesbian Psychologies Collective (Ed.), *Lesbian psychologies: Exploration & challenges.* Urbana: University of Illinois Press.

Marsella, A., & Pederson, P. (1981). *Cross cultural counseling and psychotherapy.* New York, NY: Pergamon Press.

Martin, A. (1993). *The lesbian and gay parenting handbook: Creating and raising our families.* New York, NY: HarperCollins.

Milton, M., & Coyle, A. (1999). Lesbian and gay affirmative psychotherapy: Issues in theory and practice. *British Association for Sexual and Marital Therapy, 14*, 43–59.

Mitchell, V., & Green, R. J. (2007). Different storks for different folks: Gay and lesbian parents' experiences with alternative insemination and surrogacy. *Journal of GLBT Family Studies, 3*(2–3), 81–104.

Morales, E. S. (1990). Ethnic minority families and minority gays and lesbians. In F. W. Bozett & M. B. Sussman (Eds.), *Homosexuality and family relations* (pp. 217–239). New York, NY: Harrington Park Press.

Mosher, W. D., Chandra, A., & Jones, J. (2005, September). Sexual behavior and selected health measures: Men and women 15–44 years of age, United States, 2002. *Advance Data from Vital Health & Statistics,* No. 362. Hyattsville, MD: U.S Department of Health and Human Services, Centers for Disease Control and Prevention, National Center for Health Statistics. Retrieved from http://www.cdc.gov/nchs/data/ad/ad362.pdf

Nelson, F. (1996). *Lesbian motherhood: An exploration of Canadian lesbian families.* Toronto, ON: University of Toronto Press.

Nelson, F. (2007). Mother tongues: The discursive journeys of lesbian and heterosexual women into motherhood. *Journal of GLBT Family Studies, 3,* 223–265.

Nelson, F. (2009). *In the other room: Entering the culture of motherhood.* Halifax, Canada: Fernwood.

Olyslager, F., & Conway, L. (2007, September). *On the calculation of the prevalence of transsexualism.* Paper presented at the WPATH 20th International Symposium, Chicago, IL. Submitted for publication in the *International Journal of Transgenderism* (IJT).

Pallotta-Chiarolli, M. (2006). Polyparents having children, raising children, schooling children. *Lesbian and Gay Psychology Review, 7,* 48–53.

Patterson, C. J. (1995). Families of the lesbian baby boom: Parents' division of labor and children's adjustment. *Developmental Psychology, 31,* 115–123.

Patterson, C. J., Sutfin, E. L., & Fulcher, M. (2004). Division of labor among lesbian and heterosexual parenting couples: Correlates of specialized versus shared patterns. *Journal of Adult Development, 11,* 179–189.

Perlesz, A., Brown, R., Lindsay, J., McNair, R., de Vaus, D., & Pitts, M. (2006). Families in transition: Parents, children and grandparents in lesbian families give meaning to "doing family." *Journal of Family Therapy, 28,* 175–199.

Perlesz, A., Brown, R., McNair, R., Lindsay, J., Pitts, M., & de Vaus, D. (2006). Lesbian family disclosure: Authenticity and safety within private and public domains. *Lesbian and Gay Psychology Review, 7,* 54–65.

Preto, N. G. (2005). Transformation of the family system during adolescence. In B. Carter & M. McGoldrick (Eds.), *The expanded family lifecycle: Individual, family, and social perspectives.* New York, NY: Allyn & Bacon.

Real, T. (1990). The therapeutic use of self in constructionist/systemic therapy. *Family Process, 29,* 255–272.

Reed, B., Rhodes, S., Schofield, P., & Wylie, K. (2008, September). *Gender variance: Prevalence and trend.* Paper presented at GLBT Health Summit, Brisol, England.

Ross, M. W., Fernandez-Esquer, M. E., & Seibt, A. (1996). Understanding across the sexual orientation gap: Sexuality as culture. In D. Landis & R. S. Bhagat (Eds.), *Handbook of intercultural training* (2nd ed., pp. 414–430). Thousand Oaks, CA: Sage.

Saffron, L. (1994). *Challenging conceptions.* London, England: Cassell.

Sales, J. (1995). Children of a transsexual father: A successful intervention. *European Child and Adolescent Psychiatry, 4,* 136–139.

Schacher, S. J., Auerbach, C. F., & Silverstein, L. B. (2005). Gay fathers expanding the possibilities for us all. *Journal GLBT Family Studies, 1*(3), 31–52.

Seligman, M. E. P. (1995). The effectiveness of psychotherapy. *American Psychologist, 50,* 965–974.

Shamai, M. (1999). Beyond neutrality: A politically orientated systemic intervention. *Journal of Family Therapy, 21,* 217–229.

Siegel, S., & Walker, G. (1996). Connections: Conversations between a gay therapist and a straight therapist. In J. Laird & R. J. Green (Eds.), *Lesbians and gays in couples and families.* San Francisco, CA: Jossey-Bass.

Silverstein, L. B., Auerbach, C. F., & Levant, R. F. (2002). Contemporary fathers reconstructing masculinity: Clinical implications of gender role strain. *Professional Psychology: Research & Practice, 33,* 361–369.

Simmons, T., & O'Connell, M. (2003, February). *Married-couple and unmarried-partner households, 2000.* Washington, DC: U.S. Census Bureau. Retrieved from http://www.census.gov/prod/2003pubs/censr-5.pdf

Street, E., & Rivett, M. (1996). Stress and coping in the practice of family therapy: A British survey. *Journal of Family Therapy, 18,* 303–319.

Sue, D. W., & Sue, D. (1990). *Counseling the culturally different.* New York, NY: Wiley.

Swainson, M., & Tasker, F. (2005). Genograms redrawn: Lesbian couples define their families. *Journal of GLBT Family Studies, 1*(2), 4–27.

Tasker, F., Barrett, H., & De Simone, F. (2010). "Coming out tales": Adult sons and daughters' feelings about their gay father's sexual identity. *Australian & New Zealand Journal of Family Therapy, 31,* 326–337.

Tasker, F., & Golombok, S. (1997). *Growing up in a lesbian family: Effects on child development.* New York, NY: Guilford Press.

Tasker, F., & Golombok, S. (1998). The role of co-mothers in planned lesbian-led families. *Journal of Lesbian Studies, 2,* 49–68.

Tasker, F., & Patterson, C. J. (2007). Research on gay and lesbian parenting: Retrospect and prospect. *Journal of GLBT Family Studies, 3*(2/3), 9–34.

Tripp, C. A. (1977). *The homosexual matrix*. London, England: Quartet Books.

Ussher, J. (1991). Family and couples therapy with gay and lesbian clients: Acknowledging the forgotten minority. *Journal of Family Therapy, 13,* 131–148.

Van Dam, M. A. A. (2004). Mothers in two types of lesbian families: Stigma experiences, supports, and burdens. *Journal of Family Nursing, 10,* 450–484.

Vanfraussen, K., Ponjaert-Kristoffersen, I., & Brewaeys, A. (2003). Family functioning in lesbian families created by donor insemination. *American Journal of Orthopsychiatry, 73,* 78– 90.

Vessey, J., & Howard, K. (1993). Who seeks psychotherapy? *Psychotherapy, 30,* 546–553.

Webb, D., & Wright, D. (2001). *Count me in: Findings from the Brighton and Hove lesbian, gay, bisexual, and transgender community needs assessment, 2000.* Southampton, England: University of Southampton.

Weeks, J., Heaphy, B., & Donovan, C. (2001). Same sex intimacies: Families of choice and other life experiments. London, England: Routledge.

Wyers, N. L. (1987). Homosexuality in the family: Lesbian and gay spouses. *Social Work, 32,* 143–148.

Yeung, W. J., Sandberg, J. F., Davis-Kean, P. E., & Hofferth, S. L. (2001). Children's time with fathers in intact families. *Journal of Marriage and Family, 63,* 136–154.

11

The Kids May Be All Right, but Some Might Still End Up in Your Office

Working With Children of LGBTQ Parents

KATHERINE KUVALANKA

Children with lesbian, gay, bisexual, transgender, and/or queer (LGBTQ) parents are a diverse group of individuals; likewise, the therapeutic issues they may present with are also diverse. There is no singular or universal experience of what it is like to be a child with LGBTQ parents. This is, in part, because these children vary by such social location factors as gender, race and ethnicity, socioeconomic class, age, and sexual orientation. Further, these children reside in geographic locations representing a range of social climates in terms of openness to, and acceptance of, LGBTQ people and families (Oswald, Cuthbertson, Lazarevic, & Goldberg, 2010). Moreover, the various identities of the parents themselves as LGBT and/or Q; ways in which the parents came to have children (e.g., donor insemination, surrogacy, adoption, or heterosexual intercourse); and family structures (e.g., single parent or multiparent) and transitions (e.g., parental separation or death, or stepfamily formation) contribute to the diversity of these children's experiences and perspectives. As one might imagine, a 6-year-old African American boy, growing up with two White, gay fathers in an urban East Coast community, may or may not have all that much in common with a 16-year-old White girl living in a rural midwestern state and experiencing her mother's transition from female to male.

One commonality, however, does exist among all children with LGBTQ parents: Because of the continued pervasiveness of heteronormativity, these children's families may be viewed by others as "different" or "less than ideal," given the widely perceived norm of heterosexuality and gender conformity (Oswald, Blume, & Marks, 2005). In this chapter I will touch upon several topics related to the consequences of a heteronormative society for children with LGBTQ parents, such as dealing with heterosexism and deciding whether to disclose familial or parental identities to others. I will also elaborate on the experiences of an understudied subgroup of this population that has garnered little attention in the social science literature: children of LGBTQ parents who also identify as LGBTQ themselves. Research on potential protective factors and strategies for children with LGBTQ parents as they cope with heterosexism, as well as implications for therapists and other mental health practitioners working with this population, will also be shared. First, however, an explanation of the conceptual framework of this chapter—a combined minority stress and life course perspective—is provided because context, process, and meaning are deemed important in the examination of such potential issues as heterosexism, which children with LGBTQ parents may face throughout their lives (Bengtson & Allen, 1993; Cohler, 2005).

Minority stress theory (Meyer, 2003) prompts us to consider the role that heterosexism plays in the lives of children with LGBTQ parents. In relation to their LGBTQ mothers and fathers, children of LGBTQ parents may experience "association" or "courtesy stigma" (Tasker & Golombok, 1997, p. 89), even if the children themselves do not personally identify as LGBTQ.

Indeed, the prevalence of heterosexism in the lives of children with LGBTQ parents has begun to be documented (e.g., Gartrell, Deck, Rodas, Peyser, & Banks, 2005). Thus, I posit that many children with LGBTQ parents may experience minority stress, the stress or state that results from being a part of a socially marginalized group (Brooks, 1981).

Further, a life course perspective prompts us to consider how children with LGBTQ parents interpret contextual factors, including heterosexism, that have an influence on their lives and how these children change over time as a result (Bengtson & Allen, 1993). A life course perspective also highlights the importance of "linked lives" in that social networks (e.g., families and peers) are thought to have an influence on children with LGBTQ parents, and vice versa, throughout their lifetime (Elder & Shanahan, 2006). Thus, as the development of these children carries on across the life span, their families and significant others continue to have an influence on them as they construct their own lives and their own identities separate from, yet still connected to, their families of origin. Lastly, it is important to consider the potential influence of historical context on different cohorts of children with LGBTQ parents as they (and we) interpret their individual and familial experiences (Elder & Shanahan, 2006). For example, it is very likely that children with fathers who came out as gay during the 1980s, usually in the context of heterosexual marriages and in the shadow of the newly discovered AIDS epidemic, have different interpretations of their familial experiences than do young children today, who may be adopted by already "out" gay fathers and who are growing up in a time when a diagnosis of HIV may not automatically be considered a death sentence (Newman et al., 2010). Indeed, having a "gay father" (or a "lesbian mother," a "transgender parent," etc.) may hold different meanings for adults who grew up with LGBTQ parents in decades past than for children today (Cohler, 2005). Thus, when discussing the issues faced by "children" with LGBTQ parents, adult children, adolescents, and younger children are all referred to when appropriate. I begin with an overview and summary of the social science research on how children with LGBTQ parents are faring.

The Well-Being of Children With LGBTQ Parents

Although a handful of studies do exist on children with bisexual and transgender parents, the vast majority of research in this area has focused on children in lesbian- and gay-parent families, with the number of studies involving children with lesbian mothers far outnumbering those involving children with gay fathers (Goldberg, 2010). Numerous studies conducted over the past few decades have repeatedly demonstrated that parental sexual orientation does not seem to be a relevant indicator of successful child development (Patterson, 2006). Research comparing children with lesbian and gay parents and those raised by heterosexual parents have revealed few differences in cognitive functioning and school achievement (Wainright, Russell, & Patterson, 2004), behavioral adjustment (Brewaeys, Ponjaert, Hall, & Golombok, 1997), and social and emotional development (Golombok, Tasker, & Murray, 1997).

Aspects of gender and sexual development among children with lesbian and gay parents have also been explored. These studies have found no differences regarding gender identification between children of lesbian parents and children of heterosexual parents (Golombok, Spencer, & Rutter, 1983; Gottman, 1990; Green, Mandel, Hotvedt, Gray, & Smith, 1986), and have found "appropriate" displays of gendered behaviors and attitudes among children of lesbian parents (Brewaeys et al., 1997; Golombok et al., 1983, 2003; Gottman, 1990; MacCallum & Golombok, 2004). Further, although more research is needed in order to draw definitive conclusions, the existing research on children's sexual orientation development suggests that lesbian and gay parents are no more likely than heterosexual parents to raise nonheterosexual children. Studies report that the vast majority of youth and adults with lesbian and gay parents identify as heterosexual and are no different from youth and adults with heterosexual parents in regard to experiences of same-sex attraction (Bailey, Bobrow, Wolfe, & Mikach, 1995;

Gottman, 1990; Tasker & Golombok, 1997; Wainright et al., 2004). It is important to point out that research conducted to ascertain whether children with LGBTQ parents are more likely to identify as LGBTQ than are children with heterosexual parents seems to suggest that it is "bad" if children turn out to be nonheterosexual or gender nonconforming (B. Fitzgerald, 1999). Herek (2006) noted that the relevance of sexual orientation identity research to children's psychosocial adjustment is "dubious because homosexuality is neither an illness nor a disability, and the mental health professions do not regard a homosexual or bisexual orientation as harmful, undesirable, or requiring intervention or prevention" (p. 613). That said, studies that have explored gender and sexual development among children with lesbian and gay parents have helped debunk myths about lesbian- and gay-parent families and the "harm" that might come to a child as a result of a parent's sexual identity (B. Fitzgerald, 1999; Stacey & Biblarz, 2001).

Although research on children with LGBTQ parents has helped to correct common misperceptions about LGBTQ-parent families, the emphasis on these children as "no different" than other children has also had some unintended consequences (Kuvalanka, Teper, & Morrison, 2006; Stacey & Biblarz, 2001). The message of "no difference" has been misinterpreted by some to mean that all children of LGBTQ parents "turn out fine." As a result, some children with LGBTQ parents have reported feeling a "pressure to be perfect," so as to help prove that LGBTQ people make good parents (Goldberg, 2007a; Kuvalanka et al., 2006). Obviously, there are many children of heterosexual and gender-conforming parents who are not "fine" and, likewise, not all children with LGBTQ parents exhibit positive well-being. Many of these children are dealing with familial issues more profound and pressing than their parents' sexual orientation or gender identity, such as poverty, intimate partner violence, parental separation or death, substance abuse, and mental illness. The emphasis on "no difference" in well-being between children with LGBTQ parents and children with heterosexual and gender-conforming parents has diverted attention from the examination of the struggles and hardships that some children with LGBTQ parents do, indeed, face—some of which may be connected to their parents' sexual orientation or gender identity, but most of which likely is not. Mental health practitioners working with children of LGBTQ parents should be cognizant of the fact that these youth experience and deal with many of the same challenges as children with heterosexual and gender-conforming parents (Negy & McKinney, 2006). Some children with LGBTQ parents may, however, be reticent to share their struggles for fear that others will wrongly tie their difficulties to their parents' nonheterosexual sexual orientation or gender nonconformity (Goldberg, 2007a; Kuvalanka et al., 2006). In addition, these youth may also face unique challenges in relation to their parents' sexual orientation or gender identity that result from living in a society that does not always understand or accept their families (Adams, Jaques, & May, 2004; Negy & McKinney, 2006). Some of these challenges are discussed in this chapter. Prior to delving into that discussion, however, the topic of LGBTQ parents "coming out" to their children will be broached.

Family Talk: LGBTQ Parents Coming Out to Their Children in the Midst of Homophobia

Although most heterosexual parents probably do not feel a need to formally or explicitly disclose their sexual orientation or gender identities to their children, most LGBTQ parents likely at least consider the possibility. The majority of scholarly work on lesbian and gay parents coming out to their children appears to be in regard to families where the parents adopted their nonheterosexual identities after the children were already born and were accustomed to their parents as heterosexual (Bigner, 2000; T. J. Fitzgerald, 2010; Lynch & Murray, 2000). Scholars have provided suggestions for how and when parents should disclose their sexual orientation identities to their children (e.g., Bigner & Bozett, 1990; Clunis & Green, 1995). Research has shown that children and youth may experience a range of reactions and feelings, which also are likely to change over time (Goldberg, 2010). According to Goldberg's (2010) review of the literature, young children generally seem to have the least difficulty accepting their parents' disclosure, whereas adolescent children seem to have more difficulty with the parents' news, especially if a parent's coming out coincides with a divorce. More negative reactions on the part of adolescents may also be because older children have had more time and opportunity to internalize heterosexist and homophobic messages from others (Goldberg, 2010). Regardless of a child's age, however, waiting to tell a child may be negatively interpreted by the child as the parent keeping a secret or being deceptive (T. J. Fitzgerald, 2010; Goldberg, 2010).

Research seems to indicate that most children from *de novo* families, where the parent or parents identified as nonheterosexual prior to the children's entrance into the family, report that they have always known about their parents' sexual orientation, and/or had a growing awareness of the meaning of their parents' sexual orientation identities over time (Goldberg, 2010). Clunis and Green (1995) assert that in a *de novo* family, the LGBTQ parents' task is "interpreting the situation to the child rather than making an announcement" (p. 63). Indeed, having an LGBTQ parent from a very young age, even birth, does not preclude the need for parents to provide their children with accurate information about their families and their parents' identities. Take, for example, the story of Kristy, a 21-year-old biracial daughter born to two lesbian mothers in Maryland through donor insemination. Although Kristy had two lesbian mothers from birth, she did not realize that they were lesbians, or even that they were both her parents, until she was in fifth grade. Kristy explained how it was that she never understood this, and how she finally did become aware of her mothers' sexual orientation identities:

> [My parents] sort of confused me when I was a younger kid, because they were afraid that them being gay would not be as acceptable for teachers and other parents at school. So we always labeled Kathy, my non-biological mother, as my aunt, so when she would sign permission slips or something for me for school, she would always write "aunt" next to it. And I always got kind of confused because as a little kid I wasn't sure. And then everybody sort of talked about being gay in a negative manner when (I was) younger.... And then like when I was in 5th grade, I had this huge traumatic incident, I was like "Are they gay?" because I thought this was something that might be bad.... It was sort of like a realization that sort of hit me, and then I talked to my mom about it, and she sort of looked at me like I was nuts [that] I didn't know. (Kuvalanka, 2007, p. 136)

This sudden awareness was traumatic for Kristy, very likely because she had come to equate the word *gay* with *bad* and had not been taught any other connotation of the word. Although Kristy's parents intended to protect her (and perhaps they did save Kristy from ridicule), it seems they did not adequately prepare her to successfully navigate the heterosexism she encountered. Indeed, therapists may need to inform LGBTQ parents that some children may need to be given explicit information about their families, as well as explanations of strategies parents are utilizing to combat heterosexism (T. J. Fitzgerald, 2010).

Although experts advise LGBTQ parents not to keep secrets from children about parental sexual orientation identities, the presence of heterosexism can make openness about family identity a challenge for both parents and children (Goldberg, 2010). For example, some LGBTQ parents may fear the loss of their job should their employer find out about their sexual orientation or gender identity, thus, making telling children very risky (T. J. Fitzgerald, 2010). Other parents, like Kristy's mothers, may be trying to protect their children from teasing and ostracism, especially if they live in communities that seem to have unwelcoming climates for LGBTQ-parent families. Further illustrating this point was Dana, a 25-year-old White female study participant, who grew up in New Jersey and whose mother and father divorced when she was 6 years old. Her mother kept her sexual orientation hidden from both Dana and their community. Dana found out from her father when she was in the sixth grade that her mother and her mother's female partner were lesbians; after learning this information, she talked about it with her mother and her mother's partner: "They said, 'We really don't think that this is something you talk about at school,' because it just didn't really exist in our town ... (and) they really wanted to protect me" (Kuvalanka, 2007, p. 137). When asked if she would have preferred her mother to have been more open about her sexual orientation identity, Dana addressed the complexities involved in parental coping for LGBTQ parents, such as figuring out how to be out to their children and to their communities while simultaneously protecting their families:

> There are times when I do wish she had just told me, when I was six years old and my parents got divorced and she first met Sandra. I wonder how it would have been if she had just told me then and there as a little girl, what that would have done, and if we could have educated the environment by us being out so early on.... There are definitely times where I think she should have told me right away, but then I don't know. I did have a really good high school experience in terms of having friends and being involved, even though I was unhappy, because I couldn't really talk about this, and I felt homophobia. Maybe there could have been a total flip to the story. Maybe I wouldn't have been as involved or happy in school, but I would have felt relief in being open about this. I don't know.... That's how it was in our town and it sucked, but I really can't judge her for it. (Kuvalanka, 2007, p. 137)

Thus, Dana acknowledges that there are no easy answers in regard to openness as an LGBTQ-parent family when heterosexism is present. Practitioners, though, can help families figure out how to be open with one another inside the family while also managing their parental and familial identities outside the family (T. J. Fitzgerald, 2010). I now consider more fully how heterosexism may play a role in the lives of children with LGBTQ parents.

The Influence of Heterosexism in the Lives of Children With LGBTQ Parents

Interpersonal Heterosexism: Peers and Family Members

A common assumption concerning children with LGBTQ parents is that they will face ridicule and harassment in regard to their parents' sexual orientation or gender identity, resulting in stigmatization. Although studies have revealed normative development among children with lesbian and gay parents, researchers have reported that these children may indeed experience negative social reactions from others (Patterson, 2006). For example, many children with LGBTQ parents frequently hear general antigay sentiments and remarks, and others have been overtly teased or harassed in relation to their parents' and/or their own sexuality (Kosciw & Diaz, 2008; Short, Riggs, Perlesz, Brown, & Kane, 2007; Tasker & Golombok, 1997). Gartrell and colleagues (2005) found that by the age of 10 more than 40% of the children of lesbian mothers in their study reported such experiences. Indeed, in a recent survey of 154 adolescents with LGBT parents, 23% of respondents reported feeling unsafe at school, while 40% reported having been verbally harassed at school because of their family (Kosciw & Diaz, 2008). Further, there is some evidence that experiences of heterosexism and perceptions of stigmatization may have negative effects on the well-being of children with lesbian mothers in terms of behavior problems (Gartrell et al., 2005) and self-esteem (Gershon, Tschann, & Jemerin, 1999). After reviewing the literature, Stacey and Biblarz (2001) concluded that there is "some credible evidence that children with gay and lesbian parents, especially adolescent children, face homophobic teasing and ridicule that many find difficult to manage" (pp. 171–172). Thus, a major challenge for some children with LGBTQ parents seems to be the negative reactions they may experience from the outside world. The early adolescent years in particular may present challenges to some youth with LGBTQ parents because they may encounter more heterosexist attitudes from peers than they did at younger ages (Litovich & Langhout, 2004).

Other findings, however, suggest that many children of lesbian and gay parents do not experience increased stigmatization in comparison to children with heterosexual parents, as evidenced by the quality of their peer relationships (MacCallum & Golombok, 2004; Tasker & Golombok, 1995). Investigations have also found no significant differences in levels of victimization among adolescents with two female parents and those with heterosexual parents (Rivers, Poteat, & Noret, 2008). Yet, even if children with LGBTQ parents do not actually experience teasing or rejection, many of them may have worries about losing friends and/or being judged by peers (Gartrell et al., 2005). For example, Wright (1998) reported that although the children of lesbian mothers in her study did not experience a lot of trauma overall, they still had tremendous fears about being teased; even the children who had not experienced any overt heterosexism seemed "to carry around with them a certain uneasiness and anxiety" (p. 149).

Likewise, several participants in my study (Kuvalanka, 2007) of 30 young adults with lesbian mothers recalled being concerned about losing friends as a result of others finding out about their families. For example, Denise, a 23-year-old White female participant, who grew up in Maryland and had two lesbian mothers and two gay fathers, recalled the intense feelings of concern she experienced in middle school:

> I was terrified of people knowing about my family.… In terms of this friend, I was afraid of losing her friendship or of her parents not wanting her to associate with me anymore.… And I was afraid of other people finding out. I was definitely afraid of people associating my parents' sexuality with my own. I was afraid of being teased. (Kuvalanka, 2007, p. 118)

Another 20-year-old White female participant, Tara, who grew up in Vermont and had two lesbian mothers from the time she was 2 years old, also kept her mothers' sexual orientation a secret from her peers during early adolescence. She was so worried that others would find out about her family that she left middle school for several months:

> I just had a lot of anxiety about meeting people and forming relationships … and just kind of judgment by association, that I actually ended up stopping going to school and was home schooled for a while.… I kind of made myself sick all the time just unconsciously, because I was so uncomfortable in the school environment. (Kuvalanka, 2007, p. 155)

Parents, teachers, and mental health practitioners, then, need to realize that even if children with LGBTQ parents do not experience actual teasing and/or harassment, the anticipation of such rejection may become overwhelming for some.

Although teasing and ridicule on the part of peers may pose challenges for some youth with LGBTQ parents, also as challenging may be the interpersonal heterosexism exhibited by the children's own family members. Several young adult participants in my study (Kuvalanka, 2007) reported that family members, such as fathers, stepparents, grandparents, cousins, or other extended family members, disapproved of their mothers' sexual identity or lesbian partnerships, oftentimes making disparaging comments. For example, Rita, a 20-year-old White female participant, who grew up in Pennsylvania and whose mother and father divorced when she was 2 years old, referred to her father and stepmother, who she said made her feel ashamed for having a lesbian mother:

> They were constantly, like, trying to get me to talk about, you know, that I was angry at my mom and I didn't want her to be a lesbian.… And they just made me believe that it wasn't normal and that I should be ashamed and she was a bad person. (Kuvalanka, 2007, p. 112)

Some participants also reported heterosexism in the form of a lack of recognition of some familial relationships, especially the relationships between participants and their nonbiological mothers. For example, Kristy, the previously mentioned 21-year-old female participant who was born by means of donor insemination to her two lesbian mothers and grew up in Maryland, described how her nonbiological grandparents seemed to have difficulty accepting their daughter's sexual identity and, in turn, seemed not to fully recognize Kristy as their grandchild: "I'm considered, I guess, one of their grandchildren, but they don't really send me cards on my birthday like they do my older sister, because that's their biological grandchild" (Kuvalanka, 2007, p. 98). Thus, practitioners should be aware that children with LGBTQ parents may be experiencing interpersonal heterosexism from various sources—perhaps even from inside their own families.

Institutionalized Heterosexism: Schools and Government

In addition to facing interpersonal heterosexism, children of LGBTQ parents may also be confronted with institutional heterosexism in various environments, such as schools, where LGBTQ-parent families are often rendered invisible (Gillis, 1998; Lindsay et al., 2006). That invisibility can range from the absence of any positive or even neutral information about LGBTQ-parent families to discouragement from sharing information about families or including family members in school activities (Kosciw & Diaz, 2008). Beyond invisibility, the lack of specific antiheterosexist policies or the failure of school personnel to carry out those policies may contribute to heterosexism in schools. For example, only 28% of the youth with LGBT parents in Kosciw and Diaz's (2008) survey reported that school staff intervened frequently when overhearing antigay remarks and comments. More disturbingly, 39% of the youth reported that teachers and other school staff were the perpetrators of antigay remarks. According to Snow (2004), who interviewed children of lesbian and gay parents, a daughter of a lesbian mother who faced harassment by peers noted that "some teachers knew what was going on, but no one would really say or do anything" (p. 48). As a result, children of LGBTQ parents glean meaning from the institutionalized heterosexism they witness and experience (Kuvalanka, 2007). School-level heterosexism perpetuated by teachers and administrators sends messages of disapproval and intolerance to children with LGBTQ parents, messages that are often heard "loud and clear." For example, Terry, a 22-year-old biracial genderqueer participant, who was born through donor insemination to two lesbian mothers and grew up in Oregon, stated:

> I understood that the role of lesbian parents and the value of lesbian parents in society was always very tenuous.… In a lot of places it was very clear that my family held no value. There were some people who felt that the world would be better off if my family didn't exist. (Kuvalanka, 2007, p. 116)

Conversely, teachers and other school staff can become important allies for children with LGBTQ parents. Denise, the 23-year-old participant mentioned earlier with two lesbian mothers and two gay fathers, spoke about a teacher who was helpful to her when she was dealing with another student's homophobic remarks.

> [My teacher] basically let me know that he has a lot of friends who are gay, just kind of on a personal level let me know that he would be supportive and was all for my family.… It meant the world to me.… That was a very difficult time for me, and just knowing that there was somebody there, just meant so much. (Kuvalanka, 2007, pp. 133–134)

Thus, school personnel can play a very significant role in the lives of children with LGBTQ parents, acting either as perpetuators of the interpersonal and institutionalized heterosexism that is present in schools or as sources of positive support and validation.

Institutionalized heterosexism is also perpetuated through governmental laws and policies. Goldberg (2007a) noted that incidents of institutional-level heterosexism, including political campaigns to ban marriage between same-sex couples, had personal implications for adult study participants with lesbian, gay, and bisexual parents: "In them, [participants] discerned clear messages about what is normal and what is illegitimate, as well as indirect attacks on the rights and well-being of their own parents" (p. 555). Illustrating this, Samantha, a 20-year-old White female participant from my study, who was born by means of donor insemination to her lesbian parents and grew up in Massachusetts, talked about institutional heterosexism having an impact on her family's emotional well-being:

> In high school there was the whole gay marriage battle.... Before [when] people said, "that's so gay," it was like personal, but not *that* personal. The gay marriage issue was, "My parents have been together for 25 years, and you're gonna tell them they can't get married?" Like, that was something that directly affected me and my family and my parents' happiness. (Kuvalanka, 2007, pp. 120–121)

The lack of legal recognition of same-sex partnerships poses potential problems for children of same-sex couples, especially in the absence of guaranteed access to second-parent adoptions (e.g., Pawelski et al., 2006). Given that some children of same-sex couples have only a legal relationship with one of their parents, these problems may include lack of access to a parent's health care plan, the inability of a parent to make emergency medical decisions for a child, and a child not being guaranteed a relationship with both parents in the event of parental death or separation (Pawelski et al., 2006). Thus, it seems critical that practitioners consider the role that institutionalized forms of heterosexism may play in the lives of youth with LGBTQ parents, in addition to any potential interpersonal teasing and harassment these children may endure.

Changes in Experiences of Heterosexism Over Time

In addition to experiencing different types of heterosexism, children with LGBTQ parents are also likely to experience changes in the intensity, frequency, and duration of heterosexism during their lifetimes (Kuvalanka, 2007). Likewise, the level of anxiety that some children with LGBTQ parents may feel in response to actual, or anticipated, heterosexist incidents is also likely to change (Goldberg, 2007b; Kuvalanka, 2007). For example, about half of my study participants noted that things changed positively for them between middle school and high school (Kuvalanka, 2007). Samantha, a 20-year-old White female participant from Massachusetts and born by means of donor insemination to her two lesbian mothers, recalled, "Once you get to high school, there is the Pride Alliance and there's people in high school who are coming out, so it really started to be like less and less of an issue" (Kuvalanka, 2007, p. 110). Consequently, many participants who felt vulnerable because of heterosexism in middle school expressed less fear later in their adolescence. Denise, the 23-year-old White daughter born through donor insemination to her two lesbian mothers and two gay fathers, explained why she was able to come out to her entire high school about her family, after being closeted in middle school: "I felt comfortable enough in my situation … I didn't feel threatened or afraid as much" (p. 121). Thus, for many children with LGBTQ parents, later adolescence—and also adulthood—may be less anxiety filled than early adolescence (Goldberg, 2007b; Kuvalanka, 2007).

Many of the young adult participants in my study made reference to the "passage of time" when explaining the decreasing influence of heterosexism as they got older, as well as changes in regard to how they responded to the heterosexism they experienced as adolescents (Kuvalanka, 2007). A few participants spoke about how their own growing up and maturing helped them to be more open about their families despite the existence of heterosexism. For example, Kendra, a 20-year-old White female participant from Washington and who was born by donor insemination to her two lesbian mothers, stated, "I did become much more open about it, but I think that was partly because I grew into myself.... I don't think it was anything specific. I think it was literally just growing up" (pp. 145–146). Other participants referred to the importance of their peers growing up and maturing as well. Melissa, a 20-year-old White female participant who was born to her lesbian mother and grew up in Vermont, attributed her being more open about her family in high school to other kids growing up: "I feel like kids matured more and wouldn't have such a negative outlook on it if they found out. I feel like they'd be more like, 'all right'" (p. 146). Beyond simply waiting for the passage of time to allow for growing up, there are other coping strategies that are employed by children with LGBTQ parents to deal with the heterosexism they face; two of these strategies are discussed in the next section.

Strategies for Coping With Heterosexism: (Non)Disclosure and Ally Building

(Non)Disclosure of Parental and Family Identity in Response to Heterosexism

Much is still unknown about how youth with LGBTQ parents navigate heterosexism; however, three social control strategies utilized by adolescents and young adults with gay fathers were first identified by Bozett (1987). Bozett reported that his participants' greatest concern was that they would face negative social repercussions if their fathers' sexual identity became known and others were to assume they too were gay. *Boundary control*, or attempts to control parents' behavior, their own behavior, and/or the behavior of others, served to "keep the boundary of the father's expression of his homosexuality within the limits set by the child" (Bozett, 1987, p. 42). For example, some participants asked their gay fathers not to hold hands with their male partners in front of others, or they chose not to bring certain friends home to keep the friends from seeing the fathers and their male partners together. Indeed, other scholars have also reported that some youth with lesbian and gay parents seem to report more positive feelings about their families if they have some semblance of control over how out the parents are to the rest of the world (Goldberg, 2010). A second strategy of *nondisclosure* refers to not telling others about the parents' sexual orientation, sometimes hiding such items as gay newspapers or books before visits from friends, or referring to their parents' partners as "aunts," "uncles," or "housemates" (Bozett, 1987; Goldberg 2007b; Kuvalanka, 2007). Finally, Bozett found that in an attempt to control others' reactions, some of his participants "prepared" others before meeting their parents with preemptive *disclosure* of the parents' sexual orientation. Jenny, a 20-year-old White female participant in my study who was born to two lesbian mothers through donor insemination and grew up in California, explained how she came out to her friends about her family prior to bringing them home in order to protect her family from potential homophobic reactions:

> I wouldn't have had somebody come to my house unless they had known about it before, because ... I didn't want to put someone in a position of having them feel weird or just not liking being there. I would've rather stopped being friends with them before I invited them into my home, and my family had to see that. (Kuvalanka, 2007, p. 156)

It is interesting that just as coming out is not a one-time event for LGBTQ persons, neither is it for children of LGBTQ parents, who must make decisions regarding disclosure about their family and parental identities throughout their lives (Adams et al., 2004; Goldberg, 2007b). Both Goldberg (2007a, 2007b) and Kuvalanka (2007) found that in response to heterosexist remarks, some adults with lesbian, gay, or bisexual parents verbally defended LGBTQ people in general or their own parents by coming out about their own families. For example, Kim, a 22-year-old White female participant from California whose lesbian mother divorced Kim's father when Kim was 6 years old, explained how she sometimes responded in high school when others were making offensive remarks: "If the person saying the homophobic slur was confronted and, like, just wasn't getting why he or she shouldn't be saying it, then I would be like, 'Well, because I have a lesbian mom and that like offends me'" (Kuvalanka, 2007, p. 164). Disclosure of parental sexual identity also served the function of "screening out" unaccepting heterosexist individuals and educating misinformed individuals regarding sexual orientation and diverse family forms for both adolescents and adults with nonheterosexual parents (Goldberg, 2007b). In addition, some participants seemed to cope with heterosexism through "selective association," or choosing to associate primarily with others who were seen as nonheterosexist and accepting of diverse family forms. For example, Charlie, a 22-year-old White male participant from Florida whose lesbian mother divorced Charlie's father when Charlie was 5 years old, talked about criteria he used during high school to choose his friends: "Just based on comments that were said and things, like, I kind of knew [who] would be safe" (Kuvalanka, 2007, p. 158).

In addition to learning how to be selective in regards to choosing friends, another skill that some children with LGBTQ parents learn is to develop a "thick skin," which may mean sometimes not disclosing their family identity (Kuvalanka, 2007). More than half of my study participants talked about acquiring the ability to not let heterosexism bother them (Kuvalanka, 2007, p. 156). For example, Heather, a 19-year-old White female from Massachusetts who was born through donor insemination to her two mothers, explained her strategy for dealing with heterosexism that she learned from one of her mothers:

> I mean trying to just sort of let it roll off me, my mom always says, like a duck. Like their feathers are waterproof, I guess, so when they get wet, the drops of water just roll off their backs, and she was like, you just have to be like that. (Kuvalanka, 2007, p. 157)

For many of these participants, developing a thick skin involved learning to ignore heterosexism. For example, Kara, a 19-year-old White gender-ambiguous participant born through donor insemination to two lesbian parents and who grew up in Massachusetts, described the societal messages she received about LGBTQ people and families as an adolescent, as well as her ability to ignore them: "I was told we're home wreckers and that it's a threat to the American family and … pretty much I just listen to it and just shrug it, because I—I know it's not true" (p. 157). Heather also said she is trying to work on accepting that she cannot always fight every battle against heterosexism:

> One of the things that I'm working on is … just like knowing when to just let things go and let it be ok.… If somebody says something that annoys me, I'll generally take the bait and argue with them about it. So, I'm just that way in general, so it's really hard for me to just be like, like you can't change everybody, you can't say something every single time, and so I'm still working on … letting me be ok with not saying something even though like I feel like I should. (p. 153)

It seems, then, that practitioners should be aware that although disclosure of family identity can be a sign that children with LGBTQ parents are coping positively with heterosexism, nondisclosure in certain circumstances can also be an adaptive strategy (T. J. Fitzgerald, 2010).

Ally Building: The Importance of Friends

Another strategy that seems to help some children with LGBTQ parents successfully cope with heterosexism is building or accessing a positive social support network. Having supportive friends seemed to be important for helping many participants in my study deal with the impact of heterosexism and to feel protected from it (Kuvalanka, 2007). For example, Nora, a 24-year-old White female participant from Pennsylvania whose lesbian mother divorced Nora's father when Nora was 3 years old, said:

A lot of my friends had become close to my family over time, and so one of my best friends from high school and also a bunch of my other friends from high school kept very, like, connected to my family. So, I felt a safety in that, that meant no matter how I responded to other people, like, I was doing ok. I knew that other people knew where I came from, and weren't going to let anything terrible happen to me. (p. 130)

Samantha, a 20-year-old White female participant from Massachusetts who was born by means of donor insemination to her lesbian mothers, elaborated:

I think a combination of having friends that were accepting and friends that talked about it and friends that were coming out themselves, just sort of made it less and less of an issue and more and more something to be proud of. (p. 131)

Indeed, the turning point for many of the young adult participants in my study who were not out to their friends in middle school but who opened up in high school seemed to be when they received positive feedback and support from friends (Kuvalanka, 2007, p. 131). For example, when Tara, the 20-year-old White female participant from Vermont, who had left middle school for several months because of her fear that others would find out about her family, told her high school friends about her mother; her friends responded well, which made a difference in how Tara felt about her family: "In terms of the positive feedback, it made me feel positive and unafraid about my own family. And I think towards the last few years of high school, I didn't feel hesitant about inviting people over to my house" (p. 131). Practitioners may be able to play an important role by helping some children with LGBTQ parents consider the potential benefits of a successful coming out to friends. In addition, it seems important for practitioners to concurrently educate children with heterosexual parents about the potential ally role they could play to their friends with LGBTQ parents.

It may be especially beneficial for some children with LGBTQ parents to find allies in other children with LGBTQ parents (Bos & Van Balen, 2008; T. J. Fitzgerald, 2010). In their study of 63 children born to lesbian mothers, Bos and Van Balen (2008) found that frequent contact with other children with lesbian and gay parents helped to protect study participants from the negative effects of stigmatization on their self-esteem. By sharing her experience, Denise, the 23-year-old White female participant in my study with two lesbian mothers and two gay fathers from Maryland, provided insight into the protective function of knowing others with LGBTQ parents. When Denise found COLAGE (formerly known as Children of Lesbians and Gays Everywhere; http://www.colage.org)—an organization run by and for individuals with LGBTQ parents—in high school and met other teens with LGBTQ parents, her base of social support was broadened in a uniquely significant and life-changing way:

After freshman year (of high school), I found COLAGE … and that totally changed my life. Just being in a space … with those other teens, was just mind boggling, because we all had so much in common.… It was empowering to know that there were other people out there.… Just being able to be in a space and say things or hear other people saying things that I knew exactly how they felt and what they had been through was validating for one, because none of my feelings had been validated. And, it was also, it created a support network, when I realized I wasn't the only person out there. (Kuvalanka, 2007, pp. 133, 162)

Denise realized that she was not alone, which helped her to conceptualize the heterosexism she experienced and feared in a different way than she had in the past. Likewise, Heather, a 19-year-old White female participant from Massachusetts and born by means of donor insemination to her two lesbian mothers, found it extremely helpful to have a friend with whom she could identify and consistently commiserate:

> One of my best friends also has two moms, so like we would talk about frustrations, like that, just because we could be like, "Oh my God, I know what you mean, I hate when that happens!" And so, it was just really nice to have somebody who I was close to who I could like identify with about issues like that. (p. 163)

Practitioners, then, could facilitate children with LGBTQ parents meeting other children with LGBTQ parents either informally, or through an organization such as COLAGE (T. J. Fitzgerald, 2010). This nonprofit organization provides opportunities for children with LGBTQ parents to connect with one another by providing, for example, online listservs for "COLAGErs" of different ages (Kuvalanka et al., 2006). COLAGE also provides online listservs for more specific subgroups of children with LGBTQ parents, such as children with transgender parents, and second-generation individuals, that is, LGBTQ youth and adults with LGBTQ parents.

The Experiences of Second-Generation Youth

Some social scientists, as previously noted, have explored gender and sexual identity development among children with lesbian and gay parents (e.g., Tasker & Golombok, 1997) in response to the commonly held belief that LGBTQ parents will raise children who are confused about their gender and sexual orientation. Although researchers have generally reported that a large majority of children with lesbian and gay parents identify as heterosexual and exhibit "normal" gender development, they acknowledge that a minority do report nonheterosexual and gender-nonconforming identities (Bailey et al., 1995; Kosciw & Diaz, 2008; Tasker & Golombok, 1997). This aspect of these individuals' lives, however, is rarely explored in existing studies despite the fact that nonacademic writers and queer activists have been discussing the experiences of LGBTQ youth with LGBTQ parents for more than 15 years (Garner, 2004; Kirby, 1998). Goldberg (2007b) noted that research on second-generation youth "is essential, as there may be ways in which having a gay parent eases one's own coming-out processes; alternatively, these individuals may also feel doubly marginalized and may experience greater pressure to identify as heterosexual" (p. 127). Likewise, Kosciw and Diaz (2008) noted that although LGBTQ youth with LGBTQ parents may face discrimination in relation to their own or their parents' sexual orientation or gender identity, they may have more familial support to help them cope than have LGBTQ youth with heterosexual parents.

Kuvalanka and Goldberg's (2009) secondary data analysis provided the first in-depth academic study of second-generation individuals, when they examined the experiences of 18 LGBTQ young adults with lesbian and bisexual mothers. From this initial analysis, it seems that having LGBTQ parents when one is also LGBTQ may be potentially beneficial in that some participants felt they had a less arduous coming-out process than they would have if they had heterosexual parents. Some participants said that having a lesbian or bisexual mother helped them to discover their own nonheterosexual and/or gender-nonconforming identities sooner; and many of them also did not worry about rejection upon disclosure of their identities to their parents. Perhaps, then, having an LGBTQ parent when one also is LGBTQ may provide some youth with protection against societal heterosexism. Some participants, however, discussed the unique challenges they faced, such as a delayed coming out because of fears of fulfilling critics' assertions that gay parents raise gay kids. Others reported that they did not want to be gay, having witnessing the prejudice and discrimination that their parents endured in relation to their nonheterosexual orientations. Thus, it seems that having an LGBTQ parent is not guaranteed protection against the influence of societal heterosexism. It is interesting that several participants did not seem to utilize their parents as sources of support during their sexual and gender identity formations, turning instead to friends. Further, it is perhaps surprising that some participants discussed their disappointment upon coming out to their parents. It seemed that some of the lesbian or bisexual mothers were fearful that their children would face discrimination and, thus, did not want their children to be LGBTQ; other mothers worried about being blamed for their child's nonheterosexual and/or gender-nonconforming identity. Some of the transgender (e.g., genderqueer or gender-ambiguous) participants especially seemed unhappy with their mothers' reactions to their disclosures in that their mothers seemed to have difficulty comprehending transgender identities.

Based upon these study findings, practitioners are encouraged to be sensitive to the diversity of perspectives and experiences of LGBTQ youth with LGBTQ parents and to be cognizant of youths' sensitivity about interpretations regarding the origins of their sexual orientations or gender identities (Kuvalanka & Goldberg, 2009). Although some second-generation youth might happily talk about the influence their parents have had on their sexuality and gender development, others may resent the implication that their identities are connected to that of their parents. Further, transgender second-generation youth may face certain challenges and obstacles in that their gender identities may be stigmatized or misunderstood in the larger community or social context (Wyss, 2004) and also, perhaps, within their own families.

Conclusion: Affirmative Therapy With Children of LGBTQ Parents

Therapists aiming to provide affirmative psychotherapy for individuals with LGBTQ parents need to be cognizant of the diversity of experiences that exist among these children, youth, and adults and be mindful that these individuals do not inherently need therapy as a result of their parents' sexual orientation or gender identity (Long, Bonomo, Andrews, & Brown, 2006). Even so, simply having an unrelated adult who is supportive and affirming of both the client and LGBTQ-parent families in general may be greatly helpful for individuals with LGBTQ parents. Those persons seeking therapy would likely benefit from a safe and open environment where they can share gripes about their parents—and even about their parents' sexual orientation or gender identity—without worrying that what they say will be interpreted to mean that LGBTQ people make bad parents.

Children with LGBTQ parents who enter therapy may do so for issues unrelated to their parents' sexual orientation; however, as a result of societal heteronormativity, individuals with LGBTQ parents may experience situations or feelings that they find difficult to manage (Long et al., 2006). Given that issues affecting a child also affect the entire family, a therapist working with a child of LGBTQ parents (especially if that child is under 18 years of age) very likely would also need to work with the entire family (T. J. Fitzgerald, 2010; Negy & McKinney, 2006). It is important to recognize that LGBTQ parents may need assistance with coming out to their children, strategizing with their children about how to combat heterosexism, and supporting their children through transitions and the children's explorations of their own sexual orientation and gender identities (Adams et al., 2004). Further, play therapy can provide young children with an opportunity to act out interactions with others, such as peers and teachers, and to express how they feel as a result of heterosexist interactions. Practitioners might also consider facilitating a group therapy experience in which children and youth from nontraditional families have the opportunity to build friendships and find peer allies. Older children and adults might benefit from narrative therapy, in which they have the chance to share, and perhaps (re)construct, the "story of their lives" and their identities as children of LGBTQ parents. Therapists could also role-play with children of all ages to help them think through options for dealing with heterosexism and also contemplate potentially positive and negative repercussions of disclosing their parents' identities with friends, significant others, coworkers, and other important people in their lives.

Being knowledgeable about the issues that LGBTQ-parent families might face and the resources that exist to help them (e.g., http://www.colage.org), while simultaneously being open to learning about the unique situations and experiences of each client who walks through the door, seems crucial to providing affirmative therapy to this population (Kranz & Daniluk, 2006; Negy & McKinney, 2006). Individuals with LGBTQ parents are not all happy or sad, and they are not all heterosexual or gay. They are each having their own individual journey of growing up and trying to navigate a world that is oftentimes less than accepting of them and their families.

References

Adams, J. L., Jaques, J. D., & May, K. M. (2004). Counseling gay and lesbian families: Theoretical considerations. *The Family Journal: Counseling and Therapy for Couples and Families, 12*, 40–42.

Bailey, J. M., Bobrow, D., Wolfe, M., & Mikach, S. (1995). Sexual orientation of adult sons of gay fathers. *Developmental Psychology, 31*, 124–129.

Bengtson, V. L., & Allen, K. R. (1993). The life course perspective applied to families over time. In P. G. Boss, W. J. Doherty, R. LaRossa, W. R. Schumm, & S. K. Steinmetz (Eds.), *Sourcebook of family theories and methods: A contextual approach* (pp. 469–499). New York, NY: Plenum Press.

Bigner, J. J. (2000). Gay and lesbian families. In W. C. Nichols, M. A. Pace-Nichols, D. S. Becvar, & A. Y. Napier (Eds.), *Handbook of family development and intervention* (pp. 279–298).

Bigner, J. J., & Bozett, F. W. (1990). Parenting by gay fathers. In F. W. Bozett & M. B. Sussman (Eds.), *Homosexuality and family relations* (pp. 155–175). Binghamton, NY: Haworth.

Bos, H. M. W., & Van Balen, F. (2008). Children in planned lesbian families: Stigmatisation, psychological adjustment, and protective factors. *Culture, Health, & Sexuality, 10*(3), 221–236.

Bozett, F. (1987). Children of gay fathers. In F. W. Bozett (Ed.), *Gay and lesbian parents* (pp. 39–57). New York, NY: Praeger.

Brewaeys, A., Ponjaert, I., Hall, E. V., & Golombok, S. (1997). Donor insemination: Child development and family functioning in lesbian mother families. *Human Reproduction, 12*, 1349–1359.

Brooks, V. R. (1981). *Minority stress and lesbian women*. Lexington, MA: Lexington Books.

Clunis, D. M., & Green, G. D. (1995). *The lesbian parenting book: A guide to creating families and raising children*. Seattle, WA: Seal.

Cohler, B. J. (2005). Life course social science perspectives on the GLBT family. *Journal of GLBT Family Studies, 1*(1), 69–95.

Elder, G. H., Jr., & Shanahan, M. J. (2006). The life course and human development. In R. E. Lerner (Ed.), *Theoretical models of human development* (pp. 665–715), Vol. 1 in William Damon (Series Ed.), *The handbook of child psychology* (6th ed.). New York, NY: Wiley.

Fitzgerald, B. (1999). Children of lesbian and gay parents: A review of the literature. *Marriage and Family Review, 29*, 57–75.

Fitzgerald, T. J. (2010). Queerspawn and their families: Psychotherapy with LGBTQ families. *Journal of Gay and Lesbian Mental Health, 14*, 155–162.

Garner, A. (2004). *Families like mine: Children of gay parents tell it like it is*. New York, NY: HarperCollins.

Gartrell, N., Deck, A., Rodas, C., Peyser, H., & Banks, A. (2005). The National Lesbian Family Study: 4. Interviews with the 10-year-old children. *American Journal of Orthopsychiatry, 75*, 518–524.

Gershon, T. D., Tschann, J. M., & Jemerin, J. M. (1999). Stigmatization, self-esteem, and coping among the adolescent children of lesbian mothers. *Journal of Adolescent Health, 24*, 437–445.

Gillis, J. R. (1998). Cultural heterosexism and the family. In C. J. Patterson, & A. R. D'Augelli (Eds.), *Lesbian, gay, and bisexual identities in families: Psychological perspectives* (pp. 249–269). London, UK: Oxford University Press.

Goldberg, A. E. (2007a). (How) does it make a difference? Perspectives of adults with lesbian, gay, and bisexual parents. *American Journal of Orthopsychiatry, 77*, 550–562.

Goldberg, A. E. (2007b). Talking about family: Disclosure practices of adults raised by lesbian, gay, and bisexual parents. *Journal of Family Issues, 28*, 100–131.

Goldberg, A. E. (2010). *Lesbian and gay parents and their children: Research on the family life cycle*. Washington, DC: American Psychological Association.

Golombok, S., Perry, B., Burston, A., Murray, C., Mooney-Somers, J., Stevens, M., & Golding, J. 2003. Children with lesbian parents: A community study. *Developmental Psychology, 39*, 20–33.

Golombok, S., Spencer, A., & Rutter, M. (1983). Children in lesbian and single-parent households: Psychosexual and psychiatric appraisal. *Journal of Child Psychology and Psychiatry, 24*, 551–572.

Golombok, S., Tasker, F., & Murray, C. (1997). Children raised in fatherless families from infancy: Family relationships and the socioemotional development of children of lesbian and single heterosexual mothers. *Journal of Child Psychology and Psychiatry, 38*, 783–791.

Gottman, J. S. (1990). Children of gay and lesbian parents. In F. W. Bozett & M. B. Sussman (Eds.), *Homosexuality and family relations* (pp. 177–196). New York, NY: Haworth Press.

Green, R., Mandel, J. B., Hotvedt, M. E., Gray, J., & Smith, L. (1986). Lesbian mothers and their children: A comparison with solo parent heterosexual mothers and their children. *Archives of Sexual Behavior, 15*, 167–184.

Herek, G. M. (2006). Legal recognition of same-sex relationships in the United States: A social science perspective. *American Psychologist, 61*, 607–621.

Kirby, D. (1998, June 7). The second generation. *New York Times.* Retrieved from http://query.nytimes.com/gst/fullpage.html?res=950CE1D91E3BF934A35755C0A96E958260

Kosciw, J. G., & Diaz, E. M. (2008). *Involved, invisible, ignored: The experiences of lesbian, gay, bisexual, and transgender parents and their children in our nation's K-12 schools.* New York, NY: Gay, Lesbian and Straight Education Network.

Kranz, K. C., & Daniluk, J. C. (2006). Living outside of the box: Lesbian couples with children conceived through the use of anonymous donor insemination. *Journal of Feminist Family Therapy, 18*(1/2), 1–33.

Kuvalanka, K. A. (2007). *Coping with heterosexism and homophobia: Young adults with lesbian parents reflect on their adolescence* (Unpublished doctoral dissertation). University of Maryland, College Park.

Kuvalanka, K. A., & Goldberg, A. E. (2009). "Second generation" voices: Queer youth with lesbian/bisexual mothers. *Journal of Youth and Adolescence, 38*, 904–919.

Kuvalanka, K. A., Teper, B., & Morrison, O. A. (2006). COLAGE: Providing community, education, leadership, and advocacy by and for children of gay, lesbian, bisexual, and transgender parents. *Journal of GLBT Family Studies, 2*(3/4), 71–92.

Lindsay, J., Perlesz, A., Brown, R., McNair, R., de Vaus, D., & Pitts, M. (2006). Stigma or respect: Lesbian-parented families negotiating school settings. *Sociology, 40*, 1059–1077.

Litovich, M. L., & Langhout, R. D. (2004). Framing heterosexism in lesbian families: A preliminary examination of resilient coping. *Journal of Community & Applied Social Psychology, 14*, 411–435.

Long, J. K., Bonomo, J., Andrews, B. V., & Brown, J. M. (2006). Systematic therapeutic approaches with sexual minorities and their families. *Journal of GLBT Family Studies, 2*(3/4), 1–6.

Lynch, J. M., & Murray, K. (2000). For the love of the children: The coming out process for lesbian and gay parents and stepparents. *Journal of Homosexuality, 39*, 1–24.

MacCallum, F., & Golombok, S. (2004). Children raised in fatherless families from infancy: A follow-up of children of lesbian and single heterosexual mothers at early adolescence. *Journal of Child Psychology and Psychiatry, 45*, 1407–1419.

Meyer, I. H. (2003). Prejudice, social stress, and mental health in lesbian, gay, and bisexual populations: Conceptual issues and research evidence. *Psychological Bulletin, 129*, 674–697.

Negy, C., & McKinney, C. (2006). Application of feminist therapy: Promoting resiliency among lesbian and gay families. *Journal of Feminist Family Therapy, 18*(1/2), 67–83.

Newman, C., Mao, L., Canavan, P. G., Kidd, M. R., Saltman, D. C., & Kippax, S. C. (2010). HIV generations? Generational discourse in interviews with Australian general practitioners and their HIV positive gay male patients. *Social Science & Medicine, 70*, 1721–1727.

Oswald, R. F., Blume, L., & Marks, S. (2005). Decentering heteronormativity: A model for family studies. In V. L. Bengtson, A. C. Acock, K. R. Allen, P. Dilworth-Anderson, & D. M. Klein (Eds.), *Sourcebook of family theory & research* (pp. 143–154). Thousand Oaks, CA: Sage.

Oswald, R. F., Cuthbertson, C., Lazarevic, V., & Goldberg, A. E. (2010). New developments in the field: Measuring community climate. *Journal of GLBT Family Studies, 6*, 214–228.

Patterson, C. J. (2006). Children of lesbian and gay parents. *Current Directions in Psychological Science, 15*(5), 241–244.

Pawelski, J. G., Perrin, E. C., Foy, J. M., Allen, C. E., Crawford, J. E., Del Monte, M., … Vickers, D. L. (2006). The effects of marriage, civil union, and domestic partnership laws on the health and well-being of children. *Pediatrics, 118*, 349–364.

Rivers, I., Poteat, V. P., & Noret, N. (2008). Victimization, social support, and psychosocial functioning among children of same-sex and opposite-sex couples in the United Kingdom. *Developmental Psychology, 44*, 127–134.

Short, E., Riggs, D., Perlesz, A., Brown, R., & Kane, G. (2007). *Lesbian, gay, bisexual, and transgender (LGBT) parented families: A literature review prepared for the Australian Psychological Society.* Melbourne: Australian Psychological Society.

Stacey, J., & Biblarz, T. (2001). (How) does the sexual orientation of parents matter? *American Sociological Review, 66*(3), 159–183.

Tasker, F. L., & Golombok, S. (1995). Adults raised as children in lesbian families. *American Journal of Orthopsychiatry, 65,* 203–215.

Tasker, F. L., & Golombok, S. (1997). *Growing up in a lesbian family: Effects on child development.* London, England: Guilford Press.

Wainright, J. L., Russell, S. T., & Patterson, C. J. (2004). Psychosocial adjustment, school outcomes, and romantic relationships of adolescents with same-sex parents. *Child Development, 75,* 1886–1898.

Wright, J. M. (1998). *Lesbian stepfamilies: An ethnography of love.* New York: Hawthorn Press.

Wyss, S. E. (2004). "This was my hell": The violence experiences by gender non-conforming youth in U.S. high schools. *International Journal of Qualitative Studies in Education, 17,* 709–730.

12

Raising Lesbian, Gay, or Bisexual Youth

An Affirmative Family Therapy Approach

LINDA STONE FISH and REBECCA G. HARVEY

We aim, in this chapter, to detail our therapeutic approach to family therapy with sexual minority youth (Stone Fish & Harvey, 2005). Affirmative therapy for sexual minorities (e.g., Ritter & Terndrup, 2002) is an evolving practice that is being learned as we go by those of us practicing, teaching, and writing about it. To do it well one must question basic assumptions and one's own dearly held beliefs about gender, sexuality, masculinity, and femininity and essentialist notions about identity, desire, sex, and romance. No small task. Sexual minority youth and their families arguably have the most to gain from affirmative theory and practice because they are in the midst of powerful individual identity integration as well as family developmental processes that may well set the tone for many years to come for individual and family functioning.

Our work is based in family systems theory but heavily influenced by queer theory (e.g., Butler, 1993; Sedgwick, 1993; Spargo, 1999), which simply took us where other theories could not. At the same time that the family therapy field was beginning to recognize the ways in which theorists and researchers were marginalizing sexual minority individuals in the literature, queer theorists were challenging the very assumptions that the family field was attempting to embrace. For example, Sedgwick (1993) states, "There are many people in the worlds we inhabit … who have a strong interest in the dignified treatment of any gay people who may happen to already exist. But the number of persons or institutions by whom the existence of gay people is treated as a precious desideratum, a needed condition of life, is small" (p. 76).

Queer theorists (Butler, 1993; Sedgwick, 1993; Spargo, 1999) have turned traditional notions of gender and heteronormativity on their heads and helped us understand "that being queer is not merely an issue of gender identity or sexual orientation. Being queer is also about recognizing the ways that one represents otherness, the unexplored, or the disallowed then, despite prejudice and injustice, insisting again and again that one belongs and that one is gifted, not in spite of these queer differences but because of them" (Stone Fish & Harvey, 2005, p. 4). Queer identity is interesting, necessary, and precious. This is the stance we believe affirmative therapy must take, and it is this stance that guides us as clinicians, supervisors, and teachers of affirmative therapy.

We intentionally use the word *queer* because of Sedgwick's challenge to embrace the preciousness of queer identity. *Queer* is reclaimed from hurtful language and used to embrace our valuable differences. Though we encourage youth to define and redefine themselves as often as they like, the use of the term *queer* as other than traditionally gendered and heterosexual leaves room for all sorts of ways of being. It is this idea that we most hope to pass on to clinicians, for it would be a gift to the queer youth they serve.

Background Review of the Topic Literature: Theory and Research

Psychological study of lesbian, gay, and bisexual (LGB) identity has gone through dramatic shifts in the last 30 years. Originally, it was assumed that homosexual behavior was a mental illness, and researchers were interested in exploring its etiology (Beatty, 1999; Strommen, 1989). As that view ebbed, homosexuality was taken out of the DSM, and research shifted to focus on how gays and lesbians realized, understood, and learned to manage socially stigmatized identities. Focus on sexual behavior has given way to an emphasis on sexual identity. Homosexuality became no longer simply a description of sexual behavior but an "intrinsic social identity" (Strommen, 1989, p. 249). Coming out, as it became colloquially known, was theorized as a process "by which sexual minorities come to stabilize their sense of self in family, community and societal environments which are largely hostile to their existence" (Harvey, 2007, p. 12).

Early research on LGB populations relied almost entirely on the recollections of adult, usually White, European American men who remembered their coming-out process. Out of this research a number of stage theory models were developed that identified the important milestones nonheterosexual individuals had to manage in a series of successive stages that could ultimately lead toward the desired outcome of an integrated identity as a gay or lesbian person. These stage model theories helped to organize the ways in which practitioners thought about the trajectories of the development of mature minority sexual identities. The stage models were helpful in thinking about adult development; but in large part because of the stigma associated with being queer, this early research did not look at the developmental trajectory of sexual minority youth.

Current Review of the Topic Literature: Theory and Research

We are now more firmly rooted in an age of affirmative therapy for sexual minorities (e.g., Ritter & Terndrup, 2002). Rather than theory and research looking toward tolerance of sexual minority status, lesbian, gay, bisexual, transgender and queer (LGBTQ) people and families are ubiquitous, and acceptance and acknowledgment of their lives are on the increase. Researchers focusing on sexual minority individuals are also coming of age. It is no longer true as Boxer and Cohler wrote in 1989 that "the developmental psychology of the gay and lesbian life course is in consequence, largely a psychology of the remembered past" (p. 325). The next generation of researchers (e.g., Diamond, 1998; Dube, 2000; Savin-Williams, 1998) have been able to interview youth while they are in the midst of discovering, exploring, and disclosing their nontraditional sexual identities. And what these researchers are finding is fascinating. Youth are developing more fluid, complicated gender and sexual identities and are disclosing these identities more often and at younger ages than ever before (Boxer, Cook, & Herdt, 1991; Cianciotti & Cahill, 2003; Diamond, 2008; Dube, 2000; Sanders & Kroll, 2000, Savin-Williams, 2005). What once was an internal, individual process of sexual identity development has become more overtly a family systems process, begun oftentimes while youth are still living at home (Stone Fish & Harvey, 2005).

To summarize this new gay teen, Savin-William (2005) states,

> These new teens know they're not straight, and they don't want to be. Most are okay with it. Some are thrilled with their sexuality, but don't see why they must therefore label themselves as gay. Yes, they are sexually attracted to other girls or other boys, perhaps ever so slightly. Maybe their feelings are romantic but not sexual—or sexual but not romantic. That's not bad. It's natural. It gives them an edge, a certain mystery. It sets them off from their peers—and from us adults. (p. 5)

So what is the role of families in the lives of these teens? Research confirms that disclosure of sexual identity to family members, particularly parents, is an important psychological experience and developmental milestone for queer youth, containing both risks and reward (Beals, Peplau, & Gable, 2009; Floyd, Stein, Harter, Allison, & Nye, 1999; Heatherington & Lavner,

2008; Rosario, Schrimshaw, & Hunter, 2009; Savin-Williams & Ream, 2003). Strommen (1989) wrote, "Disclosure becomes necessary because, unlike skin color, or gender, which are overt physical indicators of social group membership, homosexuality is a way of feeling and acting: homosexuals are thus 'invisible' both as individuals and as a group" (p. 249). The more positive a parent–child relationship is in general, the more likely it is that a youth will disclose sexual minority identity to parents (Heatherington & Lavner, 2008). Relationships with family members who know the sexual minority identity of a youth are rated more positively than with those family members who do not know (Beals & Peplau, 2006).

Gender seems to be an important influence in family process regarding disclosure and discussion of sexual identity. Floyd et al. (1999) found that although both parents' attitudes were significant predictors of youths' adjustment, mothers were reportedly closer and more supportive than fathers. Savin-Williams and Ream (2003) found in their research that sons who disclosed to fathers were more likely to be looking for improved connection, whereas daughters reported more likely wanting simply to "get it over with" when they disclosed. "Research on families has generally indicated that fathers are less likely to be told, less likely to be told first, and likely to react more negatively to disclosure than are mothers (Heatherington & Lavner, 2008, p. 330).

Disclosure represents a major opportunity for queer youth to be meaningfully seen and accurately known by their families. It also means they are able to invest less emotional and psychological energy in concealing their sexual identity. Family processes that encourage disclosure are seen as important protective factors for improved self-esteem, well-being, and mental health of sexual minority youth (Beals & Peplau, 2006; Elizur & Ziv, 2001; Hershberger & D'Augelli, 1995; Holtzen, Kenney, & Mahalik, 1995; Savin-Williams, 1989).

Yet these same processes also frequently produce stress both individually and for an entire family system (Crosbi-Burnett, Foster, Murray, & Bowen, 1996). Disclosing while living at home can be a catalyst for some youth to feel more connected to their families (Beals & Peplau, 2006; Savin-Williams & Ream, 2003); however, for other youth, having positive relationships with their families may lead them to be less likely to discuss their sexual identity or to attend social or support groups for gay teens because they may fear they have more to lose (Waldner & Magruder, 1999). For a variety of reasons youth may find that disclosure is not important or desired, not the least of which is that it could be unsafe precisely because living at home puts them in vulnerable positions should the reaction of their family go badly. Youth from strong traditional religious backgrounds perceived their families attitudes toward homosexuality as more negative than did youth from less religious and less traditional backgrounds and were less likely to disclose to their families (Newman & Muzzonigor, 1993; Schope, 2002). Green (2000) has disputed the importance of disclosure to families in general. As Heatherington and Lavner (2008) thoughtfully suggest, however,

> family processes may be more important in populations in which the family of origin context is particularly strong and present such as adolescents, rural gays and lesbians from small towns, and people from cultures where family members … are closely tied geographically and emotionally versus in those populations in which it is not, such as adults, urban gay and lesbian couples living far from families. (2008, p. 336)

In our own clinical experience the importance of coming out and the value of disclosure to one's family while living at home varies a great deal depending on how much one has to lose versus how much they have to gain. For those who are close to their families of origin and who have strong geographic, emotional, religious, racial identity or economic ties, there is usually much to gain and much to lose. It is important to consider the likelihood of a positive response and the capacity and resources of a young person to absorb a negative response.

The process of coming out to one's family creates pivotal moments of interaction in a queer youth's life trajectory. Whether the youth chooses to come out, is found out in an accidental way, or is not out, the negotiation itself is memorable. Development is determined to a large degree by what has previously transpired in an individual's life, including genetic predispositions, environmental events, and their interactions. Yet, within any life history, turning points or critical incidents occur that set particular developmental processes or transitions in motion. One of these for many sexual-minority youths is their parent's discovery of the youth's sexuality. (Stone Fish & Harvey, 2005, p. 64)

Understanding the family systems dynamics that influence healthy development for sexual minority youth is vitally important. Having a supportive family optimizes protective factors for youth who face layers of social stigma (Heatherington & Lavner, 2008; Savin-Williams, 2005). We also know that when youth perceive that their parents have relatively accepting attitudes regarding sexual orientation, they demonstrate closer relatedness and greater independence from parents (Floyd et al., 1999). Furthermore, there are still an alarming number of queer youth who are kicked out of their homes after parents discover their sexual identity (Clatts, Davis, Sotheran, & Atillasoy, 1998). Finally, it is increasingly obvious that families affect sexual minority children but also that the disclosure of sexual minority children inevitably affects the family system in ways that we are still discovering (Harvey, 2007).

Larger Social Issues Faced by Topic Population

Marked both by increasing cultural openness, acceptance of nontraditional relationships, and the corresponding backlash from conservative politicians and fundamentalist religious believers, queer youth are subject to all sorts of community attention. Race, culture, region of the country, and the type of community a youth is raised in all have an impact on the individual's level of acceptance and rejection. The school community, the environment in which youth spend most of their waking hours, has a direct and immediate impact on today's queer youth.

The Gay Lesbian and Straight Education Network (GLSEN) have been working on affecting change in our schools for 20 years. Their 2007 survey of 6,209 middle and high school students on national school climate found "nearly 9 out of 10 LGBT students (86.2%) experienced harassment at school in the past year, three-fifths (60.8%) felt unsafe at school because of their sexual orientation and about a third (32.7%) skipped a day of school in the past month because of feeling unsafe" (Kosciw, Greytak, Diaz, & Bartkiewicz, 2010). Furthermore, recent research suggests that rejecting responses to disclosure of sexual minority status increases a youth's marijuana, alcohol, and cigarette usage (Rosario et al., 2009).

Although the general public may, with the advent of the Logo cable TV channel, bisexual chic, *Will and Grace* reruns, the repeal of "Don't Ask, Don't Tell," and the legalization of marriage for same-sex couples in a handful of states, believe that queer youth are accepted, in fact the majority of middle and high schools in the United States continue to be hostile environments. Currently, only 12 states and the District of Columbia have antibullying policies that include sexual orientation. Furthermore, while research suggests that Gay-Straight Alliances in schools help deter bullying and harassment, only a third of students surveyed have these alliances in their school setting (Kosciw et al., 2010).

Bullying and harassment are not the only larger social issues facing today's queer youth. The National Gay and Lesbian Task Force, in collaboration with the National Coalition for the Homeless (Ray, 2006), created a white paper to summarize the research and opportunities for LGBT homeless youth. After summarizing the research, they report that 20–40% of homeless youth identify as sexual minority. These young people are kicked out of their homes or leave because of family conflict. Then, once out of the home, LGBT youth report that disclosure of their sexual identity in foster and group homes is met with rejecting reactions. More than one third of the youth questioned report that they met with violent reactions from staff and residents when discovery of their sexual identity occurred (Thompson, Safyer, & Polio, 2001). So, the most vulnerable queer youth, harassed at home and often violated by the very institutions that are supposed to keep them safe, end up on the streets, falling through the cracks in the system of supports.

Areas of Stress and Vulnerability for Queer Youth

Although all youth face challenges, sexual minority youth face particular stresses that other marginalized populations face and some that are particular to them. The stress most associated with other marginalized populations is the stress of a rejecting community. The stress particular to sexual minority youth is the stress of a rejecting family combined with rejecting communities. Even families with the best of intentions have difficulty, as a result of their own heteronormativity, helping their queer youth navigate childhood and adolescence because they have no road maps. Schools and religious communities are rejecting, clueless, or unprepared, and youth are often left without communities of support to guide them. Furthermore, LGB youth of color face additional vulnerabilities in that they are managing multiple stigmatized identities and risk the loss of important protective family and community connections if they disclose. Researchers have found that queer youth of color are less likely to come out to their families than are Caucasian youth and face conflicts between strong familial and cultural expectations and sexual minority identity (Dube & Savin-Williams, 1999; Maguen, Floyd, Bakeman, & Armistead, 2002; Merighi & Grimes, 2000).

Savin-Williams (2001) has proposed the concept of differential developmental trajectories for queer youth, meaning that the developmental process that sexual minority youth go through is both similar to and different from the developmental process heterosexual youth undergo and both similar to and different from each other's process. All youth face similar developmental tasks, and queer youth face special challenges to these tasks. The special challenges include coming in to self (Stone Fish & Harvey, 2005), coming out to others (e.g., Boxer et al., 1991; Coleman, 1982; Dank, 1971; Henderson, 1998; Herdt, 1989; Remafedi, 1987; Sanders & Kroll, 2000; Troiden, 1989), dealing with social stigma (e.g., Radkowsky & Siegel, 1997), dealing with a toxic environment (e.g., Kosciw et al., 2010; Rosario et al., 2009), and self-acceptance (Owens, 1998).

Research done over a decade ago found that rates of suicide attempts were higher for LGBT youth than for heterosexual youth (Remafedi, 1987; Remafedi, Farrow, & Deisher, 1991; Roesler & Deisher, 1972; Rotheram-Borus, Hunter, & Rosario, 1994) and that these attempts were related to such sexual milestones as self-identifying as queer (Deisher, 1991). Youth most often cited family problems as the reason for their suicide attempts (Remafedi et al., 1991). Although numerous studies suggested that queer youth were at increased risk for depression, anxiety, suicide, and substance abuse because of their experience with toxic environments, upon reaching adulthood most turned their lives around and became psychologically hardy (Elizur & Ziv, 2001). Furthermore, as growing public acceptance of LGB adults occurs, youth have more resources. With the advent of the gay and lesbian rights movement, being young and queer, for some, is not as unsafe as it was a generation ago.

Areas of Strength and Resiliency for Queer Youth

Most queer youth today are much less isolated than they were a generation ago. They see images of themselves in the media, they may know someone who is out, and they have community support by means of the Internet. Boxer et al. (1991) attribute the decreased age at which youth self-identify as sexual minority to this trend. Studies suggest that youth are coming out younger than ever before (Savin-Williams, 2005), and they are often self-identifying before they are in romantic and sexual relationships (Dube, 2000). Disclosure offers the potential of peer and family support that can build resilience within the relationship and offer protective elements that can help youth manage stigma.

A young person's family of origin's affirmative response to disclosure can be very important for the well-being of young adult sexual minorities (Heatherington & Lavner, 2008; Savin-Williams, 2005) though it is likely more important for some young people than for others. Although familial and community support are on the rise for queer youth, we cannot lose sight of the role that heteronormativity still plays in the growing-up process. With that in mind, we continue to be mindful of the strength inherent in the individual who, despite cultural mandates of fitting in, has an inherent sense of identity that soars. It is this spirit that we applaud and work toward nurturing.

Recommendations for Assessment

There are multiple individual, family, and larger cultural variables that meaningfully influence how a family handles raising a queer child. We are organized foremost by our treatment model, which developed through intersecting our knowledge of queer theory and family systems theory. Our four-part model takes what we consider the best parts of both theories to help all families work toward reaching their potential. We believe that everyone who comes to therapy is organized by unspoken rules around gender and sexuality, heterosexism and homophobia. It is not enough to create a therapeutic space that contains a family without also opening space for new ways to think about these organizing principles.

> As therapists, we must remind ourselves, despite how people may appear, that not everyone is heterosexual and that we are all constrained by traditional gender and sexual norms. In order to create space for people to allow themselves fuller access to self and other, we must try hard to close the door on our cultural mandates and welcome the family into therapy without them. (Stone Fish & Harvey, 2005, p. 88)

Treatment ideology and thorough assessment go hand-in-hand. First, at the individual level, it is important to assess the developmental trajectory of LGB youth. All youth face similar developmental tasks, and queer youth face some special challenges to these tasks. We utilize Savin-Williams's (2001) concept of differential developmental trajectories as a helpful assessment tool in seeking to understand both the similarities to and difference between our client and heterosexual youth in their area as well as similarities to and differences between our client and other queer youth in the area.

What follows is a list of questions we ask ourselves about our young clients or sometimes directly to them to assess their unique developmental process. The list focuses on identity, peer and family relationships, and social stigma or support. Though this list is not exclusive, we use it as a guide to help gather information:

1. *Identity*: How are the young persons doing at developing and integrating a gendered, social identity? How do they handle school? What interests them and how do they see themselves in the world? What is their definition of their gender? How do they understand where they fit in a world where binary categories are the norm? How do they feel about their bodies? What kind of sexual relationships are they interested in? Are there other individual variables that get in the way of their competence and agency that we should know about?

2. *Peer relationships*: How are the youth doing at developing deepening more mature peer relationships? How is their different sexual identity affecting their ability to connect with both young men and young women their age? Do they have intimate friendships?

Have they been able to talk with any peers about their sexual identity? Are they sexually active, and if so are they able to discern differences between sexual intimacy and emotional intimacy? How do they feel about their bodies?

3. *Family relationships*: How are they doing at achieving intimacy as well as increasing independence from family? What are specific things youth and/or parents would like to see as evidence of increased independence? How does being a sexual minority affect their desire and ability to establish intimacy and independence in the family? In other words, are they feeling cut off and disengaged from family and therefore more likely to always act independently even when they should reach out for support or help? Or are they feeling embattled and afraid and therefore less likely to try to establish independence from family because the family system is shielding them from larger pressures and stigma? What would intimacy and independence look like for this specific youth in this specific family? How is this youth's sexual maturation being handled?

4. *Social stigma and support*: How are they managing social stigma? What is their experience being picked on in school, and how is it the same or different from the experience of other youth? How do they handle harassment, and how do they handle being different? Do they know other LGBTQ youth at school? How likely is the specific youth to attend an LGBTQ support group? Is there one for the youth to attend?

Second, at the familial level, it is important to assess family strengths and weaknesses that work for and against nurturing environments for sexual minority youth. Although we know how important it is for youth to be known and valued by their families, we are also aware of how difficult it is for some families to accept minority sexual identity. Disclosure, then, is a risky prospect because some families truly lack the capacity to be protective or supportive and will punish queer youth for their sexual identity. How much and who knows, how disclosure occurred and how it was reacted to, are all variables that play into how much support families are capable of giving youth and must be carefully monitored as therapy progresses. Assessment and intervention work together in family therapy, a process we discuss in the next section.

Third, we are actively assessing cultural variables and their influence on families and on youth. Whereas some families live in communities that are affirmative, where school districts have Gay-Straight Alliances, and discussions about LGB people are common and positive, others live in the opposite kinds of communities. Although all families can benefit from therapy, we are more likely to see in therapy families that do not belong to affirmative, accepting communities. In these families, social stigma often permeates the lives of LGB youth, whose family members are complicit or silent on the matter. In our work, then, we begin by creating refuge from the heterosexism and homophobia that still permeate the lives of many of the families we meet with; we also work toward creating difficult dialogues, nurture queerness, and encourage transformation. We detail the stages next.

Our Model of Family Therapy

Creating Refuge

To nurture children's minority sexual identity, we must help families create refuge from the negative messages that children received and will continue to receive about their sexual identity from the culture in which they are embedded. It is not enough for families themselves to carefully monitor what they say; they must work on challenging their own socialization around gender and sexual identity and help their children navigate their worlds. Whenever a family is referred to therapy for a particular problem with a youth in the family, we set up a meeting with the youth alone and we meet with parents alone (Wachtel, 1994) to gather a detailed assessment of their child's developmental history. As we gather information, we listen for typical gender and sexual bias and work toward challenging it in a way that creates ground rules for our work when the family comes in together. For example, if in our initial session a mother said, "Our daughter has changed. She was a sweet, adorable feminine child who was always happy and pleasant but now she is always angry, acts like a man and is never around. I just don't want her to be gay. I don't think this is what God wants for her," we might say, "Sounds like you are worried and you have hopes and dreams for her. How do you think things would be different if she were your son rather than your daughter? Would you expect something different? Would you worry less or more? So you think your daughter is gay. But what does she think?"

We are also using this time to create a refuge for parents who are often confused, afraid of being blamed, and unsure. We want to understand what parents have been through, what they have tried to do to support their children, when they have felt judged, when they felt as if they have failed. We use this time to connect and build relationships with them and to assess their capacity to nurture their sexual minority youth.

Creating refuge is an ongoing process as part of our therapeutic mentality. Often people are aware of and uncomfortable with their own prejudiced beliefs, so during the first few sessions they are on their best behavior. The brilliance of family therapy is that when family dialogue heats up and impulsivity flares, people are apt to share beliefs that permeate their behavior, and therapists are right there to empathically challenge them. Creating refuge from homophobia takes hypervigilance on the therapist's part. It is an attitude that nurtures complex ideas about gender and sexuality.

How therapists create refuge is a nuanced affair, depending in large part on the therapist's preferential way of intervening and on the family's responses to those interventions. One way to help family members fight homophobia is to ask questions about their inadvertent statements around gender and sexual identity. For example:

Mom: I am frightened for him because he is so stridently gay. I just wish he would tone it down a bit. Why does he have to wear these outrageous outfits?

Therapist: What are you frightened will happen?

Mom: I'm afraid he'll get beat up at school.

Therapist: For what he wears?

Mom: Yeah.

Therapist: Do you think that's fair?

Mom: What do you mean?

Therapist: Shouldn't he feel safe enough to wear whatever he wants, to be able to express who he is, to show his brilliant, creative self in his own community? And why does that become his problem that he has to have his mom tell him to tone it down a bit? How unfair that is for you and your relationship with him. Why is it that you have to be clothes police and worry so much about his safety, and then he just gets angry with you and it becomes a battle between the two of you when really, together, we should be fighting to make the school a safer place for everyone?

Difficult Dialogues

Families who come to therapy concerned about a youth's behavior may or may not have talked about sexual identity. Comfort with the topic varies greatly within and between families. In some families, any discussion about sexual identity is fused with discomfort either because they merge sexual identity with sexual behavior or "we just don't talk about these things in our family," or because of traditional conservative family values, or because there are many taboo subjects that are not discussed. In other families, conversation flows freely between some members yet not among others. In yet other families, there is discussion but it is heated and raw, and hurt feelings keep people from resolving conflict.

Family therapy provides an opportunity for family members to engage in conversations in an enclosed space with a referee. Often, difficult conversations become stalled at home because someone leaves the room or takes up too much space or stops listening or is mean. Difficult dialogues, best facilitated by a seasoned family therapist, are interchanges in which families are helped to slowly, tentatively move toward their differences rather than away from or around them. Avoiding conflict by ignoring painful, divisive topics forces such powerful feelings as disappointment, rage, betrayal, and fear underground; stalls relationship development; isolates family members; and generally fosters a less than optimal environment. Encouraging difficult dialogues changes the dynamics in a relationship, and so the people involved in the dialogues change. This change usually occurs in small steps, in interaction, that become part of family communication long after the therapy is terminated. The goal of difficult dialogues it to help family members learn to handle differences in a way that humanizes those different and also teaches them more about themselves.

Difficult dialogues are rarely "coming-out" conversations. They are more likely to broaden and deepen family members' understanding of their and other family members' thoughts and feelings about topics related to sexual identity. More than likely, before coming to therapy family members have had fits and starts in conversation that have been uncomfortable at best and hostile at worse. For example, Stephanie (age 16) thought she wanted to tell her parents that she was a lesbian, and her parents thought they wanted to know what was going on with her and to be supportive but were unable to have a conversation at home that facilitated this level of intimacy. Stephanie's mom, Deb, had seen Stephanie's' Facebook status, which said Stephanie was into women, but had not told Stephanie that she had looked at it. Stephanie remembered, in anger, telling her parents when she was 14 that she was into girls, but neither parent remembers that conversation. And Stephanie's dad, Scott, remembered that his brother, who is gay, told him, when Stephanie was 7, that she was a lesbian, but Scott had not shared that conversation with anyone.

To facilitate difficult dialogue in the therapy office, the therapist has to understand and hold onto three concepts all at once. First, parents and children come to this conversation in different positions. Parent–child hierarchy means that parents are responsible and more accountable and that children crave for and deserves to be loved, known, and accepted. Second, homophobia and heterosexism permeate everyone's positions but to varying degrees. Whereas homophobia may be hurtful to heterosexual parents, for example, it is much more hurtful to their daughter who is a lesbian. Third, individual and relational dynamics make many conversations difficult to have. Whereas Stephanie's mother, Deb, wants to be supportive, for example, any indication that she did something wrong as a parent creates such a defensive position that she stops listening to anything that is said so that she can lick her own wounds and try to regroup. Stephanie's father, then, is critical and blaming of Stephanie's mother for not being able to handle herself and, alternately, blames Stephanie for upsetting her mother.

The therapist takes all these variables into consideration as he or she sits with the family and facilitates difficult dialogues. When Stephanie says, "You never listen to me," and her mother reacts by saying, "That's because you are always yelling at me and being disrespectful," and her father yells, "Let's just listen to what the girl has to say, can't we just do that?" it is up to the therapist to focus on what is important, which is helping Stephanie to be honest and intimate with her parents and helping her parents support her into adulthood. A therapist facilitates this conversation by calmly and ardently remembering this goal. There are multiple paths to the same goal. Here are a few things the therapist could say at this point to help move the conversation forward into a difficult dialogue:

Stephanie, I know it is really hard for you to tell your parents what is going on in your life and I know how important it is for you to share it with them because you so want them to be proud of you and you are frightened that if you share all of you with them, they will be disappointed; so instead of quietly and calmly talking about your life, you start the you-never-listen-to-me conversation so that you don't have to risk their disappointment if they were to listen. So, maybe you can start by talking about that.

Or the therapist could say,

Deb, so how Stephanie talks to you prevents you from hearing what she wants to say. I get it. I wonder, though, as her mother, and the one whose approval she really seeks, I know, it doesn't seem that way at times, but she so wants to be heard, understood, and loved, I wonder if you could let her know how much you really want to hear what she has to say?

Or the therapist could say instead,

Scott, I understand your desire to protect Stephanie from Deb and vice versa, but I wonder if you would be willing, instead, to say something directly to Stephanie about your desire to hear and support her in attempting to talk to you about what is going on, knowing she is frightened to tell you because she is afraid you will be angry with her.

The goal is to keep the conversation moving forward and to help each member of the family be his or her best self in the conversation. The therapist's facilitating difficult dialogues leads family members toward the third stage of our model, which is nurturing queerness. The research on queer youth supports what we all have known for a very long time, namely, that supportive families help sexual minority youth navigate internalized homophobia and dangerous environments. What the research is just beginning to discover, however, is how sexual minority youth are helping family members be more loving, accepting, and tolerant human beings (Harvey, 2007). We call this the gift of queerness.

Nurturing Queerness

Families who avail themselves of the opportunity to explore their youth's burgeoning development find that the integration of queerness becomes an enriching experience. Nurturing queerness goes beyond tolerating differences and works toward embracing them. Queering the family expands its worldview in unexpected ways. Some families begin to question the gender stereotyping that is the basis of their roles and expand their definition of gender, roles, and relationships. Others find that freeing themselves from restricted ways of thinking about gender and sexuality allows them more comfort to be who they want to be. Some individuals take up the cause of social justice for all, whereas others develop a newfound appreciation for their children and/or siblings. And, of course, some individuals do all of the above.

In our book *Nurturing Queer Youth: Family Therapy Transformed* (Stone Fish & Harvey, 2005), we liken this change to the invention of the game of rugby:

Rugby was created when William Webb Ellis was playing in a soccer match and picked up the ball with his hands and ran with it. The plaque that commemorates Ellis praises him for his "fine disregard for the rules of soccer." Imagine being at that soccer match. The players and fans were engrossed in the game and suddenly some guy comes along and picks up the ball. Everyone there had an investment in the status quo; many people really liked the game of soccer; some were thoroughly enjoying that specific match, and some were very good at soccer and wanted to leave well enough alone. Most were probably afraid that changing the rules would mean the end of soccer as they knew it. At the time, they probably were not able to see that there is room for all types of sports that end up enhancing each other. (pp. 173–174)

Nurturing queerness is a therapeutic stance that is taken throughout therapy, but particularly around difficult dialogues. We are overt in this value-laden approach to therapy. Although we learned in our training not to bring our own values into therapy but to attend to the values of the family and work within those confines, we take exception to this principle in our work. We believe that parents should know their children so they can guide them to the best of their ability. When families can embrace different ways of expressing gender and sexual identity and are less focused on dichotomous ways of thinking about these concepts, they allow their children to express themselves at home.

When children are different from their parents, they often receive subtle, as well as not-so-subtle, pressure to conform. When they are unable to conform, they hide. When youth hide from their parents, they do not allow the natural developmental trajectory to occur in which they continue to receive active parenting until they leave home. So, for example, if someone is being bullied at school for acting "gay," that individual might find it helpful to talk with a parent about ways to handle the bullying. If children are hiding from parents, parents cannot do their jobs.

Parenting youth is not just about support; it is also about limit setting. Although no teenager likes the limits parents set, looking back the youth often realizes that there was some wisdom in not putting oneself in situations he or she is too young to handle. When youth hide their minority sexual identity from their parents, parents lose out on the opportunity to help youth set limits that are developmentally appropriate. When youth come out to their families while still living at home, they give their family members a gift. Part of nurturing queerness in families is helping parents acknowledge the gifts their queer youth have to offer. Thus, the youth are opening the family not only to diverse ways of being but also to ways of communicating and keeping parents involved in parenting them.

Furthermore, we have found that queering the family often has a direct impact on some religious families' relationship with religion. To embrace a sexual minority youth's knowledge of self, some parents have to let go of their preconceived ideas about what is normal and healthy. Sometimes, those ideas are embedded in the religious principles they learned when very young and as adults continue to hold dear in their hearts. Religious practice can be quite comforting, yet sometimes embracing queerness goes against religious teachings. What we have noticed happening, many times, is that very religious people have to struggle with how to hold competing principles in their hearts at once. Once they have struggled with this issue by talking about it either with clergy, with us, or with each other or by silently praying about it, they seem to develop a greater relationship with religion and specifically with God. They seem to gain comfort in their faith that God knows the truth and that people are imperfect translators.

Clinical Tools for Nurturing Queerness

Supervisees often want us to tell them the right intervention to use or the right word to say to a family. They want us to tell them what to do. We have found that we are more interested in helping them learn to be with clients. Being an affirmative therapist for sexual minorities is not simply a set of interventions or something to do; it is, rather, someone to be. It is not for everyone. It requires that we question basic assumptions and wrestle with big questions. For example, we may ask our students, "How would you be different with clients if you believed that they were necessary and precious, not despite their sexual identity or orientation but because of it?" Nurturing queerness challenges us to explore our own attitudes, beliefs, biases, and preconceived notions about sex and gender, not in an academic way but in a personal one. We encourage students to ask themselves brave questions about the disavowed parts of their own identity, what they gave up to forge an identity as a man or woman, heterosexual or lesbian, gay or queer person. We challenge them, then, to think about how what they have disavowed affects their relationship with clients who have not disavowed those parts of their identity.

Encouraging personal journeys is not the only clinical tool used to help nurture queer youth. We also recommend that clinicians make it a point to never assume heterosexuality. This stance teaches both straight and queer people important ideas about diversity and also identifies the speaker as a safe person to anyone within hearing distance. We also recommend being curious about where people's beliefs about sexuality come from and asking questions that foster discussion that allows for growth and change regarding sexuality and gender. We suggest that clinicians bring up the topic of sexuality in therapy. Asking respectful, serious questions about sexuality gives permission for people to break silence and take their sexuality seriously. Respectfully clarifying what someone believes assists people to verbalize what has often never been voiced (e.g., "So you believe that same-sex relationships are wrong?") and is a great place to begin a discussion rather than an argument. Last, we recommend that clinicians mindfully develop relationships within the LGBT community.

Encouraging Transformation

We encourage family members to become active in their own communities. Often, language is political and so a little attention to language can prove useful. Instead of challenging families to be activists, we might wonder how they can actively be supportive of their children. Some families take on this mission with fervency and others do not. We routinely ask clients and supervisees how they might use their unique positions as heterosexuals, as churchgoers, as members of clubs, communities, and families, to lessen isolation for sexual minority youth and their families. For some individuals, doing this might mean thinking twice before they assume that someone is heterosexual. For others, it might mean asking questions in their church about how to be more respectful of queer people. It might mean putting up a safe-space sticker or a poster of an openly gay celebrity, or it might mean acknowledging and pointing out bias and discrimination against sexual minorities in their families or at their schools.

We continue to use ourselves and our own unique positions in therapy, in the classroom, and in our communities to actively work on encouraging transformation. For example, after moving to a more rural part of the country, one of the coauthors of this chapter (RGH) learned that in some (perhaps many) parts of the country simply being an "out" therapist and supervisor is a powerful political act that can both open up and close off opportunities, discussions, and interactions. She has learned that transformation must be encouraged in ways that honor regional and cultural dynamics of community. This often means going slower, focusing on building relationships with people who often have not worked with or perhaps even met anyone who openly identifies as a sexual minority. This also means trying to depoliticize what are often highly political interactions by personalizing the discussion and focusing on the relationships involved rather than on political debates and winning arguments.

Conclusion

We have developed a treatment model that utilizes family systems theory to best capture the resilience and strength of families. The clarity of queer theory regarding LGBQ identity enhances our systemic focus and encourages greater growth and development within individuals and between family members. We begin by creating refuge from heterosexism and homophobia that still permeate the lives of many of the families with whom we meet. Creating refuge often includes providing space for family members to speak the biased, sometimes ugly ideas they have grown up believing about LGBQ people. Then we work toward creating difficult dialogues. Out in the open these stereotypes can be challenged, personalized, and their effect on family relationships explored and neutralized through these dialogues. We nurture queerness so that families learn to embrace the positive elements of LGBQ identity and encourage their children to stop hiding and in that way allow parents to continue parenting. Finally, we encourage transformation, understanding that new ways of thinking about sexuality and gender are both threatening and freeing. We want to transform not just client family systems but also ourselves. Transformation requires that we fight the urge to separate ourselves from people who think differently. It is our hope to reach out even when it is difficult, to respectfully start and stay engaged in conversations with anyone who can also be respectfully engaged with us. It is our hope that conversations continue and that all dialogue is in the service of continuing to learn about differences rather than to change opinions. This would be a true gift to our human community.

References

Beals, K. P., & Peplau, L. A. (2006). Disclosure patterns within social networks of gay men and lesbian women. *Journal of Homosexuality, 51*(2), 101–119.

Beals, K. P., Peplau, L. A., & Gable, S. L. (2009). Stigma management and well-being: The role of perceived social support, emotional processing, and suppression. *Personality and Social Psychology Bulletin, 35*(7), 867–879.

Beatty, L. A. (1999). Identity development of homosexual youth and parental and familial influences on the coming out process. *Adolescence, 34,* 597–601.

Boxer, A. M., & Cohler, B. J. (1989). The life course of gay and lesbian youth: A immodest proposal for the study of lives. In G. Herdt (Ed.), *Gay and lesbian youth* (pp. 315–355). New York, NY: Harrington Park Press.

Boxer, A. M., Cook, J. A., & Herdt, G. (1991). Double jeopardy: Identity transitions and parent–child relations. In K. Pillemer & K. McCartney (Eds.), *Parent-child relations throughout life* (pp. 59–92). Hillsdale, NJ: Erlbaum.

Butler, J. (1993). *Bodies that matter: On the discursive limits of "sex."* New York, NY: Routledge.

Cianciotti, J., & Cahill, S. (2003). *Education policy: Issues affecting lesbian, gay, bisexual, and transgender youth.* New York, NY: National Gay and Lesbian Taskforce Policy Institute.

Clatts, M. J., Davis, W. J., Sotheran, J. L., & Atillasoy, A. (1998). Correlates and distribution of HIV risk behaviors among homeless youth in New York City. *Child Welfare, 77*(2) 195–207.

Coleman, E. (1982). Developmental stages of the coming out process. *Journal of Homosexuality, 7,* 31–43.

Crosbi-Burnett, M., Foster, T., Murray, C., & Bowen, G. (1996). Gays' and lesbians' families of origin: A social-cognitive-behavioral model of adjustment. *Family Relations, 45,* 397–403.

Dank, B. M. (1971). Coming out in the gay world. *Psychiatry, 34,* 180–197.

Diamond, L. M. (1998). The development of sexual orientation among adolescent and young adult women. *Developmental Psychology, 34,* 1085–1095.

Diamond, L. (2008). Female bisexuality from adolescence to adulthood: Results from a 10-year longitudinal study. *Developmental Psychology, 44,* 5–14.

Dube, E. M. (2000).The role of sexual behavior in the identification process of gay and bisexual males. *Journal of Sex Research, 37,* 123–132.

Dube, E. M., & Savin-Willams, R. C. (1999). Sexual identity development among ethnic sexual minority male youths. *Developmental Psychology, 35,* 1389–1398.

Elizur, Y., & Ziv, M. (2001). Family support and acceptance, gay male identity formation, and psychological adjustment: A path model. *Family Process, 40,* 25–144.

Floyd, F., Stein, T. S., Harter, K. S., Allison, A., & Nye, C. L. (1999). *Journal of Youth and Adolescence, 28*(6), 719–739.

Green, R. J. (2000). "Lesbians, gay men, and their parents": A critique of LaSala and the prevailing clinical wisdom. *Family Process, 29,* 257–266.

Harvey, R. G. (2007). *Experience of disclosure of sexual minority identity on sibling relationships: An exploratory study* (Unpublished doctoral dissertation). Syracuse University, Syracuse, New York.

Heatherington, L., & Lavner, J. A. (2008). Coming to terms with coming out: Review and recommendations for family systems focused research. *Journal of Family Psychology, 22*(3), 329–343.

Henderson, M. G. (1998). Disclosure of sexual orientation: Comments from a parental perspective. *American Journal of Orthopsychiatry, 68,* 372–375.

Herdt, G. (Ed.). (1989). *Homosexuality and adolescence.* New York, NY: Haworth.

Hershberger, S. L., & D'Augelli, A. R. (1995). The impact of victimization on the mental health and suicidality of lesbian, gay, and bisexual youths. *Developmental Psychology, 31,* 65–74.

Holtzen, D. W., Kenny, M. E., & Mahalik, J. R. (1995). Contributions of parental attachment to gay or lesbian disclosure to parents and dysfunctional cognitive processes. *Journal of Counseling Psychology, 42*(3), 350–355.

Kosciw, J., Greytak, E. A., Diaz, E. M., & Bartkiewicz, M. K. (2010). *The 2009 National School Climate Survey.* Gay Lesbian Straight Education Network. Retrieved from http://www.glsen.org/binarydata/GLSEN_ ATTACHMENTS/file/000/001/1675-1.pdf

Maguen, S., Floyd, F. J., Bakeman, R., & Armistead, L. (2002). Developmental milestones and disclosure of sexual orientation among gay, lesbian and bisexual youths. *Applied Developmental Psychology, 23,* 219–233.

Merighi, J. R., & Grimes, M. D. (2000). Coming out to families in a multicultural context. *Families in Society, 8,* 32–41.

Mohr, J. J., & Fassinger, R. E. (2003). Self-acceptance and self-disclosure of sexual orientation in lesbian, gay and bisexual adults: An attachment perspective. *Journal of Counseling Psychology, 50*(4), 482–495.

Newman, B. S., & Muzzonigor, P. G. (1993). The effects of traditional family values on the coming out process of gay male adolescents. *Adolescence, 28,* 213–226.

Owens, R. (1998). *Queer kids: The challenges and promise for lesbian, gay, and bisexual youth.* New York, NY: Haworth.

Radkowsky, M., & Siegel, L. J. (1997). The gay adolescent: Stressors, adaptations, and psychosocial interventions. *Clinical Psychology Review, 17,* 191–216.

Ray, N. (2006). Lesbian, gay, bisexual and transgenderd youth: An epidemic of homelessness. Retrieved from http://www.thetaskforce.org/downloads/reports/reports/HomelessYouth.pdf

Remafedi, G. (1987). Adolescent homosexuality: Psychological and medical implications. *Pediatrics, 79,* 331–337.

Remafeldi, G., Farrow, J. A., & Deisher, R. W. (1991). Risk factors for attempted suicide in gay and bisexual youth. *Pediatrics, 87,* 869–875.

Ritter, K. Y., & Terndrup, A. I. (2002). *Handbook of affirmative psychotherapy with lesbians and gay men.* New York, NY: Guilford Press.

Roesler, T., & Deisher, R. W. (1972). Youth male homosexuality: Homosexual experience and the process of developing homosexual identity in males aged 16 to 22 years. *Journal of the American Medical Association, 219,* 1018–1023.

Rosario, M., Schrimshaw, E. W., & Hunter, J. (2009). Disclosure of sexual orientation and subsequent substance use and abuse among lesbian, gay, and bisexual youths: Critical role of disclosure reactions. *Psychology of Addictive Behaviors, 23*(1), 175–184.

Rotheram-Borus, M. J., Hunter, J., & Rosario, M. (1994). Suicidal behavior and gay-related stress among gay and bisexual male adolescents. *Journal of Adolescent Research, 9,* 498–508.

Sanders, G. L., & Kroll, I. T. (2000). Generating stories of resilience: Helping gay and lesbian youth and their families. *Journal of Marital and Family Therapy, 26,* 433–442.

Savin-Williams, R. C. (1989).Coming out to parents and self-esteem among gay and lesbian youth. *Journal of Homosexuality, 18,* 1–35.

Savin-Williams, R. C. (1998). *"… And then I became gay."* New York, NY: Routledge.

Savin-Williams, R. C. (2001). *"Mom, dad, I'm gay."* Washington, DC: American Psychological Association.

Savin-Williams, R. C. (2005). *The new gay teenager.* Cambridge, MA.: Harvard University Press.

Savin-Williams, R. C., & Ream, G. L. (2003). Sex variations in the disclosure to parents of same-sex attractions. *Journal of Family Psychology, 17*(3), 429–438.

Schope, R. D. (2002). The decision to tell: Factors influencing the disclosure decision of sexual orientation by gay men, *Journal of Gay & Lesbian Social Services, 14,* 1–22.

Sedgwick, E. K. (1993). How to bring your kids up gay. In M. Warner (Ed.), *Fear of a queer planet: Queer politics and social theory* (pp. 69–81). Minneapolis, MN: University of Minneapolis Press.

Spargo, T. (1999). *Foucault and queer theory.* New York, NY: Totem Books.

Stone Fish, L., & Harvey, R. (2005). *Nurturing queer youth: Family therapy transformed.* New York, NY: Guilford Press.

Strommen, E. F. (1989). "You're a what?" Family member reactions to the disclosure of homosexuality. *Journal of Homosexuality, 18,* 37–58.

Thompson, S. J., Safyer, A. W., & Polio, D. E. (2001). Differences and predictors of family reunification among subgroups of runaway youths using shelter services. *Social Work Research, 25*(3), 163–172.

Troiden, R. R. (1989). The formation of homosexual identities. *Journal of Homosexuality, 17,* 43–73.

Wachtel, E. (1994). *Treating troubled children and their families.* New York, NY: Guilford Press.

Waldner, L. K., & Magruder, B. (1999). Coming out to parents: Perceptions of family relations, perceived resources, and identity expression as predictors of identity disclosure for gay and lesbian adolescents. *Journal of Homosexuality, 37,* 83–100.

13

Supporting Transgender Youth and Their Families in Therapy

Facing Challenges and Harnessing Strengths

DEBORAH COOLHART

Transgender adults and youth have a unique dependence on therapists to obtain the medical treatments they need to live life expressing their affirmed gender. Also, as families adjust to their transgender member's gender identity, they may benefit specifically from the assistance of family therapists. Despite this need for therapeutic services, many therapists lack the training that is necessary to sensitively serve transgender and transsexual clients (Coolhart, Provancher, Hager, & Wang, 2008; Lev, 2004). Erich, Boutté-Queen, Donnelly, and Tittsworth's (2007) study found that only 24% of social workers surveyed felt their education prepared them "moderately well" to work with the transgender community, whereas 35% reported their education did not prepare them well and 33% reported they were not prepared at all to work with the transgender community. Families in the process of understanding their transgender youth's gender identity may seek therapy for a number of reasons. Families may be trying to gain understanding of their child's identity, wondering if they should be trying to change the behavior, or seeking support, advocacy, or advice as they take steps in actualizing their child's gender identity (LGBT Vanderburgh, 2009). Consider the following two families that may walk into the office of a family therapist.

"Steven," a 7 year old who was assigned a male gender at birth, has been secretly dressing in his mother's clothing and getting into her makeup. Upon discovering her child's behavior, Steven's mother reacted with shock and disapproval, which resulted in Steven feeling ashamed and in tears. Steven's mother talked with him about why he was dressing in her clothing, and Steven replied, "Because I want to be a girl. That's how I feel on the inside." Steven's mother sought the assistance of a family therapist to help Steven sort through his gender "confusion."

"Julie," a 15 year old who was assigned a female gender at birth, has always hated wearing dresses and has been known as a tomboy, which her parents supported throughout Julie's childhood. As Julie has progressed into puberty, she has become increasingly uncomfortable with her body, wearing more and more layers of baggy clothing and avoiding swimsuits. Her parents have been concerned about her body image and self-esteem and have been trying to assure Julie that she is a pretty girl who should be proud of her body. After several months of feeling nagged by her parents, Julie has disclosed to them that she is transgendered and that she is really a boy. Her parents suspected that Julie might be a lesbian and were trying to come to terms with that; however, they have no real experience with or knowledge of transgendered identities. They sought family therapy for assistance in figuring out what to do.

When parents dream about their children's futures, they often think about successful careers, good health, happy marriages, and grandchildren. Part of this dream, though not often explicitly articulated, is that children will also assume gender roles that fall within society's norms and that children will be heterosexual. Although success and happiness are certainly possible for transgender children, parents may not initially believe this to be the case. Parents may believe that if their child is transgender, their child's life will be filled with pain, humiliation, harassment, isolation, discrimination, and potentially violence. Thus it is not unusual for parents to discourage gender-nonconforming behavior, react negatively to their child's transgender identity, and sometimes verbally and/or physically abuse their child because of gender nonconformity (Grossman, D'Augelli, Howell, & Hubbard, 2005). In addition, parents adjusting to their child's transgender identity may experience feelings of anxiety, embarrassment, worry, anger, concern, denial, grief, shame, self-blame, disappointment, loss, confusion, and fear for their child's safety (Brill & Pepper, 2008; Cooper, 1999; Lev, 2004; Rosenberg, 2002). In the midst of navigating this complex experience, families often seek the assistance of family therapists to help regain feelings of stability and direction. The mother of 7-year-old Steven may hope a therapist can help Steven forget about his desires to be a girl and become comfortable with his maleness so the family can go back to how things were before the discovery of the gender variance. The parents of 15-year-old Julie may hope a therapist can help them understand their child and make the right decisions to support her (or his) healthy development into adulthood.

Often therapists themselves are anxious or uncertain when a family such as one of the aforementioned walks into their practice, and they feel underprepared to assist these families. In addition to the common lack of therapist training in working with transgender adults, therapists are often uneducated about working with transgender youth specifically (Brill & Pepper, 2008). The therapeutic and medical needs of transgender youth are quite controversial within the field of transgender health care (Lev, 2004), making it even more important for therapists to be aware of the issues that are unique to working with this population. Therefore, the purpose of this chapter is to provide therapists with a framework for understanding transgender youth, awareness of the specific challenges faced by their families, and knowledge of interventions to help them uncover the unique strengths that can be discovered within families that have the courage to challenge the societal construct of gender.

Basic Concepts and Terminology

To understand gender variance and transgender youth, it is important to differentiate between two often confused concepts: gender identity and sexual orientation. *Gender identity* is one's "deep inner feelings of gender, regardless of anatomy" (Brill & Pepper, 2008, p. 13), or one's sense of self as a gendered being, usually as a female or male. People are assigned a female or male gender at birth based on the physical appearance of their genitals. This assigned gender often matches a person's internal sense of gender identity (i.e., a person assigned a female gender at birth develops a female gender identity). For transgender youth, assigned gender does not typically match gender identity. Thus, a person's internal sense of gender may be male, female, both, or neither regardless of what gender was assigned at birth. *Sexual orientation* refers to a person's sexual preference and emotional attraction (Lev, 2004). It describes the gender or genders a person is drawn to romantically, rather than how one experiences one's own gender (gender identity).

Although gender identity and sexual orientation are distinct and separate concepts, they are interrelated. In order to define one's sexual orientation (i.e., bisexual, lesbian, gay, or heterosexual), one must first locate oneself with regard to gender. For example, a person must first experience the self as male and as someone who happens to be attracted to males to be able to define himself as gay. Some transgender individuals undergo gender transition (from female to male or vice versa), which may include a shift in the perception of their sexual orientation (Coolhart et al., 2008). For example, a person assigned a female gender at birth who is attracted to females would likely be perceived as a lesbian before gender transition. However, as the individual transitions to a male gender presentation, he would be perceived as heterosexual. This newly perceived heterosexuality has implications for the person; for example, he may experience a decreased feeling of connection in the lesbian, gay, bisexual, and transgender (LGBT) communities. Conversely, a person assigned a female gender at birth who is attracted to males would be perceived as a gay male upon gender transition. Thus, some transgender people may enter into a new experience with homophobia upon gender transition (Lev, 2004).

It is also important to understand the distinction between the terms *transgender* and *transsexual*. *Transgender* is an umbrella term that is used to broadly describe people who are gender variant and do not fit into the traditionally defined gender dichotomy as male or female. The concept of transgender includes, but is not limited to, such gender expressions as *genderbender, gender outlaw, genderqueer, drag king, drag queen, androgyny, two-spirit, cross-dresser,* and *transsexual* (Carroll, Gilroy, & Ryan, 2002; Cole, Denny, Eyler, & Samons, 2000; Lev, 2004). Transsexuals, though falling under the transgender umbrella, more specifically believe that "their physical bodies do not represent their true sex" (Lev, 2004, p. 400). Transsexuals often wish to take steps to alter their physical appearance and physical bodies to more accurately reflect how they experience their gender identity internally. Typically, this gender transition is either from male to female (MTF) or female to male (FTM). Transsexuals may choose to pursue various options in gender transition, including adopting clothing and mannerisms that match their gender identity, undergoing hormone treatment and surgeries, and changing names; or they may choose not to pursue such options. There is no one right way to transition genders; rather, doing so is a process that is unique to each individual (Coolhart, Baker, Farmer, Melhaney, & Shipman, in press). Finally, for the purposes of this chapter, the term *cisgender* will be used to describe people who are not transgender. Cisgender people have a gender identity that matches the gender assigned at birth.

Development of Transgender Identity

Kohlberg's (1966) foundational theory of gender constancy involves three steps in the formation of gender identity development, which he proposed happens in the preschool years. The first stage is gender identity, in which children begin to understand themselves as a gendered person ("I am a boy"). The second stage is gender stability, in which children gain the understanding that "I will always be a boy and grow up to be a man." The third stage is gender consistency, where children realize, "I cannot change my sex. Even if I wear a dress, I will still be a boy." Although Kohlberg's (1966) theory was intended to describe the experiences of cisgender children, it also applies to transgender children, who also experience gender identity development during the preschool years. Transgender children experience Kohlberg's gender identity, though their inner experience of self does not match the messages they are being given by those around them. The transgender child may be having the internal experience of "I am a boy" while the people around the child are saying, "You are a girl." Therefore, the experiences of gender stability and gender consistency can be quite distressing for transgender children when they learn that their physical bodies will not change and that they will grow up to be their assigned gender, which does not match their internal sense of gender identity.

Brill and Pepper (2008) suggest that a child's transgender identity can be expressed as early as when the child learns to speak. During these preschool years, transgender children may verbally express their internal sense of gender, dress up in clothes that reflect their gender identity, or try to change their name to reflect their gender identity. Often parents "correct" young children about gender and disapprove of cross-gender expressions. Therefore, children learn to bury their transgender identity and may feel shame about it (Brill & Pepper, 2008). Stone Fish and Harvey (2005) discuss "gender shame" happening in three stages. First, children are socialized to control their impulses that conflict with the cultural mandates of gender. This may happen when a parent tells a child that he or she cannot or should not act on impulses of gender-variant behavior. For example, 7-year-old Steven's mom tells him he cannot dress in her clothes and should not want to; thus, Steven learns that he (she) is wrong for having this desire. The second stage in Stone Fish and Harvey's (2005) gender shame happens as humiliation is experienced when the child does not conform to gender mandates. For example, this humiliation for Steven happens when his (her) cousins tease him (her) about dressing in his (her) mother's clothes, using such hurtful gender slurs as "sissy" and "fag." This experience leads Steven to the third stage of gender shame, where he (she) learns to silence those parts that are different.

This gender shame can be devastating for transgender youth because it often pushes their true sense of a gendered self deep within. In my clinical experience, transgender clients of all ages recall specific painful childhood experiences in the gender-shame process and then describe the difficult years that followed as they tried to hide who they really were. This internal dissonance causes psychological distress, often lending itself to the development of such psychological symptoms as rage, depression, low self-esteem, self-neglect, social anxiety, and self-harming behaviors (Brill & Pepper, 2008; Coolhart et al., 2008). Although the most common time for a transgender identity to develop is in early childhood, transgender identities may emerge in prepubescent and adolescent years (Brill & Pepper, 2008). During this time, hormonal changes are happening in transgender youths' bodies, which may feel unnatural because they do not match their internal sense of gender.

Families Requesting Reorientation Therapy

Some families with transgender youth seek therapy to change their child's cross-gender behavior. For example, the mother of 7-year-old Steven may bring him to therapy saying, "My son seems to think he is a girl and has been dressing in my clothes. I want you to help him understand that he is a boy and that the behavior needs to stop." Historically, models of therapy have been utilized to "cure" homosexual or transsexual people, claiming to make individuals heterosexual or cisgender. These therapies have been called *reparative, conversion, aversion*, and *reorientation* therapies, and the techniques utilized are often based largely in religious conversion and prayer (Serovich et al., 2008). These therapies are based on the idea that there is something fundamentally wrong with LGBT identities. This author strongly opposes this assumption and asserts that the pathology associated with LGBT identities is located in the societal constructions that privilege heterosexuality and cisgenderism. These social constructs create a system of prejudice, discrimination, and oppression of LGBT people. In other words, the problem lies within the system of domination, not in the LGBT individuals themselves.

Some studies have examined the effects of sexual reorientation therapies on clients and suggest serious negative consequences on the mental health of these individuals. For example, after participation in reorientation therapies, LGBT clients have reported depression, low self-esteem, suicidal ideation, suicide attempts, difficulty sustaining relationships, sexual dysfunction, social and interpersonal harm, loss of social support, and spiritual harm (Haldeman, 2002; Shidlo & Schroeder, 2002). Reparative therapies for sexual orientation have been deemed unethical by several professional organizations, among them the American Psychiatric Association, American Psychological Association, American Counseling Association, American Academy of Pediatrics, American Medical Association, National Association of Social Workers, and Royal College of Nursing (Bright, 2004; Serovich et al., 2008). Although the American Association of Marriage and Family Therapy has not addressed the ethical appropriateness of reparative therapy, the organization has stated, "The association does not consider homosexuality a disorder that requires treatment, and as such, we see no basis for such therapy" (AAMFT, 2009).

The literature on the effects of reparative therapy has almost exclusively focused on gay men (Bright, 2004) and rarely directly addressed transgender people. However, it is likely that reorientation therapies with transgender people would produce similar negative effects. Whether the reorientation therapy is attempting to change the gender identity or the sexual orientation, it is devaluing and pathologizing a central piece of a person's self. When people are taught that what they are is wrong or bad, it is not surprising that there are negative mental health consequences. Parents' disapproval of a cross-gender identity will not change the identity (Brill & Pepper, 2008). Sending consistent messages of rejection to children will, however, change the child's experience of its identity. "Over time the child's cross-gender identity may go underground and become internalized with shame" (Brill & Pepper, 2008, p. 16).

Because of the considerable risks for the mental health and well-being of young people as well as considerations of oppressive social structures and social justice, therapists should not attempt to change youths' gender identities. When parents request reorientation therapy, therapists can discuss the risks of and ideologies behind reorientation therapies and explore parents' reasons for desiring reorientation therapy. Therapists can then encourage families to engage in trans-affirmative therapy with a willingness to respectfully work within the family's boundaries and belief systems (i.e., religion). For example, when discussing with 7-year-old Steven's mother why she desired reorientation therapy, it was discovered that she has been keeping Steven's cross-dressing behavior a secret from her husband, Steven's father. She expressed concern that her husband would reject their child, largely based on their religious beliefs that do not support homosexuality or transgenderism. With this family, there are many ways in which a therapist can begin affirmative therapy; most likely, it will be vital to engage the father in therapy sessions. Through talking with the parents, the therapist can learn more about the family's religious beliefs, seeking to discover therein elements that could be used to strengthen the family in this complex period of growth. The therapist can help the parents understand that Steven is the same child they have always known regardless of gender and can explore where within the family's belief system there exists space for growth toward the parents' increased acceptance of their child's gender variance.

Affirmative Therapy With Transgender Youth and Their Families

Most families seeking therapy after the discovery or disclosure of their child's gender variance do not specifically desire reorientation therapy. Some families, though uncomfortable with their child's gender identity, simply want guidance on how to deal with such a complex issue. Other families are accepting of their child's transgender identity, though seek therapy because they desire assistance in effectively supporting their child's gender transition or hope to obtain recommendations for medical gender transition treatments. Family therapists faced with transgender youth and their families have enormous potential to normalize, validate, and facilitate healing and growth in these families. Affirmative therapy with transgender youth and their families involves several unique tasks and roles for the therapist: supporting gender variance, educating parents, supporting the parents' process, exploring gender transition options, acting as a therapist advocate, connecting family to support systems, and being a trans-affirmative therapist.

Supporting Gender Variance

Gender-variant youth will undoubtedly come to therapy having experienced a broad range of disapproval of and opposition to how they experience and express gender. The negative messages these youth receive from parents, siblings, peers, neighbors, teachers, media, and so on can be very damaging to a youth's sense of self-esteem. Therefore, one role of the therapist is to balance these negative messages by delivering positive messages about gender variance and presenting an ideology that is grounded in "respect for the diversity of human gender expression" (Lev, 2004, p. 185). Therapists can respect a youth's internal sense of gender by finding out if the youth has a name he or she prefers that reflects gender identity and, if so, adopting the use of this preferred name as well as the youth's preferred pronouns (Coolhart et al., in press). In addition, therapists can invite the youth to use the therapy room to fully express gender identity by, for instance, dressing in the clothing of the affirmed gender. This "gender-variant safe zone" can be particularly important if the young person does not have other such safe spaces; if, for example, the youth is not currently being allowed to wear preferred clothing at home or at school. Therapists working with transgender youth and their families must use their knowledge of family systems and their clinical skills to determine how to most sensitively and effectively support a youth's gender variance within his or her presenting family. With some families, it may initially be necessary to spend time separately with the youth and parents because their tolerance for supporting gender variance may differ. For example, with 7-year-old Steven's family, the parents may not be able to tolerate, at least right away, being a part of discussions that include normalizing and validating their child's gender expression. Initial sessions with parents may need to focus heavily on supporting their process (see the later section "Supporting the Parents' Process") while only introducing the idea of respecting and supporting their child's gender identity. However, the therapist can meet alone with Steven to gain a better understanding of the youth's historical and current understanding of gender identity. Steven may express a preference for female pronouns, may want a feminine name of Jennifer, and may describe feeling this way ever since he (she) can remember. Respecting these expressions, the therapist can adopt the use of feminine pronouns and the name Jennifer while alone with Jennifer and begin to introduce these practices to the parents when appropriate.

It sometimes takes parents considerable time to adjust to new names and pronouns, particularly depending on their level of support for the gender variance, though therapists can gently explain the importance of these practices for the well-being of their child. Therapists can assist young people in expressing how hurtful it is each time their parent uses their assigned name and pronouns because youth often feel as though the assigned name and pronouns deny who they really are. Therapists can begin to coach parents to use language that respects their child's gender identity, correcting the parents when they use the assigned name and pronouns, for example, though doing so is sometimes uncomfortable. Clearly, this directive technique should be balanced with a strong therapeutic alliance built with the parents. Although supporting gender variance is an important goal, supporting the family as a whole is equally important. Thus, the therapeutic task challenges parents to look at their child's gender variance in a new way while at the same time they feel supported by the therapist in their own process of acceptance. Furthermore, therapists can assure youth that it is normal for parents to go through a time of adjustment, that parents typically become more accepting over time, and that they should not give up on their parents.

Other parents may not be as opposed to their child's gender variance, as in the case of 15-year-old Julie (Randal). Thus, with Julie's family, it may not initially be necessary to have separate sessions to discuss supporting gender variance. Julie may feel safe with her parents as she describes a painful memory about being 5 years old and being told that she had to wear a shirt outside because she was a girl. Julie may disclose feeling like a boy since early childhood, a preference for male pronouns and the name Randal, and a history of internal struggle around trying to fit into the female gender he was told to fit into. Randal's parents may be able to somewhat quickly begin using preferred names and pronouns and to explore with Randal the ways in which their behavior could be more supportive of Randal's gender expression.

Finally, it may be important to include in therapy siblings and other integral family members (e.g., grandparents) to work toward the goal of supporting gender variance. The idea is to strengthen the family as much as possible, helping the members work as a unit to deal with the transgender identity. For example, while Randal's parents are openly working toward full support of Randal's gender identity, Randal's 16-year-old brother is struggling with Randal's transgender identity. Whereas he was comfortable with the idea of a lesbian sister, he is now uncomfortable with that sister "becoming a boy" and is using derogatory names to describe Randal to his friends. Under these circumstances, it would be important for Randal's brother to engage in the therapy so that he can be exposed to an ideology that respects diverse gender expression, explore his own beliefs and emotions about gender variance, and understand the effects of his behaviors on his family members.

Educating Parents

One of the most important tasks for therapists working with the parents of transgender youth is to assist in educating them about transgenderism and transsexuality (Coolhart et al., in press; Rosenberg, 2002). Parents of transgender youth come to therapy demonstrating varying levels of support for their child's gender identity, and it is important for parents to understand that transgender youth with supportive families have the most positive outcomes for future health and well-being (Brill & Pepper, 2008). Studies indicate that parental rejection of LGBT youth may have such long-term consequences as low self-esteem and self-worth, increased rates of suicide attempts, higher levels of depression and anxiety, increased use of illegal drugs, increased engagement in unprotected sex, lack of trust, problems with knowing or showing one's feelings, being easily stressed, dissociative disorders, and reactive attachment disorders (Grossman et al., 2005; Ryan, Huebner, Diaz, & Sanchez, 2009). Therefore, therapists should coach parents in sending the most supportive messages they can to their transgender child. In addition, therapists can assist parents in working through their own process and eventually toward higher levels of acceptance of their child's gender identity (see the next section, "Supporting the Parents' Process").

Therapists should encourage parents to learn as much as they can about transgender youth outside of the therapy room as well. For example, Brill and Pepper's (2008) *The Transgender Child: A Handbook for Families and Professionals* is a useful resource for all parents of transgender youth. This book utilizes an affirmative approach to walk parents through the process of discovering that their child may be transgender and assists them in moving "from crisis to empowerment" (p. 39). It broaches such subjects as making decisions about gender transition and disclosure and discusses important issues to be considered in the educational, medical, and legal settings. Brill and Pepper's (2008) book can also be tremendously helpful for therapists working with transgender youth and their families. Because therapists do not typically receive training specific to working with this population, it is vital that therapists educate themselves in order to be most helpful in guiding families.

Supporting the Parents' Process

Although parents differ in their level of support of their child's gender variance, all of them are dealing with, or have dealt with, a variety of challenging emotions. For example, they may be wrestling with anxiety, embarrassment, worry, anger, concern, denial, grief, shame, self-blame, disappointment, loss, confusion, or fear for their child's safety (Brill & Pepper, 2008; Cooper, 1999; Lev, 2004; Rosenberg, 2002). It is normal for parents to experience such emotional processes, though sometimes the way these emotions are communicated to the transgender youth is painful and harmful for the youth to experience. By the time families come to therapy, they have typically already engaged in conversations about gender variance at home. It is often because these conversations have gone so poorly that families seek the assistance of a therapist. Furthermore, because these conversations have included how parents reject or disapprove of a core aspect of their child, transgender youth often have already been damaged by their parents' expression of their process. Therefore, sometimes the most appropriate clinical intervention is to initially have therapy sessions with parents separately from their child (Coolhart et al., in press).

In sessions with parents, the goal is to form a therapeutic alliance with the parents, provide a space where they can be supported in their process, and assist them in becoming regrounded in their role of positive parenting. Therapists can overtly recognize parents' strengths for being willing to work through this difficult process in therapy. Their commitment to grow in the process demonstrates how much they love their child and that they just want the best for their child. In this holding space for parents, they can express their raw emotions and thoughts about their child's gender variance without judgment and without hurting their child. The therapist can validate and normalize emotions and then help parents examine their reactions and beliefs as well as understand how the expressions they use impact their child. For example, in the case of 7-year-old Jennifer, her father can become engaged in sessions with his wife so that in the therapy room he can discuss his initial reactions to his child's gender variance, expressing, for instance, how he does not want a sissy boy for a child or that he believes that his child will go to hell. Clearly, these types of messages would be hurtful for Jennifer to hear; however, it is important for her father to have space to express them because they are his starting point.

Therapy can then explore with Jennifer's father what his beliefs are about gender roles and where these beliefs came from. It is often helpful to validate that society reinforces rigid rules around gender, so it makes sense that gender variance is difficult to tolerate at first because these societal messages have so much power. Jennifer's father can be challenged to imagine what it would be like to reconstruct what gender might look like were he not constrained by societal messages. With Jennifer's parents, it would also be important to examine how religion is informing their reactions, what role religion plays in their lives, and what happens when their religion is challenged. It is often helpful to explore in therapy what religious beliefs or values may be used as building blocks for further acceptance (or at least tolerance) of the youth's gender variance, such as unconditional love or the importance of family. These beliefs may provide space for Jennifer's parents to make an opening for their child's gender expression.

Because transgender youth with supportive families fare better with regard to health and well-being (Brill & Pepper, 2008), the intent of separate sessions with parents is to protect youth until parents are at some level of tolerance of the gender variance. When sessions alone with parents reach a point where parents' expressions of their process are not as hurtful to their child, family sessions should resume so that parents and children can begin to engage together around these challenging issues. Stone Fish and Harvey (2005) discuss facilitating difficult dialogues between queer youth and their families. "Difficult dialogues peel away layers of misconceptions, lies, unspoken knowledge, and damaging interactions to help family members develop new appreciation for each other so that they can love, respect, and nurture what they never did before" (p. 125). Once a refuge, or a holding place, is established for each family member, these difficult dialogues can occur, ultimately bringing family members closer together.

In some families, it is not necessary to work in sessions alone with parents on their process. Clinical judgment should govern this decision based on how parents' expression of their emotional process is affecting the youth. The expectation is not that the communication to the child will be without challenge but that ideally parents are not communicating "You are bad" or "Something is wrong with you." For example, in Randal's family, his parents are struggling to understand and support Randal's gender identity but are not communicating harmful messages to Randal. Therefore, parents may be able to be supported in their process in the context of family sessions. Randal's parents may be able to discuss their fears for Randal's safety and engage in conversations with Randal about how he can keep himself safe (i.e., whom to tell about the transgender identity or how to handle situations in which people discover the transgender identity). Randal's parents may also discuss their confusion about how to change their thinking about having a son instead of a daughter, and Randal can share his thoughts and feelings about how he understands his childhood as a "girl." During this process, therapists should continue to validate the family for confronting very challenging issues and normalize their feelings as part of a process that other families like them experience. When parents are able to engage in conversations about their process in a way that is not devaluing their child's identity, these difficult dialogues can be productive and genuine and can promote closeness in the family rather than distance.

Explore Gender Transition Options

Transgender youth typically express distress and discomfort about living in their assigned gender role. Many of them wish to take steps to transition their outward gendered appearance to match their internal gender identity. When exploring how and when youth should begin the gender transition process, there is no one-size-fits-all approach. However, when it becomes obvious that a youth is suffering because of living in the assigned gender role, it is recommended that the youth be allowed to transition (Brill & Pepper, 2008). There may be reasons for delaying decisions regarding gender transition for some youth, such as youth's confusion or ambivalence about gender transition, lack of support, or lack of psychological resilience (de Vries, Cohen-Kettenis, & Delemarre–Van de Waal, 2006). In many cases, though, it is appropriate to support youth and families in exploring gender transition options.

When youth seek medical treatments to assist with the gender transition process, therapists play an integral role in helping families decide what treatment or treatments are best for them at the time. In fact, therapists function as gatekeepers to medical treatments because most physicians require a letter of recommendation from a mental health provider to begin hormonal treatment. Coolhart et al. (in press) present an assessment tool to assist therapists in making determinations about the readiness of youth and their families for medical gender transition treatments. This assessment tool can serve as a guide through a process that is complex and, for most therapists, unfamiliar. The most common actions related to gender transition that therapists will discuss with transgender youth and their families can be grouped into three categories: nonmedical transition, pubertal delay, and initiation of hormones for the affirmed gender.

Nonmedical Transition

No medical intervention is necessary for youth transitioning before puberty because prior to the onset of secondary sex characteristics, gender transition can be achieved through the use of clothing, hairstyle, preferred name and pronouns, and gender-specific body language and behaviors. This fully reversible gender transition action allows youth to experience the effects of transition in such settings as the family and school before making physical changes that are irreversible (de Vries et al., 2006). Nonmedical transition is also a possibility for youth that have begun puberty in their assigned gender. For FTM transgender youth, this may include binding breasts, packing underwear, wearing a prosthetic penis, or applying facial hair. For MTF transgender youth, this may involve tucking genitals, removing facial hair, wearing makeup and prosthetic breasts, or practicing heightening vocal pitch.

Even though nonmedical gender transition is fully reversible, it can be challenging for parents and in such settings as school (Coolhart et al., in press). For example, Brill and Pepper (2008) suggest that it is important for parents to respond to their child's request to use a preferred name and pronouns, yet that some families are not ready to take this step. In these families, gender-neutral language (i.e., no pronouns) can be used to provide the family with time to adjust while simultaneously respecting the youth's gender identification (Brill & Pepper, 2008). In the case of 7-year-old Jennifer, her parents may not be ready to use her feminine name and pronouns. The therapist can help facilitate conversations where Jennifer can discuss with her parents how it feels when they use her masculine name and pronouns. In the interest of avoiding causing pain to their child, Jennifer's parents can be encouraged to avoid the use of pronouns and gendered language until they have had more time to move along in their process.

Pubertal Delay

As puberty draws near, some youth desire the use of hormone blockers to delay puberty. Typically, endocrinologists prescribe luteinizing hormone-releasing hormone (LHRH) agonists, medroxyprogesterone (WPATH, 2011), or GnRH inhibitors (Brill & Pepper, 2008; de Vries et al., 2006) to suppress estrogen or testosterone production that occurs during puberty. Pubertal delay is not necessarily a first step that inevitably leads to gender transition; rather it can also be a diagnostic tool (de Vries et al., 2006; Giordano, 2008). Although many youth who delay puberty do continue with gender transition, some choose not to pursue gender transition after carefully examining the transition process and all that it involves (Coolhart et al., in press). Some transgender youth may be gender variant but not be transsexual; that is, gender transition may not feel like the most genuine option to best match their internal sense of gender. Some youth blend or transcend gender categories. Brill and Pepper (2008) discuss children who are "gender fluid" and thus do not fit nicely into society's gender dichotomy. They may have shifting feelings of femaleness to maleness and back again or transcend the gender norms, feeling that neither category suits them.

Pubertal delay has multiple advantages, among them allowing the youth, family, and therapist to explore gender with little time constraint (Cohen-Kettenis & van Goozen, 1998; Giordano, 2008). During pubertal delay, youth have time to "try on" their affirmed gender before initiating less reversible treatments, and parents have time to process their child's gender transition (Coolhart et al., in press). Because transgender youth who experience the puberty of their assigned gender often experience anxiety, anguish, depression, and confusion (Coolhart et al., in press; Lev, 2004), pubertal delay may also reduce the youth's psychological distress. A further advantage to pubertal delay is that it keeps the bodies of youth from experiencing the puberty of their assigned gender and developing in the "wrong" direction; therefore youth have more body satisfaction and are more easily able to pass as their affirmed gender (Cohen-Kettenis & van Goozen, 1998; Giordano, 2008). Also, youth who delay puberty may desire fewer treatments and surgical procedures later in the transition process because their bodies have not developed the secondary sex characteristics of their assigned gender (Coolhart et al., in press). Finally, pubertal delay is fully reversible and can be discontinued at any time so the puberty of the assigned gender may begin.

Although the advantages to pubertal delay are many, there are risks, including a widening developmental gap between young people who delay puberty and their peers who are experiencing puberty. For example, such differences as stunted cognitive development that typically occurs during puberty or delaying an adolescent's growth spurt could cause ridicule from the youth's peer group (Cohen-Kettenis, & van Goozen, 1998). However, when puberty is initiated, by either discontinuing the hormone blockers or initiating hormones of the affirmed gender, these risks are reversed and typical adolescent development occurs. These advantages and risks of pubertal delay should be discussed with youth and their families who are considering this gender-transition option.

Initiation of Hormones for Affirmed Gender

As youth progress in gender transition, many of them wish to initiate hormonal treatment that matches their affirmed gender. Youth beginning feminizing or masculinizing hormonal treatment experience pubertal changes that are typical of their affirmed gender. Youth initiating female puberty may experience breast growth, feminine muscle and fat distribution, and softening of skin; and youth initiating male puberty may experience voice deepening, face and chest hair growth, masculine muscle development, and clitoral enlargement. Many youth beginning hormones for their affirmed gender experience excitement and relief because their physical bodies are becoming more congruent with their internal sense of self (Coolhart et al., in press). When initiating hormonal treatment, families should be aware that this choice is not fully reversible. Most of the youth's bodily changes, such as muscle and fat distribution and changes in emotionality and skin, will reverse if the hormonal treatment is discontinued. However, there are some changes that are not reversible, among them breast growth, voice pitch drop, and facial and chest hair growth.

Although families should also discuss the risks of hormonal treatment with the prescribing physician, such related issues as fertility can be discussed in therapy (Coolhart et al., in press). The reversibility of hormone-induced sterility is unclear (de Vries et al., 2006), and youth may have a particularly high risk of never being able to develop fertility if they never undergo the puberty of their assigned gender, even if they discontinue hormone therapy (Brill & Pepper, 2008). Thus, therapy can be utilized to discuss issues related to the potential loss of fertility and to help youth and families recreate future visions of creating their own families, perhaps considering adoption (Coolhart et al., in press). Finally, the long-term health effects of hormonal therapy are not yet known (Dahl et al., 2006), though recent research suggests that this treatment seems acceptably safe over the course of 30 years (Gooren, Giltay, & Bunck, 2008).

Therapists as Advocates

Therapists working with transgender clients may often find that their role extends outside the therapy room as educators and advocates. Transgender clients often exist within larger systems (school, places of employment, etc.) that do not understand or support transgender identities. Therapists can help these systems develop further understanding of transgender issues and therefore assist their clients in being treated with more care and consideration within these systems. In working with transgender youth, the most common system in need of education about transgender issues is the youth's school, given that sensitivity training regarding the unique needs of transgender youth among school faculty and staff is a rarity (Burgess, 1999). Thus, therapists may find themselves called to advocate in the school system, ultimately helping youth in feeling more comfortable at school (Coolhart et al., in press).

In the school setting, therapists may advocate for the following trans-friendly actions: the use of preferred name and pronouns; updating policies and forms; providing training and education for students, staff, and parents; adopting a zero-tolerance policy for discrimination; and allowing the youth to use bathrooms, locker rooms, dress codes, and gym class activities that are congruent with the student's affirmed gender (Brill & Pepper, 2008). Therapists can achieve this advocacy by talking with the youth and family to assess where further education is needed. Then, therapists can take such actions as writing letters of support, arranging meetings with key teachers and administrators, or making phone calls to school psychologists, the principal, or the youth's teacher. Brill and Pepper (2008) provide samples of letters that can be written in support of the youth's gender identity, asking that the identity be respected and treated with confidentiality and that the youth be allowed to participate in activities of the affirmed gender. When therapists advocate for youth in these ways, the youth and their families will likely feel supported by the therapist, thus aiding in the therapeutic alliance and process.

Connecting Family to Support Systems

Being a transgender youth or a family member of a transgender youth can feel like a very isolated experience. However, there are many youth and families out there who are going through similar processes, and youth, parents, and families as a whole can feel validated by connecting to others who share similar experiences. As therapists, it is helpful to know or find out about local resources that may be available for transgender youth and their families (Coolhart et al., in press). Many communities offer social or supportive groups for LGBT youth. Sometimes there are groups specifically designed for transgender youth; these groups may be helpful for youth, providing them with support while they are struggling with their transgender identity (Cooper, 1999) or trying to navigate challenges with regard to school, parents, dating, and other aspects of life.

Parents may also benefit from making connections to other parents of LGBT youth. Support groups or social events can provide parents with the opportunity to talk openly about their child (Rosenberg, 2002) and hear how other parents have handled similar situations. In addition, talking with other parents can aid parents in becoming more educated about transgender identities; ideally, parents will form a network of support outside the therapy room (Coolhart et al., in press). These connections can help parents grow toward further acceptance of their child's transgender identity by learning that their family is not the only one dealing with such issues and seeing that other families have been successful in navigating this experience. Therapists can also encourage families to reach out to support online or by connecting to organizations that organize such events for families of transgender youth as weekend retreats or youth summer camps.

The Trans-Affirmative Therapist

Transgender people are often misunderstood and treated unkindly, and thus typically they experience frequent discrimination. In order for therapists to understand transgender youth and their families, an orientation toward multicultural sensitivity and social justice is important. Therapists should seek to understand clients' experiences of injustice, validate these experiences, and support clients' emotional responses. The therapist's awareness of the societal resistance that transgender people face can also aid in the therapist–client relationship with the family, where therapists can feel compassion for these families for all they are up against and clients can feel understood. Also, it is important for therapists to be aware that the systems in which transgender youth are embedded (i.e., school) may be transphobic environments. As previously discussed, therapists often need to advocate for transgender clients in settings outside of the therapy room, essentially providing transgender sensitivity training to, for example, schoolteachers and school administrators.

Therapists should also have a strong sense of awareness about their own feelings, beliefs, and values about gender variance and LGBT identities. Approaching therapy from a trans-affirmative perspective may be difficult for a therapist who believes there is something pathological, immoral, or abnormal about LGBT expressions and identities. Therapists with these perspectives may consider referring transgender clients to trans-affirmative therapists as the most ethical decision. Therapists with trans-positive belief systems should also be aware of feelings that may arise while working with transgender clients. Because the societal gender dichotomy is so rigid, we all have been socialized to have low tolerance for gender variance. So, even therapists who are open to understanding and accepting varying gender expressions are likely influenced by the transphobic messages that are so pervasive in society. Therapist self-awareness about when these messages surface allows therapists to challenge their own transphobic thoughts in order to continue to provide trans-affirmative therapy.

Case Example

The Jackson family entered therapy for assistance dealing with the gender identity of their 12-year-old child, Jess. Jess was assigned a female gender at birth but identified internally as a male. In the first session, Jess articulated a desire to be seen as a male and for male pronouns to be used when referring to him. In order to respect Jess's gender identity and to take a trans-affirmative stance, the therapist then began using male pronouns to refer to Jess and asked about Jess's name, including where it came from and if was his preferred name. Jess, named Jessica at birth, reported preferring to use "Jess" because it is less feminine. He also said that in the future he may want to change his name to Colin, a name he had identified with for a few years, but that for the time being he was comfortable being called Jess.

Jess's parents, Natasha and Rodney, were accepting of Jess's transgender identity and were willing to support gender transition procedures if deemed appropriate in therapy. They reported knowing that their "daughter" was different from a young age and that he always preferred playing with the boys and dressing in masculine clothing. Although they were concerned about Jess being mistreated as a result of his gender expression, they also reported really just wanting their child to be happy. However, Natasha and Rodney were still using female pronouns to refer to Jess and would often slip and call him "Jessica." As well, Rodney and Natasha were concerned about how they would be accepted by their religious and racial communities. No one in their African American Baptist church community yet knew about Jess's transgender identity. Jess reported some experiences of being made fun of at school; however, Jess was also able to find community at his school in the Gay-Straight Alliance. Jess's biggest concern with school was that he wanted to be referred to as male by his teachers and also that he felt uncomfortable using the female bathrooms and locker rooms.

Because Jess's parents were quite supportive, most therapy sessions were conducted with Jess, Rodney, and Natasha together. Coolhart et al.'s (in press) clinical assessment tool for determining readiness for gender transition was used to guide much of the initial therapy. Through the use of this tool, information was gathered regarding Jess's early awareness of gender and family context, parental and family attunement to Jess's male gender identity, current gender expression, school context, sexual and relationship development, physical and mental health, support, and future plans and expectations. This clinical assessment indicated that Jess's male gender identity had been present since early childhood and had remained consistent. There were no indicators of any other mental health concerns and though having some challenges to face, the Jackson family was stable and ready to support moving toward gender transition. The therapist talked with the family about the different options regarding medical gender transition. Jess was anxious to get started on male hormones, though his parents felt it may be better to wait a while in order for the family to feel more ready. Jess had not begun a female puberty yet; because he did not want his body to develop in a feminine way, his parents agreed to allow him to hormonally delayed puberty. Thus, after several sessions the therapist wrote a letter of recommendation for pubertal delay and referred the family to an endocrinologist.

The therapist also worked with Rodney and Natasha alone for a few sessions in order to process their emotions regarding their child's gender transition. They reported feeling loss, concern for Jess's safety and happiness, and discomfort about having to explain the changes to their other children and extended family. The therapist validated these struggles as well as praised these parents for the strength and love they were demonstrating by supporting their child. The therapist talked with Natasha and Rodney about using male pronouns, which they were willing to do, though it was a struggle to make the change. When Natasha and Rodney began disclosing Jess's gender identity to their extended family, some family members were supportive and others were not. The therapist supported Natasha and Rodney as they engaged in having these difficult conversations and experiencing shifts in these important relationships. Two of Natasha's sisters and Rodney's parents agreed to attend a family therapy session to further discuss Jess's transition and their feelings about it.

When it came to Jess's siblings, his younger sister readily adapted to learning of Jess's male gender identity, though his older brother struggled more significantly. The elder boy was concerned about how he would be treated by his peers as a result. Several therapy sessions consequently included the parents and all three children. The therapist talked with all the family members about dealing with discrimination and how they may be able to utilize the strategies they already had for dealing with racism in dealing with transphobia. Therapy was also used as a place to role-play dealing with these racist and transphobic situations as well as practicing what to say when people asked questions about what it means to be transgender.

There was a lot of discussion around the Jackson's involvement in their church, what meaning their religion had in their lives, and what it might be like to lose the support of this community. Natasha and Rodney decided to begin telling the closest members in their church community about Jess' gender identity. They experienced support from some members and disapproval from others. Ultimately, they were able to stay somewhat involved in their church, though they felt more distant from this community than they had before. Natasha and Rodney talked with parents at Parents, Families, and Friends of Lesbians and Gays (PFLAG) and experienced mutuality there, though they did not rely on this support on an ongoing basis. Instead, they began exploring religious communities that were more accepting of diverse gender identities and sexual orientations. They were able to find a church where they felt supported, that was congruent with their spiritual beliefs, and that had a congregation with a large number of African Americans. As these shifts were occurring for the Jacksons, therapy often focused on providing emotional support through these challenges.

Therapy also addressed concerns about Jess transitioning at school. The therapist set up a meeting with the principal, guidance counselor, school psychologist, and Jess's teacher to educate about transgender identities and to discuss how the school may best handle this transition. Jess began being referred to as male by the school faculty and staff and had a plan with his guidance counselor about what to do if he was mistreated by his peers. Because the school principal was not comfortable with Jess using the male bathrooms and locker room, Jess was allowed to use a single-stall bathroom. Jess was able to transition at school to a male identity and eventually started male hormones at age 14, at which time the Jackson family as a whole felt ready to move forward with the medical gender transition.

Recommendations for Future Research

The unique challenges and successes of transgender youth have been underexplored in the research literature. Further studies are needed exploring what factors contribute to positive mental health outcomes for transgender youth. Studies could explore the relationship between early gender transition (during childhood or adolescence) and the youth's sense of body satisfaction, ability to pass as the affirmed gender, and social adjustment in early adulthood. Although it seems logical that transgender people experiencing gender transition earlier in life may have better mental health outcomes because of experiencing more congruence between the physical body and internal gender identity, this topic should be explored empirically. Research may also explore factors contributing to positive family adjustment to transgender youth's identities and healthy family relationships so that therapists may be better equipped to serve these families.

Conclusion: Harnessing the Family's Strengths

Through my clinical work, I have been inspired by the courage of transgender people, in general, and transgender youth, in specific. Time and time again, I have watched transgender clients trust their inner sense of self, even when the world consistently tells them not to, and take tremendous risks to live a life that is congruent with their heart. The privilege of witnessing this process has been powerful for me personally as well for my work with other clients. As therapists, is that not what we are trying to help people with? To live lives that are the most true to their heart? By making the decision to transition genders, transgender people brave challenges in every facet of their lives. They are the catalysts for change in their immediate family, extended family, school, relationships with peers, work settings, and religious institutions, and society-at-large. In therapy, this courage can be harnessed by families and drawn upon as a source of strength and pride. "Being transgender is one of the most difficult things to be because it is not understood and the binary gender system is so pervasive" (Brill & Pepper, 2008, p. 22). Transgender youth and their families have the opportunity to grow together and learn how to navigate challenging situations as a family unit. These families may, upon facing such challenges and stretching their ideas of love and acceptance of their child, so gain a new understanding of unconditional love, again adding to their bank of familial strength. While families struggle through this complex process, therapists can highlight for families the ways in which they are strong, courageous, tenacious, and bonded.

References

American Association of Marriage and Family Therapy (AAMFT). (2009). http://www.aamft.org

Bright, C. (2004). Deconstructing reparative therapy: An examination of the processes involved when attempting to change sexual orientation. *Clinical Social Work Journal, 32*(4), 471–481.

Brill, S., & Pepper, R. (2008). *The transgender child: A handbook for families and professionals.* San Francisco, CA: Cleis Press.

Burgess, C. (1999). Internal and external stress factors associated with the identity development of transgendered youth. In G. P. Mallon (Ed.), *Social services with transgender youth* (pp. 35–47). Binghamton, NY: Harrington Park Press.

Carroll, L. C., Gilroy, P. J., & Ryan, J. (2002). Counseling transgendered, transsexual, and gender-variant clients. *Journal of Counseling and Development, 80,* 131–139.

Cohen-Kettenis, P., & van Goozen, S. (1998, December). Pubertal delay as an aid in diagnosis and treatment of a transsexual adolescent. *European Child & Adolescent Psychiatry, 7*(4), 246–254.

Cole, S. S., Denny, D., Eyler, A. E., & Samons, S. L. (2000). Issues of transgender. In L. T. Szuchman & F. Muscarella (Eds.), *Psychological perspectives on human sexuality* (pp. 149–195). New York, NY: Wiley.

Coolhart, D., Baker, A., Farmer, S., Melhaney, M., & Shipman, D. (in press). Therapy with transsexual youth and their families: A clinical tool for assessing youths' readiness for gender transition. *Journal of Marital and Family Therapy.*

Coolhart, D., Provancher, N., Hager, A., & Wang, M. (2008). Recommending transsexual clients for gender transition: A therapeutic tool for assessing readiness. *Journal of GLBT Family Studies, 4*(3), 301–324.

Cooper, K. (1999). Practice with transgendered youth and their families. *Journal of Gay & Lesbian Social Services: Issues in Practice, Policy & Research, 10*(3), 111–129.

Dahl, M., Feldman, J., Goldberg, J. M., Jaberi, A., Bockting, W. O., & Knudson, G. (2006). *Endocrine therapy for transgender adults in British Columbia: Suggested guidelines.* Vancouver, BC: Vancouver Health Authority.

De Vries, A. L. C., Cohen-Kettenis, P. T., & Delemarre–Van de Waal, H. (2006). Clinical management of gender dysphoria in adolescents. In *Caring for transgender adolescents in BC: Suggested guidelines.* Vancouver, BC: Vancouver Coastal Health, Transcend Transgender Support & Education Society, and the Canadian Rainbow Health Coalition.

Erich, S., Boutté-Queen, N., Donnelly, S., & Tittsworth, J. (2007). Social work education: Implications for working with the transgender community. *Journal of Baccalaureate Social Work, 12*(2), 42–52.

Giordano, S. (2008). Lives in a chiaroscuro: Should we suspend the puberty of children with gender identity disorder? *Journal of Medical Ethics, 34*(8), 580–584.

Gooren, L. J., Giltay, E. J., & Bunck, M. C. (2008). Long-term treatment of transsexuals with cross-sex hormones: Extensive personal experience. *Journal of Endocrinology & Metabolism, 93*(1), 19–25.

Grossman, A. H., D'Augelli, A. R., Howell, T. J., & Hubbard, S. (2005). Parents' reactions to transgender youths' gender nonconforming expression and identity. *Journal of Gay & Lesbian Social Services, 18*(1), 3–16.

Haldeman, D. C. (2002). Gay rights, patient rights: The implications of sexual orientation conversion therapy. *Professional Psychology: Research and Practice, 33,* 260–264.

Kohlberg, L. (1966). A cognitive-developmental analysis of children's sex role concepts and attitudes. In E. E. Maccoby (Ed.), *The development of sex differences.* Stanford, CA: Stanford University Press.

Lev, A. I. (2004). *Transgender emergence: Therapeutic guidelines for working with gender variant people and their families.* Binghamton, NY: Haworth Clinical Practice Press.

Rosenberg, M. (2002). Children with gender identity issues and their parents in individual and group treatment. *Journal of the American Academy of Children and Adolescent Psychiatry, 41,* 619–621.

Ryan, C., Huebner, D., Diaz, R. M., & Sanchez, J. (2009). Family rejection as a predictor of negative health outcomes in White and Latino lesbian, gay, and bisexual young adults. *Pediatrics, 123*(1), 346–352.

Serovich, J. M., Craft, S. M., Toviessi, P., Gangamma, R., McDowell, T., & Grafsky, E. L. (2008). A systemic review of the research base on sexual reorientation therapies. *Journal of Marital and Family Therapy, 34*(2), 227–238.

Shidlo, A., & Schroeder, M. (2002). Changing sexual orientation: A consumer's report. *Professional Psychology: Research and Practice, 33*, 249–259.

Stone Fish, L., & Harvey, R. G. (2005). *Nurturing queer youth: Family therapy transformed.* New York, NY: Norton.

Vanderburgh, R. (2009). Appropriate therapeutic care for families with pre-pubescent transgender/gender-dissonant children. *Child and Adolescent Social Work, 26*, 135–154.

World Professional Association of Transgender Health (WPATH). (2011). *Standards of care for the health of transsexual, transgender, and gender nonconforming people* (7th version). Retrieved from http://www.wpath.org/documents/Standards%20of%20Care%20V7%20-%202011%20WPATH.pdf

14

Considerations for Assessment and Intervention With Lesbian and Gay Adoptive Parents and Their Children

MARK GIANINO and MICHELLE NOVELLE

This chapter explores life-cycle issues for gay and lesbian adoptive parents and their children as well as ways in which structures of heterosexism, homophobia, adoptism, and racism affect these families. It is estimated that of 1.6 million adopted children under age 18 years, at least 65,000 live with lesbian or gay parents (Gates, Badgett, Macomber, & Chambers, 2007; Goldberg & Gianino, 2010). There is a growing body of research on gay and lesbian adoptive-parent families (Gianino, 2008; Leung, Erich, & Kanenberg, 2005), some of which addresses the lack of scientific evidence regarding child outcomes in these families. For example, Averett, Nalavany, and Ryan (2009) investigated the association between child externalizing and internalizing behaviors and parental sexual orientation and found no association between parental sexual orientation and these behaviors. Similarly, Erich, Hall, Kanenberg, and Case (2009) found no differences in early and later adolescent attachment related to parental sexual orientation. Despite the growing scientific evidence that strongly suggests children of gay and lesbian adoptive parents are not disadvantaged by parental sexual orientation, mythologies and misinformation abound influencing laws and policies that create barriers for gay and lesbian adoptive-parent families (Averett et al., 2009; Shelly-Sireci & Ciano-Boyce, 2002).

What are the questions and challenges gay and lesbian individuals and couples face in their quest to become adoptive parents? What are the social and developmental implications for children adopted by gay and lesbian parents? What are the life-cycle issues that parents and children face throughout the adoption process, that is, from contemplation to postplacement? Does the sexual orientation of the parents matter? If so, when and how? What are some helpful strategies for clinicians to aid gay and lesbian adoptive-parent families throughout various stages of the life cycle? Many of these questions remain unanswered, or only partially answered, offering few guidelines to help practitioners who work with these families. Goldberg and Gianino (2012) note that the experiences of marginalization and stigmatization among gay men and lesbians can have a powerful influence on the development and adjustment of these parents and their children at various phases of the adoption process and the family life cycle. Consequently, the authors write, therapists who work with lesbian and gay adoptive families must be aware of the ways that lesbians and gay men have, as a group, been rejected and pathologized and understand how heterosexism and homophobia shape family members' experiences. At the same time, the authors conclude that there are ways in which gay and lesbian adoptive-parent families' experiences may also be quite similar to those of heterosexual adoptive families.

The purpose of this chapter is to provide a broad overview of assessment and intervention issues in clinical practice with gay and lesbian adoptive-parent families as well as make recommendations for practitioners. We begin by describing the life-cycle issues of gay and lesbian parents and their children at various phases of family formation from contemplation, through the transition to adoptive parenthood, to post-placement. As part of this process, we address some of the current policy issues with regard to domestic and international adoption. We then consider how individual and family identity, disclosure of family form, loss and grief, and school life affect adopted children through varied phases from early childhood to young adulthood. Recommendations for practitioners are made throughout the chapter.

Assessment and Intervention Issues in the "Contemplation" Phase

Factors Influencing a Desire to Choose the Adoption Path

Adoption by gay men and lesbians is an increasingly common social phenomenon and therefore represents an emerging issue for researchers, practitioners, and policy makers. A recent survey found that more than one half of gay men and 41% of lesbians want to have a child, and nearly half of lesbian and bisexual women have considered adoption. Further, gay and lesbian parents are raising 4% of all adopted children in the United States (Gates et al., 2007). Like their heterosexual counterparts, lesbians and gay men are motivated to become adoptive parents for various reasons. Foremost is the strong and abiding desire to parent. Among lesbians it may also be the inability to conceive that informs their choices, in contrast to gay men, for whom adoption may be the first choice (Gianino, 2008). Lesbians and gay men who choose the adoption route endorse a desire to help society while expressing little need to have a biological relationship to the child (Downing, Richardson, Kinkler, & Goldberg, 2009; Gianino, 2008; Goldberg, 2009).

In achieving their quest to become adoptive parents, lesbians and gay men face many challenges. Some of these challenges involve dynamics within the couple itself as well as unique issues for single gay or single lesbian adopters. Although some couples decide to adopt with equal levels of fervor (or trepidation), sometimes members of the couple may exhibit differing levels of motivation that might requires the help of counseling professionals. As described in the vignette that follows, what need to be explored are family-of-origin issues, among other factors, which prevent the couple from overcoming gridlock in their decision-making process (Gottman, 1999).

> Luis and Charles consulted with a social worker in order to determine whether or not they would pursue adoption. They had been struggling with this decision for months with no resolution. Luis was the driving force for the adoption, whereas Charles, who was the oldest child from a large and chaotic family, was more reluctant to become a parent. "I have taken care of kids my whole growing up and now is my time. Why would I want to give it all up?" Work with the couple involved helping them unpack their stereotypes about what adoption would or would not entail, improve patterns of communication within the couple that prevented them from coming to a decision, and develop greater empathy for each other's position. One helpful exercise consisted of the worker asking that over the intervening week between sessions the couple imagine what their lives would be like were they to choose not to adopt. They were to go about their normal activities and simply hold this thought. For Luis, this meant relinquishing his role as the "cheerleader" for adopting; as a result, presumably, Charles would be relieved of the burden of having to "defend" his position. Surprisingly, when the couple arrived for their next visit, it was Charles who conveyed a sense of sadness and grief that they might move forward in their lives without children. The next week they were now to both imagine their lives as if they proceeded with adoption, whereby Luis would not have to continually argue his position. Predictably, when the couple arrived for their next meeting, it was Luis who expressed concern about the loss of freedom and anxiety about the unpredictable twists and turns of parenthood. Through this exercise each partner was able to see the other's point of view while also being able to break out of his rigidified position.

When there are different levels of motivation between partners, it is critical that one member of the couple does not feel coerced into adoption by his or her partner or by the therapist. Work with lesbian couples may also involve addressing grief associated with years of infertility. Elaboration of motivations can be important in identifying potentially problematic or unrealistic beliefs and expectations while at the same time revealing key strengths in the couples' approach to or framing of adoption (Goldberg & Gianino, 2012).

Internalized Homophobia

No one becomes an adoptive parent by accident. Adoption is a private act that requires the assistance of myriad individuals and agencies, giving even a private adoption a very public aspect. Complexity of adoption is magnified when the petitioners are gay or lesbian and, not surprisingly, given their cultural history of marginalization, cultural heterosexism, and oppression (Elze, 2006). Lesbians and gay men may engage counselors in examining their decision to become adoptive parents through exploring a range of issues emanating from internalized homophobia, emotional and financial resources to become parents, and the need for social supports (Boyer, 2007). In addition, influenced by larger structures of patriarchy, gay male individuals and couples may seek counseling to contend with internalized sexism where they may question the appropriateness of gay men becoming fathers (Mallon, 2004).

Despite decades of progress with respect to societal acceptance of lesbians and gay men, prospective gay and lesbian adopters may feel that they are less "fit" to parent than are heterosexuals (Gianino, 2008; Goldberg, 2010). Further, they may feel that gay or lesbian parenthood is damaging to children's identity formation and psychosocial development (Mallon, 2004; Tasker & Golombok, 1997; Wainright, Russell, & Patterson, 2004). In pursuing parenthood they may feel, or may in fact have been told, that their desire to parent is selfish and unfair in subjecting children to homophobia, bullying, and other forms of maltreatment. It is critical that therapists and counselors carefully explore their clients' affects and cognitions regarding gay and lesbian parenthood and try to refrain from assuming a cheerleading role that might have the effect of driving negative stereotypes underground. At the same time, counselors need to assess clients' preparedness for the possibility that their children may be stigmatized based on their family form (Kosciw & Diaz, 2008; Ray & Gregory, 2001). The vignette that follows illustrates internal and external impediments expressed by one prospective adopter:

> A young lesbian, halfway through an adoption information session for gay and lesbian couples, threw up her hands and said, "I don't know if I can do this, I don't know if I can bring a child into our family when I feel like everyone has preconceived notions of what kind of parent I'll be just because I'm gay. I know they're thinking we'll make our child gay, that we haven't got any values, I just don't know if I can do this."

We recommend that counselors share research and evidence-based information with prospective adoptive parents to counter myths and false beliefs that sexual minorities have internalized. They can be informed that much research has indicated that lesbians and gay men are capable parents (Farr & Patterson, 2009) and that the healthy development of their children is well documented (Bos, van Balen, & van den Boom, 2007). Although the adoption process poses significant challenges to prospective gay and lesbian adopters, it is important for clinicians to identify risk and protective factors and to help predict for couples and single adopters areas of challenge and strength (Goldberg & Smith, 2008).

Other Considerations in Contemplation of Adoptive Parenthood

Prospective adopters often face other potential internal impediments to parenthood that carefully need to be explored. For example, one belief is that "coming out" as a gay man or lesbian forecloses parenting options (Bozett, 1989; Gianino, 2008). With growing numbers of gay and lesbian adoptive-parent families, there are many more models for families living integrated lives as both parents and gay men and lesbians. Counselors may also find that gay and lesbian prospective parents present such concerns and stereotypes about adoption as fears about the prohibitive cost or the inability of adopted children to form a successful attachment.

Although recent research suggests that lesbians are open to adopting African American children (Goldberg & Smith, 2009), some White lesbians and gay men may express uncertainty about adopting transracially (Farr & Patterson, 2009; Goldberg & Gianino, 2012). Some White prospective adopters may question their ability to parent a child of a different race and are fearful of piling on issues of multiple identities or inflicting on the child the double whammy of having parents of a different race or ethnicity who are also lesbian or gay. At the same time, the couple may be reluctant to share their reservations for fear of being judged or criticized by the counselor. A careful assessment will need to be conducted to determine the petitioners' willingness and preparedness for adopting transracially. For example, do they possess the resources to socialize a child of color to cope with racial discrimination (Goldberg & Smith, 2009)? Do they have personal relationships with individuals and families who are racially diverse? Would they consider moving to neighborhoods or regions that are more racially diverse? Given the controversies that still surround transracial adoption, how might they cope with potential expressions of resentment from others? Counselors should emphasize that in the interest of promoting a healthy racial identity for their children, the couple contemplating transracial adoption need to consider these questions carefully (Brodzinsky, 2008). Counselors should assume a nonjudgmental stance in order to encourage the couple to explore their own racial attitudes honestly and should help clarify racial and ethnic stereotypes that might arise for the couple as part of their parenting journey. Counselors may gently need to challenge potential adopters to consider their preparedness and to offer support for their decision should they choose finally not to adopt transracially. Roorda (2007) recommends that adoption professionals implement a systematic multicultural adoption plan for petitioners to consider. The essential elements of the plan consist of the following: (a) assessment of their reasons for adoption transracially, (b) exploration of their views of the adopted child's ethnic community of origin, (c) encouragement of building the adopters' reservoir of knowledge about the child's ethnic and cultural heritage, and (d) assessment of genuine relationships with others who share their child's racial and ethnic backgrounds. Roorda (2007) is emphatic that the child should not be the parents' primary source of information about race.

In addition to considering their access to social resources in pursuing adoption, would-be adopters need to evaluate potential extended-family reactions. Some lesbian and gay adopters anticipate a negative extended-family reaction and a general lack of family support. However, in a national study of gay and lesbian parenthood, Johnson and O'Connor (2002) reported that many family reactions of anxiety or upset were temporary and were followed by acceptance. Clinicians should try to help couples tease out whether family reactions express hostility or, as is more common, fear that the child will be stigmatized (Gianino, 2008). Nonetheless, some lesbians and gay men may indeed be at greater risk for lack of family support (Goldberg & Smith, 2008). It is important to assess risk factors for familial marginalization carefully. The following vignette illustrates the need for careful assessment of the reality and their perceptions of family reactions:

Henry and George are an African American couple who hope to marry and raise a family. George, the older of the two, has remained largely closeted within his large extended-family network. Henry, who came out several years ago to his large Pentecostal family, was severely ostracized and will not be accepted back into his family until he repents by renouncing his homosexuality. The couple are pained and struggling with what it means to adopt a child outside of a biological kinship network. The work of the therapy has been to help the couple identify and work through issues of loss and grief whether or not they adopt. If their choice is to pursue the adoption route, they will need assistance in identifying supports within and outside of their biological families. The couple also need assistance in ascertaining their level of comfort (or discomfort) with open disclosure of their family structure and, therefore, their sexual orientation.

Choosing the Path to Adoptive Parenthood: Now What?

There are numerous decisions that need to be made relative to which route to take (i.e., intercountry, domestic, foster care, or public) once the couple has decided to move forward with an adoption. Professionals who assist lesbians and gay men in their decision making (e.g., adoption consultants, child welfare workers, lawyers, and therapists) should encourage their clients to consider such factors as finances, feelings about the importance of disclosing their sexual orientation during the adoption process, and preferences regarding child age, race, ethnicity, and level and type of special needs (Goldberg & Gianino, 2012). As discussed earlier, counselors need to assess the willingness and capacity of the couple to take on a child with "special" needs. There are multiple definitions of special needs children, including those who are African American, older, and in sibling groups (Ryan, Pearlmutter & Groza, 2004). Given the frequency of transracial adoption in the lesbian and gay community, how well are individual and couple adopters prepared for the visibility they will inevitably face as a multiracial lesbian or gay household? For couples who wish to adopt older children, do they understand that the older the age of the child, the higher the likelihood is that the child will have histories of abuse and neglect (Brodzinsky & Pinderhughes, 2002)?

Implications of Being "Out" in the Adoption Process

Despite increased options for domestic adoption within the gay and lesbian community, prospective adoptive parents continue to confront institutional barriers to adoption. These obstacles include actual and perceived discrimination, as well as a lack of information about adoption resources (Brown, Smalling, Groza, & Ryan, 2009). Although the authors contend that adoption by lesbians and gay men is not a legal right, in the best interest of the many children who are awaiting adoption, petitioners should be evaluated on the merits of their character, not their sexual orientation. Practitioners need to be aware of adoption agencies that offer affirming services for lesbian, gay, bisexual, and transgender (LGBT) adoptive and foster parents and families. One invaluable guide in assessing gay-positive agency policies and practices was published by the Human Rights Campaign (HRC; 2007). This resource offers an organizational self-assessment tool in cultural competence with LGBT-parented families that can be shared with families and professionals alike.

After coming to terms with their sexual orientation and choosing to live open lives, lesbians and gay men who are uncomfortable with secrecy may be particularly drawn toward open adoption that may involve ongoing contact with the birth parent during the adoption process and postplacement (Goldberg & Gianino, 2012). Prospective adopters should be encouraged to think carefully about the level of openness they desire. Some couples may be apprehensive about disclosing their sexual orientation for fear of jeopardizing the adoption should they perceive that the birth parents would disapprove of them. Adopters should be prepared for the possibility that they may indeed face negativity from birth parents and to consider how they might contend with such reactions.

Levels of disclosure also need to be carefully considered during the home study process. Mallon (2007) cautions that writing the home study of a same-gender couple as a single-parent adoption could have severe consequences for the petitioners, the agency, and the child. If adoption agency personnel perceive that the home study has been written in an intentionally misleading way, confidence in the truthfulness of the referring agency may be undermined. Wording of the status of the relationship between the members of the couple needs to be carefully framed. For example, will the home study be modified from a "two-parent" family to a single-parent family with a "domestic partner" or "friend"? Given that agencies may send conflicting messages about disclosure, the petitioners will need to locate an agency that best fits their comfort level and, presumably, has successfully placed children with other gay and lesbian adopters.

The legal picture with regard to adoption by lesbians and gay men is a complex one represented by a vast patchwork of state laws. Understandably, practitioners may be unfamiliar with the legal issues inherent to adoptions by lesbians and gay men. Counselors and adopters can be referred to such helpful resources as the HRC, which offers a state-by-state list of adoption laws indicating whether LGBT individuals and same-sex couples are permitted to adopt and whether second-parent adoption by a same-sex partner is permitted. The range of legislation from state to state is dramatic. For example, Florida specifically bars by statute adoption of minor children by gay men or lesbians. At the other end of the spectrum is California, which permits LGBT adoption by individuals and couples as well as second-parent adoption. More common are such states such as Alabama and Delaware, which offer a hybrid approach. For example, they permit adoption by LGBT individuals and do not specifically prohibit adoption by the couple and second-parent adoption. However, HRC (2010) cautions, many of these state courts have yet to hear the issue of whether a same-sex partner can or cannot petition to adopt a partner's child. Although helpful, online resources should in no way substitute for the expertise of an adoption attorney who possesses up-to-the-minute knowledge of the ever-changing landscape of gay and lesbian adoption. Counselors will need to educate their clients and themselves about the laws and policies surrounding adoption in their state. In addition, they will need to attend to the emotional component of having one member of the couple recognized as the legal adopter because, presumably, neither partner wants to be formally left out as the legal parent.

White potential adopters who wish to form a racially homogeneous family may seek to adopt within-race. Alternatively, they might prefer to adopt from China or South Korea in the belief that children from these countries would be healthier than children from Russia or Eastern European countries (Downing et al., 2009). Counselors need to be aware of the ever-changing policy landscape governing intercountry adoption (ICA). At the time of this writing, opportunities for same-sex couples to avail themselves of ICA options are virtually nonexistent. Increasingly, ICA is under attack by such international nongovernmental agencies as UNICEF and such political organizations as the European Union (Bartholet, 2010; Dillon, 2008). The number of children who have obtained homes in the United States through ICA has plummeted from a record high of 22,990 completed adoptions in 2004 to a total of 12,753 in fiscal year 2009 (U.S. Department of State, 2010). Given that many nations have succumbed to pressures from the international community that focus primarily on the notion of heritage rights, a number of countries have changed their adoption requirements for prospective adoptive parents—in effect, all but eliminating the practice as well as eliminating particular groups of prospective parents, among them gay and lesbian couples. For example, in May 2007 China announced that all prospective parents must prove they are in a committed, heterosexual marriage and have been in that marriage for at least two years. China historically placed more than 6,000 children per year (primarily girls) in the United States; today, this program is all but closed to gay and lesbian couples.

The Impact of the Hague Convention on ICA by Lesbians and Gay Men

The U.S. implementation of the Hague Convention on Intercountry Adoption on April 1, 2008, has created new concerns as well as possible opportunities for gay and lesbian couples in the United States. While the Hague Convention was in the process of being drafted from 1988 to 1993, no country permitted the adoption of a minor by lesbians and gay men. Currently, 15 nations allow some same-sex couples to adopt children in discrete circumstances. Further, although the language within the Hague Convention does not specifically endorse or prohibit intercountry adoption by same-sex couples, its use of standard language like "eligibility" and "suitability" can create potential problems for same-sex couples. When conceptualized as moral and political, the best interest principle, a central tenet of the United Nations Convention on the Rights of the Child, can be used to foster opposition to same-sex adoptions. However, when coupled with empirical data regarding outcomes for children who find membership in these families, the best interest principle becomes an important form of international support for the expansion of adoption rights to lesbians and gay men (Tobin & McNair, 2009).

Despite the growing number of social orphans, currently defined as those children who may or may not having at least one living biological parent, UNICEF estimates that there are approximately 100 million street children worldwide, with many more children at risk. The results of the 2003 European Omnibus Survey indicate that only four European nations favored the legalization of adoption by same-sex couples, and this already minute number diminished to two when the survey was readministered in 2006 (Wardle, 2008). Opposition to adoption by same-sex couples centers upon a number of social myths. First, such adoptions deviate from the global ideal of child rearing that centers upon the traditional notion of one mother and one father. Proponents of traditional family structures express concerns about the social pathologies resulting from fatherlessness and impaired social relationships as a result of parents' sexual orientation. This thinking frames same-sex couple adoptions as adult centric rather than child centric (Blankenhorn, 1995). This argument is bolstered by strict interpretations of the best-interest standard promoted in the United Nations Convention on the Rights of the Child (Tobin & McNair, 2009). Opponents of same-sex couple adoptions promulgate further specious arguments that portray gay and lesbian life as one characterized by hypersexualism and the propensity to unduly influence children into a gay or lesbian "lifestyle" (Wardle, 2008). The fluidity of the international policies and practices surrounding adoption by gay and lesbian petitioners requires expert guidance from attorneys and practitioners intimately connected to these countries and cultures. Prospective adopters should carefully scrutinize the success of a given agency in securing placements in the current climate.

Helping Prospective Adopters in the Waiting Phase: Will It Ever Happen?

Some prospective adopters may need help from counselors in the waiting phase, a period that can span several weeks to several years. During this time, concerns about whether the prospective adopters' sexual orientation plays a role in this delay may catalyze feelings of anxiety, a feeling compounded when placements fall through. Practitioners may not know the factual basis of these events but should validate couple perceptions of the possibility that discrimination may be a factor and should help them seek adoption alternatives that might reap more satisfying results. Couples may need regular appointments to manage the anxiety during this period and to deal with any vestiges of internalized homophobia regarding their fitness to parent. Couples may also need assistance in maintaining privacy when well intentioned friends and relatives pepper them with repeated questions about the status of the adoption (Gianino, 2008; Goldberg & Gianino, 2012). In sum, it is critical to help lesbian and gay prospective parents locate LGBT-affirming agencies that exhibit cultural competence and are comfortable in the use of relevant language and are knowledgeable about legal issues facing same-sex couples or individual prospective adoptive patens through all stages of the adoption process, from the home study process, through placement, to postpermanency supports (HRC, 2007).

Transition to Adoptive Parenthood: The Early Years

The transition to parenthood, defined as the development of competency in the parenting role and comfort with parenting behavior required for child care (Hudson, Campbell-Grossman, & Fleck, 2003), represents a crisis for couples in that becoming a parent is a risk factor for individual and relational distress. There is scant research on the transition to parenthood for gay and lesbian adoptive couples (Goldberg & Smith, 2008). The changes to the couple relationship involve many of the expected challenges any couple faces, including dramatically changed priorities in their intimate relationship. As do their heterosexual counterparts, lesbian couples across the transition find patterns of decreased feeling of love and increased conflict (Goldberg & Sayer, 2006). Practitioners can help couples manage conflicts in negotiation of new roles as parents, a challenge sometimes magnified when children arrive home with trauma histories and attachment issues and other challenges that may further strain the relationship (Gianino, 2008). Some lesbian and gay couples find that enduring friendships change and shift after the arrival of a child, and sometimes friendships are lost as those who are unable to manage the complexities of the new family constellation drift away. Therapists can help clients adjust to these changes in their friendship networks while also helping them find ways of decreasing potential isolation in their new parenting roles, often by helping link them to other lesbian or gay adoptive-parenting individuals or groups.

Gay and lesbian adoptive-parent families contend with three dimensions that characterize their family life: vulnerabilities to heterosexism, adoptism, and racism (Gianino, Goldberg, & Lewis, 2010). They may face challenges of living as an adoptive and, oftentimes, multiracial family and might worry about how much attention and emphasis to place on their child's adoptive status and racial or cultural background (Goldberg & Gianino, 2012). They may seek help from counseling professionals to examine their child's need for racial or cultural socialization (Vonk, 2001) but may feel they lack the personal or social resources to meet these needs. For example, they may be unsure about how to go about facilitating a strong racial identity, especially if they live in a racially nondiverse area or have few family members or friends who share the same race as their child. Gay and lesbian adoptive parents may seek memberships in multiracial family support groups that reflect their transracial family structure but not necessarily their gay and lesbian parenting status.

Gay and lesbian adoptive parents may seek help from counseling professionals to deal with feelings of visibility and, simultaneously, invisibility as gay and lesbian adoptive parents. They may need help finding language to empower themselves and their children to deal with intrusive questions from strangers in public settings regarding their family form. Practitioners must be aware of the such resources as W.I.S.E. UP that can increase a family's ability to negotiate appropriate responses to inappropriate questions. Developed by the Center for Adoption Support and Education, W.I.S.E. UP is designed for adopted children between the ages of 6 and 12, and its goal is to provide children with concrete techniques when faced with such questions as "Where's your real mom?" or "Why do you have two dads?" Children learn to select the strategy they deem most effective in the moment: walk away, ignore, educate, or share. At the same time, members of gay- and lesbian-parent families may express feelings of invisibility as a family. For example, one youth in a large multicultural family headed by two moms noted her frustration that frequently on family excursions with her sisters and parents to encounter an adult stranger who would ask if they were a "girl scout troop."

It is most helpful in the early months postplacement to assist gay and lesbian parents in recognizing the potential impact of racism, adoptism, and heterosexism on their families. The research on adoption underscores that family communication about adoption is paramount for these families (Brodzinsky & Pinderhughes, 2002). Goldberg and Gianino (2012) note that "therapists who work with lesbian and gay adoptive parents should educate their clients about the need to develop skills in openly and comfortably discussing with their child the facts of their adoption in a way that is developmentally appropriate, sensitive, and compassionate" (p. 25). Further, racial socialization is recognized as a critical skill for transracially adoptive parents and consists of three dimensions: (1) helping children develop awareness of racism and other roles race and ethnicity will play in their lives; (2) engaging in multicultural planning that brings children in contact with their birth cultures (Paulson & Merighi, 2009); and (3) facilitating survival skills whereby children learn to externalize, not internalize, discrimination (Vonk, 2001). In addition, adoptive families should be sensitized to the importance of developing an identity of themselves as adoptive families as opposed to focusing solely and exclusively on their child's adoptive status as a factor that is relevant to their child's identity only.

Adopted Children, Adolescents, and Young Adults With Lesbian and Gay Parents

This section explores four cross-cutting themes prevalent among adopted children and their families. We discuss these themes and how they play out for adopted youth with lesbian or gay parents. We offer suggestions for assessment and intervention at several stages from early childhood to young adulthood. The cross-cutting themes to be discussed are (a) individual and family identity, (b) disclosure of adoptive status and family structure, (c) loss and grief, and (d) school life.

Individual and Family Identity

One lens through which to view the creation of adoptive family identity is *kinning*, which is the process by which the previously nonrelated child is brought into a significant and permanent relationship with his or her adoptive parents (Howell, 2003). A universal process in all societies, kinning is marked by several stages. First is the prepregnancy stage, which begins when the prospective adoptive couple (or single person) decide they would like to start a family. Pregnancy commences when the applicant is approved by the adoption agency; unlike for persons who conceive, this "pregnancy" is of an unknown duration, yet during this time the unidentified child is being incorporated into the prospective parents' sense of their own identity as expecting parents. Within this framework, birth occurs when the agency allocates the child to the adopting person or couple and extends through the allocation, arrival, and initial period after the child's entry into the home. Prospective parents actively pursue their unknown child upon their receipt of the first photo; as the photo is shared with friends, the prospective parents' social network is prepared for acceptance of the child (Howell, 2003).

As must the adoptive parents, the child too must negotiate individual and family identity. In general, typically developing children between the ages of 1 and 5 acquire language, learn simple self-care skills, and develop a socioemotional sense of self that is primarily expressed through an egocentric view of the world that centers upon such words as *no* and *mine*. At this stage, the child tends to define family as those persons who live within the boundaries of the home, and both imaginary play and exploration are hallmarks of the child's social development (C.A.S.E., 2007). For the adopted child, new complexities emerge. For example, Boss (2007) notes in her work on ambiguous loss that boundary ambiguity, understood as the inability to define who is and is not part of one's family, creates new challenges for children and adults. Children within this age range tend to ask simple questions about differences in an attempt to make sense of what is culturally acceptable; they also exhibit a readiness to learn and repeat their adoption story (Deacon, 1997), as illustrated in the following example:

Marcos, a young Colombian child, adopted at age 5, spent the first full year with his adoptive family making the same statements during dinner each night; "You came to get me in Colombia and I was with Maria and now she is in Colombia and we're here and you're my mami and she isn't, right? Why did you come and get me?" Before a response could be given, Marcos would continue with his statements. "Is Maria still my mami? Are we going back to Colombia, or are we staying here? Does Maria know where I am? Will I always stay here with you?" A child's ability to make sense of his or her adoption story and discover language to create his or her own narrative facilitates attachment as well as identity formation. Practitioners can best support this goal by providing concrete strategies for parents that include recalling the child's adoption story during such family rituals as those engaged in during dinner and at bedtime; looking at life books, photographs, and other memorabilia related to the adoption; and, finally, demonstrating increased comfort with the child's memories of parents, caregivers, and experiences that predate the adoptive parents' arrival in their child's life.

Children of same-sex couples express a desire to make sense of their story as well as locate it in the larger structures of society. Luke, who is 5 years old, has begun to ask his fathers the story of his birth mother and his actual birth and casually notes that he, too, expects that he might have a mommy someday. Practitioners and parents must be prepared to provide children with the necessary tools to create an adoption narrative that addresses the elements of the complex family structure to which the child belongs. Transracially adopted youth face unique challenges related to their adoption experience and also their experience of race and ethnicity (Gianino et al., 2010). Preliminary qualitative research findings suggest that younger children with gay and lesbian parents tend to feel less identified with their race and ethnicity. This is followed by a period where they wish their parents were of the same race as they. It is in the middle school years that youth struggled with the wish that their parents were of a different sexual orientation (Goldberg, 2010). The literature strongly suggests that the well-being of transracially adopted children rests on their parents' cultural competence related to their children's racial and cultural backgrounds (Massatti, Vonk, & Gregoire, 2004; Simon & Alstein, 2000; Vonk, 2001). Although not written specifically for gay- and lesbian-parent families, *Inside Transracial Adoption*, by Steinberg and Hall (2000), offers parents and practitioners practical suggestions to assist children through developmental processes and crises common among transracially adopted children.

The challenges that present themselves to adopted children between the ages of 6 and 12 differ dramatically from those facing younger children. In large part, the challenges are greater because of increased cognitive functioning as well as the formation of meaningful relationships outside the family. Adoption awareness for these children includes the ability to understand the implications of adoption—namely, that in order to have been adopted, the child must first have been abandoned. Thus, a sense of loss emerges as well as discomfort with difference, increased feelings of uncertainty, and the romanticization of birth parents (C.A.S.E., 2007). Furthermore, for children of gay and lesbian parents, new complexities arise as children begin to understand the concept of a biological family, and peer relationships create new pressures to conform to the dominant culture. Thus, these children may also grapple with the potential transfer of the image of parents from one of "mother and father" to one of "mother and mother" or "father and father." "It's like walking down the street and you're the only one who looks like you and then you go home and you're still the only one who looks like you" (Passmore, 2004, p. 165). This quotation illustrates the dilemma faced by transracially adopted children. The experience of these children is further complicated by having same-sex parents, for these children must cope with not only increased visibility but also a sense of "difference" based on having parents of the same gender (Boyer, 2007).

Increasingly, adolescents and young adults are speaking out about how being the child of a lesbian or gay parent is an identity in its own right (E. Castellana, personal communication, April 16, 2010); this view holds that these youth must not be regarded as allies of the LGBT community or as a step removed. The journalist Abigail Garner (2004) describes the construct of cultural queerness as an affirmation of family identity rather than an expression of one's personal sexual orientation. At the same time, the child is not the extension of the parents' identity; the child's individuation does not mean that the child disowns his or her family makeup. It does, however, mean the child's claiming his or her unique identity within it. According to Castellana, youth have their own story, their own identity, and their own "coming-out" process unrelated to that of parents. She notes that as youth mature within the context of a lesbian- or gay- parented family, they individuate, and this individuation can feel threatening or rejecting to a parent in a nonnormative family. Consequently, youth may feel pressure to defend their families because of intense public scrutiny (Garner, 2004). It is critical that the therapist explore the quality and depth of the connections that youth have within the various racial and cultural communities to which they belong, for these communities will also include other youth with lesbian or gay parents. If such connections to these diverse communities do not currently exist, it is important to support youth in considering how they envision themselves becoming more connected in order to help them integrate a healthy multicultural identity for themselves. It may also be helpful to explore their fears about how the various racial and cultural communities with which they may come in contact might perceive them because they are children of lesbian or gay parents.

Disclosure

Disclosure of family structure among youth with lesbian or gay parents is critical to development of a positive sense of self and pride in one's family (Gianino et al., 2010; Welch, 2008). Yet disclosure of their family structure is a complicated matter for the youth who live in these families because adopted youth with lesbian or gay parents must choose whether or not (and how, when, and to whom) to disclose their family structure. Early adolescence is the most challenging time for youth in disclosing their lesbian- or gay-parented family structure. Often youth at this age express a desire for a "normal" family and may attempt to hide their parents' sexual orientation. By later adolescence and early adulthood, as their multiple statuses are consolidated, youth may wish to change neither the race of their (mostly White) parents nor their parents' sexual orientation. It should be noted that children who are transracially adopted experience less privacy because of the inability to keep their adoption a secret (Brodzinsky & Pinderhughes, 2002; de Haymes & Simon, 2003; Gianino et al., 2010), which in effect "outs" them all the time. Ray and Gregory (2001) and Welch (2008) emphasize that being designated different presents difficulties and anxieties about managing disclosure. In particular, youth may fear that disclosing their parents' sexual orientation would subject them to teasing and harassment. Observed one White lesbian parent of a middle school youth,

> My son used to come home and say the other kids made fun of him because his mom is White and he's Black, but now that he's older he's coming home and saying that he got into a fight because the other kids are saying, "You have two moms." How freaky is that? No one seems to be mentioning color anymore. I know it's important that we're a biracial family, but my son is bringing different issues to the table and I feel like it's my job to attend to what he brings up.... It's really confusing and really tough to find someone to work with who understands all the complexities of adoption, of race and of same-sex parenting.

Given the ebb and flow from the child's perspective of what appears to be the most pressing concern, the practitioner, in this particular vignette, responded to the mother, "It is complex, and issues around race will resurface for your son, but let's think about where he and his peers are at developmentally and what might be some of the pressures he faces at school right now."

Practitioners carefully need to assess young people's levels of anxiety related to disclosure of their family structure, especially in the middle school years. Youth must come to terms with disclosure of their parents' sexual orientation and may experience a range of negative feelings at having to do so. Parents may engage counselors to assist their children in addressing questions about their family structure and whom to tell about it. Youth may consider such questions: Who is safe (or not safe) to tell? How do I choose? Can I trust they will keep it a secret? What will I do if they freak out? Do I have to tell—can't my friends just figure it out? It is not me—I'm not gay, so why do I need to tell anyone at all? It may be helpful for professionals to reassure youth and parents that after an initial period of wariness about disclosure, most young people do eventually choose to tell a select group of peers that their parents are lesbian or gay, and most experience a positive evolution of friendships (Gianino et al., 2010; Welch, 2008).

It is important for counselors to help youth to find language that explains their family structure to others whom they choose to tell. The counselor can facilitate role-plays where youth get to practice "telling" and work through a range of possible reactions. Further, disclosure can be complicated for youth with varied disabilities, adding another layer of difference to their and their family's story. Therapists must be able to empathize with their dilemma, affirm that they may feel angry with their parents, and finally emphasize that the decision to tell is theirs and theirs alone to make. It may be difficult for some parents to understand their child's wariness about disclosure, leaving them to feel even more excluded from the lives of their middle schoolers. This distress may be especially true for those parents who have been open about their sexuality for some time. Clinicians can emphasize that parental preparation for dealing with adoptism and heterosexism and homophobia functions to ease disclosure for youth regarding their family structure. At the same time, youth may choose not to disclose their family structure, and their desire not to disclose may lead parents to wonder if their child feels ashamed of them. The therapist can help parents understand the motivations of their child to choose to disclose or not.

Finally, there are youth who reside in homes of parents who remain closeted to varying degrees. With regard to their parents' sexual orientation, research supports the view that parents who are out to their children do model pride in their identity and self-acceptance, which facilitates youths' own acceptance of their minority family structure (Boyer, 2007; Goldberg, 2007). Challenges with regard to the parents' own coming-out process may interfere with their children feeling that they own the choice to come out, or not, about their family's structure. If the youth experience a veil of secretiveness around their families, they may not reach for support when they need it. Conversely, a parent may be so out that though the child is ready to choose to disclose, he or she may not be able to share what is essentially a family story, rather than the parents' individual story (Gianino et al., 2010; Goldberg, 2007).

Loss and Grief

Adoption is created through loss, and feelings of loss are ubiquitous among adopted children (Steinberg & Hall, 2000). A useful lens with which practitioners can view this experience is the concept of ambiguous loss, a relational disorder that describes the chronic trauma that accompanies unresolved loss. Two types of loss comprise this phenomenon: Type 1 denotes the physical absence yet psychological presence of a family member, whereas Type 2 refers to the psychological absence but physical presence of such a person (Boss, 2007). Many adopted children experience the physical absence but psychological presence of members of their families of origin and exhibit both externalizing and internalizing behaviors in an attempt to make sense of a loss they are unable to resolve. Children of same-sex couples may experience increased stress because their entry into a family that deviates from dominant cultural norms compounds feelings of impotency and helplessness in behavioral attempts to conform to a romanticized image of family.

Practitioners involved with such families may want to consider that although it is important to set limits in response to maladaptive coping behaviors, parents and child welfare workers must move away from blame, shame, and punitive behavioral management strategies that exacerbate underlying feelings of impotency, insecurity, anger, and depression (Lee & Whiting, 2007). Whereas society provides rituals for death, divorce, and other social ills, no societal ritual exists for children who have been removed from their family of origin and placed into the child welfare system, thus creating the ambiguity that potentially freezes the grief process as well as the resolution of loss (Boss, 2007).

Given that ambiguous loss is both painful and incomprehensible, its ability to immobilize people must be attended to. Regardless of the child's family structure, research suggests that practitioners must first assess children for loss rather than focus on closure. Boss (2010) recommends that practitioners help clients find meaning, temper mastery, reconstruct identity, normalize ambivalence, revise attachment, and, ultimately, discover hope. The following vignette by a young Latina named Ana illustrates this process:

> For a long time I kept thinking I was going back to my mom so I acted out and figured that if I was bad enough they would send me back there. I just didn't get what had happened. That was such a long time ago—I can't even imagine what I was thinking because this is my home, I mean, this is my mom even if we don't look anything alike and it's not how I thought it would be at first. This is my family. It's just that for a long time, when I looked at the faces of my mother and father, I kept thinking, they're strangers.... Now I get it, they don't look like me but that doesn't stop them from being my family.

School Life

In the most comprehensive survey to date investigating the experiences of school-aged children with gay and lesbian parents, a report from the Gay, Lesbian and Straight Education Network (GLSEN) concluded that for many students with LGBT parents, school is not a very safe environment. The study authors reported that half (51%) of all respondents feel unsafe in school because of a "personal characteristic, such as their actual or perceived sexual orientation, gender, or race/ethnicity. The most commonly reported reasons for feeling unsafe were because of their family constellation, i.e., having LGBT parents (23%)" (Kosciw & Diaz, 2008, p. xvi). Further, they emphasized that although students did not report victimization in their schools, a substantial minority (40%) did recount experiencing verbal harassment as well as peers' assumptions that they were gay based on parental sexual orientation. These findings corroborate the very small body of literature documenting school experiences of youth with gay and lesbian parents (Gianino et al., 2010; Ray & Gregory, 2001) by underscoring that youth with LGBT parents are subjected to teasing and harassment in schools.

Young children who are also transracially adopted have very little control regarding who in their schools knows, or does not know, about their family form, as is illustrated in the following vignette:

> Maya, who is African American, age 7, was upset that no one at her school spoke to her except to occasionally grill her about her relationship to Barbara, her White adoptive lesbian mother: "Who's that White lady?" "Is she your mom?" "Where's your real mom?" or "Who is that other lady?" Maya found herself not knowing what to say and became

increasingly withdrawn. Lately, she has been begging Barbara not to pick her up at school anymore: "It's too hard. I'm tired of having to answer all their questions!"

Although these questions may as often convey curiosity as well as hostility, such interrogations can catalyze feelings of anxiety in young children. Goldberg and Gianino (2012) urge therapists to assist lesbian and gay parents in their efforts to counteract the heterosexist messages that their children may receive in schools. When their children report problems in school related to their family form, parents should explain that there is a diverse spectrum of relationships and family structure; parents can emphasize that some women love women and some men love men, and there are many different types of families. As children grow older, parents may find it useful to teach them about the meaning of confusing or hurtful words and to introduce appropriate terminology for describing sexuality and relationships in an effort to educate their children about an acceptable range of sexual expressions.

Some useful questions can be posed to school administrators for assessing how accepting the school will be of their diverse family structure. Adapted from Steinberg and Hall (2000), such questions might include these: How many children of color attend this school? Children who have gay or lesbian parents? Children who are adopted? How important is diversity as a school value? Have there been any negative racial issues that have come up at the school? Have there been any negative issues with kids with gay or lesbian parents? In a counseling session, one gay father recounted meeting with the principal of a local Catholic school he was considering for his child. With trepidation he asked if the school would welcome lesbian- and gay-parent families like his. Clearly moved, he recounted that "she didn't bat an eye" and "she replied that there were many diverse families at this school and that all families are treated with reverence and respect!" The reality, however, is that not all gay and lesbian parents can access affirming schools. They may lack the financial resources for private school or may reside in small school districts offering limited school choice (Kosciw & Diaz, 2008). Further, where some gay and lesbian parents may choose to be actively involved in their children's schools as volunteers and so forth, others may be less inclined to do so. It is important for counselors to adopt a nonjudgmental stance with regard to parental choices. If there are few schools from which to choose, are there other opportunities for children to be in contact with affirming organizations? If there are no other lesbian- and gay-parented families in the school, what are the implications of being a "trailblazer" in this regard for the parents? For the children? The pros and cons of various decisions need to be carefully weighed to help families maximize the greatest range of empowering options as possible.

As indicated earlier, there is wide consensus across studies that it is in the middle school years where youth experience the greatest stress caused by peer reactions to their family structure. Observed one 13-year-old transracially adopted youth,

Especially in middle school I switched schools and it became really evident that people might not accept my family. So I only really told my close friends, and I think when you're at that age and you learn about different families you learn that your family is not going to be accepted by everyone and that some people in the country think it's shameful.

It is possible that boys may experience more peer taunting about their family structure; being called "homo" or faggot" is all too common (Gianino et al., 2010; Ray & Gregory, 2001). Regardless of their age at adoption, youth may struggle with acceptance and understanding of their parents' homosexuality. As they increasingly comprehend the nature of same-sex sexuality, they are also exploring issues related to their own sexuality (Goldberg & Gianino, 2012). In addition, adolescents often struggle with concerns about peer acceptance and conformity, which may heighten their concerns about their parents' sexuality and the possibility that they will be ostracized if "word gets out" at school. School counselors of youth with gay and lesbian parents will need to be especially attuned to issues of confidentiality should the youth in question not be out in the school regarding his or her family form. Therapists will also need to listen carefully to narratives of bullying and abuse in schools and ascertain the degree to which further intervention is needed by parents or school officials. Youth may feel shame about the attention this issue might draw to themselves and might minimize the bullying as "no big deal." Abuse in schools related to parental sexual orientation must be aggressively addressed by school personnel. State-level policies are beginning to address the urgent need for comprehensive safe-school legislation. For help implementing the steps in creating a safe-school climate, two valuable resources are GLSEN and the *When the Drama Club Is Not Enough: Lessons From the Safe Schools Program for Gay and Lesbian Students*, by Jeff Perrotti and Kim Westheimer (2001). One further invaluable resource for youth is Children of Lesbians and Gays Everywhere (COLAGE). With chapters in several states and as sponsor of several annual week-long retreats for people with LGBT parents, COLAGE is a youth-driven empowerment organization that offers support and advocacy by connecting youth with peers who share their experience.

Conclusion

In his chapter we have illuminated the life-cycle stages that gay and lesbian adoptive parents and their children pass through, and we have offered recommendations for direct practice. In assessment and intervention with these families and the myriad issues that parents and children may disclose to practitioners, we should remain open to the possibility that the presenting concerns may have very little to do with their lesbian- or gay-parented family form. Clinicians will need to be alert and nimble in identifying the underlying themes reviewed here and respectful of the complex tapestry woven by the family's adoptive, lesbian- and gay-parented, and often transracial and cross-cultural characteristics. Although beyond the scope of this chapter, we also strongly endorse legislation and policies designed to promote fairness and inclusiveness in all aspects of the gay- and lesbian-adoptive family's life. All legislation and polices that impede the formation and maintenance of these families should be considered antithetical to the well-being of the many children yet waiting to be placed in permanent and loving adoptive homes.

References

Averett, P., Nalavany, B., & Ryan, S. (2009). An evaluation of gay/lesbian and heterosexual adoption. *Adoption Quarterly, 12*, 129–151.

Bartholet, E. (2010). International adoption: The human rights position, *Global Policy, 1*, 91–100.

Blankenhorn, D. (1995). The state of the family and the family policy debate. *Santa Clara Law Review, 36*, 431–438.

Bos, H. M. W., van Balen, F., & van den Boom, D. C. (2007). Child adjustment and parenting in planned lesbian-parent families. *American Journal of Orthopsychiatry, 77*, 38–48.

Boss, P. (2007). Ambiguous loss theory: Challenges for scholars and practitioners. *Family Relations, 56*, 105–111.

Boss, P. (2010). The Trauma and complicated grief of ambiguous loss. *Pastoral Psychology, 59*, 137–145.

Boyer, C. (2007). Double stigma: The impact of adoption issues on lesbian and gay adoptive parents. In R. Javier, A. Baden, F. Biafora, & A. Camacho-Gingerich (Eds.), *Handbook of adoption* (pp. 228–241). Thousand Oaks, CA: Sage.

Bozett, F. (1989). Gay fathers: A review of the literature. In F. Bozett (Ed.), *Homosexuality and the family* (pp. 137–162). New York, NY: Harrington Park Press.

Brodzinsky, D. (2008). *Adoptive Parent Preparation Project: Phase 1. Meeting the mental health and developmental needs of adopted children* [Final policy and practice report]. Retrieved from http://www.adoptioninstitute.org

Brodzinsky, D. M., & Pinderhughes, E. (2002). Parenting and child development in adoptive families. In M. Bornstein (Ed.), *Handbook of parenting* (pp. 279-311). Mahwah, NJ: Erlbaum.

Brown, S., Smalling, S., Groza, V., & Ryan, S. (2009). The experiences of gay men and lesbians becoming adoptive parents. *Adoption Quarterly, 12*, 229–246.

Center for Adoption Support and Education. (2007). The adopted child's changing view: A timeline of child development. *C.A.S.E. Resources for All.* Retrieved from http://www.adoptionsupport.org/res/timeline/Timeline.pdf

Deacon, S. A. (1997). Intercountry adoption and the family lifecycle. *American Journal of Family Therapy, 25*, 245–260.

De Haymes, M. V., & Simon, S. (2003). Transracial adoption: Families identify issues and needed support services. *Child Welfare, 82*, 1–23.

Dillon, S. (2008). The missing link: A social orphan protocol to the United Nations Convention on the Rights of the Child. *Human Rights and Globalization Law Review, 1*, 39–74.

Downing, J., Richardson, H., Kinkler, L., & Goldberg, A. E. (2009). Making the decision: Factors influencing gay men's choice of an adoption path. *Adoption Quarterly, 12*, 247–271.

Elze, D. E. (2006). Oppression, prejudice, and discrimination. In D. F. Morrow & L. Messinger (Eds.), *Sexual orientation and gender expression in social work practice* (pp. 43–77). New York: Columbia University Press.

Erich, S., Hall, S. K., Kanenberg, H., & Case, K. (2009). Early and late stage adolescence: Adopted adolescents' attachment to their heterosexual and lesbian/gay parents. *Adoption Quarterly, 12*, 152–170.

Farr, R. H. & Patterson, C. J. (2009). Transracial adoption by lesbian, gay, and heterosexual couples: Who completes transracial adoptions and with what results? *Adoption Quarterly, 12*, 187–204.

Garner, A. (2004). *Families like mine: Children of gay parents tell it like it is.* New York, NY: Harper Collins.

Gates, G., Badgett, M. V. L., Macomber, J. E., & Chambers, K. (2007). *Adoption and foster care by gay and lesbian parents in the United States.* Washington, DC: Urban Institute.

Gianino, M. (2008). Adaptation and transformation: The transition to adoptive parenthood for gay male couples. *Journal of GLBT Family Studies, 4*, 205–243.

Gianino, M., Goldberg, A. E., & Lewis, T. (2010). Family outings: Disclosure practices among adopted youth with gay and lesbian parents. *Adoption Quarterly, 12*, 229–246.

Goldberg, A. E. (2007). (How) does it make a difference? Perspectives of adults with lesbian, gay, and bisexual parents. *American Journal of Orthopsychiatry, 77*, 550–562.

Goldberg, A. E. (2009). *Lesbians and gay parents and their children: Research on the family life cycle.* Washington, DC: American Psychological Association Press.

Goldberg, A. E., & Gianino, M. (2012). Lesbian and gay adoptive parent families: Assessment, clinical issues, and intervention. In D. Brodzinsky, A. Pertman, & D. Kunz (Eds.), *Gay and lesbian adoption: A new American reality* (pp. 204–232). New York, NY: Oxford University Press.

Goldberg, A. E., & Sayer, A. G. (2006). Lesbian couples' relationship quality across the transition to parenthood. *Journal of Marriage and the Family, 68*, 87–100.

Goldberg, A. E., & Smith, J. Z. (2008). Social support and well-being in lesbian and heterosexual preadoptive parents. *Family Relations, 57*, 281–294.

Goldberg, A. E., & Smith, J. Z. (2009). Predicting non–African American lesbian and heterosexual preadoptive couples' openness to adopting an African American child. *Family Relations, 58*, 346–360.

Gottman, J. (1999). *The marriage clinic: A scientifically based marital therapy.* New York, NY: Norton.

Howell, S. (2003). Kinning: The creation of life trajectories in transnational adoptive families. *Journal of the Royal Anthropological Institute, 9*, 465–484.

Hudson, D. B., Campbell-Grossman, C., & Fleck, M. O. (2003). Effects of the fathers network on first-time fathers' parenting self-efficacy and parenting satisfaction during the transition to parenthood. *Issues in Comprehensive Pediatric Nursing, 26*, 217–229.

Human Rights Campaign. (2007). *Promising practices in adoption and foster care.* Washington, DC: Author.

Human Rights Campaign. (2010). *Adoption law: State by state.* Retrieved from http://www.hrc.org/issues/parenting/adoptions/8464.htm

Johnson, S. M., & O'Connor, E. (2002). *The gay baby boom: The psychology of gay parenthood.* New York, NY: New York University Press.

Kosciw, J. G., & Diaz, E. M. (2008). *Involved, invisible, ignored: The experiences of lesbian, gay, bisexual and transgender parents and their children in our nation's K–12 schools.* New York, NY: GLSEN.

Lee, R., & Whiting, J. (2007). Foster children's expressions of ambiguous loss. *American Journal of Family Therapy, 35*, 417–428.

Leung, P., Erich, S., & Kanenberg, H. (2005). A comparison of family functioning in gay/lesbian, heterosexual and special needs adoptions. *Children & Youth Services Review, 27*, 1031–1044.

Mallon, G. P. (2004). *Gay men choosing parenthood.* New York, NY: Columbia University Press.

Mallon, G. P. (2007). Assessing lesbian and gay prospective foster and adoptive families: A focus on the home study process. *Child Welfare, 86*, 67–86.

Massatti, R. R., Vonk, M. E., & Gregoire, T. K. (2004). Reliability and validity of the Transracial Adoption Parenting Scale. *Research on Social Work Practice, 14*, 43–50.

Paulson, C., & Merighi, J. R. (2009). Adoption preparedness, cultural engagement, and parental satisfaction in intercountry adoption. *Adoption Quarterly, 12*, 1–18.

Passmore, N. (2004). Adoption and the father heart of God: Helping adoptees deal with issues of identity and loss. *Journal of Psychology and Christianity, 23*, 165–175.

Perrotti, J., & Westheimer, K. (2001). *When the drama club is not enough: Lessons from the a safe schools program for gay and lesbian students.* Boston, MA: Beacon Press.

Ray, V., & Gregory, R. (2001). School experiences of the children of lesbian and gay parents. *Family Matters, 59*, 28–34.

Roorda, R. M. (2007). Moving beyond the controversy of the transracial adoption of black and biracial children. In R. Javier, A. Baden, F. Biafora, & A. Camacho-Gingerich (Eds.), *Handbook of adoption* (pp. 133–148). Thousand Oaks, CA: Sage.

Ryan, S., Pearlmutter, S., & Groza, V. (2004). Coming out of the closet: Opening agencies to gay men and lesbian adoptive parents. *Social Work, 49*, 85–96.

Shelley-Sireci, L. M., & Ciano-Boyce, C. (2002). Becoming lesbian adoptive parents: An exploratory study of lesbian adoptive, lesbian birth, and heterosexual adoptive parents. *Adoption Quarterly, 6*, 33–43.

Simon, R., & Alstein, H. (2000). *Adoption across borders.* Lanham, MD: Rowman & Littlefield.

Steinberg, G., & Hall, B. (2000). *Inside transracial adoption.* Indianapolis, IN: Perspective Press.

Tasker, F., & Golombok, S. (1997). *Growing up in a lesbian family: Effects on child development.* New York, NY: Guilford Press.

Tobin, J., & McNair, R. (2009). Public international law and the regulation of private spaces: Does the Convention on the Rights of the Child impose an obligation on states to allow gay and lesbian couples to adopt? *International Journal of Law, Policy and the Family, 23*, 110–131.

U.S. Department of State, Office of Children's Issues. (2010, June 12). Intercountry adoption. Retrieved from http://www.adoption.state.gov

Vonk, M. E. (2001). Cultural competence for transracial adoptive parents. *Social Work, 46*, 246–255.

Wainright, J. L., Russell, S. T., & Patterson, C. J. (2004). Psychosocial adjustment and school outcomes of adolescents with same-sex parents. *Child Development, 75*, 1886–1898.

Wardle, L. (2008). The Hague Convention on Intercountry Adoption and American implementing laws and regulations for adoptions of children by gay and lesbian adults. *Indiana International and Comparative Law Review, 18*, 113–152.

Welch, M. (2008). *A phenomenological exploration of adolescents raised by same-sex parents* Unpublished doctoral dissertation. Massachusetts School of Professional Psychology, Boston, MA.

15

The Gay and Lesbian Stepfamily

Past and Present Research and Implications for Therapy

JEAN LYNCH and KATHY MCMAHON-KLOSTERMAN

If you were part of a gay or lesbian stepfamily in the 1980s and wanted to locate information on families like your own, you had one of two choices. First, you could comb through the heterosexual stepfamily literature and discover that there were indeed similarities between the challenges and strengths heterosexual stepfamily members faced and those you experienced. Second, you could review the scant material on families in the lesbian, gay, bisexual, and transgender (LGBT) research and find little, if any, evidence about different family structures. If you or your family sought counseling, you would no doubt face a similar situation—neither the training nor the materials for therapists provided them with a sufficient background to understand and treat LGBT families, especially the ways in which stepfamily status and same-sex gender composition create unique issues. Worse, most comparisons between stepfamilies and nuclear families, and certainly almost all references to same-sex families, were based on deficit comparison models, to the detriment of all same-sex and nonnuclear families (Crosbie-Burnett & Helmbrecht, 1993; Pasley, Ihinger-Tallman, & Lofquist, 1994). Heterosexist assumptions generally went unchallenged. Sexual orientation was assumed to be the problem, and therapists failed to consider the impact of homophobia on LGBT families (Baptiste, 1987; Crosbie-Burnett & Helmbrecht, 1993).

Keshel (1990) reminds us of how the early characterizations of marriage as the joint construction of reality becomes a complex process for those entering second marriages, given the lack of clear expectations and prescriptions that accompany second unions. Family construction is even further exacerbated for gay and lesbian stepfamilies, for whom there are no sources of institutionalization, definitions of roles, or even public recognition. Unlike heterosexual marriages, there are no clear guidelines delineating the rights and responsibilities of family members or the ways members relate to one another within and outside the immediate family boundaries. Stepfamily researchers have discussed "incomplete institutionalization" as characteristic of mixed-sex stepfamilies (Cherlin & Furstenberg, 1994, p. 360) and particularly the role of the stepparent. This lack of institutionalization is much broader in its consequences for the gay and lesbian stepfamily. Despite this, there are advantages and disadvantages of establishing families without preconceived ways of "becoming family." The lack of social, legal, and political recognition provides both freedom from constraints and a blank slate upon which to construct a family's own blueprint (Oswald, 2002). On the other hand, the lack of institutionalization means there are no sources of predictability and no protections for the union or its members (Keshel, 1990). In this chapter, we assume the perspective that all families—the gay and lesbian stepfamily included—create family, form interfamilial relationships, and develop ways of being from which all families can benefit.

This chapter will consider the gay and lesbian stepfamily. We define the gay and lesbian stepfamily as one in which one or both of the partners brought children to the lesbian or gay relationship from a previous heterosexual coupling. We will review the research and use the most significant findings to illustrate the stresses and vulnerabilities as well as the strengths and resiliency that can guide therapists in treating gay and lesbian stepfamilies. We promote the adoption of an "ally" identity as a particularly beneficial perspective from which to counsel gay and lesbian stepfamily members. The ally perspective is well suited to marginalized family forms subjected to ongoing stereotypes and prejudice.

Review of the Background Literature

Moral entrepreneurs typically cast gays and lesbians as "antifamily" (Bozett, 1987, p. 3). Baptiste notes that the majority of Americans believe that it is "inconceivable and inherently contradictory that a person can be both gay and a parent. The twin act of having and keeping children is still jealously reserved for heterosexual couples" (1987, pp. 223–224). The realization that increasing numbers of gays and lesbians have been heterosexually married contradicts commonly held beliefs about the rigidity of sexual orientation, gay men's and lesbian women's motivations to marry, and the desire to parent. It is not surprising, then, that the focus of the early literature responded to these issues.

The early research (until the 1990s) was devoted almost exclusively to a few topics, with the majority of studies focused on comparing children raised by LGBT parents with those raised by heterosexual parents. As expected, this area received far more attention than warranted considering the lack of any clinical indications that such children constituted a population with problems. Attention was devoted to the study of psychological adjustment and social functioning, including personality differences, peer relationships, self-esteem, and other variables that might differentiate between children raised by heterosexuals and those raised by gay or lesbian parents (Bozett, 1987; Golombok, Spencer, & Rutter, 1983; Pennington, 1987). Particular attention was paid to potential problems with gender, gender identity, and sexual orientation; but no differences were found (Golombok et al., 1983). On most scales, researchers found either no significant differences or identified problems for those children living with single mothers with a mixed-sex orientation (Bozett, 1987; Falk, 1994; Golombok et al., 1983).

A related set of studies was conducted on gay and lesbian motivations for marrying and having children, and on the parenting behaviors of gays and lesbians. Most research demonstrated that gay men and lesbians marry and have children for the same reasons heterosexuals do: love for their spouse. Whereas some homosexuals, particularly men, may have some prior same-sex experiences, many others are simply unaware of any same-sex attractions. Thus, most gays and lesbians marry with sincere love for their partners and with genuine intentions of establishing a lifelong partnership (Bigner, 1996; Lynch, 2004b). Similarly, most parents hold a firm belief that they will be good parents (Baptiste, 1987; Bigner, 1996). When differences are found between heterosexual and gay and lesbian parents, they tend to demonstrate positive parenting behaviors among homosexual parents and benefits for the children they raise (Barret & Robinson, 1994; Lynch & McMahon-Klosterman, 2007). For example, findings consistently show that children raised by gays and lesbians exhibit more tolerance and are more accepting of diversity than children reared by heterosexual parents (Lynch, 2000; Lynch & McMahon-Klosterman, 2007).

"Coming out" received significant attention in the 1980s and continues to be one of the most researched areas within LGBT family studies. Previously married lesbians and gays raised serious doubts about the traditional coming-out models. The sequential developmental-stage models posited by Cass (1984) and Troiden (1988) typically cover a period beginning at preadolescence and culminating in a final stage of identity integration at approximately the mid- to late 20s, typically 5 years after self-labeling (McDonald, 1990; Newman & Muzzonigro, 1993; Troiden, 1988). In this later stage, the person's gay or lesbian identity is no longer self-conceptualized as the master or most significant status. Although the linear progressive-stage models of the coming-out process represent a theoretical structure that may be useful for describing the experiences of many lesbian or gay individuals, as Lynch and Murray (2000) argue, the models overlook individual deviations and are inadequate to explain the experience of many gays and lesbians, particularly those who have been married within the confines of the institution of heterosexuality (Cass, 1984; Troiden, 1988). The models also fail to consider the influence of such demographic characteristics as age and the presence of children (Morris, 1997). They do not describe the experience of stepfamily members who undergo decision making about coming out as a unit. It is now generally accepted that coming out is an ongoing and lifelong process and one that may be reengaged during the process of family construction (Barret & Robinson, 1994; Lynch, 2000; Lynch & Murray, 2000).

Several conclusions emerge: (1) The majority of research failed to distinguish differences in family structure or gender composition as important for understanding family challenges and strengths; (2) Studies about parents who had previously been heterosexually married raised questions about definitions of sexual orientation. Research addressed motives for marrying and parenting and the parenting behaviors of LGBT parents; (3) Findings on parenting and the consequences of LGBT parenting on children found overwhelming evidence of successful parenting and no negative consequences for the children; and (4) Coming out was by far the single issue receiving the most attention in the early research. Most research on coming out emphasized the benefits of disclosure but also reflected the reality and dangers of homophobia and the potential negative impacts of disclosure on custody decisions. In many ways, this early research engendered a better, more progressive era in LGBT family studies. The initial studies forced a realization that parenting was not the sole purview of heterosexuals and raised serious doubts about the definitions of sexual orientation.

Review of the Current Literature

There was increasing recognition of the diversity of LGBT families following the 1980s, and researchers realized that different types of families faced unique challenges and demonstrated original strengths. We present here an overview of the current research on the gay and lesbian stepfamily, focusing on those issues most likely to confront therapists who treat gay and lesbian stepfamily members.

The integration of identities is a task that both the biological parent and the stepparent face as they become a family. Both parents are integrating parenthood identities with their gay or lesbian status, but the processes and the challenges faced are very dissimilar. The resolution of the identity challenges that confront the biological parent and stepparents in gay and lesbian stepfamilies is crucial for healthy individual growth and successful family formation. Yet with the exceptions of Lynch's (2004a, 2004b) and Bigner's (1996) studies, there has been scant attention to issues of identity integration.

Stepparents typically come to the family unit with little or no parenting experience and often hold unrealistic expectations about parenting. Most typically, the stepparents have successfully come out, with their experience of coming out similar to those traditionally outlined in the early developmental-stage models. Thus, stepparents have achieved functional integration; their gay or lesbian identity is important but no longer their most significant or master status; rather, they have successfully integrated their gay or lesbian identity with their other statuses.

For heterosexuals, the stepparent role is characterized as incompletely institutionalized (Cherlin & Furstenberg, 1994) and, because of this, a particularly difficult role to assume (Pasley et al., 1994; Visher & Visher, 1990). Heterosexual stepparents are accorded legal and social recognition and at least some of the approval that accompanies the parenthood role. For the gay or lesbian stepparent, the layering of a socially acceptable status on top of a stigmatized identity is not similarly rewarded. Gay and lesbian stepparents are marginalized and may suffer stigma at the hands of multiple sources: the heterosexual world, straight parents, and the gay or lesbian community (Berger, 2000; Power et al., 2010). Even within the home, they enter the relationship as outsiders. The biological parents and the children perceive themselves as a family; for them, the integration of the stepparent represents a change from one type of family structure (single parent) to another (stepfamily) (Nelson, 1996). The stepparent has to find place and voice within this family unit. Frequently with little or no experience in parenting, the stepparent must learn how to parent, what parenting role he or she wants and will be allowed to assume, and how to present as a gay or lesbian parent to a world that fails to recognize and, in fact, disallows gay and lesbian parents legal and social recognition and even a label.

The lack of institutionalization and freedom from normative expectations present challenges to gay and lesbian stepfamilies but also constitute advantages in allowing the unit freedom and flexibility in creating the stepfamily and assuming roles (Oswald, 2002). Decisions about stepparent roles will be based on such factors as the child's gender, age, and developmental stage; the biological parent's attitudes toward coparenting; and the stepparent's own willingness and ability to coparent. The biological parent is perceived as the expert in parenting. Much of the research finds that stepparents who are willing to learn how to parent from the biological parent, who slowly transition to the parenthood role, and who demonstrate adaptability and flexibility in assuming a variety of roles emerge as very successful stepparents (Current-Juretschko & Bigner, 2005; Lynch, 2004a). Research demonstrates that stepparents alternatively act as friends and companions, allies, teachers, and parents, changing roles depending on the specific situation and the environment (Lynch, 2004a).

The creation of a new stepfamily requires the biological parents to transition from parenting in a single-parent family to parenting in a gay or lesbian stepfamily (Nelson, 1996). They are frequently still in the process of integrating their newly realized lesbian or gay identity with their previously assumed parenthood identity. Unlike the process stepparents experience, biological parents are layering a socially stigmatized status on top of a much applauded and approved status, that of parent. Biological parents are yielding and mourning the heterosexual privilege and social approval that accompanied their previous statuses and adopting identities that are marginalized, stigmatized, and socially denigrated (Bozett, 1987; Lynch & McMahon-Klosterman, 2007).

Parenthood confers social rewards and approval and is one of the most salient roles for adults in our culture (Nelson, 1996). Parenthood is one of the roles through which adult status is confirmed. For parents, the social approval that accompanies parenthood provides them certain advantages as they integrate their homosexual identity into their parenthood status (Lynch 2004a, 2004b). The benefits that accompany parenthood may serve as an inoculation against the homophobic and heterosexist perceptions of those who become lesbian or gay parents. The confidence biological parents hold regarding their parenthood status may not be easily shaken by those who question their ability to parent by virtue of their loving a same-sex individual.

The identity integration process for biological parents is not without conflict, however. For the first time, biological parents may be confronted with external homophobia, with their rights and abilities as parents questioned. As they mourn the loss of their privileged status, they must develop both information management and stigma management strategies to protect themselves, their children, and the stepfamily from homophobia and heterosexism, with little experience to guide them. Previous sources of support—for example, families of origin—may not accept their new identity as gay or lesbian or may reject the new stepfamily. The homosexual community, which may support their lesbian and gay identity, is not a place where activities or attitudes are conducive to parenting or families (Power et al., 2010). In addition, biological gay or lesbian parents may confront threats of or actual custody suits from their ex-spouses. Finally, they have to decide whether and how much to disclose to all the significant others in their lives, including their children.

The two parents must resolve differences in their expectations of relationships and parenting. Biological parents' expectations may be based on previous relationships and what they perceived as desirous within former mixed-sex relationships. Lesbian and gay stepparents' expectations may be based on the norms of the homosexual community, where equality, freedom from gender roles, and autonomy characterize long-term partnerships and where partners construct relationships based on the needs and desires of the two adults. The expectations of the two parents may contradict each other, with the stepparent assuming that the couple relationship is primary and the biological parent assuming that the children are the primary focus. Difficulties may, consequently, arise with the stepparent and the children vying for the biological parent's attention. Stepparents frequently express surprise at the considerable involvement, intensity, and energy biological parents bestow on their offspring, whereas biological parents complain of feeling torn and exhausted in trying to meet the demands placed on them by their children and by their new partners (Furrow & Palmer, 2007; Nelson, 1996).

One of the most crucial issues immediately facing the gay or lesbian stepfamily in becoming a family is coming out. Research results unequivocally demonstrate that the benefits of coming out far outweigh those of a closeted existence (Falk, 1994; McDonald, 1990; Morrow, 1997). The relationship between parents and children is conclusive: secrecy about the parent's sexual orientation creates unnecessary distance in the parent–child relationship and interferes with parents and their children developing healthy, authentic relationships (Barret & Robinson, 1994; Bigner, 1996). Parents who fail to disclose expend unnecessary energy controlling information and maintaining secrecy (Barret & Robinson, 1994).

Lynch and Murray (2000) initially conceptualized the idea of a group coming out to describe the stepfamily process of family disclosure. That is, decisions about how out to be, what strategies would be in place, and what boundary controls would be utilized reflect family considerations rather than merely individual or couple decisions. Family members must realistically assess the impact that homophobia and a stigmatized status (Hare 1994) will have on the child or children (Barret & Robinson, 1994), as well as on the family as a whole. One of the most significant differences between gay and lesbian stepfamilies and other LGBT families is that in the former, decisions about coming out occur simultaneously with family construction. In nuclear gay and lesbian families, the parents have time to discuss issues of disclosure prior to the arrival of the children. For the stepparent who has already completed a process of coming out, coming out as a group constitutes a second coming out.

Stepparents' knowledge about coming out also helps to facilitate the other individual family members' coming-out experience. In Lynch's (2004b) research on biological parents' coming out, she discovered that biological parents often pursue some degree of recklessness in disclosing. It may be that through experiencing the privileges accompanying heterosexual marriage and parenthood, biological parents have a false sense of security as they disclose. Stepparents who have already integrated a gay or lesbian identity play the role of expert in this area, warning biological parents of the potential dangers associated with coming out. The coming-out experience is one of the ways in which the stepparents and the children cement their relationship. Stepparents are well acquainted with the experience of being marginalized and isolated and may have experienced this during their youth. Because of the stepparents have this experience, the children frequently see the stepparents as able to understand and empathize with the fears and concerns they have about being raised in a lesbian or gay household.

One consistent finding emerging from all the research on gay and lesbian stepfamilies—and particularly with respect to coming out—is that, above all else, these families are child centered. Within stepfamilies, parents' decisions about whether to come out and how out to be are based primarily on concerns for their children's well-being and comfort level. The inclusion of the children in coming-out decisions is proactive; children who are mature enough are included in the decision process, and parents encourage them to have a voice in the coming-out process. Thus, research results show that the coming-out process in these families is not only cooperative but also flexible and ongoing, one that can be adapted to circumstances, developmental stages, and specific day-to-day realities (Benkov, 1994).

It is important to note that in coming out, parents not only disclose their orientation to their children but also provide the child with information regarding the child's own disclosure about the family. The majority of parents leave disclosure decisions up to the child—specifically, about whether to disclose and who will be chosen as confidants—but they also help to protect their children from potential homophobia. Stepparents and biological parents help children through disclosure decisions, advising them of the potential problems accompanying outness and secrecy, helping them to create and adopt information management techniques when they choose nondisclosure, and assisting them in developing stigma management strategies when they choose to be open about their families (Barret & Robinson, 1994; Lynch & Murray, 2000).

Some researchers have characterized the coming-out process in families as a "revolving closet," an idea that further shows that these families are child centered. As children in a family grow and mature, their acceptance and comfort level with their parents' sexual orientation fluctuates. The timing of disclosure is clearly important, with younger children more accepting and having the least difficulty with discovering that their parent is homosexual (Barret & Robinson, 1994; Bozett 1987). Adolescence is the worst time for children to learn of their parent's gay or lesbian identity (Benkov, 1994; Crosbie-Burnett & Helmbrecht, 1993). In fact, adolescents may show difficulties with their parent's gay or lesbian identity even if the parents disclosed when the children were young. Adolescence may cause a temporary reversal in the child's comfort with membership in a gay- or lesbian-parented family. As adolescents face resolving their own sexual identity issues, parents can be confronted by requests to hide the nature of their relationship. In many of these families, parents typically acquiesce and allow the children's comfort level to determine the parents' degree of outness (Benkov, 1994; Current-Juretschko & Bigner, 2005; Lynch & Murray, 2000).

Areas of Stress and Vulnerability for Gay and Lesbian Stepfamilies

Many of the challenges confronting gay and lesbian stepfamilies are the result of external stressors rather than difficulties internal to the relationship or specific to individual family members. The lack of external recognition and support, stigma from multiple sources, and invisibility and isolation make successful family formation difficult.

Several researchers have discussed the inherent contradictions faced by gays and lesbians in stepfamilies. In this generation, there is increasing tolerance of lesbians and gays—as individuals and even in their relationships—but the idea of children being raised by lesbians and gays is still considered anathema (Campion, 1995). Homophobia continues to ensure the perceived superiority of heterosexuality, as is evident through the lack of images of gay and lesbian families. The traditional myths regarding the potential damages to the children raised by gay and lesbian parents (e.g., molestation, inappropriate gender-role socialization, and, ironically, the stigma that will confront the children; Barret & Robinson, 1994; Bigner, 1996; Campion, 1995) continue to be used to wage rigorous campaigns to deny rights to gay and lesbian families.

Gay stepfamilies are frequently isolated and lack the sources of support generally available to other gays and lesbians. As noted earlier, the gay and lesbian community is focused on serving the needs of single gays and lesbians; until recently, lesbians and gays with children were not made to feel especially welcome in this community (Bozett, 1987; Power et al., 2010). There is contradictory evidence regarding family-of-origin support, with some findings suggesting support from the families, whereas other studies suggest little recognition of the stepfamily from either extended family (Crosbie-Burnett & Helmbrecht, 1993; Power et al., 2010). In terms of finding support among peers, research on both lesbians and gays finds that for biological parents, the lesbian or gay identity is less important than is the parenthood identity. Thus, Bigner (1996) found that gay fathers find support among both straight and gay men who are fathers themselves or who approve of their family situation. Similar results have been found for lesbian woman for whom the parenthood identity trumps their lesbian status in locating support from peers (Lewin, 1993). In contrast, stepparents receive little recognition from homosexual or heterosexual parents and nonparents.

Children may also feel a sense of separateness because of being raised in a gay or lesbian stepfamily. When they are young, their fear of being seen as different may prevent them from disclosing their family situation. However, options to keep silent raise issues of information management, which is difficult for children and interferes with the development of close friendships (Bigner, 1996). Adolescents are more capable of adopting stigma management strategies and more capable of choosing friends who will accept their family situation. For adolescents who are dealing with issues about their own sexuality and identity, though, having lesbian or gay parents can present a source of stress (Bigner, 1996).

Areas of Strength and Resiliency for Gay and Lesbian Stepfamilies

Many of the strengths and benefits of gay and lesbian stepfamilies are internal; that is, they are related to the assets the individuals bring to the family or to the ways in which they become and grow as a unit. Most of these have been discussed; however, we expand on them here because they represent those issues we see as constructive for counseling gay and lesbian stepfamilies.

We discussed how the expertise of each partner brings benefits to the stepparent earlier. What we neglected is the mutuality of transformation for both partners in sharing areas of expertise. Thus, while stepparents benefit from the biological parent's knowledge of parenting, the biological parent is also positively transformed in this process. Obviously, the introduction of the stepparent lightens the load of the biological parent, but biological parents also modify their parenting and learn from the stepparent as well. Perhaps because of the equality and lack of gender-role assumptions in same-sex partnerships, there is less competition and enhanced cooperation in the parenting endeavor. Whatever the cause, the research demonstrates that biological parents credit stepparents with their own growing ability to parent.

Similarly, stepparents claim that their willingness to disclose is changed by the biological parent's assumptions about coming out. Research finds that stepparents tend to be more closeted than are biological parents and more so than are the children, except during adolescence, when children are the most closeted (Crosbie-Burnett & Helmbrecht, 1993). Stepparents' reluctance to disclose may well be a result of their past experience with coming out and their knowledge of the consequences of openness. Biological parents who are not only experiencing coming out at a different historical time but also reluctant to yield their past privileges are often more willing to disclose. Here, too, stepparents frequently experience a transformation in their perception of the fears and the benefits of disclosure and may become more receptive and willing to take risks.

There are two advantages that particularly create strength and resiliency in gay and lesbian stepfamilies: their child-centered families and their adaptability and flexibility. Several researchers have discovered that lesbian and gay stepfamilies tend to be more child centered than are mixed-sex stepfamilies (Lynch, 2000). We have discussed this previously, but some expansion is warranted. The realization of a child-centered theme in gay and lesbian families is particularly enlightening because for decades the heterosexual research and counselors advised couples to emphasize the adult relationship as primary in forming successful stepfamilies. Only recently have researchers realized that when the needs of the children are prioritized, stepfamilies fare better. Yet a number of gay and lesbian researchers had already documented the child-centered approach assumed by lesbian and gay parents regardless of structure (Barret & Robinson, 1994; Falk, 1994). Lynch and Murray (2000) found gay and lesbian stepfamilies tended to be child centered with respect to coming out. However, there is a mutual respect developed between parents and children in these families that may be initiated by having to deal with external homophobia and marginalization, but these feelings and closeness extend well beyond issues of coming out (Barret & Robinson, 1994; Lynch, 2000; Reeves et al., 2010). Gay and lesbian parents in stepfamilies treat their children with respect; as soon as they are old enough, the children have a voice in significant family decisions, a technique that helps these children mature and develop a strong sense of themselves, their value, and their abilities.

Children report that compared to their friends' parents, their own parents are more empathic and open in their relationships with them. Most of the research conducted on children raised by lesbian and gay parents, and especially children raised in stepfamilies, finds that the children express respect for their parents and admiration for their parents' courage (Lewin, 1993). Despite the hardships that may confront children who face stigma because of a parent's homosexuality, research finds that children raised in these households also develop an appreciation for diversity, are more tolerant and accepting of difference (Lynch & Murray, 2000), and develop a strong sense of morality regarding the treatment of other people (Falk, 1994) .

One of the greatest advantages in lesbian and gay families, and especially stepfamilies, is in the high level of adaptability and flexibility both parents and the unit as a whole demonstrate. Perhaps because of the particularly complex issues that confront the stepfamily members, the lack of sources of predictability, and the complete freedom they enjoy in creating their families, parents demonstrate a flexibility that is unusual in other family structures with other gender compositions. For example, previous histories mandate that each partner be willing to trust the other and take a back seat in certain areas. Stepparents evidence flexibility in the roles they alternatively adopt, whereas biological parents adapt their coming-out experience to their partners' knowledge and experience of coming out. The precarious nature of living within a culture that stigmatizes the family requires that children be given a greater power and voice to influence family decisions. Gay and lesbian stepfamilies cope with heterosexist bias and stigma from multiple sources. Despite this, most research on gay and lesbian stepfamilies finds they develop strong and healthy partnerships, engage in positive and effective coparenting, and develop strong internal support systems within the family for each member of the unit.

Recommendations for Treatment: The Therapist as Ally

Homosexuality was classified as a mental illness until 1973 by the American Psychological Association and until 1992 by the World Health Organization. It is hardly surprising, therefore, that many practicing therapists have received little appropriate training in counseling LGBT individuals or families (Buhrke, 1989; Glenn & Russell, 1986; Perosa, Perosa, & Queener, 2008; Pilkington & Cantor, 1996). Therapists and counselors admit to feeling unprepared to work with LGBT families or stepfamilies (Allison, Crawford, Echemendia, Robinson, & Knepp,1994; Bowers & Bieschke, 2005; Buhrke, 1989; Doherty & Simmons, 1996; R.-J. Green, 2000), yet the majority of therapists report that at least one in every 10 clients they serve identifies as gay or lesbian (S. K. Green & Bobele, 1994).

Most therapists' knowledge of LGBT issues comes from workshops or lectures, academic coursework, and professional journal articles (Clark & Serovich, 1997), with the latter providing the most prevalent method of developing and maintaining best practice skills in counseling this population. Most graduate counseling programs offer limited, if any, courses about diverse families, and to this day many present family counseling from an idealized but antiquated notion of the American family (Pachankis & Goldfried, 2004). This state of affairs leaves the primary methods of accessing reliable, legitimate, and objective information on LGBT families in the hands of the therapists themselves. Only those therapists who realize they have been inadequately prepared and who are motivated to alleviate this deficiency are likely to search out resources and materials on LGBT individuals and families. Unfortunately, studies reveal that many psychotherapists are prejudiced and demonstrate insensitivity in working with lesbian, gay, and bisexual people (Garnets, Hancock, Cochran, Goodchilds, & Peplau, 1991; Liddle, 1996; Nystrom, 1997). Frequently, the LGBT orientation is perceived as the problem; further, rather than acknowledging the client's voice as expert in presenting the problem, the therapist often counsels based on homophobic beliefs about LGBT lives and families (Pachankis & Goldfried, 2004).

We contend that the therapist as ally is one method through which we can ensure constructive therapy experiences for LGBT individuals, particularly those in stepfamilies. What we know about the limitations of training for therapists, coupled with possible heterosexist attitudes on the part of counselors, directs this prescription. We define an *ally* as a person from a position of privilege who acts with and is aligned with individuals or groups oppressed and marginalized. Like other identities, the ally identity encompasses both internal cognitions and external behaviors and actions. Like other identities, it cannot be adopted during therapy and then left behind when the identity of counselor becomes less salient and the therapist is engaged in his or her other roles. Adopting an ally identity is a process and a continuous journey that begins with an internal examination of the therapist's own culturally learned, homophobic stereotypes, including considerations of unequal power and privilege. The ally identity is a commitment to learning about and becoming an expert on LGBT stepfamilies through accessing resources that will enhance the counselor's ability to be an ally and an effective counselor in therapeutic encounters with LGBT stepfamily members. The ally learns all he or she can about LGBT stepfamilies using all the resources available, including the clients. The ally posture assumes the clients are experts about their lived experiences. To be an ally to the LGBT community is to make a commitment to work for social justice and to decrease the marginalization of the group based on tired, unfounded stereotypes.

To adopt this perspective, the therapist must confront various interpretations of reality. Initially, this is accomplished through therapists conducting internal examinations of their own culturally learned assumptions about homosexuality (Pachankis & Goldfried, 2004). The ally posture can be adopted only by those practitioners who are concerned with creating open discourse and who believe that alternative versions of reality are acceptable (Kendall, 2001). This perspective adheres to a poststructuralist paradigm—that is, a worldview that believes in the social creation of reality and perceives how various interpretations of it can and do emerge from those individuals who occupy different power positions within society. Poststructuralist thought and ally behaviors encourage us to critique the view that is dominated and maintained by those in power (Brod, 1989; Hooks, 1984). Adoption of this perspective allows us to understand how maintaining the heterosexual nuclear-family system benefits the power holders' patriarchal and heterosexual agenda. An ally view posits alternative definitions and interpretations of family as not only possible but also often better (Brod, 1989; Hooks, 1984; Johnson, 1997; Kendall, 2001).

The ways in which the therapists' own identities interact with the client's is crucial as therapists examine their own potential sources of bias. Adopting an ally identity and constructing that identity are essential steps for therapists regardless of their sexual orientation. For one thing, LGBT therapists are in no way immune from heterosexism; internalized homophobia can present difficulties for LGBT therapists in counseling LGBT individuals and their families. A primary key to good therapeutic relationships is to see LGBT stepfamilies as normalized and not pathological. Because the gay and lesbian community has historically focused on single persons, not parents (Power et al., 2010), it is essential for lesbian and gay therapists, as well as straight therapists, to acknowledge their feelings about family, childbearing, and LGBT families.

We cannot assume that LGBT therapists would, by virtue of their sexual orientation, necessarily provide appropriate counseling to LGBT stepfamily members. Neither can we assume that therapists who support the LGBT community in general necessarily hold positive attitudes about LGBT individuals as parents. Furthermore, we cannot assume that a LGBT therapist who is not a parent—even one who is fully committed to LGBT families—will automatically provide effective counseling to LGBT stepfamilies.

An understanding of the challenges to and benefits of LGBT family life requires more than a posture of support. The ally identity requires therapists to actively access resources on LGBT families in all their diverse structures, including scholarship in which marginalized individuals are active participants (Pachankis, & Goldfried, 2004). In this way, therapists become aware of the vulnerabilities and strengths that characterize LGBT families. For example, one dangerous assumption a therapist who is a heterosexual parent might make is in overemphasizing similarities between mixed-sex stepfamilies and LGBT stepfamilies or in assuming similarities in LGBT families regardless of structure. Some of the major challenges in the LGBT stepfamily (e.g., identity integration and coming out) are nonexistent in heterosexual stepfamilies (Lynch, 2000, 2004a, 2004b), as well as in LGBT nuclear families. In addition, unique benefits accompany LGBT stepfamily formation (e.g., the child-centered orientation). Ignorance of the challenges to and the strengths of the LGBT stepfamily restricts potential valuable sources that can be used to enhance the counseling effort and the family (Lynch & McMahon-Klosterman, 2007).

In becoming aware of the research, therapists will become attuned to crucial areas as they counsel gay and lesbian stepfamilies. Clearly, therapists will need to be aware of how the problems surrounding the lack of external and internal recognition impact all stepfamily members. Therapists must deal with the differences in relationship and parenting expectations. Therapists can help gay and lesbian families build on the egalitarian nature typical of same-sex relationships while still encouraging each partner to assume the role of expert with respect to particular issues. Thus, in parenting, the role of the biological parent predominates; but in coming out and integration of a gay or lesbian identity, the stepparent has knowledge based on prior experience.

A therapist who has read the literature can become aware of the complexities involved in integrating gay and lesbian identities with parenthood statuses for both parents. The therapist can provide support for the family and help the family members to examine the gap between idealized preconceptions, the complex realities of everyday living, and the possibilities for what the family can become (Bernstein, 2006). Therapists can make use of the intentionality and resilience that come naturally to those for whom stigma and marginalization are daily and constant realities (Oswald, 2002).

Therapists can offer help in counseling stepparents as they attempt to develop a parent identity. This process is exacerbated when the stepparent identity is unrecognized outside the family; even within the family, the stepparent is initially the outsider who must create a stepparent role within an already existing parent–child unit. It is in terms of this latter difficulty that the therapist who has studied the LGBT literature can appropriately counsel the family. For example, Lorah (2006/2007) demonstrates that in lesbian stepfamilies, participants who perceived their role within the family as valued, clearly defined, and meaningful were happy in the relationship. Therapists can encourage clear communication patterns within families with this goal in mind. Lorah (2006/2007) also stresses the therapist's role in providing recognition of and validation for the assets that lesbian stepmothers bring to stepfamilies. In addition, the therapist can advise stepparents to adopt flexibility and adaptability in parenting as they slowly transition to a parenting role.

As biological parents attempt to integrate their new stigmatized status with their parenthood identity, they may begin to mourn the loss of privilege and experience difficulty in coping with the first experience of being stigmatized. As biological parents yield previous privilege, therapists can address the advantages of the new relationship as built on an absence of gender roles and on autonomy. In addition, therapists will need to address the biological parent's inexperience with homophobia and the difficulties this lack brings to integration of the gay or lesbian identity.

Both parents will need to find systems of support as they integrate identities and strive to become family. The therapist can provide suggestions for accessing appropriate systems of support. Biological parents will need contact and support from other lesbian and gay parents. Both parents may need help in locating support alternatives so they can distance themselves from the gay and lesbian community, which may inhibit the processes of identity integration. Therapists must not only identify systems of support but also help determine the value of potential sources of support (LaSala, 2002). For example, research suggests that lack of support from families of origin may cause additional stress on LGBT stepfamilies. It may be that therapists will need to encourage space and distance from families of origin who question the value of the stepfamily (Oswald, 2002). Therapists who adopt an ally identity can help the two parents as they transition and provide the support each needs as individuals and together as a family.

The coming-out process for the family often presents difficulties for the family unit. Without a therapist who is knowledgeable about the typical coming-out processes for nonparents, parents, the family unit, and children at different ages and developmental stages, therapy cannot proceed with any clear sense of direction. If the therapist has become cognizant of the adaptability and flexibility typically characteristic of lesbian and gay families, he or she can encourage the couple in ways to use these strengths to deal with the stresses of coming out. Clearly, the therapist can also help the family benefit from the child-centered orientation that is typically adopted in gay and lesbian stepfamilies. It is important to note that LGBT stepfamilies take the children's interests seriously and include them in decision making (i.e., when to come out, how to come out) and demonstrate deep respect for the feelings of the children (Michaels, 2006, p. 59). The children learn to balance their own needs with others' needs through direct and open communication. Through this family work, children develop a great empathy and appreciation for diversity (Lynch & McMahon-Klosterman, 2007). The group coming-out experience can be a vital way in which the stepfamily becomes strengthened as a unit.

There is a fine line for the therapist to walk in not over- or underemphasizing the sexual orientation of the family (Butler, 2009). The family must determine the issues to be addressed, and the therapist must not assume the concerns are about being a member of the LGBT community. The ally therapist should not make assumptions but, rather, explore with the family members what stressors they wish to address as most important. One way this is accomplished is through the therapist's willingness to learn about the LGBT subculture and gain insight into normal patterns of behavior within the defined community. The LGBT community is the milieu within which parents and stepparents learn the norms, values, and attitudes associated with the gay or lesbian lifestyle; it is thus a reference group for the development of a gay or lesbian identity. Relating to the LGBT community contextualizes the family unit within the reference culture that is situated within the larger culture. Consequently, the therapist can redefine "normal" and understand more fully where a problem may exist but not assume it is related to sexual identity.

The ally therapist strives to create a safe therapeutic environment that supports families in creating their own "normal" in the face of external pressures. The therapist helps by identifying internal stressors versus such external stressors as the lack of civil rights or the pressure to keep the primary relationship secret. The internal issues are therapy related, whereas the external can be viewed as issues of social injustice to be addressed by the society. The ally therapist should assume an active role in working to change the conditions of the external stressors. In this way, the therapist legitimizes the LGBT stepfamily relationship as healthy and normal while identifying the source of some stress as outside the relationship.

The ally status is particularly conducive to the interaction within therapeutic encounters because it enables a person of privilege to interact with marginalized individuals without depending on heterosexually defined discourse to interpret what is said (Brod, 1989). Within therapy, counselors adopt the perspective of an empathic ally so that LGBT clients are encouraged to voice their own lived experience. Most important, the therapeutic encounter is built on a relationship of equality, with clients' voices expert in relating their lived experiences as LGBT individuals who are members of LGBT stepfamilies (Lynch & McMahon-Klosterman, 2007). The power differential between the client and the therapist must also be addressed (Bernstein, 2006, p. 443). Many therapists employ a theoretical approach that defines them as the expert, armed with the knowledge necessary to be a successful counselor. One of the advantages of adopting an ally identity, however, is that it encourages a relationship based on equity and on the ally's willingness to acknowledge the expert status of the client with respect to his or her own life and family.

The therapist who has adopted an ally identity does not leave that identity when the door to the office closes on the last gay or lesbian stepfamily member. Allies have to determine when to speak as an ally and when speaking takes away the voice of the marginalized person or group. Knowing when to speak up and when to remain silent is not always an easy determination to make. Inevitably, the ally will make errors, which raises another important ability the ally must display: willingness to acknowledge mistakes and persevere as an ally with the will to learn more and be a better ally. To be an ally to the LGBT community is to make a commitment to work for social justice and to decrease the marginalization of the group based on tired, unfounded stereotypes. The therapist, as ally, has an obligation to disrupt the professional status quo when it is heteronormative or homophobic. Our intellectual understanding generally exceeds our functional understanding of oppression. Thus therapists must persist in unraveling the complexities of oppressive counseling practices and strive for multicultural understanding to benefit all clients. Therapist should be a part of a professional group that will encourage continuous exploration of personal attitudes in a safe place where questions about the ally identity can be raised. Allies need a network of colleagues with whom to explore their own reactions in the process of acquiring a fully integrated ally identity.

As part of educating themselves, the therapists keep current on the relevant federal and state regulations that may impinge on LGBT stepfamilies and cause stress. The therapist ally must be trusted by the stepfamily to interrupt homophobic attitudes and challenge oppressive laws and practices. The therapist as ally assumes personal responsibility for acting as a LGBT ally, dismantling internalized dominance, and facilitating the power and voice of LGBT stepfamilies as legitimate and healthy families. Through this work, the therapist is able to provide a model for positive change toward social justice.

Case Study

A lesbian couple with one child presented with issues they were experiencing in their new neighborhood. The couple are highly educated people and recently moved from a relatively liberal area of the country (New England) to a very conservative midwestern Bible Belt city. They moved because the biological mother had just finished her doctorate and accepted a job offer at a large university. In their previous location they had been very comfortable with their lesbian identities, and both were out to their families of origin and in their neighborhood of residence. Their experience at the new location can only be described as culture shock.

The family opted to come to therapy to discuss a recent incident concerning their 8-year-old daughter. They were relieved when the daughter rather quickly made a new friend. Within a few weeks, however, suddenly and without warning the new friend slid a note under the front door advising the daughter that because of a number of increased school activities she would no longer have time to spend with her; added to the note was the information that the books she had borrowed were in the daughter's mailbox.

As noted earlier, a person who adopts an ally identity acts with and is aligned with individuals or groups who are oppressed and marginalized. With respect to LGBT issues and family forms, therapists who are allies adopt the belief that alternative definitions and interpretations of family and parenting are not only possible but also often better. From the very first session, the therapist's communication with the couple should emphasize that the couple and the child are the experts in determining the presenting problem and the goals for therapy. Although it might be tempting, the therapist should not automatically counsel this family as he or she might a heterosexual stepfamily in a similar situation, nor should the therapist assume that the couple's identity is the problem. Thus, in the situation presented here, a therapist might suggest that the couple act as educators and might advise them to teach the neighbors (i.e., the child's parents) about LGBT families and couples. The therapist as ally would, however, necessarily refrain from adopting any expert role and providing such advice to the couple. Whereas some LGBT stepfamily couples might opt to adopt such an educative role, others might resent the implication that they possess a responsibility to provide LGBT education to heterosexuals.

As an ally, the therapist will instead raise his or her own awareness about LGBT stepfamilies and will learn about the sources of strength and resiliency likely to be found in the present family. The therapist can help in posing what are likely to be the important issues for the couple's therapy. One issue clearly revolves around the child's loss of friendship. A second issue is whether the present situation raises an important question in the couple's relationship. The couple may need to reconsider their past behavior and level of outness and decide if they need to alter their couple presentation.

One of the therapist's roles will be to help the presenting couple parent and to determine what the child wants. In discovering information about LGBT stepfamilies, the therapist might suspect that this is one of those instances in which the stepparent can be most helpful to the child. Thus, because stepparents frequently have early experience with homophobia, they can best empathize with their child about the present situation. In the absence of an ally identity, therapists might well assume that the biological mother would be the one who adopts the primary role when her child experiences hurt. However, because the ally identity rests on accessing knowledge regarding the marginalized person's experience, the therapist will be made aware that, in this instance, the stepparent might well be the expert role model and parent.

As the second issue suggests, this couple may well need to revisit how out to be in their new conservative environment. If the therapist has done the homework, he or she will be aware that the biological parents in LGBT stepfamilies tend to be more comfortable with their LGBT identity and are more likely to argue that the family be out. In the present couple's situation, the biological parent's professional environment bolsters that view. Universities tend to encourage liberal views and acceptance of diversity. As noted earlier, the therapist will also be aware of the likelihood that the stepparent possesses greater expertise and experience with coming out and with the kind of homophobia that is currently confronting this family. One of the issues that can be problematic for the therapist as ally occurs in couple therapy: It is one thing to assume the client is the expert, but a therapist's working on this assumption is made difficult in couple therapy when the individuals hold diverse views. Nevertheless, the therapist will need to help the couple discuss their discrepant views on coming out and carefully to consider all the issues involved in this particular situation.

The therapist as ally must remain ever cognizant of and committed to the couple's role in determining the direction and the objectives for the therapeutic encounter. He or she can do so by assisting the couple members in enhancing their characteristic LGBT stepfamily assets: listening to and relying on each other's expertise and encouraging group decision making in solving problems. Particularly in a situation such as this, where the parent's LGBT identity has affected the child's experience, group decision making and respectful hearing of all family members' voices will continue to be assets to this family and to the therapist as he or she adopts an ally identity.

The therapist will continue the ally identity long after the couple determines that the therapeutic goals have been achieved. The ally identity is a continuous one. Within professional associations and in interaction with the surrounding world, the ally therapist must continue to support and to advocate for LGBT rights.

Conclusion

This chapter has considered the historical and current scholarship on gay and lesbian stepfamilies and has particularly considered those issues that are likely to confront therapists who counsel gay and lesbian stepfamily members. We have particularly focused on presenting the challenges and the strengths exhibited by gay and lesbian stepfamilies. We have recommended the ally identity as conducive to working with those individuals who have been marginalized and denied privilege, such as gay adoption of this identity, and demonstrated why this identity works in therapy with individuals who have been subjected to continual discrimination. As we have stressed here, the benefit of the ally identity is that it mitigates the therapeutic assumption that the gay or lesbian identity is what is problematic. Instead, the ally identity encourages the therapist to understand that it is our heteronormative assumptions and our homophobic environment that are responsible for many of the difficulties confronting these families and their members. The ally identity encourages therapists to view the client as expert in presenting problems and in measuring the objectives and the success of therapeutic encounters. Finally, we have presented a case study to demonstrate the way in which a therapist who adopts an ally identity can effectively work in a counseling situation with gay and lesbian stepfamily members.

References

Allison, K., Crawford, I., Echemendia, R., Robinson, L., & Knepp, D. (1994). Human diversity and professional competence: Training in clinical and counseling psychology revisited. *American Psychologist*, *49*, 792–796.

Baptiste, D. A. (1987). Psychotherapy with gay/lesbian couples and their children in stepfamilies: A challenge for marriage and family therapists. *Journal of Homosexuality*, *14*, 223–238.

Barret, R. L., & Robinson, B. (1994). Gay dads. In A. Gottfried & A. Gottfried (Eds.), *Redefining families: Implications for children's development* (pp. 151–170). New York, NY: Plenum Press.

Benkov, L. (1994). *Reinventing the family: The emerging story of lesbian and gay parents*. New York, NY: Crown.

Berger, R. (2000, September–October). Gay stepfamilies: A triple-stigmatized group. *Families in Society*, 1–4.

Bernstein, A. (2006). Re-visioning, restructuring, and reconciliation: Clinical practice with complex postdivorce families. *Family Process*, *46*, 67–78.

Bigner, J. J. (1996). Working with gay fathers developmental, postdivorce parenting, and therapeutic issues. In J. Laird & R-J. Green (Eds.), *Lesbians and gays in couples and families* (pp. 370–403). San Francisco, CA: Jossey-Bass.

Bowers, A., & Bieschke, J. (2005). Psychologists' clinical evaluations and attitudes: An examination of the influence of gender and sexual orientation. *Professional Psychology: Research and Practice*, *36*(1), 97–103.

Bozett, F. W. (1987). Gay fathers. In F. W. Bozett (Ed.), *Gay and lesbian parents* (pp. 3–22). New York, NY: Praeger.

Brod, H. (1989). Clothes and leisure suits: The class basis and bias of the men's movement. In M. S. Kimmel & M. Messner (Eds.), *Men's lives* (pp. 280–295). New York, NY: Macmillan.

Buhrke, R. A. (1989). Incorporating lesbian and gay issues into counselor training: A resource guide. *Journal of Counseling and Development*, *68*, 77–80.

Butler, C. (2009). Sexual and gender minority therapy and systemic practice. *Journal of Family Therapy*, *31*, 338–358.

Campion, M. (1995). *Who's fit to be a parent?* London, England: Routledge.

Cass, V. C. (1984). Homosexual identity formation: Testing a theoretical model. *Journal of Sex Research, 20*(2), 143–167.

Cherlin, A .J., & Furstenberg, F., Jr. (1994). Stepfamilies in the United States: Reconsideration. *Annual Review of Sociology, 20*, 359–381.

Clark, W., & Serovich, J. M. (1997). Twenty years and still in the dark? Content analysis of articles pertaining to gay, lesbian, and bisexual issues in marriage and family therapy journals. *Journal of Marital and Family Therapy, 23*(3), 239–253.

Crosbie-Burnett, M., & Helmbrecht, L. (1993). A descriptive empirical study of gay male stepfamilies. *Family Relations, 42*, 256–262.

Current-Juretschko, L., & Bigner, J. J. (2005). An exploratory investigation of gay stepfathers' perceptions of their role. *Journal of GLBT Family Studies, 1*(4), 1–20.

Doherty, W. J., & Simmons, D. S. (1996). Clinical practice patterns of marriage and family therapists: A national survey of therapists and their clients. *Journal of Marital and Family Therapy, 22*, 9–25.

Falk, P. (1994). The gap between psychosocial assumptions and empirical research in lesbian mother child custody cases. In A. Gottfried & A. Gottfried (Eds.), *Redefining families* (pp. 131–56). New York, NY: Plenum Press.

Furrow, J., & Palmer, G. (2007). EFFT and blended families: Building bonds from the inside out. *Journal of Systemic Therapies, 26*, 44–58.

Garnets, L., Hancock, K., Cochran, S., Goodchilds, J., & Peplau, L. (1991). Issues in psychotherapy with lesbians and gay men: A survey of psychologists. *American Psychologist, 46*, 964–972.

Glenn, A., & Russell, R. (1986). Heterosexual bias among counselor trainees. *Counselor Education and Supervision, 25*(3), 222–229.

Golombok, S., Spencer, A., & Rutter, M. (1983). Children in lesbian and single-parent households: Psychosexual and psychiatric appraisal. *Journal of Child Psychology and Psychiatry, 24*(4), 551–572.

Green, R-J. (2000). Introduction to special section: Lesbian, gay and bisexual issues in family therapy. *Journal of Martial and Family Therapy, 26*, 407–408.

Green, S. K., & Bobele, M. (1994). Family therapists' response to AIDS: An examination of attitudes, knowledge, and contact. *Journal of Marital and Family Therapy, 20*, 349–367.

Hare, J. (1994). Concerns and issues faced by families headed by a lesbian couple. *Families in Society, 75*(1), 27–35.

Hooks, B. (1984). *Feminist theory: From margin to center.* Boston, MA: South End Press.

Johnson, A. G. (1997). *The gender knot: Unraveling our patriarchal legacy.* Philadelphia, PA: Temple University Press.

Kendall, F. E. (2001, August). How to be an ally if you are a person with privilege. Materials from Ally Workshop, Miami University, Oxford, OH.

Keshel, J. K. (1990). Cognitive remodeling of the family: How remarried people view stepfamilies. *American Journal of Orthopsychiatry, 60*(2), 196–203.

LaSala, M. (2002). Walls and bridges: How coupled gay men and lesbians manage their intergenerational relationships. *Journal of Martial and Family Therapy, 28*, 327–339.

Lewin, E. (1993). *Lesbian mothers: Accounts of gender in American culture.* New York, NY: Cornell University Press.

Liddle, B. (1996). Therapist sexual orientation, gender, and counseling practices as they relate to ratings of helpfulness by gay and lesbian clients. *Journal of Counseling Psychology, 43*, 394–401.

Lorah, P. (2006–2007). Lesbian stepmothers: Navigating visibility. *Journal of LGBT Issues in Counseling, 1*, 59–76.

Lynch, J. (2000). Considerations of family structure and gender composition: The lesbian and gay stepfamily. *Journal of Homosexuality, 40*, 81–96.

Lynch, J. (2004a). Becoming a stepparent in gay/lesbian stepfamilies: Integrating identities. *Journal of Homosexuality, 48*, 45–60.

Lynch, J. (2004b). Identity transformation: Biological parents in lesbian/gay stepfamilies. *Journal of Homosexuality, 47*, 91–109.

Lynch, J., & McMahon-Klosterman, K. (2007). Guiding the acquisition of therapist ally identity: Research on the GLBT stepfamily as resource. *Journal of Gay, Lesbian, Bisexual, Transgender Family Studies, 2*, 123–151.

Lynch, J., & Murray, K. (2000). For the love of the children: The coming out process for lesbian and gay parents and stepparents. *Journal of Homosexuality, 39*, 1–24.

McDonald, H. B. (1990). *Homosexuality: A practical guide to counseling lesbians, gay men, and their families.* New York, NY: Continuum.

Michaels, M. (2006). Factors that contribute to stepfamily success: A qualitative analysis. *Journal of Divorce and Remarriage, 44*, 53–66.

Morris, J. F. (1997). Lesbian coming out as a multidimensional process. *Journal of Homosexuality, 33*(2), 1–22.

Morrow, D. F. (1997). Coming-out issues for adult lesbians: A group intervention. *Social Work, 41*(6), 648–659.

Nelson, F. (1996). *Lesbian motherhood: An exploration of Canadian lesbian families.* Toronto, ON: University of Toronto Press.

Newman, B. S., & Muzzonigro, P. G. (1993). The effects of traditional family values on the coming out process of gay male adolescents. *Adolescence, 28*(109), 213–225.

Nystrom, N. M. (1997). Mental health experiences of gay men and lesbians. Paper presented at the American Association for the Advancement of Science, Houston, TX.

Oswald, R. (2002). Resilience within the family networks of lesbians and gay men: Intentionality and redefinition. *Journal of Marriage and the Family, 64*(2), 374–383.

Pachankis, J., & Goldfried, M. (2004). Clinical issues in working with lesbian, gay and bisexual clients. *Psychotherapy: Theory, Research, Practice and Training, 41*(3), 227–246.

Pasley, K., Ihinger-Tallman, M., & Lofquist, A. (1994). Remarriage and stepfamilies: Making progress in understanding. In K. Pasley & M. Ihinger-Tallman (Eds.), *Stepparenting: Issues in theory, research and practice* (pp. x–xx). Westport, CT: Greenwood Press.

Pennington, S. B. (1987). Children of lesbian mothers. In F. Bozett (Ed.), *Gay and lesbian parents* (pp. 58–74). New York, NY: Praeger.

Perosa, L., Perosa, S., & Queener, J. (2008). Accessing competencies for counseling lesbian, gay, bisexual and transgender individuals, couples and families. *Journal of Lesbian Gay Bisexual Transgender Issues in Counseling, 2*, 159–169.

Pilkington, N. W., & Cantor, J. M. (1996). Perceptions of heterosexual bias in professional psychology programs: A survey of graduate students. *Professional Psychology Research and Practice, 27*, 604–612.

Power, J. J., Perlesz, A., Schofield, M. J., Pitts, M., Brown, R., McNair, R., … Bickerdike, A. (2010). Understanding resilience in same-sex parented families: The work, love, play study. *BMC Pubic Health, 10*, 1471–2458.

Reeves, T., Horne, S., Rostosky, S., Riggle, E., Baggett, L., & Aycock, L. (2010). Family members' support for GLBT issues: The role of family adaptability and cohesion. *Journal of GLBT Family Studies, 6*, 80–97.

Troiden, R. (1988). *Gay and lesbian identity: A sociological analysis.* New York, NY: General Hall.

Visher, E. B., & Visher, J. S. (1990). Dynamics of successful stepfamilies. *Journal of Divorce and Remarriage, 14*(1), 3–11.

16

Counseling Lesbian and Gay Individuals, Couples, and Families in Late Life

JOHN A. BLANDO

Cultural groups have varying attitudes toward life, death, sex, food, men, women, children, the elderly, birth and death.

—McGoldrick (1995, p. 262)

The mental health field, in general, has been slow to address the needs of lesbian and gay individuals in late life. Little has been written on the needs of older lesbians and gay men, populations who in addition to facing issues common to older adults face issues uniquely related to sexual orientation. This chapter addresses individual, couple, and family counseling of lesbians and gay men in late life. I will begin by contextualizing the experiences of U.S. lesbians and gay men in late life and then will discuss issues in counseling and the use of a strengths-based approach to working with lesbian and gay men in late life. I will end the discussion with a fictional case example. Throughout the chapter, I will discuss treatment implications.

The Context of Lesbian and Gay People in Late Life

Emotional and physical attraction to and behavior with individuals of the same gender have been documented throughout recorded history and in cultures as diverse as those present in the Americas, Europe, Africa, Asia, Southeast Asia, Melanesia, and other parts of the world. A person who experiences same-gender attraction or engages in same-gender behavior, however, will not necessarily identify as lesbian or gay. Postmodernists would suggest that identity as lesbian or gay is a sociopolitical invention describing a subset of people at a certain time and place, just as identity as *straight* or heterosexual is a sociopolitical invention that describes a subset of people at a certain time and place.

In the United States, those people who do identify as lesbian and gay in late life comprise a unique cohort with clear historical experiences (see Table 16.1). Popular history places the social visibility of the U.S. modern gay movement with the 1969 struggle at Stonewall, a popular Manhattan, between its patrons and the police. In the 1950s and 1960s, groundwork was laid for lesbian and gay identities and the struggle for civil rights through the brave work of members of the Daughters of Bilitis, the Mattachine Society, and similar organizations. Lesbian and gay people made further progress in the social recognition of their existence and acknowledgment of their right not only to exist but also to share in full civil rights through progressive philosophies associated with the sexual revolution in the 1960s and the women's and gay rights movements in the 1970s. The 1980s was a time of some setbacks and some progress in the area of lesbian and gay rights. One major setback, subsequent to the failure of the United States to pass an Equal Rights Amendment to the U.S. Constitution, was a slowing of social acceptance of full equal rights for women. Other setbacks in social acceptance of lesbian and gay people occurred subsequent to demands for heterosocial conformity under the Reagan administration as well as extremist right-wing responses to the AIDS epidemic that called for draconian

Table 16.1 Cohort Experiences of U.S. Lesbian and Gay People in Late Life

Era	Historical Event
1950s–1960s	Homosexuality as a medical disorder
	Gay and lesbian bars hidden from public
	Homosexuality treated as criminal behavior
	Homosexuality not part of social discourse
	Gay bars routinely raided
	Daughters of Bilitis, Mattachine Society
1960s–1970s	Hippies era, Summer of Love, free love movement
	Stonewall rebellion
	Feminism and women's movement
	Gay liberation movement
	American Psychiatric Association depathologizes homosexuality
	Del Martin and Phyllis Lyon advocate for lesbian rights and health care
1970s–1980s	Gay bars become more public
	HIV/AIDS epidemic
	For years, President Reagan refuses to acknowledge the epidemic
1980s–1990s	Deaths of friends and loved ones
2000s–2010s	More effective drugs for treatment of HIV
	Imposition of "Don't Ask, Don't Tell" onto military
	Fight for marriage equality
	Increased awareness of lesbian health issues
	Repeal of "Don't Ask, Don't Tell"

measures against gay men. Conversely, this era also was marked by an increase in collaboration between lesbians and gay men, as lesbians stepped into the role of caregivers for men suffering with AIDS; an increased organization by lesbian and gay people to fight for federal, state, and local acknowledgment of the epidemic and for medical and social resources to fight HIV/AIDS; and compassionate understanding by some of the public of the intense individual, couple, and family suffering caused by HIV/AIDS. The 1990s saw significant progress in medical advances to fight the syndrome; and though not particularly friendly to the lesbian and gay populace, federal administrations no longer denied the reality of AIDS. Recent social changes include the increased visibility of lesbian and gay long-term couples as well as the increased visibility of lesbian and gay families that include children, whether biological or adopted. With the decision to allow lesbian and gay people to serve openly in the military, the most current social discourse focuses on the civil right of lesbian and gay people to legally marry. As of the writing of this chapter, the Obama administration has repealed "Don't Ask, Don't Tell," and civil marriage is a right enjoyed by residents of a number of New England states and Iowa.[1]

Current events related to marriage between same-gender partners and extension of lesbian and gay families through the addition of children are particularly germane to the current chapter. Families comprising same-gender members and their children predate the fight for equal marriage rights. In fact, there are many older same-gender couples, notable among them Del Martin and Phyllis Lyon, central figures in the civil rights movement for lesbian and gay

---

[1] Also included are those lesbian and gay couples who married during the period in California when such marriages were legal and before passage of Proposition 8 in 2009 amended California's constitution to remove this right, marking the first time in California that a civil right had been revoked for a class of individuals. For more information about Proposition 8, see Reed Cowan's 8: The Mormon Proposition (Cowan, 2010).

people.[2] Some of these couples are childless; others have children from a previous heterosexual relationship or through informal adoption as *fictive kin*, that is, individuals functioning as family, though not legally recognized as family.

Lesbian and gay families in late life are varied and comprise, for example, heterosexual elders who have a lesbian or gay adult child, two lesbians or two gay men in a committed relationship, a lesbian and a gay man jointly raising a biological or adopted child, two lesbians and a gay man jointly raising a biological or adopted child, a lesbian couple and a gay male couple jointly raising children, three gay men in a committed relationship, a gay or lesbian parent with heterosexual children, and so forth. Counselors should utilize relevant historical-contextual information to provide a basis for understanding the structure, relationships, and struggles that may be present in lesbian or gay individuals, couples, and families in late life who present seeking counseling.

Cultural Sensitivity and Lesbian and Gay Families in Late Life

Just as a counselor would not expect an older Navajo woman living a traditional life in rural New Mexico to have the same experiences, attitudes, and beliefs as a young European man living in Toronto, so too counselors should not expect lesbian and gay individuals, couples, and families in late life to have the same experiences, attitudes, and beliefs as heterosexual individuals, couples, and families in late life. Further, counselors should not expect any given lesbian or gay individual, couple, or family in late life to have the stereotypical experiences, attitudes, and beliefs expected of lesbians or gay people in late life.

Generalizations about a cultural group can appear to validate stereotypes about that group (Ariel, 1999). These stereotypes function as shorthand or oversimplified mental conceptions. An example of a generalization is the belief that old gay men are lonely because they do not have families or children. A counselor who holds this belief, even if not consciously, will face greater challenges in working with a gay man in late life because such an individual is outside the counselor's *weltanschauung* and may present with nonculturally normative issues.

Stereotypes are oversimplifications, given that cultural groups comprise heterogeneous members (Ariel, 1999). Cultural groups are best understood as social constructions and what is identified as or noted about a cultural group might not be true of any given subset of that group. Ariel (1999) might say that although there may be "prevalent trends" (p. 7) in terms of beliefs, attitudes, and experiences of—in the case of this chapter—lesbian or gay families in late life, a counselor must work with the reality of the family in front of him or her and not the stereotype of such a family. According to this perspective, a counselor's perception of who comprise lesbian and gay individuals, couples or families in late life might not reflect the reality of the particular lesbian or gay individual, couple or family with whom the counselor begins to work. An older, poorer, nonurban, ethnic minority gay male family, for example, may challenge a counselor's perception that gay male families comprise younger or middle-aged, urban, affluent white men.

Counselors must be attentive to the role not only of family but also of culture in the presentation of problems, issues, or pathologies present in individuals (see Ariel, 1999). Not only can family roles, relationships, and dynamics influence what is considered problematic, but so too can culture. Consider a gay *trio*[3] in late life composed of three older males who present with

---

[2] Del Martin and Phyllis Lyon became a couple in the 1950s; they married in San Francisco, California, in 2008 preceding the death of Del Martin later that year.

[3] This type of relationship is so nonnormative in the dominant culture that there is no term to accurately describe it. The closest terms are *ménage-à-trois,* which is too overtly sexual and carries with it a sense of being salacious, or *troilism,* a technical term that refers specifically to a member of a couple enjoying seeing his or her partner engage in sexual relations with a third party.

relationship issues. North American–dominant culture would argue that a family unit consists of, at most, two adults in a romantic relationship and that, further, if there are more than two adults in a romantic relationship, it is immoral, sinful, or pathological. Normative gay male culture in the United States, however, is more accepting of romantic relationship patterns that differ from the dyadic norm of the dominant culture. Hence, a counselor who is unfamiliar with gay male culture may perceive such a relationship as pathological even though within gay male culture the relationship may be an acceptable, nonproblematic phenomenon.

Issues in Counseling Lesbians and Gay Men in Late Life

Lesbians and gay men in late life have experiences that are unique or have unique elements to them. Among these are experiencing heteronormative models of life span development and family life cycles and social expectations, experiencing lesbian or gay developmental milestones, "coming out" in late life, dealing co-occurring ageism and heterosexism, facing microaggression outside and within the family, addressing religion and spirituality, preparing for retirement, managing legal issues, dealing with sexuality in late life, and adjusting to illness and disability. Within the context of counseling, older lesbian and gay clients may have unique transference experiences with their counselor (and, vice versa, the counselor may have unique countertransference experiences with his or her client).

Limitations of Life Span and Life Cycle Models

There are many models of life span development and aging, including Hall's (1922) hill metaphor, Jung's (1933) perspective, Havinghurst's (1961) activity theory, Erikson's (1959) stages of psychosocial development, Cumming and Henry's (1961) disengagement theory, Baltes and Baltes's (1993) selective optimization with compensation theory, Salthouse's (1987) resource reduction theory Tornstam's (2005) gerotranscendence theory, Schroots's (1995) gerodynamics theory, Atchley's (1989) continuity theory, Rowe and Kahn's (1997) theory of successful aging, and others (see Blando, 2011). Some of these theories present aging as a time of decline (e.g., in Hall's hill metaphor) or compensation (e.g., in Baltes et al.'s selective optimization with compensation) or growth (e.g., in Tornstam's gerotranscendence theory). Overall, these theories tend to be focused on individual development, not couple or family development, and are Eurocentric and heteronormative. For the most part, the theories address the individual across the life course or in late life and do so without contextualizing the experiences of the aging individual. The theories, all developed by Europeans or European Americans, also tend to reflect values associated with European or North American culture, including a relative emphasis on personal independence. Further, by their lack of inclusion of issues of sexual orientation identity development over the life course, the theories also tend to be heteronormative. For this reason, these theories may have limited, though some, cachet when applied to lesbians or gay men in late life.

Family Life Cycle   Rather than looking at individual development across the life course, one may consider a multistage family life cycle model, the last stage comprising the period between retirement and death (Carter & McGoldrick, 1989, cited in Benbow et al., 1990). This last stage of life, according to the family life cycle model, is marked by adjustments to retirement, disability, illness, grandparenting or great-grandparenting, decreases in social status, and deaths of friends and of marital partners (Benbow et al., 1990). Like theories of individual life span development, the concept of the family life cycle may be more relevant to heteronormative families than to families comprising lesbian and gay people in late life. In a family life cycle model there may, for example, be an implicit assumption that a family's ability to negotiate challenges at one point in time will improve the likelihood that the family will be able to negotiate challenges later on. This assumption, however, might not hold true when the issues revolve around sexual orientation, coming out, and so forth, and in which there may be either active aggression or microaggression within the family itself.

Life Event Web   An alternative to the family life cycle model is the systemic perspective of the *life event web* (Pruchnow et al., 1979, cited in Qualls, 1999, p. 978). In this view, life events of one individual in the family affect the lives of other individuals in the family (Qualls, 1999). Because a family is interdependent, it is necessary for individual family members to negotiate and rene-gotiate roles as normative and nonnormative events occur in a family's life (Qualls, 1999). In a heteronormative family, adults in late life may become less autonomous and may need family members' assistance in daily activities or may need to move in with another family member. These options may not be available for lesbians or gay men in late life who are estranged from their families as a result of intrafamilial discrimination based on sexual orientation.

Systemic Family Development Theory   Sharing the systemic foundation of the life event web, *systemic family development theory* focuses on the common developmental process that finds unique expression in families as well as the complex, multigenerational nature of families (Bigner, 2010). The common developmental process is the experience of stressors. Stressors, however, do not manifest in every family in the same way, nor does every family respond to a stressor in the same way. Some families successfully adapt whereas others experience an inability to change, resulting in a family crisis. Families, too, may find it difficult to transition in response to the cumulative effect of multiple stressors. Families, though, can manage or mediate family crisis through stress management or external coping resources. Some families, for example, may experience as a stressor the coming out of an older adult family member, whereas other families will not experience this event as a stressor. Those families who do experience it as a stressor may adapt by educating themselves about lesbian and gay people, the process of coming out, and so forth; they too can seek external resources such as Parents, Family, and Friends of Lesbians and Gays (PFLAG) or comparable support organizations or groups. The other hallmark of systemic family development theory is the recognition of the complex, multigenerational nature of family systems (Bigner, 2010). This recognition demands that one comprehend and address the family holistically at the specific point in its development that the family comes to the attention of a counselor. It is this specificity of multigenerational family as a whole at a certain point in time that distinguishes systemic family development as a theory attuned to varied family structures (Bigner, 2010).

Most life span development models of aging are heteronormative and Eurocentric; the family life cycle model assumes a family in which intergender marriage and child rearing are the norm. The life event web demonstrates sensitivity to the interdependent nature of family member relationships. Systemic family development theory transcends heteronormative and Eurocentric bias by presenting a model that is cognizant of the unique manifestations of a common developmental process as well as the complexity of multigenerational experiences and relationships. When working with lesbian or gay male individuals, couples, or families in late life, it is incumbent upon counselors to incorporate systemic models of family develop-ment into their understanding of lesbian and gay individual, couple, or family counseling as well as into their understanding of lesbian and gay development.

Lesbian and Gay Developmental Models

Troiden (1989) proposed a stage model of sexual orientation identity development that attends to the progress of an individual's awareness and incorporation of self-identity as different from the dominant culture. Troiden (1989) posited that a sexual orientation minority individual would progress through stages (typically but not always occurring from prepubescence through early adulthood) in which he or she sensed the self as different from peers, to awareness of same-sex feelings, to movement toward same-sex communities, to incorporation of same-sex identity into the sense of self.

This model, though expected to be experienced from adolescence through early adulthood, also can be used to assist counselors in mapping the trajectory of older adults through the process of coming out in late life. Sexual orientation identity models implicitly assume a preawareness stage at which an individual identifies with heterosexual culture—an understanding that can lead to intrapsychic conflict (an intrapsychic stressor). Challenges may arise when counseling lesbian or gay clients who, though they are in late life, are at earlier stages of sexual orientation identity development; further challenges may come about when as a result of the influence of the dominant culture or cohort the client believes that his or her sexual orientation is unacceptable or should not be revealed to family or friends (external stressors), even though the result is psychological distress or lower self-esteem (Blando, 2011).

Coming Out in Late Life

Lesbian and gay people oftentimes are an invisible minority, in large part because sexual orientation is not as readily observable as race, ethnicity, or gender, for example (Lee, Blando, Mizelle, & Orozco, 2007). In fact, older lesbian and gay people are perhaps the most invisible of an invisible minority (Blando, 2001). A lack of visibility of older lesbian and gay people may result in what O'Connor (1992) described as feeling like a minority of one. This may be especially true for those older lesbian and gay people who live outside of urban areas with larger, visible lesbian and gay populations or for those older lesbian and gay people who live in lesbian and gay communities focused more on younger or middle-aged individuals.

Older lesbian and gay people who choose to come out—that is, not only self-identify but also identify to others as lesbian or gay—may benefit psychologically and socially. Research demonstrates that being out is associated with psychological well-being and satisfaction with personal relationships (Berger, 1990; DeAngelis, 1994).

Coming out may be difficult for some older people, however, because of stereotypes about lesbians or gay men, stereotypes about older people, or differences in identity based on cohort.[4] Coming out may be difficult, too, for some older people because it represents a challenge to what may have been a lifelong identity as a heterosexual. For other older adults, especially those who are secure in their family or friendship relationships, coming out may be a more emotionally manageable process. The astute counselor will enquire about not only whether an older client is out or not but also what being out means to her or him. A counselor, too, might consider role-playing coming-out scenarios, connecting clients with support groups for those coming out, and offering bibliotherapeutic resources for psychoeducation (Lee et al., 2007; Murphy, 1992).

Co-Occurring Ageism and Heterosexism

Ageism is the belief that older people are of lesser value than are younger people. Heterosexism is the belief that same-gender attraction, fantasies, and behaviors are sinful, are pathological, and destroy the social order and that they are inherently inferior to opposite-gender attraction, fantasies, and behaviors. Other forms of discrimination include racism, sexism, and ableism. Neither ageism nor heterosexism is universal. There are cultures that honor older adults and recognize age as a source of wisdom; there are cultures that tacitly or overtly incorporate same-gender experiences into the cultural milieu. In North America, whereas individuals, couples, and families in late life will to varying degrees face ageism and whereas lesbian and gay

---

[4] An example of this is some younger cohorts preferring to identify as *queer*—a term with an intense negative valence for many older people—rather than as lesbian or gay.

individuals, couples, and families will to varying degrees face heterosexism, it is lesbian and gay individuals, couples, and families in later life who will face both ageism and heterosexism, along with racism for racial and ethnic minority people, sexism for lesbians, and able-ism for people with disability. The counselor working with lesbian and gay individuals, couples, or families in later life must attend to the complex interplay between these various forms of bias; their effects on the medical, psychological, social, and religious well-being of those involved; and interventions that successfully address these multiple biases.

Managing stressors earlier in life may result in crisis competence, that is, the ability to successfully address stressors later in life (see Kimmel, 1978, 2002). Managing heterosexism by working through the coming-out process earlier in life, for example, may result in an increased ability to effectively address the ageism encountered in late life. In fact, a survey of older LGBT individuals found that 38% believed that being LGBT had been helpful as they aged and had resulted in the development of "positive character traits, greater resilience or better support networks" (MetLife Mature Market Institute, 2006, p. 14). This result was a more common experience for Latino and Latina and African American respondents than for the sample overall. Counselors might use the concept of crisis competence to help lesbian and gay individuals, couples, and families in late life to recognize that as they were able to manage stressors earlier in life, so too do they have the ability to manage stressors later in life.

Microaggression Outside and Within the Family

Microaggression is a concept arising from the study of racism in the United States and refers to subtle, everyday racism, a racism experienced by marginalized racial and ethnic communities, as opposed to overt racism (see Alvarez & Juang, 2010). This everyday racism can manifest as being ignored, ridiculed, or in some other way treated unequally.

Microaggression can be more broadly conceptualized as the subtle, everyday discrimination experienced by marginalized groups, whether they be marginalized because of race or ethnicity, sexual orientation, age, gender identity, disability status, or some other characteristic. For the purpose of our discussion, we consider microaggressions associated with heterosexism and with ageism and their impact on lesbians and gay men in late life. An example of everyday heterosexism is the experience of a lesbian or gay couple of being stared at by others while at a restaurant; an example of everyday ageism is the experience of having strangers roll their eyes at older people because they are moving slowly in the check-out lane at a supermarket.

One aspect of heterosexism that differentiates it from other forms of bias is its common manifestation within the family as well as outside the family. Unlike racial or ethnic minority family members who share a common racial or ethnic identity, lesbian or gay family members seldom share a common lesbian or gay family identity. Heterosexual parents may have a lesbian or gay child; conversely, heterosexual children may have one or more parents who are lesbian or gay. This lack of commonality may, though not necessarily will, result in intrafamilial stressors different from those stressors found in homogeneous families. Although not absolutely unique to families with lesbian or gay members (after all, it can be argued that families of mixed race and ethnicity or even mixed gender may have a similar type of experience), what can be most striking is the pervasiveness of the belief that lesbian and gay family members are qualitatively different than heterosexual family members.

An example of the convergence of everyday heterosexism and ageism is the experience of two older women who enter a restaurant holding hands, when a waitperson says, "It looks like you left the boys home to have a girls' night out." The metamessages present in this microaggression include the assumption that two older women who are together in public are heterosexual, that older women are married (or widowed), that it is socially acceptable to patronize or infantilize old people, and so forth.

Alvarez and Juang (2010), in their study of Filipino Americans, found that men who met everyday racism with active coping experienced less psychological distress and greater self-esteem than did those who met everyday racism by support seeking or avoidance, whereas women who met everyday racism with avoidance experienced greater psychological distress and lesser self-esteem. Alvarez and Juang's (2010) research findings may not be applicable to lesbian and gay people in late life, so it would be premature to suggest the use of differential coping styles to impact the psychological distress or self-esteem of lesbian or gay people in late life, yet counselors working with lesbian and gay people in late life should consider the possibility that specific coping styles (e.g., active, support seeking, or avoidant) may impact a lesbian or gay client's psychological distress and self-esteem and that specific coping styles—perhaps active or support seeking—may reduce levels of psychological distress and increase levels of self-esteem.

Religion and Spirituality

Issues of religion and spirituality oftentimes evoke strong emotional responses in clients, especially lesbian and gay clients whose religious connections were with fundamentalist groups that denied the existence of or demonized lesbian and gay people. For some lesbians and gay men in late life, the issues may have been resolved through either moving away from religion, moving away from organized religion and toward a more inclusive spirituality, or aligning with religious traditions and communities that accept the healthy expression of sexual orientation identities. The role of the counselor in these cases is to support the client in her or his healthy belief system.

Other lesbian and gay clients in late life may not have successfully resolved conflicted feelings about religion and spirituality and may present to the counselor with "feelings of confusion, self-hatred, alienation, isolation, depression, suicidal thoughts, and other negative social and psychological concerns" (Blando, 2011, p. 226.). The role of a counselor in these instances is to help a client differentiate the positive assets of his or her religious or spiritual tradition from the psychologically damaging elements of the tradition, engage in psychoeducation with the client so that the client understands that he or she is worthy of full social and civil rights, and challenge belief systems that promote sexual orientation discourse as issues of choice or morality—arguments oftentimes used to oppress sexual orientation minority individuals (see Blando, 2011).

Retirement

Older adults are increasingly remaining in the workforce (Galinsky, 2007; Nyce, 2007). By 2020, about one out of every five workers will be 55 or older (Nyce, 2007; see also Burr & Mutchler, 2007). Given a lack of accurate demographic information about lesbian and gay people, it is unclear whether lesbian or gay elders are remaining in the workforce at rates less than, comparable to, or greater than the population as a whole.

Ageism is clearly a problem in the workplace (Dennis & Thomas, 2007), manifest as hiring bias, weak enforcement of equal employment laws, and limited social support to identify age discrimination as a civil rights violation (McCann, 2003, cited in Dennis & Thomas, 2007). Ageism in the workplace can be countered, at least in part, through diversity training that includes age as a category, training manuals that address ageism, prosecution of age discrimination activity, increased scrutinizing of age discrimination instances, and intergenerational training (Dennis & Thomas, 2007). As counselors sensitive not only to age but also sexual orientation discrimination, we should advocate for diversity training that also includes sexual orientation identity, including sexual orientation as a category, training manuals that address heterosexism, prosecution of sexual orientation discrimination in the workplace, attention to sexual orientation discrimination occurrences, and training that includes heterosexual as well as lesbian and gay workers.

Lesbian and gay people in late life may find that they need to remain employed or partially employed in order to compensate for reduced financial compensation over their work lives as a consequence of discrimination that resulted in fewer opportunities for higher paying jobs. Some lesbian and gay people in late life may desire *encore careers* in one of the helping professions or para-professions or volunteering, which would allow them to engage in generative activities in late life. For other lesbians and gay men in late life, *bridge employment* may enable transition from full-time work to retirement and may comprise part-time or temporary work or self-employment with reduced hours and responsibilities (see Ulrich & Brott, 2005; Feldman, 1994, cited in Ulrich and Brott, 2005).

Older lesbians and gay men who use work as a source of generativity may face psychological challenges when their work lives end, which may occur as a result of health, family, caregiving, or other issues. Further, ageism and heterosexism may have negative impacts on career decisions. Older lesbians and gay men who have strong community and friendship networks may readily compensate for lack of social contact through work. Where strong community or friendship networks are lacking, counselors may consider exploring with older lesbian and gay clients the benefits of remaining in the workforce, rejoining the workforce or establishing or strengthening nonwork social networks.

Legal Issues

Many legal issues faced by lesbians and gay men in late life revolve around the lack of legal protections provided by marriage, blood relations between parent and child, and so forth. Lesbians and gay men in late life may have estates, large or small, that could be inherited de facto by family members (because they are next of kin) and not long-term or civil-recognized marriage partners. These individuals, couples, and families need wills and/or trusts to ensure that financial and other assets are protected and inherited by those named by the loved one.

Likewise, whereas the state grants civil-recognized marital partners durable power of attorney and/or durable power of attorney for health care, lesbians and gay men in late life need formal, legal documents that identify who is the durable power of attorney and/or durable power of attorney for health care. Without such documents, if a loved one becomes incapacitated or ill, decisions about her or his care may fall to the state or to a legal relative who may or may not have that individual's best interest at heart. Although counselors are not lawyers or legal experts, nor should they be, we can encourage lesbian or gay clients in late life to seek appropriate legal counsel to ensure their financial, familial, and other wishes are identified and granted.

Lesbian and Gay Male Sexuality in Late Life

Cultural biases demand that older adults be asexual, no longer interested in sex, no longer needing or wanting sex, no longer capable of engaging in sexual behavior, or no longer sexually appealing. Cultural biases, too, suggest that lesbians are not interested in sex and that gay men are hypersexual. When sexuality biases against older adults are added to sexuality biases regarding lesbians and gay men, it results in a compound and complex set of beliefs about aging, sexual orientation identity, and sexuality. This compounding of biases may result in a set of internalized beliefs or cultural beliefs about what it means to be a sexual being who is an older lesbian or an older gay man. For older lesbians, this may manifest in the multiple biases that women are (and should be) less sexual than men, that lesbians are less sexual than heterosexual women, and that old people are less sexual than younger people. For gay males, this may manifest in the belief that gay men are more sexually promiscuous (a concept of cultural bias and not behavior) than straight men, that old men should not be sexual, and that old men who are sexual are predatory or in some other ways creepy. Counselors who work with individuals or couples around issues of sex and sexuality may need to help clients identify their maladaptive thoughts and beliefs; engage clients with psychoeducation about sexuality in late life, lesbian sexuality, or gay male sexuality; and provide exercises for individuals or couples to strengthen their sexual self-efficacy.

Chronic Illness and Disability

Some resources may be more or less available to lesbian and gay clients in late life to manage illness and disability (e.g., HIV/AIDS), including friends and family, religious institutions, and legal benefits and protections. Many lesbians and gay men in late life will have lost friends over the last three decades to complications from AIDS and other medical illnesses, which will have resulted in a modified social network. Lesbian and gay men in late life may have family-of-origin interaction with their children, siblings, nieces, nephews, and fictive kin. Further, even though it may appear that there is a natural connection between older and younger lesbians and gay men, for some individuals interaction between these two groups may be limited because of life-span developmental differences, ageism, or differences in identity (see Fox, 2007). Counselors may need to help lesbian or gay clients in late life identify and connect with resources to enable them to adapt to illness and disability.

Transference and Countertransference With Lesbian and Gay Clients in Late Life

Although Knight (2004) did not address transference and countertransference in work with lesbian and gay clients, he did identify several types of transference (client toward counselor) and countertransference (counselor toward client) phenomena that oftentimes are present in counselor–client relationships with clients in late life. These phenomena may also be present in counselor–client relationships with lesbian and gay clients in late life. Specifically, a counselor might work with an older client who is unconsciously primed to try to replicate a parent–child, grandparent–grandchild, spousal, subordinate–authority figure, or erotic relationship (Knight, 2004). In much the same way, a counselor may unconsciously be primed to try to replicate a child–parent, grandchild–grandparent, or aging–death anxiety dynamic (Knight, 2004). Erotic transference may be a particular challenge for the counselor and the lesbian or gay client in late life, given social norms that deny elders' sexuality (Knight, 2004) and the complexities that arise around what is considered appropriate sexual or romantic expression in lesbian or gay male cultures.

Strengths-Based Lesbian and Gay Counseling in Late Life

Though some of the challenges that lesbians and gay men face in late life may be unique, lesbians and gay men may bring to their late life experience unique strengths, including "an ability to manage stigma, crisis management, role flexibility, and community, friendship, and social support" (see Anetzberger, Ishler, Mostade, & Blair, 2004, cited in Blando, 2011). Many lesbians and gay men in late life have earlier in life had the experience of identifying with a marginalized group (lesbians or gay men). The experience of working through the difficulties inherent in identifying with a marginalized group may be a strength when faced with the difficulties inherent in identifying as aged. Lesbians and gay men in late life who have survived victimization, having faced hate crimes, political repression, AIDS, and so forth, may be better able to handle the crises commonly found in late life, including loss of family and friends, loss of health, and sense of mortality. Finally, lesbians and gay men in late life who have experienced role flexibility earlier in life may more easily adopt nonstereotypical gender roles later in life. Counseling interventions may be particularly efficacious if they proceed from the strengths of the lesbian or gay client in late life.

Case Example

Shirley was a 75-year-old Canadian of European descent who was married to her husband for 50 years. She had two heterosexual children, Ron, age 49, and Rita, age 48. Shirley's husband passed away 8 years ago; Shirley passed away earlier this year. Seven years ago, a friend introduced Shirley to Marianne, a 65-year-old Latina American lesbian. Although Shirley had never been in a relationship with a woman, she and Marianne were immediately attracted to each other and began a long-distance romance in which Shirley and Marianne would travel to each other's homes for periods of months at a time. Shirley and Marianne made their relationship known to family members, even though the word *lesbian* was not uttered by either of them. Over time, Marianne became very close to Rita and Ron and their families and would spend most major holidays with Shirley and her extended family. When Shirley was diagnosed with cancer 5 years after meeting Marianne, Marianne rented out her apartment and moved to Canada to become Shirley's full-time caretaker. Shirley's children were comforted to know that their mother had someone to watch over her. When Shirley passed away 2 years later, her two children inherited her entire estate. Rita wanted to give a portion of the estate to Marianne, in her words, "as thanks for being so good to mother." Ron, however, was vehemently opposed to this. Marianne did not want to cause any hard feelings within Shirley's family, so she declined to accept any money—a position strongly argued against by Rita. Rather than turn to a lawyer, Rita, Ron, and Marianne agreed to meet with a counselor to try to work on issues that were being played out.

The counselor who initially met with this family felt "thrown off" by their presentation—an older lesbian and two adult *non*stepchildren with what appeared to be a financial issue. He referred them to another counselor, Dr. Louise Wright, who had more experience in working with older lesbians and gay men. After a period of rapport building, during which Dr. Wright informally conducted an assessment, she developed an approach to working with this family that focused on quick problem resolution and then engaged in therapy with the family until their problem was resolved. Rapport building was made easier by Dr. Wright's minimizing sexual orientation and family conception biases, allowing this family to define itself, and joining with the family on their terms. Assessment comprised observation and identification of family subsystems, alliances, rules, beliefs, and so forth, and uncovered a ruptured parental subsystem, a sibling subsystem, an alliance between Rita and Marianne, a rule that emphasized the importance of restraint in social interactions, and varied family beliefs about lesbian and gay people and about the role of religion in one's life. Through this informal assessment, Dr. Wright came to learn that Shirley, Rita, and Ron were raised in a moderately right-wing church; that Shirley had become increasingly nonreligious in her later years, as had Rita; and that Ron continued to be actively involved in his church. Ron stated that he had tolerated his mother's behavior because, in his words, "she was discreet and referred to Marianne as her 'friend'" and because "she was my mother." When Shirley died, Ron felt that he could be more open about his religious belief that homosexuality is a sin. He stated that although he sincerely liked Marianne and he appreciated what she had done for his mother, he felt that she did not deserve any money because she was a sinner. As he spoke, Rita began sobbing, apologizing to Dr. Wright and to Marianne for her brother's "hurtful words." Marianne was disappointed but not entirely surprised by Ron's revelations. After talking things through over several sessions, the three members of this family agreed to disagree about the morality of lesbian and gay people. They came to a mutual agreement that Rita would give a small sum of money to Marianne out of Rita's portion of the estate, that Marianne would accept this small sum of money, that Ron could retain his entire portion of the estate so that he need not engage in a behavior that conflicted with his strongly held religious beliefs, and that the family would continue to work to minimize hard feelings that arose or that might arise in the future. At this point, the family, along with Dr. Wright, agreed to terminate therapy.[5]

---

[5] This is a fictional case example; resemblance to any person living or dead or to anyone's personal experience is strictly coincidental.

Case Discussion

The family that presented to the counselor comprised Marianne (recently bereft of her partner, Shirley) and Shirley's two biological children from her heterosexual marriage, Ron and Rita. Reflecting on this family from a systems perspective allows us to consider the subsystems, alignments, and constraints (i.e., rules) present in the family. Subsystems present in this family included a spousal subsystem, Marianne and Shirley, and a sibling subsystem, Ron and Rita. It is unclear whether Marianne and Shirley also comprised a parental subsystem. There appeared to be clear alignments, prior to Shirley's death, between Marianne and Shirley, as well as alignments between Marianne and Rita. There too was a subsystem composed of the three women, Marianne, Rita, and—in memory—Shirley. Generic constraints included the belief that children should defer to their parents, and idiosyncratic constraints included the belief that emotions within the family should be restrained, that issues of cultural identity should not be discussed, and that family should be respected. It was clear that Ron had greater distress—quite possibly anxiety—over his mother's lesbian relationship than did Rita, and Ron was unable to demonstrate flexibility in his beliefs about same-gender relationships. The counselor, Dr. Wright, understood the subsystems, alignments, and constraints in the family as well as the rigid boundaries held by Ron, respected the differences found in the family members, and supported the family members as they mutually agreed upon a resolution.

Conclusions

There has been little in the literature addressing the counseling needs of lesbian and gay people in late life, though they represent discrete groups with unique cohort experiences. Culturally sensitive counseling uses relevant historical-contextual information related to lesbian and gay late life clients in order to provide a basis for understanding the structure, relationships, and struggles that may be present in this population. Although there may be common cohort experiences for cultural groups, including lesbians and gay men in late life, these groups also comprise heterogeneous members. Lesbians and gay men in late life have life experiences that are different from those of the dominant culture, including the presumption of heterosexuality and heterosexual life span development; such lesbian or gay developmental milestones as coming out; ageism and heterosexism; microaggression; experiences of hostile religious groups; workplace, retirement, and legal issues related to age and sexual orientation; sexuality in late life; and illness, disability, and dependency concerns. Within the context of counseling, older lesbian and gay clients may have unique transference experiences with their counselor related both to age and sexual orientation. Although there may be unique challenges faced by lesbians and gay men in late life, this group also experiences unique strengths, including strong social and community support, friendships, management of stigma and crises, and flexibility in roles. Counseling interventions that proceed from older lesbian and gay clients' strengths may be particularly successful.

References

Alvarez, A., & Juang, L. (2010). Filipino Americans and racism: A multiple mediation model of coping. *Journal of Counseling Psychology, 57*(2), 167–178.

Ariel, S. (1999). *Culturally competent family therapy: A general model.* Westport, CT: Praeger.

Atchley, R. C. (1989). A continuity theory of normal aging. *The Gerontologist, 29*(2), 183–190.

Baltes, P. B., & Baltes, M. M. (Eds.). (1993). *Successful aging: Perspectives from the behavioral sciences.* New York: Cambridge University Press.

Benbow, S., Egan, D., Marriott, A., Tregay, K., Walsh, S., Wells, J., & Wood, J. (1990). Using the family life cycle with later life families. *Journal of Family Therapy, 22,* 273–295.

Berger, R. M. (1990). Passing: Impact on the quality of same-sex couple relationships. *Social Work, 35,* 328–332.

Bigner, J. J. (2010). *Parent–child relations: An introduction to parenting* (8th ed.). Upper Saddle River, NJ: Prentice-Hall.

Blando, J. A. (2001). Twice hidden: Older gay and lesbian couples, friends, and intimacy. *Generations, 25*(2), 87–89.

Blando, J. A. (2011). *Counseling older adults.* New York, NY: Routledge.

Burr, J. A., & Mutchler, J. E. (2007). Employment in later life: A focus on race/ethnicity and gender. *Generations, 31*(1), 37–44.

Cowan, R. (2010). *8: The Mormon proposition* [Motion picture]. Los Angeles, CA: Red Flag Releasing.

Cumming, E., & Henry, W. E. (1961). *Growing old.* New York: Basic.

DeAngelis, T. (1994, September). More research is needed on gay, lesbian concerns. *APA Monitor, 25*(9), 39.

Dennis, H., & Thomas, K. (2007). Ageism in the workplace. *Generations, 31*(1), 84–89.

Erikson, E. H. (1959). *Identity and the life cycle.* New York: International Universities Press.

Fox, R. C. (2007). Gay grows up: An interpretive study of aging metaphors and queer identity. *Journal of Homosexuality, 52*(3/4), 33–61.

Galinsky, E. (2007). The changing landscape of work. *Generations, 31*(1), 16–22.

Hall, G. S. (1922). *Senescence: The last half of life.* New York: Appleton.

Havinghurst, R. J. (1961). Successful aging. *The Gerontologist, 1,* 8–13.

Jung, C. G. (1933). *Modern man in search of a soul.* New York: Harcourt.

Kimmel, D. C. (1978). Adult development and aging: A gay perspective. *Journal of Social Issues, 34*(3), 113–130.

Kimmel, D. C. (2002). Aging and sexual orientation. In B. E. Jones & M. J. Hill (Eds.), *Mental health issues in lesbian, gay, bisexual, and transgender communities* (pp. 17–36). Washington, DC: American Psychiatric Publishing.

Knight, B. K. (2004). *Psychotherapy with older adults* (3rd ed.). Newbury Park, CA: Sage.

Lee, W. M., Blando, J. A., Mizelle, N., & Orozco, G. (2007). *Introduction to multicultural counseling for helping professionals* (2nd ed.). New York, NY: Routledge.

McGoldrick, M. (1995). *You can go home again: Reconnecting with your family.* New York, NY: Norton.

MetLife Mature Market Institute, Lesbian and Gay Aging Issues Network of the American Society on Aging, & Zogby International. (2006). *Out and aging: The MetLife study of lesbian and gay baby boomers.* Retrieved from http://www.metlife.com/assets/cao/mmi/publications/studies/mmi-out-aging-lesbian-gay-retirment.pdf

Murphy, B. C. (1992). Counseling lesbian couples: Sexism, heterosexism, and homophobia. In S. H. Dworkin & F. J. Gutierrez (Eds.), *Counseling gay men and lesbians: Journey to the end of the rainbow* (pp. 63–79). Alexandria, VA: American Counseling Association.

Nyce, S. A. (2007). The aging workforce: Is demography destiny? *Generations, 31*(1), 9–13.

O'Connor, M. F. (1992). Psychotherapy with gay and lesbian adolescents. In S. H. Dworkin & F. J. Gutierrez (Eds.), *Counseling gay men and lesbians: Journey to the end of the rainbow* (pp. 3–22). Alexandria, VA: American Counseling Association.

Qualls, S. H. (1999). Family therapy with older adult clients. *JCLP/In Session: Psychotherapy in Practice, 55*(8), 977–990.

Rowe, J. W., & Kahn, R. L. (1997). Successful aging. *The Gerontologist, 37*(4), 433–440.

Salthouse, T. A. (1987). Resource-reduction interpretations of cognitive aging. *Developmental Review, 8*(3), 238–272.

Schroots, J. J. F. (1995). Gerodynamics: Toward a branching theory of aging. *Canadian Journal of Aging, 14*(1), 74–81.

Tornstam, L. (2005). *Gerotranscendence: A developmental theory of positive aging.* New York: Springer.

Troiden, R. R. (1989). The formation of homosexual identities. *Journal of Homosexuality, 17*(1/2), 43–73.

Ulrich, L. B., & Brott, P. E. (2005). Older workers and bridge employment: Redefining retirement. *Journal of Employment Counseling, 42,* 159–170.

Section IV
Special Issues, Problems, and Populations in LGBT Couple and Family Therapy

17
Helping Heterosexual Spouses Cope When Their Husbands or Wives Come Out

CAROL GREVER

My name is Kaye. I found out my husband of 39 years was gay when he was arrested for soliciting sex from a male police officer. He then revealed that for more than 12 years he had a sexual relationship with a man who was practically a member of our family. That nearly put me over the edge. After 6 months of shock, I got myself together and moved out. I have seen four therapists since the coming out. None of these therapists seemed to realize the absolute devastation that resulted from this revelation. Self-esteem, self-preservation, trust that the sun will come up in the morning—all of these are gone. I am 63 years old and feel like an infant, trying to rebuild a personality and a life from scratch.

This cry for help is real. Kaye shared her story for this chapter to help others understand the anguish of a straight spouse. Thrust into foreign territory emotionally, she needed a guide and translator to help her rebuild her devastated life. She sought professional counseling and consulted four different therapists. The results were disastrous because none of her counselors understood her special needs as a straight wife in a mixed-orientation marriage.

When a married gay person comes out, it impacts everyone in the family, but the greatest shock is borne by the unsuspecting heterosexual mate. Straight spouses are often overlooked, misunderstood, or marginalized by therapists, but relationship therapy with LGBT clients should include the whole family, especially the intimate partners who suffer with the most collateral damage. Grieved, disoriented, confused, fearful, and often enraged, straight spouses feel their trust and security are destroyed. Their self-esteem is damaged, and they feel shamed and isolated. They need informed therapy.

This chapter is intended to promote awareness of significant issues and to recommend effective counseling practices based on research and actual experiences of heterosexual spouses currently in therapy. A brief review of relevant literature demonstrates how little research has focused on men and women in this dilemma of mixed-orientation marriages and relationships. Though numerous books are available to help lesbian, gay, bisexual, and transgender (LGBT) people come out, very few focus on mixed-orientation marriages and the plight of heterosexual spouses. Even fewer address therapy techniques for people in mixed-orientation relationships. For the most part, recommendations for working with those clients who are or have been involved in mixed-orientation marriages are based on clinical experiences rather than on researched methods and techniques.

Review of the Research Literature

Very little research has been directed toward the issues facing those individuals involved in mixed-orientation marriages. For the most part, what is known has been largely derived from anecdotal material written by those who have experienced the dilemmas in these committed relationships and who have participated in quasi-therapeutic groups formed to provide informal support for both the female and the male heterosexual spouses of mixed-orientation marriages (Buxton, 2006; Wolf, 1987). A few texts have been published over the last 20 years that have served many of these individuals as the main and only source of support for coping with the traumas involving the coming out of a lexbian, gay, or bisexual spouse during these marriages. These texts are listed in an annotated bibliography found in Table 17.1.

Published Research Findings

Limited theoretical or quantitative research data are available regarding the extent, nature, and issues facing those involved in mixed-orientation marriages or relationships. Research databases reveal only a handful of such studies that have been published over the last 20 years. The general findings of these studies may be summarized as follows:

- *Extensiveness*: While it is impossible to accurately access the extensiveness of mixed-orientation marriages within the population of the United States, estimates have been made of between 2 and 4 million gay men and lesbian women (Auerback & Moser, 1989; Buxton, 2001; Pearcey, 2005, 2007) who represent one-half of these relationships. This implies an equal number of heterosexual spouses of these individuals. Many of these marriages have produced children, but there are no data that estimate how many children are involved in families based on mixed-orientation marriages. It is likely that the number of these relationships may be declining as public and societal attitudes

Table 17.1 Recommended Texts for Straight Spouses in Mixed-Orientation Marriage

The following list includes books most often recommended by related support organizations. Only one, *When Your Spouse Comes Out* (Grever & Bowman, 2008), discusses underlying psychological issues with a therapeutic approach.

- Buxton, A. P. (1994). *The other side of the closet: The coming-out crisis for straight spouses and families.* New York, NY: Wiley. Originally published in 1991, this is a study of family trauma immediately after disclosure, based on research by an experienced educator who founded the Straight Spouse Support Network after her own husband came out.
- Corley, R. (1990). *The final closet: The gay parent's guide for coming out to their children.* Miami, FL: Editech Press. This book discusses appropriate ways to talk with children about homosexuality. It addresses only that aspect of the whole family situation.
- Gochros, J. S. (1989). *When husbands come out of the closet.* Binghamton, NY: Harrington Park Press. With an academic approach focused on women with gay or bisexual partners, the book reports without offering practical solutions for long-term recovery.
- Grever, C. (2001). *My husband is gay: A woman's guide to surviving the crisis.* Freedom, CA: Crossing Press. Personal stories of 26 women illustrate guidance in facing the immediate coming-out crisis. Encouraging for women in crisis, it does not address long-term repercussions or later recovery, nor does it include male straight partners.
- Grever, C., & Bowman, D. (2008). *When your spouse comes out: A straight mate's recovery manual.* Binghamton, NY: Haworth Press. Encouraging case interpretations are reinforced by practical strategies for healing for both male and female straight spouses. Marketed both as a trade book and a university textbook in psychology and sociology, it does include suggestions for therapy.
- Whitney, C. (1990). *Uncommon lives: Gay men and straight women.* New York, NY: Plume. The author examines alternative family systems and their challenges but does not deal with married lesbians with straight husbands or with therapy.

Something important is obviously missing in this literature. These constructive books are all addressed to straight spouses themselves, but none speak directly to the counselors and therapists who guide them through their processes of discovery, crisis, and recovery. This chapter begins to address that gap in the literature.

become more accepting of homosexuality, and same-sex marriages in particular. Although why many gay men and lesbians enter into heterosexual marriages remains uncertain, it is likely that internalized homophobia and heterosexism account for the major motivation (Bigner, 2006; Corley & Cort, 2006; Higgins, 2002). It is assumed that most gay men and lesbians who come out while in heterosexual marriages are well aware of their orientation; this assumption is inaccurate as a generalization (Matteson, 1985). Although it is true that many may be aware of their same-sex attraction, others become aware of this only after years of being involved in their heterosexual marriages. This realization is upsetting and often unanticipated for these individuals, who realize that after falling in love with their best friend, for example, that this attraction and the associated feelings are what have been missing from their emotional and sexual lives for some time. Regardless of why these marriages have taken place, most individuals who are involved will require assistance from competent therapists in working through disclosure issues and other related challenges as they form new identities and new lives (Bigner, 2006).

- *Postdisclosure information*: Researchers have largely either been unable to study those involved in intact mixed-orientation marriages or have focused on recruiting participants following divorce. Those individuals who have divorced may be more visible and willing to participate in research than those who have remained married because of the perceived stigmas associated with coming out and participating in support or focus groups. For the most part, the information regarding these relationships is based on studies of both spouses following disclosure by the gay or lesbian spouse, and many are based on data gathered following divorce of these couples (Buxton, 2004; Pearcey, 2005, 2007). As such, much of the data involved are retrospective, which may skew the nature of the information provided to researchers. Since the vast majority of mixed-orientation marriages result in divorce following disclosure by the gay or lesbian spouse, we have little information to guide therapists working with those individuals who choose to remain in their marriages following disclosure (Buxton, 2006; Yarhouse, Gow, & Davis, 2009; Yarhouse & Kays, 2010). The information that is available suggests that those who remain in their marriage have different adjustments and different experiences than do those who choose to divorce (Buxton, 1994, 2001, 2005; Cram, 2008; Grever, 2001; Grever & Bowman, 2008; Tornello & Patterson, in press).
- *Gay or lesbian spouses*: The adjustment and recovery issues are likely to be different for the gay or lesbian spouses from those facing heterosexual spouses following disclosure (Bigner, 1996). For example, the majority of gay and lesbian spouses most likely have spent time, energy, and resources involved in facing disclosure issues and have most likely accepted this drastic life event and begun progress toward resolution of feelings of homophobia that are often responsible for producing their involvement in a heterosexually oriented marriage. Counter to assumption, most often report loving their spouse and children deeply and having high respect for the institution of marriage (Bigner & Jacobsen, 1989; Wolkomir, 2009). Their dilemma relates to coming to terms with their true sexual orientation, which compromises their ability to fully participate in an honest, integrated, fully functional heterosexual relationship.

A hallmark emotion that is almost universally experienced by gay or lesbian spouses is guilt (Bigner, 1996). This deep-seated feeling colors much of their ability to resolve coming-out issues and establish a new, healthy self-identity as a fully integrated gay or lesbian individual. Many of these individuals are likely to have led double lives for some time, during which they acted upon their same-sex attraction surreptitiously while attempting to maintain the charade of participating in a heterosexual relationship.

On the other hand, it is also likely that many people remain in denial regarding their feelings of same-sex attraction, which jeopardizes the health and functioning of their heterosexual relationship. Likewise, there is little information regarding any similarities or differences in adjustment issues or other challenges facing gay men or lesbians as individuals while in heterosexual relationships or following divorce from these relationships.

• *Heterosexual spouses*: Heterosexual spouses of gay men and lesbians are one of the most ignored and understudied populations. Most accounts are anecdotal or based on qualitative research methods and depict these individuals as equally victimized by the insidious nature of homophobia and heterosexism that brought their gay and lesbian mates into their relationships (Bradford, in press). Accounts have been provided that describe stages of adjustment experienced by heterosexual spouses (Buxton, 1994, 2001; Grever & Bowman, 2008). These stages are elaborated in later sections of this chapter. These experiences may be briefly described here to involve (a) initial shock following disclosure by the gay or lesbian spouse that may take varying periods of time for recovery; (b) feelings of general confusion about not truly knowing one's spouse that often develop into generalized feelings of mistrust about individuals, relationships, marriage, intimacy, and commitment; (c) deepening feelings of sexual inadequacy, questioning of one's own sexual identity, and damaged self-image; (d) serious concerns about exposure to such sexually transmitted diseases as AIDS (Klaar, in press); (e) growing anxiety about what the future holds; (f) concerns for children's welfare in their schools and communities; (g) experiencing a variety of stress-related health issues; and (h) sudden realization that they are now affected, even vicariously, by the negative stigmas attached to homosexuality by society, neighbors, churches, families of origin, and other social institutions (Buxton, 1994, 2001, 2005; Grever, in press; Grever & Bowman, 2010; Hernandez & Wilson, 2007). One support group summarizes these findings by informing heterosexual spouses that when a gay or lesbian partner comes out, the heterosexual spouse and their children go into the closet. Once there, many heterosexual spouses face the dilemmas of working through a multitude of issues not faced by parents of gay or lesbian children upon the disclosure of their sexual orientation. These additional conditions add to the already stressful problems involved in divorce for both the adult spouses and their children.

Elements of the Ordeal: Clinical Issues Facing Straight Spouses

Preparation for counseling straight spouses involves four areas: (1) the impact of related societal issues, (2) common personal challenges these spouses experience, (3) typical steps to recovery, and (4) awareness of effective therapeutic practices drawn from client reports. Information here is drawn from research in two books about straight spouse recovery (Grever, 2001; Grever & Bowman, 2008), interviews with professional counselors, and interviews with the spouses who have participated in support groups focused on mixed-orientation marriages. The chapter attempts to identify successful therapeutic approaches to help straight spouses from their crisis stage through rebuilding and healing.

External Forces

Complicating their own personal upheaval, straight spouses are pressured by larger societal forces that exacerbate their private uncertainty. Broadly categorized, the most challenging are religious condemnation, social expectations, and career and financial pressure.

Religious Condemnation   Many churches condemn homosexuality as a sin and shame or shun the whole family when a member comes out. Some religious organizations teach that homosexuality is a conscious choice and that reparative therapy can change sexual orientation. Claiming to "hate the sin and love the sinner," they attempt to repress same-sex attraction through this arcane practice, often with devastating results. The conclusion of the American Psychological Association in 1990 that these efforts to convert sexual orientation not only are unsuccessful but also do great emotional harm has so far not stopped the practice. Although religious belief may comfort families through other kinds of crises, a judgmental stance in this situation actually deepens their wounds. (The devastating effects of reparative therapy are discussed in depth in Chapters 28 and 29, this volume.)

Social Expectations   Fear of such moral judgment, along with widespread societal prejudice, drives straight spouses into the closet with their gay mates. Living in secrecy leads to intense loneliness and isolation. Life in the closet is beset with necessary lies. To meet social expectations, both partners hide their truth and pretend to be an ordinary heterosexual couple. Both partners must constantly deceive family, friends, coworkers, and social contacts. They may appear to be a perfect couple, but both partners suffer from their loss of authenticity. Social pressure of this kind creates internal conflict most people never experience. One straight spouse said she felt "violated, dirty, ashamed—even invisible." Such inner conflict is typical of the personal challenges that cause straight spouses to seek therapy.

Career and Financial Pressures   Financial fears keep some couples together. They use marriage as a cover for the gay partner in a high-profile career. If coming out means damaging or losing a lucrative professional position, they choose to remain together to maintain their social standing and lifestyle. For some parents, the expense of child support poses a formidable obstacle to separation. Their golden handcuffs may appear to be a practical solution, but marriage based only on money is seldom happy. In such cases, the straight partner is trapped for the long term in a secretive, unsatisfying, inauthentic lifestyle.

Shifting Personal Relationships

Negative community attitudes generally threaten social status and personal reputation when a married gay person comes out. Societal prejudice causes shifts in social and family ties that make straight spouses feel shamed and abandoned. Most disruptive is family breakup and resulting worry about the children's current and future well-being. If there is condemnation or lack of understanding by extended family, the breakup is particularly agonizing. Straight spouses can feel absolutely alone.

When the marriage breaks up, previous friendships often evaporate, particularly those with other couples. Rather than take sides, even old friends simply keep their distance, feeling embarrassed and uncertain. This adds to the isolation of both partners, who are too distracted to reach out for new support. They find less common ground with former friends and need to build a new social structure at a time when they are least able. With multiple institutional and societal forces impinging on mixed-orientation couples, it is no wonder so many straight spouses cry out, "My world crashed around me!"

Age also affects spouses' ability to bounce back after the shock of discovery. Those who have been married for decades before the coming out have more of their lives invested in their relationship—more history and resources, more emotional outlay. Much of their identity is tied to this partner. Separation is like cutting off a limb. Greater financial loss may also face older couples, who have had more years to accumulate wealth. Younger pairs, in contrast, may be more resilient and less invested, both emotionally and financially. With shorter history, they may be able to separate with less anguish, recover their emotional and monetary balance, and move on more quickly to another relationship.

What about the children? It is challenging to explain this adult situation to young children who have no knowledge of sexuality. Older children present an even greater quandary. Teens living at home are dealing with their own issues of emerging sexual awareness, and a parent's coming out only adds to their confusion. How can this family upheaval be faced, meanwhile safeguarding children's trust and sense of security? Grown children and other adult relatives are no less vulnerable to misunderstanding and hurt, bringing their own fully developed attitudes to the mix. Ambivalence about homosexuality, prejudice, or recalcitrant conflicts of values may surface. Religious and philosophical differences can cause condemnation and utter rifts in some families. Clearly, the intimate nature of marriage guarantees trauma when it ends, regardless of the couple's number of years together or the age of their children. Sorrow ripples in widening circles throughout their entire family. (Chapters 9, 10, and 11, this volume, discuss other aspects of coming-out issues in families.)

Internal Struggles

Even more devastating than these outer pressures are straight spouses' intense internal wars. The mate they trusted above all others has betrayed that trust. The one they thought they understood completely now seems to be someone different. Their personal sexuality comes into question, and their entire belief system wavers. Security and future plans evaporate. Identity is lost and self- esteem plummets. Life has changed forever; it seems that all is lost.

The list of personal struggles that straight spouses face is a long one. Fear is foremost and feeds smoldering rage. As well, AIDS and other sexually transmitted diseases loom as a realistic threat. Confusion about what to do causes some individuals to shut down altogether, emotionally paralyzed. Their sense of betrayal destroys trust. That loss often develops into pervasive mistrust of any relationship. Secrecy brings isolation. Loneliness follows. Reiteration of some unresolved past wound becomes complicated grief that must be unpacked in therapy, layer by layer. For some, religious and moral conflicts add more misery. Even after immediate issues are addressed, long-term psychological damage surfaces. A sense of failure fed by lowered self-esteem leads to pervasive shame. Years later, lingering and recurring anger and grief can surface. Sometimes close relationship with offspring, parents, siblings, and other relatives suffers permanent damage. The family unit is broken.

With suffering of this magnitude, therapy is sorely needed, and counselors must be educated on straight spouse issues to achieve optimum success. This education should begin with awareness of the process straight spouses experience on their way to recovery.

Stages of Recovery

Therapists who work in this field need a clear understanding of identifiable stages of straight spouse recovery. It is simplistic to assume that all individuals travel though each of these steps in order or at the same pace. The pieces get mixed up in this very human drama, but it is clear that there is a recognizable progression and that all the steps emerge and sometimes repeat. Here is a brief summary of typical stages of coping.

Shock, Relief, and Confusion

Shock to discover that the mate is gay is often followed by an odd sense of relief that previous difficulties in the relationship are not necessarily because of some inadequacy in the straight spouse. Nor did the mate "turn gay" through some fault of the straight partner. "Whew! Then it's not me!" is a familiar early response by straight spouses. Yet the world has turned upside down, and there is confusion about what this discovery means for the future. Security and future plans have vanished, leaving the person completely disoriented. Kaye's earlier quote is typical: "I am 63 years old and feel like an infant, trying to rebuild a personality and a life from scratch."

Denial, Self-Blame, and Sympathy

"This can't be true. There's some mistake. Maybe he (or she) can change. If I ignore it, maybe it'll go away." Obviously, denial is an attempt to escape the reality of the situation, but that tactic is usually short lived. Self-blame often takes its place. "It must be my fault. If I were sexier or prettier, smarter or more interesting, this wouldn't have happened." Or, "If I were a 'real man,' my wife wouldn't be interested in other women." In compassionate people, denial and self-blame may alternate with genuine sympathy for the mate's fear and anguish in coming out. A straight spouse is bombarded with these bewildering emotions. Certainly, there is plenty of pain on both sides of the closet.

Facing Reality

Eventually, denial ends and straight spouses face the reality of their mates' differing sexual orientation. Their relationship is irrevocably altered, whether they choose to stay together with some alternative arrangement or to dissolve their partnership completely. Those who remain in their marriage often do so with an unconventional agreement, such as open marriage that frees both to explore other intimate relationships. Some individuals simply stay together for companionship, with intimacy neither expected nor accepted. Others remain married for financial security or "for the sake of the children," often creating additional emotional pressures on everyone involved. Whether the couple decide to stay together with some unconventional agreement or to separate, as the majority do, the straight spouse experiences a new reality of existence.

Anger, Grief, and Despair

When their new reality is clear, three strong emotions come and go, alternating with devastating effect on the straight spouse. Anger is usually first, triggered by destruction of trust and recognition of the spouse's deception. If infidelity is apparent, disappointment, fear, and health concerns can trigger utter rage. Grief follows. Losses are huge: trust, love, family security, and plans for the future. Grief mixes with abject despair. Many spouses compare it to mourning a death, their sorrow and loss similarly deep and painful. This stage, aptly called "the black hole," is most dangerous. Getting stuck here often leads to self-destructive behaviors—clinical depression, addiction, violence, and even suicide. Though each of these emotions must be faced and overcome in order to progress toward healing, there is risk of being trapped in their cycle.

Turning Point and Resolution

If straight spouses have sufficient inner strength and resources and if they find meaning beyond themselves, they eventually accept what they cannot change, escape the black hole, and begin to heal. Sometimes it takes years to reach this turning point. Almost always, it takes wise, effective counseling in addition to encouragement from friends and family. As straight spouses begin to regain trust and hope, their anger finally abates.

Final resolution of their ordeal evades these spouses until they find it possible to forgive. As long as they harbor resentments and vestiges of anger, they cannot fully heal. Like other transformations, forgiveness is a process, not a one-time event. Forgiveness is more like a spiral staircase. One ascends slowly, one step at a time, but taking all the steps is key to full recovery. When straight spouses begin to regard their whole experience as a teacher, rather than a disaster, they can move into the next phase of their lives, welcoming a happier future.

Recovery is not a direct course. There are many turns and detours. People progress, then regress. Stages described here recur if new events trigger old responses—hooks back into grief or anger or fear. Counselors' ability to identify where a client stands on this long track to recovery informs their decisions for effective therapeutic strategies.

Counseling Options to Consider

Three distinctly different types of counseling are effective for straight spouses: peer support groups (e.g., the Straight Spouse Network [SSN]), professionally led therapy groups, and individual therapy. Each offers different possibilities, depending on the person's stage of recovery, financial resources, and felt needs at the time.

Volunteer-Led Peer Support Groups

Founded in 1991, the SSN (Buxton, 2006) is a volunteer-driven, nonprofit network that provides various services for straight spouses, notably peer support groups in many cities and an interactive, educational website. On the Web (http://www.straightspouse.org), it sponsors online support groups, some with chat rooms and web pages attached. The organization disseminates research-based information about spouse, couple, and family issues and resources. Their "Frequently Asked Questions" page contains information about disclosure, related medical questions, emotional and legal difficulties, family relations, and religious concerns. The SNN's website offers virtual support to anyone with computer access.

The organization's group meetings, often held in churches, are facilitated by a straight spouse or other volunteer, typically not a trained professional. The group varies in size but is usually small, emboldened by the promise of confidentiality. Most participants are female, perhaps because women seem more likely than men to share personal information with strangers. Each person tells her story at the meetings, surrounded by empathetic, nonjudgmental listeners. Groups are instructed to listen quietly and offer peer support but not to advise or assume that there are "right answers" for every participant. Each person is charged with finding her own path on this journey. Value lies in a safe opportunity to vent, to confide in sympathetic listeners, and to discover that one is not alone in this crisis.

Generally, SSN peer groups are most valuable in the early stages after the gay partner's disclosure, aiding participants in their initial struggles with shock, confusion, denial, and self-blame. After a few months, most spouses tire of opening old wounds repeatedly by retelling their stories. At that point they may rely entirely on Web resources or move into other kinds of personal counseling or individual therapy.

Professionally Guided Therapy Groups

Facilitated by professionally trained leaders, the strength of these groups is therapeutic guidance, not simply passive listening. Peer support among participants is also a helpful asset as they assure one other that their problems are not unique, but benefits go beyond comradeship and friendly encouragement. Professionals are trained to recognize special needs of individuals, recommend resources for specific issues, and make referrals beyond the group. Setting a specific number of meetings helps participants move into their next phase of recovery, avoiding self-perpetuated victimization. Clients who reach a turning point with a group may decide to engage a personal therapist to guide their individual course to full recovery.

Private Counseling

Individual therapy may be the most direct route to complete healing for many straight spouses. Privacy and confidentiality are assured, and evaluation is personalized and thorough. Serious underlying issues can be identified and addressed by a professional therapist after trust is established. External circumstances and special conditions that affect recovery are identified in these private sessions. Most important, a selection of therapeutic tools can be used, determined by specific needs and tailored to the individual.

Characteristics of Effective Therapists for Straight Spouses

The simplest way to learn what works best in counseling straight spouses is to ask them directly. An unusual case can demonstrate the strong influence of cultural traditions on mixed-orientation couples. It also reveals incredible courage and strength of will and the value of a competent therapist. "Lian," a Chinese American woman, was bound by the conservative Asian mores of her immigrant parents and her Chinese husband. She was married for 40 years to a gay man who brazenly brought his lovers into their home, yet she tolerated it all in silence and secrecy, following the strict precepts of her upbringing. She was compelled by custom to hold their family together and to shield their two daughters from any knowledge of their father's homosexual activities. She suffered alone in the closet of concealment for all those years.

Finally, after her daughters were grown and her parents deceased, she gathered her courage, separated from her husband, and began regular therapy with a clinical psychologist. Until she shared her history with her therapist, she had never told anyone the whole story of her isolation and anguish—not her closest friends, not even her own daughters. At last, nearing her 70th birthday, she is beginning to open to an unfamiliar freedom.

This is what she wrote about her therapist:

- I know she truly cares about me with empathy and patience.
- She has listening skills. She really hears me.
- She gives me permission to say what I haven't been able to say or don't want to say, and helps me make sense of it all.
- I totally trust her.
- She remembers what I've said in previous sessions to tie in with new events.
- She helps me see patterns in my choices and actions.
- She helps me process each stage of recovery.
- She lets me have space when I need it.
- She truly understands what being a straight spouse means and the pain involved. She is already knowledgeable about it so I don't need to explain myself.
- She doesn't judge.
- She encourages me to do the hard stuff.
- She knows when to back off when needed.

Although Lian is a long way from full recovery and still struggles with depression, she has taken significant steps toward wellness and expresses profound gratitude that the worst of her ordeal is behind her. The guidance provided by her therapist enabled this progress.

Representative reports from interviews and correspondence with countless other straight spouses suggest additional important characteristics of effective counselors in these cases.

Straight Spouse Responses to Counseling Experiences

Roger, an especially articulate man, shared his experience of the benefit he received from his therapist in only four visits. Just 8 months after his wife came out, he managed to recover his optimism about his future. Here is his story:

> We are all different, but I am a 47-year-old Australian male who was told three weeks before his 20th wedding anniversary that his wife is a lesbian and leaving. She had been in counseling for about 10 months, and I had no idea. She had never told me any of her feelings, and it was a complete surprise to me. I was completely devastated and pretty much

went into shock. I arranged a psychologist through work as a colleague pointed out that our organization provided such things.

Her name is Wendy and she saw me about a week after I found out. She was very interested in my situation, and her first and immediate concern was whether I was going to self-harm. We discussed this and I let her know that while I had thought of it, I had dismissed it as an option. I was very open with her about what had happened and she wanted to know how I thought and how the kids were and what I wanted from the sessions with her. She also talked a little about it being a new situation for her (straight guy finding out about a lesbian wife), and she suggested that I might do a little research online on lesbians and my situation. I did, and found Straight Spouse Connection at http://www.straightspouseconnection.com. It was great advice from Wendy as it got me a little control. I was doing something positive.

The next meeting was one week later. She again checked to make sure I was not going to self-harm and then we talked about the situation. This time she was quite forthright. My wife was in another city visiting her lover. Wendy pointed out what I didn't want to hear, that they were probably making love as we spoke. Very confronting but she was right and I needed to face up to this. I was then exploring a bit why my wife was doing what she was doing. I wanted to see it from her side as I genuinely wanted to know and understand. Wendy pointed out that the sessions were about ME and she was there to help me, not my wife! So we then talked of the future, how I would need to adjust to being single. I have the children (which is unusual, but so is all this, or so I thought). We talked about what I would need to do to adjust to a different lifestyle as a single father.

Our next session was again a week later. I was feeling better and was DETERMINED not to let this wreck my life. I have a number of techniques to bring myself out of problems, although this is a very deep place. I drive out bad thoughts by thinking compassionately, I force myself to smile (you would be surprised how effective that can be), and I set myself a deadline to be happy. Did it work? Well, sort of. I gave myself a month to climb out of the absolute despair I was in. It probably took about five weeks to get some balance back.

Wendy was amazed at my turnaround at our third session. We talked about pushing myself too hard and what damage that might do. I did slip backward pretty far a few times in the following weeks, but she had told me this would happen. Because I knew this, I was okay with it. In this third session we talked of the future more, how to cope with the sense of rejection and that at some time in the future I might look for companionship and love again. She expressed great confidence in my outlook. This was good, as I was struggling with the concept of a future at that time.

In our fourth and final visit, we talked about where I came from to where I was then. We talked of ongoing coping strategies and that there will be dark days to come but they would lessen. She said I had made incredible progress. When we met she was thinking I would be seeing her for a long time and that I was in a bad way. I was. At our last meeting my body language was confident and I had my cheeky, cheerful self back. So what did Wendy do for me?

1. She was there for me. She said this a couple of times: Her view was that the sessions were to help me and not for any other purpose. She was not in any way judgmental and led me to explore a whole pile of issues with calm and logic.
2. She was confronting. By that I mean she showed me in a caring way that the circumstances were what they were and I had to face that reality.

3. She explored options with me but gave no particular answer. She was very cooperative in that we worked the problem together but always with my absolute interests at heart.
4. She let me run my own pace, but warned me (very gently) not to force the pace and to care for myself. I had to be selfish in that work. I was still deeply concerned about my wife, but I needed to look after myself so I could look after the children too.
5. She gave me hope that time would take the searing pain away and that I would find my happy self again.

Could I have managed without her? Probably, but certainly not as well. I would have taken longer to get over it. She took me places I didn't want to go, and then brought me back out and set me on a good path.

Roger immediately sought individual counseling, knowing that he and his wife would end their marriage. His movement through therapy was more rapid than most, and his example is not meant to be a model for all. However, he was pleased with his result and seems realistic in his assessment of what happened in his sessions and how he was assisted.

In contrast, many couples engage in initial joint counseling as they consider their alternatives. The following case study details "Ellen's" experience during six sessions of therapy with her gay husband. Note their pragmatic approach to financial matters and establishment of ground rules while they made major decisions and worked out short-term plans.

I was numb and reeling upon my discovery that my husband of 30 years is gay. I have three children with him who are all adults, a 27-year-old son and twin 22-year-old girls. It was very important to the kids that I go to counseling with my spouse. I was reluctant, to say the least, but agreed to six sessions and then we proceeded as we felt needed from there. My experience was good and bad, but leaning a bit more to the bad side.

Good things: I was given a chance to say how I felt first. It was good to have a third party present. It relieved some fears and felt much safer. I received affirmation that I was indeed the "injured party." This was important to me to help my spouse understand that two issues were present. First, that his sexual orientation was not conducive to a marriage, and second was the infidelity. This was not dependent on orientation of the sexual partner, but more a betrayal of our marriage, trust, and loyalty. That his homosexuality was an act of omission, but his choice to cheat and lie were acts of commission. Either way, he is responsible for his actions.

We discussed financial matters. Thirty years of marriage does not unravel easily. Much was to be decided. We developed a plan to handle the money matters. We disclosed all financial records and both now have access to all records on a daily basis. We also changed our accounts to two signatures required on all withdrawals. We each established separate checking accounts for our personal expenses, which we need not explain to the other. A joint account handles the month-to-month bills and obligations. This helped both of us, I believe, to not be so worried about what the other might do. As he makes substantially more money than I, an equitable allotment is deposited into my personal account each month. This helped ease some fears while decisions such as legal separation or divorce are considered.

Because we are forced to remain in the same house for financial reasons, we agreed on some ground rules to make it bearable for both of us. No one is invited to the house unless that person is someone we both know from prior to the reveal. Weekends proved to be the toughest part. So, I must be gone from the house from Friday 6:00 p.m. until Saturday at 6:00 p.m. He must be gone from the house from Saturday 6:00 p.m. until Sunday at 6:00 p.m. It is not always convenient to be gone and to find something to do for such a long period of time, but regardless, it is much better than spending two days in the house together. That was simply awful.

Bad things: The next suggestion from the counselor remains an unknown as to whether it falls on the good or bad side. The counselor said that in relationships where an infidelity occurs, the injured party, me, benefits from knowing the extent of the infidelity. Was it online chatting, full physical, and emotional involvement, or what? So my spouse proceeded to reveal a list of his exploits. The list was extensive and involved all of the above and more. I felt disgusted and repulsed. When asked how I felt about it, I was told I was being judgmental and needed to try to understand the gay mentality. So, I guess I no longer am clinging to the thought that it was not much, but now I cannot look at him without thinking of the things he did. Many times it makes me vomit. You can decide whether this is a good or bad outcome.

I have chosen not to continue counseling with my husband. I have found that most of the activities involved my needing to try to understand the gay mentality, Not much has happened to have him understand the scope of what his actions have done to our family. I know I need to learn to cope with the situation, but I resent being viewed as the bad guy week after week. I did not do this. I have been faithful in every way for 30 years.

Ellen's mixed feelings about joint therapy with her husband may be more typical than Roger's enthusiasm. She is still raw and resentful, smarting from her husband's infidelity and deception, more than from the fact that he is gay. These two examples offer evidence that each case has unique qualities, despite common threads that run through all.

Therapeutic Outcomes

A sampling of comments from other straight spouses who recently experienced therapy further demonstrates the diversity of therapeutic outcomes. Each had differing results and commented on both effective and ineffective methods. The range of their comments also suggests the array of therapeutic approaches in use and the importance of compatibility between client and counselor.

Disappointing Experiences

- "I was in a small group with a lot of angry people who did not understand my respect and love for my ex. I was totally turned off by the approach."
- "I felt pushed to reach a preconceived conclusion (divorce). Directive counseling is not good! No single formula fits all straight spouses. We have to find our own path to recovery, and we appreciate balanced guidance from therapists. There is no 'one size fits all' solution."
- "Don't assume that every one of us will divorce. There are compelling reasons for some of us to stay together. We have to decide that ourselves!"
- "Counselors shouldn't promote their personal religion or ideology in sessions."
- "The sexual orientation of the therapist matters. Clients must feel comfortable."
- "Gay bashing of any kind is unacceptable. A therapist must be comfortable with his or her own sexual orientation and also honor 'wonderful diversity.'"
- "One counselor made me feel that I was relating juicy scandal. He made it all seem so seedy and grubby."
- "You don't want a therapist who focuses just on the negatives."
- "The therapist told me that all I needed was sex therapy! I walked out."

Successful Outcomes

- "My peer support group was really good at first to learn I'm not alone, not a freak, but I had to move past that group as healing progressed. To stay too long reopens the wound repeatedly and isn't helpful."
- "My therapist recognized that this was not just another divorce case. Issues of sexuality of the mate added another dimension, though the end result was the same for us—separation."
- "Our initial contact was immensely reassuring. My counselor treated the situation as the trauma that it was, and gave exactly what was needed—emotional first aid. My feelings were validated and I was assured that help was available. She knew the right questions to ask and gave me what I needed to look after myself. She inspired hope and confidence."
- "My therapist helped me to see that my husband's activities were not a result of me neglecting him, or anything I had done. It wasn't my fault that he is gay."
- "I was stunned when he remembered what I told him from week to week, and even from months before. I was seen. I was heard. He cared! It was a corrective emotional experience. What helped most was being believed and accompanied."
- "My therapist combines warmth and empathy with professionalism and excellent clinical skills. She helps me face the difficult questions with honesty and courage."
- "My counselor listened impartially and his only question was, 'Where is the love?' Through weekly sessions I have discovered that I was losing myself in what had become an emotional codependent relationship. The counseling has guided me through my own issues of low self-esteem and I am learning to find my own love within myself."
- "It helped me greatly to work in therapy on codependency and narcissism in order to understand my personal situation."
- "I did not have to educate my therapist about my situation. She got it! What it requires is a lot of sexual grounding so the therapist doesn't react to weird stories."
- "The most important things our therapist did were to have no preconceived ideas of how a straight–bisexual couple should live, to trust our resourcefulness, and to encourage us to 'write our own book.'"
- "What my husband and I have discovered is that our relationship is not lost just because of his sexuality. It has definitely changed and as we accept ourselves and each other as we are, we are entering into a more honest and real relationship. We still have four kids who are entitled to feel love around them, and it's our responsibility to keep that love alive. We must take responsibility for ourselves as individuals."
- "Some of my best counseling came from long-distance phone conversations with my sister, encouraged by my therapist. My sister was the only other person who knew about my problem and she was my closest confidante."
- "I only saw a therapist a couple of times, but the last time, as I was leaving, she said, 'You're going to be okay.' I remember walking across the university campus, saying over and over, 'I'm going to be okay. I'm going to be okay.' That mantra was crucial to my wellness."

These candid responses from straight spouses of varying ages, cultures, and backgrounds suggest an instructive, realistic model of therapeutic practice.

Best Practices for Straight Spouse Clients

1. *Flexible*: Rather than applying a single, rigid formula or pushing "right answers," the counselor first listens deeply to assess individual symptoms and needs.

2. *Unbiased*: Effective therapists do not bring prejudice into their work. They feel no intolerance toward homosexuality, and they do not encourage gay bashing in conversations with family members. They maintain an open, impartial mind.

3. *Exercises a broad view*: Though the focus is on the straight spouse's crisis, a good counselor sees the whole picture and brings up such related practical issues as safety, housing, needs of the family's children, and health care. If money is a problem, how can the family devise a suitable financial strategy to get through this time of hard decisions? What pressures are evident from the client's religion, extended family, and social and professional network? Are there serious underlying personal issues that need attention, like fear, guilt, shame, or anger? All this is considered.

4. *Explores other resources*: An effective therapist calls attention to sources of help already at hand. How can available resources be used to best advantage? Whom can the client trust and confide in among family and friends? Finding a confidant and/or keeping a journal while working through decisions can be extremely useful to chart a new course. How can clients be proactive to help themselves?

5. *Caring and trustworthy*: Effective counselors demonstrate empathy, patience, and genuine concern for clients. Listening carefully and without judgment, they remember details of previous conversations and put everything into context. They offer a safe space to divulge every undisclosed fact and feeling—and they help make sense of it all. Trust grows from this fertile ground.

6. *Qualified and experienced*: The best therapists are professionally educated and experienced with similar cases, therefore knowledgeable of typical patterns. Such counselors are equipped to help clients process each stage of straight spouse recovery, and they know when to step back and when to nudge clients onward.

7. *Realistic*: It takes time to achieve complete personal stability and healing. It's unrealistic for clients to expect immediate miracles or a magic pill to bring instant results. Effective therapists are therefore judicious in recommending medication that temporarily dulls emotional pain. They do not rush to a preconceived solution. They examine a client's own role in creating ongoing emotional turmoil as part of the eventual resolution. Even after successful therapy, they help clients realize that it is normal for grief or anger to be triggered occasionally—even years afterward.

8. *Encourages wellness*: Each session ends with genuine encouragement and hope. Good counselors know that their clients are fragile, and they bolster them with comforting assurance. To believe that it's possible to survive and eventually thrive has a positive influence on outcome. "I'm going to be okay" is a powerful encouragement, crucial to ultimate recovery.

9. *Celebrates healing*: Ethical therapists work themselves out of the job, urging clients in positive ways to get past their obstacles and to move on to greater happiness. The most trusted and effective counselors celebrate their own success and that of their clients.

People who choose to work with professional counselors with these qualities discover valuable tools and guidance toward recovery.

Recommendations

Straight spouses have unique issues. They are fragile. Their needs perhaps go to a deeper place than do those of individuals who seek therapy for other reasons. Ambivalent and hostile societal attitudes toward homosexuality add to their stress, and they struggle with the "outer" and "inner" issues described earlier. Their cases are complicated and multilayered. Because of this complexity, the following practical, time-tested recommendations were gathered from experienced therapists who help straight spouse clients rebuild and emerge whole from their difficulties.

- *Listen first*: Determine the client's inner condition, and then evaluate individual characteristics and personality, without any rigid formula. Is the person anxious, depressed, expressive, silent, extroverted, introverted, open to deeper work? Assess symptoms. Is the person stable, safe, depressed, suicidal? Is there indication of complicated grief, rooted in previous losses incompletely grieved? Work through the layers.
- *Determine external circumstances*: Is the home environment safe? Are there children at home? What practical issues like housing, health care, and child care are at work? Are finances a worry? Is there sufficient income to live on? Find out if there are people to confide in who can share their burden of sadness. Ask, "Is there anyone in your circle you can trust with this information?" Expressing grief helps to dissipate it and also alleviates isolation. Consider the effect of community mores on this client. What pressures are evident from religion, extended family, social network?
- *Offer a time-limited group to move people to the next stage of recovery*: A specific time frame addresses underlying ways of being that affect healing. For example, the perpetual victim cannot endlessly rerun tapes of old hurts.
- *Flexibility is paramount*: Be willing to try different techniques—cognitive behavioral, beginning with the thinking process, or Gestalt dialogue, or dream work. Open the whole tool kit of techniques and approaches to create balanced guidance.
- *Check in frequently with clients*: Also observe whether the process seems effective.
- *Watch for underlying issues, such as fear, guilt, shame, and anger*: Name the issue, surface it, and work it through individually. Women, especially, tend to turn guilt and shame back on themselves.
- *Remember that people can't forgive until they are past the deep anger stage*: Deeper personal issues have to be addressed before forgiveness is possible, so it cannot be rushed. Although forgiveness is the final step of complete healing for straight spouses, it is not a one-time act. It grows from an intention, an attitude, and a process.

People are indeed fortunate who live in locations where a wide range of therapeutic resources are available and who have the financial means to choose whatever service they need. Given these circumstances, straight spouses and their families have excellent potential to rebuild and move into a positive future. In places where that wealth of possibilities is not available, the Internet may offer the best opportunities for these special families to educate themselves about the resources that they can access. Recommended websites that relate to straight spouse issues are listed in Table 17.2.

No one has a perfect life; everyone has some burden to bear. One of the great gifts offered by competent counselors is their assurance that one is not alone and that this emotional challenge is not unique. Just knowing that others have felt the same way brings a client comfort. It is even more reassuring to discover that others have survived the straight spouse crisis and have moved through it to greater serenity.

Societal movement to more openness regarding same-sex marriage offers hope for fewer straight spouse traumas in the future. When every individual is free to be honest and open, to feel good about personal sexual orientation, the number of mixed-orientation marriages should decline. In the meantime, gays and lesbians will continue to feel compelled to marry heterosexual partners for all the reasons mentioned in this chapter, and straight spouses will continue to suffer as collateral damage.

Table 17.2 Recommended Organizations

- Children of Lesbians and Gays Everywhere (COLAGE)
  1550 Bryant Street, Suite 830
  San Francisco, CA 94103
  Phone: (415) 861-KIDS
  Internet: http://www.colage.org
  E-mail: colage@colage.org
  Support and information for children of gay, lesbian, bisexual, and transgender parents; offers parental tips for coming out to kids, a webpage, newsletter, and pen pals

- Parents, Families and Friends of Lesbians and Gays (PFLAG)
  PFLAG National Office
  1828 L Street, NW, Suite 660
  Washington, DC 20036
  Phone: (202) 467-8180
  Internet: http://www.pflag.org
  E-mail: info@pflag.org
  Source of information and advocacy for LGBT persons and family members

- Sexuality Information and Education Council of the United States (SIECUS)
  90 John Street
  Suite 402
  New York, NY, 10038
  Phone: (212) 819-9770
  Internet: http://www.siecus.org
  E-mail: siecus@siecus.org
  Distributes information on sexuality and reproductive health

- Straight Spouse Connection
  Internet: http://www.straightspouseconnection.com
  Short articles specifically addressed to straight spouses, with reader comments forming online dialogue

- Straight Spouse Network (SSN)
  P.O. Box 507
  Mahwah, NJ 07430
  Phone: (201) 825-7763
  Internet: http://www.ssnetwk.org
  E-mail: info@ssnetwk.org
  Offers resources and information specific to straight spouses or partners, current or former, of gay, lesbian, bisexual, or transgender mates

References

Auerback, S., & Moser, C. (1989, July–August). Groups for the wives of gays and bisexual men. *Social Work*, 321–325.

Bigner, J. J. (1996). Working with gay fathers: Developmental, post-divorce, and therapeutic issues. In R.-J. Green & J. E. Laird (Eds.), *Lesbian and gay couple and family relationships: Therapeutic perspectives* (pp. 370–403). New York, NY: Jossey-Bass.

Bigner, J. J. (2006). Disclosing gay or lesbian orientation within marriage. In C. A. Everett & R. Lee (Eds.), *When marriages fail: Systemic family therapy interventions and issues* (pp. 85–99). New York, NY: Haworth Press.

Bigner, J. J., & Jacobsen, R. B. (1989). The value of children to homosexual and heterosexual fathers. In F. W. Bozett (Ed.), *Homosexuality and the family* (pp. 163–172). New York, NY: Haworth Press.

Bradford, M. (in press). Couple therapy with bisexual, gay, and lesbian–straight relationships. *Journal of GLBT Family Studies.*

Buxton, A. P. (1994). *The other side of the closet: The coming-out crisis for straight spouses and families* (Rev. ed.). New York, NY: Wiley.

Buxton, A. P. (2001). Writing our own script: How bisexual men and their heterosexual wives maintain their marriages after disclosure. In B. Beemyn & B. Steinman, (Eds.), B*isexuality in the lives of men: Facts and fiction* (pp. 157–189). New York, NY: Harrington Park Press.

Buxton, A. P. (2004). Works in progress: How mixed orientation couples maintain their marriages after the wives come out. *Journal of Bisexuality, 4*(1–2), 57–82.

Buxton, A. P. (2005). A family matter: When a spouse comes out as gay, lesbian, or bisexual. *Journal of GLBT Family Studies, 1*(2), 49–70.

Buxton, A. P. (2006). Healing an invisible minority: How the Straight Spouse Network has become the prime source of support for those in mixed-orientation marriages. *Journal of GLBT Family Studies, 2*(3–4), 49–70.

Corley, M. D., & Cort, J. (2006). The sex-addicted mixed orientation marriage: Examining attachment styles, internalized homophobia, and viability of marriage after disclosure. *Sexual Addiction & Compulsivity, 13*(2–3), 167–193.

Cram, H. (2008). *You're what? Survival strategies for straight spouses.* Minneapolis, MN: Beacon Hill.

Grever, C. (2001). *My husband is gay: A woman's guide to surviving the crisis.* Freedom, CA: Crossing Press.

Grever, C. (in press). Unintended consequences: Unique issues of female straight spouses. *Journal of GLBT Family Studies.*

Grever, C., & Bowman, D. (2008). *When your spouse comes out: A straight mate's recovery manual.* Binghamton, NY: Haworth Press.

Hernandez, B. C., & Wilson, C. M. (2007). Another kind of ambiguous loss: Seventh Day Adventist women in mixed orientation marriages. *Family Relations, 56*(2), 184–195.

Higgins, D. J. (2002). Gay men from heterosexual marriages: Attitudes, behaviors, childhood experiences, and reasons for marriage. *Journal of Homosexuality, 42*(4), 15–34.

Klaar, C. (in press). Straight wives of HIV+ husbands who contracted the virus through male-to-male sexual contact. *Journal of GLBT Family Studies.*

Matteson, D. R. (1985). Bisexual men in marriage: Is a positive homosexual identity and stable marriage possible? *Journal of Homosexuality, 11*(2), 149–171.

Pearcey, M. (2005). Gay and bisexual married men's attitudes and experiences. *Journal of GLBT Family Studies, 1*(1), 21–42.

Pearcey, M. (2007). The experiences of heterosexual women married to gay or bisexual men. *Dissertation Abstracts International: Section A. Humanities and Social Sciences, 68*(4–A), 1400.

Tornello, S. L., & Patterson, C. J. (in press). Gay fathers in mixed-orientation relationships: Experiences of those who stay in their marriages and of those who leave. *Journal of GLBT Family Studies.*

Wolf, T. J. (1987). Group psychotherapy for bisexual men and their wives. *Journal of Homosexuality, 14*(1–2), 191–199.

Wolkomir, M. (2009). Making heteronormative reconciliations: The story of romantic love, sexuality, and gender in mixed orientation marriages. *Gender & Society, 23*(4), 494–519.

Yarhouse, M. A., Gow, C. H., & Davis, E. B. (2009). Intact marriages in which one partner experiences same-sex attraction: A 5-year follow up study. *Family Journal, 17*(4), 329–334.

Yarhouse, M. A., & Kays, J. L. (2010). The PARE model: A framework for working with mixed orientation couples. *Journal of Psychology and Christianity, 29*(1), 77–81.

18

Intercultural Issues in LGBTQQ Couple and Family Therapy

ANNELIESE A. SINGH and AMNEY HARPER

More often than not in the scholarship on lesbian, gay, bisexual, transgender, queer, questioning (LGBTQQ) couples and families, there are silences with regard to the inclusion of the needs and concerns of LGBTQQ people who hold additional historically marginalized identities. Instead, LGBTQQ practice and research typically neglects to explore issues of race and ethnicity, gender identity and expression, ability status, social class, immigration status, and other salient identities LGBTQQ couples and families may hold. In doing so, the overall focus of this area in psychotherapy with LGBTQQ couples and families becomes synonymous with dominant groups in society—namely, White, middle class, gay men—and a Western perspective on couples and psychotherapy. With the changing demographic in the United States, with current population trends indicating that by 2042 racial and ethnic minority groups alone will become the majority (U.S. Census Bureau, 2010), it becomes crucial that psychotherapists understand not only the diversity of clients they will work with but also how such groups as LGBTQQ couples and families have an intersection of various cultural identities within them.

As LGBTQQ identities intersect with various cultural identities, what results are "interlocking systems of power and oppression" (Tisdell, 2003, as cited in D'Amico, 2006, p. 1) that the individual must navigate and that may impact the individual's experience within the context of his or her relationships. Therefore, a major component of ethical and competent practice in this regard is ensuring an intercultural approach to counseling. An *intercultural* approach refers to an acknowledgment of the various ways that LGBTQQ couples and families communicate based on their cultural backgrounds; this approach includes a healthy respect for diverse cultural backgrounds and differences among people rather than an attempt to erase or ignore these important aspects of diverse values, worldviews, and communication styles. The purpose of this chapter is to describe some of intercultural issues about which psychotherapists should have awareness, using their knowledge and skills related to intercultural concerns in order to most effectively counsel the wide range of multicultural identities and resulting social justice issues that LGBTQQ couples and families face. In this chapter, we will describe the importance of practitioners' seeking multicultural and social justice competence in their work with diverse LGBTQQ couples and families, provide an overview of LGBTQQ diverse cultural groups, explore common presenting issues when working with this group, and present case scenarios so that counseling with diverse LGBTQQ couples and families "comes to life." In doing so, this chapter will also trouble the traditional definitions of *couple* and *family* that are used to frame practice with LGBTQQ people.

Seeking Multicultural and Social Justice Competence: A Process and an Action

An initial step in understanding diverse intercultural issues LGBTQQ couples and families face is to have a strong grasp and understanding of multicultural competencies with regard to counseling. Perhaps the most well-known multicultural competencies outline three domains in which psychotherapists should develop: awareness, knowledge, and skills (Sue, Arredondo, & McDavis, 1992).

Awareness refers to the beliefs and attitudes practitioners have about the various cultural groups in society. For instance, with LGBTQQ couples and families, developing awareness of one's beliefs and attitudes with this group would entail assessing one's own biases and assumptions about not only one's own salient cultural identities but also, and perhaps most important, the differences and similarities that exist. In order to fully explore one's beliefs and values, it is also important to understand one's personal experiences with privilege and oppression. Removing the veil of invisibility that usually accompanies privilege requires ongoing self-reflection as well as becoming aware of the systemic nature of oppression and privilege that shape the individual's experience in the world. This practitioner self-awareness is a crucial step in the process of seeking multicultural competence because these beliefs and attitudes often drive the value systems that both practitioners and clients bring into the experience of psychotherapy.

The second domain of multicultural competence, *knowledge*, is the ability to seek out information about specific cultural groups. This knowledge with LGBTQQ couples and families might, for example, involve seeking specific information about the traditions, practices, and worldviews of Chicano families and couples in order to understand how these factors may influence coping and resilience to stressors. The knowledge domain entails an active and ongoing process of gathering information. So, if one is working a LGBTQQ couple whose cultural identities are very different from those of the practitioner, the psychotherapist will want to consume the most current research and practice literature with the clients' cultural group in addition to the LGBTQQ identities. The ongoing process refers to the practitioner's seeking to be exposed to diverse cultural experiences in order to expand his or her knowledge of diverse individuals and communities.

The third domain, *skills*, aims to ensure that culturally relevant strategies are used within counseling practice that are appropriate and match the needs and concerns of clients. For instance, LGBTQQ couples and families who are negotiating issues of being immigrants in the United States would most effectively be served by a psychotherapist who not only had the awareness and knowledge of common concerns of this group but also had the skill set in order to specifically address these concerns. This skill set should not only include specific interventions used but also encompass a theoretical framework that works well with the worldview of the couple or family.

Because intercultural issues not only are based in one's own identity or the identity of one's cultural groups but also relate to specific issues of how the world responds to these identities, along with multicultural competence, psychotherapists working with diverse LGBTQQ couples and families should also understand the various social justice concerns that may be related to having diverse identities. Social justice has been called the fifth force in counseling (Ratts, D'Andrea, & Arredondo, 2004), and its proponents call for practitioners to have facility with advocacy related to social justice issues. In order to understand issues of social justice, similar to the initial step in multicultural competence, practitioners should be aware of their own identities, but as these identities specifically relate to issues of privilege and oppression. *Privilege* has been described as the "unearned advantages" that dominant groups in societies may have (e.g., being White, male, heterosexual, or able-bodied or having middle- or upper-class social status; McIntosh, 1989, p. 52). *Oppression* is defined as the experience of prejudice and discrimination as a result of being a member of a group that has historically been marginalized (e.g., women, people of color, immigrants, or LGBTQQ individuals). It is also important to understand how privilege and oppression operate together as two sides of the same coin (D'Amico, 2003). For example, whereas some persons are privileged in not having their race/ethnicity work against them in finding housing, some other persons experience oppression because based on their race/ethnicity because they do not have the same access to housing. Awareness and understanding of one's identities that have privilege or oppression statuses help practitioners focus on social justice issues (e.g., racism, sexism, heterosexism, ableism, or classism) that they might neglect to address or overly highlight based on their own experiences of privilege and oppression (Singh & Salazar, 2010).

Systems of privilege and oppression exist within institutions and also affect the access, equity, and participation of diverse LGBTQQ couples and families, who may or may not have access to various resources they need (Singh, 2010). See Table 18.1 for a listing of multicultural identities with their related privilege or oppression status.

As psychotherapists develop an active, ongoing commitment to developing multicultural and social justice competency, there are advocacy competencies for counseling that may help guide them in their advocacy (Lewis, Arnold, House, & Toporek, 2003). These advocacy competencies are organized across three large levels that are similar to Bronfenbrenner's (1977) ecological model—micro, meso, and macro—and describe advocacy strategies psychotherapists may engage in at each level.

At the *micro level*, practitioners are working specifically with clients on empowerment issues that may be done with the specific client or on behalf of the client. For instance, with diverse LGBTQQ couples and families, psychotherapists may work with these clients on developing specific self-advocacy skills related to understanding how to effectively access needed resources. When working at the *meso level*, practitioners use the awareness of various social justice issues that impact the lives of diverse LGBTQQ couples and families through their own practice with them and work with the clients to address these issues or work on behalf of them to do so. For instance, in working with diverse LGBTQQ couples and families, psychotherapists and counselors might work on behalf of diverse LGBTQQ couples and families through collaborating with a local social services agency to access these resources for the couple or family. Finally, practitioners working at the *macro level* may lobby their legislators for laws that are affirmative of LGBTQQ couples and families, for example, lobbying for adoption rights and family planning laws.

Table 18.1 Multicultural Identities and Related Privilege and Oppression Statuses of LGBTQQ Couples and Families

Multicultural Identity	Privilege Status	Oppression Status
Ability status	Able-bodied	Physical or mental health disability
Gender	Men	Women, transgender
Sex	Male	Intersex, female
Gender identity and expression	Cisgender	Transgender
Immigration status	U.S. citizen (white)	Immigrant (people of color)
Race and ethnicity	White, non-Hispanic	People of color
Sexual orientation	Heterosexual	LGBTQQ, polyamorous
Social class	Middle to upper class	Poverty, working class
Religion and spirituality	Judeo-Christian	Muslim, Eastern, Pagan, etc.
Education level	Access to higher education	High school, GED, noncompletion
Language	English as first language	English as second language
Political views	Republican, Democrat	Radical, progressive
Nationality	U.S. citizen (White), Western European	Eastern European, Asian, African, Latino, Middle Eastern, Canadian

Intercultural Practice Issues With LGBTQQ Couples and Families

Before we review the major practice issues that emerge with diverse LGBTQQ families and couples, we first must interrogate the words *couple* and *family*. In traditional psychotherapy, of course, a couple translates to a heterosexual couples where there is one person who has been assigned male at birth and one person who has been assigned female at birth, with both assignations based on anatomy. Just as traditional couple counseling that focuses on heterosexual concerns neglects LGBTQQ issues, when LGBTQQ couple counseling does not take into account diverse LGBTQQ couples, inevitably there are concerns that go unaddressed. Similarly, traditional family counseling has focused on family that is linked biologically; however, LGBTQQ families are often families of choice, formed through active efforts to build community as a result of oppression.

Yet, when diverse LGBTQQ families come to counseling, it is important to understand that because of their varied life experiences, the definition of family may be even more complicated, expansive, and defy traditional conception. For instance, the idea of family can be particularly troubled when a same-sex couple has children, for the relationship(s) the child brings to the family may involve the addition of other adults or parents to the family. There are many variations of what this may look like, from traditional (two parents with biological children from in vitro fertilization or adoption) to nontraditional. Some examples of nontraditional families follow. Some LGBTQQ families have two same-sex partners and a relationship (romantic or platonic) with a biological parent, who may also live in the home or have regular contact with the child or children. Another possible makeup of families is two sets of same-sex couples who all take equal responsibility for parenting and may or may not be biologically related to the child or children. A myth for same-sex couples is that they always either adopt or use in vitro fertilization in order to have children; however, many same-sex couples have biological children from a previous relationship, which would mean the child or children have, for example three mothers, one father, or some other combination. In families where one parent is transgender or genderqueer, a child or children may refer to the parent with a nontraditional term (e.g., a "trans man" who is the mother or a combination of the words *mother* and *father*) based on when the parent "came out" or transitioned. Another example is how the family of choice enters into relationships where a child is present. Biological relationships may or may not be present in the nuclear or extended family unit.

We can further trouble the concept of couples through thinking about it linguistically. *Couple* indicates two romantic partners. However, in polyamorous relationships, romantic relationships may involve three or more partners (e.g., three women, two women and one man, two men and a woman, or three men). These relationships take on a variety of configurations. For example, relationships may be made up of a primary couple with a secondary relationship, which may or may not include both partners of the primary relationship. However, this relationship may also include all three (or more) partners equally engaging in the relationship. Here, it is important to remember as well that queer identities can take into account heterosexual identities that trouble the heteronormative. This situation may be present particularly in such polyamorous relationships as noted here. These are just a few examples of how relationships may not follow traditional patterns. It is important when working with any LGBTQQ couples that you consider the limitless possibilities of how families and such "couples" may be constructed. In this chapter, we will hereafter use the term *couples* in quotation marks as a reminder of how this concept may differ from the heteronormative definition of couples. We also will alternatively use the term *partners*, which is more inclusive, but has not yet gained currency when referring to counseling "couples."

Regardless of the specific concerns that diverse LGBTQQ couples and families bring into counseling, Singh and Chun (2010) encouraged practitioners to use a resilience perspective when multiple salient identities and intercultural dynamics are present in the therapy room. *Resilience* is the ability an individual and/or a community has to cope positively with life's stressors (Werner, Wilson, Zimmerman, & Whalen, 2000). Despite the experiences of oppression that diverse LGBTQQ families and couples have and the potential for internalizing oppression, these groups also develop coping that may assist them in navigating experiences of prejudice and discrimination. As we explore typical presenting issues diverse LGBTQQ families and couples explore in therapy, we will simultaneously explore both the oppressive and the resilient experiences these families and "couples" have.

Multiple and Intersecting Identities of LGBTQQ Couples and Families

As noted in Table 18.1, there are many layers of privileged and/or oppressed identities that one can hold. When a person holds more than one marginalized identity, there are many considerations that one should take into account. In this chapter, we are looking specifically at how a person's LGBTQQ identity intersects with other marginalized identities. There has been much written about identity development of lesbian, gay, and bisexual people; people of color; and other marginalized identities (Atkinson, Morten, & Sue, 1989; Bleiberg, Fertmann, Todhunter Friedman, & Godino, 2005; Brown, 2002; Cass, 1979; Cross, 1991; Helms, 1995; Klein, 1993). There is also literature on biracial and multiracial identity development (Poston, 1990; Root, 2003). When you consider the identity development of someone who simultaneously holds two marginalized identities (e.g., race and sexual orientation), however, some additional considerations need to be evaluated.

In 2005, Poytner and Washington described the complex process of multiple-identity development. They describe this process as nonlinear and having two distinct trajectories: individual and group. They then identify the potential outcomes of multiple-identity development. The most optimal outcome is found when individuals are able to integrate multiple identities into their self-concept and also hold multiple group identities or memberships. Two other outcomes that are not as beneficial to well-being and sense of self are to identify with only one group while ignoring other aspects of one's identity or to identify with only one group at a time. In the next sections, we will specifically address how particular racial identities intersect with LGBTQQ identities. It is important to realize, however, that each layer of identity, visible or otherwise, presents unique variables that should be considered when working with individuals, "couples," or families with multiple identities. We will briefly cover some of these variables, according to the identities laid out in Table 18.1.

Ability Status   *Ability status* refers to an identity people may have related to physical, emotional, and mental challenges. For instance, a person who is able-bodied has fewer barriers to physical and mental health challenges than has a person with physical challenges; for example, a person living with a disability may have societal obstacles to navigate in his or her daily life (e.g., the lack of accessible buildings for people using wheelchairs, the absence of quality and accessible mental healthcare for people living with mental health challenges) as he or she attempts to live a full life. *Ableism* is the system of oppression that privileges able-bodied people. *Sex* refers to the status of male, female, or intersex that is assigned to people at birth based on anatomical and chromosomal makeup. *Gender* refers to the identity and expression of one's sense of gender and is often based on the sex assigned at birth. *Sexism* is the system of oppression that privileges men over women and boys over girls.

Race and Ethnicity   *Race and ethnicity* is a composite related to how race and ethnicity have been defined and categorized. The U.S. system of *racism* privileges White Americans over the target group of this oppression, People of Color. *Immigration status* refers to the access one has in the United States to legal documents "legalizing" one's residence in this country. *Language* is often related to race, ethnicity, and immigration status in the United States, where the privileged groups are those who have facility with English. *Nationalism* is the system of oppression that privileges those holding citizenship. *Social class* refers to the access one has to financial and other resources. *Education* is often related to social-class statuses, and the privileged groups in this regard are those who have had access to higher education, obtaining bachelor's degrees and more; whereas those who obtained a high school degree or GED, or did not complete school, are targets. *Classism* is the system of oppression that privileges social classes with higher financial resources and more access to education.

Religion and Spirituality   The identity of *Religion and spirituality* has historically received less attention from practitioners with regard to LGBTQQ couples and families; however, it is an identity that is often closely related to value systems and coping resources, so it is important. With regard to this status, Judeo-Christian religions are those that hold privileged statuses, whereas other faith traditions and those individuals who identify as agnostic, atheist, or nonbelievers are target groups. *Political views* are also an important identity status. Although we have a complicated political system that often varies by geographic region, the dominant political parties—namely, Republicans and Democrats—are privileged in the U.S. democratic system; those groups that fall outside these two parties hold less power.

African American or African Heritage

About 13.6% of the general U.S. population is African American or has African heritage (U.S. Census Bureau, 2009), currently making this group one of the largest ethnic minority communities in this country. A much neglected subgroup within this community are immigrants from African countries, who may share distinctly different experiences and worldviews than do their African American counterparts. Much of the recent literature in family therapy with individuals of African descent has focused on the importance of exploring the context of family connections, extended kinship networks, and issues of religion and spirituality affecting the lives of family members (Grimmett & Locke, 2009). For this reason, it is important to carefully assess how each of these dimensions is experienced by individuals and the related meaning they attach to them in regard to the presenting issue. For instance, in counseling an LGBTQQ African American family presenting with concerns about a teenaged daughter's relationship with her peers, exploring how extended kinship and family networks influence this issue may be important.

Gender is an important factor within any racial or ethnic group in the United States, and this is certainly true with regard to partners' and families' concerns in therapy. Avoiding assumptions and stereotypes about gender roles is a good rule of thumb; thus, practitioners might instead explore how clients' gender and race or ethnicity intersect for them. African American women may come in with concerns about shifting roles among the variety of contexts they inhabit—from work and professional relationships to family and other personal social networks (Anglin, 2006). For instance, an African American lesbian may have to shift her personality and approach to life to fit into a White norm at work, whereas in her home community she may have to shift "back" to an entirely different mode of relating to others. Another example might be working with an African American gay transgender man whose family may understand his gender identity but may not want him to tell others that he is in a relationship with another man.

A common theme in the literature with LGBTQQ African Americans is the idea of "Don't Ask, Don't Tell" (Miller & Parker, 2009). This phrase is used to describe the family dynamic wherein LGBTQQ members may feel accepted by their families, but their families ask them not share this information with others. In a study of coming-out disclosures of African American daughters to their mothers, Miller and Parker (2009) found that mothers were typically supportive of their daughters' sexual orientation, yet they asked their daughters not to disclose their orientations to others in their extended family. Church holds a particular space in the lives of African Americans because of the historical use of Black churches for political organizing during the Black freedom struggle. Even families who have a strong understanding of oppression as it relates to race (and who may not themselves be particularly active or connected to Christianity) may struggle with accepting LGBTQQ identities, which go against traditional Christian religious values (Schlosser, 2003).

Latino or Latina

According to the 2009 U.S. Census, there are approximately 48.4 million Latino[1] people living in the United States, making them the largest ethnic and racial minority group in the United States (U.S. Census Bureau, 2009). Given that there are many people living in the United States without citizenship status, this number may be higher than estimated by the U.S. Census Bureau. There are many intergroup differences among Latino peoples, who hail from many different countries and cultural groups with varied cultural practices and traditions. Important considerations related to intergroup differences when working with Latino LGBTQQ "couples" and families are language, citizenship status, country of origin and level of acculturation, class, and religion and spirituality.

In working with Latino LGBTQQ "couples" and families, it is important to consider the role of varied Latino cultural beliefs, values, and practices. Probably the most relevant and common cultural value is the central role of the family. Because of the importance placed on family in Latino cultures, it is not surprising that Latino families make up the largest group of same-sex partners who raise children and utilize adoption (Bourne, 2008). Perhaps more surprising is that in a study by Gary Gates (as cited in Tavernise, 2011), Latinos living in the South are more likely to adopt compared to Latinos in other regions of the country. Given this information, it may be particularly important when working with LGBTQQ "couples" to explore, when appropriate, the role of family and concerns related to children.

Another very important consideration in working with Latino LGBTQQ "couples" and families is the notion of traditional gender roles. After the colonization of Mexico and Latin America, the predominant religion became Christianity, particularly Catholicism (Klar, 1993). This religion played a large role in the formation of rigid gender roles, which impact the lives of Latino LGBTQQ people and contribute to their oppression in very specific ways. Within this rigid constructions of gender roles, heterosexuality and the gender binary are considered the norm, and everything else is considered abnormal. Despite this rigid division, many Latin American countries have recently legalized gay marriages and/or civil unions (Lodola & Corral, 2011). Although things seem to be shifting in some Latino cultures, many barriers still exist.

In the United States, LGBTQQ Latinos face growing discrimination. As immigration has taken a central role in national dialogue and as certain regions of the country have passed laws aimed at deporting "Mexican" immigrants and keeping them from entering the United States, Latino people face an environment in which they are even more subject to suspicion, discrimination, and possible deportation. This environment impacts all Latinos regardless of their citizenship status or country of origin. In addition to experiencing the changing climate, Latino LGBTQQ people may face barriers within both White and Latino communities when traditional roles are rigidly followed. As with any group, it is important to be aware of the current

---

[1] Note that the U.S. Census Bureau uses the term *Hispanic*. This term, however, is not currently the designation preferred by the Latino peoples whom it purports to identify. Thus the term will not be used in this chapter. Also note that when working with LGBTQQ Latino "couples" and families or any group, practitioners must be mindful to use the term preferred by each individual.

political and cultural climate when working with Latino LGBTQQ "couples" and families, yet individual differences must be considered.

Asian American and Pacific Islander LGBTQQ "Couples" and Families

Asian American and Pacific Islander (AAPI) LGBTQQ partners and families, like other ethnic minority groups, face several societal stereotypes as they attempt to lead fulfilling lives. One of the most pervasive stereotypes is the "myth of the model minority," that is, the idea that AAPI people have success at higher rates than do other ethnic minority groups (Singh, 2009). This stereotype creates additional pressure on LGBTQQ partners and families because they not only have to navigate societal heterosexism but also have to be perfect as they do so. As a result, these partners and families may not feel able to share the actual stressors present in their lives for fear of losing face (Zane & Yeh, 2002). *Losing face* is a cultural concept that refers to the importance of maintaining privacy about personal, professional, and/or family struggles, in addition to presenting an optimistic view of life. Often intersecting with the important notion of face is the cultural value that hierarchy of family relationships is paramount. For instance, there might be cultural traditions and assumptions that aging parents will be taken care of by their children in their family homes, whereas securing assisted living for aging parents would be culturally frowned upon or even considered unacceptable.

Cultural traditions and belief systems, including respect for one's parents, are often strong AAPI values that may influence how AAPI partners and families experience stressors and show resilience around their presenting concern in counseling (Singh, 2009). Therefore, understanding that there are varying views of sexual orientation and gender identity and expression within AAPI cultures, practitioners will also understand that the degree of importance AAPI partners and families may put on coming out to their families of origin may likewise vary. In addition, the myth of the model minority may make AAPI partners and families feel that their disclosure of a LGBTQQ identity may cause their families to lose face in their communities. Therefore, it is never appropriate for practitioners to pressure LGBTQQ partners and families to disclose their identities. Rather, it is more helpful to explore the stressors and resilience they experience with regard to their families and seek to connect them with other examples of AAPI partners and families (e.g., through community or social organizations and/or Internet resources).

Native American LGBTQQ "Couples" and Families

Native American people face a great many challenges in contemporary U.S. society. Many factors are important in considering the experiences of Native people, such as whether they live or have lived on or off a reservation; which tribe or tribes they are from; whether they follow Christian practices, traditional spiritual practices, another spiritual or religious path, or none at all; their experiences with alcohol and drugs, whether for the self or the family; their racial identity development; their class status; what languages they speak; and so on. There are hundreds of tribes that survived the genocide brought on by Whites of European descent, and each tribe has a unique set of beliefs, practices, and traditions, as well as variation in adherence to those practices and degree of assimilation in or acculturation to White culture. The oppression and marginalization of Native Americans have continued since Whites first invaded the Americas, as evidenced by the continued high rates of suicide, alcoholism, poverty, and other social problems that Native people face in many Native communities. One means of continuing to marginalize Native peoples is how the idea of Native American has been constructed. For example, in U.S. society's construction of the term *Native American*, native peoples of Mexico and Canada are often removed from the definition, despite the number of people living in the United States that originate from lands now known as Mexico and Canada (e.g., Aztec, Mayan, Cree, Micmac, and Squamish).

This narrative goes so far as to often include language that reflects inaccurate notions about the "extinction" of these tribes, as well as some within the United States, by referring to them in the past tense. Native identity has been historically constructed in a manner that is consistent with early attempts to assimilate and exterminate Native peoples. For example, whereas African American identity was constructed to exclude African Americans from resources, privileges, and rights—as reflected in policies that identified anyone with a single drop of African American blood as African American and therefore exempted them from White privileges—Native American identity was constructed under policies that sought the extinction of Native Americans, which meant that one had to have a high degree of Native ancestry to be labeled Native American. Native people are therefore are approaching increasing Whiteness with each new generation; that is, in each generation where Native people and White people have children together, the children are viewed as less authentically Native. Further, after a certain percentage of White ancestry is integrated, Native roots are denied by legislative bodies. This conception can be particularly challenging for same-sex partners who may wish to have children, whether the partners are of different races or if such means as adoption or in vitro fertilization are utilized.

Native people have strong historical traditions that include positive spaces for LGBTQQ people, referred to by as many different names as the tribes they come from, among them Nahdlee (Navaho) or Winkte (Lakota). In 1990, the term *Two Spirit* was coined during the third annual intertribal Native American, First Nations gay and lesbian American conference in Winnipeg (North American Aboriginal Two Spirit Information Pages; see Two Spirit Society of Denver, 2011). *Two Spirit* is an intertribal word that includes the complex intersections between gender and sexuality and was used as a means of community building between LGBTQQ people of many different tribes. The use of this term represents a new tradition, yet it is a new tradition that honors and revives older traditional conceptions of the many different ways that gender and sexuality were constructed across tribes. Although Native people have had strong histories of honoring LGBTQQ people, they are not immune to modern homophobia, biphobia, and transphobia. The consistent attempts to assimilate Native people have infused these forms of oppression into modern life.

It is important that when working with LGBTQQ Native American families and "couples," practitioners understand the cultural context of family. Although the scope of this chapter precludes space to review the intergroup differences in depth, there are some differences that might be helpful to consider. In any situation, individual differences should be attended to in understanding any couple or family's unique construction. One consideration is the importance of extended families that may or may not include nonbiological family members. Another consideration is the child-rearing principle of noninterference. This principle, practiced by many Native people, describes a process through which adults allow children to make mistakes (instead of parents immediately correcting behavior) in order to allow the children's unique personalities and life paths to emerge without undue influence from others.

A final important consideration is the role of the mental health profession in the oppression of Native people and LGBTQQ people. The mental health profession has historically been used in ways that have served to perpetuate the oppression of both of these groups (e.g., conversion or reparative therapy and the role of child and family services in the removal of Native children from the home and subsequent placement of those children in White homes until the Indian Child Welfare Act); therefore, building a trusting relationship in the therapeutic context may provide additional challenges (Sue & Sue, 2007). Allowing for the use of nontraditional methods and theoretical frameworks (e.g., the integration of spiritual leaders into the sessions), as well as the inclusion of extended families as desired by the family or "couple," may be particularly important.

White American LGBTQQ "Couples" and Families

When considering the racial identity of White Americans, it is important to consider the experiences of privilege held by Whites in U.S. society. As described by Peggy McIntosh (1989), Whites experience daily privileges that are not experienced by People of Color. In considering how these privileges are experienced by LGBTQQ individuals, the intersection of privilege and oppression is particularly important. For example, while LGBTQQ people face daily oppressions based on their sexual orientation and gender identity, White LGBTQQ people have added advantages not experienced by LGBTQQ People of Color. An example of this is in the number of White LGBTQQ characters found in television shows and movies compared to the number of LGBTQQ People of Color. Another example of this intersection is found particularly in smaller communities, where LGBTQQ communities are largely made up of White members, and their concerns are given particular weight over those of their counterparts. Similarly, the face of the LGBTQQ rights movement pivots on White figures and White concerns. A poignant example of this intersection of privilege and oppression is found in the number of White LGBTQQ suicides that have gained national attention recently, which have significantly impacted media coverage of bullying toward LGBTQQ youth in schools and universities. The increased coverage of LGBTQQ bullying is of course important—at the same time, LGBTQQ people of color become invisible in these campaigns. This invisibility is problematic, especially considering that Native Americans have the highest suicide rates in the United States (National Institute of Mental Health, 2007); this fact, though, is not reflected in the national media reporting on LGBTQQ bullying.

In working with White LGBTQQ "couples" and families, it is important to not over- or underestimate the interplay between privilege and oppression. For example, it would be faulty to pay more attention to the suicide risk of Whites because of national attention but equally dangerous to ignore it. Another important consideration is how White privilege is gendered (i.e., the intersection between male privilege and White privilege). Male privilege is experienced by gay and bisexual men differently than by their heterosexual counterparts. For example, a large part of male privilege is exclusive to heterosexuals because the definition of *man* is contingent upon the oppression and objectification of women. Gay and bisexual men who are more feminine will experience this even more acutely because traditional masculinity is required for the assumption of male privilege. In the same vein, trans and genderqueer individuals are also excluded from many aspects of White privilege because of the strict binary assumptions of gender.

Multiracial LGBTQQ "Couples" and Families

Just as we discuss the various racial and ethnic groups, it is also important to acknowledge that multiracial partners and families exist and have unique counseling needs. Although race and ethnicity may not be the focus of their presenting concerns, it is important to thoroughly assess their experience of their racial and ethnic identity. For instance, a bisexual partner with an AAPI maternal family and an African American paternal family may have been raised to value one racial or ethnic identity over another or to value both equally; on the other hand, he or she may have been raised not to think about race at all. No matter how the individual's experience of racial and ethnic identity was shaped within the family, it is important to explore both past and present experiences within and outside the individual's family to explore the development of his or her racial and ethnic identity.

Racial and ethnic identity has several components: how one is perceived by others and how one perceive one's self as a racial and ethnic being. Therefore, a component of healing and understanding within the relationships multiracial people have may entail exploring how their racial and ethnic identity development has influenced their values and worldviews, as well as how these aspects translate into their intrapersonal and interpersonal relationships. Root (1996) has written extensively on multiracial counseling, and a large component for practitioners is to explore and validate partners' and families' experiences of race and ethnicity as opposed to reinforcing racial and ethnic stereotypes these individuals may have experienced growing up (e.g., "You don't look Asian American").

Culturally Relevant Counseling Practice With LGBTQQ "Couples" and Families and Related Practice Concerns

Culturally relevant and responsive counseling with LGBTQQ couples and families entails weaving their specific concerns and life experiences throughout the course of psychotherapy. We briefly discuss some of these concerns next.

The Impact of Oppression on Intimacy

Although the literature to date has not made direct links to the impact of oppression on intimacy and desire, it is worth considering how experiences of oppression may impact partners' experiences within their relationship. Some literature exists that begins to addressed these issues, such as the role of coming out in relationship satisfaction (Jordan & Duluty, 2000) and experiences of homophobia and increased arguing and sexual problems (Green & Mitchell, 2002), which makes it easy to understand how partners with differing levels of outness may face particular struggles that their straight counterparts may not. Something that may emerge from clients' narratives is the nature of the "closet." It is important to note that LGBTQQ individuals may have varied experiences of the closet, from the idea that the secrecy involved with not being out may be particularly arousing for some, whereas for others the danger of being found out and personal safety concerns may be a barrier. We know from the minority stress model (Meyer, 2003) that the daily stressors that come from oppression add to the overall stress of individuals with marginalized identities. Considering the role that stress may have on intimacy, these issues may emerge for LGBTQQ couples with additional marginalized identities particularly strong.

Ongoing Assessment of Counselor Biases and Assumptions

A significant skill in working with diverse LGBTQQ "couples" and families entails identifying one's biases and assumptions about their cultural backgrounds and salient identities at the forefront of work with them, in addition to attending how the practitioner's worldviews will influence the course of treatment.

Intake Session

Before the intake session, practitioners should be able to connect with diverse partners and families and share the particular counseling approach and commitment to multicultural practice and concerns related to social justice. In the intake session itself, practitioners should conduct a "cultural formulation," that is, an assessment of the partners' or families' value systems related to their cultural background and salient identities. Rather than merely obtaining brief answers to these questions, practitioners can ask clients what the meaning and awareness of their background and identities hold for them. It is also important to ask specific questions about experiences with systems of oppression (e.g., racism and sexism), in addition to how these systems may influence individual, partners', and families' well-being and the presenting concern for counseling.

Assessment of Trauma

Every good intake includes a trauma assessment. With counseling of diverse LGBTQQ partners and families, however, it is important not only to ask specific questions about experiences of trauma but also to understand how these experiences may be related to systems of oppression. This trauma assessment should be ongoing throughout the course of counseling. Because of the high rates of oppression that diverse LGBTQQ persons in general experience, understanding these critical incidents will help practitioners understand the presenting issue and course of counseling more effectively, in addition to being able to collaboratively identify healthy and unhealthy coping developed in partnerships and families as a result of these experiences.

Blended Families

The general literature on couple and family counseling practice has attended to issues of blended families. However, these issues may be experienced very differently in diverse LGBTQQ partners and "couples." Interpersonal and group dynamics are influenced by cultural values and worldviews and therefore may be markedly different. For instance, there may be similar or dissimilar views on such issues as finances, dissolution of relationship, and degree of family connection. In addition, acceptance or rejection by previous partners and children of changes in the gender of new partners (e.g., for "opposite"-sexed partners who dissolve their relationship, and one partner forms a new relationship with a now same-sex partner) may prove particularly difficult when navigating such issues as custody and parenting. These issues can have an impact on new relationships as well as on the previous relationship.

Two Case Studies of Diverse LGBTQQ "Couples" and Families

In this section, this chapter presents two case studies that illustrate the chapter's focus. The first case study explores how a counselor may approach partner work with an interracial couple. The second case study highlights implications of working with diverse families in school settings.

Case Study 1: Partners Work With an Interracial Couple

Background Information   Angie, age 29, is African American and identifies as bisexual. She currently works as a bank manager at a local bank in town. She is active in the LGBTQQ community and is out in many contexts, but she is not out to her family. She is also an active member in her church, which is not supportive of same-sex relationships. Angie grew up in a working-class family, where her mother supported her and her three siblings with help from her grandmother. Angie has not had contact with her father since she was 11 years old, when he and her mother divorced. Angie and Selena met in a women's studies course at college. They began dating after studying together for the class and have been together for eight years. Selena is Angie's first same-sex partner, but Selena has been dating women only since she was in high school.

Selena, age 27, is a White American who identifies as queer. She has a master's degree in elementary education and works at an elementary school as a teacher. Selena grew up in an upper-middle-class family with her mother, father, and older brother. Her family members are devout atheists from a small town. They are supportive of Selena's identity but have had trouble accepting her relationship with Angie because of Angie's race.

Presenting Concerns   Angie and Selena have come to counseling to address their growing concerns related to intimacy and conflict related to the pressure Angie feels from Selena to come out to her family. Angie and Selena report that after an increase in bias incidents and hate crimes in their community, including a situation in which two gay men in their community were beaten severely by a group of male students on the local campus at a party, their own sense of safety has been shaken. They report that they experience more intimacy when they are able to spend time together at LGBTQQ events or with supportive friends in the LGBTQQ community. However, even this has begun to change as the holidays are approaching because Selena has been insistent that Angie come out to her family so they can spend the holidays together as partners.

Angie feels that Selena does not understand the importance of her family to her, and she worries that if she comes out, her family will disown her. In addition, she is worried that it might jeopardize her role in church, where she spends a significant amount of time, because her mother is also very active and involved in church. Selena feels that Angie's resistance is related to her bisexual identity, such that she is hesitant to commit to a same-sex relationship because she is holding onto what is left of her heterosexual privilege. Selena reports that Angie has told her she would come out to her family before this coming holiday, but that now she is backing down. Selena is concerned that if they cannot be out and proud as a couple, then their relationship will not last. Angie is already uncomfortable when they visit Selena's family because she can tell that they do not accept her race. She believes that coming out to her own family will not actually allow them to spend the holidays together comfortably anyway, since neither family is likely to fully accept the couple.

Potential Strategies and Considerations of Case Study An important first consideration for this case is to acknowledge the mounting challenges that Angie and Selena face while simultaneously building on their strengths as partners. Oftentimes it is easy to assume that people who have partners from different backgrounds than themselves are automatically knowledgeable and understanding of the differences in their lived experiences. In this case, however, it may be particularly helpful to spend some time helping each partner to understand some aspects of how they uniquely experience oppression in the world (e.g., discussing biphobia and also the role of the church community in African American identity, or the role of White privilege paired with queer identity). In addition, helping this couple collectively explore the role that oppression may have in their intimacy will be especially important. As the holidays approach, it will be important to help this couple to identify rituals and traditions that can bring them together in conjunction with helping them navigate their relationships with family and what that means to them as partners.

Case Study 2: Family Counseling With a School Counselor

Background Information Kara, age 10, is in fourth grade. She is a bright Latina girl who excels in math and science. She has always performed well in her classes and is polite and sociable. Kara's primary caregivers are her two moms, Melissa and Jessi, and her two dads, Luke and Chuck. Melissa and Luke both identify as bisexual and had Kara together, but they never married. Melissa and Luke both identify as first-generation Mexican Americans. Jessi identifies as White American, and Luke identifies as Native American. Melissa and Luke had an open relationship when they were still together, which is when Melissa met Jessi. Shortly after Melissa and Luke separated (when Kara was 4), Luke began dating Chuck. The two "couples" have maintained a positive relationship, live in the same neighborhood, share custody, and often spend weekends and holidays together as one big family. For the most part, all parties get along well, though they sometimes disagree about parenting, particularly when it comes to extracurricular activities.

Presenting Concerns Kara was referred to her school counselor after an incident with another student, where a teacher overheard another student call her a "lesbo" and a "freak." After some time in talking with Kara, she stated that the other student, along with a handful of his friends, had been bullying her for the past 2 years. Since the most recent incident, Kara has been increasingly withdrawn in the classroom and has begun to turn in work that is not at her usual level of achievement. She reports that her parents are fighting with each other about what to do now, and they have not been spending as much time together as a result.

Kara's parents were called in to come speak with the school counselor about the incident and Kara's recent withdrawal. During the meeting, Luke and Chuck were adamant that they should pull Kara out of this school and enroll her in a nearby private school known for its supportive environment. Melissa and Jessi, however, feel that the school has done a good job of addressing the issue, and they are concerned that moving Kara to a new school might cause her to withdraw more. Melissa and Luke seem to be at the core of the conflict, and Jessi has been wavering between wanting to support Melissa and trying to resolve the conflict with Luke and Chuck. This situation, however, has caused increased conflict between Melissa and Jessi. Kara seems to be caught up in the conflict, and she refuses to report any future bullying now because she does not want it to cause problems at home.

Potential Strategies and Considerations of Case Study   An important first step in working with this family is to identify the client. Given that the family has come into counseling because of concerns with Kara, the child, it will be important to balance the child's needs and concerns with the emerging issues within the family. It will be important to begin by modeling an open dialogue that encourages all members of the family to use their voices. Creating a safe environment in the sessions will reinforce the importance of speaking out in response to injustice to Kara while simultaneously allowing each partner to be a part of the conversation about what is best for the family. Individual sessions with Kara may help to facilitate this process. In individual sessions, it may important for Kara to begin to explore what her family's intersecting identities as well as her own mean to her. Helping her to find positive coping strategies to deal with whatever she may face from society will be important in order for her to have a positive and integrated sense of self.

Given the history of this family, it is clear that they have been successful in the past with resolving differences in parenting (hence their close relationships with one another). Helping family members identify how they have managed divergent viewpoints in the past may help them identify what will be most important now. It may also be important to address how each family member sees the relationship of oppression in the family as it relates to their varied identities. It may also be helpful to explore how they would like to see their child understand herself related to these aspects of herself.

Conclusion

This chapter has discussed the major factors practitioners should consider when working with diverse LGBTQQ partners and families. Overall, an attention to multicultural competence and awareness of social justice issues that influence the lives of these partners and families are paramount. Because these partners and families must negotiate not only experiences of heterosexism, homoprejudice, and transprejudice but also other systemic oppressions, it is important to use a multicultural and social justice lens through which to view clients' presenting issues in addition to an ongoing attention to counselor assumptions and biases based on the counselor's own cultural background and experiences of privileged and oppressed identities.

References

Anglin, D. M. (2006). Shifting: The double lives of Black women in America. *Journal of Black Psychology, 32*(3), 390–394.

Atkinson, D. R., Morten, G., & Sue, D. W. (1989). A minority identity development model. In D. R. Atkinson, G. Morten, & D. W. Sue (Eds.), *Counseling American minorities* (pp. 35–52). Dubuque, IA: W. C. Brown.

Bleiberg, S., Fertmann, A., Todhunter Friedman, C., & Godino, A. (2005). *The layer cake model of bisexual identity development: Clarifying preconceived notions.* Campus Activities Programming. Retrieved from http://www.unr.edu/stsv/studentactivities/leaderhints/documents/TheLayerCakeModelof BisexualIdentityDevelopment.pdf

Bourne, R. (2008). Latino gay or lesbians adopt children at highest rate. *Associated Content from Yahoo.* Retrieved from http://www.associatedcontent.com/article/593231/latino_gay_or_lesbians_adopt_children. html?cat=25

Bronfenbrenner, U. (1977). Toward an experimental ecology of human development. *American Psychologist, 32,* 513–531.

Brown, T. (2002). A proposed model of bisexual identity development that elaborates on experiential differences of women and men. *Journal of Bisexuality, 2*(4), 67–92.

Cass, V. (1979). Homosexual identity formation: A theoretical model. *Journal of Homosexuality, 4*(3), 219–235.

Cross, W. E., Jr. (1991). *Shades of Black: Diversity in African American identity*, Philadelphia, PA: Temple University Press.

D'Amico, D. (2006). Race, class, gender, and sexual orientation in ABE. *InNCSALL's Annual Review of Adult Learning and Literacy.* Retrieved from http://www.ncsall.net/?id=203

Green, R. J., & Mitchell, V. (2002). Gay and lesbian couples in therapy: Homophobia, relational ambiguity, and social support. In Alan S. Gurman & Neil S. Jacobson (Eds.), *Clinical handbook of couple therapy* (3rd ed., pp. 546–568). New York, NY: Guildford Press.

Grimmett, M. A., & Locke, D. (2009). Counseling with African Americans. In C. M. Ellis & J. Carlson (Eds.), *Cross cultural awareness and social justice in counseling* (pp. 121–146). New York, NY: Routledge Press.

Helms, J. E. (1995). An update of Helms's White and People of Color racial identity models. In J. Ponterotto, M. Casas, L. Suzuki, & C. Alexander (Eds.), *Handbook of multicultural counseling* (pp. 181–198). Thousand Oaks, CA: Sage.

Jordan, K. M., & Duluty, R. H. (2000). Social support, coming out, and relationship satisfaction in lesbian couples. From nowhere to everywhere: Lesbian geographies. *Journal of Lesbian Studies, 4,* 145–164.

Klar, N. (1993). *What was the role of the church in the conquest and colonization of Latin America? Did it vary in different areas and was there a true spiritual conquest?* Retrieved from http://klarbooks.com/ academic/catholic.html

Klein, F. (1993). *The bisexual option* (2nd ed.). New York, NY: Hawthorn Press.

Lewis, J. A., Arnold, M. S., House, R., & Toporek, R. (2003). *ACA Advocacy competencies.* Retrieved from http://www.counseling.org/Publications

Lodola, G. & Corral, M. (2011). Latin America's support for same-sex marriage. *Americas Quarterly.* Retrieved from http://www.americasquarterly.org/node/1728

McIntosh, P. (1989, July–August). White privilege: Unpacking the invisible knapsack. *Peace and Freedom.*

Meyer, I. H. (2003). Prejudice, social stress, and mental health in lesbian, gay, and bisexual populations: Conceptual issues and research evidence. *Psychological Bulletin, 129,* 674–697.

Miller, S., & Parker, B. A. (2009). Reframing the power of lesbian daughters' relationships with mothers through Black feminist thought. *Journal of Gay & Lesbian Social Services: Issues in Practice, Policy & Research, 21*(2–3), 206–218.

National Institute of Mental Health. (2007). *Suicide rates 2007.* Retrieved from http://www.nimh.nih.gov/ statistics/4SR07.shtml

Poston, W. S. C. (1990). The biracial identity development model: A needed addition. *Journal of Counseling and Development, 69,* 152–155.

Poynter, K. J., & Washington, J. (2005). Multiple identities: Creating community on campus for LGBT students. *New Directions for Student Services, 111,* 41–47.

Ratts, M., D'Andrea, M., & Arredondo, P. (2004). Social justice counseling: "Fifth force" in field. *Counseling Today, 47,* 28–30.

Root, M. P. P. (1996). *The multiracial experience: Racial borders as the new frontier.* Thousand Oaks, CA: Sage.

Root, M. P. P. (2003). Racial identity development and persons of mixed race heritage. In M. P. P. Root & M. Kelley (Eds.), *Multiracial child resource book: Living complex identities.* Seattle, WA: MAVIN Foundation.

Schlosser, L. (2003). Christian privilege: Breaking a sacred taboo. *Journal of Multicultural Counseling and Development, 31*(1), 44–51.

Singh, A. A. (2009). Counseling with Asian Americans. In C. M. Ellis & J. Carlson (Eds.), *Cross cultural awareness and social justice in counseling* (pp. 147–167). New York, NY: Taylor & Francis.

Singh, A. A. (2010). It takes more than a rainbow sticker! Using the ACA Advocacy Competencies with queer clients. In M. Ratts, J. Lewis, & R. Toporek (Eds.), *Using the ACA Advocacy Competencies in counseling* (pp. 29–41). Alexandria, VA: American Counseling Association.

Singh, A. A., & Chun, K. S. Y. (2010). From "margins to the center": Moving towards a resilience-based model of supervision for queer People of Color supervisors. *Training and Education in Professional Psychology, 4*(1), 36–46.

Singh, A. A., & Salazar, C. F. (2010). Six considerations for social justice group work. *Journal for Specialists in Group Work, 35,* 308–319.

Sue, D. W., Arredondo, P., & McDavis, R. J. (1992). Multicultural counseling competencies and standards: A call to the profession. *Journal of Counseling & Development, 70,* 477–486.

Sue, D. W., & Sue, D. (2007). *Counseling the culturally diverse: Theory and practice* (5th ed.). New York, NY: John Wiley & Sons, Inc.

Tavernise, S. (2011, January 19). Parenting by gays more common in the South, census shows. *New York Times.* Retrieved from http://www.nytimes.com/2011/01/19/us/19gays.html?pagewanted=all

Two Spirit Society of Denver. (2011). [Home page]. Retrieved from http://www.denvertwospirit.com

U.S. Census Bureau. (2009). *Population estimates.* Retrieved from http://www.census.gov/popest/national/asrh/NC-EST2009-srh.html

U.S. Census Bureau. (2010). *The census: A snapshot.* Retrieved from http://2010.census.gov/partners/materials/outreach-materials.php

Werner-Wilson, R. J., Zimmerman, T. S., & Whalen, D. (2000). Resilient response to battering. *Contemporary Family Therapy, 22,* 161–188.

Zane, N., & Yeh, M. (2002). The use of culturally-based variables in assessment: Studies on loss of face. In K. S. Kurasaki, S. Okazaki, & S. Sue (Eds.), *Asian American mental health: Assessment theories and methods. International and cultural psychology series* (pp. 123–138). New York, NY: Kluwer Academic/Plenum Publishers.

19

Issues in the Health of Lesbian, Gay, Bisexual, and Transgender People in Couple and Family Therapy

THOMAS O. BLANK, MARYSOL ASENCIO, and LARA DESCARTES

A multitude of health and health care issues affect lesbian, gay, bisexual, and transgender (LGBT) people. Some of these health concerns may be held in common by the LGBT population, such as the stigmatization and discrimination faced by gender and sexual minorities. Other health concerns may be more specific to lesbians (e.g., ovarian cancer) or gay men (e.g., prostate cancer) or transgender people (sex reassignment surgery). One major challenge in evaluating the health needs of this population is the limited research available.

Many major national and state health data collection surveillance systems do not ask about sexual orientation or gender identity. Thus, for conditions where sexual orientation is not seen as relevant—such as diabetes, cancer, respiratory diseases, heart disease, and stroke—persons with nonmajority identities are not identified. We therefore have significant gaps in information about LGBT populations, and these gaps hamper our ability to know if these populations are doing better or worse than their heterosexual counterparts in terms of their health. Instead, we must rely on a limited number of smaller scale studies and the occasional inclusion in national surveys to access the health status of LGBT individuals. The studies that are available are often unfortunately riddled with sampling and methodological issues that affect the findings' generalizability.

Boehmer (2002) performed a literature review utilizing the Medline database to gauge the amount of research on LGBT health issues. She noted that only 0.1% of the published literature focused on LGBT people, with most of those studies (85%) failing to include participants' race and ethnicity. Gay men were the subject of the most health research because of concerns about HIV/AIDS and sexually transmitted infections (STIs). Indeed, LGBT health research is framed by pathological or risk-taking models, primarily as a result of the HIV/AIDS and STI research on men who have sex with men (see later in this chapter for more discussion of this point). What is strongly lacking are data on all the other diseases, chronic and otherwise, that may affect LGBT people, as well as information about their access to health care, health and disability concerns, and general well-being.

In this chapter, we provide a brief overview of major issues and current knowledge on LGBT health to provide a framework for therapists who work with LGBT populations. We address the issues shared among LGBT people as well as those that may be more relevant to a particular group. We begin by considering the challenges facing all gender and sexual minorities in the U.S. health care system and then proceed to look at specific health concerns of lesbian and bisexual women, gay and bisexual men, and transgender women and men.

LGBT Health Care

The health care system is based on heteronormative assumptions and expectations, which can make LGBT people invisible, problematic, and vulnerable (Pugh, 2005; Trettin, Moses-Kolko, &

Wisner, 2005). Access to health care, equitable treatment by clinicians, inclusion of family members (who may not under the law be defined as family), and obtaining appropriate support services have been found to be important issues for LGBT people. In clinical settings, assumptions are made about a patient's sexual orientation, family members, sexual practices, and access to resources. These assumptions are often based on heterosexual biases: that everyone is heterosexual unless otherwise specified, that family means related by blood or marriage, and that friends are peripheral. Concerning this latter point, research (Grossman, D'Augelli, & Hershberger, 2000; Shippy, Cantor, & Brennan, 2004) indicates that sexual minorities' support networks often include partners and close friends, most of whom are also sexual minorities. These networks provide emotional, practical, financial, and social support, as well as guidance, all crucial in health care encounters.

Another area of concern is that homophobia among care-giving professionals and nurses may decrease the level of empathy and care they give to LGBT individuals (Albarran & Salmon, 2000). Therefore, the nurturing and supportive aspects of health care may be affected. In general, provider bias toward LGBT patients is a major concern (Gay and Lesbian Medical Association, 2001). Barriers to the clinical encounter for LGBT patients involve clinicians and other providers: being ignorant of the possibility that their patients may be LGBT; knowing little about LGBT people and making assumptions about their lives, sexual partners, family structures, and sexuality; creating an unwelcoming environment through verbal and nonverbal cues; and not providing sufficient access to partners and friends (Bonvicini & Perlin, 2003). Clinicians' insensitivity toward or discomfort about LGBT people may lead to patients' withholding personal information about their sexual and gender identities, sexual practices, and any behavioral health risk factors. This may reduce or eliminate opportunities for prevention or early intervention, leading to later treatment and poorer outcomes. Silvestre (2003) also reports that when patients do disclose their sexual orientation, there is the danger that their health concerns may erroneously be reinterpreted as stemming from their sexual orientation.

It has been shown that medical students given greater exposure to LGBT patients tended to hold more positive attitudes toward LGBT patients, perform more comprehensive histories, and possess a greater knowledge of LGBT concerns than do those who had little to no clinical exposure (Sanchez, Rabatin, Sanchez, Hubbard, & Kalet, 2006). As such, the proper training of medical and nursing personnel regarding LGBT patients may have a significant positive impact on the health of this population. Yet, there is a lack of attention in American medical schools to LGBT issues and sexuality in general. The average medical school spends less than half a day within the 4-year curriculum on LGBT issues (Bonvicini & Perlin, 2003). Thus, most providers get little experience with the subject and little opportunity to access their own biases or create strategies to be more sensitive to LGBT patients. The recruitment and support of LGBT-identified health and social services providers as part of the diversification of the health care delivery system comprise another strategy that can be adopted to improve the current situation (Maccio & Doueck, 2002).

There are other health-related issues specific to LGBT people. In a study on victimization, which comprised a sample of 557 lesbian and gay, 164 bisexual, and 525 heterosexual adults, Balsam, Rothblum, and Beauchaine (2005) found that lesbian, gay, and bisexual people reported more childhood psychological and physical abuse by parents and caretakers, more partner victimization in adulthood, and more sexual assault experiences in adulthood. The differences were greater among males than females. In a study of Latino gay and bisexual men, those who identified as "effeminate" (i.e., non-gender-conforming men) had higher levels of mental distress than did those who did not self-identify as such. This level was attributed to more exposure to homophobia (Sandfort, Melendez, & Diaz, 2007).

The current homophobia and heterosexism in health care delivery have potentially severe ramifications. Discrimination has been studied in terms of the stress it produces in the body and the subsequent effects on the health and well-being of minority populations, including sexual and gender minorities (Trettin et al., 2005). Researchers tend to agree that it is not a person's sexual orientation that causes psychological distress but, rather, the person's membership in a stigmatized group (Smith & Ingram, 2004, p. 57). It is interesting that those LGBT individuals and other marginalized people who deny discrimination's effects on their lives may have their physical health impacted negatively by that denial (Huebner & Davis, 2007).

Legal constraints also frame the health-related experiences of the LGBT population. Most LGBT people are unable to cover their partners on their health insurance. Partners may be denied visitation rights in a hospital or clinic setting. President Obama signed an executive order on April 15, 2010, requiring hospitals to extend visitation rights to whomever the patient designates, but this order covers only hospitals that accept Medicare and Medicaid funding (Shear, 2010). There are also such issues as parental rights regarding a nonbiological or nonadoptive child's health care and the rights of those taking care of an older nonbiological, nonadoptive parent (Bonvicini & Perlin, 2003). It remains to be seen how all these issues will be resolved.

Lesbian, gay, bisexual, and transgender people face additional health-related issues as they age. According to Schope (2002), individuals who were "gay" prior to the Stonewall riots of 1969 are less likely to disclose their sexual orientation than are individuals from succeeding generations. This means that the former may not communicate their situation to their primary caregiver or other health care personnel. This limits information provided in terms of risks or particular obstacles to care. Those who survive a long-term partner are not recognized in such federal programs as Social Security and must have their own financial support and health care in retirement. Surviving partners may find themselves in financial difficulties and, if proper estate planning was not done, may lose their property and financial resources to a late partner's biological family. These financial issues could conceivably impact LGBT elders' health, not only because of the stress generated but also because those with access to more funds are more likely to have access to quality health care. Further, LGBT elderly also are more likely than heterosexuals to live alone, which itself is correlated to "increased risk of lower income, poorer nutrition, poorer mental health, and risk of institutionalization" (McMahon, 2003 p. 591). Besides being more likely than their heterosexual counterparts to be single, some LGBT elders may not have had children. The 2006 MetLife survey of LGBT Baby Boomers indicated that nearly 20% were unsure of who would take care of them if needed, a number that rose to more than one third if the respondent was single. Although more institutions and organizations are developing to serve the particular needs of this population (e.g., Senior Action in a Gay Environment [SAGE] and LGBT retirement communities), the services and housing needs for aging LGBTs cannot be met by the current limited resources.

We now turn to overviews of issues specific to lesbian and bisexual women, followed by gay and bisexual men, and then transgendered men and women.

The Health of Lesbian and Bisexual Women

There is limited research on women who have sex with women, and the data that do exist are plagued by problems with conceptual distinctness, sampling, and validity that make generalization problematic (Malterud et al., 2009). Marrazzo (2008), for example, notes that women who identify as lesbian may have had or be having sex with men, and women who have sex with women may not identify as lesbian. Women who identify as lesbian thus may or may not engage in heterosexual sexual contact, use contraception and protection against sexually transmitted infections, and become pregnant and perhaps undergo abortion. Assumptions cannot be made about a self-identified lesbian's sexual history as it pertains to her health profile. Nor can assumptions be made about a presumptively heterosexual woman's sexual contact with other women. Such considerations are important because sex between women can result in STIs. Marrazzo, Coffey, and Bingham (2005) review the extant literature, noting that sexual contact between women may transmit trichomoniasis, genital herpes, human papillomavirus, and HIV and contribute to "an unusually high prevalence of bacterial vaginosis" (p. 6).

Despite this, lesbian women seem less likely than the general population of women to obtain regular gynecological care and screenings (Cochran et al., 2001). The Boston Lesbian Health Projects I and II provide some information on this. The first of these two national surveys was conducted in 1987, the second in 1997. Some positive findings were that lesbians in the later study were more likely than those in the first to be open with their health care providers about their lesbian identity and more likely to have had a Pap smear. The rates of Pap smears are still comparatively low (76% of the women reporting they had had one in the past 2 years), though, with lesbians less likely than the general population of women to have had them (Roberts, Patsdaughter, Grindel, & Tarmina, 2004). Adding a further layer to the issue, butch lesbians—that is, women who present a nonnormative gender identity—are less likely than more conventionally feminine lesbians to receive regular gynecological exams (Hiestand, Horne, & Levitt, 2007).

Lesbians also seem less likely than the general population to obtain regular mammographies (Cochran et al., 2001; Roberts et al., 2004). The Boston Lesbian Health Projects I and II found, however, that lesbians in the later study were more likely than those in the first to have had a mammography. In general, the impact of breast cancer and gynecological cancers on lesbians is underresearched (Bowen, Boehmer, & Russo, 2007), but there are some data (e.g., Boehmer, 2002; Dibble & Roberts, 2002; Fobair et al., 2001; Gay and Lesbian Medical Association, 2001). Lesbian women may face a higher risk for breast cancer (Kavanaugh-Lynch, White, Daling, & Bowen, 2002; Solarz, 1999), as well as other cancers that relate to their greater likelihood to be childless, overweight, and smokers and drinkers. Cochran et al. (2001) report that lesbian women manifest "greater prevalence rates of obesity, alcohol use, and tobacco use and lower rates of parity and birth control pill use" (p. 591), all factors that may relate to various forms of cancer. Bonvicini and Perlin (2003) also note that lesbians, particularly in older cohorts, may not reproduce to the extent that heterosexual women do and that there are associations between lack of childbearing and various cancers. Further, the STIs that lesbians may contract include human papillomavirus, linked to cervical cancer, yet, as noted, lesbians seem less likely than women in general to receive Pap tests.

Other studies provide further data on lesbians' health-related behaviors. The Boston Lesbian Health Project 1997 survey found rates of cigarette smoking among lesbians comparable to that of the female general population, and both drinking in general and heavy drinking more likely to occur among lesbians (Roberts et al., 2004). Other data suggest that lesbians may smoke, drink alcohol, and use some illegal drugs at higher rates than do heterosexual women (Meads, Buckley, & Sanderson, 2007; Ryan, Wortley, Easton, Pederson, & Greenwood. 2001; Tang et al., 2004; Trettin et al., 2005). As noted, lesbians have a greater likelihood than do heterosexual women of being overweight or obese (Boehmer et al., 2007; McMahon, 2003).

These negative health behaviors have consequences for an increased risk among lesbians of cancers, as well as lung and liver diseases, hypertension, stroke, diabetes, and other chronic and life-threatening health problems as the women age. For example, the Women's Health Initiative Survey of women ages 50–79 found higher rates of obesity, some cancers as noted earlier, and myocardial infarction among lesbians and/or bisexual women (McMahon, 2003).

Finally, lesbians do get pregnant, sometimes in heterosexual relationships or encounters, but often in carefully planned donor insemination processes. The time, energy, and monetary commitment required of such procedures means that when such a pregnancy is lost, that may be experienced particularly intensely—an "amplified" loss experience (Peel, 2010, p. 724). Lesbians may be more likely than heterosexual women to have both polycystic ovaries and polycystic ovarian syndrome (PCOS; Agrawal et al., 2004)—although this finding is refuted by De Sutter et al. (2008)—which could lead to difficulties in conceiving, miscarriage, and in the case of PCOS, such further health problems as coronary artery disease (Conway, Agrawal, Betteridge, & Jacobs, 1992).

More research needs to be conducted on the health issues of lesbians, including risk factors, screening, prevention, and intervention. Further, the complex nature of lesbian identity needs to be foregrounded in research and practice: the interplay of gender presentation (e.g., butch, femme), for example, with risk factors and screening rates, and the possibility that those individuals self-identified as lesbian may have had or continue to have male sexual partners.

The Health of Gay and Bisexual Men

Like all sexual minorities, gay and bisexual men are underrepresented in relation to their percentage of the population in both studies and therapeutic focus (Boehmer, 2002). Thus, much of what we present in the next section must be qualified by this lack of sound research. At the same time, gay and bisexual men have the same health issues and concerns as have heterosexual men. Yet, that would not be known by examining the relevant literature. Both research and practice have focused heavily on the relatively few issues that divide them, qualitatively or quantitatively, from the health experiences of heterosexual men—specifically HIV/AIDS and, in an often related vein, risky sexual and drug abuse behaviors.

Searches of two main databases, one specific to health and medicine (PubMed/Medline) and another general one of the widest range of published scientific material (Google Scholar), are illustrative of these two important points. On May 16, 2010, we entered several search terms into each of the search engines. These included "men" and "health," "gay men" and "health," bisexual men" and "health," and then the three gender categories combined with "HIV/AIDS," "heart disease," and "cancer." Although the numbers are highly inflated because most of the references generated using such simplistic keyword searches are either unrelated or only incidentally related (the first six citations for "gay men" and "heart disease" in Google Scholar were to articles about men and heart disease by an author with the name of Gay), the comparative magnitudes are probably relatively indicative of the results if only directly relevant publications were included. Complementing Boehmer's (2002), earlier, more systematic study, the Medline search for gay men showed 5,138 citations, 974 (19%) of which were about HIV/AIDS, 255 (5%) cancer, and 167 (3%) heart disease. There were 3,522 citations for bisexual men, of which 1,207 (34%) were about HIV/AIDS, 244 (8%) cancer, and 12 (0.3%) heart disease. When only "men" was included (with "women" excluded), there were 3,459,684 hits overall, 25,617 (0.7%) for HIV/ AIDS, 527,539 (15%) for cancer, and 279,991 (8%) for heart disease. Percentages were roughly similar on Google Scholar.

This finding demonstrates that what we know about gay and bisexual men's health is limited primarily to what is known about HIV/AIDS and other STIs; drug usage, including tobacco and alcohol; and other diseases if and only if they are causally related to behaviors that appear to be more frequent among sexual minority males, with virtually no information about larger health issues and statuses. In fact, there is a suggestion in the literature that even when HIV– gay or bisexual males present with symptoms stemming from a chronic illness, the specter of HIV/ AIDS may frame the medical encounter (Isola, 2004).

We will briefly review selected information about HIV/AIDS and risky behaviors as well as several areas that (a) pertain to all men, regardless of sexual identity; and/or (b) may have differential impacts for gay and bisexual men even though there is unlikely to be any causal relationship between the disease and behaviors that are related to sexual minorities. It is important to note first that as with lesbians, it is exceedingly difficult to categorize the population of interest, much less generalize. The lines of sexual identity are blurry. Generally, *gay* is the term used for men who are attracted sexually primarily or exclusively to other men, and *bisexual* for men who express attraction to women and men. A term often used today is *men who have sex with men* (MSM), which specifically addresses sexual behavior, which is connected to some aspects of male health. It should be kept in mind, however, that some men who identify as gay or bisexual may not express their identity through behavior. Further, the diversity of behaviors is what may be critical, and that is not encompassed well by any of the terms. For example, we will note a relationship between anal cancer and being gay or bisexual, but, in fact, the relationship has to do with being the recipient partner in anal sex; therefore, men who may be MSM but not anal receptive will not be affected differently from heterosexuals who are not anal receptive. Similarly, some findings that linked gay men and high alcohol use may be limited to a subset of men who frequent bars, whereas other findings related to STIs may be irrelevant for men who are in exclusive relationships. With those caveats in mind, we consider several health issues.

First, despite our concern about overemphasis on STIs, especially HIV/AIDS, we would obviously be grossly remiss if we did not address these issues (see various Centers for Disease Control publications for statistics; also see Sullivan & Wolitski, 2008, for a careful overview). In many ways, the gay community has borne the brunt of much of the impact of HIV/AIDS in the United States and other Westernized nations (in a way very distinct from the pandemic situation in much of Africa and other parts of the world). With the advent of better control, fortunately, AIDS has been transformed from a life-threatening illness to a chronic disease that can be managed for many years with careful attention. This is obviously a good thing; however, some gay and bisexual men may ignore appropriate precautions (e.g., as with "barebacking," unprotected anal activity; Halkitis, Parsons, & Wilton, 2003; Stolte, Dukers, Geskus, Coutinho, & deWit, 2004) because the disease does not seem as ominous as before. It is also the case that there are now sizable and growing numbers of MSM over the age of 50 with AIDS, either because of earlier exposure or by individuals' contracting HIV as they age to maintain maximum sexual activity (McMahon, 2003). It is also important to note that the impact of HIV/AIDS and the significant and serious side effects of AIDS treatment and the complications of adherence have long-term mental health implications. Thus, despite diversity within the MSM population and in HIV/AIDS transmission, with more women and older persons contracting HIV, including through drug use as well as sexual activity, for the foreseeable future HIV/AIDS retains a prominent place in discussions of the health of MSM.

Likewise, viral hepatitis (A, B, and C) and human papillovirus appear to be at higher levels among gay and bisexual men than those who are exclusively heterosexual (Rhodes & Yee, 2008). These illnesses may be acute and treatable or chronic, depending on the type. The combination of these and HIV/AIDS are the basis for the considerable attention noted on risky behaviors relating to sexual activity and drug abuse.

There are some indications that stress, depression, distress, and suicidal ideation affect gay and bisexual men more (McMahon, 2003; Mills et al., 2004) than their heterosexual counterparts, although the differences are not clear-cut. The psychosocial stresses caused by creating and maintaining a closeted life or managing the outcomes of self-disclosures also frame mental health issues (Schope, 2002). Considerable research indicates a greater level of eating disorders, especially bulimia, among gay men compared to heterosexuals (Feldman & Meyer, 2007). These levels are near those for heterosexual women, who have higher rates than do lesbians; the primary explanation for this high rate of bulimia among gay men is that eating disorders may result from body dissatisfaction, given the emphasis on muscularity and thinness to be attractive to men (Feldman & Meyer, 2007; Yelland & Tiggemann, 2003).

Abuse of illegal drugs is a concern, and it also appears that gay and bisexual men have higher rates of tobacco use than the heterosexual population (Stall, Greenwood, Acree, Paul, & Coates, 1999). Such use is not directly related to being a male sexual minority, given that it is also common among other subsets of the general population and lesbians. But the high rate is important because it means that there is a higher likelihood of such tobacco-associated diseases as lung cancer, congestive or pulmonary disease (COPD), including emphysema, and cardiovascular disease. Because gay and bisexual men have seldom been the focus of attention to these diseases, however, we have no clear information as to either morbidity or mortality disparities among these populations. Knowing the degree to which gay and bisexual men are or are not different is critical not only to being able to provide adequate services to them but also to aid in understanding the relationships of tobacco use to other disease conditions in all people.

Although some earlier studies appeared to indicate higher alcohol use and abuse by gay and bisexual men compared to heterosexuals, later research seems to suggest minor differences, at most, from general population samples that are presumptively primarily heterosexual, especially in younger cohorts (Crosby, Stall, Paul, & Barrett, 1998; Drabble, Midanik, & Trocki, 2005).

Many categories of health and the potential impact of physical health conditions within this population deserve attention. We will not review them all here because of the lack of evidence that they are differentially distributed or have different impacts on gay and bisexual men, though we do hope that future researchers systematically include sufficient categorization of sexual identities and behaviors so that we can increase our understanding. But we conclude this section by addressing two specific cancers, prostate and anal. There is no clear information as to whether prostate cancer is differentially distributed between MSM and other men, but there are reasons to think that its impact may be different for gay and bisexual men (or, more precisely, particular groups within MSM), and it is quite clear that anal cancer does have a differential likelihood of morbidity (Cress & Holly, 2003; Goldstone, Winkler, Ufford, Alt, & Palefsky, 2001) and substantial impact on MSM, specifically, individuals who are anal receptive and those who partner with them.

Prostate cancer is the most common cancer among men, with more than 200,000 cases diagnosed and about 25,000–30,000 deaths a year. It is related in a linear way to age, beginning in the late 30s or early 40s and accelerating greatly later in life. If diagnosed at an early stage, it is treatable and unlikely to result in death for many years even if primary treatment proves inadequate. Quality of life is impacted by each of the major treatments, however; the main negative impacts have to do with sexual function and, in the case of radiation, potential for rectal scarring and bowel difficulties. Until recently, no studies had been published that specifically examined prostate cancer in a gay or bisexual population. Since 2005, when Blank published a commentary in *Journal of Clinical Oncology* about the lack of attention, our research team (Asencio, Blank, Descartes, & Crawford, 2009; Blank, Asencio, Descartes, & Griggs, 2009) and several others (Allensworth-Davies & Clark, 2008; Hersom, Coon, Hart, & Latini, 2009) have attended to this population, although recruitment has proven very difficult for all teams and results are quite preliminary. Perlman and Drescher (2005) also published a book that includes chapters on scientific research and/or speculation and first-person narratives by MSM diagnosed with and treated for prostate cancer.

What has emerged is, on the one hand, that MSM approach prostate cancer in a way very similar to how heterosexual men approach it; on the other hand, the impacts of side effects, especially erectile dysfunction, may be received differently by different segments of the gay and bisexual community. This distinction appears to be a result of difference in physiological effects (e.g., radiation scarring of rectal area would be particularly problematic for someone who is anal receptive, whereas the importance of erectile function may be especially emphasized for penetrators) and the emphasis in gay culture on youth and sexual activity (again, we must keep in mind the variety within the gay and bisexual male population). Certainly, it is important for researchers and therapists to gain a better understanding of how problems with prostate health and with side effects of treatment affect both individuals and their partnered relationships.

On the other hand, anal cancer, a much rarer cancer, is one of the few diseases that does appear to be directly related to one form of sexual activity that is common within the gay and bisexual population, namely, anal sex, specifically being the recipient partner (Cress & Holly, 2003; Goldstone et al., 2001). Although a little is known about this relationship, including the connection between HPV and anal cancer and the high rates of both in MSM, there is very little guidance for health practitioners to lay a foundation for education and prevention or for enabling affected individuals to deal with the impact of the disease and its effect on sexual activity.

Despite the little that is definitively known about MSM's health issues, because of how little has been specifically investigated, several important generalities emerge from this review. Some diseases, especially HIV/AIDS and viral hepatitis, though not limited to gay and bisexual male populations, have had and continue to have considerable impact on this population; whereas to the degree that risky behaviors are higher than in the general population, negative health disparities may exist because of the connections those behaviors have to major causes of morbidity and mortality. Other diseases may or may not be differentially distributed between gay and heterosexual male populations, but they may, nonetheless, have different implications or impacts; prostate cancer is an example of this. And areas in which gay and bisexual men may have better health behaviors or outcomes have not been explored at all, certainly in part because of heterosexism and homophobia. Most important, it is not beneficial to simplistically contrast gay and bisexual populations with heterosexual ones; it is much more appropriate to look carefully within each of the overall groupings to better understand how specific subgroups, each with specific behavioral constellations, sexual and otherwise, are more or less likely to have specific health conditions.

The Health of Transgender Women and Men

The term *transgender* encompasses various groups, from those who have had complete sex reassignment with surgery and/or alteration of their breasts and genitals (in some cases, facial and other body alterations as well) to those who have had little to no surgery (Witten et al., 2003). Transgender individuals may live full or part time as the other gender or as a third gender. There are many ways in which people may identify and think about their own gender. Some individuals who have undergone sex reassignment may not identify as transgender but, rather, as either a man or woman and not be connected to the LGBT community. Each individual's particular health needs and issues may thus be unique. For transgender people, however, many of the issues previously discussed in terms of medical care may be more extreme than for other populations, since gender nonconformity and transgenderism remain highly stigmatized, pathologized, and less accepted than even lesbian, gay, or bisexual orientation (Lombardi, 2001). For major reviews of transgender health, especially for aging persons, see Witten and Eyler (2012).

There is overall less research on transgender health than there is on lesbian, gay, and bisexual health, and health care professionals do not tend to be knowledgeable about transgender individuals and their particular needs (Vanderleest & Galper, 2009). In the last decade there has been increasing focus on transgendered health needs, with some subsequent research, mostly on male-to-female (MTF) rather than female-to-male (FTM) people. Caution should be exercised in discussing that research, however, given the major methodological and conceptual limitations in defining and researching this population. Available data are often based on very small convenience samples or clinic populations.

According to Williams and Freeman (2007), the limited studies available suggest that transgender individuals are significantly more likely to have no regular source of care and to be under- or uninsured compared to other populations. Insurance companies omit coverage for such transgender-specific health procedures as hormone therapy and sex reassignment surgery and may also exclude transsexuals from treatment for other health problems even if they are unrelated to gender issues.

Understanding issues specific to transgender persons is particularly urgent in the gynecological and urological fields. According to van Trotsenburg (2009), few gynecologists are equipped to handle the gynecological care of transgender men and transgender women because of their limited knowledge of this population. He notes several areas of concern for transgender men: (a) Sex reassignment surgery for transgender men usually involves the removal of breast tissues (mastectomies) and commonly, but less frequently, the inner reproductive organs (uterus and ovaries). The external genitals are usually left intact; (b) Many transgender men may feel negatively about their remaining external female genitalia and may avoid gynecological exams completely. This is also true for transgender men who have not had surgery of any type; and (c) As transgender men age, they may experience severe vaginal atrophy as a result of androgen treatments, incontinence and pelvic floor disorders, and infections that necessitate gynecological care. Therefore, the need for continued gynecological care remains.

There are also gynecological and urological concerns for transgender women. Van Trostenburg (2009) stresses the need to maintain dilation and hygiene for the newly created vagina and tissues left vulnerable to infections that may result from surgery. He further notes that transgender women and their male sexual partners have to be advised about vaginal intercourse, since the newly created vagina is physiologically different than a biological vagina. Therefore, with both transgender men and women, health practitioners may need to spend considerable time advising and assisting their patients; yet given the limited time allotted to seeing patients in the medical care context, it is unclear whether these issues are addressed adequately.

It is important to understand that individuals who had sex reassignment surgery or medical intervention may be unaware that they retain the internal organs of the other sex (Asencio et al., 2009). As such, those tissues are at risk for disease development, including sex-specific cancers. Transgendered persons may not seek regular screening for cancer of those tissues. Also, medical care providers may be unaware that they need to screen transgender patients or may misdiagnose patient symptoms. Consequently, the likelihood of serious morbidity and death may increase.

Given the financial expense of sex reassignment, many transgendered individuals are unable to pay for procedures, medications, and medical follow-up. As a result, Williams and Freeman (2007) note, some individuals may end up obtaining medications in the streets or go outside the country for cheap surgery in clinics that provide substandard care. These measures can lead to major postsurgery problems, including those that are life threatening. Very extended hormone treatments present their own problems, whether medically provided or street based. With the latter, however, there is little to no medical supervision and follow-up. Hormones can interact with other prescription drugs. They are also associated with an increase in the risk for such health problems as diabetes, cardiovascular disease, thromboembolic events, and liver abnormalities (Williams & Freeman, 2007).

Transgendered persons may also have higher rates of other medical issues resulting from behavioral factors. In a study of patients attending a transgender health clinic, it was found that more than half of those receiving hormonal treatment were smokers—nearly two times the rate in the general population (Feldman & Bockting, 2003, referred to in Sell & Dunn, 2008). This rate is of great concern for transgender health, since smoking is contraindicated among those individuals using even low levels of estrogen. Sanchez, Sanchez, and Danoff (2009) found that the utilization of health care providers had a positive effect on reducing transgender women's risky behaviors, although there were still issues of compliance to standard-of-care protocols.

Thus, increasing access to health professionals is of critical concern in enhancing the health and well-being of this population.

Most health research with transgender women has been conducted around the issues of HIV/AIDS because of their having sex with men or engaging in sex work. In some studies, transgendered people have been identified as having a higher than normal risk for HIV infection (Kenagy, 2005; Nemoto, Operario, Keatley, & Villegas, 2004), whereas in others they have been found to be at lower risk for HIV infection (Bockting, Huang, Ding, Robinson, & Rosser, 2005). Estimates of prevalence of HIV and HIV risk on transgender populations based on a meta-analytic approach of four studies found that 27.7 % tested positive, with a high percentage of transgender women reporting risky behaviors, including unprotected receptive anal sex. In contrast, transgender men's prevalence rates of HIV and risk behaviors were found to be low (Herbst et el., 2008). Issues around sampling, including such demographic factors as race, ethnicity, socioeconomic status, and sexual work, may account for the differences in the studies. In addition, the comparison group, that is, whether the sample is being compared to MSM or the general population, may affect findings and interpretations.

There is no current research on transgendered children and youth and their particular health care needs. There have been cases of children as young as 4 identifying as transgender (Saeger, 2006). Yet, there is no way of knowing the particular access to health care issues confronted by these children. Given that the health care needs of children and youth are highly dependent on parents' health insurance and supportive attitudes, how these factors affect children's and youths' health care and prevention of later health problems needs to be investigated.

Conclusion: A Case Study and Overall Implications for Therapy

A case study of a specific situation may serve to illustrate points we have been making and how they may relate to the therapy encounter.

Emilio and George, a gay male couple, present for couple counseling. Emilio, 53, and George, 40, met through mutual friends and have been together for 2 years and cohabiting for 8 months. Both are working class; Emilio is a Mexican American who has been living in the United States for more than 30 years, and George is a non-Latino White man. Emilio has just been diagnosed with regionally advanced prostate cancer and will begin radiation treatment in the next few weeks. Emilio lacks full health insurance coverage and does not have a regular physician. He attends a walk-in clinic, which referred him to a urologist, who then referred him to a radiation oncologist. Emilio has not come out to his physicians nor is he out to family.

Throughout this intense and disruptive process of seeking health information and dealing with health outcomes, the couple has started experiencing problems in their interpersonal dynamics. George complains that Emilio is shutting him out and has become short tempered and critical. Emilio counters that George cares only about sex, which makes Emilio even more apprehensive about the upcoming treatment, since it may have a significant negative impact on his functioning and, thus, their sexual relationship.

The couple's therapist, like many therapists, did not have much experience with gay couples and even less with the nature and impact of prostate cancer treatment. She needs to pay attention to and address several interrelated issues, many of which may be specific to Emilio and George as a gay couple. These include the following concerns:

- Emilio's feelings about his sexuality and his ability to keep a relationship with George if Emilio has problems with erectile function and rectal irritation, especially as George is considerably younger than Emilio and their relationship is quite new
- George's guilt about being so concerned about their sex life

- The type of sexual activity the two men prefer, including activities that may require an erection and activities that may require being anally receptive
- The extent to which potential side effects may affect Emilio's feelings about his masculinity or self-worth, in particular as a Mexican American gay man, because both identity factors may affect expectations of how sexual prowess and erectile function relate to being a "real man"
- The sources of support that are available, including such formal support as support groups specifically for gay men with prostate cancer and gay-friendly doctors and such informal supports as friends, ex-partners, and biological family (more problematic if in need of Spanish-speaking gay-friendly resources)
- Emilio and George's emerging disagreements about the extent and comfort of being "out" as they deal with the health care system, support groups, and family
- Dealing with health providers' discrimination, discomfort, or misinformation about homosexuality

Thus, the therapist has to be aware of the potential effects of cancer treatment and how treatment-related changes in the body, sexual practices, and the relationship may be quite distinctive for what lesbian, gay, and bisexual couples experience. Knowing specific ethnic, racial, religious, and class backgrounds may also be helpful because of the variations these factors produce in self-perceptions and feelings about masculinity (or femininity), sex lives, relationships, and access to health care and health resources. The therapist should be alert to the limitations of support available to LGBT persons in mainstream venues and aware of gay-friendly options to explore, also recognizing and integrating the different kinds of informal support LGBT clients may have.

In conclusion, despite the little that is definitively known about LGBT health because of the limited numbers of studies, the studies' own limitations, and the limited number of health issues addressed, several important generalities emerge from this review. First, HIV/AIDS among gay and bisexual men (i.e., MSM) and transgender women dominates the LGBT health literature. As a consequence, there is more research available on gay and bisexual men than lesbian and bisexual women. Similarly, there is more health research on transgender women than transgender men. Second, there have been some increased risk factors connected to LGBT populations, in particular, drug, alcohol, and tobacco use. Also, third, among gay and transgender men, there are still unsafe sexual practices (e.g., unprotected anal sex) and among lesbians and transgender women are such factors as low levels of gynecological screenings that may impact health.

Homophobia and heterosexism influence risk-taking behaviors, access to health care, and even exclusion from or invisibility in research and clinical trials. Many disease and health problems among LGBT populations continue to receive little to no research. Diseases may or may not be differentially distributed between LGBT and heterosexual populations as a result of different factors or behaviors but may, nonetheless, have different implications or impacts. It is important to look carefully within each of the overall LGBT groupings to better understand how specific subgroups, each with specific behavioral constellations, sexual and otherwise, are more or less likely to have specific health conditions (the same can be said of research conducted with heterosexuals). Clearly, there have to be improvements in increasing LGBT people's health care and therapy access and, simultaneously, in more comprehensively educating health care providers on the diverse factors impacting LGBT health.

Acknowledgments

We thank Julie Griggs and Ashley Crawford for assistance with the literature review. We would also like to thank the Anthony Marchionne Foundation and the Center for Health Intervention and Prevention and Neag Comprehensive Cancer Center of the University of Connecticut for supporting the authors' work on LGBT health, particularly prostate cancer and gay men.

References

Agrawal, R., Sharma, S., Bekir, J., Conway, G., Bailey, J., Balen, A. H., & Prelevic, G. (2004). Prevalence of polycystic ovaries and polycystic ovary syndrome in lesbian women compared with heterosexual women. *Fertility and Sterility, 82*, 1352–1357.

Albarran, J. W., & Salmon, D. (2000). Lesbian, gay and bisexual experiences within critical care nursing, 1988–1998: A survey of the literature. *International Journal of Nursing Studies, 37*, 445–455.

Allensworth-Davies, D., & Clark, J. (2008, May). *Diagnosis and treatment of localized prostate cancer: The gay male experience.* Paper presented at Midwest Regional Conference of the Society for the Scientific Study of Sexuality, Cleveland, OH.

Asencio, M., Blank, T. O., Descartes, L., & Crawford, A. (2009). The prospect of prostate cancer: a challenge for gay men and their sexualities as they age. *Sexuality Research and Social Policy, 6*, 38–51.

Balsam, K. F., Rothblum, E. D., & Beauchaine, T. P. (2005). Victimization over the life span: A comparison of lesbian, gay, bisexual, and heterosexual siblings. *Journal of Consulting and Clinical Psychology, 73*(3), 477–487.

Blank, T. O., Asencio, M., Descartes, L., & Griggs, J. (2009). Aging, health, and GLBTQ family and community life. *Journal of GLBT Family Studies, 5*, 9–34.

Bockting, W., Huang, C-Y., Ding, H., Robinson, B., & Rosser, R. S. (2005). Are transgender persons at higher risk for HIV than other sexual minorities? A comparison of HIV prevalence and risks. *International Journal of Transgenderism, 8*, 123–131.

Boehmer, U. (2002). Twenty years of public health research: Inclusion of lesbian, gay, bisexual, and transgender populations. *American Journal of Public Health, 92*, 1125–1130.

Boehmer, U., Bowen, D. J., & Bauer, G. R. (2007). Overweight and obesity in sexual-minority women: Evidence from population-based data. *American Journal of Public Health, 97*, 1134–1140.

Bonvicini, K. A., & Perlin, M. (2003). The same but different: Clinician patient communication with gay and lesbian patients. *Patient Education and Counseling, 51*, 115–122.

Bowen, D. J., Boehmer, U., & Russo, M. (2007). Cancer and sexual minority women. In I. H. Meyer & M. E. Northridge (Eds.), *The health of sexual minorities: Public health perspectives on lesbian, gay, bisexual and transgender populations* (pp. 523–538). New York, NY: Springer.

Cochran, S. D., Mays, V. M., Bowen, D., Gage, S., Bybee, D., Roberts, S. J., … White, J. (2001). Cancer-related risk indicators and preventive screening behaviors among lesbians and bisexual women. *American Journal of Public Health, 91*, 591–597.

Conway, G. S., Agrawal, R., Betteridge, D. J., & Jacobs, H. S. (1992). Risk factors for coronary artery disease in lean and obese women with the polycystic ovary syndrome. *Clinical Endocrinology, 37*(2), 119 –125.

Cress, R. D., & Holly, E. A. (2003). Incidence of anal cancer in California: Increased incidence among men in San Francisco, 1973–1999. *Preventive Medicine, 36*, 1500–1510.

Crosby, G. M., Stall, R. D., Paul, J. P., & Barrett, D. C. (1998). Alcohol and drug use patterns have declined between generations of younger gay-bisexual men in San Francisco. *Drugs and Alcohol Dependency, 52*, 177–182.

De Sutter, P., Dutré, T., Vanden Meerschaut, F., Stuyver, I., Van Maele, G., & Dhont, M. (2008). PCOS in lesbian and heterosexual women treated with artificial donor insemination. *Reproductive BioMedicine Online, 17*, 398–402.

Dibble, S. L., & Roberts, S. A. (2002). A comparison of breast cancer diagnosis and treatment between lesbian and heterosexual women. *Journal of Gay and Lesbian Medical Association, 6*, 9–17.

Drabble, L., Midanik, L. T., & Trocki, K. (2005). Reports of alcohol consumption and alcohol-related problems among homosexual, bisexual, and heterosexual respondents: Results from the 2000 National Alcohol Survey. *Journal of Studies of Alcoholism, 66*, 111–120.

Feldman, J., & Bockting, W. (2003) Transgender health. *Minn Med., 86*, 25–32.

Feldman, M. B., & Meyer, I. H. (2007). Eating disorders in diverse lesbian, gay and bisexual populations. *International Journal of Eating Disorders, 40*, 218–226.

Fobair, P., O'Hanlan, K., Koopman, C., Classen, C., Dimiceli, S., Drooker, N., … Spiegel, D. (2001). Comparison of lesbian and heterosexual women's response to newly-diagnosed breast cancer. *Psycho-oncology, 10*, 40–51.

Gay and Lesbian Medical Association. (2001). *Healthy People 2010: Companion document for lesbian, gay, bisexual, and transgender (LGBT) health.* SanFrancisco, CA: Gay and Lesbian Medical Association. Retrieved from http://glma.org/policy/hp2010

Goldstone, S. T., Winkler, B., Ufford, L. J., Alt, E., & Palefsky, J. M. (2001). High prevalence of anal squamous intraepithelial lesions and squamous cell carcinoma in men who have sex with men as seen in a surgical practice. *Diseases of the Colon and Rectum, 44,* 690–698.

Grossman, A. H., D'Augelli, A. R., & Hershberger, S. L. (2000). Social support networks of lesbian, gay, and bisexual adults 60 years of age and older. *Journal of Gerontology, 55*(B), 171–179.

Halkitis, P. N., Parsons, J. T., & Wilton, L. (2003). Barebacking among gay and bisexual men in New York City. *Archives of Sexual Behavior, 32,* 351–357.

Herbst, J., Jacobs, E., Finlayson, T., McKleroy, V., Neumann, M., & Crepaz, N. (2008). Estimating HIV prevalence and risk behaviors of transgender persons in the United States: A systematic review. *AIDS and Behavior, 12,* 1–17.

Hersom, J. W., Coon, D. W., Hart, S., & Latini, D. M. (2009, April 24). *Quality of life for gay men treated for localized prostate cancer: Preliminary results from a web-based study.* Paper presented at Society of Behavior Medicine 30th Annual Meeting, Montreal, Canada.

Hiestand, K. R., Horne, S. G., & Levitt, H. M. (2007). Effects of gender identity on health care for sexual minority women. *Journal of LGBT Health Research, 3*(4), 15–27.

Huebner, D. M., & Davis, M. C. (2007). Perceived anti-gay discrimination and physical health outcomes. *Health Psychology, 26*(5), 627–634.

Isola, C. P. (2004). The impact of a non-HIV chronic illness on professional practice: Personal and professional considerations of a psychotherapist. *Journal of Gay & Lesbian Social Services, 17*(2), 97–109.

Kavanaugh-Lynch, M., White, E., Daling, J., & Bowen, D. J. (2002). Correlates of lesbian sexual orientation and the risk of breast cancer. *Journal of the Gay and Lesbian Medical Association, 6,* 91–96.

Kenagy, G. P. (2005). The health and social service needs of transgender people in Philadelphia. *International Journal of Transgenderism, 8,* 49–56.

Lombardi, E. (2001). Enhancing transgender health care. *American Journal of Public Health, 9,* 869–872.

Maccio, E. M., & Doueck, H. J. (2002). Meeting the needs of the gay and lesbian community: Outcomes in the human services. *Journal of Gay & Lesbian Social Services, 14*(4), 55–73.

Malterud, K., Bjorkman, M., Flatval, M., Ohnstad, A., Thesen, J., & Rortveit, G. (2009). Epidemiological research on marginalized groups implies major validity challenges: Lesbian health as an example. *Journal of Clinical Epidemiology, 62,* 703–710.

Marrazzo, J. M. (2008). Lesbian sexual behavior in relation to STDs and HIV infection. In K. Holmes, P. Sparling, W. Stamm, P. Piot, J. Wasserheit, L. Corey, & M. Cohen (Eds.), *Sexually transmitted diseases* (4th ed., pp. 219–235). New York, NY: McGraw-Hill Medical.

Marrazzo, J. M., Coffey, P., & Bingham, A. (2005). Sexual practices, risk perception and knowledge of sexually transmitted disease risk among lesbian and bisexual women. *Perspectives on Sexual and Reproductive Health, 37,* 6–12.

McMahon, E. (2003). The older homosexual: Current concepts of lesbian, gay, bisexual, and transgender older Americans. *Clinical Geriatric Medicine, 19,* 587–593.

Meads, C., Buckley, E., & Sanderson, P. (2007). Ten years of lesbian health survey research in the UK West Midlands. *BMC Public Health, 7,* 251. doi:10.1186/1471-2458-7-251

Mills, T. C., Paul, J., Stall, R., Pollack, L., Canchola, J., Chan, Y. J., … Catania, J. A. (2004). Distress and depression among men who have sex with men: The urban men's health study. *American Journal of Psychiatry, 161,* 278–285.

Nemoto, T., Operario, D., Keatley, J., & Villegas, D. (2004). Social context of HIV risk behaviours among male-to-female transgenders of colour. *AIDS CARE, 16*(6), 724–735.

Peel, E. (2010). Pregnancy loss in lesbian and bisexual women: An online survey of experiences. *Human Reproduction, 25,* 721–727.

Perlman, G., & Drescher, J. (2005). *Gay man's guide to prostate cancer.* New York, NY: InformaHealthcare.

Pugh, S. (2005). Assessing the cultural needs of older lesbians and gay men: Implications for practice. *Social Work in Action, 17*(3), 207–218.

Rhodes, S. D., & Yee, L. J. (2008). Hepatitis A, B, and C virus infections among men who have sex with men in the United States: Transmission, epidemiology, and intervention. In R. J. Wolitski, R. Stall, & R. O. Valdiserri (Eds.), *Unequal opportunity: Health disparities affecting gay and bisexual men in the United States* (pp. 194–219). New York, NY: Oxford University Press.

Roberts, S. J., Patsdaughter, C. A., Grindel, C. G., & Tarmina, M. S. (2004). Health related behaviors and cancer screening of lesbians: Results of the Boston Lesbian Health Project II. *Women & Health, 39*(4), 41–55.

Ryan, H., Wortley, P. M., Easton, A., Pederson, L., & Greenwood, G. (2001). Smoking among lesbians, gays and bisexuals: A review of the literature. *American Journal of Preventive Medicine, 21*(2), 142–149.

Saeger, K. (2006). Finding our way: Guiding a young transgender child. *Journal of GLBT Family Studies, 2*, 207–245.

Sanchez, N. F., Rabatin, J., Sanchez, J. P., Hubbard, S., & Kalet, A. (2006). Medical students' ability to care for lesbian, gay, bisexual, and transgendered patients. *Family Medicine, 38*(1), 21–27.

Sanchez, N. F., Sanchez, J. P., & Danoff, A. (2009). Health care utilization, barriers to care, and hormone usage among male-to-female transgender persons in New York City. *American Journal of Public Health, 99*, 713–719.

Sandfort, T. G. M., Melendez, R. M., & Diaz, R. (2007). Gender nonconformity, homophobia, and mental distress in Latino gay and bisexual men. *Journal of Sex Research, 44*(2), 181–189.

Schope, R. D. (2002). The decision to tell: Factors influencing the disclosure of sexual orientation by gay men. *Journal of Gay & Lesbian Social Services, 14*(1), 1–22.

Sell, R. L., & Dunn, P. M. (2008). Inclusion of lesbian, gay, bisexual and transgender people in tobacco-related surveillance and epidemiological research. *Journal of LGBT Health Research, 1*, 27–42.

Shear, M. D. (2010, April 16). Obama extends hospital visitation rights to same-sex partners of gays. *The Washington Post*. Retrieved from http://www.washingtonpost.com/wp-dyn/content/article/2010/04/15/AR2010041505502.html

Shippy, R. A., Cantor, M. H., & Brennan, M. (2004). Social networks of aging gay men. *Journal of Men's Studies, 13*, 107–120.

Silvestre, A. J. (2003). Ending health disparities among vulnerable LGBT people: A commentary. *Clinical Research and Regulatory Affairs, 20*(2), ix–xii.

Smith, N. G., & Ingram, K. M. (2004). Workplace heterosexism and adjustment among lesbian, gay, and bisexual individuals: The role of unsupportive social interactions. *Journal of Counseling Psychology, 51*, 57–67.

Solarz, A. L. (1999). *Lesbian health: Current assessment and directions for the future.* Washington, DC: National Academy Press.

Stall, R. D., Greenwood, G. L., Acree, M., Paul, J., & Coates, T. J. (1999). Cigarette smoking among gay and bisexual men. *American Journal of Public Health, 89*, 1875–1878.

Stolte, I. G., Dukers, N. H., Geskus, R., Coutinho, R. A., & deWit, J. B. F. (2004). Homosexual men change to risky sex when perceiving less threat of HIV/AIDS since availability of highly active anti-retroviral therapy: A longitudinal study. *AIDS, 18*, 303–309.

Sullivan, P. S., & Wolitski, R. J. (2008). HIV infection among gay and bisexual men. In R. J. Wolitski, R. Stall, & R. O. Valdiserri (Eds.), *Unequal opportunity: Health disparities affecting gay and bisexual men in the United States* (pp. 220–247). New York, NY: Oxford University Press.

Tang, H., Greenwood, G. L., Cowling, D., Lloyd, J. C., Roeseler, A. G., & Bal, D. G. (2004). Cigarette smoking among lesbians, gays and bisexuals: How serious a problem? (United States). *Cancer Causes and Control, 15*, 797–803.

Trettin, S., Moses-Kolko, E. L., & Wisner, K. L. (2005). Lesbian perinatal depression and the heterosexism that affects knowledge about this minority population. *Archives of Women's Mental Health, 9*, 67–73.

Vanderleest, J. G., & Galper, C. Q. (2009). Improving the health of transgender people: Transgender medical education in Arizona. *Journal of the Association of Nurses in AIDS Care, 20*, 411–416.

Van Trotsenburg, M. A. A. (2009). Gynecological aspects of transgender healthcare. *International Journal of Transgenderism, 11*, 238–246.

Williams, M. E., & Freeman, P. A. (2007). Transgender health: Implications for aging and caregiving. *Journal of Gay & Lesbian Social Services, 18*(3/4), 93–108.

Witten, T. M., Benestad, E. E. P., Berger, I., Ekins, R., Ettner, R., Harina, K., … Sharpe, A. N. (2003). Transgender and transexuality. In C. R. Ember & M. Ember (Eds.), *Encyclopedia of sex and gender* (pp. 216–229). New York, NY: Springer.

Witten, T. M., & Eyler, A. E. (2012). *Gay, lesbian, bisexual, and transgender aging: Challenges in research, practice, and policy.* Baltimore, MD: Johns Hopkins University Press.

Yelland, C., & Tiggemann, M. (2003). Muscularity and the gay ideal: Body dissatisfaction and disordered eating in homosexual men. *Eating Behavior, 4*, 107–116.

20

Spirituality and Religion in Same-Sex Couples' Therapy

SHARON SCALES ROSTOSKY, STEVEN D. JOHNSON, and ELLEN D. B. RIGGLE

Spirituality is the universal human pursuit of meaning, purpose, and committed action in response to such existential questions as "Why are we here?" and "What is worth living for?" (Helminiak, 2005). Although many same-sex couples may enact their spirituality through specific religious traditions and belief systems, spirituality, as a facet of human experience, does not require religion or a belief in any metaphysical entity. Although the psychological literature frequently conflates the two constructs or even uses them interchangeably, it is important for clinicians to disentangle these constructs in their conceptualization, assessment, and treatment of spirituality in same-sex couples' therapy.

For many same-sex couples, religious beliefs and traditions may provide comfort and support or may pose challenges to healthy functioning. In counseling or psychotherapy, a same-sex couple may need to address both sides of this coin. That is, many (but certainly not all) same-sex couple members are likely to have had experiences in which religious beliefs were used as a justification for discriminating against and even rejecting their individual and couple identities. Whereas religion takes many forms that can be either helpful or hurtful to same-sex couples, spirituality, which may or may not be expressed through religious belief and practice, addresses questions of meanings and values related to dealing with human limitation and finitude (Pargament & Mahoney, 2005). Therefore, regardless of whether same-sex couple members have rejected all forms of religion or are working to integrate their sexual identities and religious identities, spirituality can serve as a resource to enhance their lives together and their sense of well-being.

A primary goal of this chapter is to give clinicians some conceptual and practical tools for conceptualizing, assessing, and facilitating couples' spirituality (i.e., shared values and commitments in response to existential questions) as a resource for healthy relational functioning. We draw on a strengths-based or positive psychological perspective (e.g., Peterson & Seligman, 2004) to address this aim. First, however, we briefly describe minority stress theory as the framework for understanding experiences of religion-based discrimination and stigma that may negatively affect lesbian, gay, and bisexual (LGB) couple members' relational functioning. We also use case examples to illustrate how the spirituality and spiritual values of same-sex couples can be used to decrease minority stress and facilitate their relational goals.

Case Example 20.1

Lisa and Michelle come to a counselor because of issues surrounding their spirituality. Lisa grew up attending a small African Methodist Episcopal (AME) church in a small town in Ohio. Her uncle was the minister of the congregation, and her family attended church several times a week. The church was central in the family and a dynamic part of Lisa's childhood. Michelle, on the other hand, attended church only a few times each year. She was from Cincinnati, Ohio, and was raised Catholic. She attended a parochial school run by the local parish. Michelle admits that she never really connected with the Catholic faith, and her memories of church are more about how controlling and punitive the church could be. Neither church is open and affirming of same-sex couples. Lisa and Michelle have a 2-year-old son whom they adopted 6 months ago. Lisa feels strongly that they should raise their son in a church. Michelle sees no reason to give up her Sundays being around a bunch of people who think it is wrong to be gay and who do not support their relationship. Their differing perspectives are putting a significant strain on their relationship.

Religion-Based Sources of Minority Stress

The American Psychological Association (APA) has recognized that religion can be both a target and a source of prejudice and discrimination and has encouraged psychologists to act to eliminate discrimination that is "based on or derived from religion and spirituality" (APA, 2008, p. 432). Disempowered groups, including racial minorities and women, have historically found religiousness to be a source of strength and hope and thus have participated in religious institutions at high rates (Pargament, 2002). However, the use of religious doctrine and authority as a mechanism to maintain the oppression of minorities and women is also a social reality. Sexual minorities have likewise frequently endured condemnation and rejection in their religious communities and families.

Minority stress is the chronic stress that accompanies a stigmatized identity (Brooks, 1981). As applied to LGB individuals, minority stress includes experiences of discrimination and prejudice, anticipation of rejection, concealment of the stigmatized identity, the internalization of negative societal views (commonly known as *internalized homophobia*), and the efforts expended to cope with these stressors (Meyer, 2003, 2007). In Case Example 20.1, Lisa and Michelle are faced with minority stress manifested in their concern that they will be rejected as a couple and family because of their sexual identities. Same-sex couples experience this and other types of minority stress that impact their daily lives and their relationships (Dudley et al., 2005; Herek & Garnets, 2007; Otis, Hamrin, Riggle, & Rostosky, 2006; Rostosky, Riggle, Gray, & Hatton, 2007).

For some same-sex couples, religious institutions are a source of minority stress to the extent that religion has been used to justify prejudice and discrimination against sexual minorities and their committed partnerships. As in the case of Lisa and Michelle, forming a committed relationship with a same-sex partner and/or becoming parents may represent a developmental milestone that intensifies any conflict between religious identity and sexual identity. In many religion-based institutions, scriptures and doctrines are interpreted in ways that support the condemnation of nonheterosexual identities, the disapproval of nontraditional gender roles and expressions, and the rejection of same-sex couples and their families.

Same-sex couple members who have been raised in a nonaffirmative religious context may internalize these negative views and experience shame to the point of hiding their same-sex relationship from religious family members and others in an effort to cope with the anticipated rejection. All too commonly, couple members from religious families report histories that include pressures to renounce their same-sex attractions under threat of eternal damnation and social isolation from family and community (see Barton, 2010) and may struggle with guilt, shame, and high levels of internalized homophobia (Sherry, Adleman, Whilde, & Quick, 2010). Higher levels of internalized homophobia and religious fundamentalism often motivate sexual minorities, especially men and Persons of Color, to participate in sexual reorientation therapies (Maccio, 2010), which have been challenged by the American Psychological Association as having harmful rather than helpful psychosocial effects.

To reconcile and reclaim their religious and spiritual selves, couple members who have suffered as a result of their nonaffirming religion-based experiences may need to work through the parts of their past experiences that have been detrimental to their individual and couple identity. Because

Lisa and Michelle have vastly different experiences with religion, spirituality, and acceptance of their sexuality, their therapy sessions will likely first focus on understanding how their past religion-based experiences have shaped their thoughts and feelings as individuals and as a couple.

Same-Sex Couples' Coping With Minority Stress Through Spiritual and Religious Involvements

At present, few research studies are available to inform therapists about the role of religiosity and faith communities in the relationships of same-sex couples. Although having the same religious tradition was not shown to be related to the relationship satisfaction of female same-sex couples (Smith & Horne, 2008a), other evidence suggests that same-sex couples who share similar levels of intrinsic religiosity report higher relationship satisfaction (Rostosky, Otis, Riggle, Kelly, & Brodnicki, 2008). In interviews exploring religiosity and spirituality in same-sex couple relationships, both male and female couples asserted that their shared spiritual worldview was an important touchstone or foundation for their relationship (Rostosky, Riggle, Brodnicki, & Olson, 2008). Thus, it may be important to help couples to discuss their religious or spiritual similarities and differences and negotiate meaningful religious or spiritual activities that they can share together. In working with Lisa and Michelle, a clinician might help the couple to identify their spiritual values, manage any conflict associated with their differences in spiritual values, and facilitate a process of generating creative solutions that meet their family's needs.

To cope with the minority stress generated by religion-based institutions and communities, couples report using several strategies (Rostosky, Otis, et al., 2008). Couples may refuse to participate in institutions that do not support their relationship and thus may reject religion and religious practice (Halkitis et al., 2009; Sherry et al., 2010). Halkitis et al.'s (2009) convenience survey of 498 LGB adults found that only 25% of the sample currently affiliated with a religious institution even though the majority was raised in a Christian or Jewish faith. Participants in this survey also reported that they were more spiritual, which they collectively defined as pursuit of meaning, transcendence, and connection, than religious, which they defined as structured belief systems and organized worship.

Thus, as a second strategy, couples may adopt a subjective and private spirituality. In interviews, couples identified a number of joint activities that they consider spiritual, including engaging in prayer and meditation, traveling to other countries and cultures, enjoying nature, or reading inspirational texts (Rostosky, Riggle, et al., 2008). Any activity or sphere of life can be infused with spiritual meaning. Couples may, thus, imbue their relationship, their parenting, their work lives, and/or their social activism with transcendent meanings and values. Consider the following example.

Case Example 20.2

A therapist, while working with a gay couple, brought up the topic of emotional connection. She asked the couple to identify how they felt they were able to stay emotionally connected through the years. The couple, together for 13 years, reported that they attribute part of the success of their relationship and emotional connection to activities and projects that they do together that they feel link them spiritually. They both are passionate about the environment and volunteer once a month with a local organization that organizes community cleanup and recycling. One of the partners had also been a long-time supporter of the local humane society. Her partner is now also involved, and they foster rescue animals when needed. They both discuss how these activities enhance their individual and shared spirituality.

Imbuing their relationship with spiritual meaning has helped some same-sex couples to cope with difficulties and challenges brought on by others' religion-based prejudice agains them while maintaining a positive focus on the spiritual ideals of authenticity and generosity (Rostosky, Riggle, et al., 2008). Furthermore, as a source of connection, purpose, and meaning in life, spirituality has also been shown to be associated with higher levels of sexual satisfaction in same-sex-partnered women (Smith & Horne, 2008b). With Lisa and Michelle, a clinician might help the couple to find a common spiritual activity they can share, such as a faith community or a family ritual (e.g., sharing a morning walk each week or perhaps reading affirming devotional material together). Creating special rituals and traditions that have unique spiritual meaning strengthens identities and family relationships and "touch[es] us at the core of our humanity" (see Imber-Black, 2009, p. 230).

Another strategy that same-sex couples have used involved rejecting or reinterpreting the religious views of their past, letting go of destructive religion-based views and beliefs, and adopting new interpretations of sacred texts and new affirmative beliefs (Rostosky, Riggle, et al., 2008). This strategy has allowed some couples a way to continue a meaningful participation together in congregational activities. For these couples, religion and spirituality continues to be a source of support that may diminish the negative effects of minority stress and enhance relationship satisfaction. In Case Example 20.1, Michelle might discover that by being open to Lisa's positive experiences and understanding their value to Lisa, she can redefine some of the negative messages of her own religious past.

For sexual minority individuals, such welcoming and affirming congregations as the Metropolitan Community Church and Unitarian Universalist Church or earth-spirited religious or spiritual communities (see Smith & Horne, 2007) offer social support and stress-buffering effects for integrating positive sexual and religious identities (Rodriguez, 2010; Rodriguez & Ouellette, 2000). These and other affirmative faith-based groups support and validate same-sex couples by performing commitment ceremonies, recognizing same-sex couples' anniversaries, and providing faith-based couple and family enrichment programs that are fully inclusive. Experiencing such affirmation in one's faith community has been shown to be related to lower levels of internalized homonegativity in LGB individuals (Lease, Horne, & Noffsinger-Frazier, 2005).

Taken together, findings on same-sex couples' religiosity and spirituality are consistent with findings from studies of religiosity in general samples. That is, "sanctifying" one's life and relationships with spiritual meaning and significance is a positive religious coping strategy that is associated with psychological well-being (Pargament, 2002). At the conclusion of his review, Pargament (2002) notes that

> at its best, religiousness is smoothly integrated in the search for significance, offering diverse and distinctive resources that assist the individual in the discovery, conservation, and transformation of sacred values throughout life's ups and downs. At other times, however, religion may be part of a process out of kilter, marked by conflicts between the individual and the larger social context. (p. 177)

Certainly much empirical work remains to be done to understand how different religious or spiritual involvements and commitments function to either help or hinder same-sex couples' relationships. To the extent that it provides social support, a sense of meaning and purpose, and coping resources and fosters such positive emotions as hope and optimism, religion or spirituality may contribute to relationship quality and stability. In conceptualizing and assessing religion and spirituality, therapists should remember that these constructs can be highly related, partially related, or unrelated for any particular couple.

Case Example 20.3

Ethan and Jacob met a year ago at the gay pride parade in Boston. They are now living together and are planning a wedding ceremony in the next few months. Ethan, who moved to Boston for a job after graduating from Berkeley, describes his spiritual beliefs as mostly Buddhist. He is connected with a mindfulness meditation group and studies and practices Zen principles. He describes his spiritual pursuits as more of a life philosophy than a religion. Jacob grew up in Brooklyn as a Modern Orthodox Jew. When he came out last year at age 24, he affiliated with Reformed Judaism, a more liberal branch of the religion. He continues to explore this transition and how to interpret and integrate Jewish traditions in his life as a gay man.

Ethan's sister, who is a psychotherapist in California, suggested that the couple get some premarital counseling before their upcoming wedding. Both partners feel that it is important to have an understanding of each other's spiritual beliefs; however, their interactions often seem more like debates rather than intimate sharing. They thought about talking with a rabbi, but Ethan thought he would feel more comfortable talking with a counselor first.

Assessing Religiosity and Spirituality in Couples' Therapy

Clinicians need to be culturally competent to help same-sex couples attain the highest level of relational functioning and satisfaction, and for many same-sex couples this process will involve assessing their religious and spiritual values and how they express those in ways that are affirming to their relationship. Pargament and Krumrei (2009) recommend a comprehensive approach to spiritual assessment that includes assessing (a) the place of spirituality in the clients' lives (central to peripheral); (b) the location of the clients in their individual spiritual journeys, that is, whether the clients are engaged, disengaged, conserving or transforming, stuck or struggling; (c) the content of the client's spirituality and how it is expressed; (d) the context of the clients' spirituality; (e) the impact of the clients' spirituality on health and well-being; and (f) the appropriate place of spirituality in the clients' treatment.

A brief spiritual assessment allows the clinician to determine what role religion and spirituality play for each couple member and if spirituality issues are perceived to be connected to the presenting issue. In the case of Ethan and Jacob, sharing and understanding their religious and spiritual values comprise a primary motive for seeking counseling. For the clinician, the assessment is not so much an exploration into the couple's theology or worldviews but, rather, a way to gain an understanding of how spirituality and religion-based beliefs impact the couple's relationship and their life together. The overarching assessment task is to explore ways that religion or spirituality may have contributed to the couple's distress as well as the ways that spiritual resources may be drawn upon to increase well-being (Walsh, 2009). Examples of a brief spiritual assessment might include such questions as the ones listed here, which were adapted from Hodge (2005) and Sperry (2001):

- How does religion or spirituality play a part in your life as an individual and as a couple?
- How does your spirituality help you in your life?
- What challenges does your spirituality pose in your life?
- Do you or your partner attend a church, synagogue, temple, sangha, or other type of spiritual community? Do you attend together or separately?
- Do you occasionally or regularly engage in any spiritual activities?
- Do you feel you and your partner have similar views on religion and spirituality?
- Would you like to address your religious or spiritual beliefs and practices in our sessions?

The foregoing types of questions will help the clinician to understand if religion or spirituality is an area that is pertinent to the presenting issue or issues. Because some clinicians prefer to do individual assessments with each partner, the questions are formatted so that they can be done individually or asked at the same time to the couple. If the results of the brief spiritual assessment suggest that religion or spirituality are salient issues for the couple, particularly an area of conflict, then a full spiritual assessment could be performed in following sessions.

A full assessment might include taking a spiritual history from the couple, either individually or together. For same-sex couples, a full spiritual assessment includes asking couples how their religious or spiritual identities have been influenced by other important aspects of their identities (e.g., gender, race, ethnicity, national origin, sexual orientation, or class). What follow are suggested prompts for taking a spiritual history, adapted from Hodge (2005) and Sperry (2001), encouraging partners to describe the religious or spiritual tradition in which they grew up.

- How did your parents and their families express spiritual beliefs?
- How important was religion or spirituality to your family?
- Did your parents share the same religion or spirituality? If not, how did they negotiate differences in their beliefs?
- What were some of their most important spiritual beliefs? Did they pass these on to you?
- Do you recall any significant experiences (either positive or negative) while growing up that had to do with religion or spirituality?
- Have religious or spiritual issues caused any problems between you and your family?
- Has your sexual orientation affected your spiritual or religious beliefs? How?
- Is your current spiritual orientation different from that of your family of origin? How? Does this difference cause any kind of problems or distress for you or your family?
- If you have children, do you and your partner agree or disagree on the spiritual orientation with which they are being raised?

For couple members who indicate that they are involved or committed to a particular institutional religious tradition, it is also important to ask how their religious beliefs support their lives. Couple members should be asked to provide the clinician with the appropriate term(s) for addressing their theological beliefs (e.g., God, Goddess, Higher Power, Life Force, or any other label supplied by the couple). These beliefs can be an important resource for coping with the stress and challenges of life. Some important assessment questions in this area may include the following:

- How do you understand your place in or relationship to the world? In the universe?
- What religion-based or spirituality-based beliefs and practices do you draw on in times of stress or challenge?

Such other assessment tools as spiritual genograms, spiritual journey maps, and spiritual inventories may also be helpful in assessing same-sex couple members' religious heritage and spiritual evolution across time. In his discussion of spiritual assessment with couples, Hodge demonstrates ways to use these tools and also lists quantitative inventories of spiritual development and spiritual well-being (Hodge, 2005). Walsh (2009) suggests that clinicians assess possible spiritual resources, including personal faith, contemplative practices, faith community, creative arts expression and appreciation, nature, service to others, and activism.

Including a spiritual assessment in a holistic biopsychosocial-spiritual assessment model will help clinicians touch on all domains that might be relevant to therapy. This holistic approach will help the clinician understand each couple member's individual spiritual orientation and how these values have shaped the individual's life experiences. Also of primary importance will be to understand the extent to which spiritual and religious issues have resulted in perceived connection or disconnection in the couple relationship. As noted by Rostosky, Riggle, et. al. (2008), spirituality and religiosity can be sources of strength and support in same-sex relationships. Or, as with other issues, they can be areas of disconnection, resentment, and confusion. An in-depth understanding of how spirituality and religion impact each individual and the relationship can increase awareness within the couple and help the partners to begin to generate goals and build solutions that will support their relationship. For Ethan and Jacob, interventions that increase their ability to communicate their thoughts, feelings, beliefs, and needs with each other would be particularly important. Given that they have taken different spiritual paths up to this point, helping them find common elements and possible areas of concern would likely help them build intimacy and connection as a couple.

Therapeutic Interventions With Same-Sex Couples

Although clinicians generally acknowledge the importance of assessing the spiritual backgrounds and values of their clients, according to their own reports, they are "reluctant to act" on this assessment information (Frazier & Hansen, 2009, p. 85). This reluctance may come from a lack of training in appropriate and effective interventions (Frazier & Hansen, 2009; Post & Wade, 2009). Once clinicians have assessed the degree to which couple members' religion-based backgrounds and current religious or spiritual activities are sources of support or sources of minority stress for them, the next step is to collaborate with them on strategies for addressing any aspects of minority stress that are exacerbated by experiences with religion-based institutions and family members or others who convey nonaffirmative religion-based attitudes.

As the working phase of therapy commences, before disclosing their religion-based or spiritual concerns clients may test the waters to see if their therapist will be sensitive and respectful. This initial reticence on the part of clients may partially explain why these issues are more likely to emerge gradually over the course of therapy (Post & Wade, 2009). In the case of Ethan and Jacob, early therapy sessions should focus on creating a safe therapeutic alliance where each partner can explore and understand his own and his partner's religion-based experiences and spiritual values and meanings to understand how differences are impacting their relationship.

With very few role models or "scripts" to follow, same-sex couples are often left on their own to figure out how to deal with religion-based or spiritual issues that might arise in their relationship. Combining spiritual beliefs and practices with family traditions has generated internal and interpersonal conflict for Lisa and Michelle, who as new parents have concerns about child rearing and their relationship to spiritual communities. When a same-sex couple presents for couples' therapy with these concerns, clinicians should be prepared and comfortable in offering guidance and support as couples forge their paths to health and well-being.

In working with the couples in the previous case examples, clinicians should help their clients to discover the meaning of religion and spirituality in their lives as these constructs intersect with other social identities such as race, gender, and class. Assessing and addressing how religion-based institutions and beliefs have contributed to minority stress in the couples' lives helps to externalize the problem so that Lisa and Michelle and Ethan and Jacob are not caught up in blaming themselves or each other for their difficulties. The therapist can serve as an effective "witness" to any discrimination or rejection that the couple may have experienced in the past or that they anticipate experiencing in a religious setting.

Therapists can also help couples to identify any negative impacts of religion-based prejudice that may have been internalized. To identify internalized negative beliefs about their sexual identities or their same-sex couple relationship, clinicians can assign journaling exercises or thought-monitoring tasks. Interventions to replace negative beliefs with more self-accepting and affirming beliefs may include such spiritually based interventions as loving kindness and other mindfulness meditations. In general, research is demonstrating the power of positive emotions in health and well-being; thus, interventions to increase such positive emotions as love and acceptance should be part of couples' therapy (Fredrickson, 2003).

The clinician should seek to facilitate discussions and explorations without judgment. For example, drawing on the basic principles of emotionally focused therapy (Greenburg & Johnson, 1988), the clinician can help the couple members to see where they are becoming disconnected and then facilitate new connections as they increase their awareness of the meaning of religion or spirituality in each of their lives. Positive relational practices can be assigned as homework to encourage couples to deepen the spiritual component of their relationship. For instance, couples might develop letter-writing rituals in which they express appreciation and gratitude to each other. The partners can be encouraged to use positive narratives about how they met, an adventure they had, a time they laughed, or a time they felt lucky to be together. Drawing on the positive aspects of their relationship can strengthen their sense of connection.

Creating new patterns of thinking and behavior will allow couples like Lisa and Michelle and Ethan and Jacob to develop and practice their unique spiritual values and enhance their spiritual growth toward wholeness and connection. Counselors can teach couples such positive practices as breathing exercises to decrease anxiety, stress, and reactivity; deep, empathic listening skills; and authentic and loving speech. To help couples explore the meaning of spirituality in their lives, the clinician may wish to incorporate exercises for the couple to do at home. Whitman and Boyd's (2003) *The Therapist's Notebook for Lesbian, Gay, and Bisexual Clients* has several exercises that can be helpful in working with same sex-couples. Suggestions specific to LGBT clients include writing a spiritual autobiography, creating and using rituals, and completing a spiritual needs inventory.

Along with identifying specific interventions, Serlin (2005) suggests several ways to include the spiritual strengths and resources that couples bring to therapy and that may come to light as part of the assessment phase. These strengths and resources can be marshaled in the couples' therapy by using a discovery-oriented, collaborative approach that honors the specific spiritual values and resources of each couple. Spiritual resources can be found in nature, in music, and in social activism, as well as in religious or spiritual communities and traditions (Walsh, 2009).

Transcendent values of compassion, generosity, and forgiveness may also be practiced and reinforced as couples proceed through the process of identifying and negotiating solutions to any internal and external sources of minority stress that may be causing them distress. Helping couples create meaning and construct spiritual support systems can help couples develop psychological maturity (Serlin, 2005) and enhance well-being. Therefore, clinicians need to be aware of affirmative spiritual resources for same-sex couples and their families. A partial list of affirmative organizations is included in Table 20.1.

Training Therapists to Be Effective With Same-Sex Couples' Religious and Spiritual Issues

The fields of psychology, family therapy, and social work avoided spirituality and religion in clinical training until recently (Walsh, 2009). Believing that clinicians might somehow offend clients or unprofessionally share their bias with clients, most trainers instructed their students to tread lightly in this domain. Unfortunately, this lack of attention to spirituality has led to a shortage of empirical research that could help guide clinicians in addressing an area that is often significant to both individuals and couples. The extant research base specific to the spiritual issues of LGBT clients, and hence evidence-based training recommendations, is meager.

Establishing a Therapeutic Alliance

Therapists in training must be effective in establishing a strong therapeutic alliance with same-sex couples. Engaging the couple members so that they feel equally heard and understood by the clinician should be the priority in the therapeutic process. Findings from a recent qualitative study of same-sex couples suggest that respondents are concerned about their therapist's knowledge about and comfort level with their identities. In addition, same-sex couples are concerned when they suspect that their therapist may be overcompensating for negative attitudes toward them as a couple (Grove & Blasby, 2009). Problematic therapist behaviors include being overly

Table 20.1 Spiritual Assessment Tools for Clinicians

Reference	Title	Description
Hall and Edwards (1996)	Spiritual Assessment Inventory	43-item scale used to measure spiritual development (awareness of God and quality of relationship with God) from a Judeo-Christian perspective
Korinek and Arredondo (2004)	Spiritual Health Inventory	28-item scale used to measure three spiritual domains: spiritual experience, spiritual locus of control, and spiritual well-being (i.e., how strongly a person feels a sense of harmony with the world)
Paloutzian and Ellison (1982)	Spiritual Well-Being Scale	20-item instrument used to measure the client's spiritual well-being; can easily be scored (see http://www.lifeadvance.com)
Piedmont (1999)	Spiritual Transcendence Scale	24-item scale used to explore how spirituality might be a motivational force in someone's life; includes three subscales: prayer fulfillment, universality, and connectedness

tentative, overly cautious, or avoidant of exploring or challenging possible negative aspects of the couple relationship. In the following example, the therapist is probably being overcautious:

Case Example 20.4

The therapist is meeting with Thad and Calvin for their first couple therapy session. As he inquires into their histories, he finds information with which he appears to be uncomfortable:

Therapist: *Thad, you were telling me about your life before you met Calvin. Could you tell me some more about it?*

Thad: *Well, before I met Calvin, I was involved with a group of guys that liked to party together. We would travel together to different circuit events and often engage in group sex activities.*

Calvin: *I was never involved with anything like that and don't really understand how you could just have sex with different people. I'm trying really hard to trust Thad, but sometimes I feel weird that he has had sex with so many different people in the past. My religious belief is that couples should be monogamous. I believe God wants us to be faithful to each other. I know that was in the past, but I still feel funny about it at times.*

Therapist: *Well, since that was in the past, perhaps it would be best for us to focus on your relationship now and how to make things better in the future.*

In this example, the therapist may be uncomfortable with either or both of the topics of sexuality and spirituality in this case. This discomfort may lead to his wanting to move away from Thad's disclosure, even though Calvin is obviously troubled by it and expresses a desire to work through some of his feelings about it. This avoidance on the therapist's part could likely be damaging to the therapeutic relationship with the couple.

Much has been written about building a therapeutic relationship with individuals and couples; however, specific actions on the part of the therapist can send the message that the therapist is affirming of sexual minority identities and same-sex couples. Therapists should, for example, provide LGBT-related reading materials in their waiting room and routinely use inclusive language that does not make heterosexist assumptions.

A strong therapeutic alliance characterized by caring, trust, open-mindedness, and hope will facilitate couples' comfort with sharing potentially emotionally laden information about the intersection of sexual orientation, spirituality, and religion. The couple members need to feel that the clinician truly understands their situation and their past struggles. They should also feel assured that the therapist is nonjudgmental, agenda free, and unconditionally supportive of both partners, thus creating a strong therapeutic alliance (Burckell & Goldfried, 2006).

Competence in Addressing Spirituality and Religion

In addition to developing competence related to same-sex relationship issues, clinicians should also develop competence in the spiritual and religious issues that couples encounter. A recent review of religion and spirituality in therapy concluded that one of the most important things therapists can do is to make an explicit statement at the beginning of therapy that communicates openness to discussing religious and spiritual issues (Post & Wade, 2009). Unfortunately, many clinicians are polarized on these issues (Duba & Watts, 2009). Some feel that they are not qualified to discuss spiritual concerns with individuals or couples and thus avoid the topic. On the other hand, some clinicians who draw upon the importance of the self of the therapist (e.g., Sperry, 2005), consider the clinician's own spiritual journey to be vital to the interpersonal process of guiding others. From this perspective, clinicians should have firsthand experience with finding spiritual meaning in their own lives before they assist others.

If because of personal history the clinician has a strong bias against organized religion or disregards spirituality as important in working with clients, he or she should seek supervision or individual psychotherapy to resolve these issues so they do not interfere with treatment. As with other aspects of diversity, clinicians should examine their own religious or nonreligious beliefs to ensure that their personal biases to do not interfere with an ability to understand, respect, and effectively treat diverse clients (APA, 2008). Suggested interventions for helping therapists in training to become aware of their own beliefs and biases in the area of religion and spirituality include writing their own spiritual autobiography (Wiggins, 2008).

The Role of the Therapist

Clinicians do not have to share the sexual identity or sexual orientation of their clients. A study of bisexual and lesbian women found that the competence of the therapist was more important than the sexual orientation of the therapist (Saulnier, 2002). Clinicians must, however, have a frame of reference to be able to convey genuine empathy.

Clinicians who are religious should also be aware that because of possible negative experiences with religion in the past, some same-sex couples may make very negative comments about religion, church, and those who attend church. The therapist must be able to remain empathic with these emotions and perceptions. Clinicians and trainees should also ensure that they are familiar with religious and spiritual resources in their local communities and on the Internet. Some useful resources are included in Table 20.2. Some clinicians further recommend that therapists familiarize themselves with the scriptures, rituals, traditions, and spiritual reading materials the clients mention in therapy (Sperry, 2005).

Another training issue is appropriate self-disclosure. It would not be uncommon for a couple to want to find out the spiritual beliefs of the clinician. As with any personal self-disclosure, the clinician must determine if sharing personal information is in the best interest of the client or couple. If sharing personal information will inhibit the therapeutic process by making the couple members feel uncomfortable in sharing spiritual information because they feel it to be incongruent with the clinician's personal beliefs, then the clinician would be advised not to

Table 20.2 Resources

Affirmative religious organizations

Affirmation United Methodist Church for Lesbian, Gay, Bisexual, and Transgender Concerns: http://www.umaffirm.org

Al Fatiha (Islam): http://www.al-fatiha.org

Association of Welcoming and Affirming Baptists: http://www.wabaptists.org

Dignity/USA (Catholic): http://www.dignityusa.org

Friends for Lesbian, Gay, Bisexual, Transgender, and Queer Concerns (Quaker): http://www.flgbtqc.quaker.org

Gay and Lesbian Vaishnava Association (Hindu): http://www.galva108.org

GLAD Alliance (Disciples of Christ): http://www.gladalliance.org

Integrity (Episcopalian): http://www.integrityusa.org

Lutherans Concerned/North America: http://www.lcna.org

Metropolitan Community Church: http://www.mcchurch.org

More Light Presbyterians: http:/www.mlp.org

UCC Coalition for LGBT Concerns (United Church of Christ): http://www.ucccolition.org

QueerDharma (Buddhist): http://www.queerdharma.org

World Congress of Gay, Lesbian, Bisexual and Transgender Jews: http://www.glbtjews.org

Additional resources

Human Rights Campaign: Faith and Religion: http://www.hrc.org/issues/religion/religion_introduction.asp

National Gay and Lesbian Taskforce: Faith: http://www.thetaskforce.org/issues/faith

Documentaries

For the Bible Tells Me So (Karslake, 2007): http://firstrunfeatures.com/forthebibletellsmesodvd.html

Fish Out of Water (Dickens, 2009): http://www.fishoutofwaterfilm.com

All God's Children (Mosbacher, Reid, & Rhue, 1996): http://www.womanvision.org/all-gods-children.html

Trembling Before G-d (Dubowski, 2001): http://www.hulu.com/watch/76545/trembling-before-g-d

A Jihad for Love (Sharma, 2007): http://firstrunfeatures.com/jihadforlovedvd.html

disclose too much information. If, on the other hand, briefly sharing one's common struggles and faith journey may foster an environment of openness and understanding that may improve the therapeutic alliance, doing so may in turn normalize aspects of the couple's experience and ultimately improve therapy outcome. In the following example, the therapist offers appropriate self-disclosure to help reassure a couple and normalize their struggle.

Case Example 20.5

Couple: We feel that we would like to be involved in a church, but not a church like the ones we grew up in that are not welcoming of LGB folks. We miss going to church, but are not sure it is even worth the effort to try and find a welcoming congregation.

Therapist: I have worked with several couples that have had similar struggles with wanting to be involved with a congregation but felt tentative about visiting churches. When I first moved to the area several years ago, I remember struggling with this issue as well. Even though my husband and I are a straight couple, we wanted to attend a church that was welcoming and affirming of all people. We looked online at several churches and decided to visit a few. I remember how awkward it was to visit and wondering if it was worth the effort. I remember feeling a little intimidated at times. We can certainly talk more about your feelings about exploring churches if you feel that would be helpful.

Trainees also need to learn how the interpersonal process of discussing such emotional and possibly sensitive topics as spirituality and sexuality may trigger feelings in the client that are projected onto the therapist (transference) or, alternately, may trigger feelings in the therapist that interfere with effective therapeutic responding (countertransference). For example, if one member of the couple becomes defensive when describing his or her faith background or beliefs, that individual may project onto the therapist (as well as onto the partner) the ridicule experienced in the past. Likewise, when one of the clients unknowingly berates the therapist's religious tradition or faith, the therapist might respond defensively by inappropriately challenging the client. If the couple and clinician share the same religious beliefs, there might be personal differences in how each approaches certain specific issues. Assumptions and differing expectations may lead to conflicts within the therapy sessions, and therapists must learn how to address these conflicts and use them as part of an effective therapeutic process.

Conclusion

At its best, the process of therapy is "a spiritual well-spring for healing and resilience" (Walsh, 2009, p. 51) as same-sex couples rise to meet the challenges they face and forge lives of meaning, connection, and purpose. Same-sex couples can draw on spirituality and spiritual resources to support the health and happiness of their relationship and their individual sense of wholeness and belonging. A spirituality-based relationship can help couples to join together in practicing compassion for each other, for their communities, and for the world, thus healing the profound disconnection that has become epidemic in modern society and perhaps acutely in the lives of those whose identities are stigmatized. The couple relationship can, thus, be a safe haven for cultivating empowering love, spiritual growth, and self-transcendence. Clinicians can help same-sex couples in this endeavor through a two-pronged approach that addresses religion-based experiences of minority stress (i.e., stigma, prejudice, discrimination, and internalized homophobia) and facilitates the positive spiritual values and meanings that serve as resources as they confront the challenges of life. Understanding the social context of same-sex couples' lives, which includes their religious and spiritual backgrounds and values, is important to facilitating their health and well-being.

References

American Psychological Association (APA). (2008). Resolution of religious, religion-based and/or religion-derived prejudice. *American Psychologist*, *63*, 431–434.

Barton, B. (2010). "Abomination"—life as a Bible Belt gay. *Journal of Homosexuality*, *57*, 465–484.

Brooks, V. R. (1981). *Minority stress and lesbian women*. Lexington, MA: Lexington Books.

Burckell, L. A., & Goldfried, M. R. (2006). Therapist qualities preferred by sexual-minority individuals. *Psychotherapy: Theory, Research, Practice, Training*, *43*(1), 32–49.

Dickens, K. (Director). (2009). *Fish out of water* [Motion picture]. United States: Yellow Wing Productions.

Duba, J. D., & Watts, R. E. (2009). Therapy with religious couples. *Journal of Clinical Psychology*, *65*(2), 210–223.

Dubowski, S. A. (Director). (2001). *Trembling before g-d* [Motion picture]. Israel: Simcha Leib Productions.

Dudley, M. G., Rostosky, S. S., Riggle, E. D. B., Duhigg, J. M., Brodnicki, C., & Couch, R. (2005). Same-sex couples' experiences with homonegativity. *Journal of GLBT Family Studies*, *1*(4), 68–93.

Frazier, R. E., & Hansen, N. D. (2009). Religious/spiritual psychotherapy behaviors: Do we do what we believe to be important? *Professional Psychology, Research, and Practice*, *40*, 81–87.

Fredrickson, B. (2003). The value of positive emotions. *American Scientist*, *91*, 330–335.

Grove, J., & Blasby, S. (2009). The therapeutic encounter in same-sex couple counseling—the client's perspective. *Counseling and Psychotherapy Research*, *9*(4), 257–265.

Greenberg, L. S., & Johnson, S. M. (1988). *Emotionally focused therapy for couples*. New York, NY: Guilford Press.

Halkitis, P. N., Mattis, J. S., Sahadath, J. K., Massie, D., Ladyzhenskaya, L., Pitrelli, K.,…Cowie, S.-A. E. (2009). The meanings and manifestations of religion and spirituality among lesbian, gay, bisexual, and transgender adults. *Journal of Adult Development*, *16*, 250–262.

Hall, T., & Edwards, K. (1996). The initial development and factor analysis of the Spiritual Assessment Inventory. *Journal of Psychology and Theology, 24*(3), 233–246.

Helminiak, D. A. (2005). A down-to-earth approach to the psychology of spirituality a century after James's Varieties. *Humanistic Psychologist, 33*, 69–86.

Herek, G. M., & Garnets, L. D. (2007). Sexual orientation and mental health. *Annual Review of Clinical Psychology, 3*, 353–375.

Hodge, D. (2005). Spiritual assessment in marital and family therapy: A methodological framework for selecting from among six qualitative assessment tools. *Journal of Marital and Family Therapy, 31*(4), 341–356.

Imber-Black, E. (2009). Rituals and spirituality in family therapy. In F. Walsh (Ed.), *Spiritual resources in family therapy* (pp. 229–246). New York, NY: Guilford Press.

Karslake, D. G. (Director). (2007). *For the bible tells me so* [Motion picture]. United States: Atticus Group.

Korinek, A., & Arredondo, R. (2004). The Spiritual Health Inventory (SHI): Assessment of an instrument for measuring spiritual health in a substance abusing population. *Alcoholism Treatment Quarterly, 22*(2), 55–66.

Lease, S. H., Horne, S. G., & Noffsinger-Frazier, N. (2005). Affirming faith experiences and psychological health for Caucasian lesbian, gay, and bisexual individuals. *Journal of Counseling Psychology, 52*, 378–388.

Maccio, E. M. (2010). Influence of family, religion, and social conformity on client participation in sexual reorientation therapy. *Journal of Homosexuality, 57*, 441–458.

Meyer, I. H. (2003). Prejudice, social stress, and mental health in lesbian, gay, and bisexual populations: Conceptual issues and research evidence. *Psychological Bulletin, 129*, 674–697.

Meyer, I. H. (2007). Prejudice and discrimination as social stressors. In I. H. Meyer & M. E. Northridge (Eds.), *The health of sexual minorities: Public health perspectives in lesbian, gay, bisexual and transgender populations* (pp. 242–267). New York, NY: Springer.

Mosbacher, D., Reid, F., & Rhue, S. (Producers and Directors). (1996). *All God's children* [Motion picture]. United States: Woman Vision.

Otis, M. D., Hamrin, R., Riggle, E. D. B., & Rostosky, S. S. (2006). Stress and relationship quality in same-sex couples. *Journal of Social and Personal Relationships, 23*, 81–99.

Paloutzian, R. E., & Ellison, C. W. (1982). Loneliness, spiritual well-being and the quality of life. In L. A. Peplau & D. Perlman (Eds.), *Loneliness: A sourcebook or current theory, research, and therapy.* New York, NY: Wiley.

Pargament, K. I. (2002). The bitter and the sweet: An evaluation of the costs and benefits of religiousness. *Psychological Inquiry, 13*, 168–181.

Pargament, K. I., & Krumrei, E. J. (2009). Clinical assessment of clients' spirituality. In J. D. Aten & M. M. Leach (Eds.), *Spirituality and the therapeutic process: A comprehensive resource from intake to termination* (pp. 93–119). Washington, DC: American Psychological Association.

Pargament, K. I., & Mahoney, A. (2005). Spirituality: Discovering and conserving the sacred. In C. R. Snyder & S. J. Lopez (Eds.), *Handbook of positive psychology* (pp. 646–659). New York, NY: Oxford University Press.

Peterson, C., & Seligman, M. E. P. (2004). *Character strengths and virtues: A handbook and classification.* Washington, DC: American Psychological Association.

Piedmont, R. (1999). Does spirituality represent the sixth factor of personality? Spiritual transcendence and the five-factor model. *Journal of Personality, 67*(6), 985–1013.

Post, B. C., & Wade, N. G. (2009). Religion and spirituality in psychotherapy: A practice-friendly review of research. *Journal of Clinical Psychology: In session, 65*, 131–146.

Rodriguez, E. M. (2010). At the intersection of church and gay: A review of the psychological research on gay and lesbian Christians. *Journal of Homosexuality, 57*, 5–38.

Rodriguez, E. M., & Ouellette, S. C. (2000). Gay and lesbian Christians: Homosexual and religious identity integration in the members and participants of a gay-positive church. *Journal for the Scientific Study of Religion, 39*, 333–348.

Rostosky, S. S., Otis, M. D., Riggle, E. D. B., Kelly, S., & Brodnicki, C. (2008). Religiosity and same-sex couple relationships. *Journal of GLBT Family Studies, 4*, 17–36.

Rostosky, S. S., Riggle, E. D. B., Brodnicki, C., & Olson, A. (2008). An exploration of lived religion in same-sex couple relationships. *Family Process, 47*, 389–403.

Rostosky, S. S., Riggle, E. D. B., Gray, B. E., & Hatton, R. L. (2007). Minority stress experiences in committed couple relationships. *Professional Psychology: Research and Practice, 38*, 392–400.

Saulnier, C. F. (2002). Deciding who to see: Lesbians discuss their preferences in health and mental health care providers. *Social Work, 47*, 355–365.

Serlin, I. (2005). Religious and spiritual issues in couples therapy. In M. Harway (Ed.), *Handbook of couples therapy* (pp. 352–369). Hoboken, NJ: Wiley.

Sharma, P. (Director). (2007). *A jihad for love* [Motion picture]. United States: Channel Four Films.

Sherry, A., Adleman, A., Whilde, M. R., & Quick, D. (2010). Competing selves: Negotiating the intersection of spiritual and sexual identities. *Professional Psychology: Research and Practice, 41*, 112–119.

Smith, B., & Horne, S. (2007). Gay, lesbian, bisexual and transgendered (GLBT) experiences with earth-spirited faith. *Journal of Homosexuality, 52*(3–4), 235–248.

Smith, B., & Horne, S. (2008a). The role of faith affiliation for women in same-sex relationships. *Journal of GLBT Family Studies, 4*(2), 165–179.

Smith, B. L., & Horne, S. G. (2008b). What's faith got to do with it? The role of spirituality and religion in lesbian and bisexual women's sexual satisfaction. *Women & Therapy, 31*(1), 73–87. doi:10.1300/02703140802145243

Sperry, L. (2001). *Spirituality in clinical practice: Incorporating the spiritual dimension in psychotherapy and counseling.* Philadelphia, PA: Brunner-Routledge.

Walsh, F. (2009). Integrating spirituality in family therapy: Wellsprings for health, healing, and resilience. In F. Walsh (Ed.), *Spiritual resources in family therapy* (2nd ed., pp. 31–61). New York, NY: Guilford Press.

Whitman, J. S., & Boyd, C. J. (2003). *The therapist's notebook for lesbian, gay, and bisexual clients: Homework, handouts, and activities for use in psychotherapy.* New York, NY: Hawthorn Clinical Practice Press.

Wiggins, M. I. (2008). Therapist self-awareness of spirituality. In J. D. Aten & M. Leach (Eds.), *Spirituality and the therapeutic process* (pp. 53–74). Washington, DC: American Psychological Association.

21

Treatment of Partner Violence in Gay and Lesbian Relationships

DEANNA LINVILLE, KRISTA CHRONISTER,
MARY MARSIGLIO, and TIFFANY B. BROWN

The prevalence of partner violence in adult same-sex lesbian and gay relationships is well documented; however, our understanding of the unique abuse dynamics, concerns, social service needs, and effective interventions for this population is not as clear. This chapter provides an overview of the current literature regarding violence in adult same-sex lesbian and gay relationships and includes recommendations for effective and culturally sensitive therapeutic assessment and intervention strategies. We outline progress made by researchers in the conceptualization and examination of this topic and identify areas in need of future attention. In addition, we provide recommendations for screening, assessment, and treatment specific to same-sex lesbian and gay couples who are experiencing partner violence.

Treatment of Partner Violence in Gay and Lesbian Relationships

Partner violence affects more than 1 million people in the United States each year, and the familial, economic, and social consequences are significant (Murray & Mobley, 2009; Rennison & Welchans, 2000). Current data suggest that partner violence occurs at similar or higher rates in lesbian and gay same-sex relationships than in heterosexual relationships (Balsam, 2001; Greenwood et al., 2002; Seelau, Seelau, & Poorman, 2003). In fact, partner violence is considered the third-largest problem facing gay men today after substance abuse and AIDS, and some researchers estimate between 25% and 33% of same-sex couples experience partner violence (Peterman & Dixon, 2003; Wallace, 1996). Despite the fact that partner violence occurs at similar rates among all couples, same-sex couples are underrepresented in studies investigating the prevalence, incidence, and dynamics of partner violence (Peterman & Dixon, 2003; Stanley, Bartholomew, Taylor, Oram, & Landolt, 2006).

In this chapter we review the literature published on adult same-sex partner violence and provide assessment and treatment recommendations for practitioners working with lesbian and gay couples who have experienced or who are experiencing partner violence. We acknowledge that our literature review and recommendations reflect many of the same strengths and limitations present in the extant literature. We hope that this chapter will, however, help researchers and practitioners identify the research and treatment gaps in this area and devote more attention to studying and understanding same-sex partner violence.

Key topics addressed in this literature review include domestic violence, interpersonal violence, intimate partner violence, and domestic abuse in lesbian and gay relationships. Existing literature on same-sex partner violence tends to focus on three main areas: (1) personal accounts written by survivors and activists describing their partner violence experiences, (2) estimates of the prevalence rates of violence in lesbian and gay relationships, and (3) descriptions of barriers lesbian and gay individuals and couples face while accessing support services, as well as recommendations for services (Bornstein, Fawcett, Sullivan, Senturia, & Shiu-Thornton, 2006).

Our literature review focuses on books, chapters, and journal articles published between 2000 and 2010. We examined research from the areas of couple and family therapy, psychology, nursing and medicine, and social work by searching databases relevant to these fields. Our search initially yielded 480 articles; we narrowed the search by excluding articles that did not focus primarily on the topic (e.g., if partner violence was a peripheral aspect of the article or the focus was primarily on heterosexual partnerships). We also excluded articles written in response to previous articles and omitted studies that yielded low response rates to data collection or were conducted internationally and with limited generalizability.

In this chapter we use the term *partner violence* to describe a pattern of coercive control consisting of physical, sexual, or psychological acts of aggression committed by a current or former partner (Flitcraft, Hadley, Hendricks-Matthews, McLeer, & Warshaw, 1992; Saltzman, Fanslow, McMahon, & Shelley, 2002). Partner violence occurs among opposite-sex and same-sex couples, among those who do and do not cohabitate, and among couples who are and are not sexually intimate. We use the term *same-sex partner violence* to define partner violence between romantic partners who are of the same sex. Partner violence also occurs among couples from diverse economic, racial, ethnic, national, and other cultural backgrounds (Krug, Dahlberg, Mercy, Zwi, & Lozano, 2002), although it is important to acknowledge that specific individual and contextual factors significantly increase an individual's risk for partner violence victimization and perpetration (e.g., acculturative stress and socioeconomic risk; Aldarondo, Kantro, & Jasinski, 2002; Espín, 1999; Falicov, 1998; Heise & Garcia-Moreno, 2002; Perilla, 1999; West, 2002; Wilson & Brooks-Gunn, 2001). Partner violence is conceptualized as a continuum of abuse that includes physical, sexual, threat of physical or sexual, and psychological or emotional abuse (Saltzman et al., 2002; VAWA, 2005). Our review of partner violence also examines economic and spiritual abuse (Brown, Salomon, & Bassuk, 1999; Chronister & McWhirter, 2003; Kanuha, 1994; Lyon, 2000).

Although our focus is on partner violence among adult same-sex couples, we acknowledge that several other communities are at high risk for partner violence, most often because of the sociocultural marginalization that various communities experience (Aldarondo et al., 2002; Kanuha, 1994; West, 2002). For example, adolescents are at particular risk for dating violence, which in turn increases their risk for violence and other negative health outcomes in adulthood (Banyard & Cross, 2008; Eaton, Davis, Barrios, Brenner, & Noonan, 2007; Halpern, Young, Waller, Martin, & Kupper, 2004; Roberts & Klein, 2003; Silverman, Raj, Mucci, & Hathaway, 2001). The scope of this chapter does not allow us to devote focused attention on adolescent same-sex partner violence and same-sex partner violence in specific communities, but we encourage scholars to develop empirically based, affirmative, and culturally inclusive assessments, treatments, and preventive interventions for the numerous and diverse populations that experience partner violence.

Critical Review of the Literature

The following major themes emerged from our literature review of same-sex partner violence and couple intervention: problems with accessing services, issues involved in reporting violence, theory and models of violence related to lesbian and gay concerns, risk and protective factors unique to the lesbian and gay community, and internal and external homophobia. Significant limitations are associated with extant same-sex partner violence research, and they have reduced the usefulness and generalizability of empirical findings (Murray & Mobley, 2009; Renzetti, 1992; Waldner-Haugrud, Gratch, & Magruder, 1997). These limitations include (a) use of nonrepresentative samples, (b) lack of a standard definition of partner violence across studies, (c) lack of appropriate strategies to account for potential inclusion of partners in the same relationship in study examples, (d) failure to specify the timing of data collection, and (e) failure to describe the exclusion criteria for study participation (Burke & Follingstad, 1999; Murray & Mobley, 2009).

In 2009, Murray and Mobley conducted a methodological review of empirical research on same-sex partner violence and identified the strengths and weaknesses of existing literature on this subject. They identified the following strengths: (a) use of appropriate statistical analyses, (b) clarification of the types of abuse measured within the studies, (c) development of appropriate conclusions on the basis of study results, (d) description of the manner in which sexual orientation was measured and categorized, (e) detailed explanation of the eligibility criteria for study participation, and (f) provision of sufficient detail about the methodologies used in order to permit replication. As such, Murray and Mobley suggested a research foundation for clinicians to draw upon as they provide research-informed services to gay and lesbian persons dealing with partner violence. In addition to using Murray and Mobley's research foundation, it is important that treatment providers are critical consumers of the literature and examine their own beliefs and values when interpreting and applying research findings to their work with same-sex couples. Such critical thinking and self-examination will significantly increase the likelihood that treatment providers make accurate, cautious conclusions from research findings and deliver culturally sensitive and inclusive services.

In spite of research design limitations and the concern that, by studying violence in same-sex relationships, social stigmatization and marginalization of same-sex couples and lesbian and gay communities will increase, numerous researchers have attempted to document prevalence rates. Studies of prevalence rates have focused more on lesbian relationships because there are few studies documenting rates of gay male partner violence (Ristock, 2002). Researchers have estimated that approximately one quarter to one half of all same-sex intimate partnerships are abusive (Alexander, 2002; McClennen, 2005; Pitt, 2000). The etiology of same-sex partner violence and abuse patterns and dynamics are similar to those identified with heterosexual couples such that the abuse tends to recur, escalate, and become increasingly violent over time (Island & Letellier, 1991; Renzetti, 1992). A detailed list of abuse tactics specific to same-sex partnerships is provided in the power and control wheel for lesbian, gay, and bisexual individuals found at http://www/ncdsv.org/publications_wheels.html (available in both English and Spanish). Risk factors for same-sex partner violence victimization are (a) prior physical violence by an intimate partner, (b) controlling behaviors on the part of the perpetrator, (c) alcohol and drug use, (d) depression, and (e) termination of the relationship (Glass et al., 2008). Unfortunately, the majority of existing theories and models about partner violence risk and prevention and intervention strategies have been developed with heterosexual couples and then applied to same-sex couples; this blanketing approach fails to capture the distinct stress, oppression, marginalization, and abuse dynamics that increase same-sex couples' risk for partner violence (Balsam & Szymanski, 2005; Hassouneh & Glass, 2008).

In general, researchers studying partner violence in same-sex lesbian and gay relationships have provided important information about the barriers to reporting abuse and subsequently accessing services and help (Freedberg, 2006). Most of the barriers identified are related to larger social issues and injustices facing lesbian and gay same-sex couples and to gender stereotypes about "who" is violent and "what" is violence. For example, if gay men and lesbians reveal their sexual orientation to health care providers, they may face rejection, judgment, discrimination, and substandard care (Freedberg, 2006; I. Meyer, 2001; Rondahl, Innala, & Carlsson, 2004). The following section details the larger social issues faced by same-sex couples who have experienced or are experiencing partner violence.

Larger Social Issues

Same-sex gay and lesbian couples may face additional social issues that heterosexual couples likely do not face; these challenges may make their experiences with partner violence that much more complex. One overarching social issue is that same-sex couples live in a heterosexist and homophobic society and thus may experience significant isolation and increased risk for losing employment, housing, or family if they share that they are in a same-sex partnership or experiencing abuse (Pharr, 1997). *Heterosexism* is defined as an ideological system privileging heterosexuality and heterosexual values as universal (Herek, 1990). *Homophobia*, which is created by heterosexism, is an emotional reaction of fear, disgust, and aversion to gays and lesbians (Berkman & Zinberg, 1997). There are clearly documented negative consequences to both lesbian and gay individuals and couples living in a heterosexist society, including increased rates of depression, anxiety, suicide, and alcohol and drug use (Bernhard & Applegate, 1999; Cheng, 2003; Lewis, Derlega, Griffin, & Krowinski, 2003; Mays & Cochran, 2001). Each of these consequences also increases couples' risk for partner violence.

Heterosexism and traditional gender roles create a specific image of partner violence. Thus, many people have difficulty imagining that males can be survivors of partner violence and that females can be perpetrators of partner violence, or they assume that violence must be mutual among same-sex partners (Brown, 2008). Consequently, violence in same-sex partnerships is often not legitimized or taken seriously and may be viewed as less intense or less hurtful than violence in heterosexual partnerships. Such assumptions are often fueled by biological theories that suggest that men are more aggressive and that same-sex partnerships must not experience the same power differentials as heterosexual partnerships (Brown, 2008; Burke & Follingstad, 1999). The battered women's movement has also conceptualized the problem of partner violence in terms of a male–female phenomenon, linking violent behavior to the male-gender socialization process and adherence to specific male and female gender roles (Miller, Greene, Causby, White, & Lockhart, 2001; Ristock, 2002). This conceptualization has led to several misconceptions about same-sex partner violence, including: (a) lesbian partner violence does not occur because women are not violent, (b) power dynamics do not exist because power and control are traditionally defined in the context of a man exerting power and control over a woman, and (c) because the partners are of the same gender, it is mutual violence with each perpetrating equally (Brown, 2008). These misperceptions make it more difficult and dangerous for individuals in violent same-sex couple relationships to report abuse and seek help. Further, such misconceptions lead to greater isolation for individuals in violent same-sex partnerships and reinforce community inattentiveness, apathy, and ignorance related to same-sex partner violence.

Additional social issues faced by same-sex partners act as barriers to reporting same-sex violence. First, males are more likely believed to be perpetrators and females to be victims (Wise & Bowman, 1997). Consequently, practitioners often fail to complete a thorough and accurate assessment of partner violence, stigmatize men for being victims of partner violence, and negate the seriousness of women's perpetration of violence. Many partner violence treatment programs, for example, offer male-only anger management groups and women-only support groups and allow only heterosexual couples to participate in treatment. Similarly, treatment providers often make assumptions about the level of danger on the basis of the gender of the perpetrator; they are more likely to screen for violence against a woman than against a man and will work to protect female victims more than male victims (Feather, 1996; Harris & Cook, 1994; Seelau & Seelau, 2005). In addition, researchers have found that higher sentences are often recommended for male perpetrators than for female perpetrators (Poorman, Seelau, & Sealau, 2003), and police may be less likely to intervene with same-sex partner violence situations because of gender stereotypes (e.g., women cannot be abusers and men cannot be abused; Island & Letellier, 1991). These larger social issues may make gay and lesbian individuals more likely to stay with their abusive partners and not access services (Peterman & Dixon, 2003).

A second social issue specific to same-sex partner violence has to do with cycle of abuse and power theory. The cycle-of-violence model (Walker, 1979) proposes that there are three critical phases in the patterns of violent relationships: tension building, acute battering incidence, and honeymoon phases. This model of violence, however, is defined in heterosexual terms and does not account for the unique aspects of same-sex abuse dynamics, such as the perpetrator threatening to "out" his or her partner, questioning the victim's sexual orientation and lesbian and gay community allegiance, or making claims of "mutual abuse." Being "outed" may have serious and detrimental occupational, financial, and social consequences. A lesbian or gay batterer may use fear of sexual orientation disclosure as a unique manipulation tool, intimidating his or her partner into remaining silent about the abuse (Helfrich & Simpson, 2006). Moreover, lesbian and gay individuals may find it difficult to identify the abuse that they have experienced or perpetrated when treatment providers are using heterosexist language to explain partner violence or the cycle of violence (Patzel, 2006). The nonviolent partner may also struggle with accessing local support services, worried about having to out himself or herself in order to talk about the abuse or worried about how the provider will respond to the disclosure. In addition, gay men and lesbian women may feel pressure not to reveal the abuse in order to protect the perpetrator and other lesbian and gay community members from (a) being cut off from family, friends, and church as a result of their sexual orientation; and/or (b) being considered disloyal, a traitor to the lesbian and gay communities, or antifeminist (Akpodiete, 1993; Island & Letellier, 1991).

A third, and perhaps one of the most unique, issues faced by same-sex partners is the influence of negative social attitudes and heterosexist beliefs on the lesbian or gay individual (Balsam, 2001; Irwin, 2008). Researchers have adopted the minority stress perspective as a framework for understanding the strain lesbian and gay individuals face by living in a heterosexist social environment (I. H. Meyer, Schwartz, & Frost, 2008). Developing a healthy self-concept becomes difficult within an environment that represents same-sex couples in a shameful manner and marginalizes their romantic partnerships and families. Heterosexist beliefs and attitudes are often self-generated and persist at an individual level, and they are reinforced by societal discrimination (Frost & Meyer, 2009). Although internalized homophobia is common to the formation of a lesbian or gay identity, it is not a personal trait or internal pathology; rather, it is the application of heterosexism to the self (Russell & Bohan, 2006).

Researchers have consistently shown that internalized homophobia has a negative effect on romantic relationship quality and is associated with violence perpetration and victimization in same-sex relationships (Balsam & Szymanski, 2005; Bartholomew, Regan, White, & Oram, 2008; Frost & Meyer, 2009; C. Meyer, 1995). Overcoming internalized homophobia is an essential part of forming a healthy self-concept and correspondingly healthy relationships (Ciliberto & Ferrari, 2009; Frost & Meyer, 2009; Mayfield, 2001; Rowen & Malcolm, 2002). Perpetrators can be fueled by their internal rejection of a self based on cultural influence and may simultaneously use the same negative societal messages to further degrade and berate their partners. Further research is needed to thoroughly understand the interaction between internalized homophobia and partner violence perpetration and victimization.

Assessment and Intervention Recommendations

Researchers have demonstrated that once violence begins in a relationship, it is likely to continue and escalate without intervention (Lawson, 2003; O'Leary et al., 1989). Yet, many clinicians have not had formal training about how to assess and intervene with partner violence (Hamberger & Ambuel, 1997). This lack of training has left clinicians without a guide for how to assess and intervene in a supportive, affirming, and culturally competent way with same-sex couples. In the following sections we make general practice recommendations that are based on our review of the literature and on our clinical experiences, and we provide specific recommendations for each aspect of couples practice with same-sex couples who are experiencing or who have experienced partner violence.

First, clinicians should seek training and continuing education that is generally relevant to domestic violence and is specifically relevant to same-sex partner violence (A. Miller, Bobner, & Zarski, 2000). A solid understanding of domestic violence in same-sex partnerships will increase clinicians' competency with regard to asking relevant assessment questions, interpreting couples' verbal responses, and selecting assessment methods and instruments that capture the context of abuse, that are culturally sensitive and appropriate for each couple, that keep both partners safe, and, if possible, that are grounded in normative data collected from same-sex couples (Stith, Rosen, & McCollum, 2002, 2003; Stith, Rosen, McCollum, & Thomsen, 2004). Second, clinicians should use contextual and culturally inclusive frameworks to interpret assessment findings. Examples of such models include the ecological model (Bronfenbrenner, 1979), an empowerment model of counseling (McWhirter, 1994), and relational-cultural theory (Comstock et al., 2008). Each of these frameworks helps reduce clinicians' risk of pathologizing couples and helps them conceptualize couples' behavior in context, identify couples' resources and strengths across each level of their ecologies, and identify targets for intervention. Third, clinicians should use caution when interpreting assessment results because for most assessment instruments, psychometric data have been gathered with predominantly heterosexual couples and/or small samples of same-sex couples (Renzetti, 1997). The following sections provide more specific recommendations for various aspects of same-sex partner violence.

Screening for Same-Sex Partner Violence

Scholars debate whether or not to screen universally for partner violence in clinical settings (Moracco & Cole, 2009; Richardson et al., 2002) even though emerging evidence has shown that universal screening can increase rates of violence disclosure, be conducted safely, and lead to more appropriate handling of presenting concerns (Phelan, 2007). We recommend that clinicians screen universally for partner violence to avoid screening biases and assumptions about who fits the mold of a perpetrator and a victim of violence. Unfortunately, partner violence–screening instruments and methods often use heterosexist language that can alienate lesbians and gay individuals and may reinforce their silence (Hammond, 1989; Renzetti, 1996). For example, even though the power imbalance within lesbian relationships is considered the primary correlate of partner abuse (Hart, 1986; Margolies & Leeder, 1995; Morrow, 1994), partner violence-screening tools do not measure power balance in lesbian relationships (McClennen, Summers, & Daley, 2002).

Practitioners typically do not conduct partner violence screenings because they lack training and fear clients' reactions (e.g., damaging the therapeutic alliance). Yet clients are likely to support universal partner violence screening when they feel the environment is private, nonjudgmental, nonpressured, and supportive (Todahl & Walters, 2011). As such, practitioners should provide clients with information about why the screening is being conducted, who will have access to the information, and how the information will be used (McNutt, Waltermaurer, McCauley, Campbell, & Ford, 2005; Thackeray, Stelzner, Downs, & Miller, 2007). Moreover, practitioners should critically review their intake forms and other screening instruments to identify heterosexist language. Todahl and Walters (2011) identify the following components of a successful partner violence screening:

> In our view, although disclosure of violence can be one outcome of a successful IPV [interpersonal violence screen], markers of a successful screen should be extended to include (a) harm reduction and an increase in well-being, (b) setting the stage for future disclosures or help seeking, (c) normalizing and giving legitimacy to the discussion of IPV, (d) creating a connection (i.e., reducing isolation), (e) interruption of internalized emotionally abusive messages (e.g., "you're crazy"), and (f) an opportunity to provide practical

information, including handouts, local resources, and referrals—even when abuse is not disclosed. (p. 10)

We also recommend that practitioners conduct a first-session conjoint meeting with the couple and then immediately follow up with a conversation with each individual to assess for partner violence (Bograd & Mederos, 1999). During the initial part of the first session, therapists should spend time joining with the couple and assessing the relationship history and strengths. A principal goal of this first session is to ask what the clients believe are strengths and protective buffers to normative couple conflict in their relationship. In addition to normalizing couple conflict during the first session, the therapist should clarify that the individual session is a routine part of therapy and explain the therapeutic utility of understanding each partner as an individual in addition to understanding the couple as a unit. This discussion sets the stage for the separate sessions and diminishes defensiveness that can occur from scheduling individual meetings. The therapist should refer to the individual meetings as *overall health screenings* rather than overtly refer to them as *violence screens*. It is advisable that therapists use open-ended questions regarding the couple's arguments and common couple conflicts as a nonthreatening precursor to specific screening questions about violent behavior that may be occurring within the relationship.

Assessment of Same-Sex Partner Violence

Assessment of partner violence in same-sex couples should follow the recommendations of Todahl and Walters's (2011) model and include information about the (a) type and frequency of the violence, (b) lethality and imminence of the violence, and (c) involved parties' beliefs about the violence. Todahl and Walters further recommended that prior to the first appointment, the first tier of assessment should involve clients writing their answers to four questions (adapted by Freyd, Klest, & Allard, 2005) typically obtained from intake paperwork: (1) Have you ever witnessed someone deliberately attack one of your family members in a way that resulted in injuries such as scratches, bruises, bleeding, or broken bones? (2) Have you ever been deliberately attacked by an intimate partner in a way that resulted in injuries such as scratches, bruises, bleeding, or broken bones? (3) Have you ever been emotionally mistreated in a significant and ongoing way by an intimate partner, such as being told you were ugly or stupid, or being restricted from activities that are very important to you? and (4) Have you ever been made to have some form of unwanted sexual contact? These questions are then asked orally in the follow-up individual conversation with each partner (Todahl & Walters, 2011). At this point, further violence assessment and inquiry are conducted if the results of this initial screen suggest that violence is presently occurring or if the client indicates feeling unsafe in the relationship (Todahl & Walters, 2009). Some therapists may decide to assess through the individual interview only, and others may want to also administer commonly used domestic violence assessment instruments that are designed to measure each partner's behavior and relationship experience and the context of the abuse. In addition, it is essential that the therapist assess each partner's substance abuse, depression, and suicidality and the extent of psychological abuse because these factors are commonly linked and reciprocally influenced by partner violence (Stith, 2000).

We also recommend that therapists ask about partner violence in a nonjudgmental, routine way using their own words and ask about specific acts of violence because many clients will define violence differently (Stith, 2000). Therapists might ask, for example, "Specifically, how do you resolve conflicts?" and "Have you ever slapped, pushed, kicked, etc., your partner or had these done to you?" (Lawson, 2003). It is also important to ask about each partner's perception of danger and fear in the relationship. Weisz, Tolman, and Saunders (2000) found that the victim's perceived risk for severe assault is a significant predictor of the level of danger in the relationship. In addition, assessing the level at which the perpetrator is willing to take responsibility for the violence is essential in determining if conjoint treatment is safe and indicated. Information gained from these types of assessments helps clinicians decide whether it is appropriate to see the couple as a unit or to recommend individual therapy for both. If it is determined that conjoint therapy is not appropriate because of ongoing violence in the relationship, we recommend the therapist have an open conversation with the clients individually or as a couple regarding concerns about meeting conjointly. The therapist may say, for example:

> At this time, I recommend individual meetings for a while versus meeting as a couple. I want to let you know up front that in order for us to work together and come up with new, more effective ways for both of you to communicate and to meet each other's needs, the abuse, physical and verbal, has to stop. I cannot work effectively with you if any abuse continues because I do not believe a healthy, loving relationship is possible when abuse is happening or when one or both partners are afraid they may be abused.

We recommend that the clinician be this direct with the couple only if it is clear that neither partner is in imminent danger and that discussing the abuse with the couple would not place one or both partners in greater danger. If the therapist decides that conjoint therapy would not be safe and thus recommends individual meetings, we suggest the therapist offer clear, specific steps for clients to follow before they can be considered appropriate for conjoint sessions. Rather than turn the couple away, we recommend working with clients toward their goals if they are both willing to engage in creating change in the relationship and agree to follow the therapist's recommendations. For example, the therapist can require the offending partner to take anger management classes, engage in groups that focus on anger, or participate in partner violence classes when available. The therapist can also suggest that clients consistently and successfully implement a time-out contract before conjoint sessions are considered. In addition, we recommend the therapist maintain individual sessions until conjoint therapy is indicated (i.e., the perpetrator takes responsibility for the violence, and the violence decreases).

Treatment of Same-Sex Partner Violence

If, after conducting a thorough assessment of relationship safety and violence in the relationship, the therapist determines that it is appropriate to do couple therapy, we recommend the therapist follow the treatment model developed and tested by Stith, Locke, Rosen, and McCollum (2001). These researchers recommend this conjoint couples treatment modality for those couples who (a) engage in low-level partner violence, (b) are not substance abusers, (c) want to remain a couple, and (d) want to end the violence. Conjoint couples treatment for partner violence may be controversial, but not all violent couples are alike; as such, different treatment approaches are warranted. We also maintain that conjoint treatment is warranted in some cases because (a) it is common for both partners in the relationship to be violent, and cessation of partner violence by one partner is highly dependent on whether the other partner also ceases; and (b) separate groups (e.g., anger management groups and support groups) often do not address the underlying relationship dynamics that may affect each partner's decision to remain in the relationship (Stith et al., 2001).

Therapeutic Framework and Strategies

We recommend that therapists use a solution-oriented, strengths-focused framework to guide therapy with same-sex couples dealing with partner violence (Lipchik & Kubicki, 1996; Stith, 2000). Thus it is essential that during the first session therapists collect information from the couple about what they see as buffers to stress and strengths in their relationship and community. Therapists should focus on helping couples see the possibilities for their relationship, determine if they can manage conflict in a nonviolent way, and understand how their individual, couple, and community or cultural competencies can help them develop more healthful patterns in their relationship. We recommend supporting couples as they create a shared vision for the relationship, one that includes a positive sense of intimacy and communication and a positive sense of the other important aspects of their environment. For example, extended family, religion and spirituality, and/or ethnic community ties may be very important to each partner, who they may consider them essential to his or her individual and/or relational health. This meaning making can be developed from the conversation about what the couple see as their inherent strengths and what fosters these strengths. McWhirter's (1994) empowerment model of counseling is especially useful for identifying and nurturing couples' strengths. McWhirter defined empowerment as "the process by which people, organizations, or groups who are powerless or marginalized (a) become aware of the power dynamics at work in their life context, (b) develop the skills and capacity for gaining some reasonable control over their lives, (c) which they exercise, (d) without infringing on the rights of others, and (e) which coincides with actively supporting the empowerment of others in their community" (1994, p. 12). The five Cs of empowerment are collaboration, context, competence, critical consciousness, and community (McWhirter, 1998). Practitioners may use each of these Cs of empowerment to help couples identify and describe their individual, relational, and community strengths and resiliencies.

When therapists focus on what is working well in the relationship and amplify change (O'Hanlon & Weiner-Davis, 1989) while not minimizing the violence or its impact, it is likely that couples will feel more valued for their strength and coping skills (Green, 2004), less judged, and more open to working on their relationship. This sense of acceptance and openness seems particularly important for same-sex couples, who may already feel stigmatized and discriminated against by the larger society. As recommended by Stith (2000), we also suggest that cotherapy teams work with same-sex couples who want to end the violence in their relationship. A cotherapy arrangement enables therapists to meet individually with each partner, both before and after the session, so that they can do "safety checks," ask whether violence has occurred between sessions, discuss the perceived risk level, and conduct safety planning as needed. Creative brainstorming with clients in terms of safety planning may be especially warranted in a same-sex partnership because the partners may have fewer "safe places and people" to access.

We also recommend developing a negotiated time-out procedure with the couple early in treatment (Rosen, Matheson, Stith, McCollum, & Locke, 2003), which includes the following components: (a) being aware of internal cues that anger is escalating, (b) deciding when anger is escalating past either partner's safety zone and a time-out is needed, (c) initiating a time-out with an agreed-upon signal, (d) acknowledging time-out, (e) disengaging by going to separate locations, (f) engaging in calming activities, and (g) returning and reconnecting if calm. Therapists are encouraged to have each partner sign a "no violence contract" at the beginning of therapy; this contract should be revisited as needed throughout the therapy process.

Finally, it is important for therapists to know about other resources for dealing with violence in their local community. It is essential to know which shelters, treatment programs, and legal and law enforcement professionals are open and able to competently address same-sex partner violence. For example, it should not be assumed that local domestic violence shelters are a safe and available resource for gay and lesbian individuals because the design and operation of most shelters are grounded in a heterosexual paradigm. Knowledge about community resources and collaborative partnerships will help therapists develop realistic safety plans with their clients and help clients access the services they need. Therapists may also need to provide consultation about same-sex partner violence to other professionals in the community to dispel myths that hinder practitioners' ability to provide affirming and healing services. In addition, we recommend that practitioners provide couples and other professionals with same-sex partner violence psychoeducational materials, including, for example, the website address for Stop Abuse for Everyone (http://www.safe4all.org) and for Abuse, Rape, and Domestic Violence Aid and Resource Collection (http://www.aardvarc.org/dv/gay.shtml). Also potentially helpful is the E. Weiss (2003) book *Family and Friends' Guide to Domestic Violence: How to Listen, Talk and Take Action When Someone You Care About Is Being Abused.*

Role and Guidelines for Therapists

We recommend that the therapist's role include being a relationship consultant, collaborator, and facilitator of effective conflict management, communication, critical consciousness raising, and relationship enhancement. As a relationship consultant, the therapist learns from clients what would make therapy worthwhile and effective. The therapist supports each individual in the couple relationship while also supporting the couple as a unit. Moreover, the therapist facilitates couples' critical awareness and self-reflection about how their life experiences and multiple contexts affect their individual and relationship development.

Creating a Safe Therapeutic Environment

The therapist is charged with providing a nonjudgmental, safe, and open environment for same-sex couples who are dealing with violence. It is essential that therapists examine the ways in which heterosexism has shaped their own personal and professional lives (McGeorge & Carlson, 2011). This self-examination will help them become aware of biases that may be influencing their work and clarify how they might provide more lesbian- and gay-affirmative therapy. McGeorge and Carlson described a three-step process for heterosexual therapists to critically explore the influence of their heteronormative assumptions, heterosexual privilege, and heterosexual identity. We agree that participating in this process of self-reflection and exploration is essential for heterosexual therapists who are attempting to provide affirmative therapy for lesbian and gay couples dealing with partner violence. We concur with Wetchler (2004) that it is important for heterosexual therapists to recognize that they can never be completely free from the influence of heteronormative assumptions. Critical self-reflection, however, is crucial for all therapists, given the dominance of heterosexist culture.

We do not assume that therapists who identify as lesbian or gay will be inherently competent at providing affirmative and inclusive therapy for lesbian and gay couples who are experiencing partner violence. Helpful strategies for therapists providing affirmative therapy for same-sex couples experiencing partner violence include "coming out" as a lesbian- and gay-affirmative therapist, communicating a lesbian- and gay-affirmative stance in therapy, and helping same-sex couples deconstruct the influence of heterosexism on lesbian and gay clients and the therapy process (McGeorge & Carlson, 2011). Asking questions about the gender of a person's partner rather than making assumptions (Matthews, 2007), ensuring that there are materials (i.e., magazines and books) in the waiting room that are relevant for lesbian and gay individuals and relationships, and helping same-sex couples give voice to how living in a heterosexist society affects them as individuals and affects their relationships are examples of affirming practices (McGeorge & Carlson, 2011).

We also recommend that therapists reflect on and increase their self-awareness regarding biases they may have about partner violence. It is important for them to examine their beliefs and underlying assumptions about same-sex partner violence because it is generally assumed that violent couples are heterosexual, with the male partner as the abuser (Brown, 2008; Burke & Follingstad, 1999). Therapists must be able to facilitate disclosure of the abuse and then be able to handle the disclosure in a way that fosters safety and hope. It is paramount, therefore, that therapists be patient and empathetic and recognize that the victim of the partner violence may choose to stay in the relationship (Peterman & Dixon, 2003).

Supervision and Consultation

In addition to the recommendations we have described, it is imperative for therapists to seek regular consultation with supervisors and/or peers to address normative issues of countertransference that can arise when working with violent couples. Consultation can also provide the therapist with key support, knowledge, and experiences, which can in turn enable the therapist to better support clients. For example, clinicians can use cross-cultural consultation experiences to increase their awareness of their sexist, heterosexist, and homophobic biases and assumptions.

Case Study

Jess and Laurie presented for couples therapy. Jess reported on the intake forms that she is European American, female, age 38 years, and presented for counseling with concerns about their arguments over the past year and how they are negatively affecting their relationship. Laurie reported on her intake forms that she is biracial, European American and African American, female, age 37 years, and presented for counseling primarily at Jess's urging, but she is also concerned about her relationship with Jess.

The therapist explained that they would first all meet together and, as is routine procedure for working with couples, would then each meet individually the following session for an overall health screen. During their first meeting, using an ecological framework and empowerment approach, the therapist explored the couple's concerns and easked about the buffers to conflict within the relationship. The therapist enquired how they both handled tension and conflict in their relationship and the couple reported that they typically do not talk about conflictual topics until there is a "blow out."

The therapist used the individual session time following the joint session to explore further each woman's concerns, individual and relationship history, and current contextual supports and barriers. Most important, the therapist assessed for partner violence by exploring the couple's conflicts, gathering data regarding their behaviors during an argument, and determining the level of danger in the relationship. During their individual meetings, the therapist learned that there were significant differences in outness for each partner, which had created a significant amount of stress for the couple.

In response to partner violence screening questions, Jess shared that she has always felt safe with Laurie, but that sense of safety wavered a bit 2 months ago when Laurie was drinking, got angry, and threw a plate at the wall near where Jess was standing. Upon further questioning, Jess did not disclose any other incidents that concerned her, noting the argument with the plate as the worst it has been. Upon the therapist's further questioning, both partners expressed feeling safe and willing to discuss their arguments in the couple's sessions.

After considering information from the couples and individual sessions, the therapist determined that it would be appropriate to continue treating the couple in joint sessions because (a) Jess and Laurie each consented to continue couple therapy, (b) each expressed feeling safe talking with each other about their relationship and their conflicts, (c) assessment results of substance use by both partners was minimal, and (d) intake and interview assessment results evidenced that the level of abuse experienced in their relationship was minimal. The therapist informed Jess and Laurie that her approach would involve conducting ongoing safety checks throughout their argument cycle. In addition, the therapist also developed a time-out contract for the remainder of treatment. Finally, by asking the couple if they had any questions or concerns about her or the counseling process that they would like to talk about, the therapist created an open, collaborative, and safe environment.

Ongoing treatment considerations for Jess and Laurie include regular assessment of partner violence and substance use during the course of treatment, ongoing assessment of the use and success of the time-out contract, the role that outness has within their relationship, and acknowledgment and amplification of what is working well within the relationship. In addition, it will be imperative for the therapist to receive ongoing consultation and supervision and be aware of any developing countertransference with this client system.

Recommendations for Future Research

Murray and Mobley (2009) provided seven recommendations for researchers planning future studies of same-sex partner violence: (1) Develop creative strategies for recruiting representative samples; (2) use clear, consistent definitions to describe the type of violence studied; (3) include strategies to control for the potential influence of social desirability; (4) use appropriate assessment instrumentation and provide psychometric properties of instruments used; (5) account for variables unique to the lesbian and gay population; (6) replicate previous studies in order to validate their findings; and (7) seek out, and advocate for, funding sources to help support future research examining same-sex partner violence. We agree with these recommendations for the conduct of quantitative studies and support rigorous qualitative inquiry into the topic of same-sex partner violence.

Some important areas of inquiry for future research studies are the following: (a) an exploration of the possible combinations of sexual identity stages in same-sex couples and how they affect the therapy process (A. Miller et al., 2000); (b) an examination of the complexities and heterogeneity of relationships as they relate to partner violence and arise from differently gendered, racialized, sexualized, and personal relations between two women or two men (versus examining one totalizing theory; Ristock, 2003); (c) an investigation of the effectiveness of treatment models specific to same-sex couples dealing with partner violence; and (d) an evaluation of the practitioner's assessment practices of same-sex couple partner violence.

Conclusion

Given that prevalence rates and the etiology of same-sex partner violence are similar, but that these couples face additional social stigmas and injustices, it is imperative that researchers, clinicians, and policy makers break down the barriers for gay and lesbian couples seeking the necessary support and treatment. We recommend utilizing a universal screening protocol for partner violence among lesbian and gay couples and employing a strengths-focused, empowerment approach to treatment. We believe that focusing on strategies that increase safety, healthy communication, and positive social support is essential. Screening, assessment, and treatment of partner violence with same-sex couples require therapists to be knowledgeable of the sociocultural needs of a marginalized group that is dominated by heteronormative standards. Researchers need to include same-sex couples in the ongoing study of the most effective approaches to assessment, treatment strategies, and therapeutic modalities in order to end partner violence. In addition, specifically exploring the unique assessment and treatment needs of gay and lesbian couples is important.

References

Akpodiete, T. (1993). Opening the door on lesbian violence. *Horizons, 7*(1), 13.

Aldarondo, E., Kantro, G. K., & Jasinski, J. L. (2002). A risk marker análisis of wife assault in Latino familias. *Violence Against Women, 8*(4), 429–454.

Alexander, C. J. (2002). Violence in gay and lesbian relationships. *Journal of Gay and Lesbian Social Services, 14*, 95–98.

Balsam, K. (2001). Nowhere to hide: Lesbian battering, homophobia, and minority stress. In E. Kaschak (Ed.), *Intimate betrayal: Domestic violence in lesbian relationships* (pp. 25–37). New York, NY: Haworth Press.

Balsam, K., & Szymanski, D. (2005). Relationship quality and domestic violence in women's same-sex relationships: The role of minority stress. *Psychology of Women Quarterly, 29*, 258–269.

Banyard, V. L., & Cross, C. (2008). Consequences of teen dating violence: Understanding intervening variables in context. *Violence Against Women, 14*, 998–1013.

Bartholomew, K., Regan, K. V., White, M. A., & Oram, D. (2008). Patterns of abuse in male same-sex relationships. *Violence and Victims, 23*(5), 617–636.

Berkman, C. S., & Zinberg, G. (1997). Homophobia and heterosexism in social workers. *Social Work, 42* (4), 319–332.

Bernhard, L., & Applegate, J. (1999). Comparison of stress and stress management strategies between lesbian and heterosexual women. *Health Care for Women International, 20*, 335–347.

Bograd, M., & Mederos, F. (1999). Battering and couples therapy: Universal screening and selection of treatment modality. *Journal of Marital and Family Therapy, 25*, 291–312.

Bornstein, D. R., Fawcett, J., Sullivan, M., Senturia, K. D., & Shiu-Thornton, S. (2006). Understanding the experiences of lesbian, bisexual and trans survivors of domestic violence: A qualitative study. *Journal of Homosexuality, 51*(1), 159–181.

Bronfenbrenner, U. (1979). *The ecology of human development.* Cambridge, MA: Harvard University Press.

Brown, C. (2008). Gender-role implications on same-sex intimate partner abuse. *Journal of Family Violence, 23*, 456–462.

Browne, A., Salomon, A., & Bassuk, S. S. (1999). The impact of recent partner violence on poor women's capacity to maintain work. *Violence Against Women, 5*, 393–426.

Burke, L. K., & Follingstad, D. R. (1999). Violence in lesbian and gay relationships: Theory, prevalence, and correlational factors. *Clinical Psychology Review, 19*, 487–512.

Cheng, Z. (2003). Issues and standards in counseling lesbians and gay men with substance abuse concerns. *Journal of Mental Health Counseling, 25*(4), 323–336.

Chronister, K. M., & McWhirter, E. H. (2003). Applying social cognitive career theory to the empowerment of battered women. *Journal of Counseling and Development, 81*(4), 418–424.

Ciliberto, J., & Ferrari, F. (2009). Interiorized homophobia, identity dynamics, and gender typization: Hypothesizing a third gender role in Italian LGB individuals. *Journal of Homosexuality, 56*(5), 610–622.

Comstock, D. L., Hammer, T. R., Strentzsch, J., Cannon, K., Parsons, J., & Salazar, G., II. (2008). Relational–cultural theory: A framework for bridging relational, multicultural, and social justice competencies. *Journal of Counseling and Development, 86*, 279–287.

Eaton, D. K., Davis, K. S., Barrios, L., Brenner, N. D., & Noonan, R. K. (2007). Associations of dating violence victimization with lifetime participation, co-occurrence, and early initiation of risk behaviors among U.S. high school students. *Journal of Interpersonal Violence, 22*, 585–602.

Espín, O. M. (1999). *Women crossing boundaries: A psychology of immigration and transformation of sexuality.* New York, NY: Routledge.

Falicov, C. J. (1998). *Latino families in therapy: A guide to a multicultural practice.* New York, NY: Guilford Press.

Feather, N. T. (1996). Domestic violence, gender, and perceptions of justice. *Sex Roles, 35*, 507–519.

Flitcraft, A. H., Hadley, S. M., Hendricks-Matthews, M. K., McLeer, S. V., & Warshaw, C. (1992). *Diagnostic and treatment guidelines on domestic violence.* Chicago, IL: American Medical Association.

Freedberg, P. (2006). Health care barriers and same-sex intimate partner violence: A review of the literature. *Journal of Forensic Nursing, 2*(1), 15–41.

Freyd, J., Klest, B., & Allard, C. (2005). Betrayal trauma: Relationship to physical health, psychological distress, and a written disclosure intervention. *Journal of Trauma and Dissociation, 6*(3), 83–104.

Frost, D. M., & Meyer, I. H. (2009). Internalized homophobia and relationship quality among lesbians, gay men, and bisexuals. *Journal of Counseling Psychology, 56*(1), 97–109.

Glass, N., Perrin, N., Hanson, G., Bloom, T., Gardner, E., & Campbell, J. C. (2008). Risk for reassault in abusive female same-sex relationships. *American Journal of Public Health, 98*(6), 1021–1027.

Green, R. (2004). Risk and resilience in lesbian and gay couples: Comment on Solomon, Rothblum, and Balsam (2004). *Journal of Family Psychology, 18*(2), 290–292.

Greenwood, G., Relf, M., Huang, B., Pollack, L., Canchola, J., & Catania, J. (2002). Battering victimization among a probability-based sample of men who have sex with men. *American Journal of Public Health, 92*, 1964–1969.

Halpern, C. T., Young, M. L., Waller, M. W., Martin, S. L., & Kupper, L. L. (2004). Prevalence of partner violence in same-sex romantic relationships in a national sample of adolescents. *Journal of Adolescent Health, 35*, 124–131.

Hamberger, L., & Ambuel, B. (1997). Training psychology students and professionals to recognize and intervene into partner violence: Borrowing a page from medicine. *Psychotherapy, 34*, 375–385.

Hammond, N. (1989). Lesbian victims of relationship violence. *Women & Therapy, 8,* 89–105.

Harris, R. J., & Cook, C. A. (1994). Attributions about spouse abuse: It matters who the batterers and victims are. *Sex Roles, 30,* 553–565.

Hart, B. (1986). Lesbian battering: An examination. In K. Lobel (Ed.), *Naming the violence: Speaking out about lesbian battering* (pp. 173–189). Seattle, WA: Seal Press.

Hassouneh, D., & Glass, N. (2008). The influence of gender role stereotyping on women's experiences of female same-sex intimate partner violence. *Violence Against Women, 14,* 310–325.

Heise, L., & Garcia-Moreno, C. (2002). *Violence by intimate partners. World report on violence and health.* Geneva, Switzerland: World Health Organization.

Helfrich, C., & Simpson, E. (2006). Improving services for lesbian clients: What do domestic violence agencies need to do? *Healthcare for Women International, 27,* 344–361.

Herek, G. (1990). The context of anti-gay violence: Notes on cultural and psychological heterosexism. *Journal of Interpersonal Violence, 5*(3), 316–333. .

Irwin, J. (2008). (Dis)counted stories: Domestic violence and lesbians. *Qualitative Social Work: Research and Practice, 7*(2), 199–215.

Island, D., & Letellier, P. (1991). *Men who beat the men who love them: Battered gay men and domestic violence.* Binghamton, NY: Haworth.

Kanuha, V. (1994).Women of color in battering relationships. In L. G. Comas-Diaz & B. Greene (Eds.), *Women of color: Integrating ethnic and gender identities in psychotherapy* (pp. 428–454). New York, NY: Guilford.

Krug, E. G., Dahlberg, L. L., Mercy, J. A., Zwi, A. B., & Lozano, R. (Eds.). (2002). *World report of violence and health.* Geneva, Switzerland: World Health Organization.

Lawson, D. (2003). Incidence, explanations and treatment of partner violence. *Journal of Counseling and Development, 81*(1), 19–32.

Lewis, R., Derlega, V., Griffin, J., & Krowinski, A. (2003). Stressors for gay men and lesbians: Life stress, gay-related stress, stigma consciousness, and depressive symptoms. *Journal of Social and Clinical Psychology, 22*(6), 716–729.

Lipchik, E., & Kubicki, A. (1996). Solution-focused domestic violence views: Bridges toward a new reality in couples therapy. In S. D. Miller, M. A. Hubble, & B. L. Duncan (Eds.), *Handbook of solution-focused brief therapy* (pp. 65–97). San Francisco, CA: Jossey Bass.

Lyon, E. (2000). *Welfare, poverty, and abused women: New research and its implications. Building comprehensive solutions to domestic violence.* Harrisburg, PA: National Resource Center on Domestic Violence.

Margolies, L., & Leeder, E. (1995). Violence at the door: Treatment of lesbian batterers. *Violence Against Women, 1*(2), 139–157.

Matthews, C. (2007). Affirmative lesbian, gay, and bisexual counseling with all clients. In K. J. Bieschke, R. M. Perez, & K. A. DeBord (Eds.), *Handbook of counseling and psychotherapy with lesbian, gay, bisexual and transgender clients* (2nd ed., pp. 201–219). Washington, DC: American Psychological Association.

Mayfield, W. (2001). The development of an internalized homonegativity inventory for gay men. *Journal of Homosexuality, 41*(2), 53–76.

Mays, V., & Cochran, S. (2001). Mental health correlates and perceived discrimination among lesbian, gay and bisexual adults in the United States. *American Journal of Public Health, 91*(11), 1869–1876.

McClennen, J. C. (2005). Domestic violence between same-gender partners: Recent findings and future research. *Journal of Interpersonal Violence, 20,* 149–154.

McClennen, J., Summers, A., & Daley, J. (2002). The lesbian partner abuse scale. *Research on Social Work Practice, 12*(2), 277–292.

McGeorge, C., & Carlson, T. (2011). Deconstructing heterosexism: Becoming an LGB affirmative heterosexual couple and family therapist. *Journal of Marital and Family Therapy, 37*(1), 14–26.

McNutt, L., Waltermaurer, E., McCauley, J., Campbell, J., & Ford, D. (2005). Rationale for development of the computerized intimate partner violence screen for primary care. *Family Violence Prevention & Health Practice, 3,* 1–13.

McWhirter, E. H. (1994). *Counseling for empowerment.* Alexandria, VA: American Counseling Association.

McWhirter, E. H. (1998). An empowerment model of counsellor training. *Canadian Journal of Counselling, 32*(1), 12–26.

Meyer, C. (1995). Assessment. In R. L. Edwards (Ed.), *Encyclopedia of social work* (19th ed., pp. 260–270). Washington, DC: NASW Press.

Meyer, I. (2001). Why lesbian, gay, bisexual and transgender public healthy? *American Journal of Public Health, 9*(16), 856–859.

Meyer, I. H., Schwartz, S., & Frost, D. M. (2008). Social patterning of stress and coping: Does disadvantaged social status confer more stress and fewer coping resources?. *Social Sciences and Medicine*, *67*(3), 368–379.

Miller, A., Bobner, R., & Zarski, J. (2000). Sexual identity development: A base for work with same-sex couple partner abuse. *Contemporary Family Therapy*, *22*(2), 189–200.

Miller, D., Greene, K., Causby, V., White, B., & Lockhart, L. (2001). Domestic violence in lesbian relationships. In E. Kaschak (Ed.), *Intimate betrayal: Domestic violence in lesbian relationships* (pp. 107–128). New York, NY: Haworth Press.

Moracco, K., & Cole, T. (2009). Preventing intimate partner violence: Screening is not enough. *Journal of the American Medical Association*, *302*(5), 568–570.

Morrow, J. (1994). Identifying and treating battered lesbians. In *San Francisco Medicine*. San Francisco, CA: San Francisco Medical.

Murray, C. E., & Mobley, A. K. (2009). Empirical research about same-sex intimate partner violence: A methodological review. *Journal of Homosexuality*, *56*, 361–386.

O'Hanlon, W., & Weiner-Davis, M. (1989). *In search of solutions: A new direction in psychotherapy*. New York, NY: Norton.

O'Leary, K., Barling, J., Arias, I., Rosenbaum, A., Malone, J., & Tyree, A. (1989). Prevalence and stability of physical aggression between spouses: A longitudinal analysis. *Journal of Consulting and Clinical Psychology*, *57*, 263–268.

Patzel, B. (2006). What blocked heterosexual women and lesbians in leaving their abusive relationships. *Journal of the American Psychiatric Nurses Association*, *12*(4), 208–215.

Perilla, J. L. (1999). Domestic violence as a human rights issue: The case of immigrant Latinos. *Hispanic Journal of Behavioral Sciences*, *21*(2), 107–133.

Peterman, L., & Dixon, C. (2003). Domestic violence between same-sex partners: Implications for counseling. *Journal of Counseling and Development*, *81*(1), 40–47.

Pharr, S. (1997). *Homophobia: A weapon of sexism*. Berkley, CA: Chardon Press.

Phelan, M. (2007). Screening for intimate partner violence in medical settings. *Trauma, Violence, & Abuse*, *8*(2), 199–213.

Pitt, E. L. (2000). Domestic violence in gay and lesbian relationships. *Gay and Lesbian Medical Association Journal*, *4*, 195–196.

Poorman, P., Seelau, E., & Seelau, S. (2003). Perceptions of domestic abuse in same-sex relationships and implications for criminal justice and mental health responses. *Violence and Victims*, *18*, 659–669.

Rennison, C., & Welchans, S. (2000). *Intimate partner violence* (NCJ 178247). Washington, DC: Bureau of Justice Statistics.

Renzetti, C. (1992). *Violent betrayal: Partner abuse in lesbian relationships*. Newbury Park, CA: Sage.

Renzetti, C. (1996). The poverty of services for battered lesbians. In C. M. Renzetti & C. H. Miley (Eds.), *Violence in gay and lesbian domestic partnerships* (pp. 61–68). New York, NY: Haworth.

Renzetti, C. M. (1997). Violence in lesbian and gay relationships. In L. L. O'Toole & J. R. Schiffman (Eds.), *Gender violence* (pp. 285–293). New York, NY: New York University Press.

Richardson, J., Coid, J., Petruckevitch, A., Chung, W. S., Moorey, S., & Feder, G. (2002). Identifying domestic violence: Cross sectional study in primary care. *British Medical Journal*, *324*, 274–281.

Ristock, J. (2002). *No more secrets: Violence in lesbian relationships*. London, England: Routledge.

Roberts, T. A., & Klein, J. (2003). Intimate partner abuse and high-risk behavior in adolescents. *Archives of Pediatrics and Adolescent Medicine*, *157*, 375–380.

Rondahl, G., Innala, S., & Carlsson, M. (2004). Nursing staff and nursing students' emotions towards homosexual patients and their wish to refrain from nursing, if the option existed. *Scandinavian Journal of Caring Sciences*, *18*, 19–26.

Rosen, K., Matheson, J., Stith, S., McCollum, E., & Locke, L. (2003). Negotiated time-out: A de-escalation tool for couples. *Journal of Marital and Family Therapy*, *29*(3), 291–298.

Rowen, C. J., & Malcolm, J. P. (2002). Correlates of internalized homophobia and homosexual identity formation in a sample of gay men. *Journal of Homosexuality*, *43*(2), 77–92.

Russell, G. M., & Bohan, J. S. (2006). The case of internalized homophobia. *Theory and Psychology*, *16*(3), 343–366.

Saltzman, L. E., Fanslow, J. L., McMahon, P. M., & Shelley, G. A. (2002). *Intimate partner violence surveillance: Uniform definitions and recommended data elements, Version 1.0*. Atlanta, GA: National Center for Injury Prevention and Control, Centers for Disease Control and Prevention.

Seelau, S., & Seelau, E. (2005). Gender-role stereotypes and perceptions of heterosexual, gay and lesbian domestic violence. *Journal of Family Violence*, *20*(6), 363–371.

Seelau, E., Seelau, S., & Poorman, P. B. (2003). Gender and role-based perceptions of domestic abuse: Does sexual orientation matter? *Behavioral Sciences and the Law, 21*, 199–214.

Silverman, J. G., Raj, A., Mucci, L. A., & Hathaway, J. E. (2001). Dating violence against adolescent girls and associated substance use, unhealthy weight control, sexual risk behavior, pregnancy, and suicidality. *Journal of the American Medical Association, 286*, 572–579.

Stanley, J., Bartholomew, K., Taylor, T., Oram, D., & Landolt, M. (2006). Intimate violence in male same-sex relationships. *Journal of Family Violence, 21*(1), 31–41.

Stith, S. (2000). Clinical update: Domestic violence. *American Association for Marriage and Family Therapy, 2*(3), 1–7.

Stith, S., Locke, L., Rosen, K., & McCollum, E. (2001, August/September). Domestic violence focused couples treatment. *American Association for Marriage and Family Therapy*, 10–12.

Stith, S. M., Rosen, K. H., & McCollum, E. E. (2002). Developing a manualized couples treatment for domestic violence: Overcoming challenges. *Journal of Marital and Family Therapy, 28*(1), 21–25.

Stith, S. M., Rosen, K. H., & McCollum, E. (2003). Effectiveness of couples treatment for spouse abuse. *Journal of Marital and Family Therapy, 29*(3), 407–426.

Stith, S. M., Rosen, K. H., McCollum, E. E., & Thomsen, C. J. (2004). Treating intimate partner violence within intact couple relationships: Outcomes of multi-couple versus individual couple therapy. *Journal of Marital and Family Therapy, 30*(3), 305–318.

Thackeray, J., Stelzner, S., Downs, S., & Miller, C. (2007). Screening for intimate partner violence: The impact of screener and screening environment on victim comfort. *Journal of Interpersonal Violence, 22*(6), 659–670.

Todahl, J., & Walters, E. (2009). Universal screening and assessment for intimate partner violence: The IPV screen and assessment tier (IPV-SAT) model. *Journal of Feminist Family Therapy, 21*, 247–270.

Todahl, J., & Walters, E. (2011). Universal screening for intimate partner violence: A systematic review. *Journal of Marital and Family Therapy, 37*(3), 355–369.

Violence Against Women and Department of Justice Reauthorization Act of 2005 (H.R. 3402). Public Law Number 109-162.

Waldner-Haugrud, L. K., Gratch, L. V., & Magruder, B. (1997). Victimization and perpetration rates of violence in gay and lesbian relationships: Gender issues explored. *Violence and Victims, 12*, 173–184.

Walker, L. (1979). *The battered woman.* New York, NY: Harper & Row.

Wallace, H. (1996). *Family violence: Legal, medical, and social perspectives.* Needham Heights, MA: Allyn & Bacon.

Weiss, E. (2003). *Family and friends' guide to domestic violence: How to listen, talk and take action when someone you care about is being abused.* Volcano, CA: Volcano Press.

Weisz, A., Tolman, R. M., & Saunders, D. (2000). Assessing risk of severe domestic violence. *Journal of Interpersonal Violence, 15*, 75–90.

West, C. M. (2002). *Battered, black, and blue: An overview of violence in the lives of Black women.* New York, NY: Haworth Press.

Wetchler, J. L. (2004). A heterosexual therapist's journey toward working with same-sex couples. *Journal of Couple and Relationship Therapy, 3*, 137–145.

Wilson, M., & Brooks-Gunn, J. (2001). Health status and behaviors of unwed fathers. *Children and Youth Services Review, 23*(4–5), 377–401.

Wise, A., & Bowman, S. (1997). Comparison of beginning counselors' responses to lesbian vs. heterosexual partner abuse. *Violence and Victims, 12*, 127–134.

22

Treatment of Substance Use Disorders in LGBT Couples and Families

SANDRA C. ANDERSON

Most of the problems presented by same-sex couples are identical to those presented by heterosexual couples, and the therapist needs to distinguish when they are related to LGBT-specific challenges.[1] Similarly, LGBT clients with substance abuse problems experience many of the same issues that all substance abusing clients experience, and the therapist must distinguish between those that do and do not pertain to sexual orientation (Matthews & Selvidge, 2005). As summarized by Connolly (2004), "As therapists we must discern how much of the presenting problem stems from societal oppression and internalized homophobia versus normal and universal couple dynamics" (p. 10).

Although the majority of LGBT individuals are well adjusted and do not suffer from substance use disorders, stress resulting from the internalization of homo-, bi-, and transphobia and victimization significantly increases their risk for these disorders (Hughes & Eliason, 2002). For a detailed discussion of incidence and prevalence of substance use disorders in this population, see Anderson (2009). Although it is clear that these disorders have profound negative effects on intimate relationships (Fals-Stewart, Lam, & Kelley, 2009), the inclusion of LGBT clients in rigorous clinical trials is still quite rare (Gillespie & Blackwell, 2009).

There is consensus in the literature that LGBT substance abusers fare better when programs are designed to address their unique needs, yet only 7.4% of substance abuse treatment programs can identify a service specifically tailored to the needs of LGBT clients (Cochran, Peavy, & Robohm, 2007). Although the involvement of significant others increases the likelihood that clients will enter and complete treatment, only 27% of community-based outpatient programs in the United States actually provide couple-based treatment (Fals-Stewart & Birchler, 2001).

Outcome studies involving predominantly heterosexual clients need to be replicated with LGBT client populations. For example, numerous studies have shown that treatment duration is a reliable predictor of positive substance abuse treatment outcomes (Marsh, Cao, & Shin, 2009; Woodward, Raskin, & Blacklow, 2008), but treatment duration has never been studied with LGBT couples. Two groups of addiction experts (Miller & Carroll, 2006; National Quality Forum, 2005) have identified couple and family therapy as empirically supported practices with clients who have substance use disorders; most of these studies include only heterosexual couples.

More specifically, a growing number of studies support the use of behavioral couples therapy (BCT) and community reinforcement and family training (CRAFT) with clients who have substance use disorders. This chapter will review these two models with attention to their relevance to use with LGBT clients. In addition, the chapter will include a discussion of critical assessment

---

[1] Portions of this chapter are from Chapter 10 of *Substance Use Disorders in Lesbian, Gay, Bisexual, and Transgender Clients* by Sandra C. Anderson. Copyright © 2009 Columbia University Press. Reprinted with permission of the publisher. Portions of the case material are adapted from *Journal of Feminist Family Therapy*, 7(3/4), 87–113, 1995.

issues, other family-based treatment models that have not as yet been adequately studied, and therapeutic issues unique to the lives of LGBT couples. Finally, this chapter will address counter-transference issues and future treatment and research needs specific to work with LGBT couples with substance use disorders.

Assessment

There are a number of theoretical explanations for the heightened risk of substance use disorders among LGBT populations. To date, no evidence exists suggesting biological differences that would inordinately predispose LGBT individuals to develop dependence on alcohol or other drugs (Anderson, 1996). When they are equally predisposed, however, the added stress of unresolved "coming-out" issues and dealing with discrimination and a stigmatized social status could produce higher rates of substance abuse or dependency. Substances can be used to cope with depression, often resulting from loss and alienation from family and friends (Berg, Mimiaga, & Safren, 2008). Substances can also be used to deal with internalized homo-, bi-, and transphobia. Other risk factors include partner substance use and intimate partner violence (Fals-Stewart, O'Farrell, & Lam, 2009). In addition, Weber (2008) notes that discriminatory family laws and lack of equal social and legal rights are very stressful to same-sex couples, often resulting in their social invisibility as a couple.

Large population-based studies consistently show that women who identify as lesbian and bisexual report higher levels of alcohol, marijuana, and tobacco use and misuse than do heterosexual women (see, e.g., Drabble, Midanik, & Trocki, 2005). Rosario, Schrimshaw, and Hunter (2008) point out that one factor that may explain this greater risk is gender expression atypicality. They note that between 33% and 85% of lesbian women self-identify as butch or femme, and those with a more butch self-presentation use and misuse larger quantities of tobacco, alcohol, and marijuana over time than do femmes. Their study found that both internalized homophobia and environmental stressors accounted for their higher level of tobacco and marijuana use. Because they are more easily identified as lesbian than are femmes, butch lesbians are more likely to experience antigay prejudice and violence.

Lesbians encounter stressors that differ from the stressors faced by heterosexual women in other ways that can increase their risk for developing substance use disorders. They start drinking earlier in adolescence (Ziyadeh et al., 2007) and have a higher rate of sexual victimization than do heterosexual women (Roberts, Grindel, Patsdaughter, DeMarco, & Tarmina, 2004). Lesbians also have less decline of alcohol use with age (Hughes & Eliason, 2002), have a greater prevalence of substance use in their families of origin, and report more psychopathology in their mothers (Crothers, Haller, Benton, & Haag, 2008). Although some research suggests that bisexual individuals may have more alcohol-related problems than do lesbians, gay men, and heterosexual individuals, they are frequently deleted from studies because of low numbers (Amadio, Adam, & Buletza, 2008).

When assessing LGBT couples, the therapist should be aware that although same-sex couples are underrepresented in studies of intimate partner violence, it appears that the prevalence of intimate partner violence is equal to that found in heterosexual couples (Owen & Burke, 2004). And intimate partner violence is significantly higher among clients in treatment for substance use disorders than among the general population (Galvani, 2007). Alcohol is a common precipitant to intimate partner violence (Dube et al., 2001), and reduced alcohol consumption following treatment is associated with reductions in intimate partner violence (Hellmuth, Follansbee, Moore, & Stuart, 2008).

It should be noted that the use of couples treatment with domestically violent partners is very controversial. For a review of this issue, the reader is referred to Fals-Stewart, Kashdan, O'Farrell, and Birchler (2002) and Galvani (2007).

Treatment Models

Many LGBT clients have been strengthened by years of dealing with the stresses of homo-, bi-, and transphobia and discrimination (Anderson & Sussex, 1999). The "strengths perspective" acknowledges this strengthening by applying an empowerment focus to whatever treatment model is being utilized with individuals or couples. The strengths perspective is collaborative, builds upon the strengths of clients and their families, and respects clients' goals in relation to their substance use and misuse.

More than 25 years ago, Zweben and Pearlman (1983) noted that problem drinkers were more likely to remain in treatment and have more positive outcomes when their spouses were involved in sessions. McCrady (2006) reported the importance of the presence in treatment of a partner who is clear and direct about drinking. Predictors of poorer treatment outcome include high levels of emotional reactivity and a partner who withdraws, tolerates, or is passive about substance misuse. In recent years, BCT has emerged as the most effective couple therapy method of treating substance use disorders.

BCT

The most widely used model in substance abuse treatment programs continues to be the family disease approach, which involves separate, parallel programs for the patient and family member. Partners are offered individual or group therapy, educational groups, and referral to Al-Anon or Nar-Anon. They are urged to give up attempts to change the patients' substance use, but relationship issues are not directly addressed. On the other hand, BCT focuses on both substance use and relationship issues, with the assumption that substance abuse and relationship functioning are reciprocal. In essence, substance abuse damages relationship functioning, and severe relationship distress combined with partner attempts to control substance use can reinforce use and trigger relapse (Fals-Stewart, Klostermann, Yates, O'Farrell, & Birchler, 2005). It is assumed that partners can reward abstinence and that patients in happier relationships with better communication will have a lower risk of relapse (O'Farrell & Fals-Stewart, 2002).

In BCT, the substance-misusing patient and partner are seen together for 12–20 outpatient sessions over 5–6 months. During the first two sessions, the partners negotiate a verbal sobriety contract in which the patient states her or his intent not to drink or use drugs and the partner expresses support for the patient's efforts to stay abstinent. For patients taking a recovery-related medication (e.g., disulfiram or naltrexone), daily ingestion witnessed by the partner is part of the contract. The partner records the results of the daily contract on a calendar provided by the therapist. Both partners agree not to discuss past substance misuse or fears about future misuse at home, which can trigger conflict and relapse, but reserve these discussions for the therapy sessions. At the beginning of each session, the therapist reviews the contract calendar as well as relevant drug screens and self-help meetings attended that work week. Progress is rewarded verbally at each session (O'Farrell & Fals-Stewart, 2006).

In addition to the sobriety contract are behavioral assignments used to teach such effective communication skills as active listening and expressing feelings directly. Partners are encouraged to acknowledge positive behaviors and engage in shared recreational activities. For example, each partner is asked to address one pleasing behavior performed by the other each day and both are encouraged to surprise each other by doing something special to show their caring. They must also plan an activity that involves both, either by themselves or with their children or other adults. Finally, at the end of their sessions, each couple completes a continuing recovery plan that specifies continuing activities to support abstinence as well as how to cope with a relapse (Fals-Stewart, Birchler, & Kelley, 2006; O'Farrell & Fals-Stewart, 2002). For a comprehensive guidebook and session-by-session BCT treatment manual, the reader is referred to O'Farrell and Fals-Stewart (2006).

As mentioned, BCT is currently the family-centered model with the strongest research support for effectiveness with substance use disorders. Numerous randomized clinical trials have demonstrated that among substance-abusing patients and their partners, those who received BCT reported significantly fewer days of substance use, longer periods of abstinence, fewer arrests, lower levels of intimate partner violence, and higher relationship satisfaction at follow-up than do patients receiving treatment-as-usual or a partner-involved attention control intervention (Fals-Stewart, O'Farrell, Birchler, Cordova, & Kelley, 2005). When compared with clients who get only individual substance abuse counseling, BCT patients are less likely to relapse, are more compliant with recovery-related medications, and report more improvement in their children's functioning. These positive findings have involved substance-abusing heterosexual men and their partners (Fals-Stewart et al., 2002; O'Farrell & Fals-Stewart, 2002; Rotunda, O'Farrell, Murphy, & Babey, 2008), children of heterosexual couples (Kelley & Fals-Stewart, 2002, 2007; Lam, Fals-Stewart, & Kelley, 2008, 2009), and heterosexual substance-abusing women and their partners (Fals-Stewart et al., 2006; McCrady, Epstein, Cook, Jensen, & Hildebrandt, 2009; Winters, Fals-Stewart, O'Farrell, Birchler, & Kelley, 2002).

Overall, it can be concluded that BCT shows better outcomes than do individual-based treatment for heterosexual couples seeking treatment for substance use disorders. A recent meta-analysis of 12 well-controlled randomized trials of BCT found it superior to individual treatments on all three outcome domains: frequency of use, consequences of use, and relationship satisfaction (Powers, Vedel, & Emmelkamp, 2008). Other promising uses of BCT include improving compliance with such medications as methadone (Fals-Stewart, O'Farrell, & Birchler, 2001) and disulfiram for alcoholic patients (O'Farrell, Choquette, & Cutter, 1998).

Lesbian and Gay Couples

The most rigorous trial of BCT with these groups to date was conducted by Fals-Stewart, O'Farrell, et al. (2009). Lesbian ($n = 48$) and gay ($n = 52$) patients with alcohol use disorder and their non-substance-abusing partners were randomly assigned to BCT plus individual treatment or individual treatment only. Treatment was provided by self-identified lesbian and gay therapists. For both lesbian and gay patients, those who received BCT had a significantly lower percentage of heavy drinking days and higher levels of relationship adjustment in the year after treatment than did those who received individual treatment only. These findings are consistent with those of BCT with heterosexual couples, making the relative lack of couple-based treatment in agencies even more surprising. According to O'Farrell and Fals-Stewart (2006): "With by far the largest number of studies supporting its effectiveness . . . BCT is well known among substance abuse researchers. Unfortunately, BCT is virtually unknown and unused by practitioners" (p. vii).

CRAFT

Another effective family-based model is CRAFT, which involves therapists teaching significant others behavioral techniques that allow them to give nonantagonistic feedback to the substance abuser. Family members learn to withhold reinforcement for substance-using behavior and increase positive reinforcement for clean and sober behavior. Miller, Meyers, and Tonigan (1999) found that significant others assigned to CRAFT were much more successful in having their loved one enter alcohol treatment (64%) than were those assigned to the Johnson Institute Intervention (30%) or Al-Anon (13%). With illicit substance-abusing populations, Meyers, Miller, Hill, and Tonigan (1999) found that 74% of individuals trained in CRAFT methods were successful in engaging the resistant individual in treatment. In addition, all concerned family members showed significant reduction in their own anger, depression, anxiety, and physical symptoms. In summary, CRAFT is a relatively inexpensive outpatient treatment model that is consistently superior to other approaches in engaging in treatment resistant individuals with substance use disorders (J. E. Smith, Meyers, & Miller, 2001). Studies of effectiveness of CRAFT with LGBT couples may show similar outcomes.

Family Therapy

Family therapy can be invaluable in helping members of the current family, family of origin, and family of choice understand and support the client's recovery. Unfortunately, the families of LGBT clients are often rendered invisible by clinicians, and "the full integration of family therapy into standard substance abuse treatment is still relatively rare" (CSAT, 2004, p. xvii). In spite of this, substance abuse treatment and family therapy can be integrated to increase effectiveness, and a growing body of data is demonstrating the cost-benefits of doing so. Such inclusion requires an integrated model, a large number of which have been discussed in the literature (McCrady, 2006; McIntyre, 2004).

The stages-of-change model (Prochaska & DiClemente, 1992) can be used to assess the family's readiness to change and used as a framework for treatment. Not every family member will necessarily be at the same stage of change, however, so a family's readiness needs to be carefully evaluated. Van Wormer and Davis (2003) have reviewed these stages as they apply to families, but again, their review is not specific to LGBT families.

There are now convincing data that family therapy is effective for adolescents as well as adults with substance use disorders, and family intervention is associated with higher rates of treatment retention than is treatment without family involvement (Rowe & Liddle, 2003; Szapocznik & Williams, 2000; Waldron & Selsnick, 1998). When family members understand their role in the substance abuse and are willing to support recovery, the likelihood of long-term recovery improves (CSAT, 2004). According to McCrady (2006), successful family treatment can be predicted by the absence of substance problems in other family members, a more severe substance abuse problem in the identified client, some degree of social and relationship stability, and receptivity to treatment after a crisis. McCrady notes that there is strong empirical support for focusing on improving daily family interactions, increasing positive exchanges, and teaching constructive communication and problem solving.

In adolescents, as with adults, family therapy is strongly associated with better retention and treatment outcomes (D. C. Smith & Hall, 2008). Burkstein (2000) found family interventions empirically well supported for youth with a substance use disorder. And for adolescents with co-occurring disorders (e.g., substance use and conduct disorder), family therapy is among the most effective interventions (Waldron, 1997).

As mentioned, a number of integrated models of family therapy have been described in the literature. Unfortunately, there are still many unanswered questions about their utility. As summarized by CSAT (2004):

> At present, research cannot guide treatment providers about the best specific matches between family therapy and particular family systems or substances of abuse. Research to date suggests that certain family therapy approaches can be effective, but no one approach has been shown to be more effective than others. (p. 16)

It follows that research is also insufficient to suggest the efficacy of any one model of family therapy over another for use with LGBT families. Lev (2004) has discussed the emergence stages of family members of gender-variant people but notes that "clinically, little guidance is available on how to work with partners, spouses, children, and other family members" (p. 271).

It is clear, however, that many LGBT clients have unresolved issues with their families of origin, often related to their sexual orientation or gender identity. It is important to explore any unresolved family issues because they can act as emotional triggers to relapse. In some cases, clients may be hiding their sexual orientation, and treatment may or may not involve coming out to the family of origin. In other cases, the family may experience guilt about the client's homosexuality and/or substance abuse or blame each for the other's existence (Senreich & Vairo, 2004). Many clients may be reluctant to include family-of-origin members in therapy because they fear rejection and an increase in their own anxiety.

When LGBT clients do agree to engage in family-of-origin therapy, it can be a very powerful experience for them. Juhnke and Hagedorn (2006) point out that "even minute insights from one's family of origin can create major self-perception shifts" (p. 280). Bowen (1978), the originator of family systems theory, posited that substance abuse is one way that individuals and families attempt to manage anxiety. Bowen noted that emotional responses are passed down from one generation to another, and that clients can be helped to become more differentiated and less enmeshed in the family emotional system.

Family Systems Model With LGBT Clients

Alcohol treatment agencies have been reluctant to adopt family systems models, even though a number of unpublished studies have found them to be effective (Flynn, 2008). These models can integrate a number of practice theories and perspectives with knowledge of substance use disorders. For example, the author (Anderson, 1995) uses a model of couple therapy with lesbian, gay, and bisexual clients that is strengths-based and utilizes techniques from motivational interviewing, cognitive-behavioral therapy, and family systems therapy. The model reflects the integration of my own experience and the adapted models of Wetchler, McCollum, Nelson, Trepper, and Lewis (1993) and Bepko (1989). An assumption of the model is that relationship patterns are repeated multigenerationally and that current relationships play a role in maintaining substance abuse. Thus, treatment focuses on both historical and present family processes (Wetchler et al., 1993). The model has four stages.

Stage I

Stage I focuses on developing a collaborative therapeutic alliance and involves active questioning about substance use history and relationship issues. An attempt is made to determine whether substance abuse is central to the couple's problems or concurrent with or secondary to an underlying psychiatric disorder. There is exploration of what solutions have been attempted by the couple and discussion of how typical responses to drug abuse, usually controlling or protective behaviors, can contribute to the maintenance of the problem. Feelings of anger, depression, and anxiety are normalized. Education about substance abuse and dependency is provided if appropriate. The focus is on coping skills that are working, and severe relationship problems are not addressed until abstinence is well established. In the second and third sessions, a multigenerational family genogram is completed for each partner. In this process the clients tell their stories about family emotional relationships, substance abuse, physical and sexual abuse, family rituals, family strengths, and other important relationships. Since some clients may need to deal initially with issues around their sexual orientation, it is important to explore both internalized heterosexism and other sources of stress. The therapist validates the couple's relationship, recognizes the oppression they face, and actively helps them deal with it (Fassinger, 1991).

When clients are substance dependent (i.e., showing evidence of tolerance, withdrawal symptoms, or a pattern of compulsive use), abstinence is the most appropriate goal. Many substance-dependent clients are not capable of doing this immediately, however, and need ongoing therapeutic support. I do not refuse to work with couples when one or both are having trouble abstaining, but if there are numerous relapses without increasing intervals of sobriety between episodes, clients are encouraged to consider an intensive outpatient or residential treatment program.

The first stage of treatment involves encouraging clients to avoid situations that trigger drug use and develop activities that reinforce abstinence and replace time spent in drug use. Involvement in some type of sobriety support group is usually helpful in achieving and maintaining abstinence. As clients begin the shift to a more sober lifestyle, their defenses are supported and redirected instead of interpreted and confronted, in order to keep anxiety and the subsequent risk of using to a minimum.

Stage II

Stage II focuses on challenging behaviors and expanding alternatives. This stage usually begins when clients have less conscious conflict about abstinence, are taking responsibility for their own drug use behavior, and are beginning to resolve grief around losses resulting from drugs and the loss of drugs themselves. Focus is on the improvement of communication and conflict resolution skills and making explicit the connection between present and past family patterns (Wetchler et al., 1993). Clients may need to grieve the loss of "heterosexual privilege" in the family of origin and learn ways to challenge parental homophobia (Murphy, 1989). Clients often need to change patterns of underfunctioning and overfunctioning that serve to maintain substance abuse problems (Bepko, 1989). The therapist needs to assess the adaptive consequences of the substance abuse for the relationship, with the objective of attaining relationship goals without the use of drugs. It is a mistake to assume, however, that shifting the system will eliminate the need for drugs. As noted by Bepko: "The relationship between the addict and the drug needs to be disrupted as well. Systemic change is a necessary, but not sufficient, response to an addiction" (p. 407).

Stage III

Stage III focuses on consolidating change. In this phase of treatment clients become more aware of the early warnings of relapse and of methods of coping with potential problems (Wetchler et al., 1993). Because the need for abstinence has been internalized, more difficult relationship problems, which often elicit anxiety, may now be addressed. This phase of treatment continues to focus on the needs of clients as individuals as well as on the needs of the relationship.

Stage IV

Stage IV focuses on maximizing sustained change by involvement in longer term Bowen-based family systems interventions. Although some couples choose to terminate therapy at the end of Stage III, most wish to strengthen their relationship by focusing on unresolved family-of-origin issues. As Freeman (1992) notes, unresolved loss issues with the family of origin often lead to relationship problems in adulthood because it is difficult to give a partner what has not been received from one's original family. Clients' stories about their unmet needs in their families of origin are replicated in some form in their current relationships. In order to rewrite their own stories, they must hear their parents' stories and observe their parents' anxiety without needing to fix, control, or distance from them. When doing this is mastered, they will be less anxious and needy in their current relationships and much less likely to relapse into drug use in times of stress.

For those clients who have not come out to their family, this phase of therapy often involves continued discussion of the implications of secrecy and disclosure, the recognition of different timetables for coming out, and preparation for disclosure. The risks involved in coming out should never be underestimated, and the dynamics of the process vary by age, race, ethnicity, social class, and geography (Anderson, 2001). Some well-differentiated clients will choose not to come out to their families (Anderson & Holliday, 2004), and their wisdom in this decision needs to be respected. Even in these cases, however, the therapist should avoid comments that could serve to solidify distance from family and preclude connections that could be important to long-term recovery.

When clients are out to their parents and less reactive to them, it is my preference to invite parents in for at least one session during the last stage of treatment. The purpose of such sessions is to challenge the family mythology by asking the parents to tell stories about their lives. As Freeman (1992) notes, these stories inform adult children about how events shaped their parents' responses to them and can be used as positive legacies. The client observes but does not participate, and the session is videotaped for future viewing and as a gift to subsequent generations. The rationale for the client's silence in the interview is based on Freeman's observations that adult children often have emotional reactions to their parents' sad stories, and the parents worry about these reactions. The therapist is more likely to be able to ask less reactive questions, stay calm, and find aspects of the story that emphasize survival, connections, and competence. In telling their stories, parents are encouraged to talk about their personal losses and loss of expectations for their child. In some instances parents can be helped to revise their self-blaming stories into more empowering ones. Such sessions are usually preceded and followed by Bowen-based visits home by each client to reposition with the family and begin to broaden the story about parents and siblings. Attention is given to the grieving of family-of-origin losses and finding a way, even if imperfect, to stay connected to family.

Case Example: Family Systems Model

Sarah, a 36-year-old attorney, and Cate, a 34-year-old medical illustrator, were referred by their internist because of Cate's alcohol problem and couple communication problems, both of which had worsened over the course of the couple's 2-year relationship. A genogram of each woman began the process of understanding how current problems were related to past losses.

Sarah stated that she no longer felt close to Cate, that Cate drank excessively and was rarely there for her. Sarah periodically tried to control Cate's drinking but typically just withdrew. She described a distant relationship with her older sister and a very tense relationship with her 68-year-old mother, whom she described as extremely quiet, never initiating conversations or expressing feelings. She described her father as having been uninvolved with the family. He had died unexpectedly 6 years earlier, and his death had never been discussed. Sarah stated that she was angry about having always been invisible to both parents.

Cate described a pattern of alcohol use that had become of increasing concern to her over the past 10 years. In the past 2 years she had noticed increased tolerance and mild withdrawal symptoms on Mondays. She had made several unsuccessful attempts to control her drinking, avoided social activities that were alcohol free, and recognized that her drinking was destroying her relationship with Sarah. Cate viewed her mother as an angry, anxious, cold woman with whom she had never connected, whereas she described her father as an alcoholic who was physically abusive to her mother. She had a distant relationship with two older brothers, both alcoholic.

Stage I of our work together focused on developing activities that would substitute for the time Cate spent drinking and respectfully challenging her denial about the consequences of her drinking. Cate was supported in her attempts to avoid going to bars to drink with friends and in her participation in such positive activities as yoga and joining a lesbian self-help group. The couple were advised to avoid all anxiety-provoking situations. Both talked at length about the hurt they experienced from not having their relationship taken seriously by relatives.

In Stage II of our work, it became clearer that Sarah and Cate had similar types of unfinished business with their original families. Both had reactively distanced from their families and looked to the relationship to make up for earlier losses and provide feelings of being safe and special. Although both complained of too much distance in the relationship, their tendency to alternate pursuing and distancing behaviors indicated that they both needed the distance to stay safe.

In the first few months of treatment, Cate had two brief relapses, which were framed as opportunities to learn more about herself and her grief around the loss of alcohol. As she began to take more responsibility for her drinking behavior, our work began to focus more on the connections between the current relationship, alcohol problems, and families of origin. I began to talk about how the distance they felt in their relationship was more about the sadness and anxiety each brought into the relationship than about what the other was doing. As we moved toward exploring the impact of unfinished business on their current needs for distance and on Cate's use of alcohol, I continued to focus my questions on self issues (Freeman, 1992). I asked, for example: What do you want from your partner that you feel you did not get from your original family? What gets stirred up in you (how do you explain it to yourself) when your partner is not there for you? What losses does this remind you of? How do you take care of yourself when you feel you are not good enough? What is different about you when your needs are met? How do you teach your partner what you need when you feel sad and alone? What is going on with you when you need your partner to be different? If you changed the way you perceived your partner, how would you have to be different in the relationship?

As we moved into Stage III of our work, Cate had been abstinent for 4 months and had a sound understanding of early warning signs of relapse. She had very effective ways of dealing with anxiety and craving and was an active member of her lesbian Alcoholics Anonymous group. In this stage, she spent a great deal of time discussing chronic feelings of self-hatred and shame about being a lesbian. I continued to validate their lifestyle as well as their legitimate concerns around coming-out issues. As alcohol was removed as a distancing issue, anxiety in the relationship temporarily increased, and both expressed new concerns about the future of their relationship. It was at this point that I began to question and gently challenge their stories about their original families. I asked each what the loss would be to them of changing their story about their mother or father. What would they each lose by giving up their old issues with their parents? How would they go about discovering new stories about their families?

Stage IV of our work, which began 6 months after Cate achieved sobriety, focused on active repositioning with the families of origin. I continued to ask questions that introduced doubt into their theories about their parents and wondered how their parents' losses, what they did not get, affected their parenting. As Sarah and Cate developed more curiosity about their own histories, each decided on different methods of repositioning with her parents. Two examples of their initial efforts will be described.

Sarah's mother was planning a visit from the East Coast and was invited for an interview. Sarah agreed to observe without participating, and the session was videotaped. Her mother's story was one of profound loss and sadness. She was quite young when her family lost everything in the Great Depression, and her father subsequently developed a serious drinking problem. As an only child, she felt responsible for taking care of her mother's fairly constant sadness. She described herself as a quiet, good child who tried to stay out of the way of her parents' conflicts. She said that she had only wanted Sarah and her sister to have everything she did not have. She did not want to interfere with their lives or burden them in any way. She viewed her distancing from them as protecting them from her sadness. Sarah commented in the next session that she had reviewed the videotape, and it was a great relief to realize that her mother's parenting of her was about her mother's own losses and not about lack of love for her.

Cate chose to initiate repositioning with her father through letters and phone calls. She worked several weeks on a letter in which she came out to him and expressed curiosity about his family. Over the course of several letters, her father acknowledged her lesbianism (although he disapproved) and thanked her for telling him. For the first time, he began to tell her his own story. He carried a great deal of shame throughout his life for being born out of wedlock to an alcoholic mother in Germany. As a small child he was abandoned a number of times; he was also abused by his stepfather. He left Nazi Germany and came to New York alone at age 12, surviving but struggling his whole life with loneliness, depression, and alcoholism. As Cate began to let her father back into her life, she shared with him her sadness about not having a relationship with him for so many years. She also began to make phone calls to her brothers, came out to them, and had the first visit from her mother without her father. The visit went well, and she began to gradually change her story about her mother as well.

As Sarah and Cate made peace with their original family losses, they were able to change their stories about themselves and each other. They no longer needed to use distance and alcohol to stay safe with each other or to deal with the stresses related to being lesbian in this society.

Contraindications

There are a few instances in which family therapy is contraindicated, the major one being a history of significant domestic violence. McCrady (2006) also notes that some family interactions are so "toxic" that family therapy is inappropriate. In her view, toxic families may

> (1) [c]ommunicate in such cruel and destructive ways that involving them in therapy will increase the user's negative experience; (2) be unable to harness their hostility enough to be able to support the user's efforts to change; (3) be largely unresponsive to the therapist's interventions to teach constructive communication skills; or (4) have significant alcohol or drug problems themselves that they do not want to change. (pp. 178–179)

Therapeutic Issues

Therapeutic issues relevant to practice with LGBT individuals include coming out; managing violence; dealing with internalized homo-, bi-, and transphobia; managing co-occurring disorders and HIV disease; addressing family-of-origin issues; and dealing with parenting issues. Couples and families deal with all these therapeutic issues as well as some that are more specific to relationships. These issues must be addressed when treating LGBT clients with substance use disorders because they often act as triggers for substance abuse. Clinicians need to assess how relationships with families of origin, partners, and families of choice contribute to substance abuse problems and/or serve as resources in supporting recovery.

Clinicians may become involved with couples during a personal transition, such as when a spouse comes out as lesbian, gay, bisexual, or transgender. This often, but not always, leads to the dissolution of the marriage. In some cases, these clients knew their gender orientation before entering the marriage; in others, they considered themselves heterosexual before marriage. The straight spouse is usually shocked and angry about the disclosure, feeling confused and betrayed. When a partner is coming out as transsexual, the nontranssexual partner must reexamine his or her own sexuality and make decisions about continuing as an intimate or non-intimate partner or dissolving the relationship (Brown & Rounsley, 1996). These situations are even more difficult to resolve when substance abuse is involved.

When working with lesbian and gay couples presenting with a substance use disorder, it is important that the clinician not use heterosexual relationship models. There is often more role flexibility in gay and lesbian relationships; for example, monogamy is not always the norm in gay relationships (Senreich & Vairo, 2004). The majority of lesbian couples prefer monogamy, however, and an affair is often the crisis event that brings lesbian couples into therapy. Lesbian and gay couples also differ from heterosexual ones in that they must deal with homophobia and heterosexism, issues around coming out, and complicated family-of-origin and family-of-choice issues. Gay men report a significantly higher level of internalized homophobia than do lesbians (Span & Derby, 2009). Partners may differ on how "out" they are to their families of origin and are frequently conflicted around loyalty to their partners and families. These discrepancies can result in distancing from partners or cutting off from families of origin. Finally, it is not unusual for gay and lesbian couples to include former lovers in their current social networks. Although these patterns of behavior differ from those of heterosexual couples, such behavior should not be viewed as pathological (Bepko & Johnson, 2000).

In working with gay male couples, the clinician must appreciate their lack of legal recognition and role models as well as their male-gender acculturation that can make male-to-male intimacy difficult (Tunnell & Greenan, 2004). Because of their male socialization, gay men may have trouble showing emotional vulnerability to other men and may attempt to avoid direct conflict. Tunnell and Greenan (2004) suggest that substance abuse "can be reframed by the therapist as [a way] of disengaging from the partner in order to avoid open conflict through power struggles" (p. 19). In spite of these dynamics observed in some couples seen in clinical settings, Green, Bettinger, and Zacks (1996) found that the gay couples in their sample had higher ratings of couple cohesion than did the heterosexual couples.

In working with lesbian couples struggling with substance abuse, it is important to recognize that problems with closeness are much greater when there is a history of trauma or addiction (Bepko & Johnson, 2000). Further, many lesbian partners are at different life-cycle stages, have different racial and ethnic identifications, and vary greatly in financial status. These imbalances in professional status and power often cause considerable stress and can lead to affairs and substance misuse. In spite of these potential difficulties, high levels of intimacy are found in many lesbian relationships (Green, Bettinger, & Zacks, 1996), and parental disapproval does not appear to negatively affect these relationships (LaSala, 2005).

In both gay and lesbian couples, the term *enabler* has been used to describe the ways nonaddicted partners perpetuate substance abuse by removing consequences of the abuse or attempting to control the addicted person's behavior. It should be pointed out that this behavior is also observed in heterosexual couples. Rotunda, West, and O'Farrell (2004) found that heterosexual partners took over chores for alcoholic clients, drank or used other drugs with them, and lied or made excuses to others to cover for them. As Zelvin (2004) points out, nonaddicted partners may also deny their partner's substance abuse, minimize its extent, and deny their own problems. As a result, these nonaddicted partners gradually develop an unnaturally high tolerance for unacceptable behavior.

Initially, this enabling behavior of partners was labeled by those in the chemical dependency field as *codependency*, a concept that has since been applied to all kinds of families. Codependency is described as a primary disease present in every member of an addictive family, often worse than the substance dependence itself. Although men can theoretically be codependent, the literature refers almost exclusively to women as having the disease. The origins are thought to be found in early childhood, at which time the individual learns a tendency to enter into addictive relationships. The codependency movement does, in fact, pathologize behaviors associated with female qualities and overlook the significance of oppressive social and political structures in shaping the personalities of women. Females are overtly and covertly trained in excessive caretaking of others and taught to deny their own well-being to feel connected with others. Van Wormer and Davis (2006) suggest that instead of using the pejorative term *codependent*, "the more positive term *survivor* be applied to women (and men) who have done whatever is necessary to protect themselves and their families from the consequences of their partners' drinking and drug use" (pp. 293–294). For a more extensive critique of the concept of codependency, the reader is referred to Anderson (1994).

Clients who are in bisexual relationships (i.e., those in which at least one of the individuals is bisexual) deal with all the therapeutic issues gay and lesbian couples face as well as some unique ones. Although there is no one model for a successful bisexual relationship, there must be agreement between partners about what will be exclusive to the primary relationship and what, if anything, will occur with other relationships. Because many bisexual men engage in unprotected sex with both men and women, the threat of HIV/AIDS and other sexually transmitted diseases is a major issue. Given that substance use is often involved in this unprotected sex, the clients' sexual behavior needs to be openly acknowledged in therapy. Once the bisexual couple have negotiated some degree of sexual "openness," the partners must face issues of jealousy, boundaries, and communicating needs to each other (McLean, 2004). Although it can be assumed that many of these therapeutic issues are experienced by transgender couples who are lesbian, gay, or bisexual, there are no empirical data to confirm this is so.

In summary, LGBT couples and families with substance abuse problems present an array of therapeutic issues in addition to those presented by individuals. The clinician always needs to assess the degree of internalized homo-, bi-, and transphobia in each partner, since a poor sense of self can be related to problems with intimacy (LaSala, 2001). When the presenting problems result from the projection onto partners of unresolved family-of origin-issues, differentiation is increased by achieving autonomy from the family of origin while also maintaining connections with family members (Bowen, 1978). The Bowen approach with gay and lesbian couples involves handling conflicts around distance regulation, linking couple and family-of-origin functioning, and encouraging extended family work (Bepko & Johnson, 2000). Again, these issues are most productively addressed after the attainment of sobriety.

Heterosexist Attitudes and Countertransference Issues

Heterosexist bias, reflections of a belief system in which heterosexuality is seen as superior to and/or more natural than homosexuality, is common among mental health providers (Anderson & Holliday, 2007; Liddle, 1999; Long & Lindsey, 2004; Mohr, Israel, & Sedlacek, 2001) and substance abuse counselors (Eliason, 2000). Eliason (2000) found that substance abuse counselors lacked critical information about lesbians' and gay men's experiences and that although many counselors were accepting, a large percentage were ambivalent or negative. They also found that these counselors expressed the greatest negativity about transgender clients and also knew the least about this group. Matthews and Selvidge (2005) found that "at best, addiction counselors engage in affirmative behavior with LGB clients only some of the time" (p. 87), and Cochran, Peavy, and Cauce (2007) found that substance abuse practitioners' negative biases regarding LGBT individuals were stronger for heterosexual counselors and for those with few LGBT friends. Buloff and Osterman (1995) note that the therapist's unexamined heterosexism is potentially more damaging to clients than overt prejudice.

In addition to dealing with their own homo-, bi-, and transphobia, therapists must recognize and work through countertransference reactions that could negatively affect their clients. Lesbian, gay, bisexual, and transgender therapists are just as susceptible as straight therapists to countertransference issues and homo-, bi-, and transphobia, and some countertransference issues might have a greater effect on lesbian and gay therapists than on heterosexual therapists (Milton, Coyle, & Legg, 2005). For example, lesbian and gay therapists may be in more danger of colluding with unhealthy subculture issues or overidentifying with their lesbian and gay clients. Similar countertransference issues arise when any therapist treats members of groups to which the therapist belongs. Therapists who are in recovery from substance dependence must also be concerned about overidentifying with clients with substance use disorders (Anderson &

Wiemer, 1992). Overidentification can lead to inflexibility, mutual blind spots, and an overinvestment in outcome. There is no evidence that recovering counselors produce any better (or worse) outcomes when compared with counselors not in personal recovery (McLellan, Woody, Luborsky, & Goehl, 1988).

Conclusions and Future Practice and Research Needs

It is now clear that involving the family in the patient's treatment is an effective way to promote recovery from substance use disorders, and families should be included in the assessment and treatment processes (McCrady et al., 2009; O'Farrell, Murphy, Alter, & Fals-Stewart, 2007). At present, both CRAFT and BCT have significant empirical support. To date, BCT is positively associated with reductions in substance use, improvements in relationship adjustment, reductions in intimate partner violence, and fewer behavioral problems of the couples' children (Fals-Stewart, O'Farrell, et al., 2005). Overall, BCT shows better outcomes than does individual treatment for couples seeking help for substance use disorders (Powers et al., 2008). The use of BCT with gay and lesbian couples with alcohol use disorders is promising, consistent with what has been observed with heterosexual couples (Fals-Stewart, O'Farrell, et al., 2009).

In the future, the efficacy of BCT for couples in which both partners misuse psychoactive substances needs to be tested (Powers et al., 2008). In addition, more attention needs to be given to sustaining gains after BCT by adding posttreatment relapse prevention sessions (Fals-Stewart, et al., 2006). Finally, more clinical trials comparing BCT to other promising interventions are greatly needed. This is a difficult challenge, since BCT and other family-based treatments are quite underutilized in substance abuse treatment programs (Carroll & Rounsaville, 2006; Fals-Stewart & Birchler, 2001). As noted by Lambert, Garfield, and Bergin (2003), only a limited number of treatment approaches have been adequately studied.

Cochran and Cauce (2006) point out that providing effective treatment for LGBT substance abusers may require administrative and staff adjustments in treatment agencies. For example, inclusive language needs to be used in all forms and brochures, contacts must be established within the LGBT community, and specialized programs provided to LGBT clients. Since lesbian, gay, and bisexual counselors are considered more affirmative than heterosexual counselors, efforts to hire more LGBT counselors openly should be accelerated (Matthews & Selvidge, 2005).

There is a critical need for family-based therapy to merge with substance abuse treatment. Such a merger will require policy changes in insurance reimbursement as well as a considerable investment in staff training and supervision. The most significant question related to LGBT clients with substance use disorders is whether treatment models that have demonstrated effectiveness with heterosexual clients will be as effective with LGBT individuals without culturally appropriate modifications. To date, the field has not developed adequate LGBT-specific practice guidelines for substance abuse treatment services, and it remains to be determined whether LGBT-specific treatment is more effective than mainstream treatment for these clients. When we find answers to these questions, we must still face the large gap between what research shows to be effective and what is actually practiced in substance abuse treatment settings. According to Miller and Carroll (2006):

> What is different now from even 20 years ago is that scientific research has revealed a great deal about the nature of drug problems and how they can be prevented and treated. Thousands of new reports appear each year in the scientific literature, so many that it is impossible for any one person to digest them all. That's the good news. The bad news is that very little of this science has found its way into practice. (p. xi)

References

Amadio, D. M., Adam, T., & Buletza, K. (2008). A clinical comparison of lesbian and heterosexual women in a psychiatric outpatient clinic. *Journal of Gay & Lesbian Social Services*, *20*(4), 315–327.

Anderson, S. C. (1994). A critical analysis of the concept of codependency. *Social Work*, *39*(6), 677–685.

Anderson, S. C. (1995). Addressing heterosexist bias in the treatment of lesbian couples with chemical dependency. *Journal of Feminist Family Therapy*, *7*(3/4), 87–113.

Anderson, S. C. (1996). Substance abuse and dependency in gay men and lesbians. *Journal of Gay & Lesbian Social Services*, *5*(1), 59–76.

Anderson, S. C. (2001). Lesbians and bisexual women: Relevant policy and practice issues. In K. J. Peterson & A. Lieberman (Eds.), *Building on women's strengths: A social work agenda for the twenty-first century* (pp. 219–252). New York, NY: Haworth Press.

Anderson, S. C. (2009). *Substance use disorders in lesbian, gay, bisexual, and transgender clients*. New York, NY: Columbia University Press.

Anderson, S. C., & Holliday, M. (2004). Normative passing in the lesbian community: An exploratory study. *Journal of Gay & Lesbian Social Services*, *17*(3), 25–38.

Anderson, S. C., & Holliday, M. (2007). How heterosexism plagues practitioners in services for lesbians and their families: An exploratory study. *Journal of Gay and Lesbian Social Services*, *19*(2), 81–100.

Anderson, S. C., & Sussex, B. (1999). Resilience in lesbians: An exploratory study. In J. Laird (Ed.), *Lesbians and lesbian families* (pp. 305–329). New York, NY: Columbia University Press.

Anderson, S. C., & Wiemer, L. E. (1992). Administrators' beliefs about the relative competence of recovering and nonrecovering chemical dependency counselors. *Families in Society: Journal of Contemporary Human Services*, *73*(10), 596–603.

Bepko, C. (1989). Disorders of power: Women and addiction in the family. In M. McGoldrick, C. M. Anderson, & F. Walsh (Eds.), *Women in families* (pp. 406–426). New York, NY: Norton.

Bepko, C., & Johnson, T. (2000). Gay and lesbian couples therapy: Perspectives for the contemporary family therapist. *Journal of Marital and Family Therapy*, *26*(4), 409–419.

Berg, M. B., Mimiaga, M. I., & Safren, S. A. (2008). Mental health concerns of gay and bisexual men seeking mental health services. *Journal of Homosexuality*, *54*(3), 293–306.

Bowen, M. (1978). *Family therapy in clinical practice*. New York, NY: Aronson.

Brown, M. L., & Rounsley, C. A. (1996). *True selves: Understanding transsexualism for families, friends, coworkers, and helping professionals*. San Francisco, CA: Jossey-Bass.

Buloff, B., & Osterman, M. (1995). Queer reflections: Mirroring and the lesbian experience of self. In J. M. Glassgold & S. Iasenza (Eds.), *Lesbians and psychoanalysis: Revolutions in theory* (pp. 93–106). New York, NY: Free Press.

Burkstein, O. G. (2000). Disruptive behavior disorders and substance use disorders in adolescents. *Journal of Psychoactive Drugs*, *32*(1), 67–79.

Carroll, K. M., & Rounsaville, B. J. (2006). Behavioral therapies. In W. R. Miller & K. M. Carroll (Eds.), *Rethinking substance abuse* (pp. 223–239). New York, NY: Guilford Press.

Center for Substance Abuse Treatment (CSAT). (2004). *Substance abuse treatment and family therapy: Treatment improvement protocol (TIP) 39* (DHHS Pub. No. [SMA] 06-4219). Rockville, MD: Substance Abuse and Mental Health Services Administration.

Cochran, B. N., & Cauce, A. M. (2006). Characteristics of lesbian, gay, bisexual, and transgender individuals entering substance abuse treatment. *Journal of Substance Abuse Treatment*, *30*, 135–146.

Cochran, B. N., Peavy, K. M., & Cauce, A. M. (2007). Substance abuse treatment providers' explicit and implicit attitudes regarding sexual minorities. *Journal of Homosexuality*, *52*(3), 181–207.

Cochran, B. N., Peavy, K. M., & Robohm, J. S. (2007). Do specialized services exist for LGBT individuals seeking treatment for substance misuse? A study of available treatment programs. *Substance Use and Misuse*, *42*, 161–176.

Connolly, C. M. (2004). Clinical issues with same-sex couples: A review of the literature. *Journal of Couple and Relationship Therapy*, *3*(2/3), 3–12.

Crothers, L., Haller, E., Benton, C., & Haag, S. (2008). A clinical comparison of lesbian and heterosexual women in a psychiatric outpatient clinic. *Journal of Homosexuality*, *54*(3), 280–292.

Drabble, L., Midanik, L. T., & Trocki, K. (2005). Reports of alcohol consumption and alcohol-related problems among homosexual, bisexual, and heterosexual respondents: Results from the 2000 National Alcohol Survey. *Journal of Studies on Alcohol*, *66*, 111–120.

Dube, S., Anda, R. F., Felitti, V. J., Croft, J. B., Edwards, V. J., & Giles, W. H. (2001). Growing up with parental alcohol abuse: Exposure to childhood abuse, neglect, and household dysfunction. *Child Abuse and Neglect*, 25, 1627–1640.

Eliason, M. J. (2000). Substance abuse counselors' attitudes regarding lesbian, gay, bisexual, and transgender clients. *Journal of Substance Abuse*, 12, 311–328.

Fals-Stewart, W., & Birchler, G. R. (2001). A national survey of the use of couples therapy in substance abuse treatment. *Journal of Substance Abuse*, 20(40), 277–283.

Fals-Stewart, W., Birchler, G. R., & Kelley, M. L. (2006). Learning sobriety together: A randomized clinical trial examining behavioral couples therapy with alcoholic female patients. *Journal of Consulting and Clinical Psychology*, 74(3), 579–591.

Fals-Stewart, W., Kashdan, T. B., O'Farrell, T. J., & Birchler, G. R. (2002). Behavioral couples therapy for drug-abusing patients: Effects on partner violence. *Journal of Substance Abuse Treatment*, 22, 87–96.

Fals-Stewart, W., Klosterman, K., Yates, B. T., O'Farrell, T. J., & Birchler, G. R. (2005). Brief relationship therapy for alcoholism: A randomized clinical trial examining clinical efficacy and cost-effectiveness. *Psychology of Addictive Behaviors*, 19(4), 363–371.

Fals-Stewart, W., Lam, W., & Kelley, M. L. (2009). Learning sobriety together: Behavioral couples therapy for alcoholism and drug abuse. *Journal of Family Therapy*, 31, 115–125.

Fals-Stewart, W., O'Farrell, T. J., & Birchler, G. R. (2001). Behavioral couples therapy for male methadone maintenance patients: Effects on drug-using behavior and relationship adjustment. *Behavior Therapy*, 32, 391–411.

Fals-Stewart, W., O'Farrell, T. J., Birchler, G. R., Cordova, J., & Kelley, M. L. (2005). Behavioral couples therapy for alcoholism and drug abuse: Where we've been, where we are, and where we're going. *Journal of Cognitive Psychotherapy*, 19, 229–246.

Fals-Stewart, W., O'Farrell, T. J., & Lam, W. K. K. (2009). Behavioral couple therapy for gay and lesbian couples with alcohol use disorders. *Journal of Substance Abuse Treatment*. 37, 379–387.

Fassinger, R. E. (1991). The hidden minority: Issues and challenges in working with lesbians and gay men. *Counseling Psychologist*, 19, 157–176.

Flynn, B. (2008). Using couple and family therapy to treat people experiencing alcohol problems. *Nursing Times*, 104(50/51), 40–42.

Freeman, D. S. (1992). *Family therapy with couples*. Northvale, NJ: Aronson.

Galvani, S. A. (2007). Safety in numbers? Tackling domestic abuse in couples and network therapies. *Drug and Alcohol Review*, 26, 175–181.

Gillespie, W., & Blackwell, R. L. (2009). Substance use patterns and consequences among lesbians, gays, and bisexuals. *Journal of Gay and Lesbian Social Services*, 21, 90–108.

Green, R. J., Bettinger, M., & Zacks, E. (1996). Are lesbian couples fused and gay males disengaged? Questioning gender straightjackets. In J. Laird & R. J. Green (Eds.), *Lesbians and gays in couples and families: A handbook for therapists* (pp. 185–230). San Francisco, CA: Jossey-Bass.

Hellmuth, J. D., Follansbee, K. W., Moore, T. M., & Stuart, G. L. (2008). Reduction of intimate partner violence in a gay couple following alcohol treatment. *Journal of Homosexuality*, 54(4), 439–448.

Hughes, T. L., & Eliason, M. (2002). Substance use and abuse in lesbian, gay, bisexual, and transgender populations. *Journal of Primary Prevention*, 22(3), 263–298.

Juhnke, B. A., & Hagedorn, W. B. (2006). *Counseling addicted families*. New York, NY: Routledge.

Kelley, M. L., & Fals-Stewart, W. (2002). Couples-versus individual-based therapy for alcohol and drug abuse: Effects on children's psychosocial functioning. *Journal of Consulting and Clinical Psychology*, 70(2), 417–427.

Kelley, M. L., & Fals-Stewart, W. (2007). Treating parental alcoholism using Learning Sobriety Together: Effects on adolescents versus preadolescents. *Journal of Family Psychology*, 21, 435–444.

Lam, W. K., Fals-Stewart, W., & Kelley, M. L. (2008). Effects of parent skills training with behavioral couples therapy for alcoholism on children: A randomized clinical pilot trial. *Addictive Behaviors*, 33, 1076–1080.

Lam, W. K., Fals-Stewart, W., & Kelley, M. L. (2009). Parent training with behavioral couples therapy for fathers' alcohol abuse. *Child Maltreatment*, 14(3), 243–254.

Lambert, M. J., Garfield, S. L., & Bergin, A. E. (2003). Overview, trends and future issues. In M. J. Lambert (Ed.), *Bergin and Garfield's handbook of psychotherapy and behavior change* (5th ed., pp. 139–193). New York, NY: Wiley.

LaSala, M. C. (2001). Monogamous or not: Understanding and counseling gay male couples. *Families in Society*, 82(6), 605–611.

LaSala, M. C. (2005). The importance of partners to lesbians' intergenerational relationships. In F. J. Turner (Ed.), *Social work diagnosis in contemporary practice* (pp. 149–157). New York, NY: Oxford Press.

Lev, A. I. (2004). *Transgender emergence: Therapeutic guidelines for working with gender-variant people and their families*. New York, NY: Haworth Press.

Liddle, B. J. (1999). Gay and lesbian clients' ratings of psychiatrists, psychologists, social workers, and counselors. *Journal of Gay and Lesbian Psychotherapy, 3*, 81–93.

Long, J. K., & Lindsey, E. (2004). The sexual orientation matrix for supervision: A tool for training therapists to work with same-sex couples. *Journal of Couple and Relationship Therapy, 3*(2/3), 123–135.

Marsh, J. C., Cao, D., & Shin, H. (2009). Closing the need-services gap: Gender differences in matching services to client needs in comprehensive substance abuse treatment. *Social Work Research, 33*(3), 183–192.

Matthews, C. R., & Selvidge, M. M. D. (2005). Lesbian, gay, and bisexual clients' experiences in treatment for addiction. *Journal of Lesbian Studies, 9*(3), 79–90.

McCrady, B. S. (2006). Family and other close relationships. In W. R. Miller & K. M. Carroll (Eds.), *Rethinking substance abuse* (pp. 166–181). New York, NY: Guilford Press.

McCrady, B. S., Epstein, E. E., Cook, S., Jensen, N., & Hildebrandt, T. (2009). A randomized trial of individual and couple behavioral alcohol treatment for women. *Journal of Consulting and Clinical Psychology, 77*(2), 243–256.

McIntyre, J. R. (2004). Family treatment of substance abuse. In S. L. A. Straussner (Ed.), *Clinical work with substance-abusing clients* (pp. 237–263). New York, NY: Guilford Press.

McLean, K. (2004). Negotiating (non)monogamy: Bisexuality and intimate relationships. *Journal of Bisexuality, 4*(1/2), 83–97.

McLellan, A. T., Woody, G. E., Luborsky, L., & Goehl, L. (1988). Methamphetamine-dependent gay men's disclosure of their HIV status to sexual partners: Treatment success among four counselors. *Journal of Nervous and Mental Disease, 16*, 423–430.

Meyers, R. J., Miller, W. R., Hill, D. E., & Tonigan, J. S. (1999). Community reinforcement and family training (CRAFT): Engaging unmotivated drug users in treatment. *Journal of Substance Abuse, 10*(3), 291–308.

Miller, W. R., & Carroll, K. M. (2006). Drawing the science together. In W. R. Miller & K .M. Carroll (Eds.), *Rethinking substance abuse* (pp. 293–311). New York, NY: Guilford Press.

Miller, W. R., Meyers, R. J., & Tonigan, S. J. (1999). Engaging the unmotivated in treatment for alcohol problems: A comparison of three strategies for intervention through family members. *Journal of Consulting and Clinical Psychology, 67*, 688–697.

Milton, M., Coyle, A., & Legg, C. (2005). Countertransference issues in psychotherapy with lesbian and gay clients. *European Journal of Psychotherapy, Counseling, and Health, 7*(3), 181–197.

Mohr, J. J., Israel, T., & Sedlacek, W. E. (2001). Counselors' attitudes regarding bisexuality as predictors of counselors' clinical responses: An analogue study of a female bisexual student. *Journal of Counseling Psychology, 48*, 212–222.

Murphy, B. C. (1989). Lesbian couples and their parents: The effects of perceived parental attitudes on the couple. *Journal of Counseling and Development, 68*, 46– 51.

National Quality Forum. (2005). *Evidence-based treatment practices for substance use disorders*. Washington, DC: Author.

O'Farrell, T. J., Choquette, K. A., & Cutter, H. S. G. (1998). Couples relapse prevention sessions after behavioral marital therapy for alcoholics and their wives: Outcomes during three years after starting treatment. *Journal of Studies on Alcohol, 59*, 357–370.

O'Farrell, T. J., & Fals-Stewart, W. (2002). Behavioral couples and family therapy for substance abusers. *Current Psychiatry Reports, 4*, 271–376.

O'Farrell, T. J., & Fals-Stewart, W. (2006). *Behavioral couples therapy for alcoholism and drug abuse*. New York, NY: Guilford Press.

O'Farrell, T. J., Murphy, M., Alter, J., & Fals-Stewart, W. (2007). Brief family treatment intervention to promote aftercare among male substance abusing patients in inpatient detoxification: A quasi-experimental pilot study. *Addictive Behaviors, 32*, 1681–1691.

Owen, S. S., & Burke, T. W. (2004). An exploration of prevalence of domestic violence in same- sex relationships. *Psychological Reports, 95*(1), 129–132.

Powers, M. B., Vedel, E., & Emmelkamp, P. M. G. (2008). Behavioral couples therapy (BCT) for alcohol and drug use disorders: A meta-analysis. *Clinical Psychology Review, 28*, 952–962.

Prochaska, J. O., & DiClemente, C. C. (1992). Stages of change in the modification of problem behaviors. In M. Herson, R. M. Eisler, & P. M. Miller (Eds.), *Progress in behavior modification* (pp. 184–214). Sycamore, IL: Sycamore Press.

Roberts, S. J., Grindel, C. G., Patsdaughter, C. A., DeMarco, R., & Tarmina, M. S. (2004). Lesbian use and abuse of alcohol: Results of the Boston Lesbian Health Project II. *Substance Abuse, 25*(4), 1–9.

Rosario, M., Schrimshaw, E. W., & Hunter, J. (2008). Butch/femme differences in substance use and abuse among young lesbian and bisexual women: Examination and potential explanations. *Substance Use and Misuse, 43,* 1002–1015.

Rotunda, R. J., O'Farrell, T. J., Murphy, M., & Babey, S. H. (2008). Behavioral couples therapy for comorbid substance use disorders and combat-related posttraumatic stress disorder among male veterans: An initial evaluation. *Addictive Behaviors, 33,* 180–187.

Rotunda, R. J., West, L., & O'Farrell, T. J. (2004). Enabling behavior in a clinical sample of alcohol-dependent clients and their partners. *Journal of Substance Abuse Treatment, 26,* 269–276.

Rowe, C. L., & Liddle, H. A. (2003). Substance abuse. *Journal of Mental and Family Therapy, 29,* 97–120.

Senreich, E., & Vairo, E. (2004). Treatment of gay, lesbian, and bisexual substance abusers. In S. L. A. Straussner (Eds.), *Clinical work with substance-abusing clients* (pp. 392–422). New York, NY: Guilford Press.

Smith, D. C., & Hall, J. A. (2008). Strengths-oriented family therapy for adolescents with substance abuse problems. *Social Work, 53*(2), 185–188.

Smith, J. E., Meyers, R. J., & Miller, W. R. (2001). The community reinforcement approach to the treatment of substance abuse disorders. *American Journal on Addictions, 10,* 51–59.

Span, S. A., & Derby, P. L. (2009). Depressive symptoms moderate the relation between internalized homophobia and drinking habits. *Journal of Gay & Lesbian Social Services, 21,* 1–12.

Szapocznik, J., & Williams, R. A. (2000). Brief strategic family therapy: Twenty-five years of interplay among theory, research, and practice in adolescent behavior problems and drug abuse. *Clinical Child & Family Psychology Review, 3*(2), 117–134.

Tunnell, G., & Greenan, D. E. (2004). Clinical issues with gay male couples. *Journal of Couple and Relationship Therapy, 3*(2/3), 13–26.

Van Wormer, K., & Davis, D. R. (2003). *Addiction treatment: A strengths perspective.* Pacific Grove, CA: Brooks/Cole.

Waldron, H. B. (1997). Adolescent substance abuse and family therapy outcome: A review of randomized trials. *Advances in Clinical Child Psychology, 19,* 199–234.

Waldon, H. B., & Selsnick, N. (1998). Treating the family. In W. Miller & N. Heather (Eds.), *Treating addictive behaviors* (pp. 259–270). New York, NY: Plenum Press.

Weber, S. (2008). Parenting, family life, and well-being among sexual minorities: Nursing policy and practice implications. *Issues in Mental Health Nursing, 29,* 601–618.

Wetchler, J. L., McCollum, E. E., Nelson, T. S., Trepper, T. C., & Lewis, R. A. (1993). Systemic couples therapy for alcohol abusing women. In T. J. O'Farrell (Ed.), *Treating alcohol problems* (pp. 236–260). New York, NY: Guilford Press.

Winters, J., Fals-Stewart, W., O'Farrell, T. J., Birchler, G. R., & Kelley, M. L. (2002). Behavioral couples therapy for female substance-abusing patients: Effects on substance use and relationship adjustment. *Journal of Consulting and Clinical Psychology, 70*(2), 344–355.

Woodward, A. M., Raskin, I. E., & Blacklow, B. (2008). A profile of the substance abuse treatment industry: Organization, costs, and treatment completion. *Substance Use & Misuse, 42,* 647–679.

Zelvin, E. (2004). Treating the partners of substance abusers. In S. L. A. Straussner (Ed.), *Clinical work with substance-abusing clients* (pp. 264–283). New York, NY: Guilford Press.

Ziyadeh, N. J., Prokop, L. A., Fisher, L. B., Rosario, M., Field, A. E., Camago, C. A., et al. (2007). Sexual orientation, gender, and alcohol use in a cohort study of U.S. adolescent girls and boys. *Drug and Alcohol Dependence, 87,* 119–130.

Zweben, A., & Pearlman, S. (1983). Evaluating the effectiveness of conjoint treatment of alcohol-complicated marriages: Clinical and methodological issues. *Journal of Marital and Family Therapy, 9,* 61–72.

23

LGBT Couple Enrichment

SHOSHANA D. KEREWSKY

The 2009 comedy *Couples Retreat* (Fox, Riedel, Isbell, & Mason) provides a useful summary of the accurate as well as inaccurate assumptions many people have about couple enrichment activities. Most of the couples depicted in the movie initially reject the idea of attending such an event, raising concerns about privacy and asserting that they do not need (or believe in) therapy. The workshop is expensive and lasts several days at a location away from home. When the couples arrive, they discover that the advertising was deceptive and, far from being a rest and relaxation retreat, the program is coercive and includes mandatory couple skill building, embarrassing group experiential activities, sexualized body work, and strange directives from the guru-like group leader. Whereas some of the couples have empathic counselors, others receive confrontational and disturbing interventions. The couples themselves demonstrate many of the negative behaviors familiar to family therapists as Gottman's Four Horsemen of the Apocalypse (Gottman & Gottman, 1999). By participating in the activities, albeit sometimes reluctantly, the couples' communication improves and their marriages are saved.

An important factor that is missing from this portrayal of couple enrichment workshops is religion, which is often an explicit or underlying component in this work. Also important, and also missing from the movie, is the inclusion of couples with lesbian, gay, bisexual, transgender, or queer (LGBT) partners. No same-sex couples are shown in the 2-minute opening montage of male–female couples; all the characters, whether primary or in the background, are in male–female pairs and (with the exception of one identified gay masseuse) appear to be heterosexual. Even the name of the resort, Eden, suggests the prelapsarian bliss of the first male–female couple, Adam and Eve. Unfortunately, this omission is a more accurate portrayal than not.

From their religion-based origin to contemporary options, few couple enrichment programs have welcomed LGBT couples and even fewer have been designed to be specific to the needs of LGBT partnerships. This chapter reviews the literature on couple enrichment, describing the history of the activity and the structures of typical programs and characterizing the intended participants in early programs. I then describe contemporary issues, including efforts to develop empirical support for couple enrichment, as well as the increasing availability of research findings on LGBT individuals and couples. This literature includes social issues and areas of vulnerability and strength relevant to the intersection of LGBT people and couple enrichment activities. Few resources exist for LGBT people seeking couple enrichment. Fortunately, a small handful of LGBT-welcoming and population-specific programs is now available. I describe available and potential couple enrichment options for LGBT couples, as well as ways that therapists can be helpful. Finally, I suggest that much of the couple enrichment research to date may be flawed as a result of heteronormative and gender-normative assumptions, omission and elision of bisexual and transgender partners' experiences, and long-term, dyadic relationships as the focus of intervention and research.

Because the literature on this topic spans not only decades but also worldviews, I will use the term *couple enrichment* (henceforth CE) when I refer generally to couples' activities and workshops that include psychoeducation, prevention strategies, skill building, and related activities. I will refer to lesbian, gay, bisexual, transgender, and queer (henceforth LGBT) people when greater specificity is not required.

Overview of CE Programs

A number of authors have described and reviewed CE programs (e.g., Halford, 2004, Hunt, Hof, & DeMaria, 1998; Jakubowski, Milne, Brunner, & Miller, 2004; Larson, 2007). The present chapter is not exhaustive but includes representative material and examples. Until recently, the literature on this topic has been based on a male–female couple.

A Brief History of CE

Couple enrichment programs evolved from the premarital counseling sessions some religious communities offered to engaged couples (Halford, 2004; Hunt et al., 1998). These sessions appeared in something approaching their present form by 1952, when Fr. Gabriel Calvo, a Spanish Roman Catholic priest, created the "Encuentro Conyugal" (Rest Stop, 1999). This religious origin still informs and permeates many CE programs explicitly (Halford, 2004), as in the case of Worldwide Marriage Encounter (http://www.wwme.org) and the Hope Focused approach (Worthington, Ripley, Hook, & Miller, 2007). It may also be implicit in the values that guide particular programs or in more general descriptions of CE's utility, goals, and participants. For example, many writers describe the goal of CE as stabilizing marriages for the sake of the children and, ultimately, society (e.g., Hunt et al., 1998).

Halford (2004) reports that "by the late 1990s, between one quarter to one third of marrying couples in the United States, Australia, and Britain were attending some form of relationship education" (p. 559). Over time, CE has been promoted as a prevention strategy (Halford, 2004; Hunt et al., 1998) to keep couples from divorcing and as a form of skill enhancement for couple relationships (Halford, 2004; Larson, 2007).

Typical CE Programs

The delivery of CE programs varies considerably, ranging from in-person group programs engaged in over many weeks (e.g., Hawes, 1982) to in-person weekend groups (e.g., Hawes, 1982; Marriage Encounter, http://www.wwme.org), to brief questionnaires (e.g., RELATE and READY, http://www.relate-institute.org), videos, and 90-minute webinars administered online (e.g., ContemporaryCouples.com, http://www.contemporarycouples.com).

Larson (2007) reports, "The goals of these programs include providing information about creating a successful relationship, increasing self and partner awareness, providing feedback, initiating cognitive changes, and improving relationship skills" (p. 200). Many programs blend relationship education and enrichment or enhancement (Halford, 2004; Larson, 2007); some may include a therapeutic component (Larson, 2007). Although other components (e.g., group discussions or religious education) may be added, these are the primary goals and are typically accomplished through two major forms of activity, inventories and skill building. The appeal of these activities is they are more likely to be evidence based (Halford, 2004) as compared to other activities associated with CE (e.g., couple enrichment study groups; see, e.g., Hawes, 1982).

Inventories   Some CE programs use inventories as all or part of their intervention. This approach uses questionnaires that are completed by the individuals in the couple (Halford, 2004). These are typically self-report inventories related to communication skills and relationship functions, not instruments that assess personality or psychopathology. The couple receives the results and sometimes further intervention (Halford, 2004). Halford (2004) identifies widely used inventory-based programs: PREmarital Preparation and Relationship Enhancement (PREPARE), the Facilitating Open Couple Communication Understanding and Study (FOCCUS), and RELATionship Evaluation (RELATE).[1]

As strengths of the inventory, Halford (2004) reports, these programs "[assess] factors relevant to relationship outcomes" (p. 560) and "provide the opportunity for couples to assess their personal risk and resilience profiles" (p. 560). Research on the lasting effects of this type of intervention is lacking, however, and self-report inventories are not objective (Halford, 2004).

Skills Training   According to Halford (2004), skills training refers to "approaches that focus on active training of skills, although these approaches typically also include significant emphasis on building awareness and cognitive change" (p. 560). Halford gives as examples the Relationship Enhancement program (RE), the Premarital Relationship Enhancement Program (PREP), the Couple Commitment and Relationship Enhancement program (Couple CARE), the Couples Communication Program (CCP), and Couples Coping Enhancement Training (CCET), which have in common "positive communication, conflict management, and positive expression of affection," though they have "significant variations" (p. 560) as well.

The strengths of the skills-training approach include its focus on communication, effectiveness, and standardization (Halford, 2004, p. 560). Weaknesses include their uniformity, that is, their "one size fits all" approach (Larson, 2007, p. 203) and the paucity of sufficiently rigorous research (Larson, 2007).

Intended or Assumed Participants   Many CE programs are based on assumptions about, and research on, engaged or married heterosexual dyads. The man and woman in this relationship are presumed to have been born in their present or apparent biological sex. These assumptions are understandable, given the premarital counseling origins of the intervention, the preponderance of heterosexual people in the world, and the dearth of ways for LGBT couples to legally declare or solemnize their partnerships. However, it is surprising that more contemporary CE programs still do not clearly name the populations that they hope will participate in the program or for whom the program is appropriate.

Similarly, though some contemporary researchers and authors do articulate that their focus is restricted to male–female couples (Halford, 2004), many do not, and most if not all seem to presume that none of the participants are bisexual or transgender.

Descriptions of the potential CE participant couple's concerns and developmental stage vary considerably. Halford (2004) suggests that "it is probably easier for couples with no or mild distress to enhance their relationship than it is for couples who have severe relationship problems to alter entrenched negative patterns and feelings" (p. 559), though others have found greater gains for couples presenting in greater distress (Stanley, Markman, & Jenkins, 2002, cited in Reardon-Anderson, Stagner, Macomber, & Murray, 2005). Developmentally, Halford (2004) sees the beginning of a marriage (cf. Baucom, Hahlweg, Atkins, Engl, & Thurmaier, 2006), the first 2 years of a marriage, and such transitional events as "parenthood, relocation, and major illness" (p. 560) to be times when CE programs could assist couples. The target couple may vary as to

---

[1] For ease of reading, sources for CE programs and instruments are generally not identified but may be found by consulting the reference list of the primary author cited.

whether they are engaged, married, or cohabiting (Halford, 2004; for examples, see Hunt et al., 1998; Larson, 2007).

Unfortunately, some authors articulate their focus in a way that may be problematic for LGBT clients and affirmative therapists alike. Hunt et al., whose book *Marriage Enrichment: Preparation, Mentoring, and Outreach* (1998) might otherwise engage a broader audience, includes the following alienating statements: "There is no other human relationship like a man-woman dyad sanctioned by their society" (p. xii); "In studying marriages, both healthy and unhealthy, we will newly discover the wisdom of the woman-man dyad that cannot be fully matched by other arrangements" (p. xii); and "All of the alternatives to marriage (and/or to family) begin with persons who, for one reason or another, have been unable or unwilling to find satisfaction and success in a woman-man marriage" (p. xiii). Although the authors state that their focus is only on marriage enrichment because of the vastness of the field and that they "applaud those who are addressing these populations" (p. xii), the former comments imply that the reason for their exclusion of same-sex couples is less a consequence of space constraints than of placing a higher value on heterosexual couples. Their tone is not neutral and may dissuade therapists and couples from utilizing CE interventions out of a belief that these authors represent the stance of the field.

Other issues of language and tone seem unintentional but may still be alienating or perplexing. Although an increasing number of programs indicate that lesbian and gay or LGBT couples are welcome, the use of such words as *marital* may be confusing or send a message of exclusion to potential participants. It is thus likely that LGBT couples may feel invisible when researching such sites as the Coalition for Marriage, Family, and Couples Education (CMFCE; http://www.smartmarriages.com/index.html), which sponsors the Smart Marriages Conference. Although the conference is described as appropriate for gays and lesbians, this information is found on the singles page (http://www.smartmarriages.com/singles.html). Furthermore, although another page asserts that the courses brokered by CMFCE "work for gay/lesbian couples" (http://www.smartmarriages.com/first.person.html), nothing more is said and no evidence is provided. Of the site search results returned for the term *gay*, several links include vaguely negative appraisals of lesbian and gay people.

Many people are familiar with Worldwide Marriage Encounter (http://www.wwme.org), one of the oldest CE programs. Although there is no site-specific search function, it is relatively easy to determine that participants are expected to be married (http://www.wwme.org/new.html, as well as from the description on the "Common Questions" page). The registration form on this site also makes this expectation clear, since it asks for the names of the husband and wife (http://www.wwme.org/register.html). Questions about the program's religious orientation are easily found under the heading "Is there a specific religious orientation to the weekend?" The answer is very clear: "Marriage Encounter does present God as a focus for successful marriage. There are many faith expressions of Marriage Encounter Weekends— Catholic, as well as several Protestant denominations" (http://www.wwme.org/new.html). Similarly, the Hope-Focused approach (Worthington et al., 2007) clearly identifies itself as a Christian intervention.

As opportunities for same-sex marriages, civil unions, legal domestic partnerships, and religious ceremonies become more widespread, unclear nomenclature will only be more problematic for researchers as well as potential clients seeking CE experiences. Does a workshop advertised for married couples include married same-sex couples? Legally married couples where one partner is transsexual? It would behoove all programs, regardless of their inclusion and exclusion criteria, to identify themselves and their criteria explicitly and in neutral language in order to facilitate appropriate referrals and provide accurate descriptions of their intended participant bases.

Best Practices for CE Programs

Jakubowski et al. (2004) found that "marital education programs consistently lead to an improvement of communication skills and relationship satisfaction" (p. 528). They go on to say the following:

> Halford and colleagues presented seven guidelines for best practice in marital education. These seven guidelines included assessing the risk profile of couples, encouraging high-risk couples to attend relationship education, assessing relationship aggression, offering marital education at change points, promoting early presentation of relationship problems, matching content to couples with special needs, and enhancing accessibility of evidence-based marital education programs. (p. 528)

All these suggestions are relevant to CE programs serving LGBT couples.

Research on CE Outcomes and on Lesbian and Gay Couples

It is important to consider the general findings on the outcomes of CE participation as well as contemporary research on normative lesbian and gay couples in order to determine appropriate CE interventions for this group. Unfortunately, there is still a great deficit in the literature on couples with at least one bisexual or transgender partner, suggesting a need for much more extensive work in this area.

CE Findings

The research on CE programs' efficacy is generally positive. These positive outcomes suggest that a range of CE programs have some utility for male–female couples and potentially for other couples or partnerships as well.

Several reports have characterized CE outcomes. Jakubowski et al. (2004) evaluated 13 programs, finding four "efficacious" (PREP, Relationship Enhancement, Couple Communication Program, Strategic Hope-Focused Enrichment), three "possibly efficacious" (Couple Care, ACME, CCET), and six "empirically untested" (Structured Enrichment, Marriage Encounter, PAIRS, Imago, Traits of a Happy Couple, SYMBIS; pp. 528–530). Jakubowski et al. (2004) describe these programs in more detail in their useful and clear report. Further, they describe Gottman's Marriage Survival Kit (Gottman & Gottman, 1999) as insufficiently studied as an intervention but as having "a strong research component in its content" (p. 533).

Larson (2007) provides a helpful summary of program types and clarifies that some of the programs that Jakubowski et al. (2004) described as empirically untested have in fact been evaluated, but not sufficiently stringently. Larson also describes short CE activities that have promise but have not yet been well evaluated, such as Marriage Checkups or Tuneups (Gee, Scott, Castellani, & Cordova, 2002; Larson, 2003, cited in Larson, 2007). Sullivan and Goldschmidt (2000) report on client satisfaction with a short CE program within a managed-care setting. Although Hawley and Olson's (1995) findings were equivocal, participants in the programs they studied were highly satisfied with their program.

Baucom et al. (2006) summarize findings that such relationship education programs as PREP can help prevent marital distress among newlyweds. Studies of some CE programs, among them the Minnesota Couple Communication Program, found mixed results (Wampler & Sprenkle, 1980). Reardon-Anderson et al. (2005) assert that "generally there is promising evidence that couples can learn specific skills to improve their relationships" (p. 3).

In addition to these generally positive findings are some barriers and problems that have been identified. Halford (2004) notes that longer term outcome evaluations are needed. Eminent marital researcher Robert L. Weiss agrees that most evaluation has occurred relatively soon after the intervention, probably resulting in overinflated positive outcomes or a "workshop effect"

(R. L. Weiss, personal communication, May 23, 2010). Doss, Rhoades, Stanley, and Markman (2009) founds that although it was common for couples to seek relationship help in the first 5 years of their marriages, participation in CE events was related to demographic factors. Doherty and Walker (1982) found that some Marriage Encounter participants experienced distress.

Since none of the studies summarized in these reports appear to have included LGBT couples, it is not possible to assert that the research to date supports the efficacy of CE for these populations. However, as I will describe, there is reasonably good evidence from the Gottman Relationship Institute/Gottman Institute (http://www.gottman.com) and from the work of Lawrence Kurdek (2004) and others cited below to support the use of CE interventions with LGBT couples based on characteristics of couple communication that hold across sexual and affectional orientations.

Lesbian and Gay Couple and Family Findings

In recent years, researchers have devoted considerably more attention to LGBT people's lives and experiences. It is now possible for therapists to find information on supportive counseling as well as therapeutic interventions for LGBT clients. There continues to be a deficit of research on bisexual and transgender people, particularly as they experience and participate in their partnerships. The following summary is by no means comprehensive; rather, it serves to highlight some aspects of lesbian and gay (and to a much lesser extent, bisexual and transgender) people's couple and family experiences that are similar to those of heterosexuals.

Burgoyne (2001), citing Bell and Weinberg (1978), reported that at that time about half of gay men were in a primary relationship, and Harry (1979) wrote about the characteristics of what he called subinstitutional gay men's "marital" liaisons in 1979. Kurdek (2004) cited studies showing that "between 40% and 60% of gay men and between 45% and 80% of lesbians are currently involved in a romantic relationship" (p. 880). Patterson (2000) noted that "many if not most lesbians and gay men express the desire for an enduring love relationship with a partner of the same gender" (p. 1053), with the survey data she examined showing that "40 to 60% of gay men and 45 to 80% of lesbians are currently involved in steady romantic relationships" (p. 1503). Lesbian and gay relationships show low separation rates (pp. 1504, 1505).

Koepke, Hare, and Moran (1992) found that though all the lesbian relationships they studied were "solid and happy" (p. 224), couples with children scored higher on some measures. Bos, van Balen, and van den Boom (2004) found many similarities between lesbian and heterosexual parents. Kurdek (2004) took a different tack, examining cohabiting gay and lesbian couples without children. He found that for half the comparisons, there were no significant differences between the three groups; and that for most of the differences, the heterosexual couples scored worse. Kurdek had previously studied relational conflict across these groups (1994b) and heterosexual parent couples (1994a), finding all the groups similar or equivalent in their scores. In 2004, Kurdek summarized his results:

> The overall pattern of findings across the range of issues studied here is clear: Relative to heterosexual parents, partners from gay couples and partners from lesbian couples do not function in ways that place their relationships at risk for distress. In particular, there is no evidence that gay partners and lesbian partners were psychologically maladjusted, that they had high levels of personality traits that predisposed them to relationship problems, that they had dysfunctional working models of their relationships, and that they used ineffective strategies to resolve conflict. The only area in which gay and lesbian partners fared worse than heterosexual parents was in the area of social support: Gay partners and lesbian partners received less support for their relationships from family members than heterosexual parents did. (p. 886)

The Gottman Institute conducted a 12-year study and concluded the following:

> [A]ll couple types—straight or gay—have many of the same problems and the same paths to staying happy together.... [T]here are also some qualities of strength (like humor and ability to calm down during a fight) that are especially key to [i.e., more frequently found in] same-sex couples. (The 12 Year Study, n.d.)

Although LGBT couples may have some between-group differences and may face social issues and stressors that differ from those faced by heterosexual couples, it also appears that they are similar to heterosexual couples in many aspects (Patterson, 1994) that suggest that CE interventions, appropriately tailored to LGBT people's areas of risk and resilience, would be appropriate and potentially useful.

Larger Social Issues Faced by LGBT Couples

The Gottman Institute nicely articulates the relationship between general couples' concerns and specific lesbian and gay couples' concerns:

> Gay and lesbian couples, like straight couples, deal with every day ups-and-downs of close relationships.... We know that these ups-and-downs may occur in a social context of isolation from family, workplace prejudice, and other social barriers that are unique to gay and lesbian couples. (The 12 Year Study, n.d.)

Even a normal, healthy LGBT relationship takes place in a broad cultural context that poses stressors. Meyer (1995) found that gay men experience minority stress, and it is clearly and broadly documented that experiences of discrimination, threats, and other social stressors are present in many LGBT people's lives. As noted, Kurdek (2004) found lack of social support to be an area of deficit relative to heterosexual couples. In addition, LGBT people face unique social stressors related to their partner relationships. For example, Penn (August, 2009) reports the case of a Mexican lesbian couple seeking asylum in Canada "in hopes of being married and escaping alleged harassment and beatings from police" (p. 8). Patterson (1994) suggests that "the concept of gay and lesbian families is viewed as an oxymoron" (p. 62) and comments as follows:

> [I]n view of obstacles to lasting relationships (e.g., stigmatization of gay relationships, denial of marriage rights to same-sex couples), it is perhaps remarkable that most gay and lesbian adults say that they are involved in a relationship at any given moment, and that at least some of these relationships are sustained over a period of many years. (p. 63)

Even as the increasing opportunity for same-sex couples to enter into a publicly sanctioned legal status resolves such stressors as difficulties with hospital visitation rights, that opportunity may create unexpected stresses as well. Although publicity was desirable, when *The New York Times* and other newspapers began to print notices of same-sex couples' domestic partnerships, civil unions, and commitment ceremonies (e.g., "'Times' OKs gay-couple notices, stirs debate," 2002, August 20), the publicity also created an opportunity for highly visible notices of same-sex relationships, potentially raising concerns about privacy, disclosure, and threats. Patterson (2000) notes, "When a couple disagrees about the extent to which they should disclose the lesbian or gay nature of their relationship, problems in their relationship can ensue" (p. 1054).

Similarly, when Multnomah County, Oregon, began to issue marriage licenses to same-sex couples, several local therapists who work with LGBT clients made the same observation. We noticed that though some of our clients were happy and rushed to Portland, others reported that the option to marry was causing a strain in their partnerships. Couples who had not previously discussed the nature of their relationship were now faced with a difficult and sometimes conflictual conversation about each partner's vision of the partnership. In addition, some LGBT people in polyamorous relationships expressed both happiness for same-sex dyads and distress at being excluded (N. T. Kemp and members of the Oregon Psychological Association, personal communication, May 7, 2004).

Thus, even attaining more rights and freedoms may be a source of stress for LGBT couples. For those individuals in jurisdictions that do not recognize their union or where there is an active threat of violence, these stressors are, of course, significant. All forms of social stress increase the need for an adequate understanding of risk and resilience, good assessment, and interventions that are a useful match for the couple's presenting issues.

Areas of Stress and Vulnerability

In addition to these larger social stressors, there are specific vulnerabilities and risks that may be relevant for members of LGBT couples. These should be assessed within each partnership when determining the relevance and utility of a CE referral.

Since LGBT couples may be similar to heterosexual couples along many dimensions, it is not surprising that all partnerships may suffer from similar stressors. Patterson (2000) describes "different religious, racial, ethnic, or socioeconomic backgrounds" and differences of values as general couple stressors, as well as "problems at either partner's job, financial pressures on the couple, [and] friction with members of extended family networks" (p. 1054). She cites Kurdek's finding that "the top five areas of conflict for lesbian and gay couples were finances, driving style, affection/sex, being overly critical, and division of household tasks" (p. 1054), certainly a list that would be familiar to U.S. heterosexual couples.

In the FAQ "What are the negative behavior patterns that can predict divorce?" the Gottman Relationship Institute summarizes its research findings on behaviors that destroy relationships (http://www.gottman.com/49853/Research-FAQs.html). They are the well-known "Positive-to-Negative Ratio of 0.8 or Less" and "The Four Horsemen of the Apocalypse": criticism, contempt, defensiveness, and stonewalling. The Gottman Relationship Institute has identified a gender difference that is relevant to same-sex couples:

> Our studies have found that men tend to react with more signs of physiological stress than do women during disagreements, and therefore, men are more likely to withdraw (stone-wall). (It is interesting to note that we have also followed same-sex couples, and stonewall-ing occurs between them as well.) (http://www.gottman.com/49853/Research-FAQs.html)

Again, there may be other stressors that are relevant to LGBT relationships, even if they also affect some heterosexual couples. These might include HIV/AIDS (Patterson, 2000, p. 1055) and Kurdek's finding (1998) that gay men and lesbians reported more frequent ends to their relationships (presumably because they also reported fewer barriers to leaving).

Areas of Strength and Resiliency

Research has also identified many areas of strength for LGBT couples. These areas include more autonomy for gay and lesbian partners and more intimacy and equality in lesbian couples (Kurdek, 1998). Turning the relationship dissolution finding on its head, Kurdek muses:

> Perhaps a positive side of not having same-sex marriage is that gay and lesbian partners confront no formal institutionalized barriers and obstacles to leaving unhappy relation-ships…. As a result, the relatively high rate of dissolution for gay and lesbian couples might indicate that gay and lesbian cohabiting partners are less likely than heterosexual married partners to find themselves trapped in empty relationships…. Given the current lack of formal institutionalized barriers to leaving a same-sex relationship, perhaps the

most remarkable finding from this project … is that gay men and lesbians nonetheless build and sustain durable relationships. At the time of the last available assessment, 52% of the 125 gay stable couples and 37% of the 100 lesbian stable couples had been together for more than 10 years. Further, 14% of the 125 gay stable couples and 10% of the 100 lesbian stable couples had been together for more than 20 years. (p. 886)

Similarly, Halford (2004) inverts the usual statistic that about 50% of U.S. marriages end in divorce, stating that "in most Western countries, 50% or more of couples who marry remain together for the rest of their lives" (p. 563).

Patterson (2000) found that the research on same-sex couples showed overall "positive adjustment, even in the face of stressful conditions" (1052). In the studies she reviewed, most lesbians and gay men reported happiness and positive relationships. The Gottman study of gay and lesbian couples (The 12 Year Study, n.d.) characterized gay and lesbian couples as more "upbeat," (para. 4) affectionate, humorous, and positive during and after conflict. Indeed, "'Straight couples may have a lot to learn from gay and lesbian relationships,' explains Gottman" (para. 4). Gay and lesbian couples "use fewer controlling, hostile emotional tactics … [thereby suggesting] that fairness and power-sharing between the partners [are] more important and more common in gay and lesbian relationships than in straight ones" (para. 5); they also "accept some degree of [interpersonal] negativity without taking it personally" (para. 6); and reversing the pattern of heterosexual couples, they are physically calmer, though "lesbians are more emotionally expressive" (para. 7) and "[g]ay men need to be especially careful to avoid negativity in conflict" (para. 9) (The 12 Year Study, n.d.).

In addition to maintaining their dyadic partner relationships, Patterson (1994) reminds us that "lesbian and gay individuals and couples are believed to be more likely than heterosexuals to count close friends and ex-lovers as family members" and, in fact, "ex-lovers are particularly likely to be represented in such networks, especially among lesbians" (p. 63; see also Burgoyne, 2001). It would be important to consider the strengths of such extended "family" networks on LGBT couple functioning.

Ideally, these areas of LGBT resilience would be used to shape strengths-based interventions not only for LGBT couples but for heterosexuals as well.

Recommendations for Assessment and Referral

Although the LGBT affirmative therapist may not be the person offering the CE experience, the therapist may still be the person who makes the referral. Jakubowski et al. (2004) "think that it may be advisable to assess individual psychopathology" (pp. 321–322), though they are referring to screening research participants, not necessarily all CE participants. Particularly because many CE programs (especially Web-delivered inventories such as RELATE, http://www.relate-institute.org) do not engage in prescreening, it is important for the therapist to evaluate the appropriateness of the referral.

Although such instruments as Burgoyne's (2001) Relationship Assessment Measure for Same-Sex Couples (RAM-SSC) might have utility for evaluating couples for CE referral, it may be easier to assess each partner's interpersonal risk and resilience through an informal interview. Burgoyne (2001) suggests that exploring

the availability of role models and social support for the couple, the history of family interactions and degree of closeness versus emotional cut-off from extended family, self-image in the context of gay identity, habitual responses to stress, style of seeking information and help, role flexibility, and the impact of concordant or discordant HIV status (where relevant) on sexuality and the relationship in general. The effects of cumulative losses within the couple's network because of HIV/AIDS should also be assessed. (pp. 285–286)

An interview based on Bronfenbrenner's ecological self-in-context model may also be useful (Chronister, McWhirter, & Kerewsky, 2004). This interview format assesses clients' risk and resilience factors at each level of their social ecologies, including physical characteristics, close relationships, intersecting or diverging relationship systems, policies and media, cultural beliefs, and changes over time. This structure reminds the therapist to evaluate the client's strengths and vulnerabilities at both interpersonal and sociocultural levels and not to neglect the client's identities and group memberships in addition to being lesbian, gay, bisexual, or transgender. This format helps the therapist adhere to the standards of the American Psychological Association's (APA) *Guidelines for Psychological Practice With Lesbian, Gay, and Bisexual Clients* (2011) and *Guidelines for Providers of Psychological Services to Ethnic, Linguistic, and Culturally Diverse Populations* (1990), as well as attending to the observation that issues of minority status may decrease help seeking as compared to majority culture–identified people.

Screening may also serve as a preliminary CE intervention. Halford (2004) describes Cordova, Warren, and Gee's 2001 report of using a relationship checkup with positive outcomes. The Center for Family Therapy at University of Oregon offers an annual Valentine's Day relationship checkup ("UO program offers free counseling," 2008), which can serve as a freestanding CE experience or an assessment for referral.

It should go without saying that intake forms, interviews, or instruments administered as part of an evaluation for services or referral should not include questions that assume heterosexuality, biological sex as target sex, or a dyadic adult family structure. If these types of questions cannot be edited because of norming or other constraints, this issue should be discussed with the clients.

Ethically and legally, the therapist must be familiar with the varieties of legal status available to LGBT clients in that jurisdiction. It may be necessary for the therapist to clarify the clients' legal relationship, if any, since this may have a bearing on privacy and access to information or records.

Based on the literature reviewed in the foregoing discussion, it is possible to make several critical recommendations to therapists seeking to refer their clients to CE activities:

1. Evaluate the clients' readiness for a CE experience.
2. Become familiar with CE programs that may be a good match for your clients' needs (i.e., ones with a particular focus or philosophy, a low-cost program, an in-person workshop, or a religious affiliation, among other factors).
3. Review the identified program thoroughly. If materials are available online, check all the pages and skim the links if it is necessary to preview the program's content or tone. This could also be a homework assignment for clients.
4. If possible, refer the couple to a program with expertise in meeting the needs of LGBT clients. If this is not feasible, refer to a program that states clearly that it welcomes LGBT participants.
5. If the program's online materials make no reference to LGBT participants and an Internal search yields no results, try using a search engine such as Google. For example, an Internet search for *lesbian* at http://www.gottman.com returns the note "There are no search results for lesbian," but a search for *Gottman lesbian* on Google directs the searcher to http://dev.gottman.com/research/gaylesbian, where useful information is available.
6. Discuss with couples that have at least one bisexual or transgender partner the scarcity of available information about CE programs specifically geared to their needs. Discuss the affirmative programs that are available to see if one may be a good fit.
7. If the clients are interested in a CE program that has not been studied for efficacy, explain what this means and discuss how the clients might informally evaluate the

goodness of fit and the potential outcomes. For example, a program such as Hawes's (1982) might appeal to some clients because it has a strong emphasis on assets and on discussion with other couples.

8. If no formal CE program is available, feasible, or attractive to your clients, consider meeting some of the same needs through bibliotherapy. Useful resources include such books as Berzon (1988), *Permanent Partners: Building Gay and Lesbian Relationships That Last*; Erhardt (1997), *Journey Toward Intimacy: A Handbook for Lesbian Couples*; Isensee (2005), *Love Between Men: Enhancing Intimacy and Resolving Conflicts in Gay Relationships*; and Leonhard and Mast (1997), *Feathering Your Nest: An Interactive Workbook and Guide to a Loving Lesbian Relationship*.

Recommendations to and for CE Programs

Before identifying several CE programs with an explicit and specific focus on LGBT clients, it is important to make several key recommendations to the creators and trainers who administer CE programs.

1. In published materials, state clearly whether LGBT couples are welcome and whether or not your program is relevant to their needs (Halford, 2004).
2. If LGBT couples are welcome, be sure that the registration form reflects this and does not ask for the names of the husband and wife.
3. If an inventory or other materials used include heterosexist bias or exclude LGBT people, consult about whether this can be changed without affecting the norming if the data will be used for research.
4. If you are not familiar with acceptable nomenclature, have an LGBT consultant review your materials for possible misstatements or problems. For example, the terms *gay women* and *homosexual* are not in favor, *transgender* and *transsexual* have related but distinct meanings, and *marital* is not a neutral term.
5. If necessary, revise program materials to show same-sex couples as well as male–female pairs. If the program uses videos or webinars that present case studies of couples, be sure that some are LGBT. It may be useful to link these to the LGBT resilience factors and relational strengths described earlier.
6. Consider creating materials that reflect the relational concerns of couples with bisexual or transgender partners.
7. Periodically review website links. Links that are confusing, dead, or use automated news feeds that may capture objectionable articles may discourage clients who are not sure that this CE program is a good fit for them.
8. If your CE program includes in-person activities, consider the impact of other couples' potential homophobia on LGBT participants. Make sure that materials reflect the mixed nature of the group and that trainers are alert to the possibility of bias or inappropriate statements by participants.
9. Consider conducting focus groups with LGBT community members to determine whether your program's content, inventories, or skills training are a good fit for them.
10. Consider conducting outcome research with LGBT CE participants, especially if you are able to conduct long-term studies.

Fortunately, several CE programs now exist that may be appropriate for LGBT clients. First, though not an LGBT-specific program, RELATE (http://www.relate-institute .org) is an inventory that returns results in generally gender-neutral language. As do all programs administered at a distance, it raises fewer concerns about couples' privacy and potential stigma.

Second, Gay Couples Institute (http://www.gaycouplesinstitute.org) offers weekend workshops for gay men and lesbians. Its program is based on Gottman's work. Bisexual and transgender couples do not appear to be a focus at the time of this writing.

Third, ContemporaryCouples.com (http://www.contemporarycouples.com) is an online CE program that uses PAIRS and research-based webinars. In-person workshops can be arranged. The site identifies LGBT couples as its focus, although content specific to bisexual and transgender people has not yet been added. As the program expands, it will add webinars specific to these groups, as well as other LGBT-related content. Jeff Lutes worked with the PAIRS Foundation to revise their PowerPoint presentation for use with same-sex couples (J. Lutes, personal communication, May 22, 2010).

Since some organizations offer a mix of CE and other couple-related education and activities, it would be worthwhile to examine additional interventions and research to identify activities that may be particularly relevant to LBGT couples. For example, Picucci (1992) described a weekend workshop for lesbians and gay men focused on psychological wounds and healing through experiential activities. Page (2009) discusses the utility of a group intervention using gift theory to promote psychological health and community building for gay, bisexual, and transgender men.

Helpful Therapist and Trainer Characteristics

Although therapist and CE trainer will have diverging foci and responsibilities in relation to LGBT clients who participate in CE programs, some characteristics and practices will be useful for people in both roles.

First, the professional should be up to date on the literature, both research and theoretical, on couples work with LGBT clients, as well as the broader categories of couples work and LGBT considerations. This self-education includes reviewing assumptions about couples as well as LGBT people and checking previous learning against current knowledge. Do we still believe in lesbian bed death? The professional cannot be sure without reading contemporary sources and consulting knowledgeable peers.

It would also be helpful to be familiar with the general wellness literature in each field and to consider an assets- or strengths-based approach to the couple's presenting issues. Overemphasizing the problem description of the couple may make it more difficult to identify their strengths. In conjunction with this focus, it is important not to misinterpret the literature on couples' or LGBT people's problems. For example, Halford (2004) states, "Individuals who cohabit before marriage have certain personal characteristics that make them more likely to divorce after marriage" (p. 562). The particular circumstances of LGBT couples may render this statement meaningless, however, since marriage is generally not an option. Laird and Green's (1996) handbook, *Lesbians and Gays in Couples and Families* is a useful resource if the material is supplemented with more contemporary research.

Professionals should seek out resources that illuminate aspects of bisexual and transgender people's couple experiences, such as Reinhardt's (2002) article "Bisexual Women in Heterosexual Relationships," Israel's (2004) chapter "Supporting Transgender and Sex Reassignment Issues: Couple and Family Dynamics," and Kins, Hoebeke, Heylens, Rubens, and De Cuypere's (2008) article "The Female-to-Male Transsexual and His Female Partner Versus the Traditional Couple: A Comparison." Again, focus groups with bisexual and transgender people could be very helpful for both therapists and CE trainers.

As we know, being an LGBT therapist or trainer is no guarantee that the professional will not have countertransference or other responses to LGBT couples. In addition to LGBT issues, such couple issues as sexual discussion, violence, monogamy, multiple partners, or the army of ex-lovers living with the couple may evoke the professional's emotional responses and irrational beliefs. Consistent consultation should always be a priority.

Recommendations for Future Research on Couple Enrichment

As Larson (1997) reminds us, a weakness of CE programs can be the idea that "one size fits all" (p. 203). This weakness is even more true of CE for LGBT couples who may not be similar to the presumptively heterosexual couples on whom the instruments and interventions were normed and whose outcomes have been studied. Further, there are within-group differences between lesbian, gay, bisexual, and transgender individuals. For that matter, this chapter has not even touched on the issues of queer identity as distinct from LGBT identification. Sometimes a couple may be not a couple but a triad or a couple plus friends. These identifications and variations in identity and relationship composition may or may not be relevant to CE program development and research on their effectiveness, but we will not know until they are studied.

Research on both CE and LGBT people has typically been conducted with participants who do not adequately represent the range of human diversity. We know a reasonable amount about White, middle-class participants but much less about other groups.

Similarly, we do not know that the male–female couples represented in the literature to date would identify themselves as heterosexual, though researchers have presumed them to be. This assumption alone suggests the strong need for more rigorous screening in which potential CE research participants are asked about their sexual orientation and gender identity. Without this data, it is difficult to know whether the demographics and hence the norms generated by the research are even accurate.

Conclusion

It is important to note that CE programs began as a religiously inspired premarital intervention for heterosexual couples, without reference to LGBT couples or other relational constellations. Over time, CE has broadened its methods and scope. With the increasing visibility and cultural acceptance of LGBT people has come a commensurate increase in research on LGBT relationships and, in some cases, greater flexibility or welcome to LGBT couples from CE programs. Notably, some programs now explicitly invite LGBT couples to participate or, more ambitiously, include activities intended to meet the specific needs of LGBT couples.

Extant CE programs still vary considerably in the extent to which they explicitly address the needs of LGBT couples. Lack of specificity and clarity presents a marketing problem for programs trying to reach their intended participants and a customer problem for all couples trying to find a salutary intervention that will support and enrich their relationship. The lack of clear information and population-specific considerations is particularly acute for couples with bisexual or transgender partners, as well as for polyamorous relationships.

In addition to such processes as assessing the couple's readiness for a CE experience, referral sources will serve LGBT couples best by helping the couple to be proactive. Given the variability in programs, potential LGBT participants in such programs should carefully consider the goodness of fit between a program and the couple's needs.

Finally, any study of the experiences of, and outcomes for, LGBT people in any form of CE program would be a welcome and significant contribution to our understanding of the potential utility and efficacy of CE activities for these populations.

References

American Psychological Association. (1990). *Guidelines for providers of psychological services to ethnic, linguistic, and culturally diverse populations.* Retrieved from http://www.apa.org/pi/oema/resources/policy/provider-guidelines.aspx

American Psychological Association. (2011) *Guidelines for psychological practice with lesbian, gay, and bisexual clients.* Retrieved from http://www.apa.org/pi/lgbt/resources/guidelines.aspx

Baucom, D. H., Hahlweg, K., Atkins, D. C., Engl, J., & Thurmaier, F. (2006). Long-term prediction of marital quality following a relationship education program: Being positive in a constructive way. *Journal of Family Psychology, 3,* 448–455.

Bell, A., & Weinberg, M. (1978). *Homosexualities: A study of diversities among men and women.* New York, NY: Simon & Schuster.

Berzon, B. (1988). *Permanent partners: Building gay and lesbian relationships that last.* New York, NY: Dutton.

Bos, H. M. W., van Balen, F., & van den Boom, D. C. (2004). Experience of parenthood, couple relationship, social support, and child-rearing goals in planned lesbian mother families. *Journal of Child Psychology and Psychiatry, 45,* 755–764.

Burgoyne, R. W. (2001). The Relationship Assessment Measure for Same-Sex Couples (RAM-SSC): A standardized instrument for evaluating gay couple functioning. *Journal of Sex & Marital Therapy, 27,* 279–287.

Chronister, K. M., McWhirter, B. T., & Kerewsky, S. D. (2004). Prevention from an ecological framework. In R. K. Coyne & E. P. Cook (Eds.), *Ecological counseling: An innovative approach to conceptualizing person–environment interaction* (pp. 315–338). Alexandria, VA: ACA Press.

Doherty, W. J., & Walker, B. J. (1982). Marriage Encounter casualties: A preliminary investigation. *American Journal of Family Therapy, 10*(2), 15–25.

Doss, B. D., Rhoades, G. K., Stanley, S. M., & Markman, H. J. (2009). Marital therapy, retreats, and books: The who, what, when, and why of relationship help-seeking. *Journal of Marital & Family Therapy, 35,* 18–29.

Erhardt, V. (1997). *Journey toward intimacy: A handbook for lesbian couples.* Atlanta, GA: Couples Enrichment Institute.

Fox, D., Riedel G., Isbell, J., & Mason, M. (Producers) & Billingsley, P. (Director). (2009). *Couples retreat* [Motion picture]. Hollywood, CA: Universal Studios.

Gee, C. B., Scott, R. L., Castellani, A. M., & Cordova, J. V. (2002). Predicting 2-year marital satisfaction from partners' discussion of their marriage checkup. *Journal of Marital and Family Therapy, 28,* 399–407.

Gottman, J. M., & Gottman, J. S. (1999). The marriage survival kit: A research-based marital therapy. In R. Berger & M. T. Hannah (Eds.), *Preventive approaches in couples therapy* (pp. 304–330). Philadelphia, PA: Brunner/Mazel.

Halford, W. K. (2004). The future of couple relationship education: Suggestions on how it can make a difference. *Family Relations, 53,* 559–566.

Harry, J. (1979). The "marital" liaisons of gay men. *The Family Coordinator, 28,* 622–629.

Hawes, E. C. (1982). Couples growing together: Couple Enrichment programs. *Individual Psychology, 38,* 322–331.

Hawley, D. R., & Olson, D. H. (1995). Enriching newlyweds: An evaluation of three enrichment programs. *American Journal of Family Therapy, 23,* 129–147.

Hunt, R. A., Hof, L., & DeMaria, R. (1998). *Marriage enrichment: Preparation, mentoring, and outreach.* Philadelphia, PA: Brunner/Mazel.

Isensee, R. (2005). *Love between men: Enhancing intimacy and resolving conflicts in gay relationships.* Retrieved from http://www.iuniverse.com/Bookstore/BookDetail.aspx?BookId=SKU-000082152

Israel, G. E. (2004). Supporting transgender and sex reassignment issues: Couple and family dynamics. In J. E. Bigner & J. L. Wetchler (Eds.), *Relationship therapy with same-sex couples* (pp. 53–63). New York, NY: Haworth Press.

Jakubowski, S. F., Milne, E. P., Brunner, H., & Miller, R. B. (2004). A review of empirically supported marital enrichment programs. *Family Relations, 53,* 528–536.

Kins, E., Hoebeke, P., Heylens, G., Rubens, R., & De Cuypere, G. (2008). The female-to-male transsexual and his female partner versus the traditional couple: A comparison. *Journal of Sex & Marital Therapy, 34,* 429–438.

Koepke, L., Hare, J., & Moran, P. B. (1992). Relationship quality in a sample of lesbian couples with children and child-free lesbian couples. *Family Relations, 41,* 224–229.

Kurdek, L. A. (1994a). Areas of conflict for gay, lesbian, and heterosexual couples: What couples argue about influences relationship satisfaction. *Journal of Marriage and Family, 56,* 923–934.

Kurdek, L. A. (1994b). Conflict resolution styles in gay, lesbian, heterosexual nonparent, and heterosexual parent couples. *Journal of Marriage and Family, 56,* 705–722.

Kurdek, L. A. (1998). Relationship outcomes and their predictors: Longitudinal evidence from heterosexual married, gay cohabiting, and lesbian cohabiting couples. *Journal of Marriage and Family, 60,* 553–568.

Kurdek, L. A. (2004). Are gay and lesbian cohabiting couples *really* different from heterosexual married couples? *Journal of Marriage and Family Therapy, 66*, 880–900.

Laird, J., & Green, R. J. (Eds.). (1996). *Lesbians and gays in couples and families.* San Francisco, CA: Jossey-Bass.

Larson, J. H. (2007). Couple enrichment approaches. *Journal of Couple and Relationship Therapy, 6*, 197–206.

Leonhard, G., & Mast, J. (1997). *Feathering your nest: An interactive workbook and guide to a loving lesbian relationship.* Huntington Station, NY: Rising Tide.

Meyer, I. H. (1995). Minority stress and mental health in gay men. *Journal of Health and Social Behavior, 36*, 38–56.

Page, K. (2009). Gift theory: A new theoretical construct and its application to gay, bisexual, and transgender men in large-group retreats. *Group, 33*, 235–244.

Patterson, C. J. (1994). Lesbian and gay families. *Current Directions in Psychological Science, 3*(2), 62–64.

Patterson, C. J. (2000). Family relationships of lesbians and gay men. *Journal of Marriage and the Family, 62*, 1052–1069.

Penn, D. (2009). Lesbian couple seek asylum in Canada. *Lesbian News Magazine, 35*(1), 8.

Picucci, M. (1992). Planning an experiential weekend workshop for lesbians and gay males in recovery. *Journal of Chemical Dependency Treatment, 5*(1), 119–139.

Reardon-Anderson, J., Stagner, M., Macomber, J. E., & Murray, J. (2005). *Systematic review of the impact of marriage and relationship programs.* Retrieved from http://www.urban.org/url.cfm?ID=411142

Reinhardt, R. U. (2002). Bisexual women in heterosexual relationships. *Journal of Bisexuality. 2*(2–3), 2002, 163–171.

Rest Stop. (1999). *The history of marriage encounter.* Retrieved from http://www.reststop.com/info/marriage/history.html

Sullivan, K. T., & Goldschmidt, D. (2000). Implementation of empirically validated Interventions in managed-care settings: The prevention and relationship enhancement program. *Professional Psychology: Research and Practice, 31*, 216–220.

"Times" OKs gay-couple notices, stirs debate. (2002, August 20). *USA Today*, p. 03d.

The 12-year study. (n.d.). Retrieved from http://www.gottman.com/SubPage.aspx?spdt_id=2&sp_id =100842&spt_id=1

UO program offers free counseling. (2008, February 14). *The Register Guard*. Retrieved from http://www.thefreelibrary.com/UO+program+offers+free+counseling.-a0175094405

Wampler, K. S., & Sprenkle, D. H. (1980). The Minnesota Couple Communication Program: A follow-up study. *Journal of Marriage and Family, 42*, 577–584.

Worthington, E. L., Jr., Ripley, J. S., Hook, J. N., & Miller, A. J. (2007). The hope-focused approach to couple therapy and enrichment. *Journal of Psychology and Christianity, 27*(2), 132–139.

24

Therapeutic Considerations in Same-Sex Divorce

KEVIN P. LYNESS

Whereas same-sex couples in committed relationships have been breaking up for as long as there have been same-sex relationships, only recently have same-sex couples had the opportunity to legally marry, and thus legal divorce is now a consideration. This chapter will start with a summary of the recent legal landscape in the United States and Canada. Following this review will be a discussion of what is known about relationship dissolution in same-sex couples. Briefly discussed will be risk and resiliency considerations, though very little has been written in these areas related to divorcing same-sex couples. Finally, therapeutic considerations will be discussed, focusing on how the literature on divorce therapy applies to same-sex couples.

It should be noted at the outset that there are those in the lesbian, gay, and bisexual (LGB) community who do not believe that gays and lesbians should aspire to marriage (Card, 2007; Felicio & Sutherland, 2001; Rothblum, 2006). Card (2007) makes that case that marriage is so riddled with injustices that it should not be the standard for durable relationships. She goes on to discuss the further complications of legal divorce:

> A dash of realism needed in the debate over same-sex marriage might be to think of it as the gay divorce issue, for part of the baggage of marriage is the liability to being divorced and the requirement of getting a divorce in order to signify similarly one's eternal commitment to a new partner.... Marriage and divorce can be such nightmares that I have difficulty wrapping my mind around the evident fact that so many same-sex couples in the United States have demonstrated their desire to marry by participating in public ceremonies. (Card, 2007, p. 28)

This chapter focuses particular attention on the therapeutic issues of those LGB individuals who have decided to marry and who are now contemplating divorce (or similar legal dissolution of a civil union or domestic partnership). However, as will also be noted, many same-sex couples have participated in religious marriage or commitment ceremonies that are not legally recognized, and many of the concepts in this chapter (particularly the nonlegal ones) apply to these couples as well.

Background and Review of the Literature

It is difficult to know how many same-sex couples there are in the United States. United States Census data showed approximately 594,000 same-sex couples in 2000 (O'Connell & Lofquist, 2009). It is likely that U.S. Census estimates are low because of underreporting, given that not all committed couples live together, and because of measurement error (Oswald & Clausell, 2006). There are a large number of same-sex couples who are reporting themselves as married (on the 2007 American Community Survey conducted by the U.S. Census Bureau, there were 341,000 same-sex couples reporting as married) even though they are not legally recognized as such either because they were married in a church or religious ceremony not recognized by the state or they identified as spouses for other reasons—what O'Connell and Lofquist call "socially defined" (p. 8) marriages. (Note that all these data were collected prior to more recent legal recognition of same-sex marriage in several states.)

One implication of this demographic description is that there are a number of same-sex couples who identify as married even though their marriage is not legally recognized. Although legally these couples cannot divorce (although those couples who are in legally recognized civil unions or domestic partnerships will likely require legal action to dissolve their relationships), they may seek services of couple therapists substantively similar to divorce therapy.

Legal Context

Little has been written on either the legalities or the emotional dynamics of same-sex divorce because this is a very new phenomenon, though there has been one recent book published on the subject (*The Complete Gay Divorce*; Sember, 2006) and Hertz, Wald, and Shuster (2009) provide a nice recent summary of the changing legal landscape (Patterson's 2007 summary is also useful, but was published before the recent legalization of same-sex marriage in all but Massachusetts and does not address divorce). Massachusetts was the first state in the United States to legalize same-sex marriage, enacted in 2004 based on a state supreme court decision in 2003, although Vermont had legalized civil unions in 2000 (Samar, 2006, discusses the context for how this came about and about potential future struggles). Five other states in the United States allow same-sex marriage: Connecticut (2008), Iowa (2009), Vermont (2009), New Hampshire (2009), and New York (2011), as well as the District of Columbia (2010). New York is both the most recent and most populous state to legalize same-sex marriage. Several other states have had some other relationship recognition laws: Vermont (2000) and New Hampshire (2007) both had civil unions before they enacted same-sex marriage. New Jersey also allows civil unions. Domestic partnership laws are in place in California (2005), Oregon (2007), Washington (2008), and Nevada (2009). Maine (2004), Maryland (2008), and Wisconsin (2009) all have more limited domestic partnership laws. Colorado (2009) has a law allowing designated beneficiaries and Hawaii (1997) has a law allowing reciprocal beneficiaries. New York (2008) and Maryland (2010) recognize same-sex marriages performed in other states (and California recognizes same-sex marriages registered inside or outside of California prior to November 5, 2008, as marriage and those relationships registered outside of the state on or after November 5, 2008, as domestic partnerships). Rhode Island has a mixed set of legal opinions on same-sex marriage—in 2007 the state attorney general issued an opinion that same-sex marriages performed in Massachusetts be recognized in Rhode Island, but later in 2007 the Rhode Island supreme court stated that the family court lacks jurisdiction to hear a divorce petition involving same-sex couple who were married in Massachusetts. Maine had legalized same-sex marriage in 2009, but a ballot measure passed overturning the law the same year. California had legalized same-sex marriage in 2008, but a ballot measure passed amending the constitution of the state to define marriage as a union between a man and a woman. Most recently, the California amendment was declared unconstitutional and this decision is under appeal. The overturning of the California amendment will have major implications if upheld.

On the other side, several other states have passed constitutional amendments defining marriage as a heterosexual union, and several states have even broader prohibitions against same-sex relationships (typically banning same-sex couples from domestic partnerships and/or civil unions as well). Of course, overlaying all this is the federal Defense of Marriage Act, signed into law in 1996, which has two effects: No state needs to treat same-sex relationships as marriage, even if another state has recognized the relationship as such; and the federal government defines marriage as a union between one man and one woman only. It is interesting that even though the federal government in the United States does not recognize same-sex marriage, "the 2010 Census will be the first to report counts of both same-sex partners and same-sex spouses.

The person filling out the form (Person 1) is asked to identify how all other individuals in the household are related to him or her." (U.S. Census Bureau, 2010). The 2003 U.S. Supreme Court decision overturning state sodomy laws as unconstitutional has also had an effect on the legal landscape (Samar, 2006). It is important to note that in 2011 the Obama administration decided that they could no longer defend the Defense of Marriage Act, though they would continue to enforce the law. Another notable event in 2011 was the overturn of the military "Don't Ask, Don't Tell" policy which restricted gays and lesbians serving in our armed forces.

The situation in Canada is starkly different. In 2005, with passage of the Civil Marriage Act, Canada legalized same-sex marriage across the country. Several court decisions had led to legalization of same-sex marriage in eight of the 10 provinces starting in 2003, and since 1999 many of the benefits of marriage had been extended to cohabiting same-sex couples. To round out North America, Mexico City recently passed a law legalizing same-sex marriage. Same-sex civil unions are also performed in the northern Mexican state of Coahuila. Given the legal status of same-sex marriage is greatly in flux around the world, the interested reader might consult online sources (e.g., Lambda Legal maintains an up to date directory of state laws affecting same-marriage at http://www.lambdalegal.org/states-regions) for the most up-to-date information. Another helpful website is that of the National Gay and Lesbian Task Force (http://www.theTaskForce.org), which has a number of maps showing the legal landscape in the United States.

One of the reasons that it is important to start with this discussion of the patchwork of laws in the United States is that one of the difficulties lies in how to get divorced in a state that does not recognize the marriage in the first place (Hertz et al., 2009; Sember, 2006). Many couples have married in states like Massachusetts but have then found many legal challenges when they have decided to end their relationship. Whereas Massachusetts has had few residency requirements for marriages, they do have a one-year residency requirement for divorce. Canada has a similar residency requirement for divorce.

Another legal contextual area to briefly mention is that related to custody and the adoption of children (see Appell, 2003, and Patterson, 2007, for fairly recent reviews of developments in lesbian and gay adoption law). Several states have passed laws restricting adoptions by gays and lesbians, and in many other states the status is unclear. Dodge (2006) notes that "generally, second parent adoption affords the non legal parent legal rights to the child" (p. 89) and can be an important protection for the nonbiological parent in the case of relationship dissolution. Child custody issues are among the most challenging to manage in same-sex divorce cases, particularly in states that do not recognize same-sex marriage (Hertz et al., 2009; Matthews & Lease, 2000; McIntyre, 1994). Sember (2006) also makes that point that even same-sex couples who are not legally married or in some other legally recognized relationship often have other legal entanglements (e.g., purchasing a house together and comingling finances), and these issues will have to be resolved. Many couples are not aware of some of the consequences of the current legal situation:

> To a high degree, many lesbians or gay men have had limited awareness of how the marital rules could play out in a dissolution, especially where such rules may be at odds with how they organized their financial lives, and where the circumstances of registration or marriage may have had little to do with the private understandings or intentions of the parties. (Hertz et al., 2009, p. 125)

One of the legacies of homophobia in the United States is that many courts have operated under heterosexist myths in court proceedings (McIntyre, 1994). Among these are assumptions that homosexuals (particularly gay men) will sexually abuse their children and that children in same-sex households will be damaged somehow (by their "deviant" parents, by societal discrimination, by exposure to HIV/AIDS, etc.) or that children will develop homosexual preferences because they grew up with gay parents (the concern itself is inherently homophobic, assuming that developing homosexual preferences is a bad outcome). A good deal of literature has thus been devoted to debunking these myths (see Patterson, 2006, 2009). In study after study, children of gay and lesbian parents have been shown to be at least as well adjusted as children from opposite-sex relationships.

The legal issues are particularly complicated for those couples who were legally married but now live in a state that does not recognize same-sex marriage, as noted earlier and by Hertz et al. (2009). Hertz et al. (2009) and Sember (2006) warn, first, that a legal divorce may not be possible in such a state and, second, that even if you get divorced in the state you were married in, the state you currently live in may not recognize any terms of the divorce, including custody and financial arrangements. Same-sex divorce or annulment has no legal standing in a state that does not recognize the same-sex marriage in the first place. There are many test cases working their way through the legal system, however, and precedents may be set at any time (Sember, 2006).

A recent study by Shapiro, Peterson, and Stewart (2009) found that lesbian mothers in the United States are more likely to have worries about legal problems and custody issues, and to report higher levels of depressive symptoms, than are lesbian mothers in Canada, where the legal climate is more supportive. Hertz et al. (2009) also address this dynamic:

> Laws motivated by homophobia and hostility often frame the dissolution so as to be particularly harmful to one or both parties. In states where marriage or domestic partnership is not allowed, there is often a resulting sense of delegitimization of the relationship, and for partners whose relationships have not been honored by their friends or family or coworkers a dissolution can be a painful reminder of this invisibility.... [I]n some instances the dissolution serves as perceived confirmation of the impossibility of making a long-term gay relationship work, combined with a sense of having been betrayed by one's only "comrade." It is rare for "the law" to be experienced as a *disempowering* force, but for many lesbians and gay men this is precisely the case.... For many years the law was rarely on the side of lesbians and gay men; rather, it was a tool of oppression.... Ironically, therefore, the requirement of a court divorce has for some couples become a new form of legal nightmare. (p. 127, italics in original)

Patterson (2007) also points out that "what was once a unitary experience of discrimination and oppression for same-sex couples in the United States has now been transformed into many different experiences" (p. 362) that depend on the particular legal climate of the state.

Another consequence of the muddled legal situation is that others may not recognize the seriousness of same-sex relationship dissolution when marriage is not legally recognized (Sember, 2006). Sember (2006) suggests that same-sex couples in committed relationships should use the term *divorce* when referring to their breaking-up process so that others understand the depth of the commitment and have a frame for understanding the process. Therapists should not minimize the difficulties in adjustment to relationship dissolution even in states where same-sex marriage is not legally recognized (Matthews & Lease, 2000).

Understanding Relationship Dissolution in Same-Sex Couples

Because same-sex marriage is such a new legal construct, to date there have been no empirical studies of same-sex couples who legally divorce (i.e., who legally end state-sanctioned marriage). However, Balsam, Beauchaine, Rothblum, and Solomon (2008) did a 3-year follow-up of same-sex couples who had civil unions in Vermont in the first year these were legal in that state. This follow-up appears to be the only study of relationship dissolution of legally sanctioned same-sex relationships to date, and so it is worth summarizing here. The authors followed up with 65 male and 138 female same-sex couples who had civil unions in Vermont in 2000. Note that 80% of those couples came from outside Vermont, and they had been in non–legally sanctioned relationships, many of them long-term, prior to the civil unions, making them different from many newly married couples. The comparison groups in the Balsam et al. study were 55 heterosexual married couples (one member of each of these couples was a sibling to a member of a civil union couple). In addition, there was a group of same-sex couples from the friendship circles of the civil union couples who did not have civil unions (23 male and 61 female same-sex couples). One of the initial analyses by Balsam et al. was to compare the same-sex couples in civil unions with those not in civil unions at Time 1 of their study. Of particular interest here are findings related to relationship terminations. Same-sex couples not in civil unions were more likely to have ended their relationships at the third year than were both civil union couples and heterosexual married couples. The difference between same-sex civil union and heterosexual married couples' dissolution rates was not significant. Similar to other research (e.g., Kurdek, 2004), these authors found that same-sex couples reported higher levels of relationship satisfaction in this sample than did heterosexual married couples. Also of interest were Time 1 predictors of relationship quality at follow-up: For men in same-sex relationships, these included being more out, being in a relationship of shorter duration, and having less conflict; for women in same-sex relationships, these included greater frequency of sex and less conflict. There were no significant measured predictors of relationship satisfaction at follow-up for the heterosexual married couples.

One of the most significant findings of this study (Balsam et al., 2008) was the lack of difference in relationship dissolution rates for same-sex couples with civil unions. Past research (e.g., Kurdek, 2004) had shown that same-sex couples ended their relationships sooner than did opposite-sex couples, so it may be that such legal contracts as civil unions and marriage are protective. It should be noted again that over 80% of these same-sex couples did not live in Vermont, where the legal protections would hold. In addition, these couples were among the first to take advantage of civil unions and may not be representative of all same-sex couples who marry or engage in civil unions. However, the authors did quote one of their participants discussing how the civil union had affected her relationship:

> Having a civil union has been good for us. Relationships can be hard at times and having at least one formal barrier helps make you think about splitting up…. Even though our civil union doesn't give us any real rights in (our home state), we love that we have it. In the past few years (since the civil union) it's seemed as if it was O.K. to have some separate interests. (Balsam et al., 2008, p. 112)

Perhaps the most comprehensive review of same-sex relationship dissolution was conducted by Oswald and Clausell (2006), in the *Handbook of Divorce and Relationship Dissolution* (Fine & Harvey, 2006), though given the recent expansion in marriage rights for same-sex couples, this chapter is now somewhat out of date. The following information from their review describes what was known about same-sex relationship dissolution before the legal recognition of same-sex marriage in the United States and Canada. The authors also note that the majority of research on same-sex couples has been conducted with "White, highly educated, and financially secure, 'homosexually identified' urban people who are connected to gay and lesbian organizations" (p. 500) and who do not have children.

There are not many empirical estimates of the number of same-sex relationships that break up or at what point in the relationship this might happen. The best data to date are by Balsam et al. (2008), as reported earlier. Other estimates of relationship dissolution are from studies that do not include legal marriage or civil unions and range from 4% to 31% of couples in the studies reported. In summarizing the state of research, Oswald and Clausell (2006) state, "We do not know the extent to which having a civil union or other legal or ritual marker has an impact on relationship stability—nor do we know anything in depth about the impact of children on same-sex dissolution" (p. 504).

Oswald and Clausell (2006) note, "Virtually everything we know in answer to the question of why and how same-sex couples break up has come from the research program of Kurdek" (p. 504; e.g., see Kurdek, 1991, 1992, 2004, 2006, 2008, 2009). Again, these data were gathered in a context where there was no legal recognition of same-sex marriage.

> Kurdek's research suggests that same-sex and opposite-sex couple are similar in that partners seem to stay together when they find the relationship rewarding and perceive fewer alternatives to being together. In contrast to heterosexual couples, partners in same-sex couples perceive fewer barriers to leaving, and this is perhaps largely due to their lack of institutionalization. (Oswald & Clausell, 2006, p. 506)

For couple therapists working with same-sex couples considering divorce or other form of relationship dissolution, it is likely that the reasons given for the divorce will be similar to those given by heterosexual couples. For example, in Kurdek's early research (1991), he found that the top reasons for ending same-sex relationships were nonresponsiveness and partner problems (e.g., drug or alcohol problems). Other contributors were frequent absence, sexual incompatibility, and mental cruelty. Emotional responses to separation included personal growth, loneliness, and relief from conflict; managing relationships with ex-partners and financial stress were the top problems experienced after breakup. Managing well after the breakup was associated with higher education, less time in relationship with the ex-partner, maintaining independent finances, and lower reported levels of love and attachment to the partner. No differences were found between lesbian and gay male couples.

Additional reasons for ending relationships include such financial issues as arguing about money, having discrepant income levels, and not pooling finances (Oswald & Clausell, 2006). Couples where work intruded on the relationship were more likely to break up, as were sexually dissatisfied couples. Additional factors in relationship dissolution include higher levels of reported negative emotions, less relationship satisfaction, less emotional commitment, less time invested in the relationship, and higher values on personal autonomy. Over time, couples whose relationship ended reported a decrease in positivity and an increase in relationship conflict and an increase in personal autonomy. It is important to note that most of these patterns held for opposite-sex as well as same-sex couples.

Although many of the issues leading to relationship dissolution are very similar for same-sex and opposite-sex couples, there are some areas of unique stress in same-sex couples. Ritter and Terndrup (2002) summarize several areas of potential conflict in same-sex couples that may lead to relationship dissolution if not addressed. These include partner differences, including discrepancies in age, ethnicity, and income. Many authors (Connolly, 2004; Green, 2004; Green & Mitchell, 2002; Ritter & Terndrup) also note that homophobia (external and internalized) and heterosexism are particular stressors on or challenges for same-sex couples.

One area where gender-role socialization and lack of legal recognition have combined to create risk for relationship dissolution is with gay male couples, who often see separation and dissolution of the relationship as the first option when faced with conflict (see Greenan & Tunnell, 2003). It is not known if this dynamic will carry over to relationships that are legally sanctioned, though the evidence from Balsam et al. (2008) that the couples from Vermont with civil unions did not separate more than did heterosexual couples is promising. When there are no legal bindings, separation can often be a knee-jerk response for gay couples, and therapists should be aware of this inclination.

Very little is known about relationship dissolution in same-sex couples with children. Oswald and Clausell (2006) summarize an unpublished dissertation (Turteltaub, 2002) on relationship dissolution in lesbian couples with children, focusing on the experiences of the children. It should be noted that the children were all conceived through donor insemination and only the biological mother was legally recognized as the parent. The children in these relationships experienced many of the stresses of children of divorce in opposite-sex couples but also several stressors unique to having lesbian mothers. These additional stressors included having difficulty talking with others about their experience because others assumed they had a mother and a father (sometimes they lied about having two mothers and then felt bad "because they did not want people to think they were ashamed of their families," Oswald & Clausell, 2006, p. 507). The children also reported feeling protective of their mothers, seeing them as vulnerable to prejudice. The children expressed appreciation for being raised in affirming households, and this was a protective factor. One challenge, then, in same-sex divorce is protecting the children from the dual threats of divorce and perceived deviancy of the family, and this challenge often requires the parents to join forces in coparenting, a task that can be a great difficulty for divorcing couples whether they be same sex or heterosexual (Morton, 1998).

In the Turteltaub (2002) study, the reasons for relationship breakup included disagreement about parenting, weak couple communication exacerbated by the demands of parenting, and conflict worsened by poor extended family support or acceptance. Legal barriers to becoming parents contributed to the couples' conflict. One theme that came up with these mothers, a theme echoed across other reports (e.g., Dodge, 2006; Hertz et al., 2009; Morton, 1998), is the fear of losing contact with their children because of a lack of legal parental rights. From a power perspective, the parent without legal standing is seriously disadvantaged, often feeling at the mercy of the biological or legal parent.

Emotional Dynamics of Same-Sex Relationships Relevant to Divorce

Much of the literature reviewed for this section was published before marriage was legally sanctioned for same-sex couples in the United States and Canada; however, many of these dynamics are relevant to this discussion. In general, while there are many commonalities with opposite-sex couple divorce, there are also several unique dynamics in same-sex relationship divorce and dissolution. The unique dynamics are related to a number of issues, but primarily these can be seen as attributable to discrimination, bias, and homophobia and to the nature of same-sex relationships. As has been noted earlier, social supports are extremely important in adjustment to same-sex divorce, and these supports are often affected by homophobia and lack of acceptance, both in one's family of origin and in society at large (Green, 2004; Green & Mitchell, 2002; Hertz et al., 2009; Morton, 1998; Oswald & Clausell, 2006; Ritter & Terndrup, 2002).

Several authors (e.g., Green, 2004; Greenan & Tunnell, 2003; Ossana, 2000; Ritter & Terndrup, 2002) discuss how gender-role socialization may provide challenges for same-sex couples in an ongoing relationship and in divorce. One issue is emotional fusion and avoidance of conflict in lesbian couples (see Green, 2004). Similarly, for gay men, gender-role socialization may lead to problems of emotional disengagement or competition (Green, 2004). Male socialization typically rewards individuality and stoic behavior that may lead to intimacy challenges in gay male couples and may make postdivorce adjustment challenging as well, particularly in situations where coparenting is necessary. Although therapists have relied on gender-role socialization as an explanation for stress in same-sex couples, the reality may be different than assumed—Ritter and Terndrup (2002) report findings that lesbians and gay men incorporate gender constructs differently, and much of Kurdek's research has not shown relationship deficits in areas assumed to be related to gender-role socialization. On the other hand, some research shows that relationship problems in gay male couples are linked to "an overdevelopment of skills and values associated with traditional masculinity" (Ossana, 2000, p. 279). Similarly, the evidence that fusion or female socialization creates problems in lesbian couples is also more complex than that simple assumption. As summarized by Ossana (2000): "Many of the relational features characterized as fusion … are related to the high levels of relationship satisfaction reported by lesbian couples. This kind of intense intimacy may encourage personal growth and risk taking by creating deeper trust and safety" (p. 281). Morton also talks about the construct of merger, or the high levels of emotional closeness that are often typical in these relationships. According to Morton (1998), merger may result in difficulties in tolerating difference after divorce or may make it difficult to differentiate after the divorce. On the other hand, in many lesbian communities, partners continue to remain close after relationship dissolution, and some authors have posited that the emotional closeness of lesbian relationships should not be pathologized but is instead a source of strength (Felicio & Sutherland, 2001; Matthews & Lease, 2000; Morton, 1998). So, gender-role socialization may be both a strength and a challenge for lesbian and gay male couples, but therapists working with these couples would be well advised to assess and attend to how gender plays a part in the relationship dissolution and subsequent postdivorce adjustment.

One of the consequences of societal and political pressure is that there may be a perception that divorcing couples have to be especially careful to not have a "messy" divorce; that is, there is pressure to act in a way that does not further tarnish societal views of same-sex relationships (Morton, 1998). Additional emotional dynamics in same-sex divorce can be found in literature focusing on risk and resiliency.

Therapeutic Considerations in Issues of Risk and Resiliency

There does not appear to be any direct research looking at risk and/or resiliency factors in divorcing same-sex couples to date. Prouty Lyness's (2006) edited volume *Lesbian Families' Challenges and Means of Resiliency: Implication for Feminist Family Therapy* does not have any references to divorce but does have chapters with relevance. Connolly (2006) explores feminist perspectives of resilience in lesbian couples, including stressors. Overall stressors for all LGBT people includes deprivation of civil and legal rights as well as discrimination, bias, and violence. Kurdek (2006) notes that in both lesbian and gay cohabiting couples, partners report receiving more support from friends than from family. Kurdek (2004, 2009) also reports that supports are important for relationship satisfaction in same-sex couples (as it is for opposite-sex couples). It is likely particularly the case during divorce and relationship dissolution that support of family of origin will be a protective factor. Afifi and Hamrick (2006) note that social support in general, and family support specifically, is a protective factor in divorce among opposite-sex couples. It is likely that social supports play an even more important role in postdivorce adjustment for partners from same-sex relationships, given the hostile nature of the overall culture (Connolly, 2006; Morton, 1998).

Several specific constructs have been linked to lesbian couples' resiliency, including community resources, public programs, and community institutions (Connolly, 2006). Connolly suggests that therapists can utilize prior responses to stressors when looking for ways to build resiliency in same-sex couples. Long and Andrews (2007) also provide general considerations for strengthening resiliency in same-sex couples, but their focus is on intact couples not divorcing couples.

Afifi and Hamrick (2006) provide an excellent review of risk and resiliency in postdivorce families. However, none of this research was done with members of same-sex couples, so it is unknown how much of the findings applies to this group. On the other hand, Kurdek's body of research shows that in many of the processes that regulate relationship commitment and satisfaction, same-sex couples are similar to opposite-sex couples, so it is reasonable to assume that some of the risk and resiliency factors are similar as well. Briefly, Afifi and Hamrick identify the following risk factors for poor postdivorce adjustment: poor communication skills and negativity; lack of flexibility and a certainty orientation (i.e., being more comfortable when there is a great deal of clarity); engaging in avoidant coping behaviors; parents' hostility and aggression toward each other (this is one of the strongest predictors of children's well-being in postdivorce opposite-sex families, particularly when children are caught in the middle of parental conflicts); and poor conflict management strategies (e.g., escalation, negativity, avoidance, and aggression).

Afifi and Hamrick (2006) note that many of these challenges can then lead to difficulty with appropriate boundaries. The discussion of poor boundaries in postdivorce families involving children focuses on enmeshment and emotional overreliance on the children and the negative effects this lack of boundaries has on children (Afifi & Hamrick, 2006). As noted earlier, children in same-sex divorce may feel even more pressure to protect their parents because of societal hostility creating additional loyalty binds. Research on the effects of this boundary ambiguity on children is somewhat equivocal. Some research contradicts the notion that emotional reliance on children is detrimental. For example, in qualitative interviews Arditti (1999) found that children experienced their mother's reliance on them positively and reported that they felt closer to their mothers. The majority of research from heterosexual divorce, however, does support the notion that role enmeshment can pose psychological risks for children.

Afifi and Hamrick (2006) focus attention on the importance of effective coparenting in postdivorce adjustment, as well as the negative effects of ongoing partner conflict. As clinicians we are aware of the loyalty conflicts that are often manifested in divorced families where there is a great deal of conflict—children are often forced to pick sides and cannot maintain equitable relationships with both parents. Although there is no research that explores whether this situation is exacerbated in divorce in same-sex couples, it is very likely that the additional legal confusion created by nonbiological parents, second-parent adoptions (or the unavailability of such), and potential discrimination in the courts will have negative effects on children as well as their parents and should be carefully attended to by therapists working with divorcing same-sex families.

Finally, Afifi and Hamrick (2006) discuss the importance of family rituals in positive postdivorce adjustment. Rituals may actually be a strength of divorcing same-sex partners in that since same-sex couples have been denied legal marriage and the rituals associated with that, they have been free to develop their own sets of rituals marking relationship transitions, and many groups of gays and lesbians have developed breaking-up rituals that may help to mark this transition for them and their families and friends (Felicio & Sutherland, 2001; Matthews & Lease, 2000). Afifi and Hamrick discuss the construct of *family making* (from the work of Bella as cited in Afifi and Hamrick, 2006). Active engagement in family making postdivorce has been found to help members reconstruct a sense of family after divorce. Again, because gay and lesbian couples have had to actively engage in family making because they have been denied the traditional cultural family markers, they may have skills in this area that therapists and others can utilize. A focus on rituals in couple therapy with gay and lesbian families, whether intact or divorcing, may be particularly important because gay and lesbian families are so often excluded from other rituals marking and resolving major life events (Ossana, 2000).

There are a number of factors that have been shown to be protective for children in opposite-sex divorce (Hetherington & Stanley-Hagen, 2000). These factors include personal characteristics of intelligence, an easy temperament, high academic achievement, self-worth, ego strength, and internal locus of control. In addition, a harmonious, supportive family environment with a residential parent who demonstrates high levels of warmth, responsiveness, control, and monitoring (i.e., an authoritative parenting style), as well as low conflict between coparents, are all important factors in promoting resiliency in these divorcing families. There is no reason to suspect that these factors would not also be important considerations in adjustment to same-sex divorce.

Additional Treatment and Intervention Considerations

General Considerations

It is important that therapists working with same-sex couples have an understanding of same-sex couple relationship dynamics, a full review of which is clearly beyond the scope of this chapter. I direct the readers to several excellent sources on working with same-sex partners other than this volume: Bigner and Wetchler's (2004) *Relationship Therapy With Same-Sex Couples;* Bieschke, Perez, and DeBord's (2007) *Handbook of Counseling and Psychotherapy With Lesbian, Gay, Bisexual, and Transgender Clients*; Greenan and Tunnell's (2003) *Couple Therapy With Gay Men;* Ritter and Terndrup's (2002) *Handbook of Affirmative Psychotherapy With Lesbians and Gay Men*; as well as specific articles and chapters by Alonzo (2005), Green and Mitchell (2002), Long and Andrews (2007), Long and Lindsey (2004), and Wallace and Lyness (2004).

Applications From Divorce Therapy

Much of the initial work in divorce therapy was by Sprenkle (see Sprenkle's *Divorce Therapy*, 1985). More recently, Adams (2007), Emery and Sbarra (2002), Rice (2005), and Sprenkle and Gonzalez-Doupé (1996) have published chapters on divorce therapy or couple therapy with divorcing couples. None of these chapters focuses on same-sex couples; only Adams's (2007) chapter was published after any legal recognition of same-sex marriage, and Rice is the only author to even mention same-sex divorce in her chapter. Nonetheless, much of this clinical wisdom is useful for working with divorcing same-sex couples. Readers should familiarize themselves with this literature on divorce therapy, given that here there is room only to highlight important considerations.

Divorce therapy "can be defined as relationship treatment that focuses on decreasing the function of the marital bond, with the eventual goal of dissolving it" (Sprenkle & Gonzalez-Doupé, 1996), though the process itself is often not that clear-cut. Many therapists utilize a stage model to conceptualize the divorce process, the most general of which involves three stages: (1) predivorce decision making, (2) divorce restructuring, and (3) postdivorce recovery (Adams, 2007; Rice, 2005; Sprenkle & Gonzalez-Doupé, 1996), though all these authors note that this model is simply a heuristic and the process may not proceed linearly through the stages.

The decision-making phase may be the most important phase in working with same-sex couples for a number of reasons. First, as has been noted already, for gay male couples breaking up or divorce may be a knee-jerk reaction to conflict or difficulty, and couple therapists should be particularly aware of this. Also, considerations of the legal context may be particularly important here. Therapists working in this area should be well informed of the legal contexts affecting the couple (Patterson, 2007). The therapist will need to assess the clients' level of knowledge about the legal contexts described here in addition to more standard considerations of divorce therapy.

The restructuring phase is often complicated and stressful, particularly for couples with children (Sprenkle & Gonzalez-Doupé, 1996). The confused legal context for same-sex couples will likely lead to fear, anxiety, and stress in divorcing couples beyond that experienced by heterosexual divorcing couples. The restructuring phase may be affected by the reasons for divorce, but perhaps in different ways than in opposite-sex couples. For example, infidelity is often a key reason for divorce in opposite-sex couples (Emery & Sbarra, 2002) but may not be an issue for many gay male couples (Greenen & Tunnell, 2003). This areas is where a thorough understanding of same-sex couple dynamics will be important in helping the therapist determine how these dynamics are affecting the divorce process.

Rice (2005) takes a developmental approach to divorce and focuses on issues of intimacy and identity, noting that dangers of divorce include a retreat from intimacy or commitment, in addition to challenges to identity (e.g., identity diffusion as a result of defining oneself by one's relationship and incomplete self-differentiation). Also focused on identity, Morton (1998) notes that divorce for lesbians may also lead to challenges in homosexual identity development. Therapists should be aware of their clients' level of homosexual identity development, as well as their level of outness, which can vary between partners and may be an issue in divorce in a number of ways, as noted earlier in this chapter.

Mediation

One of the primary tools mentioned throughout the literature on same-sex divorce is mediation (Dodge, 2006; Felicio & Sutherland, 2001; Hertz et al., 2009; McIntyre, 1994). A key consideration in mediation is that unbiased mediation requires attention to internalized homophobia (Dodge, 2006; Felicio & Sutherland, 2001; Hertz et al., 2009; McIntyre, 1994), as well as an understanding of the relationship dynamics of same-sex couples. Dodge (2006) makes several recommendations for mediation programs: (1) Provide training for mediators on the varied familial constructs they might confront in same-sex married couples' families; (2) support joint custody resolutions involving interaction between the two parents, but still respect the biological origins of the child; (3) if demonstrable, recognize the de facto parental role a same-sex partner had in raising the child; and (4) show respect for prearrangement agreements.

Mediation is particularly important in cases where child custody is an issue (Dodge, 2006; Hertz et al., 2009). Traditionally, parentage has been established by giving birth (for women), by being married to a woman who gave birth (for men), and by adoption, as well as by contractual arrangements that have been deemed valid; but for same-sex parents where egg or sperm donation or surrogacy have been used, challenges to the status quo have resulted. Legal parentage involves four factors: (1) biology and genetics, (2) procreative intent, (3) parental conduct, and (4) marital or domestic partnership or civil union; furthermore, nearly half of states recognize parentage based on parental conduct and bonding with the child (Hertz et al., 2009).

Disputes over parentage are far more common in same-sex dissolutions than in opposite-sex dissolutions (Hertz et al., 2009) because of necessary reliance on adoption or assisted reproduction. These disputes typically arise in three instances: (1) where same-sex partners have functioned as parents, but only one partner is a legal parent; (2) when a third party (e.g., sperm or egg donor, surrogate mother, involved family member) seeks parental rights; and (3) where a legal judgment has rendered both partners parental rights, but one partner is now trying to disavow this arrangement or set aside an adoption. Mediation is likely to be the best way of addressing these disputes, particularly because partners can typically choose mediators who are LGB-friendly (Dodge, 2006).

A Case Study

Derek and Gary are a married couple who live in Massachusetts. They had been together for many years prior to the legalization of gay marriage in their state, and they were excited to take advantage of a legal marriage. Massachusetts has long allowed adoptions by same-sex couples, and Derek and Gary had adopted an infant, a son, in 2001. They believed that the legal recognition of marriage would help with Gary's family, who were strongly opposed to their relationship on religious grounds. This conflict with Gary's family was a long-standing source of stress for the couple. Unfortunately, over the years Gary and Derek have grown apart and have now presented to a couple therapist with the desire to end their relationship.

The therapy starts with a discussion of the recent emotional climate in the relationship. Both Gary and Derek report that their interactions in the past few years have trended toward more negative interactions and fewer positive ones. They report increased arguing over a number of issues, but particularly about money. The stress related to Gary's lack of family support has been an increasing source of conflict between the partners. They also report that their frequency of sex has decreased markedly. Neither partner reports any infidelity. They live in a welcoming community and do not experience much external homophobia. As part of the predivorce decision-making phase, the therapist works with the partners to make sure that this is not a knee-jerk reaction to conflict, though it is apparent from the history that this is not the case for this couple. One area that the therapist explores is where the couple plans to live after the divorce—both partners intend to stay in the state, making the legal context easier to deal with.

The partners present with significant conflict over parenting and custody. The therapist believes that mediation may be particularly helpful for this couple and refers them for several sessions of mediation with someone trained in working with same-sex couples. The mediation focuses on building effective coparenting and coming up with a joint custody plan. The therapist works to supplement the mediation by focusing the couple on developing some end-of-relationship rituals that will help to mark the transition for both them and their son. The therapist also helps them with family making, particularly Gary, who cannot rely on his family for social support. Over several months they work toward developing a solid coparenting relationship, decreasing conflict between them, and setting appropriate boundaries. When the divorce is final, the therapist recommends that both Derek and Gary each see someone individually to work on issues of loneliness and the stresses of coparenting. In addition, they both intend to work on identity issues, trying to redefine themselves post divorce.

Recommendations for Future Research and Conclusions

The gaps in the research literature are easy to summarize: There has been no research on same-sex divorce as a legal entity and very little research overall on the dynamics of relationship dissolution in same-sex couples. We need research investigating the effects of institutionalization on relationship dissolution. It is important, too, that this research "move beyond gay–straight comparisons that privilege heterosexual relationships as the dominant referent ... and instead document ... the unique ways that same-sex relationship dissolutions may progress" (Oswald & Clausell, 2006, p. 510).

What research has been done has involved mostly White, educated, middle-class same-sex couples. Clearly, research is needed that explores how and why same-sex couples divorce, the unique dynamics associated with same-sex divorce, and the effects of the legal context on these dynamics and the divorce process and on the utility and efficacy of divorce therapy with same-sex couples. All this research needs to include diverse samples in diverse locations, thereby representing the diverse ethnicity in couples (e.g., as evident in the work of Blumer, 2008, who has studied gay men's experiences of couplehood in Alaska; also in the work of Farmer, 2004, who studied gay Mexican American men). This need for study of diverse couples is particularly important because members of unmarried same-sex couples (and unmarried opposite-sex couples) report higher proportions of interracial relationships than do married opposite-sex couples (O'Connell & Lofquist, 2009).

Another influence on same-sex relationship dissolution that needs addressing empirically is domestic violence (Oswald & Clausell, 2006). Although some researchers (e.g., Sember, 2006) imply that domestic violence is related to same-sex divorce, there is no empirical foundation for this assertion. Ritter and Terndrup (2002) summarize the state of research on domestic violence in same-sex couples, and note that prevalence estimates vary widely, though they conclude that rates are likely to be similar to those in opposite-sex couples. They do note that same-sex partners are less likely to seek help from the legal system for problems of relational violence. As an example of how violence in same-sex relationships is not recognized, they cite gay male violence, which is often invisible because of assumptions that the relationships of gay males are not intimate, that the violence involves a fight between equals, and that men are free to simply leave a violent relationship (Ritter & Terndrup, 2002). As is true in opposite-sex couples, it is important to screen for violence in working with couples who are seeking divorce, particularly as the partners may not volunteer this information. Oswald and Clausell (2006) also wonder how help seeking might be constrained by legal vulnerabilities faced by abused gay or lesbian fathers and mothers.

Same-sex divorce, from a legal perspective, is a new phenomenon in North America. The legal context is rapidly evolving, often confusing and contradictory, and saddled with heterosexist norms, beliefs, and laws that result in continued oppression and discrimination while at the same time opening up opportunities for legally recognized same-sex marriage in certain jurisdictions. Although public acceptance of gay and lesbian committed relationships is clearly growing (Rothblum, 2006), there is still discrimination and oppression at many levels of society— from the micro level of one's family of origin or community to the macro-level influence of the Defense of Marriage Act and "Don't Ask, Don't Tell"—which affect couples in myriad ways. Therapists need to understand the changing legal context, their local legal context, and the contexts affecting the couple in question (Patterson, 2007).

Therapists' beliefs and attitudes are extremely important for therapists working with same-sex couples (Alonzo, 2005; Bieschke, Paul, & Blasko, 2007; Emery & Sbarra, 2002; Green & Mitchell, 2002; Patterson, 2007). When considering same-sex divorce, therapists must consider not only their own attitudes and beliefs about gay and lesbian relationships but also their beliefs about separation and divorce (Emery & Sbarra, 2002; Rice, 2005). Therapists working to help same-sex couples with divorce or relationship dissolution must attend to not only the common experiences of all couples experiencing divorce but also the unique considerations for same-sex couples. When children are involved, complex legal issues related to custody must be attended to; therapists must also attend to unique loyalty binds of children in these relationships, as well as the social supports from community and families of origin. The issue of social support is complicated as well for divorcing couples who do not have children. Issues of gender-role socialization are likely to be important. Finally, therapists working with same-sex couples must always be aware of heterosexist assumptions and of the potential for effects of oppression and discrimination. Therapists are well advised to go beyond this introductory chapter to familiarize themselves with the literature on same-sex relationships and divorce therapy.

Acknowledgment

The author would like to thank Alicia Bosley for her assistance in developing materials for this chapter.

References

Adams, J. F. (2007). Divorce therapy in context. *Journal of Couple and Relationship Therapy*, 6(1/2), 109–123.

Afifi, T. D., & Hamrick, K. (2006). Communication processes that promote risk and resiliency in postdivorce families. In M. A. Fine & J. H. Harvey (Eds.), *Handbook of divorce and relationship dissolution* (pp. 435–456). Mahwah, NJ: Erlbaum.

Alonzo, D. J. (2005). Working with same-sex couples. In M. Harway (Ed.), *Handbook of couples therapy* (pp. 370–385). Hoboken, NJ: Wiley.

Appell, A. R. (2003). Recent developments in lesbian and gay adoption law. *Adoption Quarterly*, 7(1), 73–84.

Arditti, J. A. (1999). Rethinking relationships between divorced mothers and their children: Capitalizing on family strengths. *Family Relations*, 48, 109–119.

Balsam, K. F., Beauchaine, T. P., Rothblum, E. D., & Solomon, S. E. (2008). Three-year follow-up of same-sex couples who had civil unions in Vermont, same-sex couples not in civil unions, and heterosexual married couples. *Developmental Psychology*, 44, 102–116.

Bieschke, K. J., Paul, P. L., & Blasko, K. A. (2007). Review of empirical research focused on the experience of lesbian, gay, and bisexual clients in counseling and psychotherapy. In K. J. Bieschke, R. Perez, & K. DeBord (Eds.), *Handbook of counseling and psychotherapy with lesbian, gay, bisexual, and transgender clients* (2nd ed., pp. 293–315). Washington, DC: American Psychological Association.

Bieschke, K. J., Perez, R., & DeBord, K. (Eds.). (2007). *Handbook of counseling and psychotherapy with lesbian, gay, bisexual, and transgender clients* (2nd ed.). Washington, DC: American Psychological Association.

Bigner, J. J., & Wetchler, J. L. (Eds.). (2004). *Relationship therapy with same-sex couples*. New York, NY: Haworth.

Blumer, M. L. C. (2008). *Gay men's experiences of Alaskan society in their coupled relationships*. Unpublished dissertation, Iowa State University. Ames

Card, C. (2007). Gay divorce: Thoughts on the legal regulation of marriage. *Hypatia, 22*, 24–38.

Connolly, C. M. (2004). Clinical issues with same-sex couples: A review of the literature. In J. J. Bigner & J. L. Wetchler (Eds.), *Relationship therapy with same-sex couples* (pp. 3–12). New York, NY: Haworth.

Connolly, C. M. (2006). A feminist perspective of resilience in lesbian couples. In A. M. Prouty Lyness (Ed.), *Lesbian families' challenges and means of resiliency: Implications for feminist family therapy* (pp. 137–162). New York, NY: Haworth Press.

Dodge, J. A. (2006). Same-sex marriage and divorce: A proposal for child custody mediation. *Family Court Review, 44*, 87–103.

Emery, R. E., & Sbarra, D. A. (2002). Addressing separation and divorce during and after couple therapy. In A. S. Gurman & N. S. Jacobson (Eds.), *Clinical handbook of couple therapy* (3rd ed., pp. 508–530). New York, NY: Guilford Press.

Farmer, S. (2004). *A phenomenological study of gay, Mexican-American men who disclose their HIV+ status to their family*. Unpublished Doctoral dissertation, St. Mary's University, San Antonio, TX.

Felicio, D., & Sutherland, M. (2001). Beyond the dominant narrative: Intimacy and conflict in lesbian relationships. *Mediation Quarterly, 18*, 363–376.

Fine, M. A., & Harvey, J. H. (Eds.). (2006). *Handbook of divorce and relationship dissolution*. Mahwah, NJ: Erlbaum.

Gartrell, N., Banks, A., Reed, N., Hamilton, J., Rodas, C., & Deck, A. (2000). The national lesbian family study III: Interviews with mothers of 5-year-olds. *American Journal of Orthopsychiatry, 70*, 542–548.

Green, R-J. (2004). Forward. In J. J. Bigner & J. L. Wetchler (Eds.), *Relationship therapy with same-sex couples* (pp. xiii–xvii). New York, NY: Haworth.

Green, R.-J., & Mitchell, V. (2002). Gay and lesbian couples in therapy: Homophobia, relational ambiguity, and social support. In A. S. Gurman, & N. Jacobson (Eds.), *Clinical handbook of couple therapy* (pp. 546–568). New York, NY: Guilford Press.

Greenan, D., & Tunnell, G. (2003). *Couple therapy with gay men*. New York, NY: Guilford Press.

Hertz, F., Wald, D., & Shuster, S. (2009). Integrated approaches to resolving same-sex dissolutions. *Conflict Resolution Quarterly, 27*, 123–143.

Hetherington, E., & Stanley-Hagan, M. (2000). Divorce. In A. Kazdin (Ed.), *The encyclopedia of psychology* (Vol. 3, pp. 61–65). Washington, DC: American Psychological Association.

Kurdek, L. A. (1991). The dissolution of gay and lesbian couples. *Personal Relationships, 8*, 265–278.

Kurdek, L. A. (1992). Relationship stability and relationship satisfaction in cohabiting gay and lesbian couples: A prospective longitudinal test of the contextual and interdependence models. *Journal of Social and Personal Relationships, 9*, 125–142.

Kurdek, L. A. (2004). Are gay and lesbian cohabiting couples *really* different from heterosexual married couples? *Journal of Marriage and Family, 66*, 880–900.

Kurdek, L. A. (2006). Differences between partners from heterosexual, gay, and lesbian cohabiting couples. *Journal of Marriage and Family, 68*, 509–528.

Kurdek, L. A. (2008). A general model of relationship commitment: Evidence from same-sex partners. *Personal Relationships, 15*, 391–405.

Kurdek, L. A. (2009). Assessing the health of a dyadic relationship in heterosexual and same-sex partners. *Personal Relationships, 16*, 117–127.

Long, J. K., & Andrews, B. V. (2007). Fostering strength and resiliency in same-sex couples: An overview. *Journal of Couple and Relationship Therapy, 6*(1/2), 153–165.

Long, J. K., & Lindsey, E. (2004). The Sexual Orientation Matrix for Supervision: A tool for training therapists to work with same-sex couples. In J. J. Bigner & J. L. Wetchler (Eds.), *Relationship therapy with same-sex couples* (pp. 123–135). New York, NY: Haworth.

Matthews, C. R., & Lease, S. H. (2000). Focus on lesbian, gay, and bisexual families. In R. M. Perez, K. A. DeBord, & K. J. Bieschke (Eds.), *Handbook of counseling and psychotherapy with lesbian, gay, and bisexual clients* (pp. 249–273). Washington, DC: American Psychological Association.

Mclntyre, D. H. (1994). Gay parents and child custody: A struggle under the legal system. *Mediation Quarterly, 12*(2), 135–149.

Morton, S. B. (1998). Lesbian divorce. *American Journal of Orthopsychiatry, 68*, 410–419.

O'Connell, M., & Lofquist, D. (2009). *Counting same-sex couples: Official estimates and unofficial guesses.* Paper presented at the annual meeting of the Population Association of America, Detroit, MI.

Ossana, S. M. (2000). Relationship and couples counseling. In R. M. Perez, K. A. DeBord, & K. J. Bieschke (Eds.), *Handbook of counseling and psychotherapy with lesbian, gay, and bisexual clients* (pp. 275–302). Washington, DC: American Psychological Association.

Oswald, R. F., & Clausell, E. (2006). Same-sex relationships and their dissolution. In M. A. Fine, & J. H. Harvey (Eds.), *Handbook of divorce and relationship dissolution* (pp. 499–514). Mahwah, NJ: Erlbaum.

Patterson, C. J. (2006). Children of lesbian and gay parents. *Current Directions in Psychological Science, 15,* 241–244.

Patterson, C. J. (2007). Lesbian and gay family issues in the context of changing legal and social policy environments. In K. Bieschke, R. Perez, & K. DeBord (Eds.), *Handbook of counseling and psychotherapy with lesbian, gay, bisexual, and transgender clients* (2nd ed., pp. 359–377). Washington, DC: American Psychological Association.

Patterson, C. J. (2009). Children of lesbian and gay parents: Psychology, law, and policy. *American Psychologist, 64,* 727–736.

Prouty Lyness, A. M. (Ed.). (2006). *Lesbian families' challenges and means of resiliency: Implications for feminist family therapy.* New York, NY: Haworth Press.

Rice, J. K. (2005). Divorcing couples. In M. Harway (Ed.), *Handbook of couples therapy* (pp. 405–430). Hoboken, NJ: Wiley.

Ritter, K., & Terndrup, A. (2002). *Handbook of affirmative psychotherapy with lesbians and gay men.* New York, NY: Guilford Press.

Rothblum, E. D. (2006). Same-sex marriage and legalized relationships: I do, or do I? In J. J. Bigner (Ed.), *An introduction to GLBT family studies* (pp. 203–214). Binghamton, NY: Haworth.

Samar, V. J. (2006). Same-sex marriage: The difficult road ahead. In J. J. Bigner (Ed.), *An introduction to GLBT family studies* (pp. 215–219). Binghamton, NY: Haworth.

Sember, B. M. (2006). *The complete gay divorce.* Franklin Lakes, NJ: Career Press.

Shapiro, D. N., Peterson, C., & Stewart, A. J. (2009). Legal and social contexts and mental health among lesbian and heterosexual mothers. *Journal of Family Psychology, 23,* 255–262.

Sprenkle, D. H. (1985). *Divorce therapy.* New York, NY: Haworth.

Sprenkle, D. H., & Gonzalez-Doupé, P. (1996). Divorce therapy. In F. P. Piercy, D. H. Sprenkle, J. L. Wetchler, & Associates (Eds.), *Family therapy sourcebook* (2nd ed., pp. 181– 219). New York, NY: Guilford Press.

Turteltaub, G. (2002). *The effects of long-term primary relationship dissolution on the children of lesbian parents.* Unpublished clinical dissertation, Alliance University, San Francisco, CA.

U.S. Census Bureau. (2010). *The census: A snapshot.* Washington, DC: Author. Retrieved from http://2010.census.gov/partners/pdf/factSheet_General_LGBT.pdf

Wallace, D., & Lyness, K. P. (2004). Resources on same-sex couples for therapists and clients. In J. J. Bigner & J. L. Wetchler (Eds.), *Relationship therapy with same-sex couples* (pp. 147–155). New York, NY: Haworth.

Section V
Training Issues

25

LGB-Affirmative Training Strategies for Couple and Family Therapist Faculty

Preparing Heterosexual Students to Work With LGB Clients

THOMAS STONE CARLSON and CHRISTI R. MCGEORGE

The literature clearly highlights the need for couple and family therapists (CFTs) to be prepared to work with lesbian, gay, and bisexual clients (LGB; Bepko & Johnson, 2000; Bernstein, 2000; Clark & Serovich, 1997; R. J. Green, 1996; S. K. Green & Bobele, 1994; Henke, Carlson, & McGeorge, 2009; Rock, Carlson, & McGeorge, 2010). For instance, the research suggests that LGB individuals seek therapy services at a rate of 25% to 77%, which is two to four times the rate of heterosexual individuals (Bell & Weinberg, 1978; Bradford, Ryan, & Rothblum, 1994; Liddle, 1997). Specifically, in the CFT field, S. K. Green and Bobele (1994) found that 72% of the 457 clinical members of the American Association for Marriage and Family Therapy (AAMFT) they surveyed reported that approximately 10% of their client population identified as LGB and that 80% reported that they were currently working with lesbian and gay clients. Given these findings it is apparent that CFTs will have LGB clients in their caseloads and must be prepared to provide competent services to this population.

It is important to note, however, that researchers and educators have been critical of the lack of training that CFTs receive to work with LGB clients (Bepko & Johnson, 2000; Bernstein, 2000; Godfrey, Haddock, Fisher, & Lund, 2006; Long, 1996; Long & Serovich, 2003). For example, Doherty and Simmons (1996) found that in their sample of AAMFT clinical members, nearly half the respondents reported that they felt incompetent to treat lesbian and gay clients. Several studies have found that graduate students in clinical training programs also reported feeling inadequately prepared to provide competent therapy to LGB clients (Anhalt, Morris, Scotti, & Cohen, 2003; Rock et al., 2010; Savage, Prout, & Chard, 2004). For instance, Rock et al. (2010) found that 60.5% of their sample of 190 students in accredited CFT programs reported that they received no training on affirmative therapy practices with LGB clients. This lack of LGB-affirmative training is problematic given that these researchers also found that the amount of LGB-affirmative training CFT students received was predictive of their self-reported clinical competence with LGB clients. In another study, Phillips and Fischer (1998) found that nearly half the 107 clinical graduate students in their sample reported that they had not been encouraged to explore their heterosexist biases. This finding is important because research has also found that the exploration of heterosexist biases predicted students' readiness to work with LGB clients (Phillips & Fischer, 1998). Given that "therapists typically receive the most intensive part of their training in graduate school…if graduate programs do not address gay, lesbian, and bisexual issues, most therapists will probably be inadequate in this area" (Dworkin & Gutierrez, 1989, p. 7). Therefore, LGB clients who seek the services of CFTs "are essentially at the mercy of the therapist's own struggles, prejudices, and intolerance" (McCann, 2001, p. 80).

In addition to this overall lack of training on LGB topics in clinical programs, Clark and Serovich (1997) found, there were few resources for CFTs in the form of journal articles that address working with LGB clients. In particular, they found that only 77 (0.006%) of the 13,217 articles published from 1975 to 1995 in the 17 main family therapy and related discipline journals addressed topics related to LGB clients, utilized an LGB sample, or considered sexual orientation as a variable. Clark and Serovich (1997) also explored other training opportunities that were available to CFTs by examining the number of presentations and posters that addressed LGB topics at annual AAMFT conferences. They found that at the 1996 AAMFT conference only five of the 146 presentations (3.4%) and none of the 75 posters addressed LGB topics. In order to determine if the lack of training opportunities on LGB topics at AAMFT conferences has continued, we reviewed the conference presentations for the 2009 conference and found that only four of the 113 presentations (3.5%) and only five of the 121 posters (4.1%) focused on sexual orientation. Given the limited increase in training opportunities for CFTs at the AAMFT conferences and the limited training that students report receiving on affirmative therapy practices with LGB clients, "the need for special training [on LGB topics] appears to be widespread and urgent" (R. J. Green, 1996, p. 390).

We propose that the "special training" needed involves not only teaching students about topics related to LGB clients but also helping CFT students develop positive beliefs and attitudes about LGB individuals. Given that affirmative therapy is defined as "an approach to therapy that embraces a positive view of LGB identities and relationships and addresses the negative influences that homophobia and heterosexism have on the lives of LGB clients" (Rock et al., 2010, p. 175), this chapter focuses on helping CFT faculty ensure that heterosexual students gain the self-awareness and skills necessary to provide competent therapy services to LGB clients. Although lesbian, gay, bisexual, and transgender individuals are often grouped together, we discuss working with just LGB clients because our focus is on sexual orientation rather than gender identity and expression. We recognize that in the CFT literature, topics related to working with transgender clients have been marginalized and, to some extent, entirely absent. It is not our intent to add to this marginalization; however, it is important to us that the differences between sexual orientation and gender identity are recognized and that they are seen as two distinct yet interrelated factors of a person's identity. Furthermore, although many of the ideas discussed in this chapter can be applied to transgender clients, we will not be addressing the additional oppressions that transgender clients can experience as a result of their gender identity and expression because this subject is beyond the scope of this chapter. Thus, we acknowledge that to prepare CFT students to work with transgender clients, additional scholarly literature is needed in order to ensure that topics related to working with transgender clients receive the detail and attention they deserve.

Before further defining the scope of this chapter, it is important for us to acknowledge that we are married and heterosexually identified CFT faculty members. Although we are both committed to being out as allies in our personal and professional lives, we recognize that our heterosexual privileges blind us to many of the challenges and oppressions faced by the LGB community. Because of our position as heterosexual individuals, we focus this chapter on helping heterosexual CFT faculty members train heterosexual CFT students to competently and ethically work with LGB clients. Although we work with LGB student therapists, we want to acknowledge that because of our heterosexual privilege we cannot take a stand as experts regarding the education of LGB students.

Literature Review

Before reviewing the literature on LGB-affirmative training practices, it seems important to first summarize the process of becoming an LGB-affirmative therapist because this process informs the training literature. Given the lack of literature and empirical research on LGB-affirmative therapy and training in the CFT field, we extended this review to include literature from other clinical disciplines (e.g., psychology and counseling).

Becoming an LGB-Affirmative Therapist

The literature on becoming an LGB-affirmative therapist highlights the need for therapists to engage in a process of critical self-reflection and develop specific skills in their work with LGB clients (Bepko & Johnson, 2000; Bernstein, 2000; Long & Lindsey, 2004; Matthews, 2007; McCann, 2001; McGeorge & Carlson, 2011). Affirmative therapy goes beyond working with LGB clients and is about a belief system and attitude that is applied to our work with all clients regardless of sexual orientation. Therefore, "affirmative counseling with gay, lesbian, and bisexual clients begins before we know the client's sexual orientation" (Matthews, 2007, p. 201). It is important for affirmative therapists to not assume that every client is heterosexual and be open to the possibility that any client may be LGB (Matthews, 2007).

Therapists who are LGB-affirmative believe that all sexual orientations are "valid and rich orientations in their own right and … perceive homophobia, not diverse sexualities, as pathological" (Davies, 2000, p. 40). In addition to believing in the legitimacy of all sexual orientations, the literature suggests that heterosexual therapists must conduct a thorough exploration of their attitudes and values related to LGB relationships. This exploration should include an examination of the "family therapist's family values" (Bernstein, 2000, p. 446) in order to determine if those values are inclusive of LGB individuals, couples, and families. Thus, heterosexual therapists must work to identify and label homophobic and heterosexist beliefs within themselves to begin the process of becoming an LGB-affirmative therapist (Bepko & Johnson, 2000; Bernstein, 2000; McGeorge & Carlson, 2011).

Although heterosexual therapists need specific training on self-of-the-therapist issues related to their own homophobia, becoming an LGB-affirmative therapist also involves gaining knowledge of issues relevant to the lives of LGB clients and current research on LGB topics (McCann, 2001). In particular, the literature suggests that heterosexual therapists need to be knowledgeable about internalized homophobia, the "coming-out" process, LGB models of identity development, gay-related stress, legal and political issues important to the LGB community, resources for the LGB community, and heterosexual bias and privilege (Bernstein, 2000; R. J. Green, 1996; Greene, 2007; McGeorge & Carlson, 2011). Knowledge and awareness of each of these issues are essential because it is impossible to provide ethical therapy to LGB clients without being able to fully affirm LGB individuals, couples, and families (Murphy, 1991).

Preparing Students to Provide LGB-Affirmative Therapy

The majority of the literature reviewed in this section represents theoretical or nonempirical articles that provide important guidance for preparing students to become LGB-affirmative therapists. It should also be noted, however, that the research studies that do exist have found that clinical students consistently report a lack of training on LGB topics in their graduate programs (Pilkington & Cantor, 1996; Rock et al., 2010; Savage et al., 2004). For instance, in one study, sexual orientation issues were covered in less than 25% of all graduate courses reviewed (Pilkington & Cantor, 1996). In response to this overall lack of training, R. J. Green (1996) wondered, "In a culture with widespread antipathy toward lesbian and gay relationships, what messages do silence, neutrality, and omission of lesbian and gay family topics convey to students in our classes?" (p. 395). Thus, educators have an ethical obligation to break their silence on these issues (Long & Lindsey, 2004).

An important component of this obligation on the part of clinical faculty members is to teach students the knowledge and skills necessary to work with LGB clients (Long, 1996). Phillips and Fischer (1998) argue that "generalist training will not result in LGB affirmative therapists as it is usually provided in a heterosexual/heterosexist worldview" (p. 713) and that preparing students to become LGB affirmative requires specialized training. One study that sought to identify the specialized training required to help students become LGB-affirmative was a Delphi study conducted by Godfrey et al. (2006). These researchers found that their panel of experts thought that the two most important factors in preparing students to be LGB-affirmative therapists were to help them develop an awareness of their own values, biases, and prejudices regarding sexual orientation and to teach them about the concepts of internalized and institutional homophobia. Moreover, this Delphi study found that faculty members need to help students develop the ability to name examples of heterosexism and acquire the skills to overcome internalized and externalized heterosexism in their work with LGB clients. In addition, Godfrey et al. (2006) found that faculty members needed to teach students to identify examples of their own heterosexual privileges. The importance of having students explore their own beliefs is further supported by research that has found that this critical self-exploration is an essential component of training students to become LGB-affirmative therapists (Lidderdale, 2002).

Another important area addressed in the affirmative training literature is the need to train students to avoid seeing LGB individuals as a homogenous group but instead see the diversity that exists within the LGB community (Greene, 2007). Thus, it is important to teach students about intersectionality and the multiple forms of oppression that LGB clients can experience as a result of the relationship between their sexual orientation and their gender, race, ability status, socioeconomic status, and the like. Greene (2007) also argues not only that specialized skills are needed to address the homophobia and heterosexism LGB clients experience in the larger society and in their families but also that we need to prepare students to understand that LGB clients seek therapy for many of the same reasons that heterosexual clients seek therapy.

Although there are many things that individual faculty members can do to prepare students to work with LGB clients, the literature also highlights the need for training programs themselves to become LGB affirmative. For example, Phillips (1999) argues that "training environments should be characterized by the absence of homophobia and heterosexism and the presence of LGB-affirmative attitudes and behaviors" (p. 340). Furthermore, it is important that programs actively seek to include the presence of LGB students and faculty and ensure that topics and events significant to the LGB community are "naturally integrated into the daily training environment for students" (Phillips, 1999, p. 340).

Much of the literature appears to assume that faculty already possess the knowledge and skills necessary to prepare students to work with LGB clients, yet researchers have found that students report knowing more about LGB topics than their faculty members do (Phillips & Fischer, 1998). The need for educators to explore their own biases and assumptions about sexual orientation and gain the knowledge necessary to work competently with LGB clients should not be overlooked. Thus, an important first step for CFT faculty members is to explore their own heterosexual biases before beginning the process of helping their students to address their own heterosexist bias (Long, 1996; Long & Lindsey, 2004). In addition to exploring their own biases and assumptions about sexual orientation, educators have a responsibility to seek out learning opportunities to increase their knowledge about working with LGB clients through "formal coursework, attending workshops on LGB topics, and joining professional LGB organizations" (Godfrey et al., 2006, p. 502).

Larger Societal Issues Faced by Heterosexual Faculty and Students

Before presenting a series of strategies for faculty members to use to prepare students to become LGB-affirmative therapists, it is important to address the larger societal issues that heterosexual faculty members and students face as they prepare themselves to work affirmatively with LGB clients. If left unexplored, these larger societal issues could become a barrier for faculty members in their own pursuits to become LGB-affirmative therapists and educators. In addition to exploring these larger societal issues in their own lives, heterosexual CFT faculty members need to ensure that their heterosexual students also examine these issues for themselves. In particular, three larger societal issues have been identified in the literature as barriers to becoming an LGB-affirmative heterosexual therapist: (1) heterosexism, (2) heteronormative assumptions, and (3) heterosexual privilege (Long, 1996; Long & Lindsey, 2004; Matthews, 2007; McCann, 2001; McGeorge & Carlson, 2011).

Heterosexism involves two interrelated societal processes: the devaluing and disadvantaging of LGB individuals, couples, and families and, at the same time, the privileging of heterosexual individuals, couples, and families (Herek, 1990; Ritter & Turndrup, 2002). Although it is important to be aware of the oppression and discrimination faced by the LGB community, many heterosexual educators may fail to see the corollary process of heterosexism that establishes heterosexuality as superior to all other sexual orientations. Spaulding (1999) argues that heterosexism represents "a form of social control" that seeks to establish and maintain heterosexual dominance (p. 13). It is important for heterosexual CFT faculty members and students to be aware of the negative influence of heterosexism on the lives and relationships of LGB individuals and families and on the therapy process itself (Bepko & Johnson, 2000; Bernstein, 2000; Long, 1996; Long & Lindsey, 2004; Long & Serovich, 2003). It is of particular importance that heterosexual faculty members and students acknowledge having been socialized in a heterosexist culture and, therefore, cannot escape the shaping influence that heterosexism has had on their lives. It is also important that heterosexual faculty members and students become aware of the many ways that heterosexism has shaped their view of what constitutes a "healthy" relationship.

Another barrier experienced by all heterosexual faculty members and students is the tendency to rely on and apply heteronormative assumptions to their personal and professional lives (Oswald, Blume, & Marks, 2005). Heteronormative assumptions are a product of heterosexism and represent the "automatic unconscious beliefs and expectations that reinforce heterosexuality and heterosexual relationships as the ideal norm" (McGeorge & Carlson, 2011, p. 15). Thus, heteronormative assumptions create a situation where heterosexual relationships are the standard from which all other relationships are judged. It is important to note that since heteronormative assumptions operate at the unconscious level, well-intentioned heterosexual CFT faculty members and students unknowingly apply these assumptions in ways that are harmful to their LGB clients.

Heterosexual privilege, unearned advantages given to heterosexuals based solely on their sexual orientation, is another barrier that heterosexual faculty members and students experience as they work to become LGB-affirmative therapists. Heterosexuals are often unaware that they experience daily advantages and societal benefits that make their lives easier and affirm their sexual orientation as the idealized norm. Whereas the negative impacts of oppression on the self-worth of LGB individuals receives much attention, little attention is focused on heterosexual privilege, which has the opposite effect on heterosexual individuals by creating an increased sense of self-worth (McGeorge & Carlson, 2011). This increased sense of self-worth comes from the sense of belonging that heterosexual individuals receive as members of the dominant socially sanctioned group and is one of the primary privileges associated with being a heterosexual person.

Strategies for Preparing LGB-Affirmative Student Therapists

The literature highlights three areas that should be addressed in order to prepare students to become competent to provide affirmative therapy to LGB clients. The first area involves the need for heterosexual CFT faculty members to engage in self-of-the-faculty work to explore their own heteronormative assumptions, heterosexual privileges, and heterosexual identity development. The second area focuses on training strategies that faculty members can use to prepare their heterosexual students. The final area involves the need for CFT programs to develop affirmative policies and practices that guide the overall structure of their training.

Self-of-the-Faculty Work

Most of the literature on preparing students to work with LGB clients appears to make the assumption that heterosexual faculty already are affirmative themselves and possess the necessary knowledge and skills to competently work with LGB clients. However, since there appears to be a lack of training in the CFT field around working affirmatively with LGB clients, it seems safe to assume that heterosexual faculty members themselves have not received the training needed to prepare their students to provide therapy to LGB clients (Long & Serovich, 2003; Phillips, 1999). Therefore, a logical first step in preparing students to work with LGB clients would be to make sure that heterosexual CFT faculty members engage in the self-of-the-faculty work necessary to explore their own beliefs and biases related to sexual orientation.

To assist heterosexual faculty members in this important self-of-the-faculty work, we have adapted a three-step self-exploration model that was created for heterosexual CFTs to use in becoming affirmative therapists (McGeorge & Carlson, 2011). The three steps of this model involve the exploration of (1) heteronormative assumptions, (2) heterosexual privileges, and (3) heterosexual identity development.

Step 1: Exploring Heteronormative Assumptions   The first step in this self-of-the-faculty work involves a critical reflection on the beliefs that heterosexual CFT faculty members personally hold with regard to normative and healthy relationship practices. Since we are all socialized in a heterosexist society, it is impossible for heterosexual faculty members to be completely free of heteronormative assumptions. Therefore, it is critical that heterosexual CFT faculty members acknowledge that they hold unconscious heteronormative assumptions and work to make conscious the ways in which their beliefs about sexual orientation, sexuality, and intimate relationships have been shaped by these heteronormative assumptions. This awareness process involves examining the societal and familial messages that faculty members learned about the normality of a heterosexual sexual orientation and the abnormality of an LGB sexual orientation. An important aspect of this exploration process involves an awareness that heteronormative assumptions lead to the unconscious belief in the superiority of heterosexual relationships. Thus, acknowledging the presence of these unconscious heteronormative assumptions is important in helping heterosexual CFT faculty members examine the extent to which heterosexism has shaped their perceptions about the LGB community in ways that may go against their personal values and beliefs (Pope, 1995). A series of self-reflection questions to help heterosexual CFT faculty examine their unconscious heteronormative assumptions can be found in McGeorge and Carlson (2011). Examples of these self-reflection questions include:

- Were sexual orientation and same-sex and bisexual relationships talked about in my family? If so, what values were communicated? If not, what did that silence communicate?
- What are my beliefs about how a person "becomes" gay, lesbian, or bisexual? What are my beliefs about why I did not "become" gay, lesbian, or bisexual?
- When I first meet someone, how often do I assume that person is heterosexual? What values and beliefs inform this assumption?

It is important that as members of the dominant socially sanctioned group, heterosexual CFT faculty members review such questions frequently in order to examine the impact of their heteronormative assumptions about their personal and professional lives.

Step 2: Exploring Heterosexual Privileges The second step in this self-of-the-faculty work involves becoming aware of the heterosexual privileges that we hold as members of a dominant socially sanctioned group. This process of exploring heterosexual privilege is vital because "the discrimination experienced by the LGB community is inherently linked to and amplified by the advantages granted to heterosexual persons by a heterosexist society" (McGeorge & Carlson, 2011, p. 18). Thus, the process of becoming LGB affirmative requires heterosexual CFT faculty members to acknowledge their privileged status and work to dismantle the unearned benefits we receive on a daily basis. Heterosexual CFT faculty members can begin this process of acknowledging and dismantling heterosexual privileges by reflecting on the questions found in McGeorge and Carlson (2011). Sample questions include:

- How has your involvement in heterosexual relationships been encouraged, rewarded, acknowledged, and supported by your family, your friends, and the larger society?
- Have you ever worried about being removed from a spiritual, religious, civic, or professional organization because of your heterosexuality?
- Have you ever worried that a therapist would refuse to see you based on your heterosexuality or that a therapist might try to change your heterosexuality?

In addition, it may be helpful for heterosexual CFT faculty members to create their own list of heterosexual privileges they experience in their roles as faculty members, supervisors, and therapists and in their professional associations (e.g., AAMFT).

Step 3: Exploring the Development of a Heterosexual Identity The third step in this self-of-the faculty work for heterosexual faculty involves acknowledging that they have a sexual orientation and exploring how they came to develop a heterosexual sexual orientation (McGeorge & Carlson, 2011). In recent years, researchers have begun to address the importance of examining the identity development of heterosexual individuals in an effort to highlight that all people have a sexual orientation and to more fully understand the development of heteronormative assumptions and heterosexual privilege (Mohr, 2002; Worthington, Savoy, Dillon, & Vernaglia, 2002). When heterosexual therapists explore the development of their heterosexual identity, for example, they tend to have greater acceptance of all sexual orientations, which reduces their reliance on heteronormative assumptions (Dillon et al., 2004). Furthermore, the process of exploring the development of a heterosexual identity "appropriately shifts the focus from exclusively examining the identity development of the marginalized group to examining the identity development of the dominant socially sanctioned group" (McGeorge & Carlson, 2011, p. 19). This process is critical given that heterosexism is "an expression of who the therapists are as heterosexual-identified people" (Mohr, 2002, p. 534). A list of questions that heterosexual faculty members may find helpful as they begin to explore the development of their heterosexual sexual orientation can be found in McGeorge and Carlson (2011). Examples of these questions include:

- How do you explain how you came to identify as a heterosexual? What factors were most important or influential to your development of a heterosexual identity?
- Have you experienced attraction to members of the same sex? If so, how did you make sense of those attractions? If not, how do you make sense of not having attractions to members of the same sex?
- How does your identification as a heterosexual influence how you make sense of how a person comes to identify as an LGB individual?

As heterosexual faculty engage in this exploration, "heterosexuality thus becomes not simply an assumption, but a sexual orientation identity that people develop, just as people develop a gay, lesbian, bisexual, or other identity" (Matthews, 2007, p. 206).

There are several ways that heterosexual CFT faculty members could use the self-reflection questions associated with each of these three steps. First, we recommend that individual faculty members attempt to answer each of these questions on their own using a critical journaling process. After completing this individual self-examination process, CFT faculty members should identify another heterosexual colleague to serve as an accountability partner. We recommend that with this partner they review the questions a second time in an effort to be more honest about their progress toward being more aware of the ways heterosexism has influenced their personal and professional lives. In addition, we believe it important for all the heterosexual CFT program faculty members to meet regularly to discuss these questions, thereby collectively raising awareness of the influence of heterosexism in their training program. Finally, it is important that once heterosexual faculty have engaged in this important self-of-the-faculty work, they guide their heterosexual students through this same process.

Training and Educational Strategies

Much of the literature on LGB-affirmative therapy is focused on educational and training strategies to prepare students to work with LGB clients. These strategies for training students to work competently with LGB clients can be divided into three main sections, namely, suggestions for course content, assignments, and class activities.

Course Content   This section focuses on topics that need to be addressed in academic courses to prepare heterosexual CFT students to provide LGB-affirmative therapy. A general suggestion is that before discussing specific topics that need to be addressed, CFT faculty should include readings in each course that focus on issues relevant to working with LGB clients (Bepko & Johnson, 2000; Long, 1996; Long & Serovich, 2003). In particular, the literature highlights the need to include readings that explore the heterosexist biases that exist in the foundational theoretical approaches of the field (Matthews, 2007; Phillips, 1999). In addition, faculty members could invite students to discuss ways that these theories could be altered to be more LGB affirmative. For example, faculty members could assign students to write a paper or give a presentation reconstructing one of the foundational theories from a perspective that is informed by an awareness of heterosexism and heteronormative assumptions (McGeorge & Carlson, 2010).

Diagnosis and Assessment   In addition to understanding the heterosexist bias in the foundational CFT theories, it is also important to teach students about the heterosexist biases that exist in the diagnosis and assessment process and in the *Diagnostic and Statistical Manual of Mental Disorders* (American Psychiatric Association, 2000). Moreover, faculty members should teach students how heterosexism, gay-related stress, and internalized homophobia negatively influence the lives and relationships of LGB people (Phillips, 1999). For example, the literature documents that LGB individuals experience increased rates of depression and anxiety as well as alcohol and drug misuse (Bos, van Balen, van den Boom, & Sandfort, 2004; Lewis, Derlega, Griffin, & Krowinski, 2003; Mays & Cochran, 2001). Researchers have also found, however, that gay-related stress (i.e., the additional stress that LGB individuals experience as a consequence of their minority status) appears to be the cause of these increased rates of depression, anxiety, and drug misuse (Meyer, 1995). Thus, it is essential for faculty members to teach students about the role that gay-related stress may play in the emotional and relationship struggles experienced by LGB individuals.

Ethics   Another important topic to include is the unique ethical considerations related to working with LGB clients. For instance, the literature clearly highlights the need for faculty members to teach students about the unethical nature of conversion therapy and the research that highlights its damaging effects on LGB clients (Greene, 2007; Phillips, 1999; Serovich et al.,

2008). Considering that conversion therapy is based on the belief that LGB sexual orientations are pathological and/or immoral, Serovich and colleagues (2008) argue that "the theory and practice of conversion therapy violates principles of competence, integrity, respect for individual rights and dignity, and social responsibility" (p. 235). In addition to teaching students about existing research on conversion therapy, CFT faculty members have an ethical responsibility to familiarize students with the AAMFT board's position on the practice of conversion therapy, which states that the AAMFT "does not consider homosexuality a disorder that requires treatment, and as such, we see no basis for such therapy" (2009). Considering that the AAMFT has yet to develop guidelines related to the ethical treatment of LGB clients, it seems important for CFT faculty members to teach students about the American Psychological Association's *Guidelines for Psychotherapy With Lesbian, Gay and Bisexual Clients* (APA, 2000).

Research Methods   The literature on LGB-affirmative training also highlights the need to include LGB topics in research methods courses (Anhalt et al., 2003; Phillips, 1999). Particularly, faculty members can use examples from published studies on LGB topics as models for how to design research studies (Anhalt et al., 2003). Faculty could also introduce students to queer theory as a legitimate research methodology. Oswald et al. (2005) argue that queer theory methodologies provide an effective mechanism to decenter traditional heteronormative assumptions that are present in many existing approaches to theory and research.

Life-Span Development   In addition to clinical and research courses, content on LGB individuals and families should also be included in life-span development courses (Greene, 2007). It is important that LGB-affirmative therapists have the knowledge they need to work with LGB clients across the life-span. For example, since children can be aware of their sexual orientation at an early age and may struggle with feelings of being different from their peers, it is important that therapists be open to the possibility that children may have diverse sexual orientations and be prepared to work with children in nonheterosexist ways. Another important topic to address in life-span development courses is the diversity that exists between and within the LGB community (Greene, 2007). Highlighting the diversity that exists within the LGB community decreases the likelihood that students will apply monolithic stereotypes to LGB clients.

Advocacy Skills   Finally, a key aspect of preparing heterosexual students to become LGB-affirmative therapists involves the teaching of advocacy skills and sociopolitical awareness (Dillon et al., 2004; McGeorge & Carlson, 2010). Since many of the struggles experienced by LGB individuals are the result of living in a heterosexist society, CFT faculty need to teach heterosexual students how to advocate for their LGB clients effectively both inside and outside the therapy room. For example, heterosexual students need to learn how to deconstruct the influence of heterosexism in the everyday lives and relationships of LGB clients (McGeorge & Carlson, 2011). This deconstruction process can involve helping LGB clients explore the possible impact that heterosexism has on the presenting issues that brought them to therapy. Another advocacy skill to teach students is to be aware of resources that exist within the local community that serve the LGB individuals in order to help LGB clients confront the isolation that can be associated with belonging to a marginalized group (Bernstein, 2000; R. J. Green, 1996; Long & Serovich, 2003).

Course Assignments   In addition to proposing LGB-relevant course content, the literature on LGB-affirmative training also suggests a number of course assignments that CFT faculty members can use to prepare students to work with LGB clients. One of the primary purposes of these assignments is to help heterosexual students engage in their own self-reflection work to explore their heteronormative assumptions and heterosexual privilege. One mechanism for this self-reflection work is the use of writing assignments. For example, faculty members can assign heterosexual students to write about their "journeys around sexual orientation and goals for development in reducing heterosexism in their own lives" (Godfrey et al., 2006, p. 498). Faculty can also assign heterosexual students to write an ally coming-out paper, which can help strengthen the students' identities as LGB-affirmative therapists (Lidderdale, 2002). Similarly, McGeorge and Carlson (2010) recommend that faculty require heterosexual students to write an LGB-affirmative statement, which involves the students' articulating their commitments to becoming LGB-affirmative therapists and describing their own unique model of LGB-affirmative therapy.

In addition to having students engage in these self-reflection writing assignments, it would be helpful for CFT faculty to assign projects that assist heterosexual students in developing their advocacy skills. One example of such an assignment is for faculty to assign students to write the AAMFT or their state professional organizations to request that these groups adopt policies indicating their support of equal rights for the LGB community. Another example involves having students write letters to the editor supporting the rights of LGB individuals, couples, and families.

Along with suggesting these writing assignments, the literature also discusses the need to expose students to the lives and relationships of LGB individuals. For example, faculty can assign heterosexual students to read books and magazines as well as watch movies or television shows geared to an LGB audience (Long & Serovich, 2003; Matthews, 2007). It is important for CFT faculty to assign students to watch videos or movies of healthy LGB couples and families, not just clinical examples, because most heterosexual students will not have everyday experiences with LGB individuals and families (Brown, 1991; R. J. Green, 1996). Another assignment to help expose students to nonclinical LGB individuals is to have students interview an LGB couple about their coming-out experiences, relationship history, and advice for family therapists (R. J. Green, 1996).

Although it is important to expose students to the lives of LGB individuals, Matthews (2007) argues these assignments should not be restricted to the classroom. In order to teach students to provide affirmative therapy, CFT faculty members could assign heterosexual students to become involved in their local LGB community by attending events or activities by, for example, marching in a local pride parade as a part of a group of affirmative therapists (Matthews, 2007). These personal interactions and contacts can decrease the level of heterosexist bias that students possess and increase their advocacy skills. As heterosexual students increase their familiarity to the LGB community, it is important that they not simply rely on their LGB clients for this personal contact but, instead, become actively involved in the larger LGB community.

Course Activities   There are several course activities that are recommended in the LGB-affirmative training literature. For example, faculty members can have students engage in role-plays with LGB client scenarios in order to help students practice the skills associated with LGB-affirmative therapy prior to working with LGB clients (Godfrey et al., 2006; Long & Serovich, 2003; Phillips, 1999). Members of the CFT faculty could also invite LGB therapists to guest-lecture in their classes or participate in a panel discussion about issues relevant to working with LGB clients (Godfrey et al., 2006; Long, 1996; Long & Serovich, 2003). In addition, a small-group activity could involve showing a video clip of an LGB person coming out to family members and having each small group develop and present a treatment plan showing how they would work affirmatively with the family (R. J. Green, 1996).

Strategies for Programs

Researchers have found that the LGB-affirmative nature of clinical agencies is predictive of therapists' ability to practice LGB-affirmative therapy (Bieschke & Matthews, 1996; Matthews, Selvidge, & Fisher, 2005). Thus, perhaps the most important way to prepare students to become LGB-affirmative therapists is for CFT programs to develop and implement LGB-affirmative policies and practices. In this section, we focus on how to develop an affirmative CFT program through strategies that shape the identity and structure of the program.

Assessment   In an effort to begin the process of structuring an LGB-affirmative program, it may be important for CFT programs to perform an initial assessment. Long and Serovich (2003) offer a series of assessment questions to help CFT training programs evaluate their effectiveness in preparing students to work with LGB clients:

> (1) "Are we training students to be competent in working with LGBT clients?" (2) "Is our program adequately inclusive of sexual minority training materials?" (3) "Do trainees have adequate exposure to working with LGBT individuals, couples, and families? If not, why, and what can be done to improve the learning atmosphere?" and (4) "What struggles do we experience in cultivating an inclusive environment?" (p. 60)

Finally, programs should also ask themselves, "Would gay, lesbian, and bisexual trainees feel comfortable disclosing their sexual orientation within the environment of this program?" (Long & Serovich, 2003, p. 65). These questions are helpful because they encourage CFT faculty to intentionally examine the overall training environment they have created and identify areas in which they can become more LGB affirmative.

Policies   There are several ways that CFT programs can implement LGB-affirmative policies. For instance, programs could include LGB related policies and resolutions adopted by the AAMFT in their student handbooks (Phillips, 1999). Programs could also develop antiharassment policies that would ban the use of homophobic language and behaviors (Long & Serovich, 2003). In addition to banning homophobic language, it would be important to provide students with information on the appropriate use of terms related to sexual orientation as found in section 3.13 of the *Publication Manual of the American Psychological Association* (APA, 2009) in their student handbooks. Moreover, CFT programs should consider having a policy stating their affirmative beliefs toward LGB sexual orientations and their commitment to preparing students to serve LGB clients competently. Furthermore, programs may want to create a policy explaining that students are expected to hold LGB-affirmative beliefs and a procedure for handling situations where students do not hold affirmative beliefs about LGB sexual orientations (Long & Serovich, 2003).

On-Site Clinic   Another strategy to create a more LGB-affirmative program environment is to ensure that training programs with on-site clinics include in their intake paperwork the option for clients to identify whether they are in a long-term committed relationship instead of simply providing the choices of single or married (Long & Serovich, 2003; Matthews, 2007). Also, programs could add wording in their informed consent documents that disclosures related to sexual orientation will be kept confidential (Long & Serovich, 2003). It is also important that all clinic advertising materials include a nondiscrimination statement that specifically includes sexual orientation because "such a statement lets LGB clients know that the agency has considered the possibility that LGB individuals may be clients" (Matthews, 2007, p. 204). Programs should also consider including images of LGB people in their clinic marketing materials and making their waiting rooms LGB friendly by including magazines and other resources directed at the LGB community (Long & Serovich, 2003; Matthews, 2007). Beyond creating a welcoming clinical environment for LGB clients, training programs need to establish relationships with agencies that serve the LGB community in order to actively recruit LGB clients for their clinics, as CFT programs have a responsibility to ensure that students have the opportunity to provide direct therapy services to LGB clients (Long & Serovich, 2003).

Recruitment   In addition to recruiting LGB clients, CFT programs also need to develop specific strategies to recruit LGB students. For example, CFT programs could send recruitment materials locally, regionally, and nationally to LGB studies programs, campus LGB student service centers, and campus organizations that serve LGB students. Additionally CFT programs might consider advertising their programs through listservs focused on LGB scholarship or for LGB professionals and in LGB magazines or service directories. In recruitment materials, it is important to highlight the program's involvement in LGB events or activities as well as research on LGB topics by faculty and students (Phillips, 1999). Such actions can communicate to potential LGB students that the program is welcoming and affirmative.

It is essential that CFT faculty recognize that because we live in a heterosexist society, it is impossible for programs to ever arrive at a place where they are fully affirmative. Therefore, CFT programs continually need to evaluate their policies, processes, and structures (Phillips, 1999). These programs may want to consider asking local members of the LGB community to participate in annual evaluations of the program's efforts to be more LGB affirmative. These local members of the LGB community could also serve on an ongoing advisory board that regularly reviews all policies and practices associated with the program.

Recommendations for Future Research on Affirmative Training

There are limited empirical data that provide insight into what CFT programs are actually doing to prepare their students to work with LGB clients. Therefore, a systematic study of how CFT programs are attempting to address sexual orientation and implement LGB-affirmative training practices is needed. For example, researchers could explore both the amount and the type of LGB content being taught in accredited CFT programs. Researchers could also develop tools and measures to assess students' actual competence working with LGB clients, and not just students' perceptions of their competence. These measures could be based on clinical observations of students' work or survey instruments for LGB clients to assess their therapist's knowledge and competence. Finally, considering the importance of the training environment in preparing students to work with LGB clients, researchers could assess the degree to which CFT programs demonstrate an LGB-affirmative environment. The Nonheterosexist Organizational Climate Scale developed by Bieschke and Matthews (1996) could be a good resource to assist researchers in this process.

Conclusion

The literature documents the need for CFT programs to prepare students to provide competent therapy services to LGB clients. The process of training CFT students to become LGB-affirmative therapists begins when faculty members commit to engaging in their own self-of-the-faculty work to address the influence of heterosexism on their personal and professional lives. Until heterosexual CFT faculty members gain the knowledge, skills, and beliefs that are associated with LGB-affirmative therapy, it is unlikely that CFT students will ever be prepared to provide competent therapy services to LGB clients. Preparing students to provide LGB-affirmative therapy requires a significant level of commitment on the part of CFT faculty members and students. This commitment requires that CFT faculty members "cease to define [LGB-affirmative therapy] as a political issue and instead realize that this is a matter of ethics, standard of care, and psychotherapy effectiveness" (Brown, 1996, p. 54).

References

American Association for Marriage and Family Therapy. (2009). Reparative/conversion therapy. Retrieved from http://www.aamft.org/iMIS15/AAMFT/MFT_Resources/MFT_Resources/Content/Resources/Position_On_Couples.aspx

American Psychiatric Association. (2000). *Diagnostic and statistical manual of mental disorders* (4th ed., text revision). Arlington, VA: American Psychiatric Publishing.

American Psychological Association (APA). (2000). Guidelines for psychotherapy with lesbian, gay, and bisexual clients. Retrieved from http://www.apa.org/pi/lgbt/resources/guidelines.aspx

American Psychological Association (APA). (2009). *Publication manual of the American Psychological Association* (6th ed.). Washington, DC: APA.

Anhalt, K., Morris, T. L, Scotti, J. R., & Cohen, S. H. (2003). Student perspectives on training in gay, lesbian, and bisexual issues: A survey of behavioral clinical psychology programs. *Cognitive and Behavioral Practice, 10,* 255–263.

Bell, A. P., & Weinberg, M. S. (1978). *Homosexualities: A study of diversity among men and women.* New York, NY: Simon & Schuster.

Bepko, C., & Johnson, T. (2000). Gay and lesbian couples in therapy: Perspectives for the contemporary family therapist. *Journal of Marital and Family Therapy, 26*(4), 409–419.

Bernstein, A. C. (2000). Straight therapists working with lesbians and gays in family therapy. *Journal of Marital and Family Therapy, 26*(4), 443–454.

Bieschke, K. J., & Matthews, C. R. (1996). Career counselor attitudes and behaviors toward GLB clients. *Journal of Vocational Behavior, 48,* 243–255.

Bos, H. M. W., van Balen, F., van den Boom, D. C., & Sandfort, T. G. M. (2004). Minority stress: Experience of parenthood and child adjustment in lesbian families. *Journal of Reproductive and Infant Psychology, 22*(4), 291–304.

Bradford, J., Ryan, C., & Rothblum, E. D. (1994). National lesbian health care survey: Implications for mental health care. *Journal of Consulting and Clinical Psychology, 62,* 228–242.

Brown, L. (1991). Commentary on the special issue of *The Counseling Psychologist*: Counseling with lesbians and gay men. *The Counseling Psychologist, 19*(2), 235–238.

Brown, L. (1996). Preventing heterosexism and bias in psychotherapy and counseling. In E. D. Rothblum & L. A. Bond (Eds.), *Preventing heterosexism and homophobia* (pp. 36–58). Thousand Oaks, CA: Sage.

Clark, W. M., & Serovich, J. M. (1997). Twenty years and still in the dark? Content analysis of articles pertaining to gay, lesbian, and bisexual issues in marriage and family therapy journals. *Journal of Marital and Family Therapy, 23*(3), 239–253.

Davies, D. (2000). Towards a model of gay affirmative therapy. In D. Davies & C. Neal (Eds.), *Pink therapy: A guide for counselors and therapists working with lesbian, gay, and bisexual clients* (pp. 24–40). Philadelphia, PA: Open University Press.

Dillon, F. R., Worthington, R. L., Savoy, H. B., Rooney, S. C., Schutte, A. B., & Guerra, R. M. (2004). On becoming allies: A qualitative study of lesbian, gay, and bisexual affirmative counselor training. *Counselor Education and Supervision, 43,* 162–177.

Doherty, W. J., & Simmons, D. S. (1996). Clinical practice patterns of marriage and family therapists: A national survey of therapists and their clients. *Journal of Marital and Family Therapy, 22*(1), 9–25.

Dworkin, S. H., & Gutierrez, F. (1989). Counselors be aware: Clients come in every size, shape, color, and sexual orientation [Introduction to special issue]. *Journal of Counseling and Development, 68,* 6–8.

Godfrey, K., Haddock, S. A., Fisher, A., & Lund, L. (2006). Essential training components of curricula for preparing therapists to work with lesbian, gay, and bisexual clients: Adelphi study. *Journal of Marital and Family Therapy, 32*(4), 491–504.

Green, R. J. (1996). Why ask, why tell? Teaching and learning about lesbians and gays in family therapy. *Family Process, 35,* 389–400.

Green, S. K., & Bobele, M. (1994). Family therapists' response to aids: An examination of attitudes, knowledge, and contact. *Journal of Marital and Family Therapy, 20*(4), 349–367.

Greene, B. (2007). Delivering ethical psychological services to lesbian, gay, and bisexual clients. In K. J. Bieschke, R. M. Perex, & K. A. DeBord (Eds.), *Handbook of counseling and psychotherapy with lesbian, gay, bisexual, and transgender clients* (2nd ed., pp. 181–199). Washington, DC: American Psychological Association.

Henke, T., Carlson, T. S., & McGeorge, C. R. (2009). Homophobia and clinical competency: An exploration of couple and family therapists' beliefs. *Journal of Couple and Relationship Therapy, 8*(4), 325–342.

Herek, G. M. (1990). The context of anti-gay violence: Notes on cultural and psychological heterosexism. *Journal of Interpersonal Violence, 5,* 316–333.

Lewis, R. J., Derlega, V. J., Griffin, J. L., & Krowinski, A. C. (2003). Stressors for gay men and lesbians: Life stress, gay-related stress, stigma consciousness, and depressive symptoms. *Journal of Social and Clinical Psychology, 22*(6), 716–729.

Lidderdale, M. A. (2002). Practitioner training for counseling lesbian, gay, and bisexual clients. *Journal of Lesbian Studies, 6* (3/4), 111–119.

Liddle, B. J. (1997). Gay and lesbian clients' selection of therapists and utilization of therapy. *Psychotherapy, 34*, 11–18.

Long, J. K. (1996). Working with lesbians, gays, and bisexuals: Addressing heterosexism in supervision. *Family Process, 35*(3), 377–388.

Long, J. K., & Lindsey, E. (2004). The sexual orientation matrix for supervision: A tool for training therapists to work with same-sex couples. *Journal of Couple & Relationship Therapy, 3*(2–3), 123–135.

Long, J. K., & Serovich, J. M. (2003). Incorporating sexual orientation into MFT training programs: Infusion and inclusion. *Journal of Marital and Family Therapy, 29*(1), 59–67.

Matthews, C. R. (2007). Affirmative lesbian, gay, and bisexual counseling with all clients. In K. J. Bieschke, R. M. Perex, & K. A. DeBord (Eds.), *Handbook of counseling and psychotherapy with lesbian, gay, bisexual, and transgender clients* (2nd ed., pp. 201–219). Washington, DC: American Psychological Association.

Matthews, C. R., Selvidge, M. M. D., & Fisher, K. (2005). Addiction counselors' attitudes and behaviors toward LGB clients. *Journal of Counseling and Development, 83*, 57–65.

Mays, V. M., & Cochran, S. D. (2001). Mental health correlates and perceived discrimination among lesbian, gay, and bisexual adults in the United States. *American Journal of Public Health, 91*(11), 1869–1876.

McCann, D. (2001). Lesbians, gay men, their families and counseling: Implications for training and practice. *Educational and Child Psychology, 18*(2), 78–88.

McGeorge, C. R., & Carlson, T. S., (2010). Social justice mentoring: Preparing family therapists for social justice advocacy work. *Michigan Family Review, 14*(1), 42–59.

McGeorge, C. R., & Carlson, T. S. (2011). Deconstructing heterosexism: Becoming an LGB affirmative heterosexual couple and family therapist. *Journal of Marital & Family Therapy, 37*(1), 14–26.

Meyer, I. (1995). Minority stress and mental health in gay men. *Journal of Health and Social Behavior, 36*, 38–56.

Mohr, J. (2002). Heterosexual identity and the heterosexual therapist: An identity perspective on sexual orientation dynamics in psychotherapy. *The Counseling Psychologist, 30*(4), 532–566.

Murphy, B. C. (1991). Educating mental health professionals about gay and lesbian issues. *Journal of Homosexuality, 22*, 229–246.

Oswald, R. F., Blume, L. B., & Marks, S. R. (2005). Decentering heteronormativity: A model for family studies. In V. L, Bengtson, A. C. Acock, K. R. Allen, P. Dilworth-Anderson, & D. M. Klein (Eds.), *Sourcebook of family theory & research* (pp. 143–165). Thousand Oaks, CA: Sage.

Phillips, J. C. (1999). Training issues and considerations. In R. M. Perez, K. A. DeBord, & K. J. Bieschke (Eds), *Handbook of counseling and psychotherapy with lesbian, gay, and bisexual clients* (pp. 337–358). Washington, DC: American Psychological Association.

Phillips, J. C., & Fischer, A. R. (1998). Graduate students' training experiences with lesbian, gay, and bisexual issues. *The Counseling Psychologist, 26*(5), 712–734.

Pilkington, N. W., & Cantor, J. M. (1996). Perceptions of heterosexual bias in professional psychology programs: A survey of graduate students. *Professional Psychology: Research and Practice, 27*(6), 604–612.

Pope, M. (1995). The "salad bowl" is big enough for us all: An argument for the inclusion of lesbians and gay men in any definition of multiculturalism. *Journal of Counseling and Development, 73*, 301–304.

Ritter, K. Y., & Turndrup, A. I. (2002). *Handbook of affirmative psychotherapy with lesbians and gay men.* New York, NY: Guilford Press.

Rock, M., Carlson, T. S., & McGeorge, C. R. (2010). Does affirmative training matter? Assessing CFT students' beliefs about sexual orientation and their level of affirmative training. *Journal of Marital & Family Therapy, 36*(2), 171–184.

Savage, T. A., Prout, H. T., & Chard, K. M. (2004). School psychology and issues of sexual orientation: Attitudes, beliefs, and knowledge. *Psychology in the Schools, 41*(2), 201–210.

Serovich, J. M., Craft, S. M., Toviessi, P., Gangamma, R., McDowell, T., & Grafsky, E. L. (2008). A systematic review of the research base on sexual reorientation therapies. *Journal of Marital and Family Therapy, 34*(2), 227–238.

Spaulding, E. (1999). Unconsciousness-raising: Hidden dimensions of heterosexism in theory and practice with lesbians. In J. Laird (Ed.), *Lesbians and lesbian families: Reflections of theory and practice* (pp. 11–26). New York, NY: Columbia University Press.

Worthington, R. L., Savoy, H. B., Dillon, F. R., & Vernaglia, E. R. (2002). Heterosexual identity development: A multidimensional model of individual and social identity. *The Counseling Psychologist, 30*, 496–531.

26
Queer Supervision

JANIE K. LONG and JACK GROTE

Why queer supervision? Perhaps you grew up when the first author did and the word *queer* is one that makes you cringe. These days, however, working in a job that is focused on students who identify as gay, bisexual, transgender, pansexual, intersexed, lesbian, questioning, transsexual, and queer, we have learned that for many of them using the word *queer* is empowering. For them, it usually means that you cannot put them in a stereotypical box and think that you can figure them out because of whom they date, whom they have sex with, how they perform their gender, and so on. How the word is used also acknowledges the existence of fluidity in sexual attraction, one's sex, and one's gender identity. Today, the first author finds the use of the word *queer* to be, in fact, refreshing. A person who identifies as intersexed has medically established physical and/or hormonal attributes of both the male and female sex. Someone who is attracted to people regardless of their sex or gender may identify as pansexual. Pansexuality differs from bisexuality in that pansexuals are attracted to the entire range of sexual and gender identities.

There has always been more than male and female, gay and straight, and masculine and feminine. As a culture, we have worked hard to maintain that illusion, but students are saying no more! So we choose the title "Queer Supervision" to honor our students and what they teach us every day and also to acknowledge that the times they are a'changin'! Thus, if we believe in reciprocal process, we as supervisors will change. So know that in this chapter when we use the word *queer*, you may plug in any number of sexual and/or gender identities. If we are highlighting a particular subset of queer, we will use the more specific labels, knowing that even as we do, they may not be the label our supervisee embraces. Thus, for example, if we are talking about a supervisee who is attracted to both men and women, we may use the term *bisexual* or *pansexual* but that supervisee may actually identify as queer. However, keep in mind as you read that we are assuming that both supervisor and supervisee identify somewhere in the sexual orientation and/or gender-identity spectrums.

It is not surprising that there is a paucity of literature examining the relationship between queer supervisors and queer supervisees. Previously, Long acknowledged some of the complexities of this particular supervision pairing; however, this is the first time she has focused solely on the challenges and opportunities of such pairings (Long & Bonomo, 2007; Long and Serovich, 2003; Storm, McDowell, & Long, 2003). In addition to highlighting the joys and the challenges of this supervisory dyad, we will provide case examples throughout the chapter to illustrate at least one possible scenario in each area of discussion.

Why is it important to examine the pairing of a queer supervisor with a queer supervisee? Research that has reviewed what is effective in therapy has consistently shown that therapeutic alliance, not the models and techniques used in therapy, accounted for the majority of the variance in treatment outcome. Extratherapeutic conditions related to the client often have more to do with outcome than anything that happens in the therapy room (Miller, Duncan, & Hubble, 2004). Clients' assessments of the therapeutic relationship have been shown to be highly predictive of outcome. Congruence between clients' beliefs about the causes of their problems and the treatment approach offered resulted in stronger therapeutic alliance, less early dropout, and improved treatment outcomes (Duncan, Miller, Wampold, & Hubble, 2009).

Although no studies have shown that strong supervisory alliance is key to successful therapeutic outcome, many authors writing about supervision have noted that the quality of relationship between the supervisor and supervisee is crucial to the process of supervision. Alderfer and Lynch (1986) suggest that the supervisory relationship has more influence on the success of the process of supervision than does any other factor. Kaiser (1992, p. 284) notes, "The supervisory relationship interacts in a dynamic way with what is taught in supervision…[and] it is, in fact, the medium through which how to do therapy is taught." Yet, Kaiser and others have noted that the supervisory relationship has been an underdeveloped area of focus in research and writing.

Factors to Consider

Openness

Your degree of openness about your own sexuality and/or gender identity can influence the experience of supervision in several ways. Let us consider first that you are very open about your identity. If the queer supervisee has a choice of supervisors, it is likely that they choose you, in part, because you are queer. They may be looking for someone who will provide queer-informed supervision or someone who can model for them what it means to be an "out" professional. When we write about queer-informed supervision, we are referring to someone who is both knowledgeable of and sensitive to the complexities of queer identities and queer lives.

If the supervisee is questioning or not open about identity and you are, if that individual did not have a choice, he or she may be somewhat fearful of working with you. Perhaps you will figure out the person's identity, perhaps you will "out" the person to other supervisors or supervisees, or perhaps you will judge the person lacking because he or she is not open. Another possibility if the supervisee did choose you is that person wants to come out to someone else whom he or she believes will understand.

Perhaps one of the most damaging things a queer supervisor can do is to simply ignore that sexual orientation and/or gender identity is important to the queer supervisee. If an open context is not modeled in supervision, it can give the queer supervisee one or more of the following messages: that issues of sexuality and gender are off-limits in supervision; that the supervisor is uncomfortable with who they are and, thus, who the supervisee is; or that one's personal attributes never make a difference in the therapy room. Any of these messages can create an unsafe environment for both supervisees and clients because important issues that could bring harm to clients may be ignored. It also sends a message to supervisees that openness in supervision is neither required nor important.

> **Case Example 26.1:   Queer-Informed Supervision**
>
> Erika arrives for her first supervision session with a tape in hand. "I can't wait for you to start supervising this case because I know you are going to be so much more helpful to me than my last supervisor. You see, she was straight, and I'm working with a lesbian couple. My last supervisor kept saying, 'Just treat them like any other couple,' but they are not just any other couple!"

> **Case Example 26.2:   Ignoring One's Identity**
>
> Manny, your queer supervisee, is preparing for supervision and reviewing his tape. (Thinks to himself:) "I wonder if this teen could be struggling with his gender identity? I know Kieran (his supervisor) identifies as trans, but we never discuss it in supervision. I wonder why…maybe he's not comfortable with discussing personal issues or maybe he thinks it is not appropriate to talk about himself or maybe he's not comfortable talking about

his identity. I guess I best not "go there" when we meet. I don't want him to think I am getting too personal."

Attributing Too Much Knowledge to Oneself or to a Queer Supervisee

The lesbian, gay, bisexual, transgender, and queer (LGBTQ) community is a very diverse community. The research knowledge base related to the community is also ever growing and evolving, bringing us new information. What we think we know today may no longer be true tomorrow. These facts are good news in that we know more about gender and sexuality than we have ever known before, but they also present a challenge to supervisors to stay abreast of a shifting landscape. For this reason, it would be understandable that there are likely gaps in queer supervisors' knowledge base. At times, supervisees may even have a more current knowledge base.

The other likely scenario is that queer supervisors may assume that queer supervisees know more than they do about the LGBTQ community and relationships. We are often surprised at how little one subgroup of the community knows about another. Naively, we assume that because we are living a queer existence, others have the same experiences. Stereotyping happens as well because even members of the queer community have grown up in a biased culture. We are not immune to heterosexism, homonegativity, biphobia, transphobia, sexism, racism, ageism, and the like. Heterosexism is a system of beliefs that favors and privileges heterosexual relationships over all others. Biphobia is prejudice and discrimination against people who identify as bisexual, and transphobia is prejudice and discrimination against people who identify as transgender or transsexual. Like many other supervisees, queer supervisees are also often fearful of allowing supervisors to know that they do not possess a broad knowledge base.

Case Example 26.3:   A Lack in the Supervisor's Knowledge Base

You are working with a queer supervisee who begins to refer to the client as "ze." *Ze* is a gender-neutral pronoun similar in use to the traditional *he*. At first you think the supervisee is simply trying to be humorous, but as you try to follow the conversation without becoming too distracted you realize the supervisee is talking in a very serious way about a potentially suicidal client. You sense that the supervisee is using this word on purpose, but you are uncertain why. You do not want to appear ignorant, so you say nothing. You continue to use the male pronouns you believe to be appropriate for the client. Later you look up the word on the Internet and find that the supervisee was probably being very purposeful about the use of the word as a gender-neutral pronoun to describe the client who identified as gender nonconforming and that by not doing likewise you could have offended the client and/or the supervisee.

Case Example 26.4:   Supervisee's Lack of Knowledge

Your supervisee who identifies as a queer woman is discussing her case. She says that her client identifies as intersex but says that she is confused because the client's name is Ralph. She explains that he looks like a man, dresses like a man, and seems interested sexually only in women, yet he identifies as a lesbian. Your supervisee cannot understand why (by her definition) a man would call himself a lesbian. She then says that he must be transsexual. This supervisee is not aware that she lacks knowledge and that she is exposing her lack of knowledge both in her description of the client and in her conceptualization of the problem. As her supervisor, you are shocked that she seems to know so little about intersex individuals as well as about the differences between gender identity and sexual orientation.

Over- or Underemphasizing Difference

Hare-Mustin (1987, p. 15) warns against "alpha bias" (the exaggeration of differences between people) and "beta bias" (ignoring differences that do exist). This type of binary thinking minimizes the complexity of relationships. In the context of the supervisory relationship, assumptions on the part of queer supervisors could include that the experiences of the supervisees mirror those of their own or that because they identify with different parts of the queer spectrum, their experiences may be completely different. The supervisees could, of course, do likewise.

Case Example 26.5: Beta Bias

Supervisor: "So this client is obviously struggling, like we all have, with his relationship with his parents and acceptance. How might your own struggles with your parents influence how you view these parents?" Perhaps the supervisee did not struggle with parents. Do supervisees tell supervisors they did not have the same experience? Will revealing that their path has been less challenging make the supervisor think differently of them?

Case Example 26.6: Alpha Bias

Ramone is discussing his lesbian supervisor with another supervisee: "Yea, you know Julie, she doesn't get it. Lesbians just don't understand gay male sex and open relationships, so she can't help me with this couple."

Forms of Bias

Bias is present in supervision whether we acknowledge it or not. We all have bias. Long has noted in the past that she is less afraid of the bias within herself or within her supervisee than she is about the bias that could go unexamined in either or both of them (Long & Bonomo, 2007). In this section, we are particularly interested in all forms of bias against clients, supervisees, and supervisors based on their sexual identities, sexual orientation, and/or their gender identity.

It has long been noted that mental health professionals are ill prepared for working with LGBTQ individuals, couples, and families (Laird & Green, 1995; Long, 1996; Long & Serovich, 2003; Ritter & Terndrup, 2002). Recently, Henke, Carlson, and McGeorge (2009) measured couple and family therapists' levels of homophobia and self-perceived levels of competence in working with lesbian and gay clients. Their findings support the notion that training programs must incorporate various forms of LGBTQ awareness and information in order to decrease levels of bias and enhance clinical competency.

Even as recently as 2010, when teaching psychology doctoral students and psychiatric residents who were already seeing clients-patients, Long discovered that almost all of them had little to no content or specific training related to working with members of the LGBTQ community. They even lacked basic information related to the myriad differences within the community. Some of these trainees also identify as LGBTQ. Long's conversations with these queer trainees revealed that when they had information, it was because they sought out the information themselves, not because it was shared with them by the persons responsible for training them.

If part of combating bias is to be exposed to updated knowledge, then we are grossly underpreparing our trainees, including our queer trainees. As we continue to expand the knowledge base related to queer families (Bos & Gartrell, 2010), there is also much to be learned about individuals who are intersex, gender nonconforming, pansexual, and transgender. In addition to building our knowledge, we must incorporate time for both our own self-examination of bias and reflection with the queer supervisee of his or her potential areas of bias (Long & Bonomo, 2007).

Bias comes in many forms, so we will highlight several ways that bias might be present in queer supervision:

1. We sometimes assume that because we are queer, we know or are familiar with all things queer. Yet how does a lesbian really understand the world of someone who is transitioning, or how does someone who is White and queer understand the life of a

person of color who is queer, or how does someone who is Jewish and queer understand the life of someone who is Muslim and queer? Our community is so diverse no one can completely understand the life of another.

2. We assume that because we are oppressed, we do not also hold other forms of bias, that somehow being queer exempts us from sexism, racism, classism, ageism, ethnocentrism, anti-Semitism, and the like. As examples, gay men can be sexist, queer women can discriminate based on age, and someone who is pansexual can discriminate based on class.

3. Even within the LGBTQ community one often finds stereotyping among the various subgroups, and likely the targets are the community members one knows the least about or with whom one has the least experience. For example, Weiss (2004) provided us with a lengthy history of gays and lesbians exhibiting biphobia and transphobia.

4. Sometimes we hold bias against others in the queer community based on how out they are, their relationship status, their HIV status, their lack of or involvement in advocacy, their politics, and other issues.

5. Another way in which we often hold bias is when we are "allergic" to anything that is too gay, too queer, too butch, too gender conforming, too essentialist, and so on. When others do not embody their sexual orientation or gender identity in the way with which we are comfortable, we sometimes judge them for being too much or too little.

Case Example 26.7:   Bias

You have gathered a group of queer supervisees to discuss the potential for starting a support group for gay males in your clinic. Supervisee 1 identifies as a gay male, Supervisee 2 identifies as a lesbian, Supervisee 3 identifies as a gender-nonconforming gay male, and Supervisee 4 identifies as a gay male. Supervisee 4 is also a student of color. You highlight that you have added in the past 2 years a support group for queer women and one for persons who identify with the trans community. You note that there have been recent requests for a group for gay men as well. Supervisee 1 says he does not think a group for gay men is necessary because they have so much privilege. Supervisee 2 quickly agrees that there is no need for a group for gay men. They already dominate our clientele. Supervisee 4 wonders aloud what the problem is, Why would we not also offer a group for gay men? Supervisee 3 says he agrees that White gay men have a lot of power but that saying that all gay men have more power than all lesbian women is misleading and simply not true.

This particular example offers an opportunity to explore issues of many forms of bias, including sexism, racism, and classism.

Case Example 26.8:   Bias

You identify as a lesbian and are currently supervising a trans man, that is, is someone who was originally identified as a woman but who now identifies as a man.

This is the first time you have supervised someone who chose to transition from female to male. You notice during your first supervision session that you keep wondering why someone would decide to no longer be a woman. You are very distracted by these thoughts and realize that your discomfort is getting in the way of providing fully present supervision. You decide after the session that you want to look for more information about the transitioning process and that it would be a good time to seek some peer supervision.

Case Example 26.9:   Bias

Your supervisee who identifies as a gay male reports that he is seeing a client who identifies as bisexual, or, as he says in supervision, "Yet another bisexual woman." You ask what he means by that framing, and he replies, " It seems like most of the women I see these days identify as bisexual. I wish they would just get over themselves and admit that they are lesbian. Everyone knows that people who say they are bisexual are just hiding from or masking the fact that they are attracted to people of the same sex."

Case Example 26.10: Bias

Lindon is a 63-year-old queer supervisor. Andrew is his 24-year-old queer supervisee, and Risa is his 36-year-old queer supervisee. One day after their third supervision session together, Risa and Andrew are talking.

Risa:	You know he has a thing for you, right?
Andrew:	Who?
Risa:	Lindon, of course.
Andrew:	You're kidding, right?
Risa:	Not at all....I see the way he looks at you.
Andrew:	You're crazy.
Risa:	I bet he has a thing for young ones like you; all older gay men want a young trick!
Andrew:	Stop. Now you're just being disrespectful.
Risa:	Oh come on, you know guys his age are pretty much just sexual predators. He grew up in the age of free love and bathhouses!
Andrew:	Okay enough—how did you get to be so ageist?
Risa:	Okay, naive one, just wait till he gropes you behind the one-way mirror!

Suddenly Andrew has a new thought in his head about Lindon that he did not have before. Could Risa be right? Did he need to be careful with Lindon?

As Fong and Lease (1997) note, the majority of supervisors in this country are White. For this reason, queer supervisees of color will most likely not be paired with a supervisor from a similar racial background. There are clear issues that may come up as a result of the racial difference between the supervisor and supervisee, namely, "unintentional racism" (Fong & Lease, 1997, p. 389). This issue may occur when well-intentioned supervisors ignore or avoid racial issues because they are uniformed about them. However, there are further sets of issues that occur because the supervisee is both queer and a racial minority.

Suppose, for example, that John, a therapist, has a client, Susie, of a similar racial background who expresses the idea that her status as queer threatens her position within her respective racial group because "non-reproductive sexual practices may be perceived as a threat to the group's survival" (Greene & Boyd-Franklin, 1996, p. 51). John may feel uncomfortable approaching his White supervisor about this topic because he may feel that his supervisor will not be able to address this issue adequately. Furthermore, he may fear that his supervisor will assume that John can address the topic sufficiently just because he is a member of the minority group.

In both of these cases, the supervisees' multiple minority identities play a role in the alliance with the supervisor. If undiscussed, these issues could lead to a negative effect on the supervisory alliance.

Power

Supervisors hold power over supervisees in numerous ways. As a supervisor, you may hold the key to the supervisees' grade or employment, for example. As supervisees, they likely have less knowledge or clinical experience than you do, they often have insufficient information to negotiate their rights, they may lack the skills to evaluate your competence, and they may be limited in their choice of supervisors. Further, you have the potential to affect their future in numerous ways, especially in terms of licensing and employment. You have the power of your position, expert power, knowledge power, skills power, network power, and sometimes power related to personal attributes (e.g., age, sex, or physical ability). In addition to having these potential sources of power, you are queer.

As a queer supervisor, you may be the first out professional with whom the queer supervisee has contact. This fact alone can give you immense influence in the life of the supervisee. If you add to this scenario that you are more experienced and hold privilege in other ways (e.g., sex, class, or education), a less experienced supervisee may hold you on a pedestal. This place of power can be of help in your guiding the supervisee, but it may also mean there is greater potential for you to either fall from grace or disempower the supervisee in some way, especially if you are unaware of your power.

An important source of power for the queer supervisor is the potential difference in power related to one's identity development, especially if the supervisee is new to recognizing a queer identity. If you are not comfortable in your own skin, you can be either a role model or a threat, as evidenced by Case Example 26.11.

Case Example 26.11:   Power

Elena has recently fallen in love with a trans woman, and she has recently learned that people are now identifying as pansexual. The more Elena has learned about this identity, the more she feels that it fits the individual she has fallen in love with. A trans woman, Elena has discovered, is someone who was originally identified as a man but who now identifies as a woman. Elena has heard that her supervisor is a hardcore feminist lesbian who has a reputation for challenging supervisees who question their own sexual orientation. Elena is certain that if the supervisor does not value who she is as a sexual being, she will also not validate her clinical work. So before even meeting with the supervisor, Elena decides that she must never let the supervisor know anything about her orientation because the supervisor will likely think less of her. Elena will just not be open to who she is because the supervisor appears to be "like those women at the Michigan Womyn's Music Festival" who include and welcome only "womyn born womyn" (Spaulding, 2010).

Before even meeting the supervisor, the supervisee has formed opinions of her based on hearsay, stereotypes, ageism, and like variables. Whether any of the supervisee's fears are valid remains in question, yet the supervisee nonetheless fears that the supervisor will use her power to somehow invalidate her clinical abilities.

Boundaries

Multiple role relationships are prevalent and inevitable in supervision, at times evolving naturally from the nature of the supervisory context. We often function as not only clinical supervisors but also supervisees' employers, professors, or signatories on their hours for licensure. There are inherent dangers in these multiple role relationships, yet there is also the potential to enhance supervision. The dangers include the following:

- *Exploitation*: When a supervisor takes advantage of the supervisory relationship for another purpose beyond that of the training agenda, supervisees are exploited. Example: Assigning a supervisee the task of reviewing the literature in a specific area as a part of the individual's supervision assignment and then using that literature review for your own writing purposes.
- *Hierarchy*: Supervisees are unable to freely and equally consent to the nonprofessional aspects of multiple relationships. Example: Calling on a supervisee to offer you emotional support related to your relationship difficulties.
- *Secrecy*: A dual agenda develops, and one agenda is kept covert, under the guise of an official relationship. Example: You have your supervisee housesit for you while you take a month away for vacation.

- *Reduction of power*: Holding multiple roles with a supervisee can reduce the supervisor's power and alter the supervisor's capacity to evaluate. Example: While house sitting for you, your supervisee discovers that you are in financial trouble when a bill collector calls. The supervisee promises not to tell others, and you feel secrecy is contingent upon the grade you give the supervisee.

It is important to remember that multiple role relationships also have the potential to enrich supervision. Among the benefits, having multiple role relationships can do the following:

- Increase the supervisor's sense of connection and personal responsibility toward the supervisee.
- Encourage both parties to be more honest.
- Provide an opportunity for the supervisee to learn to manage complexity in relationships, which can be very helpful to learn within a safe setting.
- Help make the supervisory relationship more egalitarian than authoritative; the latter is a supervisory style that the research suggests can inhibit the supervision process (Long, Lawless, & Dotson, 1996).
- Demystify the supervisor and thus make the supervisory relationship more authentic.

Managing multiple roles can, however, increase the chance for boundary violations to occur. When we only downplay our power, boundary violations are more likely to occur. According to Peterson (1992), the four motifs of boundary violations are (1) a reversal or altering of roles, (2) a secret, (3) a double bind, and (4) indulgence of professional privilege. Let us take a look at a potential boundary violation that could be complicated by the supervisor's sexual orientation or gender identity.

Case Example 26.12: Boundary Violation

Suppose you are a trans man who is also a supervisor. You've been on hormones for 5 years and hope to soon be cutting back your dosage. You have been employed in your current position about 3 months. You were able to change your sex on your birth certificate just before you took this position, so your employers know you as male but not as a trans man. You are new to the area, having moved here to take your new position, and are happy to find a trans support group. When you attend the group the first time, you are very surprised to discover one of your queer supervisees is one of the facilitators of the group. The supervisee also seems surprised to see you and explains that she transitioned about 12 years ago. She assures you that she will never reveal your presence in the group. You feel stuck. You feel that you cannot tell your employers at this juncture that you are trans, and you also cannot simply quit supervising the supervisee. You also worry that if you continue to supervise this supervisee, doing so could alter your ability to evaluate her honestly because of your fear that she may reveal your "secret." You continue to supervise her, though, and do indeed find yourself checking constructive criticism you would offer other supervisees.

Another type of boundary violation that might occur in clinical supervision between a queer supervisee and a queer supervisor is a supervisee who believes that the queer supervisor should "go easier" on him or her because they are both queer. Queer supervisees could believe that because you share a "background of oppression," you should not hold them to the same standards as other supervisees. It is also true that some supervisees who are not queer may feel that because you share a sexual orientation and/or gender identity with a supervisee, you may show some type of favoritism to that supervisee.

Another scenario could be the queer supervisor who unconsciously tends to be less lenient with a queer supervisee. This can happen as a result of wanting the supervisee to succeed in the future or wanting to make sure that you pass along particular bits of queer knowledge that you know the supervisee is unlikely to get elsewhere, or perhaps you are simply keenly aware of your role as a mentor in this instance and want to live up to that role. Although not a boundary violation per say, such a situation reflects unequal treatment.

Finally, in regard to boundaries, within training programs, "faculty members are in a unique position of frequently being called on to offer counsel or guidance to students or trainees on personal matters" (Long & Serovich, 2003, p. 65). This request is very likely to happen between queer supervisors and queer supervisees. It would not be uncommon for a supervisee who is struggling with some aspect of his or her queer identity to reach out to a queer supervisor for guidance. Although this action alone does not constitute a boundary violation, a supervisor may need to be wary because boundary violations are "a process rather than a single event" (Peterson, 1992, p. 72).

Because queer communities are often small, it can be the case that queer supervisees may lack strong, positive queer role models. In such a small community, the queer supervisee may increasingly rely on the queer supervisor for support in a way in which heterosexual and gender-conforming supervisees would not because they likely have better access to support networks. Throughout this process, it is possible for the natural power dynamic to be altered. It is also highly possible that a queer supervisor may know a queer supervisee through nonprofessional channels. This likelihood increases opportunities for boundary violations to occur. It is probable that they will both be in attendance at queer social events, for example, forcing a merger of professional and personal lives. It is important that supervisors always remember their role as the supervisee's supervisor and act appropriately. Thus, with increased personal life interaction, it is important for all queer supervisors to be particularly aware of boundary violations and how to approach them cautiously.

Conclusion

There are many advantages to pairing queer supervisors with queer supervisees. It should not be assumed, however, that there are no potential negative effects of such an alliance. As with any alliance, nothing should be taken for granted, such as assuming an adequate knowledge base or assuming sameness based on identity, and queer supervisors should make sure to minimize bias and reduce the likelihood of abuses of power. Queer supervisors should acknowledge the role that queer identities play in the alliance between them and their supervisees and work to ensure queer supervisees' professional growth. At the same time, by making sure to include issues related to identity, sexuality, and gender, the queer supervisor is aiding in the development of professionals who are proficient in their ability to work with sexual and gender minorities "and in the creation of therapists who are comfortable with ambiguities and questions regarding sexuality and gender" (Brown, 1991, p. 237). In fact, we believe that the greatest growth ahead for supervisors is in the area of the construction of gender, and we hope the many examples offered throughout the chapter have helped to further queer supervisors on this journey of discovery.

References

Aldefer , C. J., & Lynch, B. (1986). Supervision in two dimensions, *Journal of Strategic and Systemic Therapies*, *5*, 70–73.

Bos, H., & Gartrell, N. (2010). Adolescents of the USA National Longitudinal Lesbian Family Study: Can family characteristics counteract the negative effects of stigmatization? *Family Process, 49*, 559–572.

Brown, L. S. (1991) Commentary on the special issue of *The Counseling Psychologist*: Counseling with lesbians and gay men. *The Counseling Psychologist, 19*, 235–238.

Duncan, B. L., Miller, S. D., Wampold, B. E., & Hubble, M. (2009). *The heart and soul of change: What works in therapy* (2nd ed.). Washington, DC: American Psychological Association.

Fong, M. L. & Lease, S. H. (1997). Cross-cultural supervision: Issues for the white supervisor. In D. B. Pope-Davis & H. L. K. Coleman (Eds.), *Multicultural counseling competencies* (pp. 387–405). Thousand Oaks, CA: Sage.

Greene, B., & Boyd-Franklin, N. (1996). African American lesbian couples: Ethnocultural considerations in psychotherapy. In M. Hill & E. D. Rothblum (Eds.), *Women and therapy* (pp. 49–60). New York, NY: Haworth Press.

Hare-Mustin, R. T. (1987). The problem of gender in family therapy theory. *Family Process, 26*, 15–27.

Henke, T, Carlson, T. S., & McGeorge, C. R. (2009). Homophobia and clinical competency: An exploration of couple and family therapists' beliefs. *Journal of Couple and Relationship Therapy, 8*, 325–342.

Kaiser, T. L. (1992). The supervisory relationship: An identification of the primary elements in the relationship and in the application of two theories of ethical relationships. *Journal of Marital and Family Therapy*, 18, 283–296.

Laird, J., & Green, R. J. (1995). Introduction. *Journal of Feminist Family Therapy, 7*, 3–13.

Long, J. K. (1996). Working with lesbians, gays, and bisexuals: Addressing heterosexism in supervision. *Family Process, 35*, 1–6.

Long, J. K., & Bonomo, J. (2007). Revisiting the Sexual Orientation Matrix for Supervision: Working with LGBTQ families. In J. J. Bigner & A. Gottlieb (Eds.), *From the inside out: Clinical interventions with families of lesbian, gay, bisexual, and transgender people* (pp. 151–166). New York, NY: Haworth Press.

Long, J. K., Lawless, J., & Dotson, D. (1996). Supervisory Styles Index: Examining supervisees' perceptions of supervisory style. *Contemporary Family Therapy, 18*, 589–606.

Long, J. K., & Serovich, J. M. (2003). Incorporating sexual orientation into MFT training programs: Infusion and inclusion. *Journal of Marital and Family Therapy, 29*, 59–68.

Miller, S. D., Duncan, B. L., & Hubble, M. A. (2004). Beyond integration: The triumph of outcome over process in clinical practice. *Psychotherapy in Australia, 10*, 2–19.

Miller, S. D., Hubble, M. A., & Duncan, B. L. (2008). Supershrinks: What's the key to their success? *Psychotherapy Networker, 4*, 14–22.

Peterson, M. R. (1992). *At personal risk: Boundary violations in professional–client relationships*. New York, NY: Norton.

Ritter, K. Y., & Terndrup, A. I. (2002). *Handbook of affirmative psychotherapy with lesbians and gay men*. New York, NY: Guilford Press.

Spaulding, P. (2010, March 4). *Michigan women's music festival: Lesbian and feminist musical artists supporting segregation*. Retrieved from http://www.pamshouseblend.com/diary/15398/michigan-womyns-music-festival-lesbian-and-feminist-musical-artists-supporting-segregation

Storm, C. L., McDowell, T., & Long, J. K. (2003). The metamorphosis of training and supervision. In T. L. Sexton, G. R. Weeks, & M. S. Robbins (Eds.), *Handbook of family therapy* (pp. 431–446). New York, NY: Brunner-Routledge.

Weiss. J. T. (2004). GL vs. BT: The archaeology of biphobia and transphobia within the U.S. gay and lesbian community. *Journal of Bisexuality, 3*, 35–55.

Section VI
Ethical Issues in LGBT Couple and Family Therapy

27

Ethical Issues in LGBT Couple and Family Therapy

DAMIEN W. RIGGS

One of the roles of the professional bodies that regulate the varying forms of mental health practice (which include, but are not limited to, social work, psychology, psychiatry, and counseling) is to enforce the ethical principles adopted by each profession. There are, of course, subtle differences between each of these professions in terms of the ethical principles they espouse, differences that are the product of the historical development of each profession and the role of ethics in its formation. For example, Brown (1997) suggests that psychological associations and societies developed ethical guidelines for psychological practice a considerable time after the discipline of psychology itself was well established. By contrast, and as McCartt Hess and Feldman (2008) suggest, the discipline of social work was concerned much earlier in its formation with constituting itself as a discipline centered upon discussing what constitutes ethical practice. Today these differing histories are reflected to some degree in the ethical codes of psychological and social work associations and societies, with the former primarily enshrining approaches to practice that emphasize the Hippocratic injunction to do no harm, whereas social work ethics tend to go further to include "aspirational ethics" that encompass a call for social change.

There is, of course, more to the story of mental health professional ethics than the simple binary presented in the foregoing introduction. Psychology as a discipline too has a history of striving for radical social change, albeit a history that is largely hidden by the dominant narrative of the discipline itself as one striving to be a science (Bradley & Selby, 2001). And it is equally important to acknowledge that the discipline of social work has as much at times enacted normative social values as it has sought to challenge them (consider, for example, early social work discourses about "moral hygiene"). These competing histories of two of the mental health professions, and their relationship to notions of what constitutes ethical practice, highlight what will be the central argument of this chapter, namely, that what is understood as ethical practice is highly contingent upon the social and cultural context in which mental health disciplines and practitioners operate, contexts that often function to close down consideration of the normative role that ethical codes play in perpetuating, rather than challenging, marginalization.

In order to more thoroughly explicate some of the divergent ways in which ethics are understood within the mental health professions, two distinct discussions of ethical practice with LGBT couples and families are presented in this chapter. The first outlines some of the core ethical concerns identified in previous literature and in so doing highlights the particular conceptualization of ethics that underpins this literature and the model of practice that it emphasizes. The second account of ethical practice provided in this chapter goes beyond the do-no-harm approach and asks the question "What would it mean to take as our starting place the ethical standpoints of LGBT people?" Such an approach, of course, does not discount the need for ethical codes that provide information about the minimal standards required to work with LGBT clients. Rather, it emphasizes the accompanying need for aspirational ethics that hold the potential to combat some of the significant social stressors that LGBT communities face living in social contexts that contribute to negative mental health outcomes. As a whole, then, this chapter provides clear information for practitioners working with LGBT couples and families as to how, at the very least, to recognize the needs of these populations, while also providing practitioners with an injunction to go beyond simple service provision and instead incorporate a reflexive examination of the role that ethical codes play in perpetuating marginalization, and the accompanying need to engage in a mental health praxis that creates the possibility for social change.

Standard Ethical Concerns

As Brown (1997) has so cogently argued, existing ethical guidelines across mental health professions largely focus on fiduciary relationships between clients and practitioners. Brown, of course, acknowledges that this has become the case as a result of the increasingly litigious nature of Western societies. The byproduct of this need for caution, as Brown again suggests, has been the development of specific ethical guidelines or the extension of standard guidelines aimed at providing clear checklists for practitioners working with LGBT clients so as to best protect all parties from harm. Existing literature on ethical practice with LGBT people (e.g., Janson, 2002; Sobocinski, 1990) suggests three key areas of concern that require attention when attempting to provide adequate services to this population:

1. An understanding of the contexts in which LGBT people live
2. Reflexivity about the practitioner's own beliefs, values, and location
3. Specific skills for working with LGBT people

In regard to the first point, Meyer's (2003) social stressor model provides key insight as to some of the reasons why LGBT people come into contact with mental health professionals. Meyer suggests that as a result of living in social contexts in which nonheterosexuality and nongender normativity are constructed at best as diverse and at worst as deviant, LGBT people face many forms of discrimination that often occur on a daily basis; furthermore, such negative contexts are detrimental to the mental health of LGBT people. In regard to LGBT couples, for example, certain sectors of the media along with politicians and some religious groups continue to depict LGBT relationships as inherently unstable, just as LGBT-headed households continue to be represented as unhealthy places for children to live. Although research and the lived experiences of LGBT couples and families clearly indicate that this is not the case (see Short, Riggs, Perlesz, Brown, & Kane, 2008, for a summary), such negative representations can weigh heavily upon LGBT people and thus negatively shape individual mental health as well as the well-being of couples and families. To practice ethically in this regard thus requires practitioners to understand the multiple sources from which marginalization occurs for LGBT people, to be mindful of the impact marginalization may have, and to take this into account when engaging with LGBT clients.

Brown (1996) sums up the second point about reflexivity well when she states that "any mental health professional working with sexual minorities inherits the history of collaboration between the mental health professions and the oppression of individuals who are sexual minorities" (p. 899). In other words—and as a consequence of the historical pathologization of homosexuality that was endorsed by the mental health professions—mental health practitioners are presented with the requirement not simply to claim to engage in ethical practice but also to actively examine their own complicity with marginalizing practices, intentional or otherwise.

Braun (2000) provides a useful framework for undertaking such an examination: She suggests that practitioners working with LGBT people may engage in heterosexism (or, indeed, gender normativity) by either omission (i.e., failing to challenge discrimination) or commission (i.e., explicit acts of discrimination, whether intended or not). An example of the former might occur if a practitioner is aware of a coworker making disparaging remarks about an LGBT client but fails to challenge this. Examples of commission include assuming that a client is heterosexual, assuming that a client's child was conceived through heterosexual intercourse, or making comments about members of LGBT communities that rely upon stereotypes.

Peel (2001) has usefully coined the term *mundane heterosexism* to refer to some of the foregoing examples that may often pass by routinely without comment by LGBT people, but which are no less discriminatory or hurtful (e.g., presuming that a client's partner is of the opposite sex). Riggs and Patterson (2009) have similarly elaborated the term *mundane transphobia* to refer to the ways in which discrimination against trans people is often couched in inclusive terms (e.g., asking trans people to talk about their lives in their sex assigned at birth). The tools provided by these authors can equip practitioners with skills for examining both subtle and explicit ways in which they may inadvertently make statements or ask questions that contribute to the marginalization of LGBT clients. Although the existing ethical codes that prohibit against explicitly homophobic, biphobic, or transphobic assumptions about LGBT people (e.g., the belief that LGBT are deviant and in need to therapy to "cure" them) have done much to improve service delivery to these populations (see Chapter 28, this volume, however, for a discussion of conversion therapy as an ongoing practice of explicit discrimination), it continues to be the case that practitioners must assess and challenge the assumptions they bring to working with LGBT people.

Of course, a large part of the work of addressing the first two key areas, stated earlier, requires mental health practitioners to undertake training specific to working with LGBT people. Although reflecting upon one's own assumptions and beliefs is an important aspect of providing adequate services to LGBT people, so that such services are not impacted upon by discrimination on the part of practitioners, it is also important to recognize, as Greene (2007) states, that "heterosexist thinking and behavior can be exacerbated by training that either ignores LGB issues or attends to them but reinforces old distortions" (p. 182). Research (see Greene, 2007, for a summary) continues to highlight that students in mental health–related graduate programs receive little if any exposure to issues related to working with LGBT people yet, it is important to note, that even minimal exposure can greatly increase the cultural competency of future practitioners (Riggs & Fell, 2010).

Undertaking professional development prior to working with LGBT couples and families is thus a vital component of ethical practice. The reasons for this preparation are at least twofold. First, it is unreasonable for practitioners to expect that LGBT clients will educate them about their lives as sexual and gender minorities. Although it is, of course, fair for clients to outline aspects of their own life histories germane to the presenting issue, it is not appropriate for practitioners to call upon clients to educate them about, for example, LGBT relationship forms or the dynamics of LGBT-headed families. Learning about such issues as these should be undertaken by all practitioners before working with LGBT clients. The earlier chapters in this volume serve as an excellent resource for undertaking this work. The second reason why developing knowledge about LGBT communities is a vital component of ethical practice is that a practitioner may often not know at the initial meeting, or even for several appointments, that a client identifies as nonheterosexual and nongender normative. For example, a client may present in regard to relationship or parenting issues but may not mention his partner's gender. This may be because the client is wary to disclose as a result of being fearful of the practitioner's response. By the time trust is developed and the disclosure is made, however, it may be detrimental for the client if the practitioner, feeling inadequately skilled to work with LGBT clients, then refers him to another practitioner. Although there may be some instances where referral is acceptable, on the whole it is important that all practitioners have at least some knowledge enabling them to work with a diverse range of populations.

In addition to the three key areas about ethical practice with LGBT couples and families identified earlier, previous literature identifies several other issues that are typically referred to in codified ethical guidelines. These include the following:

- Multiple relationships for LGBT practitioners working with LGBT clients
- Ways in which LGBT identities are understood
- Specific aspects of practice settings that require extra attention when working with LGBT clients

In regard to the first point, previous literature presents contradictory claims about LGBT practitioners coming out as such to LGBT clients. On the one hand, such authors as Dworkin (1992) suggest that coming out to clients may potentially introduce overt sexuality into the therapeutic space. Especially with regard to transference, this situation can mean that any attractions between the client and practitioner are heightened and may thus interfere with the therapeutic alliance. When occurring with LGBT couples, for example, this transference can add a problematic dimension to counseling that could be avoided if the practitioner does not come out as nonheterosexual or nongender normative. On the other hand, a greater number of authors advocate for the strategic utility of coming out in the counseling space (e.g., Kane, 2004; Morrow, 2000; Riggs, 2010a). Morrow summarizes this position well when she states, "By not disclosing, the therapist collaborates with the larger culture in perpetuating a norm of secrecy and may inadvertently encourage the client to remain in the closet" (p. 142). It must be recognized, of course, that supporting clients to come out should occur only if it is likely that coming out will be supported by the client's broader social network (Davison, 2001). In some instances, coming out may, in reality, be antithetical to meeting the mental health needs of some clients. Nonetheless, for many clients having an LGBT-identified therapist may assist in developing a positive sense of self that challenges negative social representations of LGBT people.

As the foregoing points about disclosure to clients suggest, LGBT practitioners are faced with unique ethical issues in working with LGBT clients. These issues include the fact that there will be an increased likelihood of overlapping roles (e.g., seeing clients at social gatherings or knowing clients through partners or extended networks). As a result, it is incumbent upon LGBT practitioners to take the lead in facilitating conversations with LGBT clients in regard to the best responses for the client should overlaps occur in their everyday lives (i.e., how will the practitioners introduce themselves to friends of a client should they meet in a social setting). In addition, although all practitioners must adhere to ethical guidelines relating to intimate relationships with clients, LGBT practitioners must be especially careful about boundary issues with clients that may arise as a result of being members of the same community. Brown (1989, 1996) elaborates this well in relation to lesbian therapists working with lesbian clients in communities where the degrees of separation may be few between clients and former or current lovers or partners. Such dilemmas as these should not prevent practitioners working with clients—and certainly not in small communities where they may be only one LGBT-friendly or identified mental health practitioner available—but must be constantly assessed by the practitioner and openly discussed with clients.

Kane (2004) provides an excellent case example of the foregoing point relating to LGBT practitioners working with LGBT clients. In a chapter cleverly entitled "The Unintended Use of a Pronoun," Kane outlines his work with a client named Geoffrey, who had first come to see him in regard to issues relating to substance use and the relationship difficulties the client was experiencing with his female partner. As a product of the work undertaken, the client displayed a marked reduction in his consumption of cannabis and alcohol, though no considerable reduction in his general levels of anxiety, which had been the driving factor behind his substance use as way of managing his feelings of distress. At this point, the client shared with

Kane the fact that it was difficult to continue working toward sobriety while his female partner was continuing to consume alcohol and offer it to him. Kane responding by noting that this situation is often a challenge for couples and that he himself had experienced a similar issue with his male partner. In using the pronoun *he*, Kane made visible his identity as a gay man, an unintended action that produced a powerful effect on his client: Arriving at the following appointment in a visible state of distress, the client disclosed his same-sex attractions to Kane. This eventually led the client to decide to leave his female partner and then to a first sexual encounter with a male and later to a relationship with a male, all of which occurred while the client continued to see Kane.

In "outing" himself to his client, even if unintentionally, Kane (2004) was faced with a number of challenges that do not typically present themselves to heterosexual practitioners working with nonheterosexual clients. First, Kane was forced to reevaluate his own ethics regarding disclosing to clients details about his personal life and to examine what this meant for him both as a gay man and as a practitioner. Second, Kane had to negotiate with the client how they would maintain boundaries between their lives and, specifically, what they would do in the likely situation that they saw each other in a gay venue. Finally, Kane had to be proactive in considering what it would mean if Geoffrey entered into a relationship with someone who was a part of Kane's own circle of friends. Although this scenario did not eventuate, Kane was keenly aware of the conflicting position such a scenario would place him in, not only as a practitioner bound by confidentiality laws but also as a gay man who though wanting to support a gay client in his journey through coming out also had the right to his own privacy. Again, these issues are ones that heterosexual practitioners are typically unlikely to face, not because similar issues cannot come up between heterosexual practitioners and their heterosexual clients but because the relatively small size of LGBT communities and the typically small number of practitioners who actively service such communities often means that LGBT practitioners are far more likely to be required to have a much smaller gap between their private life and their public practice. The case presented by Kane highlights these issues clearly and provides specific guidance for responding to these issues (as is also examined in detail throughout this chapter).

To return to the second point raised earlier in terms of ethical guidelines for working with LGBT clients, it is also important that practitioners speak with clients as to their preferred terms of reference and understandings of identity. As has been elaborated in other chapters in this volume, it is important that practitioners recognize that LGBT clients will inhabit a range of identities, and thus a homogenous model of LGBT identities cannot be assumed. Previous research (Riggs, 2007) has found that research on LGBT communities often presumes that the categories used within primarily White middle-class LGBT communities can be simplistically applied to other LGBT communities without regard for the differences between communities and the differing meanings of key terms. Practicing ethically with LGBT couples and families thus requires practitioners to determine through either explicit questions or observation not just the terms that clients use but also the meanings of the terms and their specific application to their lives. For example, some lesbian mother-couples make reference to a distinction between birth mothers and nonbirth mothers (who may be referred to as biological mothers and social mothers, mother and comothers, etc.), whereas other lesbian mother-couples may find such distinctions unnecessary or even offensive. Practitioners may in the first instance attempt to identify from the literature the most common terms used, but they should ideally attempt to ascertain from clients their own terms and to make use of those. Of course, it may well be the case that part of the work of therapy may involve examining or indeed challenging some of the terminology used by clients, particularly if it is negatively self-referential for LGBT clients; but in general, practitioners should aim to develop a client-centered approach to language, self-definition, and identity.

In regard to the final key point noted earlier, specific aspects of the physical space in which practice occurs, it is important for practitioners to understand commonplace strategies that exist for engendering a positive and welcoming therapeutic space. Although considerations of space often do not fall within ethical guidelines, they are increasingly recognized as vital to providing a respectful space within which to work with LGBT clients. Examples of maintaining respectful space include displaying LGBT-specific posters or community newspapers or magazines in the waiting room; including books for children in LGBT-headed families in the toy basket; and ensuring that all registration forms are inclusive of all relationship and family forms, which includes not simply recognizing same-sex partnerships and preferred gender identities but also recognizing a wider range of relationships and family forms, including polyamorous relationships and families with multiple parents. Other space-related issues include consideration of the special need for privacy among some LGBT clients (e.g., those accessing HIV-specific services or those LGBT clients who are not out but who access mainstream services and who do not wish to be potentially identified as nonheterosexual or nongender normative by other clients or by practitioners accessing the same service). Addressing these issues may involve having multiple entrances to consulting spaces, ensuring that appointment scheduling does not place clients in direct view of one another, and ensuring that clients can feel trust in the record-keeping practices of the service.

The understanding of ethical practice presented in this section has been primarily informed by literature that emphasizes the goals of protecting clients and practitioners from harm and ensuring that at minimum LGBT clients receive adequate service. Such goals are certainly a progression from past practices of either at worst pathologizing LGBT clients or at best expecting them to make use of mainstream services with no adaptations made. Yet as will be elaborated in the following section, ethical guidelines as they are currently adopted by most mental health professions still function to reinforce a relatively normative understanding of gender and sexuality and thus potentially do very little to challenge discrimination against LGBT people within the broader community and culture.

Aspirational Ethics

Any discussion of what are referred to here as aspirational ethics must start by acknowledging the dilemmatic nature of LGBT-affirmative therapy itself. On the one hand, the seminal work of Kitzinger and Perkins (1993) suggests the impossibility of a lesbian feminist psychology (on the basis that psychological modalities as a whole treat the individual and thus fail to challenge the social determinants of negative mental health outcomes within LGBT communities).

Increasingly, however, practice approaches across the mental health professions have been developed that take as central the impact of the social and, indeed, the thorough imbrication of the individual and the social. Langdridge (2007) makes a useful distinction, then, in relation to this new wave of potentially LGBT-affirmative therapies in his suggestion that though the approaches to practice described in the previous section may be understood as ethically affirmative in that they affirm standard ethical principles that should be taken as given for all practitioners, LGBT-affirmative approaches go beyond this in seeking both to affirm LGBT identities and experiences and to challenge marginalizing social structures. Morrow (2000) summarizes the latter approach well when she asks, "How would affirmative therapy for lesbian, gay, or bisexual (LGB) clients look if its primary goal, beyond repairing the damage caused by a heterosexist and homophobic society, were the creative enhancement of the identities of LGB people? What would this creative enhancement look like? And what qualities of LGB-affirmative therapists might contribute to creative enhancement of the identities, lives, and communities of LGB individuals?" (p. 137). This section summarizes literature that indicates some of the considerations that might inform such an affirmative approach to therapy.

Central to an LGBT-affirmative approach to working with couples and families is an acknowledgment of the operations of power, both between clients and practitioners and within relationships and families. In regard to the former, Brown (1989, 1996) makes the important point that although all practitioners must be mindful of how they potentially wield the power they are apportioned in the role of the knowing practitioner, this awareness is equally as true for LGBT practitioners as for heterosexual and gender-normative practitioners. Brown suggests, for example, that just because a lesbian therapist and a lesbian client may have similar experiences of misogyny from the broader culture, this does not mean that their experiences are the same. It could similarly be suggested that a White middle-class gay practitioner who is a parent of three children through surrogacy may have little insight into the experiences of an African American gay client with two children from a previous heterosexual marriage. Although similarities between the lives of practitioners and clients may provide opportunities for connection, practitioners should, regardless of the modality they operate within, be mindful of the ways in which power operates through the authorizing function of the mental health professions and the considerable social value accorded to those positioned as holders of knowledge.

Further to these points about disciplinary power, it is important for practitioners to consider the norms that play out through specific modalities and assessment tools. As Kitzinger and Perkins (1993) suggest, many psychological modalities individualize mental health issues to the client and may, indeed, locate problems within clients. So, for example, a gay couple who presents with issues relating to extrarelationship sex may be treated in ways that construct this issue as a problem of infidelity, rather than considering mononormativity's negative impact upon the relationship. More recently, Riggs (2010a) has critiqued postmodern approaches to therapy for similarly failing to provide an account of the individual that is mutually constituted with the social.

Further to these concerns about examining the assumptions undermining therapeutic modalities is the need to question the utility of standard assessment tools when working with LGBT people. In some instances, such tools may function in relatively mundane ways to marginalize LGBT people (i.e., measures that refer only to heterosexual families or presume congruency between natal sex and gender identity), whereas other measures may be more explicitly and dangerously marginalizing (i.e., the inclusion of gender-identity disorder in the DSM-IV and the requirements it places upon trans people for recognition of their gender identity through a pathologizing diagnosis). Mental health practitioners seeking to undertake ethical practice that is LGBT-affirmative must thus be very careful when using diagnostic tools and be reflexive about the likely impact of their chosen therapeutic modality.

Equally as true for an ethical LGBT-affirmative practice, however, is the need for a critical eye upon the practices of LGBT communities. At least three reasons compel this need. First, as Greene (2007) suggests, "whilst ethical practice requires practitioners to be sensitive to cultural and religious norms, this does not mean that such norms should be accepted blindly without regard for whether or not they are causing harm" (p. 188). A good example supporting this need appears in the case of working with clients who are members of an organized religion. Although practitioners should aim to respect the religious beliefs of clients and their family members, doing so not mean that practitioners must support discrimination against LGBT people. Furthermore, although as suggested in the previous section there may be times when coming out may not be the best option for certain clients (e.g., if doing so is likely to result in exclusion from support networks), this does not mean that it is automatically appropriate for a client to be supported to stay living in a homophobic familial and/or religious context. Practitioners must work with clients to weigh, for example, the negative psychological effects of homophobia from birth family against the loss of support should the clients come out to their family members.

The second form of critical examination of LGBT communities involves recognizing that some LGBT communities may be wary of airing dirty laundry about the community itself (Hillier, Edwards, & Riggs, 2008). Of course, this caution be understandable, given the propensity within society more broadly toward assuming a pathologizing view of LGBT communities. Yet regardless of this reasoning, it is important that practitioners do not buy into the view that LGBT communities are perfect. So, for example, though we might wish to acknowledge research that indicates "strikingly lower" rates of child abuse within lesbian-headed families as compared to heterosexual families (Gartrell, Deck, Rodas, Peyser, & Banks, 2005, p. 523), we must also acknowledge that domestic violence does occur in LGBT relationships and that LGBT individuals may be especially prone to substance abuse. Of course, an LGBT-affirmative approach will acknowledge that social prohibition on LGBT relationships potentially contributes to violence within relationships, just as minimal opportunities for social contact may lead LGBT people to socialize primarily in venues that promote alcohol consumption (Adams, McCreanor, & Braun, 2007). Regardless of recognition of these factors, however, it is important for practitioners to understand that negative events do occur within LGBT communities, relationships, and families.

Finally, it is important that practitioners recognize that marginalization occurs within LGBT communities. Research continues to find, for example, that bisexual people experience discrimination from lesbians and gay men (Israel, 2007), that non-White LGBT people experience discrimination from White LGBT people (Han, 2006), and that LGBT people with physical or intellectual impairments experience discrimination from mainstream LGBT communities (Bennett & Coyle, 2007). Thus, though it is important that practitioners support LGBT clients in making connections to LGBT communities, this must be done cautiously so as not to further contribute to experiences of marginalization.

One way of addressing the issues raised in this section about how to best engender an LGBT-affirmative approach to ethical practice with couples and families is to center the ethical norms that inform specific LGBT communities. One example occurs in relation to gay men who engage in unprotected anal intercourse. Controversy arose over this topic when an internalizing and relatively pathologizing view of this practice was reported in the *British Journal of Social Psychology*, to which a group of LGBT psychologists responded by asserting the need to value the ethical and moral frameworks within some sectors of gay communities (see Barker, Hagger-Johnson, Hegarty, Hutchison, & Riggs, 2007). Although it is of course important that practitioners work with all clients to understand HIV transmission, it may be equally important that practitioners recognize that some gay men, among other groups of LGBT people, will engage in unprotected anal intercourse; thus the best approach may be to also undertake discussions related to negotiated risk. To do otherwise would be to dismiss gay men's moral frameworks and thus run the risk of not assisting gay men in developing skills for making informed decisions about their sexual practices. In this sense, acknowledging LGBT-specific ethical and moral frameworks is affirming not solely because doing so recognizes the rights of LGBT people to make decisions about their own bodies but also because it affirms that such decisions often represent healthy and productive choices about how to best live in a relationship, presenting a range of factors that influence the options that LGBT people have available to them.

Relatedly, it is important that practitioners seeking to undertake ethical LGBT-affirmative practice not just value the decisions that LGBT people make but also clearly acknowledge the detrimental effects of living in a heteronormative and gender-normative society and their differential impact on LGBT people. Lev (2004) makes an insightful point in her book on lesbian and gay parenting when she reports an instance where her own child, as well as the child of a heterosexual friend, ran along the street naked. Lev reports feeling anxious, as a lesbian mother, that people would be watching and that her child's naked body would be read as reflecting badly upon her as a lesbian mother. In relating this story, Lev discusses ways in which anxieties about how LGBT parents are read by the broader society are not typically representative of pathology; being anxious about potential discrimination is not a sign of neuroticism but, rather, a normal response to the fact that in many instances discrimination, stereotyping, and negative judgments about LGBT parents are made by such people.

Recognizing the cumulative negative impact of experiences of discrimination upon LGBT people is thus an important aspect of ethical practice that seeks to correctly diagnose or treat LGBT people and in so doing avoid attributing pathology when in fact the problem is the society in which LGBT people live. Furthermore, it is important to recognize the differential ways in which social norms impact upon a range of LGBT people. For example, feminism has long demonstrated the importance of acknowledging the daily violence that occurs against women as a result of living in a patriarchal society. What is being increasingly acknowledged, however, is that trans women will have a unique experience of misogyny. Although, as some biological women have suggested, trans women are natally assigned a male identity and thus experience relative privilege during some portion of their lives, having been accorded such male privilege does not mitigate against the potential fact that some trans women may be unprepared for the discrimination they may face as women in addition to discrimination they may face as trans people. Of importance, then, is that ethical practice requires acknowledgment of the many ways in which LGBT individuals experience the effects of social norms; practitioners must recognize that a one-size-fits-all model will fail to examine the complexities of the lives of individual LGBT people.

Finally, research has increasingly recognized the specific impact of social norms and discrimination upon LGBT youth (Sobocinski, 1990). Supporting LGBT youth in a therapeutic context requires active consideration of how children and young people are represented in society more broadly and how heteronormativity and gender normativity negatively affect the development of gender and sexual identities among LGBT youth. Bond Stockton (2004) states this issue well when she refers to the "tendency to treat all children as straight whilst we culturally consider them asexual" (p. 283). When it is assumed that there are "naturally" two sexes and that gender identity matches with particular body parts taken as signifying male or female, then children are from birth forced into narrow categories that potentially fail to validate their experiences of embodiment and identity (Goethals & Schwiebert, 2005). Furthermore, discourses of childhood innocence and the need for adults to protect children, though important in some specific instances, also fail to recognize that it is particular children who are protected by particular adults with the expectation that they will adopt a normative gender identity (Riggs, 2010b). Such expectations of children fundamentally fail to recognize the differing desires and experiences of LGBT youth, as is reflected in reports of the provision of mainstream sex education to LGBT youth (Hillier & Mitchell, 2008).

As has been suggested throughout this section, then, part of the work of ethical practice with LGBT people requires challenging broader cultural assumptions about what constitutes, for example, our notions of children, youth, gender, sexuality, and identity more broadly. Otherwise, there is every chance that ethical practice that simply follows any given ethical code enshrined by a mental health professional body will actually fail to do no harm. In other words, although codified ethics may attempt to ensure no malfeasance, they may do nothing to ensure beneficence—namely, that LGBT couples and families actually benefit from therapy in their everyday life, rather than just addressing the specific problems that may bring them to therapy. Affirming LGBT couples and families thus requires going beyond the couple or family unit that presents for therapy and encompassing the need for advocacy for social change on the part of the practitioner. This work must, of course, be done with the knowledge and permission of the client: Practitioners must give due consideration to the visibility of the clients and their wish for privacy in regard to advocacy (McCartt Hess & Feldman, 2008). Nonetheless, an ethical

LGBT-affirmative approach to practice requires practitioners to speak out in their everyday lives about discrimination in general and to affirm the rights of LGBT clients to therapeutic approaches that do more than just no harm.

Summary

This chapter has presented two views of ethical practice with LGBT clients: one that is ethically affirmative (i.e., that provides the minimal ethical standards LGBT clients should expect to receive) and one that is LGBT affirmative (i.e., that affirms the values and experiences of LGBT communities and which recognizes and challenges broader social discrimination). There are similarities between the two approaches in that both ideally adopt a strengths-based approach, where LGBT communities are recognized as healthy, in some instances even thriving, despite living in a heteronormative and gender-normative social context. Riggs, McLaren, and Mayes (2009) suggest this view in their research among a sample of lesbians and gay men on attitudes toward lesbian and gay parents, where the researchers propose that "viewing lesbian and gay parents who continue to thrive in the context of heterosexism and homophobia as enacting positive forms of parenting in comparison to heterosexual parents is not the product of exaggeration, but rather one of celebration and recognition" (p. 60). In other words, there is nothing delusional or fake about LGBT communities making positive claims; these reflect recognition that it takes considerable strength to thrive in the face of social marginalization. We need only consider what it could be like for LGBT couples and families to live in a context of adequate social support and recognition to understand that a strengths-based approach recognizes the achievements of LGBT communities.

Another important focus of this chapter has been to consider the experiences of LGBT clients as those of an LGBT person, someone who lives life as such in a context where LGBT identities are politicized and made to matter, but not to make therapy with LGBT couples and families all about sexuality. Acknowledging that some LGBT clients may present with issues relating to sexual dysfunction or concerns about sexual practices is, of course, important, but equally important is recognizing that sexuality will be but one of many presenting issues. Indeed, most other presenting issues will have nothing to do with the sexual orientation or the gender identity of the client per se even though living in a context of heteronormativity and gender normativity means, by default, that many of the mental health problems of LGBT people arise from the effects of social marginalization based on gender and/or sexuality. Understanding this approach to therapy requires practitioners to have the capacity to work with clients to clearly understand the specific contexts they live in, to determine what is personal and what is social in regard to determining factors, and to challenge the conflation of LGBT identities with pathology while not failing to diagnose disorders as appropriate among LGBT communities.

Finally, it is important for ethical practice to maintain a focus on what social functioning means for LGBT people, given that the goal of many mental health interventions is to increase the capacity of clients to function within the broader community. Although this is a laudable goal, it is equally important to consider the messages we give to LGBT clients when we create an injunction to function. Does functioning in society mean that LGBT people have to accept the existence of heteronormativity and gender normativity and not rock the boat? And does such an account of functioning render LGBT people, as well as those who work with them, complicit with marginalization and thus the perpetuation of mental health problems? These are particularly vexing questions, and the responses to them will likely differ according to the view of therapy and society held by individual practitioners. Nonetheless, ethical mental health practice in any form should at its simplest do no harm; and though functioning in terms of, say, being able to leave the house is likely a definition most practitioners could agree upon, in reality for some LGBT people even this definition may seem unachievable in the face of potential violence against LGBT people. Ethical practice with LGBT people must thus be keenly aware of the specific implications of a range of mental health concepts in the lives of this population. It must strive to assist the functioning of LGBT couples and families both from within the unit itself and also by making the world they live in more viable for them.

References

Adams, J., McCreanor, T., & Braun, V. (2007). Alcohol and gay men: Consumption, promotion and policy responses. In V. Clarke & E. Peel (Eds.), *Out in psychology: Lesbian, gay, bisexual, trans and queer perspectives* (pp. 369–390). Chichester, UK: Wiley.

Barker, M., Hagger-Johnson, G., Hegarty, P., Hutchison, C., & Riggs, D. W (2007). Responses from the BPS Lesbian & Gay Psychology section to Crossley's "Making sense of barebacking." *British Journal of Social Psychology, 46,* 127–133.

Bennett, C., & Coyle, A. (2007) A minority within a minority: Experiences of gay men with intellectual disabilities. In V. Clarke & E. Peel (Eds.), *Out in psychology: Lesbian, gay, bisexual, trans and queer perspectives* (pp. 125–145). Chichester, UK: Wiley.

Bond Stockton, K. (2004). Growing sideways, or versions of the queer child: The ghost, the homosexual, the Freudian, the innocent, and the interval of the animal. In S. Bruhm & N. Hurley (Eds.), *Curiouser: On the queerness of children* (pp. 277–315). Minneapolis: University of Minnesota Press.

Bradley, B. S., & Selby, J. M. (2001). To criticise the critic: Songs of experience. *Australian Psychologist, 36,* 84–87.

Braun, V. (2000). Heterosexism in focus group research: Collusion and challenge. *Feminism and Psychology, 10,* 133–140.

Brown, L. S. (1989). Beyond thou shalt not: Thinking about ethics in the lesbian therapy community. In E. D. Rothblum & E. Cole (Eds.), *Lesbianism: Affirming nontraditional roles* (pp. 13–26). New York, NY: Haworth Press.

Brown. L. S. (1996). Ethical concerns with sexual minority patients. In T. Stein & R. Cabaj (Eds.), *Textbook of homosexuality and mental health* (pp. 897–916). Washington, DC: American Psychiatric Association.

Brown, L. S. (1997). Ethics in psychology: *Cui bono?* In D. Fox & I. Prilleltensky (Eds.), *Critical psychology: An introduction* (pp. 51–67). London, UK: Sage.

Davison, G. C. (2001). Conceptual and ethical issues in therapy for the psychological problems of gay men, lesbians, and bisexuals. *Journal of Clinical Psychology, 57,* 695–704.

Dworkin, S. H. (1992). Some ethical considerations when counseling gay, lesbian, and bisexual clients. In S. H. Dworkin & F .J. Gutierrez (Eds.), *Counseling gay men and lesbians: Journey to the end of the rainbow* (pp. 325–334). Alexandria, VA: American Association for Counseling and Development.

Gartrell, N., Deck, A., Rodas, C., Peyser, H., & Banks, A. (2005). The National Lesbian Family Study 4: Interviews with the 10-year-old children. *American Journal of Orthopsychiatry, 75,* 518–524.

Goethals, S. C., & Schwiebert, V. L. (2005). Counseling as a critique of gender: On the ethics of counseling transgendered clients. *International Journal for the Advancement of Counselling, 27,* 457–469.

Greene, B. (2007). Delivering ethical psychological services to lesbian, gay, and bisexual clients. In K. J. Bieschke, R. Perez, & K. A. DeBord (Eds.), *Handbook of counseling and psychotherapy with lesbian, gay, and bisexual clients* (2nd ed., pp. 181–199). Washington, DC: American Psychiatric Association.

Han, A. (2006). "I think you're the smartest race I've ever met": Racialised economies of gay desire. *ACRAWSA, 2*(2). Retrieved from http://www.acrawsa.org.au

Hillier, L., Edwards, J., & Riggs, D. W. (2008). Mental health and LGBT communities [Editorial]. *Gay and Lesbian Issues and Psychology Review, 4,* 65–68.

Hillier, L., & Mitchell, A. (2008). "It was as useful as a chocolate kettle": Sex education in the lives of same-sex-attracted young people in Australia. *Sex Education: Sexuality, Society and Learning, 8,* 211–224.

Israel, T. (2007). Training counselors to work ethically and effectively with bisexual clients. In B. A. Firestein (Ed.), *Becoming visible: Counseling bisexuals across the lifespan* (pp. 381–394). New York, NY: Columbia University Press.

Janson, G. R. (2002). Family counseling and referral with gay, lesbian, bisexual and transgendered clients: Ethical considerations. *Family Journal, 10,* 328–333.

Kane, G. (2004). "The unintended use of a pronoun": Coming out in the counseling environment. In D. W. Riggs & G. A. Walker (Eds.), *Out in the antipodes: Australian and New Zealand perspectives on gay and lesbian issues in psychology* (pp. 85–96). Perth, Australia: Brightfire Press.

Kitzinger, C., & Perkins, R. (1993). *Changing our minds: Lesbian feminism and psychology.* New York, NY: New York University Press.

Langdridge, D. (2007). Gay affirmative therapy: A theoretical framework and defence. In E. Peel, V. Clarke, & J. Drescher (Eds.), *British lesbian, gay, and bisexual psychologies: Theory, research, and practice* (pp. 27–44). New York, NY: Haworth Press.

Lev, A. I. (2004). *The complete lesbian and gay parenting guide*. New York, NY: Berkley Books.

McCartt Hess, P., & Feldman, N. (2008). Values and ethics in social work practice with lesbian, gay, bisexual, and transgender people. In G. P. Mallon (Ed.), *Social work practice with lesbian, gay, bisexual, and transgender people* (2nd ed., pp. 25–39). New York, NY: Routledge.

Meyer, I. (2003). Prejudice, social stress and mental health in lesbian, gay and bisexual populations. *Psychological Bulletin, 129*, 674–697.

Morrow, S. L. (2000). First do no harm: Therapist issues in psychotherapy with lesbian, gay, and bisexual clients. In R. Perez, K. A. DeBord, & K. Bieschke (Eds.), *Handbook of counseling and psychotherapy with lesbian, gay, and bisexual clients* (pp. 137–156). Washington, DC: American Psychiatric Association.

Peel, E. (2001). Mundane heterosexism: Understanding incidents of the everyday. *Women's Studies International Forum, 24*, 541–554.

Riggs, D. W. (2007). Recognising race in LGBT psychology: Privilege, power & complicity. In V. Clarke & E. Peel (Eds.), *Out in psychology: Lesbian, gay, bisexual and transgender perspectives* (pp. 59–76). London: Wiley.

Riggs, D. W. (2010a). Queering evidence-based practice. *Psychology and Sexuality, 2*, 87–98.

Riggs, D. W. (2010b). *What about the children! Masculinities, sexualities and hegemony.* Cambridge, UK: Cambridge Scholars Press.

Riggs, D. W., & Fell, G. R. (2010). Teaching cultural competency for working with lesbian, gay, bisexual and trans clients. *Psychology Learning and Teaching Journal, 9*, 30–38.

Riggs, D. W., McLaren, S., & Mayes, A. (2009). Attitudes toward parenting in a lesbian and gay community convenience sample. *Journal of Gay and Lesbian Mental Health, 13*, 51–61.

Riggs, D. W., & Patterson, A. (2009). The smiling faces of contemporary homophobia and transphobia. *Gay and Lesbian Issues and Psychology Review, 5*, 185–190.

Short, L., Riggs, D. W., Perlesz, A., Brown, R., & Kane, G. (2008). *Literature review on lesbian, gay, bisexual and transgender (LGBT) parented families.* Melbourne, Australia: Australian Psychological Society.

Sobocinski, M. R. (1990). Ethical principles in the counseling of gay and lesbian adolescents: Issues of autonomy, competence, and confidentiality. *Professional Psychology: Research and Practice, 21*, 240–247.

28

Research on Reorientation Therapy

JULIANNE M. SEROVICH, ERIKA L. GRAFSKY, and RASHMI GANGAMMA

Couple and family therapists are faced with treating clients who present with discomfort accepting a lesbian, gay, or bisexual identity or seek assistance with changing their sexual orientation. Therefore, therapists should be prepared to effectively and ethically provide services to persons who are struggling with a lesbian, gay, or bisexual (LGB) identity. This chapter provides a summary of the results of a recent review of the science of reorientation therapies (Serovich et al., 2008) that revealed an inadequate scientific basis to warrant the use of reorientation therapies by couple and family therapists. This chapter also reviews the challenges faced by individuals struggling with accepting their sexual orientation and provides a brief overview of affirmative approaches to therapy. Finally, provided here are suggestions for the production of high-quality scholarship in the area of ethical approaches to working with clients who are experiencing conflicts regarding their sexual orientation.

The Science of Reorientation Therapies

During the past few years, clinicians in a variety of mental health disciplines have engaged in a discourse as to the necessity and effectiveness of sexual reorientation therapies. The conversation and debates have focused on such questions as these: What are sexual reorientation therapies? Do these therapies work to modify sexual orientation? Can these therapies be harmful to individuals or families? In 2005, our team began an investigation into the research literature addressing such therapies. The purpose of this research was to investigate the scientific rigor of the studies supporting the conclusions claimed by those individuals who believe sexual orientation can be changed and those who argued that it could not (Serovich et al., 2008). Those in support of reorientation therapies argue that sexual orientation can be changed and should, for religious, social, and health reasons, be "fixed" (Nicolosi, 1991; Socarides & Kaufman, 1994). The latter disagree, stating that whereas sexual desire and behavior can be altered, a person's enduring attraction to members of the same sex is not malleable (Socarides & Kaufman, 1994). One way to address this issue is by comprehensively critiquing the available literature base on sexual reorientation therapies. Our focus was not just on the outcomes of these studies (i.e., did change occur) but, rather, on revealing the strengths and weaknesses of the research underlying this literature.

In general, sexual reorientation approaches can be categorized as "reparative" or "aversive" in nature. In our previous work, and this chapter, we contend that "reparative therapy," also known as "conversion therapy," involves a group of techniques utilized with the purpose of permanently altering a person's sexual orientation (Nicolosi, 1991; Socarides & Kaufman, 1994). Based on a psychoanalytic interpretation of homosexual behavior, Nicolosi (1991) suggested that the pathological sexualization was in need of "repairing," thus the term *reparative therapy* (Morrow & Beckstead, 2004). Reparative approaches, as a program of psychotherapy, attempt to "cure" LGB individuals by transforming them into heterosexuals (Hicks, 1999). These therapies can include myriad techniques, including prayer, religious conversion, and individual or group counseling.

Aversion therapies are techniques that share the same goal but are primarily behavioral. These include such approaches as electro-convulsive shock treatments, injections of drugs to induce nausea or vomiting, use of noxious stimuli, hypnotic suggestions, or orgasmic reconditioning using visual stimuli. These interventions range in intensity from mild to severe. In particular, orgasmic reconditioning involves instructing the participant to arouse himself manually with the aid of pictures or videos. When orgasm is imminent, the visual stimulus is changed from male to female to allow for the pairing of pleasure with desired arousal content. Electro-convulsive shock treatments are diverse in nature but generally pair shocks to the genital area with undesirable visual images. Traditional methods of aversion techniques have been termed "cruel" (Haldeman, 2002) and would not pass current Institutional Review Board standards for acceptable ethical research practices. As in our previous work, for the purposes of this chapter, the term *sexual reorientation* will be utilized as an umbrella term to describe therapies that are either aversive (behavioral) or reparative (psychosocial).

The primary aim of our 2008 work was to examine the manner in which research on the topic of reparative therapy had been conducted and reported. Of interest was the evaluation of the rigor in which the science supporting each study had been conducted. The project was carried out in a number of steps. First, relevant academic databases, including PsycINFO, Social Science Citation Index, Academic Search Premier Database, and Sociological Abstracts, were searched for articles using such terms as *conversion therapy*, *reparative therapy*, and *sexual reorientation therapy*. In addition, the websites of such organizations as the National Association for Research and Treatment of Homosexuality (NARTH), Exodus International, and Focus on the Family were also searched for citations of empirical research. Articles, books, and book chapters addressing reparative therapies were carefully reviewed for citations of additional works.

The search yielded 182 pieces of literature that addressed the topic of reorientation therapies. In order to be included in the analysis, the research needed to be empirically based and directly address the topic of reparative therapy. Not included were editorials and letters to editors, commentaries, book chapters, cases studies, literature reviews, articles not verified or located within the academic library system, those that were not about sexual reorientation therapies, and articles that only described ethical issues or clinical procedures. After our thorough review of each article, the final sample of data for this study included 28 empirically based, peer-reviewed full-length articles and brief reports addressing the efficacy of reparative therapies.

Second, the research team designed a coding sheet that included issues and variables deemed relevant to the investigation. Items included the research topic, theoretical orientation of the study, sample characteristics, and study design. Third, a randomly assigned primary and secondary reviewer coded each article. The primary reviewer was responsible for the initial written coding of the article, which was confirmed, refuted, or accentuated by the second reviewer.

Overall, results suggested that the rigor in which both reparative and aversive studies were conducted and reported was poor. Most notable problems included the degree to which important omissions in the data occurred, including the lack of demographic characteristics of the available samples, the absence of control groups or longitudinal follow-up designs, and the absence of theory. These sampling limitations affect the degree to which a consumer of research can evaluate the generalizability of the outcomes to demographically and geographically diverse populations. Further, the design limitations of the majority of these studies question the degree to which claims regarding change can be accurately made.

It was perhaps the most striking that in these studies the assessment of sexual orientation tended to reflect sexual activity or functioning versus any dimension of identity. In fact, 75% of the reparative therapy studies and 60% of the aversion therapy studies did not report the use of any measure of sexual orientation. Of those that did, these instruments varied considerably in quality. The Kinsey Scale (Kinsey, Pomeroy, & Martin, 1948), the most highly regarded measure of sexual orientation, was used in only three studies. Researchers seemed to prefer participants' self-identification as gay or not gay as a measure of sexual orientation. This approach is highly problematic, given the complexities of sexual identity (Klein, Sepekoff, & Wolf, 1985), and thus minimizes the usefulness of the research base. Sexual reorientation research that is absent of a strong measure of outcome (i.e., change in sexual orientation) should be considered peculiar at best. In studies that allowed participants to self-identify as gay or not, the definition was primarily behaviorally oriented. That is, questions probed sexual activity (one's behavior) versus identity (who one believes one is). In addition, the outcomes often focused only on the decrease or elimination of "homosexual" thoughts and behaviors. This narrow focus is problematic because not engaging in same-sex behaviors does not necessarily change partner preferences or emotional attraction. The equivalent would be to assume that individuals engaging in abstinence are neither homosexual nor heterosexual. The use of the plethesmograph, which assesses penile engorgement, has long been considered the gold standard outcome measure. This too, however, is problematic because equating arousal with identity is erroneous. Furthermore, it has been well established that a person's sexual orientation can change remarkably through the lifetime, and that no one set of sexual behaviors is sufficient to identify a person's sexual orientation (Klein et al., 1985). Therefore, competent measures of sexual orientation should include behaviors, thoughts, fantasies, and affective responses.

As a whole, one strength of the studies was ample sample sizes. The aversion studies were based on a total sample of just over 400 cases, whereas the reparative samples totaled over 2,100 cases. Typical sampling strategies included advertising or recruiting at large conferences, soliciting support group attendees, therapist referrals, print- and web-based media advertising, and word-of-mouth (Nicolosi, Byrd, & Potts, 2000; Schaeffer, Hyde, Kroencke, McCormick, & Nottebaum, 2000; Shidlo & Schroeder, 2002; Spitzer, 2003). Limited information regarding inclusion criteria and respondent tracking, however, created difficulty in determining how many men and women would have been eligible to participate in these studies or how many were approached or recruited more than once. Informed consent procedures were rarely mentioned; in addition, often in order to limit duplicate sampling there was no mention of maintaining a list of individuals who had been approached and had completed the study.

Overall, it was concluded that the research base on reorientation therapies was severely compromised in scope and quality. This finding suggests that any claims of effectiveness of reorientation therapies are impossible to substantiate and could constitute unethical practice. Although strategies for future researchers to consider in strengthening the literature base were recommended, it was also noted that critical ethical and moral issues must first be addressed. Of primary consideration is the attempt to "fix" something that not only is not "broken" but cannot be altered. On the surface, reorientation appears to offer an outcome that is unlikely to be achieved.

Ethical Couple and Family Therapy for Persons Experiencing Sexual Orientation Conflicts

Given the lack of credible scientific evidence supporting the use of reorientation therapies, couple and family therapists should be cautioned against utilizing any sort of therapeutic practice that is based on the premise that a homosexual orientation can be reoriented to a heterosexual orientation. Rather, couple and family therapists who are adequately informed and aware of their own values regarding sexual orientation are in a position to provide ethical treatment to persons who are struggling with their sexual orientation. In the remainder of this chapter, we review some of the challenges faced by someone who is struggling with sexual orientation and provide a brief overview of gay-affirmative therapy. Finally, we make suggestions for the production of high-quality scholarship in the area of ethical approaches to working with clients who are experiencing sexual orientation conflicts.

Sexual Orientation Conflicts

According to sexual orientation identity models (i.e., Cass, 1979; Troiden, 1988, 1989), most individuals who identify as lesbian, gay, or bisexual have experienced some degree of conflict regarding their sexual orientation. For example, according to Cass (1979), the first stage of forming a gay or lesbian identity includes feelings of *identity confusion*, which involve becoming aware of same-sex attractions and usually finding them unacceptable given the heterocentric cultural norms. Cass also posits that in Stage 2, *identity comparison*, that one may accept homosexual attraction but reject a homosexual identity or vice versa. This incongruence between identity and attraction involves conflicted feelings about one's self. Similarly, Troiden's (1998, 1989) first two stages, *sensitization* and *identity confusion*, include recognition of being different as well as feeling confused or conflicted regarding one's identity. This conflict typically decreases once the individual has formed a consolidated identity as a gay man, lesbian women, or bisexual man or woman.

For some individuals, however conflicts regarding identity may be more prominent and enduring (Beckstead & Israel, 2007). This may be especially true when family members have trouble accepting that a loved one is experiencing same-sex attractions. In this situation, individuals with same-sex attractions may struggle with issues of loyalty. Specifically, stressors may arise from having to choose between family of origin and family of choice or between one's perception of self-identity and others' construction of it. Although resolution of this conflict depends largely on acceptance of one's sexual orientation, family dynamics also play a key role. Individuals who are, in most circumstances, comfortable with identifying as gay, lesbian, or bisexual may find it difficult to discuss their orientation or intimate relationships with their parents, siblings, and other family members; or they may, in extreme cases, be forced to pass as straight (Dooley, 2009). This spilt in identity, as well as the need to maintain it, may increase interpersonal as well as intrapersonal angst.

Although there are a variety of potential sources of conflict regarding one's sexual orientation, the prevailing heterosexist social context and also cultural and religious conflicts are the most commonly identified in the literature (Beckstead & Israel, 2007). These macro-level value systems influence multiple aspects of people's lives. One way to understand these sources of conflict is to situate them as competing identities. That is, it may, for example, be difficult for someone to reconcile being a lesbian woman and a devout Catholic. Further, the woman's Mexican heritage may further complicate her ability to successfully establish a positive identity as a lesbian woman. Conflicts between competing identities (e.g., being gay, African American, and Baptist; or being bisexual and heterosexually married) can lead to such symptoms as emotional distress, negative self-concept, and isolation from others (Beckstead & Israel, 2007). These symptoms may be further exacerbated if the person is situated in a close relational context, whether a family or other intimate partnership.

In the case of conflicts regarding one's sexual orientation, clients who seek the services of couple and family therapists could be in various family forms and developmental life-cycle stages. For example, a family may present in crisis because a son was unexpectedly found kissing a male friend in his bedroom; the female partner in a middle-aged heterosexual couple reveals that she was having an affair with her best female friend; or a soon-to-be heterosexually married man seeks services because he is having problems with intimacy and shares that he cannot tell his partner that he is attracted to men. Regardless of the composition of the client system that seeks services for issues related to confusing or unwanted same-sex sexual attraction, couple and family therapists should be prepared to respond responsibly and ethically to these clients.

If clinicians working with individuals who experience same-sex attractions are to assist these clients, they must understand the context of social stigmatization, multiple layers of identities, and potential conflicts faced by these individuals. Unfortunately, members of LGB populations have been recipients of long-standing discrimination and controversy in the mental health field, which continues to complicate the delivery of services to this population (Brown, 1996). A few of the complicated factors that could affect the receipt of quality services for individuals who are experiencing conflicts in regard to their sexual orientation include the clinician's competence in treating this population and the ethics of sexual reorientation therapies (Greene, 2007).

Emerging research on psychotherapy practices reveals the existence of unique therapeutic and therapist factors that significantly influence successful treatment. For instance, Pixton (2003) discussed six factors identified in her interviews with gay and lesbian clients that were markers of a meaningful therapeutic experience. These factors—including communication of a nonpathological stance toward homosexuality, providing a space for open exploration of sexuality, having levels of knowledge and awareness of LGB issues, and being able to connect fully with a gay client without prejudices—suggest that therapists working with sexual minority populations have to actively consider and reflect upon their own thoughts about the nature of human sexuality. Endorsing a neutral stance or merely expressing a lack of bias is not sufficient for a therapist to remain effective (Liddle, 1997).

Gay-Affirmative Therapy

Gay-affirmative therapy, as a framework of practice that depathologizes homosexuality and embraces diversity in expressions of sexuality, is often deemed appropriate for working with individuals, couples, and families (Crisp, 2006). Malyon (1982) is credited with first coining the term and proposing a stage model for gay-affirmative psychotherapy. Training in gay-affirmative therapy is a significant factor in therapists' ability to work with sexual minority populations (Kilgore, Sideman, Amin, Baca, & Bohanske, 2005). Davies and Neal (1996) provide extensive detailed guidelines for clinicians on what it means to be a gay-affirmative therapist. In addition, other authors in this volume also elaborate on a gay-affirmative approach for couple and family therapy. For example, Tunnell (Chapter 2, this volume) describes an approach for working with gay males in couple therapy and Connolly (Chapter 3, this volume) describes affirmative therapy with lesbian couples.

Milton and Coyle (1999) suggest that there are two ways in which a gay-affirmative framework can be incorporated in practice. The first, which perhaps falls under the purview of the critical theory paradigm, is for therapists to challenge their own levels of comfort with homosexuality and to raise false consciousness surrounding oppressive experiences of LGB individuals. The second is to incorporate an affirmative attitude into all existing frameworks of psychotherapeutic practices. The American Psychological Association (APA) has adopted the latter approach as its recommendations for professionals working with clients who are experiencing sexual orientation conflicts. The APA (2009) describes an affirmative approach as "supportive of clients' identity development without an a priori treatment goal for how clients identify or live out their sexual orientation" (p. 60). The APA (2009) elaborates,

> Affirmative client-centered approaches consider sexual orientation uniquely individual and inseparable from an individual's personality and sense of self (Glassgold, 1995, 2008). This includes (a) being aware of the client's unique personal, social, and historical context; (b) exploring and countering the harmful impact of stigma and stereotypes on the client's self-concept (including the prejudice related to age, gender, gender identity, race, ethnicity, culture, national origin, religion, sexual orientation, disability, language, and socioeconomic status); and (c) maintaining a broad view of acceptable life choices. (p. 63)

These guidelines provide clinicians with a lens "through" which to work with clients that avoids the historically perceived choices between conversion therapy and gay-affirmative therapy that excluded a large group of individuals who found neither model entirely satisfactory (Haldeman, 2002).

Although most literature on affirmative practices has focused on psychotherapeutic approaches, very little is available as guidelines for family therapists working with LGB populations and their families. Malley and McCann (2002) note that an individual's assumptions about family relationships are based on norms of the dominant culture, which is, in this context, heterosexist. Gay and lesbian individuals face unique issues that may be missed in an uneducated imposition of knowledge about traditional family systems onto gay and lesbian families. For instance, the issue of disclosure of sexual orientation or seropositive status may significantly impact an individual's relationship with a partner, parent, and/or child; balance of power among gay couples may involve such factors as degree of "outness" in one's social network; children of gay parents may have more than two significant caregivers. These issues could be overlooked if a therapist fails to comprehensively understand the contributions of unique life experiences and circumstances that affect families of LGB individuals.

Incorporating an Affirmative Framework Into Existing Couple and Family Therapy Models

As mentioned earlier, Milton and Coyle (1999) suggest that another way psychotherapists can ethically serve LGB clients is to incorporate an affirmative stance into existing models of practice. Further, incorporating an affirmative approach is the recommended approach to working with clients who are experiencing sexual orientation conflicts according to the APA (2009). However, there is limited literature in the field of couple and family therapy that describes how therapists can ethically respond to clients who present with sexual orientation conflicts. As clinicians who practice from a variety of family therapy models (e.g., Bowenian, contextual, experiential, strategic, structural, and solution focused), the field should challenge itself in critically examining and broadening the understanding of how models of family therapy can be applied effectively to such diverse issues as these.

For instance, for clinicians using the contextual therapy approach (Boszormenyi-Nagy & Krasner, 1986), situating sexual orientation conflicts would involve understanding that LGB individuals, as a minority group, face discrimination at various levels that could influence relationship dynamics with significant others. This understanding could be conceptualized under two interrelated dimensions of the approach: "facts" and "relational ethics." Using the contextual therapy techniques of acknowledgment and multidirected partiality, clinicians could discuss the unfairness and its implications to help clients move beyond destructive entitlements, filters that prevent individual and relational growth.

Recently Greenan and Tunnell (2003) elucidated the use of structural family therapy with gay male couples. Adapting the basic model to the needs of gay male couples, the authors emphasize the importance of "joining" with their clients by becoming familiar with their culture. The process of joining, or developing a working therapeutic alliance, is not new to family therapists. Numerous studies have pointed to the importance of therapeutic alliance in treatment outcome for individuals, couples, and families (i.e., Knobloch-Fedders, Pinsof, & Mann, 2007; Martin, Garske, & Davis, 2000; Shelef, Diamond, Diamond, & Liddle, 2005). We believe that developing an alliance with LGB individuals requires therapists to make a conscious effort to acknowledge and understand the intersection of competing identities that complicate development of relationships with significant others. This requires the therapist, regardless of the approach used, to be in a position to explore, acknowledge, accommodate, and work with apparent incongruencies that LGB clients may present in therapy (i.e., being devoutly religious and gay; being in a significant intimate relationship but not "out" to family members), and not impose a "correct" way of life. The process of understanding begins with training therapists in issues related to sexuality and sexual orientation and challenging impositions of heteronormative ideas of individual and family development. The therapist should avoid invalidating a client's beliefs and value systems and instead convey empathy and recognition of the client's commitment to their religion, culture, or other heterocentric values that are likely a key part of that person's conflict regarding their sexual orientation.

Future Research

The development of couple and family therapy–oriented gay-affirmative therapies will require rigorous research support. These researchers should not repeat the mistakes made by reorientation researchers, thereby creating results that are uninterpretable or inconclusive. Instead, researchers should include the assessment of pertinent demographic variables; clearly defined methods of recruitment, as well as retention data and inclusion criteria; and a well-articulated theoretical framework and methods of data collection, as well as the use of longitudinal research designs.

Complete and comprehensive demographic information includes gender, age, race or ethnicity, religiosity or spirituality, participants' place of residence (e.g., rural or urban location, and area of the country), and such constructs of socioeconomic status as education, income, and employment. These data are important because, without adequate information on study participants, generalization of study data is limited. For example, 79% of reorientation studies did not report the race of their samples, and only one aversion therapy study included women. If these studies had shown successful outcomes, consumers of the research could not apply them appropriately to persons of varying demographic backgrounds (e.g., women, minorities).

Researchers should adequately describe their methods of participant recruitment, how many individuals approached agreed to participate, and how many completed treatment. These data provide more detail about the sampling procedures and can provide a contextualized perspective on the demographics of the sample. Furthermore, clearly outlined and articulated inclusion criteria allow other researchers to assess generalizability and replicate studies to target other types of persons to further establish the effectiveness of particular approaches or treatments with diverse populations.

Studies can be conducted as randomized clinical trials, small- to large-scale observational studies of particular approaches, or case studies. The most desirable designs are longitudinal and include well-timed and adequate follow-up assessments, which allow clinicians to evaluate the impact of the therapy over time. Therapeutic dosage should be accounted for, and the fidelity of therapist to treatment should be measured and included in subsequent analyses.

Conclusion

The empirical research underlying the effectiveness of reorientation therapies is diminutive and lacking in quality and capacity. Therefore, claims of effectiveness and a call for the usage of these techniques are unsubstantiated. Couple and family therapists should heed the warnings by such reputable mental health organizations as the American Psychological Association, American Psychiatric Association, American Academy of Pediatrics, American Medical Association, American Counseling Association, National Association of School Psychologists, National Association of Social Workers, and Royal College of Nursing against utilizing these strategies. Rather, the field would be well served by the development of gay-affirmative therapies or the adaptation of our theories of change to address issues facing LGB persons seeking therapy.

Acknowledgment

The authors would like to thank Wiley-Blackwell Publishing for granting permission to reproduce parts of the following original manuscript: Serovich, J. M., Craft, S. M., Toviessi, P., Gangamma, R., McDowell, T., & Grafsky, E. L. (2008). A systematic review of the research base on reparative therapies. *Journal of Marital and Family Therapy, 34*(2), 227–238.

References

APA Task Force on Appropriate Therapeutic Responses to Sexual Orientation. (2009). *Report of the task force on appropriate therapeutic responses to sexual orientation.* Washington, DC: American Psychological Association.

Beckstead, L., & Israel, T. (2007). Affirmative counseling and psychotherapy focused on issues related to sexual orientation conflicts. In K. J. Bieschke, R. M. Perez, & K. A. DeBord (Eds.), *Handbook of counseling and psychotherapy with lesbian, gay, bisexual, and transgender clients* (2nd ed., pp. 221–244). Washington, DC: American Psychological Association.

Boszormenyi-Nagy, I., & Krasner, R. B. (1986). *Between give and take: A clinical guide to contextual therapy.* New York, NY: Brunner/Mazel.

Brown, L. S. (1996). Ethical concerns with sexual minority patients. In R. Cabaj & T. Stein (Eds.), *Textbook of homosexuality and mental health* (pp. 897–916). Washington, DC: American Psychiatric Press.

Cass, V. C. (1979). Homosexual identity formation: A theoretical model. *Journal of Homosexuality, 4,* 219–235.

Crisp, C. (2006). The Gay Affirmative Practice Scale (GAP): A new measure for assessing cultural competence with gay and lesbian clients. *Social Work, 51,* 115–126.

Davies, D., & Neal, C. (1996). *Pink therapy: A guide for counselors and therapists working with lesbian, gay, and bisexual clients.* Bristol, PA: Open University Press.

Dooley, J. (2009). Negotiating stigma: Lessons from the life stories of gay men. *Journal of Gay & Lesbian Social Services, 21,* 13–29.

Greenan, D. E., & Tunnell, G. (2003). *Couple therapy with gay men.* New York, NY: Guilford Press.

Greene, B. (2007). Delivering ethical psychological services to lesbian, gay, and bisexual clients. In K. J. Bieschke, R. M. Perez, & K. A. DeBord (Eds.), *Handbook of counseling and psychotherapy with lesbian, gay, bisexual, and transgender clients* (2nd ed., pp. 181–199). Washington, DC: American Psychological Association.

Haldeman, D. C. (2002). Gay rights, patient rights: The implications of sexual orientation conversion therapy. *Professional Psychology: Research and Practice, 33*(3), 260–264.

Hicks, K, A. (1999). "Reparative" therapy: Whether parental attempts to change a child's sexual orientation can legally constitute child abuse. *American University Law Review, 49,* 506–547.

Kilgore, H., Sideman, L., Amin, K., Baca, L., & Bohanske, B. (2005). Psychologists' attitudes and therapeutic approaches toward gay, lesbian, and bisexual issues continue to improve: An update. *Psychotherapy: Theory, Research, and Practice, 42,* 395–400.

Kinsey, A. C., Pomeroy, W. B., & Martin, C. E. (1948). *Sexual behavior in the human male.* Philadelphia, PA: Saunders.

Klein, F., Sepekoff, B., & Wolf, T. (1985). Sexual orientation: A multi-variable dynamic process. *Journal of Homosexuality, 11*(1–2), 35–49.

Knobloch-Fedders, L. M., Pinsof, W. M., & Mann, B. J. (2007). Therapeutic alliance and treatment progress in couple psychotherapy. *Journal of Marital and Family Therapy, 33,* 245–257.

Liddle, B. (1997). Gay and lesbian clients' selection of therapists and utilization of therapy. *Psychotherapy, 34,* 11–18.

Malley, M., & McCann, D. (2002). Family therapy with lesbian and gay clients. In A. Coyle & C. Kitzinger (Eds.), *Lesbian and gay psychology: New perspectives* (pp. 198–218). Oxford, UK: Blackwell.

Malyon, A. K. (1982). Psychotherapeutic implications of internalized homophobia in gay men. *Journal of Homosexuality, 7*(2/3), 59–69.

Martin, D. J., Garske, J. P., & Davis, K. M. (2000). Relation of the therapeutic alliance with outcome and other variables: A meta-analytic review. *Journal of Consulting and Clinical Psychology, 68,* 438–450.

Milton, M., & Coyle, A. (1999). Lesbian and gay affirmative psychotherapy: Issues in theory and practice. *Sexual and Marital Therapy, 14,* 43–59.

Morrow, S. L., & Beckstead, A. L. (2004). Conversion therapies for same-sex attracted clients in religious conflict: Context, predisposing factors, experiences, and implications for therapy. *Counseling Psychologist, 32*(5), 641–650.

Nicolosi, J. (1991). *Reparative therapy of male homosexuality.* Northvale, NJ: Aronson.

Nicolosi, J., Byrd., A. D., & Potts, R. W. (2000). Retrospective self-reports of changes in homosexual orientation: A consumer survey of conversion therapy clients. *Psychological Reports, 86,* 1071–1088.

Pixton, S. (2003). Experiencing gay affirmative therapy: An exploration of client's views of what is helpful. *Counselling and Psychotherapy Research, 3,* 211–215.

Schaeffer, K. W., Hyde, R. A., Kroencke, T., McCormick, B., & Nottebaum, L. (2000). Religiously motivated sexual orientation change. *Journal of Psychology & Christianity, 19,* 61–70.

Serovich, J. M., Craft, S. M., Toviessi, P., Gangamma, R., McDowell, T., & Grafsky, E. L. (2008). A systematic review of the research base on reparative therapies. *Journal of Marital and Family Therapy, 34*(2), 227–238.

Shelef, K., Diamond, G. M., Diamond, G. S., & Liddle, H. A. (2005). Adolescent and parent alliance and treatment outcome in multidimensional family therapy. *Journal of Consulting and Clinical Psychology, 73*(4), 689–698.

Shidlo, A., & Schroeder, M. (2002). Changing sexual orientation: A consumers' report. *Professional Psychology: Research and Practice, 33,* 249–259.

Socarides, C. W., & Kaufman, B. (1994). Reparative therapy [Letter]. *American Journal of Psychiatry, 151,* 157.

Spitzer, R. (2003). Can some gay men and lesbians change their sexual orientation? 200 participants reporting a change from homosexual to heterosexual orientation. *Archives of Sexual Behavior, 32*(5), 403–417.

Troiden, R. R. (1988). Homosexual identity development. *Journal of Adolescent Health Care, 9,* 105–113.

Troiden, R. R. (1989). The formation of homosexual identities. In G. Herdt (Ed.), *Gay and lesbian youth* (pp. 43–73). New York, NY: Hayworth.

29

Helping Individuals and Families Recover From Sexual Orientation Change Efforts and Heterosexism

JEFF LUTES and MARSHA MCDONOUGH

Once a society loses this capacity [to dialogue], all that is left is a cacophony of voices battling it out to see who wins and who loses. There is no capacity to go deeper, to find a deeper meaning that transcends individual views and self-interest. It seems reasonable to ask whether many of our deeper problems in governing ourselves today, the so-called "gridlock" and loss of mutual respect and caring … might not stem from this lost capacity to talk with one another, to think together as part of a larger community.

Peter Senge (cited in Stanfield, 2000)

To work ethically with lesbian, gay, bisexual, and transgender (LGBT) persons, family therapists must examine and respond to the pervasive influence of heterosexism. Heterosexism is a force behind past and current efforts to change sexual orientation and gender identity. This chapter provides a comprehensive review of sexual orientation change efforts (SOCE) and the harmful effects of SOCE on LGBT people and their families. Collaborative Therapy (CT) is proposed as an ethical model of treatment that challenges the practices and assumptions of heterosexism. This chapter describes how collaborative therapists join clients in relationships and conversations that reduce shame and increase self-agency. Using examples from both inside and outside the therapy office, the authors demonstrate therapy, community building, and social justice actions that effectively challenge prejudice, discrimination, and heterosexual privilege.

Understanding SOCE

A Brief History

Sexual orientation change efforts encompass an array of methodologies that endeavor to transform a person's ego-dystonic homosexuality or bisexuality to heterosexuality. These efforts originated in the middle of the 19th century during a period in which homosexuality was considered both a crime and a medical illness (J. Katz, 1995). Pathologizing perspectives, influenced by psychoanalytic theories and social stigma, continued until the middle of the 20th century (Drescher, 1998). A landmark study by psychologist Evelyn Hooker (1957) used projective measures to compare heterosexual and homosexual men on levels of functioning. Hooker's findings counter the notion of homosexuality as a mental disorder. Follow-up research on personality and mental illness, conducted throughout the 1960s and 1970s, found heterosexuals and homosexuals to be relatively indistinguishable on levels of stability, social and vocational adaptiveness, judgment, and psychological adjustment (Freedman, 1971; Gonsiorek, 1982, 1991; Hart et al., 1978; Reiss, 1980).

Nonetheless, SOCE using psychoanalytic, cognitive, and behavioral techniques remained prevalent within mainstream psychology and psychiatry until the preponderance of research resulted in the removal of homosexuality from the American Psychiatric Association's *Diagnostic and Statistical Manual of Mental Disorders* in 1973 (Drescher, 2003). Following the declassification of homosexuality as a mental disorder, the number of published research studies on SOCE declined as mainstream mental health professionals and social scientists began to view homosexuality as normal and positive expression within the continuum of human sexuality (APA, 2009).

The accumulation of empirical evidence led to resolutions, opposing the depiction of homosexuality as a mental illness, by the American Psychiatric Association (1973), the American Psychological Association (Conger, 1975), the American Counseling Association Governing Council (1998), the National Association of Social Workers (1998), and the American Psychoanalytic Association (1991). The American Medical Association (2004) and the American Academy of Pediatrics (1993) issued similar statements and the World Health Organization removed homosexuality from its list of disorders in 1992 (Nakajima, 2003). In November 1999, a primer on sexual orientation included a warning on the potential harm caused by reparative therapy (Just the Facts Coalition, 2008). This primer was endorsed by the following organizations:

- American Academy of Pediatrics
- American Association of School Administrators
- American Counseling Association
- American Federation of Teachers
- American Psychological Association
- American School Counselor Association
- American School Health Association
- Interfaith Alliance Foundation
- National Association of School Psychologists
- National Association of Secondary School Principals
- National Association of Social Workers
- National Education Association
- School Social Work Association of America

Contemporary SOCE and Heterosexism

Despite the affirmative position taken by contemporary mental health professionals toward LGBT persons, SOCE continue to proliferate. These efforts are largely fueled by religious groups (APA, 2009) and are referred to as faith-based "ex-gay" ministries, reorientation therapy, conversion therapy, or reparative therapy. It is important to note that SOCE are rooted in the larger problem of heterosexism—namely, the widespread social and religious assumption that heterosexuality is superior and preferable to homosexuality. Unlike other forms of prejudice, heterosexism eludes scrutiny and leads lawmakers to vote against equality, employers to fire their LGBT workers, parents to disown their children, clergy to teach untrue stereotypes, and self-hatred to be sowed among LGBT people (Hunt, 2007). By necessity, reparative therapists and leaders of ex-gay ministries reinforce heterosexuality as normative. They promote a disease model that views same-sex attraction as psychopathology, developmental immaturity, and a deficit in moral character (Drescher, 1998). The SOCE leaders discount the important contributions of LGBT persons within culture and throughout history, ignoring the reality of well-adjusted, long-term same-sex couples and families who live, work, worship, and raise children within every community (Besen, 2003).

Ex-gay ministries attempt to conquer same-sex attraction through a mix of prayer, Bible study, church attendance and worship sessions, group activities, self-help exercises, and educational classes. They forbid any form of intimate coupling or human sexuality other than heterosexual expression (Erzen, 2006). Ex-gay ministries range in modality from weekly individual and group sessions to such residential programs as Love in Action, New Hope, and Desert Stream. Residential programs require clients to live communally for up to several months while undergoing a process geared to heal sexual "brokenness."

Two outspoken proponents of ex-gay ministries include the conservative Christian organizations Focus on the Family and Exodus International. Focus on the Family sponsored a conference entitled Love Won Out (1998–2009) across the United States. Love Won Out attempted to "promote the truth that change is possible for those who experience same-sex attractions" (Burroway, 2007). By the end of 2005, Love Won Out conferences had reached 25,000 people across the United States (Gilgoff, 2007). In 2009, citing budget cuts, Focus on the Family turned Love Won Out over to Exodus International. According to the Focus on the Family website (http://www.exodusinternational.org), Exodus International includes more than 230 ex-gay ministries in the United States and Canada. Through the Exodus Global Alliance, they promote the messages "change is possible" and "freedom is possible through Jesus Christ." Whereas most ex-gay ministries are rooted in fundamentalist Christianity, other programs are tied to different faith traditions, among them JONAH for the Jewish community (http://www.jonahweb.org), Courage for Catholics (http://www.couragerc.net), and Evergreen International for followers of the Church of Jesus Christ of Latter-day Saints (http://www.evergreeninternational.org).

Programs to address specific populations have emerged, among them Witness Freedom Ministries for African Americans (http://www.witnessfortheworld.org); Exodus Latinoamerica (http://www.exoduslatinoamerica.org), Courage Latino (http://www.courage-latino.org), and Camino de Salida (http://www.caminodesalida.blogspot) for Latin Americans; as well as Exodus Youth (http://www.exodusyouth.net). Support groups include Homosexuals Anonymous, modeled after 12-step programs (http://www.ha-fs.org), and Parents and Friends of Ex-Gays and Gays (http://www.pfox.org). Many churches in the United States and abroad offer various forms of self-help and ex-gay ministries through the Exodus Church Association (http://www.exoduschurchassociation.org).

In contrast to faith-based programs, there are licensed mental health professionals claiming to change same-sex attraction or to eliminate same-sex sexual behavior using psychotherapy. Despite social science research indicating otherwise, these practitioners routinely conceptualize homosexuality as a form of mental illness, developmental disorder, gender deficit, or addiction. Treatment protocols are predicated on disproven etiological theories that same-sex attraction results from family dysfunction, failure to establish healthy bonding with parental figures (particularly the same-gender parent), early traumatic events, or developmental arrest and intrapsychic conflict (Drescher, 1998). Those LGBT persons who struggle with guilt and shame may be drawn to these theories, hoping that resolution will remove unwanted homoerotic feelings, redeem them from mortal sin, and create a heteronormative future with loved ones.

Joseph Nicolosi is a well-known figure within the SOCE movement. As founder of the National Association for the Research and Therapy of Homosexuality (NARTH), he coined the term *reparative therapy* to eliminate unwanted homosexuality (Nicolosi, 1991). Nicolosi, along with others, further suggestd that reparative therapy is a viable option for changing a person's gender identity (Psychvideos, 2009). Reparative therapists like Nicolosi often present themselves as secular psychologists. In fact, they are connected to fundamentalist religious leaders and organizations (Besen, 2003). For example, Nicolosi served as a popular keynote speaker at Focus on the Family's Love Won Out conference. Nicolosi's extreme claims about homosexuality include these statements:

- "The mother is over-emotionally involved; a dominant, strong personality … the father is quiet, withdrawn, non-expressive, and/or hostile."
- "I've never met a homosexual man that had a loving respectful relationship with his father."
- "Homosexuality is a gender identity disorder."
- "There is no such thing as a homosexual…. We are all heterosexual, but some heterosexuals have a homosexual problem."
- "Homosexual behavior is always prompted by an inner state of emptiness."
- "We advise parents to use clear and consistent messages: 'We do not accept your effeminacy. You are a boy. God made you a boy. Being a boy is special.' When parents do this, especially fathers, they can turn their boys around."
- "The further gay argument is to say 'efforts to modify,' which is to say 'treat' gender identity disorder in children, is equal to 'homosexual genocide,' and they are right. It [reparative therapy] is a way to eliminate future individuals who identify as gay or lesbian" (Nicolosi, 2003).

Proponents of SOCE hailed a 2003 Columbia University study by Robert Spitzer, MD, claiming 200 individuals changed their orientation from homosexual to heterosexual (Spitzer, 2003). The story received wide media coverage, in part because Spitzer played a key role in removing homosexuality from the list of mental disorders (Drescher, 2003). A number of researchers were critical of Spitzer's methodologies (Besen, 2006), and in 2004 Spitzer expressed concern regarding the distortions of his research in a videotaped interview:

> I think anybody that has any familiarity with gay people knows that it is not something one chooses, and it is also something that is very difficult to change. The difficulty I had in doing my study was finding 200 subjects that met the criteria, and that was after extensive notices in Christian and other groups that do this kind of therapy. So, finding it difficult to find 200 individuals, my own guess is that it is a relatively rare phenomenon for those who enter that kind of therapy. It's relatively rare that they are successful. One concern I have is that the study is being used as part of a general effort by these organizations to deny gays civil rights, and it is part of that agenda. I am not sympathetic with their efforts to do that. I think it also makes many homosexuals even more uncomfortable with being homosexual, rather than accepting themselves as they are. (Lutes, 2005)

In 2009, the American Psychological Association published a comprehensive review of SOCE studies. According to the *Report of the Task Force on Appropriate Therapeutic Responses to Sexual Orientation*, sexual orientation change is rare, whereas adaptation in sexual orientation identity is a more common result of SOCE. *Sexual orientation* is defined as patterns of sexual, romantic, and affectional arousal. According to the report, *sexual orientation identity* "refers to acknowledgment and internalization of sexual orientation and reflects self-exploration, self-awareness, self-recognition, group membership and affiliation, culture, and self-stigma" (APA, 2009, p. 30).

Harmful Effects of Sexual Orientation Change Efforts

Licensed mental health professionals aspire to the Hippocratic injunction to "do no harm." Mandated by the ethical guidelines of their respective professional associations, mental health professionals are required to reject interventions, interpretations, and techniques that might negatively impact the emotional, cognitive, and spiritual well-being of those under their care (AAMFT, 2001; ACA, 2005; APA, 2009; American Psychological Association, 2002; NASW, 2008).

Individuals who enter SOCE often leave treatment with a clear conviction that they were harmed. In a newspaper interview, Peterson Toscano discussed his experience of 17 years and $30,000 spent trying to change his sexual orientation:

> One day I woke up exhausted from it all. It was like I woke up out of a coma, and for the first time in years, I was thinking with my own mind. I asked myself the critical question, "What the hell are you doing? This is crazy. You're destroying yourself. It's not working." I realized I was in a coma all those years—a Biblically induced, culturally Christian coma. (Moore, 2007)

As further evidence of harm, on June 27, 2007, former leaders of the ex-gay movement came together in Los Angeles to issue a public apology for the damage they inflicted on others. Michael Bussee (cofounder of Exodus International), Darlene Bogle (former director of an Exodus ministry), and Jeremy Marks (founder of Courage UK) include the following in their remarks:

> As former leaders of ex-gay ministries, we apologize to those individuals and families who believed our message that there is something inherently wrong with being gay, lesbian, bisexual, or transgender. Some who heard our message were compelled to try to change an integral part of themselves, bringing harm to themselves and their families. Although we acted in good faith, we have since witnessed the isolation, shame, fear, and loss of faith that this message creates. We apologize for our part in the message of broken truth we spoke on behalf of Exodus and other organizations. We call on former ex-gay leaders to join the healing and reconciliation process by adding their names to this apology. We encourage current leaders of ex-gay programs to have the courage to evaluate the fruit of their programs. We ask them to consider the long-term effects of their ministry. (*Soulforce & Beyond Ex-Gay*, 2007)

In addition to personal accounts, the literature describes such harmful effects of SOCE as anxiety, depression, fear of intimacy, sexual dysfunction, negative self-concept and personal unworthiness, shame, self-destructive behavior, posttraumatic stress disorder, and suicidal ideation (Haldeman, 2001; Nicolosi, Byrd, & Potts, 2000; Shidlo & Schroeder, 2002; Tozer & Hayes, 2004). These negative effects are exacerbated by the stigma impacting the daily lives of LGBT people (Herek, 2009) and are perpetuated by heterosexual privilege. For example, in 2007 the president of the Southern Baptist Theological Seminary wrote,

> If a biological basis is found, and if a prenatal test is then developed, and if a successful treatment to reverse the sexual orientation to heterosexual is ever developed, we would support its use as we should unapologetically support the use of any appropriate means to avoid sexual temptation and the inevitable effects of sin. (Mohler, 2007)

Another example of stigma and harm unfolded in March 2009, when two proponents of reparative therapy, Don Schmierer (Exodus International) and Caleb Lee Brundidge (International Healing Foundation), took part in a conference in Uganda promoting Christianity and the ex-gay movement. Schmierer and Brundidge joined conservative preacher Scott Lively. Lively and Abrams's book *The Pink Swastika: Homosexuality in the Nazi Party* revisions the Holocaust to claim that "there was far more brutality, rape, torture and murder committed against innocent people by Nazi deviants and homosexuals than there ever was against homosexuals" (1995, p. iv). The presence of these Americans influenced a bill introduced in Uganda's parliament calling for the prosecution of and death penalty for homosexuals (Alsop, 2009).

The promotion of genocide against LGBT persons is not an exaggeration. Scholars Sue Spivey and Christine Robinson of the Department of Sociology and Anthropology at James Madison

University conducted a comprehensive and systematic analysis of written and oral material from NARTH, Exodus International, Exodus Global Alliance, and Focus on the Family. Their findings in the international journal *Genocide Studies and Prevention* indicate that the rhetoric of these organizations is consistent with the definition of genocide listed in Articles II(b)–(e) of the 1948 United Nations Convention on the Prevention and Punishment of the Crime of Genocide (UNCG). Included among the strategies employed to eliminate groups of unwanted persons are aims to create "us–them" thinking that divides the world into "us" (Christians) and "them" (homosexuals) and to define members of a community as if they are objects or in terms of behaviors or conditions that can then be demonized and blamed for a variety of social evils (Spivey & Robinson, 2010).

The APA Task Force report examines SOCE and encourages affirmative therapists to reduce harm by grounding their professional actions in the following scientific facts:

- Same-sex sexual attractions, behavior, and orientations per se are normal and positive variants of human sexuality—in other words, they are not indicators of mental or developmental disorders.
- Same-sex sexual attractions and behavior can occur in the context of a variety of sexual orientations and sexual orientation identities.
- Gay men, lesbians, and bisexual individuals can live satisfying lives and form stable, committed relationships and families that are equivalent to those of heterosexual individuals in essential respects.
- No empirical studies or peer-reviewed research supports theories attributing same-sex sexual orientation to family dysfunction or trauma. (APA, 2009, p. 54)

The practice of reparative therapy and the international proliferation of ex-gay ministries will continue until societies and religions worldwide refuse to tolerate prejudice, and sexual minorities are allowed to express their identities openly without fear of coercion, oppression, and discrimination. Until then, therapists working with SOCE survivors and other victims of heterosexual supremacy should provide client education on the scientific facts, engage in social justice advocacy, and promote empowerment strategies to develop the client's capacity for self-advocacy (Crethar, Bradley, Lewis, Toporek, & Tripp, 2006). Practitioners must, according to Goodman et al. (2004), use "scholarship and professional action designed to change societal values, structures, policies, and practices such that disadvantaged or marginalized groups gained increased access to the tools of self-determination" (p. 795). Since the majority of SOCE survivors come from conservative religious backgrounds (Wolkomir, 2006), affirmative therapists can provide information about religious communities in their local area that welcome and affirm sexual minorities (Dahl & Galliher, 2009). To assist clients in the full integration of their sexual and religious identities, an egalitarian and relational approach to therapy that promotes dialogue and shared inquiry is highly recommended.

Helping Individuals and Families Heal From SOCE and Heterosexism

Survivors of SOCE are a unique population presenting for therapy. Literature is scant on best practices for providing therapy for ex-gay ministry survivors and other victims of sexual oppression. The literature is clear that conversion therapy has potential for harm and the research on its efficacy is flawed (Serovich et al., 2008; Shidlo & Schroeder, 2002). What is efficacious and ethical when it comes to working with ex-gay survivors and with persons who are struggling with dilemmas of living as a sexual or gender minority?

Family Therapy With SOCE Survivors and Others Impacted by Heterosexism

The distinctive therapeutic needs of LGBT persons have been increasingly addressed in the marriage and family therapy (MFT) literature, including the comprehensive nature of this present volume. Literature on family therapy with LGBT persons supports reducing heterosexist bias and increasing sensitivity, education, and training (Adams & Benson, 2007; Benson, 2005; Bernstein, 2000; Clark, 1997; Coolhart & Bernal, 2007; Godfrey, Haddock, Fisher, & Lund, 2006; Long & Serovich, 2003). Green (2003) addresses the complexities of working with LGBT persons who seek to change their sexual orientation. According to Green, when clients seek therapy to change certain human traits, they often present with a great deal of ambivalence that cannot be dismissed. The 2005 AAMFT Code of Ethics and standards for accreditation (see http://www.aamft.org) address nondiscrimination on the basis of sexual orientation and require training programs to address diversity and discrimination, as well as addressing discrepancies in "power and privilege" in therapeutic relationships (Long & Serovich, 2003).

Complexity and Conversation, Not Certainty and Conversion

In the latter part of the 20th century, family therapy has been at the forefront of developing models of therapy that flatten the hierarchy between client and therapist; privilege client experience over diagnosis; affirm the value of multiple perspectives; and foster personal meaning making by emphasizing relationship, conversation, and narrative. Family therapists Harlene Anderson, Tom Andersen, Lynn Hoffman, and Michael White, among others, have turned to postmodern philosophy and social constructionism in breaking new ground with therapies referred to as dialogical, narrative, and collaborative (Anderson & Goolishian, 1988; Hoffman, 2002; A. Katz & Shotter, 1996; Seikkula & Trimble, 2005; Strong & Pare, 2004).

CT (Anderson, 1997; Anderson & Gerhart, 2007) is suited for ex-gay survivors and others who are struggling because of heterosexual supremacy. A hallmark of CT is to welcome complexity into therapeutic dialogue. Rather than striving to strategically condense a person's dilemma, the intent of a collaborative therapist is to foster the richest possible shared inquiry among the therapist, the client, and those whom the client deems important. According to Anderson (1997), therapy is conversation that takes place in relationships in which stories of people's lives are cocreated and coconstructed. The outcome of collaborative conversations is self-agency or a client's readiness to "go on" independently without the therapist until further conversation is needed (Andersen, 1990; McNamee, 2004).

CT deemphasizes diagnosis and is keenly attuned to therapist power and privilege, making it a preferred approach for those individuals wounded by SOCE tactics or rejected for their sexuality or gender identity. Collaborative therapists position themselves as experts on dialogue and relationship rather than experts on the lives of others. They come from a "not-knowing" perspective, not allowing any one perspective or story to totalize the conversation, holding biases in abeyance in order to make room for all points of view and to connect deeply with clients. Not knowing does not mean a therapist dismisses her own knowledge. Collaborative therapists transparently share thoughts and feelings with the intention of fostering genuine connection. As described by McDonough and Koch (2007),

> Collaborative Therapy embraces the following premises: the therapist facilitates therapy from a non-hierarchical, not-knowing position; she invites multiple perspectives into conversations to promote a shared inquiry into clients' dilemmas; and she creates space for rich dialogue and conversation, both in and out of the consultation room. The therapist is a conversational partner who fosters mutual relationships and who values conversations that are multi-voiced and multi-storied. The collaborative therapist is less concerned with diagnosis or pathology, and more interested in communicating respect for clients through heartfelt curiosity about their stories. To guide reflections on and contributions to therapeutic conversations, the collaborative therapist listens carefully to her own inner dialogue created in response to the dialogue among all conversational partners. To sustain

and enliven therapy, a collaborative therapist joins with clients and others to reflect on their work, sometimes through co-research. This shared inquiry promotes belonging as well as diversity, leading to changes in language and relationships. (p. 168)

CT offers the opportunity for growth and healing that conversion therapy destroys. Inspired by McNamee's writings about CT (2004), the following distinctions can be made between CT and SOCE. Examining these distinctions brings their glaring differences into view and illustrates the healing potential of CT for SOCE survivors and other oppressed persons (see Table 29.1).

Collaborative Therapy With Darren: From Hierarchy to Shared Inquiry

As I (Marsha) greeted Darren in the waiting room, I smiled warmly and invited him into my office. After we shook hands and walked together toward my cozy sofa and chairs, I urged Darren

Table 29.1 Examining Distinctions Between Collaborative Therapy and SOCE

Collaborative Therapy	SOCE
Curiosity about differences.	Judgment about differences.
Inviting multiple, conflicting perspectives into the conversation.	Limiting the number of perspectives invited into the conversation.
Uncertainty about ideas and experiences.	Certainty about ideas and experiences.
Fostering dialogue or coordinated action around topics.	Fostering debate on topics.
Inviting many possible competing "truths" about a situation, without privileging one over the other.	Preferring one "reality" or "truth" about the situation.
"Going on" together amid various truths, sometimes without agreement.	Seeking agreement in order to "go on."
Therapy as a natural human process of shared inquiry and crisscrossing of ideas.	Therapy as an expert-driven process.
Therapist's attention to relational, conversational, and narrative processes.	Therapist's attention to facts, behaviors, and gathering data.
Resources emerge from within the conversation and relationship.	Resources are provided by the therapist to the client.
Therapy as a philosophical stance about relationships and conversation in action in the moment.	Therapy as a set of techniques for certain circumstances.
Problems considered part of everyday living.	Problems seen as pathology.
Conversational partners talk "with" each other.	Therapist and client talk "to" each other.
Therapist and client are colearners and coexplorers of dilemmas.	Client learns from therapist more than therapist learns from the client.
Atmosphere of improvisation.	Atmosphere of an "agenda" or scripted conversation.
Client and therapist shaped, reshaped, and transformed in the conversation and relationship.	Focus on client change, not mutual change.
Energetic, engaged, and responsive atmosphere, filled with shared human emotion.	Shame-filled and blaming atmosphere.
Shared power, talked about with transparency.	Hierarchical power, with therapist dominating client.
Client and therapist knowledge privileged.	Therapist knowledge privileged.
Ethics is a process within as well as outside the room, based on mutual relational responsibility and accountability.	Ethics from outside the relationship take precedence.

to sit where he felt most comfortable. His smile was wide, yet as with most people, there was a slight nervousness about how our meeting would play out. I felt eager to learn how we might work together. Darren said he heard me speak about social constructionism and CT, 7 months earlier, at the employee assistance program (EAP) where he worked. During the workshop, he thought to himself: "She's really smart. And, she seems nice." Also, I was on his insurance plan, and money was tight because of recent medical bills. I suddenly recognized Darren from the workshop, remembering him as participatory, a leader among his peers, and very helpful to me as I gathered my materials to leave.

I invited Darren to tell me everything he thought I needed to know to help him. As he talked, I listened with openness and curiosity. For a brief moment, I was struck by his small stature for a man in his early 30s. Since I am only 5 feet tall, I made a mental note to ask, should an opening arise, if he had ever been bullied, as is so often the case. I held that thought in abeyance, however, not to be detoured from listening to what he wanted to tell me. At this first meeting, Darren did not reveal that he was a transgender person.

His presenting dilemma was that he was in the midst of a breakup of a 3-year relationship. At best, his girlfriend was not going to make it easy for him to move out; at worse, she might become suicidal, as she had previously. He also wanted to talk about "going over core issues such as shame, self-worth, and narcissism," which he described as being overly tied up with other people and judging them. As a corollary, he said he was "too caught up in worrying about what other people thought about him." He wished to gain a sense of "really being able to say what I think and feel and not fly by the seat of my pants." I remember thinking, "I like talking with Darren. I don't yet know what all of this means, but I hope I made him feel comfortable and conveyed that I was open to a good working relationship—one that would allow us to puzzle together, effectively, over these concerns."

This opening conversation led to a series of talks over one year. Within the first few meetings, Darren told me he was beginning to live as a transgender person; he was born female. He had been named Elizabeth but decided to take the name of his grandfather, whom he admired greatly. He was speaking with his doctor about gender transformation and taking testosterone. He was reading books about this change. Darren was not talking with many people about his gender transformation, however, other than his family and a few close friends. I felt open to learning and talking about this part of his life, with him taking the lead. I told Darren I was a heterosexual woman and asked him to let me know if this ever became a problem for him.

I noticed I felt my internal dialogue reminding me to be responsive to the ethical processes within our relationship. I was keenly aware of the tacit power bestowed on me by a society and a profession that frequently devalues difference. I felt grateful my CT philosophy would help me take a not-knowing, curious, and respectful stance. I trusted I would neither push nor pull my client in any one direction but, rather, would walk alongside him in focused conversation about parts of his life he believed were important. My contributions to the dialogue could be strong, as long as my intentions were to keep the conversation going in ways that would be useful to Darren and would keep our relationship both lively and safe. I felt a responsibility to review the therapy literature on gender transformation and LGBT persons. If I shared "expert" ideas with Darren, I used the collaborative principle of "uncertainty," presenting those ideas in a tentative manner, asking about their relevance to him. Darren often replied that research and practice information did not apply to his situation. I was pleased that he trusted me enough to set me straight.

Darren wanted to talk about making a clean break from his old relationship, making new friends, making a fresh start in his new house, beginning to date, and moving up the ladder in his job. Darren made great strides in all areas during our year together. As time passed, the tenor of our talks became deeper and more emotional, compared to initial visits. We became engaged in a process of constructing meaning, together, about where Darren had come from and where he was going.

Once, when an opening arose, I asked Darren if he was interested in constructing a genogram together. I expressed a sincere interest to know more about Darren's roots. As his unique story unfolded, I became enthralled. As with all good stories, Darren's narrative was filled with joy, sorrow, pain, pleasure, anger, love, fear, good and bad luck, gain, loss, troubles, and miracles. Sharing the story of his legacy was a turning point for Darren. Our mutual engagement in the story of his life provided new knowledge and inspiration—he felt renewed connection rather than loneliness. As conversational partners, we were participating in a crisscrossing of ideas or dialogue, rather than a fact-gathering process. I was aware that as long as we kept this mutually influential process and relationship going along CT lines, Darren would inevitably discover possibilities.

One example of how collaborative conversations led to a difference in Darren's life took place in the realm of spirituality. Darren was raised with strong ties to the Methodist Church, including relatives who were missionaries. Darren practiced Buddhism, influenced by his previous therapist, who was Buddhist. Rather than revisit her, Darren decided to see me, a secular therapist, and to continue his Buddhist practice, finding insight in some aspects and struggling with others.

Christianity had been a big part of Darren's life growing up in a close-knit, multigenerational family and community. The young and vibrant Elizabeth was an active participant and youth leader in the church. Darren missed being part of a Christian community and missed the familiar rituals of his youth. Darren was not interested in the local LGBT-affirming Christian churches. Miraculously, when Darren began dating, he met and became close to a woman who shared his love of Christianity. Together, they attended Methodist services. This was another emotional turning point in our work because Darren's sense of belonging was palpably increasing, having found not only a girlfriend but also someone who shared his Methodist roots. When he told me about going to church with his girlfriend, I felt deeply moved and happy for him.

As we progressed in therapy, I felt a strong pull for more voices and more perspectives to be part of our conversation—especially the voices of peers, including other transgender persons. Darren did not know any other transgender people, and occasionally he posed heartbreaking dilemmas about relationships and sexuality that I felt could be better understood by peers. I was "public" or transparent about my wish to help, expressing my heartbreak, and puzzling with him on how to find greater connection with others about these dilemmas.

When we first began to talk about ways to connect with a supportive peer group, Darren was not interested in a transgender group facilitated by a well-known transgender therapist in our town. Over time, and through a growing sense of self-agency, Darren began investigating groups. One day, to my surprise, Darren talked about attending a group that fit for him. This group, led by a transgender therapist, both talked about relational issues and had of a mixture of members: gay, straight, transgender, and partners of LGBT persons. This mix provided the solution for adding voices into our therapeutic conversation. We decided to pause on our journey together. Our conversations would roll into further conversations with others. He made a promise to keep me posted, and I reminded him "my door is always open."

A year later, I spoke with Darren again. When we spoke, Darren shared that he was doing well, that he was still with his girlfriend, and that the group continued to be an immense resource. I invited him to join in a coresearch project about CT. On a videotape for professional colleagues, Jeff, Darren, and I conversed about the question "What stands out for you about your work with Marsha?" Darren gave us permission to use the videotape in a presentation on ethical therapy with LGBT people (McDonough & Lutes, 2008). On the videotape, he made the following remarks about the process and effectiveness of CT with Marsha:

- "I remember when I told you I was trans[gender], born female … you were just interested in that while at the same time you acknowledged that you did not know what that was like and you asked a lot of questions and I just appreciated your curiosity."

- "Something about you—you weren't going toward me a lot or running away from me too much. You were just really there."
- "You asked lots of questions; all therapists ask a lot of questions, but there is something different about some of the questions you asked or the energy with which you asked … it seemed very genuine, very much you."
- "Those were questions that were like a conversation, not a conversation about you, not at all, but it was very conversational and I wouldn't be able to predict what kind of question you would come up with."
- "Several times you had come back to my childhood and my teenage years. I had minimized that stuff—the pain, but—you were intrigued. It kept piquing your curiosity."
- "It felt right … the relationship allowed me to be more myself, which was the core thing I wanted, and it felt like I was in a conversation with a whole person … we were still guided by our roles as therapist and client, but it really felt like more than other therapy relationships I've been in."

Collaborative Conferences: Moving Beyond the Therapy Office Into the World

I (Jeff), as a collaborative therapist and social justice advocate, initiated work with SOCE survivors and others at two unique conferences. The Ex-Gay Survivor Conference (2007) and the Anti-Heterosexism Conference (2009) brought survivors and allies together to create space for storytelling, healing, and community building and to educate the public about harm caused by SOCE.

At the Ex-Gay Survivor Conference, we talked with and listened to nearly 200 survivors from the United States, United Kingdom, and Australia as they coconstructed new possibilities for their lives. Since our intention was to follow the lead of the survivors, we began with a "chalk talk" in which conference participants engaged in a "visual conversation," writing words, phrases, or images about their SOCE on a wall-sized piece of paper. I remember feeling deeply moved as I watched this silent exercise unfold. Here is some of the poignant dialogue shared by survivors:

- "I thought I was changing. In reality, I had walled away my sexuality."
- "I helped create Exodus in 1976. Please forgive me."
- "I failed God."
- "I bore false witness."
- "My family can only love the mask they give me to wear."
- "I was 16 when my small-group leader molested me."
- "I talked to him again last night. I think I'm falling in love … guess my exorcism didn't work."

Stories told at the conference had a clear, consistent theme: Reparative therapies and ex-gay ministries cause more harm than good. Although outweighed by the harm, survivors reported a few benefits to their SOCE: decreased social isolation, increased empathy, and spiritual support. These claims are consistent with both the literature on SOCE (Beckstead & Morrow, 2004), and the literature on the common beneficial factors across psychotherapy models (Norcross, 2002).

We invited ex-gay leaders and reparative therapists to sit down for dialogue and shared inquiry about SOCE, welcoming complexity and all relevant voices into the conversation, despite differences in perspective. Survivors Peterson Toscano and Christine Bakke sent the following invitation to Exodus leaders:

It is no coincidence that we scheduled the Ex-Gay Survivor Conference at the same time and in the same city as Exodus' Freedom Conference. Although we do not wish to interrupt your gathering, we do long for the opportunity to connect with you. Many of us have spent months and years under your care in your ministries. We turned to you for help and received some good from our time under your care. Sadly our ex-gay experiences caused more harm than good, and for many of us we have needed years to recover.

We understand that this was not your intent. From knowing quite a few of you personally, we know that you have a heart to help people and to serve God. You meant to bless us.

Too often once we leave your programs, you never hear about our lives and what happens to us. Most ministries do not have aftercare programs or any formal means to follow-up on participants. Some stories you do not get to hear. If you do, our stories can be simplified by the press or infused with anger or hurt. In hopes of giving you the opportunity to hear about our experiences and the harm that we felt came to us as a result of our pursuit of an ex-gay life, we would like to invite you to join us for a private dinner on Friday, June 29, 2007.

The purpose of the dinner is to give you an opportunity to hear our stories. We do not wish to bash you, attack you or shame you. We simply desire to share our stories with you. No members of the press will be allowed into the dinner and it will not be recorded or filmed. We are hoping for a small gathering with a few ex-gay leaders and some ex-gay survivors. At the dinner a few of us will tell you our stories. If you are interested in attending this dinner, please RSVP to bxg@beyondexgay.com (*Soulforce & Beyond Ex-Gay*, 2007).

A small number of Exodus leaders accepted this invitation and heard the painful survivor stories.

In November 2009, colleagues and I organized the Anti-Heterosexism Conference concomitant with the annual NARTH meeting. Our intention was to highlight, examine, and deconstruct the heterosexist attitudes inherent in SOCE and in society. As a collaborative therapist, my intention was to facilitate generative conversations with survivors, LGBT persons, and allies, knowing that when space is made for dialogue and storytelling, that healing and social justice will occur. Writing on a large sheet of paper posted in the lobby of the conference hotel, participants from around the globe set the agenda for the conference by responding to the following prompts: "I am here because," "This conference is meaningful because," "Heterosexism means," "I feel welcome here because," and "When I leave here." Here are some of the moving responses that set the tone for our conference conversation:

- "I am here because young people are taught to be uncomfortable in their own skin and fear what will become of their lives."
- "Heterosexism is the indirect, unconscious ideology that we breathe in like poison in the air, telling us that heterosexuality is somehow superior or more desirable than any other way of being. By the way, I love heterosexuals!"
- "Heterosexuality is not 'normal'; it's just more common. Normal is a cycle on your washing machine."
- "I am here because if I stay silent and do not speak the truth, more lives will be harmed."
- "One hundred years from now they will look to us and say, 'They broke new ground'!"

Survivor Jallen Rix, in his book *Ex-Gay No Way* (2010), writes, "Although life is always full of challenges and I'm still learning to let go and receive, I can now go days, weeks, and whole seasons feeling great about myself, with little shame in sight" (p. 232). Jallen's story, along with those of others, reminds me of my ethical obligation to serve dual roles. Inside the psychotherapy office, my job is to assist in the healing of those traumatized by SOCE and heterosexual privilege. Outside the therapy office, my duty is to advocate for those who have been marginalized and oppressed.

Conclusions

It is our position that CT can help SOCE survivors reauthor their personal stories, reduce the impact of social and religious stigma, and assist in the development of healthy self-respect and an aptitude for self-advocacy. We believe that LGBT-affirmative therapists of all therapeutic orientations have a professional and ethical responsibility to serve as social change agents in and out of the therapy office. Furthermore, LGBT-affirmative therapists have an important role in actively challenging prejudice, discrimination, and the inequitable distribution of social power that favors heterosexuality and gender conformity over homosexuality, bisexuality, or gender variance.

References

Adams, A., & Benson, K. (2007, May/June). Transgender in family therapy. *Family Therapy Magazine*, 36–41.

Alsop, Z. (2009, December). Uganda's anti-gay bill inspired by the U.S. *Time*. Retrieved from http://www.time.com/time/world/article/0,8599,1946645,00.html

American Academy of Pediatrics. (1993). *Policy statement on homosexuality and adolescence* (RE9332). Elk Grove Village, IL: Author.

American Association for Marriage and Family Therapy (AAMFT). (2001). *AAMFT code of ethics*. Alexandria, VA: Author.

American Counseling Association (ACA). (2005). *ACA code of ethics*. Alexandria, VA: Author.

American Counseling Association Governing Council. (1998). *Affirmative resolution on lesbian, gay, and bisexual people*. Alexandria, VA: Author.

American Medical Association (AMA). (2004). Statement on homosexuality. In *Policy on the health care needs of the homosexual population* (H-160.991). Implementation of resolutions and report recommendations, AMA House of Delegates annual meeting, June 12–16. Retrieved from http://www.amaaama-assn.org

American Psychiatric Association (APA). (1973). *Homosexuality and civil rights*. Position statement approved by the Board of Trustees. Retrieved from http://www.psych.org/Departments/EDU/Library/APAOfficialDocumentsandRelated/PositionStatements/197310.aspx

American Psychiatric Association (APA). (2009). *The principles of medical ethics: With annotations especially applicable to psychiatry*. Arlington, VA: Author.

American Psychoanalytic Association. (1991). *Position statement: Homosexuality*. Retrieved from http://www.apsa.org/ABOUTAPSAA/POSITION-STATEMENTS/HOMOSEXUALITY/tabid/473/Default.aspx

American Psychological Association. (2002). *Ethical principles of psychologists and code of conduct*. Retrieved from http://www.apa.org/ethics/code/index.aspx

Andersen, T. (1990). *The reflecting team: Dialogues and dialogues about dialogues*. Broadstairs, UK: Bormann.

Anderson, H. (1997). *Conversations, language, and possibilities: A postmodern approach to therapy*. New York, NY: Basic Books.

Anderson, H., & Gerhart, D. (Eds.). (2007). *Collaborative therapy: Relationships and conversations that make a difference*. New York, NY: Routledge.

Anderson, H., & Goolishian, H. (1988). Human systems as linguistic systems: Evolving ideas about the implications for theory and practice. *Family Process, 27*, 371–393.

APA Task Force on Appropriate Therapeutic Responses to Sexual Orientation. (2009). *Report of the Task Force on appropriate therapeutic responses to sexual orientation*. Washington, DC: American Psychological Association.

Beckstead, A. L., & Morrow, S. L. (2004). Mormon clients' experiences of conversion therapy: The need for a new treatment approach. *Counseling Psychologist, 32*, 651–690.

Benson, K. (2005, November/December). T is for transgender. *Family Therapy Magazine*, 39–40.

Bernstein, A. (2000). Straight therapists working with lesbians and gays in family therapy. *Journal of Marital and Family Therapy, 26*(4), 443–454.

Besen, W. (2003). *Anything but straight: Unmasking the scandals and lies behind the ex-gay myth*. Binghamton, NY: Harrington Park Press.

Besen, W. (2006). Political science. In J. Drescher & K.J. Zucker (Eds.), *Ex-gay research: Analyzing the Spitzer study and its relation to science, religion, politics, and culture* (p. 291–307). Binghamton, NY: Haworth Press.

Beyond Ex-Gay. (2007). *An open invitation to Exodus International for dinner and dialogue.* Retrieved from http://www.beyondexgay.com/DearExodusLeaders

Burroway, J. (2007). *Prologue: Why I went to "Love Won Out."* Retrieved from http://www.boxturtlebulletin.com/2007/02/12/220

Clark, W. (1997). Twenty years and still in the dark? Content analysis of articles pertaining to gay, lesbian, and bisexual issues in marriage and family therapy journals. *Journal of Marital and Family Therapy, 23*(3), 239–253.

Conger, J. J. (1975). Proceedings of the American Psychological Association, Incorporated, for the year 1974: Minutes of the annual meeting of the Council of Representatives. *American Psychologist, 30*, 620–651.

Coolhart, D., & Bernal, A. (2007, May/June). Transgender in family therapy. *Family Therapy Magazine*, 36–42.

Crethar, H. C., Bradley, L. J., Lewis, J., Toporek, R., & Tripp, F. (2006, April). *Promoting systemic change through advocacy competence.* Presented at the annual American Counseling Association convention, Montreal, Canada.

Dahl, A. L., & Galliher, R. V. (2009). LGBQQ Young adult experiences of religious and sexual identity integration. *Journal of LGBT Issues in Counseling, 3*, 92–112.

Drescher, J. (1998). *Psychoanalytic therapy and the gay man.* Hillsdale, NJ: Analytic Press.

Drescher, J. (2003). The Spitzer study and the culture wars. *Archives of Sexual Behavior, 32*, 431–432.

Erzen, T. (2006). *Straight to Jesus: Sexual and Christian conversions in the ex-gay movement.* Berkeley, CA: University of California Press.

Freedman, M. (1971). *Homosexuality and psychological functioning.* Belmont, CA: Brooks/Cole.

Gilgoff, D. (2007). *The Jesus machine: How James Dobson, Focus on the Family, and evangelical Americans are winning the culture war.* New York, NY: St. Martin's Press.

Godfrey, K., Haddock, S., Fisher, A., & Lund, L. (2006). Essential components of curricula for preparing therapists to work effectively with lesbian, gay, and bisexual clients: A Delphi study. *Journal of Marital and Family Therapy, 32*(4), 491–504.

Gonsiorek, J. C. (1982). Results of psychological testing on homosexual populations. *American Behavioral Scientist, 25*, 385–396.

Gonsiorek, J. C. (1991). The empirical basis for the demise of the illness model of homosexuality. In J. C. Gonsiorek & J. D. Weinrich (Eds.), *Homosexuality: Research implications for public policy* (pp. 115–136). Newbury Park, CA: Sage.

Goodman, L. A., Liang, B., Helms, J. E., Latta, R. E., Sparks, E., & Weintraub, S. R. (2004). Training counseling psychologist as social justice agents: Feminist and multicultural principles in action. *Counseling Psychologist, 32*, 793–837.

Green., R. J. (2003). When therapists do not want their clients to be homosexual: A response to Rosik's article. *Journal of Marital and Family Therapy, 29*(1), 29–38.

Haldeman, D. C. (2001). Therapeutic antidotes: Helping gay and bisexual men recover from conversion therapies. *Journal of Gay and Lesbian Psychotherapy, 5*(3–4), 117–130.

Hart, M., Roback, H., Tittler, B., Weitz, L., Walston, B., & McKee, E. (1978). Psychological adjustment of nonpatient homosexuals: Critical review of the research literature. *Journal of Clinical Psychiatry, 39*, 604–608.

Herek, G. M. (2009). Sexual stigma and sexual prejudice in the United States: A conceptual framework. In D. A. Hope (Ed.), *Nebraska Symposium on Motivation: Vol. 54. Contemporary perspectives on lesbian, gay, and bisexual identities* (pp. 65–111). New York, NY: Springer.

Hoffman, L. (2002). *Family therapy: An intimate history.* New York, NY: Norton.

Hooker, E. A. (1957). The adjustment of the male overt homosexual. *Journal of Projective Techniques, 21*, 18–31.

Hunt, M. E. (2007). Eradicating the sin of heterosexism. In M. M. Ellison & J. Plaskow (Eds.), *Heterosexism in contemporary world religion: Problem and prospect* (pp. 155–176). Cleveland, OH: Pilgrim Press.

Just the Facts Coalition. (2008). Just the facts about sexual orientation and youth: A primer for principals, educators, and school personnel. Washington, DC: American Psychological Association. Retrieved from http://www.apa.org/pi/lgbc/publications/justthefacts.html

Katz, A., & Shotter, J. (1996). Hearing the patient's voice: Toward a social poetics in diagnostic interviews. *Social Science and Medicine, 43*, 919–931.

Katz, J. (1995). *Gay American history: Lesbians and gay men in the United States.* New York, NY: Thomas Crowell.

Lively, S., & Abrams, K. (1995). *The pink swastika.* Keizer, OR: Founders.

Long, J. K., & Serovich, J. M. (2003). Incorporating sexual orientation into MFT training programs: Infusion and inclusion. *Journal of Marital and Family Therapy, 29*(1), 59–67.

Lutes, J. (Prod.). (2005). *Dear Dr. Dobson: An open video letter to focus on the family* [DVD]. Available from http://www.soulforce.org

McDonough, M., & Koch, P. (2007). Working with children and families in private practice: Shifting and overlapping conversations. In H. Anderson & D. Gerhart (Eds.), *Collaborative therapy: Relationships and conversations that make a difference* (pp. 167–181). New York, NY: Routledge.

McDonough, M., & Lutes, J. (2008, November). *Ethics and conversion therapy: From hierarchy to inquiry.* Presented at the AAMFT annual conference, Memphis, TN.

McNamee, S. (2004). Therapy as social construction: Back to basics and forward toward challenging issues. In T. Strong & D. Pare (Eds.), *Furthering talk: Advances in the discursive therapies.* New York, NY: Kluwer/Plenum.

Mohler, A. (2007, March 2). Is your baby gay? What if you could do something about it? [Blog post]. Retrieved from http://www.albertmohler.com/2007/03/02/is-your-baby-gay-what-if-you-could-know-what-if you-could-do-something-about-it-2

Moore, S. (2007, January 25–31). Ex-ex-gay: Peterson Toscano—a survivor of the ex-gay movement. *The Portland Mercury.* Retrieved from http://www.portlandmercury.com/portland/Content?oid=110772 &category=34029

Nakajima, G. A. (2003). The emergence of an international lesbian, gay, and bisexual psychiatric movement. *Journal of Gay & Lesbian Psychotherapy, 7*(1/2), 165–188.

National Association of Social Workers (NASW). (1997). Policy statement: Lesbian, gay, and bisexual issues [approved by NASW Delegate Assembly, August 1996]. In *Social work speaks: NASW policy* (4th ed., pp. 198–209). Washington, DC: Author.

National Association of Social Workers (NASW). (2008). *Code of ethics.* Washington, DC: Author.

Nicolosi, J. (1991). *Reparative therapy of male homosexuality.* Northvale, NJ: Aronson.

Nicolosi, J. (2003). Love Won Out conference [Tape recording], Focus on the Family, Oklahoma City, OK.

Nicolosi, J., Byrd, A. D., & Potts, R. W. (2000). Retrospective self-reports of changes in homosexual orientation: A consumer survey of conversion therapy clients. *Psychological Reports, 86,* 1071–1088.

Norcross, J. C. (2002). *Psychotherapy relationships that work: Therapist contributions and responsiveness to patients.* New York, NY: Oxford University Press.

Psychvideos. (2009, January 26). *Dr. Phil Show: Little boy lost—Sparks fly among guests* [Video file]. Retrieved from http://www.youtube.com/watch?v=bXue5IknI2U&NR=1

Reiss, B. F. (1980). Psychological tests in homosexuality. In J. Marmor (Ed.), *Homosexual behavior: A modern reappraisal* (pp. 296–311). New York, NY: Basic Books.

Rix, J. (2010). *Ex-gay no way: Survival and recovery from religious abuse.* Forres, Scotland: Findhorn Press.

Seikkula, J., & Trimble, D. (2005). Healing elements of therapeutic conversation: Dialogue as an embodiment of love. *Family Process, 44*(4), 461–475.

Serovich, J., Craft, S., Toviessi, P., Gangamma, R., McDowell, T., & Grafsky, E. (2008). A systematic review of the research base on sexual reorientation therapies. *Journal of Marital and Family Therapy, 34*(2), 227–238.

Shidlo, A., & Schroeder, M. (2002). Changing sexual orientation: A consumers' report. *Professional Psychology: Research and Practice, 33,* 249–259.

Soulforce & Beyond Ex-Gay. (2007). Retrieved from http://www.soulforce.org/article/1277 [Video] or see http://www.beyondexgay.com/article/apology

Spitzer, R. L. (2003). Can some gay men and lesbians change their sexual orientation? Two hundred participants reporting a change from homosexual to heterosexual orientation. *Archives of Sexual Behavior, 32,* 403–417.

Spivey, S. E., & Robinson, C. M. (2010). Genocidal intentions: Social death and the ex-gay movement. *Genocide Studies and Prevention, 5*(1), 68–88. doi:10.3138/gsp.5.1.68

Stanfield, R. B. (2000). *The art of focused conversation.* Retrieved from http://www.ica-associates.ca/resources/AFC.pdf

Strong, T., & Pare, D. (2004). *Furthering talk: Advances in the discursive therapies.* New York, NY: Kluwer/Plenum.

Tozer, E. E., & Hayes, J. A. (2004). Why do individuals seek conversion therapy? The role of religiosity, internalized homonegativity, and identity development. *Counseling Psychologist, 32,* 716–740.

Wolkomir, M. (2006). *Be not deceived: The sacred and sexual struggles of gay and ex-gay Christian men.* New Brunswick, NJ: Rutgers University Press.

30

A Little Bit Pregnant?

The Ethics of Same-Sex Marriage

CORINNE RECZEK and ESTHER ROTHBLUM

Debates over legalizing same-sex marriage have continued to rage within U.S. culture at large, as well as within the lesbian, gay, bisexual, transgender, and queer (LGBTQ) communities. In this chapter, we present research from a variety of academic traditions related to same-sex marriage. We begin by providing a historical and contemporary overview of the battle over legalizing same-sex marriage, outlining the important legal and demographic contexts that frame debates on same-sex marriage. Following this overview, we examine the implications for promoting, or denying, same-sex marriage at the individual and societal levels. To do so, we demarcate two opposing positions on legal same-sex marriage—the perspective that advocates for same-sex marriage, and the contrasting one that critiques the fight for same-sex marriage. In the final sections of this chapter, we outline empirical research on same-sex couples' perceptions of the same-sex marriage movement and provide a case vignette for therapists of same-sex couples.

A Brief History of the Marriage Movement and a Review of Same-Sex Union Demographics

The political and popular movement aimed at ending discrimination of LGBTQ-identified individuals gained momentum and visibility throughout the 1980s (Hull, 2006). By the last decade of the 20th century, the fight to extend civil rights protections to LGBTQ individuals, most notably including the legalization of same-sex marriage rights, became a national and international conversation. At the broadest level, advocates of same-sex marriage utilized civil rights discourses to argue that like other disadvantaged groups, LGBTQ individuals were being discriminated against on the basis of their sexual orientation. In contrast, those who opposed same-sex marriage argued for viewing marriage as a sacred institution between one man and one woman. The same-sex marriage debates in the United States have continued to carry political and social relevance in political and legal arenas into the 21st century.

The history of same-sex marriage legislation in the United States is a relatively short one. At the time of this writing, no federal legislation exists to legally recognize same-sex marriages. Internationally, Denmark was the first nation to legalize same-sex unions in 1989 (Soland, 1998), and same-sex marriage is now legal in Argentina, Belgium, Canada, Iceland, the Netherlands, Norway, Portugal, South Africa, Spain, and Sweden. In addition, more than 20 other countries recognized registered nonmarital same-sex unions at the national level (Eskridge, 2002; Eskridge & Spedale, 2006; Hull, 2006). Because no federal legislation recognizes same-sex marriages in the United States today, states have independently enacted legal marriage rights for same-sex couples through a variety of avenues. The first state to attempt to legalize same-sex marriage—Hawaii—did so in 1993 through a State Supreme Court decision that ruled the state's refusal to allow same-sex marriage was unconstitutional. In response, in 1998 a ballot measure was passed creating a constitutional amendment banning same-sex marriage (Hull, 2006). This early loss for same-sex marriage rights launched the current marriage equality movement, setting the tone for the next 15 years of legal battles over same-sex marriage (Wolfson, 2001). Shortly after the Hawaii marriage initiatives, Congress passed the Defense of Marriage Act (DOMA) in 1996 under the Clinton administration. The DOMA was initiated in response to apprehension that if same-sex marriage were to become legal in Hawaii, other states would be legally bound to recognize same-sex marriages conducted in Hawaii (Hull, 2006). With the passing of DOMA, marriage became legally defined as a union between one man and one woman, and no state is legally bound to recognize a same-sex marriage from another state (Cahill, 2004; Hull, 2006).

After Hawaii and DOMA, Massachusetts legalized same-sex marriage in 2003, followed by Connecticut, Iowa, New Hampshire, Vermont, and New York. The District of Columbia also now grants full marriage rights. Twelve states—California, Delaware, Hawaii, Illinois, Maine, Maryland, Nevada, New Jersey, Oregon, Rhode Island, Washington, and Wisconsin—grant iterations of legal marriage to same-sex couples, including civil unions and domestic partnerships. The rights granted to same-sex couples through civil unions or domestic partnerships vary; in some states civil partners have nearly identical rights to married partners, whereas in other states partners have "near spousal" legal rights (Chambers, 2000). Maryland and Rhode Island legally recognize same-sex marriages from other states, but they do not grant same-sex marriage licenses. To complicate matters, the 13,000 same-sex couples who married in California during the short period in 2008 when it was legal to do so are still legally married, but no other same-sex couples can marry in California at this time.

In contrast to advances toward marriage equality from 1998 to 2008, residents of 30 states voted on initiates to ban same-sex marriage (McVeigh & Diaz, 2009). To date, 37 states prohibit same-sex marriages through either legal statute or constitutional amendments, and several of these states further prohibit the recognition of same-sex marriages from other states. Many of these ballot initiatives took place during the 2004 and 2008 presidential and local political campaigns. In fact, some scholars argue that the "culture wars" over same-sex marriage were a significant force in President George W. Bush's 2004 reelection victory (Hull, 2006). These culture wars played a less significant role in the 2008 campaigns of Barack Obama and John McCain, yet the ballot initiative to ban same-sex marriage in California—known as Proposition 8—received significant media attention. Proposition 8 was a response to the California State Supreme Court's decision that the ban against same-sex marriage was unconstitutional. This decision was overturned by the passing of Proposition 8—which enacted a constitutional amendment defining marriage as a union between one man and one woman. Proposition 8 most clearly epitomizes continued same-sex marriage debates. In the media coverage of Proposition 8, the pro–same-sex marriage camp was framed with a discourse of equality and human rights, where as anti–same-sex marriage position rested upon notions of traditionalism and conservative religious and family values.

These political and legal battles fought throughout the past 2 decades have cultivated unprecedented attention on the lives LGBTQ-indentified people. As unparalleled changes continue to affect the legal status of members of the LGBTQ community, demographers and other social scientist have attempted to take count of same-sex couples in legal and non-legal unions. Because the legal status of same-sex partners varies by state and union type (i.e., marriage, civil union, or domestic partnership), and because national data on nonmarried couples are virtually nonexistent, defining the number—as well as sociodemographic characteristics—of individuals in same-sex unions is complex. Recent data suggest that approximately 32,000 same-sex couples are legally partnered in some way in the United States, although nearly 150,000 same-sex couples identify themselves as married in a recent American Community Survey (ACS), the yearly supplement to the U.S. Census (Gates, 2009). Estimates of nonmarried same-sex couples are far more difficult to ascertain. Data from the

2010 U.S. Census suggest that there are approximately 646,000 cohabiting same-sex partners (U.S. Census, 2011).

Estimates suggest important demographic differences among same-sex couples who marry. In the United States, women are more likely to enter into same-sex marriages than men. For example, in Vermont, nearly twice as many female as male same-sex couples entered into civil unions (Solomon, Rothblum, & Balsam, 2004); and in Massachusetts in the first year same-sex marriages were made legal, 65% of unions were of lesbian couples (Belge, 2005). In a study of same-sex partners in California, Carpenter and Gates (2008) found that whereas nearly half of lesbian partners were legally registered in California, less than a quarter of gay partners were registered. However, the opposite is found internationally; in fact, two men are almost three times more likely to marry than two women (Waaldijk, 2001). In a study comparing married same-sex couples in Massachusetts, legally domestic partners in California, and partners in civil unions in Vermont, Rothblum, Balsam, and Solomon (2008) found that men, as compared to women, were more likely to be older, were less likely to have children, and had been in their relationships for longer periods of time before becoming legally partnered. The vast majority of same-sex couples in U.S. legalized relationships are White, and this demographic has been explained by the fact that couples of color are faced with homophobia as well as racism and so may not choose the very public step of a marriage or civil union (Rothblum et al., 2008). Other differences between same-sex married couples have been uncovered. For example, according to 2000 U.S. Census data, about 10% of gay male couples lived with children, whereas 22% of lesbian couples lived with children. Using the same data, we see that nearly 90% of gay partners and 85% of lesbian couples lived in an urban area, and gay- and lesbian-partnered individuals are better educated than their heterosexual counterparts (Black, Sanders, & Taylor, 2007).

In sum, a bourgeoning literature draws attention to important changes in the legal status of same-sex couples over the past 2 decades. Because of the political contention over same-sex marriage, this topic has received substantial attention from news and popular media. In media portrayals of these debates—most recently seen in relation to the 2008 California Proposition 8 ballot initiative—dichotomous boundaries are drawn. On one side is a monolithic LGBTQ community fighting for the right to marry; on the other side are traditional straight conservatives with the aim to preserve a view of marriage as a union between one man and one woman. This simplified, bifurcated version of the same-sex marriage debate obscures the complexity of nuanced positions on the topic. Most notably, scholars argue that the LGBTQ community is not a monolithic force that unilaterally agrees with the pursuit of same-sex marriage. Instead, a close examination of the same-sex marriage movement suggests that within the LGBTQ community, a variety of voices not only argue in favor of the legalization of same-sex marriage but also express positions against attempts to legalize same-sex marriage.

In an attempt to outline the multifaceted viewpoints on same-sex marriage within the LGBTQ community, Yep, Lovaas, and Elia (2003) describe what they call two competing "sexual ideologies." They argue that individuals within the LGBTQ, or what they refer to as "queer," community who view same-sex marriage as an important civil right critical for the stabilization of same-sex relationships are *assimilationists*. In contrast, individuals who view same-sex marriage as an oppressive institution that the queer community should work to dismantle, not partake in, adhere to a *radical* view. These opposing views are themselves not monoliths, as a variety of positions are expressed within each. However, we believe that these contested ideologies have real implications for individuals' everyday relationships in that "conceptions of how to seek, pursue, develop, define, maintain, and represent loving sexual relationships invariably occur in an ideological context" (Yep et al., 2003, p. 48). In the remainder of the chapter, we aim to underscore how these ideological standpoints shape the costs and benefits of same-sex marriage on individual, relational, and community levels.

The Case for (Same-Sex) Marriage

> Marriage is a fundamental institution in American culture that rewards participants with social advantages in multiple forms. Unlike mixed-sex couples in the United States, same-sex couples are denied the tangible and intangible benefits of marriage, a deprivation that restricts their citizenship and hinders their mental health and well-being. (Herdt & Kertzner, 2006, p. 1)

In one of the prevailing views on same-sex marriage, an assimilationist or "normalizing" approach frames same-sex marriage as an equal rights issue, wherein the legal right to marry marks the final step toward full and legal citizenship (Wintemute & Andenaes, 2001). Scholars and activists who adhere to this approach suggest that being LGBTQ identified is a discriminated status because these individuals do not have access to the same rights other citizens have (Bell & Binnie, 2000; Calhoun, 2000; Cott, 2000). As outlined by Yep and colleagues (2003), assimilationists argue that legalizing same-sex marriage not only would provide equal citizenship rights for same-sex couples but also would be beneficial to society generally and to same-sex intimate couples specifically. In the remainder of this section, we outline an assimilationist view of the benefits of same-sex marriage in these two arenas.

On the societal level, assimilationists argue that allowing same-sex couples to marry will normalize same-sex relationships as similar to heterosexual married ties. This normalization would, in turn, reduce the stigma and minority stress of LGBTQ individuals in society at large (Meyer, 2003). In this view, visibility and legal equality are the keys to undermining pervasive homophobic, heteronormative culture in the United States. Research shows that LGBTQ individuals may have higher rates of psychological distress and face stigma on account of their nonnormative sexual orientation (King & Bartlett, 2006). Thus, if same-sex marriage is legal, there will be less social stigma associated with being LGBTQ identified, in turn reducing the incidence of mental health problems of LGBTQ people. Moreover, according to this frame, access to marriage would moderate sexually promiscuous behavior and promote monogamy. Some scholars suggest that lower levels of sexually promiscuous or nonmonogamous behavior will lead to greater respectability and lower levels of stigma against LGBTQ individuals (Rotello, 1997).

Assimilationists propose that legalizing same-sex marriage will foster greater benefits to society at large. Because one of the main critiques of same-sex marriage is that it will destroy the meaning of traditional, opposite-sex marriage (Badgett, 2009), some individuals supporting the assimilationist approach emphasize that same-sex marriages will not denigrate but will actually work to bolster different-sex marriages. In a study on the impact of legalizing same-sex marriage on different-sex marriage in Europe, Badgett (2004, 2009) finds that extending marriage rights to same-sex couples in Denmark, Norway, Sweden, Iceland, and the Netherlands had no impact on trends in different-sex marriages or nonmarital birth rates. Badgett argues,

> The legal and cultural context in the United States gives many more incentives for heterosexual couples to marry than in Europe, and those incentives will still exist even if same-sex couples can marry. Giving same-sex couples marriage or marriage-like rights has not undermined heterosexual marriage in Europe, and it is not likely to do so in the United States. (2004, p. 8)

Here, Badgett emphasizes that same-sex marriages in the United States pose no threat to the institution of marriage. Badgett further suggests that same-sex marriage may make the institution of marriage better by challenging patriarchal gendered norms and family roles of husband and wife in marriage (Badgett, 2009).

Aside from the proposed benefits of same-sex marriage on society in general, assimilationist scholars suggest that gay marriage will benefit LGBTQ individuals, as well as same-sex partnerships, in numerous ways. First, scholars who argue from an assimilationist framework point to potential benefits that partners and couples would accrue if able to legally marry. Marriage and family scholars have long suggested that transitioning from cohabiting or dating relationships to marriage makes unions stronger and more stable (Waite & Gallagher, 2000). Assimilationists believe that, as is theorized for different-sex couples, participating in the institution of marriage would bolster relationship quality, make same-sex relationships more stable, and induce stronger feelings of long-term commitment (Hull, 2006; King & Bartlett, 2006; Sullivan, 1995). Moreover, assimilationists believe that being legally bound may deter same-sex couples from obtaining a divorce due to the legal, social, and emotional complications (Badgett, 2009; Kurdek, 2004).

There is some empirical evidence supporting the importance of legal marriage on these dimensions, at least for different-sex couples. Married couples are qualitatively different than other intimate couples, such as cohabiting couples, in a variety of ways (for a review, see Smock, 2000). For example, research shows that there is less commitment in cohabiting relationships (Stanley, Whitton, & Markman, 2004), and cohabiters are more likely to break up and are less likely to pool financial resources than are married partners (Brines & Joyner, 1999; Bumpass & Lu, 2000). Thus, same-sex couples who participate in marriage may accrue these same benefits. Green (2004) argues that there is "commitment ambiguity" experienced by nonmarried same-sex couples, wherein same-sex partners do not have a shared understanding of what to expect from each other in their relationships, causing distress (p. 291). Green suggests that the commitment of marriage may foster more concrete, long-term plans together (e.g., having children or buying a home). Access to marriage, then, may promote greater financial security, provide partners with a sense of pride for their sanctioned commitment, and provide individuals with a template of what to expect as they pass through various life stages (Green, 2004; Slater, 1995).

Recent research suggests that these dimensions of same-sex relationships may indeed benefit from marriage. A recent study compared same-sex unmarried partners, legally married different-sex partners, unmarried different-sex partners, and single gay, lesbian, and heterosexual individuals and suggests that same-sex partners reported less happiness than did married different-sex partners, but no other differences on health outcomes were found between these two groups (Wienke & Hill, 2009). Research on same-sex civil unions in Vermont suggests that there was not a significant difference in break-up rates between same-sex couples in civil unions and heterosexual married couples but that both same-sex couples in civil unions and heterosexual married couples had lower break-up rates than did same-sex couples who were not in civil unions (Balsam, Beauchaine, Rothblum, & Solomon, 2008). In Sweden, however, same-sex couples were more likely to end their registered partnerships than were married different-sex couples likely to divorce (Andersson, Noack, Seierstad, & Weedon-Fekjaer, 2006). This research suggests that access to same-sex marriage may shape the relationship of same-sex couples in important ways.

In addition to pointing out the proposed benefits of legal marriage on relationship stability and quality, scholars argue that married people gain physical and mental health benefits from entering into marriage (Waite & Gallagher, 2000). Marital partners regulate and manage each other's health habits and overall health (Umberson, 1992), have increased social and emotional support, and receive an income boost with marriage (Heck, Randell, Sell, & Gorin, 2006; King & Bartlett, 2006; Waite & Gallagher, 2000). Assimilationists believe that much like different-sex couples, same-sex couples who marry would also accrue these benefits. For example, King and Bartlett (2006) write, "The social respectability conferred by state sanction of same sex relationships combined with the financial benefits of such unions and the necessary commitment to share a future may have positive health effects" (p. 189). King and Bartlett go on to suggest that access to same-sex marriage will "reduce the tendency" (p. 189) to have sex with multiple partners as part of the cultural transmission of monogamy related to marriage, and subsequently gay communities will witness lower rates of sexually infectious diseases. Moreover, recent research suggests that men and women in same-sex relationships have lower rates of health insurance than do men and women in different-sex relationships (respectively) and are also more likely to have more unmet medical needs (Buchmueller & Carpenter, 2010; Heck et al., 2006). The inability to gain insurance benefits from one's partner is viewed as one reason for this gap. For example, because 40% of women in the United States obtain their health care from their husbands, women who do not have husbands or access to their partner's health care are less likely to have coverage (Heck et al., 2006). Recent research suggests that people with same-sex partners are nearly twice as likely than married spouses to be uninsured (Badgett, 2009). King and Bartlett (2006) argue that legal marriage will increase access to health care. Access to same-sex marriage may alleviate some of this disparity.

In sum, an assimilationist perspective suggests that marriage is a social institution that has not only legal but also symbolic benefits, and that the extension of legal marriage will influence society in general and same-sex relationships specifically in positive ways. However, questions remain as to the extent to which same-sex couples will accrue the benefits of marriage seen by straight couples and how influential same-sex marriage will be on a homophobic U.S. culture. In this vein, several scholars suggest that the fight for same-sex marriage has important detriments to same-sex relationships and to society in general. We explore this position next.

Queer Critiques of the Movement for Same-Sex Marriage

> But marriage—forget the "gay" for a moment—is intrinsically conservative. It does not just normalize, it requires normality as the ticket in. Assimilating another "virtually normal" constituency, namely monogamous, long-term, homosexual couples, marriage pushes the queerer queers of all sexual persuasions—drag queens, club-crawlers, polyamorists, even ordinary single mothers or teenage lovers—further to the margins. "Marriage sanctifies some couples at the expense of others," wrote cultural critic Michael Warner. "It is selective legitimacy." (Levine, 2003)

Perhaps it is surprising, given the media's bifurcated portrayal of the same-sex marriage debates, that opposition to same-sex marriage has arisen not only among conservative marriage traditionalists but also among queer scholars and activists who aim to highlight inherent differences between LGBTQ and heterosexual people (Lewin, 2009). This view, understood in opposition to an assimilationist approach, is what Yep and colleagues call a "radical" approach and what Badgett (2009) terms a "dissenter" approach. Radicals or dissenters argue that the movement for same-sex marriage is harmful to the larger queer community, to queer relationships, and to all families in the United States, straight or queer. We outline each of these areas here.

First, radical scholars argue that the quest for same-sex marriage is harmful to the larger queer community. For some individuals, focusing the time, money, and energy of the LGBTQ rights movement distracts from other issues in the queer community, depoliticizing a larger, more diverse movement for a variety of interests of all queer people regardless of marital status (Ettelbrick, 1992; Weston, 2005). Since the beginning of the movement for same-sex marriage rights in the United States, the push for such rights has been at the forefront of legal and political action. While other legal battles have raged, including the repealing of sodomy laws and "Don't Ask, Don't Tell" in the military, and battles to obtain legal protection against discrimination on the basis of sexual orientation, these legal efforts have been dwarfed by efforts to legalize same-sex marriage (Hull, 2006).

Moreover, queer scholars believe that LGBTQ culture is intrinsically unique, and thus view the fight for same-sex marriage as an attempt to assimilate "to mainstream, middle-class values, [that are] intrinsically distinctive from what it means to be lesbian or gay" (Lewin, 2009, p. 6). At the core of this approach, scholars argue that queer culture is oppositional to normative heterosexual culture, and that this distinct culture is at risk of dissolution when queer individuals gain the right to marriage. This critique of same-sex marriage has been defined by the term *homonormativity*, wherein the efforts to gain access to same-sex marriage fail to "contest dominant heteronormative assumptions and institutions" but instead work to sustain them while demobilizing queer culture "anchored in domesticity and consumption" (Duggan, 2003, p. 50). For these scholars, same-sex marriage is part of the mainstreaming of queer culture, stripping the progressive potential of queer politics. Any attempt made to attain access to the quintessential feature of heterosexual life—marriage—is a disloyalty to the larger queer movement's emphasis on difference and opposition (Bronski, 1984; Warner, 1999). Most notably, radical scholars view the fight to challenge homophobia and resistance to heteronormativity through subversive queer culture as an imperative aspect of queerness (Halberstam, 2005; Polikoff, 2008).

In a similar way, queer scholars further argue that the quest for same-sex marriage works to marginalize individuals in the queer community who do not choose normative relationship configurations that would be sanctioned by marriage. The quest for same-sex marriage, then, depoliticizes queerness, shifting it from a community with the aim to radically resist and critique the institution of marriage to one that values marriage above all other forms of intimate ties (Polikoff, 2008; Robson, 1994; Vaid, 1995). These scholars warn of a new hierarchy of queer relationships, wherein the presence of respectable married queer individuals further marginalizes those queer individuals who chose alternative relationships (Butler, 2001; Walters, 2001). Michael Warner (1999) argues that efforts for gay marriage work to promote "normal" and "respectable" same-sex couples who want marriage and nuclear families much as do different-sex couples, consequently framing "abnormal" queer families as disrespectable, "bad" gays (Walters, 2001). Similarly, some lesbian scholars argue that the quest for same-sex marriage disregards long-standing feminist and lesbian critiques "of the oppressive and political nature of the family in favor of advocating recognition for 'our' families" (Robson, 1994, p. 977). In this approach, same-sex marriage acts to make queer individuals who are not in two-person intimate relationships and works to demonize nonmonogamous, polyamorous relationships (Saalfield, 1993; Warner, 1999). Moreover, an emphasis on the tie between two intimate partners through legal marriage works to obscure other nonsexual family relationships that are theorized to be unique to LGBTQ communities. For example, Weston's (1991) families of choice, along with other alternative, nonbiological family relationships, will be obscured (Bronski, 1998). Such books as *That's Revolting! Queer Strategies for Resisting Assimilation* (Mattilda, 2004), *I Do, I Don't: Queers on Marriage* (Wharton & Philips, 2004), and *Same-Sex Marriage Pro and Con: A Reader* (Sullivan, 2004) portray these radical approaches through personal narratives and queer theory.

Scholars from a radical perspective argue that participating in marriage will not only harm the queer community but also have specific negative implications for same-sex intimate relationships (Warner, 1999). This approach draws from feminist critiques of marriage that argue the institution is inherently flawed because of its foundation on women's subordination to men (Bernard, 1972). In this view, this flawed institution will also detrimentally influence the intimate relationships of same-sex partners by perpetuating inequality (Walters, 2001). Whereas some scholars suggest that same-sex couples are revolutionaries, promoting a new vision of marriage that dismantles norms of inequality that govern intimate relationships (Cherlin, 2004; Stacey, 2000), others are less optimistic. In a radical view, same-sex couples who marry must interface and construct gendered selves within the context of long-standing inequality of marriage. Thus, because marriage is linked to patriarchy (Ettelbrick, 1992), even queer marriages will reinforce hegemonic, unequal models of intimate relationships. In a similar vein, some argue that marriage invites the state's intrusion on the intimate relationships of queer people, fostering a loss of individuality and independence (Clarkberg, Stolzenberg, & Waite, 1995). These scholars suggest that legal same-sex marriage sanctions state interference in the intimate lives of those people who participate (Warner, 1999), rather than attempting to subvert the state's hold on personal relations.

In the article "Is Gay Marriage Racist?" (Bailey, Kandaswamy, & Richardson, 2004), the authors argue that marriage—for both same-sex and different-sex couples—benefits couples with privilege. Black families have been marginalized regardless of legal marital status, and Black parents have children removed by child protection authorities more than any other demographic group. Marriage can provide both spouses with health benefits, but only if one spouse has access to a stable job with health insurance (Bailey et al., 2004).

Finally, scholars of a radical approach extend their critiques of same-sex marriage beyond its effect on the queer community or on same-sex relationships to argue that same-sex marriage will actually do harm on a broader societal level. Although same-sex couples may benefit by gaining access to other legal aspects of marriage, queer radicals believe, health care, tax credits, and other benefits of marriage should be delinked from the institution of marriage. Radical queer scholars argue that legalizing same-sex marriages works to reinforce inequality in all relationships because the fight to legalize same-sex marriage obscures efforts to dismantle the institution of marriage. In this view, queer efforts against same-sex marriage and marriage in general may decouple the long-synonymous relationship between any intimate relationship and state- or religion-sanctioned legal marriage. Further, the effort toward moving away from recognizing just one form of relationships in favor of emphasizing a choice of partners and commitments may create "more opportunities for discovering new social arrangements that work in ways we have yet to conceive" (Yep et al., 2003, p. 58).

In sum, scholars who adhere to a radical approach argue that the fight for same-sex rights works to the detriment of queer culture, queer intimate relationships, and society at large. In the next section, we move beyond accounts of assimilationist and radical approaches in order to gain a view of the opinions and beliefs that same-sex couples themselves have on the fight for same-sex marriage and on getting married.

Do Same-Sex Couples Want to Get Married?

In the previous sections, we worked to explore the opposing discourses on same-sex marriage within the queer community, highlighting the potential consequences of same-sex marriage on U.S. culture, the queer community, and same-sex relationships. Now, we turn to a brief discussion of empirical studies that focus on queer individuals' and same-sex couples' beliefs about same-sex marriage. Relatively few studies attempt to systematically ascertain the beliefs about same-sex marriage from the perspective of same-sex couples and queer individuals. Here, we outline recent research on this topic, highlighting how demographic differences may shape perceptions of same-sex marriage.

Overall, U.S. attitudes toward LGBTQ individual rights have become increasingly liberal over time (Loftus, 2001). Opinion polls indicate that despite increasing numbers of people who believe same-sex couples should be able to marry, most remain against same-sex marriage (Hull, 2006; Loftus, 2001). Although most large-scale survey research focuses on U.S. perceptions in general, some studies—mostly smaller scale qualitative studies—ascertain what same-sex couples themselves think about same-sex marriage. At the broadest level, this research area reveals that same-sex couples believe that they should, as a matter of equality, have the option to legally marry (Badgett, 2009; Lannutti, 2005; Porshe & Purvin, 2008; Reczek, Elliott, & Umberson, 2009). Yet a closer reading of same-sex couples' perceptions of same-sex marriage reveals more ambivalent understandings of this issue.

Although studies show that most same-sex couples believe they should be able to legally marry, the symbolic meaning of marriage is articulated as a point of contention. Taking an assimilationist approach, some couples see marriage as the epitome of the symbolic commitment two individuals can make to each other; those individuals who adhere to this view express their desire to access to this symbol. The importance of symbolic marriage for some couples is seen in the popularity of commitment ceremonies (Hull, 2006; Lewin, 1998). In an attempt to understand the relationship between commitment ceremonies and marriage, Hull (2006) interviewed same-sex couples who had been together for more than 2 years or who had undergone a commitment ceremony. Her findings suggest that ceremonies are embraced by some same-sex couples as symbolic of legal marriage in that they are a way to bind the couple together in a profound marriage-like union. Hull further argues, as do scholars who study the effects of marriage on relationships (Waite & Gallagher, 2000), that those who have taken part in commitment ceremonies change their behaviors in relationship-enhancing ways. Similarly, in a study of married Dutch couples, Badgett found that "even those who believed they were already committed before marriage expressed that sharing their commitment in front of others in the form of a marriage ceremony changed their relationship in important ways" (Badgett, 2009, p. 124). These findings point to the continued symbolic importance of marriage and commitment ceremonies for some same-sex couples.

In contrast, aligned with the radical approach, some same-sex couples express hesitancy and concern with the symbolic meaning same-sex marriage holds for their relationships. These couples vocalize underlying tensions regarding the potential negative consequences same-sex unions may have on their intimate relationships, as well as on the queer community in general. Several qualitative studies highlight this nuanced approach to same-sex marriage, finding that though most couples desire the right to be able to legally marry, they view the institution of marriage as problematic (Lannutti, 2005; Reczek et al., 2009). For example, Badgett (2009) and Lannutti (2005) both call attention to same-sex couples'—especially lesbian couples'—hesitation about the institution of marriage as a patriarchal, outdated institution ripe for inequality.

There is reason to suspect that the age and relationship length of a couple shape beliefs about marriage. Same-sex couples have interfaced with tremendous historical changes in the legal and social status of their intimate ties over the past half-century (Cook-Daniels, 2008; Marcus, 2002). As a result of these rapid changes, younger cohorts of queer individual may have more positive beliefs and perceptions of same-sex marriages than do older cohorts. In a study of same-sex couples together 8 years or longer, Reczek et al. (2009) found that for couples who established their relationships before the gay marriage debates of the 1990s, marriage was not viewed as symbolically important to their relationships, even though nearly all couples believed that same-sex couples should have the right to marry (also see Porsche & Purvin, 2008). Survey research suggests that younger and less educated lesbian, gay, and bisexual people are more likely than their older counterparts to say they would marry if they could. For example, an 18-year-old person identified as nonstraight is 31% more likely to want to legally marry than is a 65-year-old lesbian, gay, or bisexual person, and 61% of young gay men and 78% of young lesbian women want to legally marry at some point (D'Augelli, Rendina, Sinclair, & Grossman, 2008).

Gender may also influence couples' decisions to marry. As discussed earlier, in the United States lesbian couples are more likely to participate in state-sanctioned unions than are gay couples (Belge, 2005; Carpenter & Gates, 2008; Solomon et al., 2004); whereas internationally, gay couples are more likely to marry than are lesbian couples (Waaldijk, 2001). In addition, studies suggest that lesbian cohabiting relationships break up at a higher rate than do gay cohabiting relationships and that the average relationship duration of gay partnerships is significantly longer than that of lesbian partnerships (Kurdek, 1998, 2004). Research from Scandinavia suggests that the risk of divorce is more than two times higher in lesbian registered partnerships than in gay registered partnerships in Norway and Sweden (Andersson et al., 2006; Noack, Seierstad, & Weedon-Fekjaer, 2005), as well as Denmark (Wockner, 1997).

Research and theory explaining these gender differences in legal partnership and dissolution rates are far from conclusive. Scholars suggest that gay men are much more likely than lesbians to marry in countries other than the United States because there are more gay male couples in the population (Laumann, Gagnon, Michael, & Michaels, 1994) or because of men's greater financial benefit from marriage, given men's higher incomes. In contrast, within the United States, scholars argue that because partnership rights do not include any of the federal benefits of different-sex marriage (e.g., Social Security, inheritance, and retirement), there may be less legal incentive to marry (for a review of these theories, see Rothblum, 2005). Those couples who do marry view their marriage primarily as a symbolic event, and "it is possible that women are socialized to value the symbolism of marriage more so than men" (Rothblum, 2005, p. 27). In terms of divorce rates, marriage scholars suggest, the higher relationship dissolution rates of lesbian compared to gay unions may reflect an underlying gender dynamic in which women have higher expectations for relationships and are more likely to exit unsatisfying relationships (Sweeney, 2002). Research suggests that women are more likely than men to perceive a heterosexual marriage as strained, to express dissatisfaction with their marriage (Umberson, Williams, Powers, Chen, & Campbell, 2005), and to file for divorce (Sweeney, 2002). It may be that like straight women, lesbians are more likely to have higher expectations for their marriages and, when expectations are not met, be more likely to dissolve these unions.

Taken together, studies of same-sex couples' views on getting married themselves mirror— and, in some ways, complicate—the broader assimilationist and radical debates outlined earlier in this chapter. The ambivalence about same-sex marriage among same-sex couples points to the tensions between assimilationist and radical arguments. Future research should continue to explore the perceptions of same-sex marriage of LGBTQ populations with a focus on how the fight for marriage may shape the everyday lives of these individuals.

Case Vignette

Roger Kirkpatrick, age 49, and Carlos Garcia, age 41, met 15 years ago when Roger was coaching his son's high school baseball team at a local park in Los Angeles and Carlos was playing on a gay and bisexual men's softball team. At the time, Roger was heterosexually married, had three young children, and self-identified as bisexual. He worked as a civilian contractor in the navy, and knew he would lose his job if he came out as gay or bisexual. Consequently, he was extremely closeted and had told no one about his attractions to men. He admitted later that he agreed to coach high school baseball because he knew about the gay softball team playing at the same time.

Carlos had been attracted to boys as long as he could remember. A very athletic child, he participated in several sports leagues and had sex with other boys in middle school and high school while sharing motel rooms at regional sports tournaments. He joined a theater club at his high school; as a star athlete he could get away with membership in a club that had the reputation of being a "gay club." Many students in the theater club were planning to attend small, liberal arts colleges, and Carlos applied to and received a scholarship from a college known for its nontraditional curriculum, its progressive policies on the environment, and, not surprisingly, its large LGBT student population. Carlos's parents, first-generation immigrants from the Dominican Republic, would have preferred him to attend the local state college near home. Since graduation, Carlos has stayed in the college town, working part time as a waiter in a gay bar, volunteering at an advocacy group for immigrant rights, and participating in a number of amateur sports teams. He has a lot of gay and bisexual friends but is not out to his family of origin, which lives 500 miles away.

Roger and Carlos were immediately attracted to each other and began to meet frequently. It was a time when Roger's children were about to leave for college, and so Roger came out to his family, divorced his wife, and found a job with a progressive firm. This is the first long-term relationship for Carlos (who has had many gay sexual partners) and the first same-sex relationship for Roger. Yet despite their differences in age, relationship history, and degree of outness, they have had a very positive relationship with few conflicts.

When their state legalized same-sex marriage, Roger wanted them to get married, but Carlos did not. This difference has led to a number of arguments, and both men have been urged by friends—both Carlos's and Roger's—to seek counseling.

Roger and Carlos face a dilemma shared by many same-sex couples: One partner wants marriage and the other does not. Among heterosexual couples, who have always had the option of marriage, a partner who is opposed to marriage (or children) would bring up this topic early on. For same-sex couples who met prior to the present century, legal marriage was not an option, and so even long-term couples did not discuss this issue until marriage became a possibility in their state, in the case of Roger and Carlos, 15 years into their relationship.

Of the couples who had civil unions when Vermont became the first U.S. state to grant any type of legalized relationships, 40% had previously been heterosexually married (Solomon et al., 2004). Thus Roger, previously married, may gravitate to the institution of marriage in order to solidify his relationship with Carlos. However, the majority of same-sex couples getting married in the United States are female, so Roger may not receive support from the gay male community for his choice. As a Latino, Carlos may avoid the public process of marriage to a man, given that he is already a member of an ethnic minority group and may not want the added stress of having the state government know about his sexual orientation. Furthermore, marriages are public information, and Carlos is worried that his family may obtain access to his marriage certificate.

Case Discussion

It is important that therapists stay informed about the ever-changing laws about same-sex marriage and such other legal statuses as civil unions and domestic partnerships. Some states are establishing such laws, whereas others are trying to take them away. Furthermore, many same-sex couples go out of state or to Canada to get married, so same-sex marriage is not just an issue for therapists in progressive states.

It also important that therapists are aware of the various viewpoints held about marriage in LGBTQ communities. Just as some people are fighting for same-sex marriage and would get married as soon as they could, others are opposed to marriage on principal. Furthermore, some individuals get married on a whim and are then surprised how meaningful and symbolic the marriage is; others are disappointed that their family, coworkers, or religious leaders do not recognize the institution (see Rothblum, Balsam, & Solomon, 2011a, 2011b).

Conclusion: Implications for Therapists

Although it is not possible to be a little bit pregnant, it is certainly possible for LGBTQ individuals to be a little bit married. A married gay male couple living in Massachusetts has the same legal benefits at the state level as their heterosexual married neighbors but none of the federal benefits. Furthermore, they will not be legally recognized as a couple when they travel to most other U.S. states. Even in Massachusetts, their family, religious institution, and workplace may not give them the same psychological validation that heterosexual married couples receive. It is thus important that couple and family therapists understand the precarious emotional and legal status of same-sex relationships today.

We also urge couple and family therapists not to assume that marriage is the desire of all LGBTQ couples. As this chapter has shown, there are various radical voices in the LGBTQ communities who feel marginalized by the media focus on marriage. It is ironic that same-sex couples who are politically against marriage may now feel pressure to marry by their family and friends (e.g., Badgett, 2009). Therapists will see same-sex couples where one partner wants to get married but the other does not.

Scholarly, political, and social debates over the legalization of same-sex marriage continue into the 21st century. With a focus on the perspectives of queer activists and scholars, this chapter draws attention to the competing notions of the importance of same-sex marriage within the queer community itself. Instead of painting a monolith of a unified queer community whose joint aim is to legalize same-sex marriage, we have emphasized how same-sex couples interface with multiple ideas about their relationships and lives and show the consequences of these discourses on same-sex intimate relationships and the queer community.

Acknowledgment

The authors acknowledge the Mentoring Program of the Center for Population Research in LGBT Health, supported by the Eunice Kennedy Shriver National Institute of Child Health and Human Development (NICHD) under Award Number R21HD051178. The content is solely the responsibility of the authors and does not necessarily represent the official views of the NICHD or the National Institutes of Health.

References

Andersson, G., Noack, T., Seierstad, A., & Weedon-Fekjær, H. (2006). The demographics of same-sex marriages in Norway and Sweden. *Demography, 43*, 79–98.

Badgett, M. V. L. (2004). Will providing marriage rights to same-sex couples undermine heterosexual marriage? *Sexuality Research and Social Policy: Journal of NSRC, 1*(3), 1–10.

Badgett, M. V. L. (2009). *When gay people get married: What happens when societies legalize same-sex marriage?* New York, NY: New York University Press.

Bailey, M. M., Kandaswamy, P., & Richardson, M. U. (2004). Is gay marriage racist? In Mattilda, aka M. B. Sycamore (Ed.), *That's revolting! Queer strategies for resisting assimilation* (pp. 87–93). Brooklyn, NY: Soft Skull Press.

Balsam, K. F., Beauchaine, T.P., Rothblum, E.D., & Solomon, S.E. (2008). Three-year follow-up of same-sex couples who had civil unions in Vermont, same-sex couples not in civil unions, and heterosexual married couples. *Developmental Psychology, 44*(1), 102–116.

Belge, K. (2005). *Gay marriages in Massachusetts: One year later. May 2005.* Retrieved from http:lesbianlife. about.com/od/weddings/a/MassOneYear.htm.

Bell, D., & Binnie, J. (2000). *The sexual citizen: Queer politics and beyond.* Cambridge, England: Polity Press.

Bernard, J. (1972). *The future of marriage.* New York, NY: World Publishing.

Black, D. A., Sanders, S. G., & Taylor, L. J. (2007). The economics of lesbian and gay families. *Journal of Economic Perspectives, 21*, 53–70.

Brines, J., & Joyner, K. (1999). The ties that bind: Principles of cohesion in cohabitation and marriage. *American Sociological Review, 64*, 333–355.

Bronski, M. (1984). *Culture clash: The making of gay sensibility.* Boston, MA: South End Press.

Bronski, M. (1998). *The pleasure principle: Sex, backlash, and the struggle for gay freedom.* New York, NY: St. Martin's Press.

Buchmueller, T., & Carpenter, C. S. (2010). Disparities in health insurance coverage, access, and outcomes for individuals in same-sex versus different-sex relationships, 2000–2007. *American Journal of Public Health, 100*, 489–495.

Bumpass, L. L., & Lu, H. (2000). Trends in cohabitation and implications for children's family contexts in the United States. *Population Studies, 54*, 29–41.

Butler, J. (2001). "There is a person here": An interview with Judith Butler (compiled by M. S. Breen, W. J. Blumenfeld, et al.). *International Journal of Sexuality and Gender Studies, 6*, 7–23.

Cahill, S. (2004). *Same-sex marriage in the United States: Focus on the facts.* Lanham, MD: Lexington Books.

Calhoun, C. (2000). *Feminism, the family, and the politics of the closet: Lesbian and gay displacement.* Oxford, UK: Oxford University Press.

Carpenter, C., & Gates, G. (2008). Gay and lesbian partnerships: Evidence from California. *Demography, 45*, 573–590.

Chambers, D. L. (2000). Couples: marriage, civil unions, and domestic partnership. In J. D'Emilio, W. B. Turner, & U. Vaid (Eds.), *Creating change: Sexuality, public policy, and civil rights* (pp. 281–304). New York, NY: St. Martin's Press.

Cherlin, A. (2004). The deinstitutionalization of American marriage. *Journal of Marriage and Family, 66*, 848–861.

Clarkberg, M. E., Stolzenberg, R. M., & Waite, L. J. (1995). Attitudes, values, and entrance into cohabitational versus marital unions. *Social Forces, 74*, 609–634.

Cook-Daniels, L. (2008). Living memory GLBT history timeline: Current elders would have been this old when these events happened. *Journal of GLBT Family Studies, 4*, 485–497.

Cott, N. F. (2000). *Public vows: A history of marriage and the nation*. Cambridge, MA: Harvard University Press.

D'Augelli, A. R., Rendina, H. J., Sinclair, K. O., & Grossman, A. H. (2008). Lesbian and gay youth's aspirations for marriage and raising children. *Journal of LGBT Issues in Counseling, 1*(4), 77–98.

Duggan, L. (2003). *The twilight of equality? Neoliberalism, cultural politics, and the attack on democracy*. Boston, MA: Beacon Press.

Eskridge, W. N. (2002). *Equality practice: Civil unions and the future of gay rights*. New York, NY: Routledge.

Eskridge, W. N., & Spedale, D. R. (2006). *Same-sex marriage: For better or worse? What we've learned from the evidence*. New York, NY: Oxford University Press.

Ettelbrick, P. L. (1992). Since when is marriage a path to liberation? In S. Sherman (Ed.), *Lesbian and gay marriage: Private commitments, public ceremonies*. Philadelphia, PA: Temple University Press.

Gates, G. J. (2009). *Same-sex spouses and unmarried partners in the American Community Survey, 2008*. Los Angeles, CA: Williams Institute, UCLA. Retrieved from http://www.escholarship.org/uc/item/72t806m7

Green, R. J. (2004). Risk and resilience in lesbian and gay couples: Comment on Solomon, Rothblum, and Balsam. *Journal of Family Psychology, 18*, 290–292.

Halberstam, J. (2005). *In a queer time and place: Transgender bodies, subcultural lives*. New York, NY: New York University Press.

Heck, J., Randell, M., Sell, R., & Gorin, S. (2006). Health care access among individuals involved in same-sex relationships. *American Journal of Public Health, 96*, 1111–1118.

Herdt, G., & Kertzner, R. (2006). *I do, but I can't: The impact of marriage denial on the mental health and sexual citizenship of lesbians and gay men in the United States* [Policy paper]. San Francisco, CA: National Sexuality Research Council.

Hull, K. E. (2006). *Same-sex marriage: The cultural politics of love and law*. Cambridge, UK: Cambridge University Press.

King, M., & Bartlett, A. (2006). What same sex civil partnerships may mean for health. *Journal of Epidemiology and Community Health, 60*, 188–191.

Kurdek, L. A. (1998). Relationship outcomes and their predictors: Longitudinal evidence from heterosexual married, gay cohabiting, and lesbian cohabiting couples. *Journal of Marriage and the Family*, 553–568.

Kurdek, L. A. (2004). Are gay and lesbian cohabiting couples "really" different from heterosexual married couples? *Journal of Marriage and Family, 66*(4), 880–900.

Lannutti, P. (2005). For better or worse: Exploring the meanings of same-sex marriage within the lesbian, gay, bisexual and transgendered community. *Journal of Social and Personal Relationships, 22*, 5–18.

Laumann, E. O, Gagnon, J. H, Michael, R. T., & Michaels, S. (1994). *The social organization of sexuality: Sexual practices in the United States*. Chicago, IL: University of Chicago Press.

Levine, J. (July 22, 2003). Stop the wedding! Why gay marriage isn't radical enough. *The Village Voice*. Retrieved from http://www.villagevoice.com/2003-07-22/news/stop-the-wedding

Lewin, E. (1998). *Recognizing ourselves: Ceremonies of lesbian and gay commitment*. New York, NY: Columbia University Press.

Lewin, E. (2009). *Gay fatherhood: Narratives of family and citizenship in America*. Chicago, IL: University of Chicago Press.

Loftus, J. (2001). America's liberalization in attitudes towards homosexuality, 1973–1988. *Sociological Review, 63*, 27–38.

Marcus, E. (2002). *Making gay history: The half-century fight for lesbian and gay equal rights*. New York, NY: Perennial.

Mattilda, aka M. B. Sycamore. (2004). *That's revolting! Queer strategies for resisting assimilation*. Brooklyn, NY: Soft Skull Press.

McVeigh, R., & Diaz, M. D. (2009). Voting to ban same-sex marriage. *American Sociological Review*, *74*, 891–915.

Meyer, I. H. (2003). Prejudice, social stress, and mental health in lesbian, gay, and bisexual populations: Conceptual issues and research evidence. *Psychological Bulletin*, *129*(5), 674–697.

Noack, T., Seierstad, A., & Weedon-Fekjaer, H. (2005). A demographic analysis of registered partnerships (legal same-sex unions): The case of Norway. *European Journal of Population*, *21*, 89–109.

Polikoff, N. D. (2008). *Beyond (straight and gay) marriage: Valuing all families under the law*. Boston, MA: Beacon Press.

Porsche, M., & Purvin, D. (2008). "Never in our lifetime": Legal marriage for same-sex couples in long-term relationships. *Family Relations*, *57*, 144–159.

Reczek, C., Elliott, S., & Umberson, D. (2009). Commitment without marriage: Union formation among long-term same-sex couples. *Journal of Family Issues*, *30*, 738–756.

Robson, R. (1994). Resisting the family: Repositioning lesbians in legal theory. *Signs*, *19*, 975–996.

Rotello, G. (1997). *Sexual ecology: AIDS and the destiny of gay men*. New York, NY: Dutton.

Rothblum, E. D. (2005). Same-sex marriage and legalized relationships: I do, or do I? *Journal of GLBT Family Studies*, *1*, 21–31.

Rothblum, E. D., Balsam, K. F., & Solomon, S. E. (2008). Comparison of same-sex couples who were married in Massachusetts, had domestic partnerships in California, or had civil unions in Vermont. *Journal of Family Issues*, *29*, 48–78.

Rothblum, E. D., Balsam, K. F., & Solomon, S. E. (2011a). The longest "legal" U.S. same-sex couples reflect on their relationship. *Journal of Social Issues*, *67*, 302–315.

Rothblum, E .D., Balsam, K. F., & Solomon, S. E. (2011b). Narratives of same-sex couples who had civil unions in Vermont: The impact of legalizing relationships on couples and on social policy. *Sexuality Research and Social Policy, 8*, 183–191.

Saalfield, C. (1993). Lesbian marriage … (k)not! In A. Stein (Ed.), *Sisters, sexperts, queers: Beyond the Lesbian Nation* (pp. 187–195). New York, NY: Penguin.

Slater, S. (1995). *The lesbian family life cycle*. New York, NY: Free Press.

Smock, P. J. (2000). Cohabitation in the United States: An appraisal of research themes, findings, and implications. *Annual Review of Sociology*, *26*, 1–20.

Soland, B. (1998, Spring). A queer nation? The passage of the gay and lesbian partnership legislation in Denmark, 1989. *Social Politics*, 48–69.

Solomon, S. E., Rothblum, E. D., & Balsam, K. F. (2004). Pioneers in partnership: Lesbian and gay male couples in civil unions compared with those not in civil unions, and married heterosexual siblings. *Journal of Family Psychology*, *18*, 275–286.

Stacey, J. (2000). Gay and lesbian families are here; All our families are queer: Let's get used to it. In C. L. Williams & A. Stein (Ed.), *Sexuality and gender* (pp. 382–394). Malden, MA: Blackwell.

Stanley, S. M., Whitton, S. W., & Markman, H. J. (2004). Maybe I do. *Journal of Family Issues*, 25, 496–519.

Sullivan, A. (1995). *Virtually normal: An argument about homosexuality*. New York, NY: Knopf.

Sullivan, A. (2004). *Same-sex marriage: Pro and con: A reader*. New York, NY: Vintage Books.

Sweeney, M. M. (2002). Remarriage and the nature of divorce: Does it matter which spouse chose to leave? *Journal of Family Issues*, *23*(3), 410–440.

Umberson, D. (1992). Gender, marital status, and the social control of health behavior. *Social Science and Medicine*, *34*, 907–917.

Umberson, D. J., Williams, K., Powers, D. A., Chen, M. D., & Campbell, A. M. (2005). As good as it gets? A life course perspective on marital quality. *Social Forces*, *84*, 493–511.

U.S. Census. (2011). *Census Bureau releases estimates of same-sex married couples*. Retrieved October 6, from http://www.census.gov/newsroom/releases/archives/2010_census/cb11-cn181.html

Vaid, U. (1995). *Virtual equality: The mainstreaming of gay and lesbian liberation*. New York, NY: Doubleday.

Waaldijk, K. (2001). Small change: How the road to same-sex marriage got paved in the Netherlands. In R. Wintemute & M. Andenaes (Eds.), *Legal recognition of same-sex partnerships: A study of national, European and international law* (pp. 437–464). Oxford, UK: Hart.

Waite, L. J., & Gallagher, M. (2000). *The case for marriage: Why married people are happier, healthier, and better off financially*. New York, NY: Doubleday.

Walters, S. D. (2001). Take my domestic partner, please: Gays and marriage in the era of the visible. In M. Bernstein & R. Reimann (Eds.), *Queer families, queer politics: Challenging culture and the state*. New York, NY: Columbia University Press.

Warner, M. (1999). *The trouble with normal: Sex, politics, and the ethics of queer life*. Cambridge, MA: Harvard University Press.

Weston, K. (1991). *Families we choose: Lesbians, gays, kinship*. New York, NY: Columbia University Press.

Weston, K. (2005). Families in queer states: The rule of law and the politics of recognition. *Radical History Review, 93*, 122–141.

Wharton, G., & Philips, J. (2004). *I do, I don't: Queers on marriage*. San Francisco, CA: Suspects Thoughts Press.

Wienke, C., & Hill, G. J. (2009). Does the "marriage benefit" extend to partners in gay and lesbian relationships? Evidence from a random sample of sexually active adults. *Journal of Family Issues, 30*, 259–289.

Wintemute, R., & Andenaes, M. T. (2001). *Legal recognition of same-sex partnerships: A study of national, European and international law*. Oxford, UK: Hart.

Wockner, R. (1997). *New statistics on Danish gay marriage*. Retrieved from http://gaytoday.badpuppy.com/garchive/world/040497wo.htm

Wolfson, E. (2001). The Hawaii marriage case launches the US freedom-to-marry movement for equality. In R. Wintemute & M. T. Andenaes (Eds.), *Legal recognition of same-sex partnerships: A study of national, European, and international law* (pp. 169–176). Oxford, UK: Hart.

Yep, G. A., Lovaas, K. E., & Elia, J. P. (2003). A critical appraisal of assimilationist and radical ideologies underlying same-sex marriage in LGBT communities in the United States. *Journal of Homosexuality, 45*, 45–67.

Index

Page numbers followed by "n" refer to footnotes